DIVIDED LOYALTIES:
THE LIBERAL PARTY OF CANADA, 1984–2008

The Liberal Party has governed Canada for much of the country's history. Yet over the past two decades, the 'natural governing party' has seen a decrease in traditional support, finding itself in opposition for nearly half of that time. In *Divided Loyalties*, Brooke Jeffrey draws on her own experience as a party insider and on interviews with more than sixty senior Liberals to follow the trajectory of the party from 1984 to the leadership of Stéphane Dion in 2008.

Riven by internal strife, leadership disputes, and financial woes, the Liberal Party today faces unprecedented challenges that threaten its very future. Conventional wisdom attributes the origins of the disarray to personal conflict between Jean Chrétien and Paul Martin. However, Jeffrey argues that this divisiveness is actually the continuation of a dispute over Canadian federalism and national unity that began decades earlier between John Turner and Pierre Trudeau. This dispute, as evidenced by recent leadership crises, remains unresolved to this day. An insightful examination of the federal Liberal Party, *Divided Loyalties* sheds much-needed light on an increasingly fissured party.

BROOKE JEFFREY is an associate professor and director of the Master of Public Policy and Public Administration program in the Department of Political Science at Concordia University. She has been actively involved in Liberal politics since 1984, including roles as director of the Liberal Caucus Research Bureau, secretary of the party's Platform Committee, and secretary general of the Leadership Forums.

ALSO BY BROOKE JEFFREY

Breaking Faith: The Mulroney Legacy of Deceit, Destruction and Disunity
Strange Bedfellows, Trying Times: The Charlottetown Accord and the Defeat
  of the Power Brokers
Hard Right Turn: The New Face of Neo-Conservatism in Canada

BROOKE JEFFREY

Divided Loyalties

The Liberal Party of Canada, 1984–2008

UNIVERSITY OF TORONTO PRESS
Toronto Buffalo London

© University of Toronto Press Incorporated 2010
Toronto Buffalo London
www.utppublishing.com
Printed in Canada

ISBN 978-0-8020-3848-7 (cloth)
ISBN 978-1-4426-1065-1 (paper)

Printed on acid-free paper

Library and Archives Canada Cataloguing in Publication

Jeffrey, Brooke
Divided loyalties : the Liberal Party of Canada, 1984–2008 / Brooke Jeffrey.

Includes bibliographical references and index.
ISBN 978-0-8020-3848-7 (bound). – ISBN 978-1-4426-1065-1 (pbk.)

1. Liberal Party of Canada – History.   2. Canada – Politics and
government – 1984–1993.   3. Canada – Politics and government –
1993–2006.   I. Title.

JL197.L5J44 2010   324.27106   C2010-905239-0

University of Toronto Press acknowledges the financial assistance to its
publishing program of the Canada Council for the Arts and the Ontario
Arts Council.

University of Toronto Press acknowledges the financial support of the
Government of Canada through the Canada Book Fund for its publishing
activities.

In Memory of
Charles Caccia
(1930–2008)

Contents

Illustrations follow page 376

Preface

I have been asked many times by publishers and interested observers to write about my experiences with the Liberal Party. My answer was always the same, that the time was not right. Recently, though, a number of events have conspired to change my mind.

First, at the 2003 leadership convention I was approached by many of the key players during the Turner era, who actively encouraged me to produce a record of those times. Several suggested enough time had passed to make it possible for an objective analysis, and they believed almost all of those involved would be willing to cooperate. A few urged it should be done sooner rather than later, before too much time had passed and no one could remember important details. One individual, former national policy chair Rodger Schwass, made another compelling point, namely that this would not be a simple account of one of the party's rare failures. It would also reveal that the Turner years were a testament to the determination of many fine Liberals to persevere in spite of difficulties and rebuild the party, making a number of important changes which helped to pave the way for the party's return to power in 1993.

Of course those years also served as a cautionary tale, and one whose lessons the Liberals of the Chrétien era took to heart for much of the time. But as the party descended into internecine warfare the sense of history repeating itself was striking. Indeed, many of the players engaged in the Chrétien-Martin conflict of the recent past were actually involved in the Turner-Trudeau and Turner-Chrétien feuds two decades earlier. Outside observers have tended to focus on the personalities involved in these conflicts. In those few instances where any more detailed analysis was offered, it almost always centred quite predictably on the traditional division between business and social Liberals, that is, between the philosophical right and left wings of the party.

Yet it has seemed obvious to me for some time that a new factor has entered the debate. Providing an explanation for this new development is the second and even more important reason for my decision to proceed with this book. In it, I argue the introduction of the Meech Lake Accord by Prime Minister Brian Mulroney in 1984 served as a catalyst for the emergence of a new cleavage in the Liberal Party along the federalism axis, pitting traditional Trudeau federalists against a new breed of Liberal decentralists. In short, while many of the players are the same, I conclude the issues underlying the party's internal conflict are now more complex and possibly are becoming more intractable because they remain largely unrecognized and therefore unresolved.

Interestingly, not one of the individuals I interviewed disagreed with this analysis of the situation, regardless of which side of the Liberal divide they occupy. Some felt the federalist cleavage was of less importance than other issues, but none denied its existence, and many agreed quite vigorously with my assessment of its significance. Above all, there was a nearly unanimous recognition that the divisions in the party have not been resolved and continue to plague rebuilding efforts.

This leads me to the third and final reason for agreeing to undertake this study. Unlike the Progressive Conservatives, or even the new Conservative Party, there have been almost no academic analyses of the Liberal Party in recent years. Since the publication two decades ago of Joseph Wearing's *The L-Shaped Party* and Stephen Clarkson and Christina McCall's excellent two-volume work, *Trudeau and Our Times*, both of which conclude before the end of the Trudeau era, or John English's superb recent biography of Trudeau in power, *Just Watch Me*, no serious study of the party has been produced.

One of the reasons for this striking gap in the literature, I feel sure, is the great difficulty in trying to understand the internal operations of a political party from the outside. At the same time I believe it is important for academics to acquire such understanding. Many of the textbooks to which I was exposed as an undergraduate were woefully inadequate in this regard, as I later learned first-hand. One example serves to illustrate this point beautifully. I will never forget my first day in my new job as director of the Liberal Research Bureau. My invaluable administrative assistant, the incomparable Lise Pelletier, asked me what I was doing in my office first thing on Monday morning. Unsure how to reply, I asked where she thought I should be. 'At the Tactics

Committee meeting of course' was her immediate response. Having learned where it was taking place, I made a hasty beeline for this event which I had never heard of before, despite my doctorate in political science and my decade of experience working in the federal government and on Parliament Hill for the Parliamentary Research Service. I quickly learned it was the most important event in the parliamentary day for opposition parties, and much of the Bureau's activities would revolve around it. Chastened by my experience and realizing I had much to learn, I returned to my office. The next morning, to my complete surprise, I was asked the same question by Mme Pelletier. 'But this is Tuesday!' I replied, thinking the Monday meeting had been intended to organize caucus activities and Question Period for the week. 'Surely they don't do this *every day*?' The look on her face made it clear that Lise believed the caucus executive had made a horrible mistake in hiring me, and I had to work hard to dispel that notion.

I was reminded again of the importance of first-hand experience when an old acquaintance and I were observing the Liberals' 2006 leadership race in Montreal. 'The Conservatives have Tom Flanagan,' she said. 'Why don't you ever write about us? You actually understand what is going on.' While she may have been somewhat overconfident in her assessment, it is certainly true that I have been privileged to observe the party from the inside in a variety of capacities over much of the past twenty-five years.

Beginning with my recruitment from the public service in 1985 to become the director of the Liberal Caucus Research Bureau, during the darkest hours of the party after the crushing 1984 election defeat, I was not only present for, but directly involved in, many of the most crucial events of the next six years. A lack of other senior personnel meant I was often asked to take on tasks no director before, or likely since, has ever filled, and I recognized even at the time that this was a most unusual situation. During those years, for example, I attended all national caucus meetings and was appointed by the leader to serve as a member of the party's emergency task force on the constitution, which ultimately drafted the amendments tabled in the House of Commons and Senate on the Meech Lake Accord. I also met on a weekly basis with my counterparts in OLO (the chief of staff or principal secretary) and at the party headquarters (secretary general, later national director). In 1987 I served as co-secretary of the Canada Conferences and then as co-secretary of the Platform Committee that drafted the first real 'red book.' In 1988 I was a member of the National Campaign Committee, and in

1990 I was appointed secretary general of the Leadership Forums. In 1993 I was the party's candidate in my riding of Okanagan-Shuswap in British Columbia, where I was privileged to receive visits of support during the campaign from both Jean Chrétien and Paul Martin. Having failed in my bid for election in spite of their visits, I returned to full-time teaching at Concordia University but retained many informal ties to the party. During the first Chrétien mandate, for example, I directed the Western Communications Project referred to in chapter 8. Since then I have served as a policy adviser to a number of caucus and party committees, most recently as a member of the party's Red Ribbon policy committee on the constitution chaired by the Hon. Martin Cauchon, which published its landmark report before the 2006 leadership convention. I also provided policy advice to the leadership campaigns of Sheila Copps (2003) and Gerard Kennedy (2006), primarily but not exclusively on the constitution and Quebec.

Not surprisingly, perhaps, I have accumulated a tremendous amount of material about the party and its activities over the years. Much of this material is in the form of internal memos, confidential documents, and letters that were never published, although fragments of some of them may have found their way into the press. Some of this material I produced myself. Some I received as a normal consequence of the positions I held at the time. Some of it was given to me by friends and former colleagues, either at the time or later. As a result, although I have made every effort to indicate the source of all material referred to in this text, in some cases these sources may not be publicly available, but all are in my possession. Similarly, throughout the text I have referred to my own involvement not by name but by simply indicating the involvement of the position which I held at the time.

Finally, I should note that when I began my formal involvement with the party I was not even a card-carrying member. Nor had I been involved in the 1984 leadership race. I did, however, know quite well a number of key Liberals of the day who were instrumental in convincing me to make the leap from the security of the public service, chief among them Jean-Luc Pépin and Doug Frith. Since then I have become good friends with many fine Liberals on both sides of this unfortunate internal divide. Many of the Liberals I interviewed for this book were kind enough to mention that it was precisely because they knew me, and by extension my work, that they were willing to discuss these issues so frankly and in such detail. I am deeply indebted to all of them, but no one more so than my longtime friend and mentor, Charles Caccia, to whom this book is dedicated.

Brooke Jeffrey
Ottawa
July 2010

Acknowledgments

This book was over four years in the making. During that time I spoke informally with countless party organizers, campaign workers, candidates, parliamentarians, and journalists about the history of the Liberal Party over the past quarter-century. All of those conversations contributed immeasurably to my understanding of the party and its operations. Nearly seventy individuals graciously consented to interviews, most of which were lengthy and very detailed. Many also answered numerous written requests for additional information. Some of them were interviewed on several occasions, and always without complaint. In addition, ten senior public servants and a small number of senior Liberals agreed to be interviewed on the condition of anonymity. To all of them I owe a significant debt and am very grateful for their patience and understanding.

I would, however, be remiss if I did not single out the exceptional assistance provided to me by certain individuals who not only encouraged me to undertake this project but followed through with continuous assistance, counsel, and thoughtful analysis, often providing material from their personal files, filling in some of the blanks in my own recollection of certain events, and agreeing to review various chapters about events in which they were most implicated. Despite my urging, two insisted on remaining anonymous for reasons I can easily understand.

Sadly, the list also includes two dear friends and former colleagues, the late Hon. Doug Frith and Hon. Charles Caccia, whose sound advice, enthusiasm, and encouragement were crucial to the completion of this manuscript and who will be sorely missed. In addition, the Hon. Richard Stanbury, Dan McCarthy, and Mark Resnick cheerfully agreed to far more than their fair share of interviews and provided valuable assistance on a range of issues.

As always I am indebted to the staff of the Reference Branch of the Library of Parliament, who provided prompt and reliable responses to detailed queries, and to various officials of the Liberal Caucus Research Bureau and party headquarters, all of whom were most cooperative in providing information and assistance. At Concordia University I was ably assisted over time by several graduate students, including Kris Einerson, Justin Leclair, Caitlin O'Boyle, Valerie Goodhue, and Mohamad Bazzi. In addition, I am most grateful to longtime Liberal photographer Jean-Marc Carisse, who generously provided all of the photos for this book, and to Joanne Rycaj Guillemette of the Photo Archives Division of Library and Archives Canada, who ably assisted him in locating them.

I would also like to thank the many individuals at University of Toronto Press who have worked so hard to make this project a reality, including Managing Editor Wayne Herrington, who shepherded the text through its final stages, my editor Daniel Quinlan, who cheerfully took on the daunting task of reducing a huge manuscript to a somewhat more manageable size, and copy editor James Leahy, who did an excellent job of turning my sometimes turgid prose into a more reader-friendly final version.

Last but hardly least, thanks are once again due to my long-suffering but always supportive husband, family, and friends, who probably thought that this time I really had taken on too much and this book would never see the light of day. To them I can only repeat my promise that this will be my last such endeavour!

DIVIDED LOYALTIES:
THE LIBERAL PARTY OF CANADA, 1984–2008

Introduction

The Liberal Party has no dogma. Its creed is unity – national unity and party unity.

– Senator Michael Pitfield

The Liberal Party is the most successful political machine in the Western world. Widely referred to as the 'natural governing party,' it dominated the political landscape in Canada throughout the twentieth century. With only one exception, every Liberal leader to contest a federal election since Confederation became prime minister.

Between 1945 and 2000 the Liberal Party received more votes than any other party in all but four of seventeen national elections. In more than half of those elections it obtained more seats than all other parties taken together. The domination of the Liberal Party at the national level was so complete that prominent Canadian scholar John Meisel once wrote 'the line between the government and the Liberal Party has become tenuous.'[1]

One of the most commonly cited reasons for the party's success was its ability to take advantage of its brief periods in opposition – or infrequent changes in leadership – to renew its policies and organization. Another was its remarkable degree of internal cohesion. Liberals, it was well known, did not wash their dirty linen in public like the Progressive Conservatives. Also unlike the Tories, they did not destroy their leaders. In exchange, successful Liberal leaders reached out to their defeated leadership opponents, and their opponents' supporters, to keep the party united. This show of solidarity translated into public confidence in the party's competence to govern.

Most important, the Liberal Party's dominance has been attributed to its ability to shape and define Liberal values as *Canadian* values, positioning itself as the party of national unity. Liberals were long seen by Canadians as the party best able to manage the country's cultural and regional diversity, through a combination of nation-building social programs and commitment to strong central government. As Senator Michael Pitfield famously summed up, 'The Liberal Party has no dogma. Its creed is unity – national unity and party unity.'[2] This reality has long been recognized by politicians as well as academics, and once prompted a frustrated Alliance Leader Stephen Harper to exclaim 'You can be a good Canadian and not vote Liberal!'[3]

Given the Liberal Party's unparalleled record of success, the last twenty-five years represent a unique era in party history, and one about which surprisingly little has been written. For nearly half that time the country's natural governing party has found itself out of power, relegated to the ranks of the Official Opposition. And the party did not simply lose power. The 1984 federal election decimated the Liberals, reducing them to a mere forty seats in Parliament as Brian Mulroney's Conservatives won the biggest majority in Canadian history.

Difficult as it was for most Liberals to believe, shortly after the 1984 election the very future of the natural governing party was called into question. Some political pundits predicted the Liberals would be reduced to third-party status like their counterparts in Britain. Others speculated, even more incredibly, that the Liberal Party could disappear altogether from the Canadian political scene.

Adding to the Liberals' woes were a number of serious practical problems. Their party was deeply in debt. Their vaunted electoral Red Machine was hopelessly disorganized and out of date. Worse still, the party's membership was badly split by the divisive leadership race held only a month before the election call, when heir apparent John Turner had triumphed over Trudeau protégé Jean Chrétien.

Then the Liberals in opposition under John Turner did the unthinkable. They abandoned virtually every guiding principle that had ensured the party's success in the past. A dramatic shift in the Liberals' approach to national unity, brought about by the Conservative government's proposed Meech Lake Accord, marked the beginning of a period of painful and highly public infighting. Open dissension in the ranks was followed by two unprecedented attempts to remove the leader against his will, one of which took place in the middle of an election campaign. This astonishing collapse in internal party cohesion was an important factor in the party's failure to return to power in the 1988 election, in spite of the public's profound dissatisfaction with the Mulroney government.

Yet despite these potentially insurmountable problems, the Liberal Party of Canada was able to return from the brink of bankruptcy and political oblivion in 1993 to win a substantial majority. The Herculean rebuilding efforts of a small band of party stalwarts in achieving this dramatic turnaround are an important chapter in the party's history, and a remarkable accomplishment by any standard. Yet few ordinary Canadians, and even longtime Liberal Party supporters, are aware of the difficulties faced or, indeed, how close the party came to political oblivion.

When the Liberals returned to power in 1993 it was widely assumed the natural governing party would resume its traditional policy agenda and winning ways, closing ranks to present a united front to the world. For some time this appeared to be the case and the party reaped the benefits. Jean Chrétien delivered two more Liberal majority governments in 1997 and 2000, each larger than the last. The magnitude of the Liberals' victory in 2000 stunned their opponents. Many observers concluded the party's dominance was likely to continue for the foreseeable future. As political scientist Bruce Doern declared, 'Jean Chrétien stands astride the Canadian political scene without much effective opposition at the federal level.' For Doern, the key question after the election was 'the extent to which a one-party state is congealing at the federal level (under the Liberals).'[4]

Behind the scenes, however, the Liberals' return to power had not been as seamless or harmonious as it appeared. The party continued to struggle with the organizational problems that had plagued the Turner era. More significant still, it soon became apparent the internal divisions which had overwhelmed the party in opposition had not disappeared with the return to power. They had merely gone underground. The division in Liberal ranks was kept under control and out of sight for much of the Chrétien era, aided by the party's return to power. It was not, however, resolved. Instead, this internal disagreement continued to fester and eventually contributed to the unprecedented removal of a sitting prime minister as leader of the party.

The significance of this palace coup occurring when the party was in power can hardly be overemphasized. Despite record high levels of public support for the party after nine years in power, and Jean Chrétien's equally unprecedented delivery of three straight majority governments, the 'discipline of power' for which the Liberal Party had always been famous began to dissolve surprisingly quickly. Ignoring the lessons from the Turner era on the political price to be paid for disunity, disgruntled caucus members and party officials were challenging Chretien's authority as early as 1998. Supporters of Paul Martin, whose leadership aspirations had not dimmed, became ever more vocal. By 2000 the discontent had become open warfare, and, in August 2002, for the first time ever, a Liberal leader was effectively deposed. For a party whose leaders had always served lengthy terms in office and chosen their own departure dates, this development was nothing short of revolutionary.

Nor was it the end of the story. To the great surprise of most Liberals – and most Canadians – Paul Martin's victory in the subsequent leadership race did not resolve the party's divisions. His brief stewardship of the party exacerbated rather than healed the rift. Journalist Susan Delacourt's prediction that the 'tension' between Martin and Chrétien supporters would disappear once Martin took over would prove to be wildly inaccurate. 'Grudges are a big part of politics,' Delacourt wrote optimistically in December 2003, 'but they usually evaporate upon victory.' Citing the legendary Liberal reputation for coming together for the good of the party once a leadership contest was over, she concluded: 'There will be a huge temptation on the part of Liberals – and especially Martin and his supporters – to simply forget a struggle that was a fascinating and important all-but-inevitable ingredient of his success.'[5]

Instead, the Martin Liberals ignored the basic principles that had stood the party in good stead for so long. No attempt was made to reconcile defeated leadership opponents, and one – Sheila Copps – was effectively hounded out of public life. Martin's first cabinet saw twenty-two former Chrétien ministers replaced with his own leadership supporters. In the run-up to the June 2004 election, a record number of sitting Liberal MPs either resigned or lost nomination battles to challenges by Martin supporters. The national media began to speak of an apparent Martin 'vendetta' against any Liberals who had supported Jean Chrétien or failed to actively support Martin, a vendetta which seemed to continue throughout Martin's eighteen-month tenure as prime minister.

The Martin Liberals' rapid fall from grace, turning majority into minority in the 2004 election and then losing power in early 2006, was punctuated by repeated public displays of internal party dissent. Within days of the party's return to the opposition wilderness, Martin had resigned, after spending barely two years in the position he had sought for nearly twenty.

Any notion the Martin-Chrétien feud would die with the departure from public life of the two principals was soon proven wrong. The 2006 leadership race to succeed Martin provided ample evidence of the ongoing feud and its consequences for party unity. For many Liberals, even the unexpected outcome of that race was seen as the result of the ongoing internal divisions.

Since then, the Liberals have spent nearly four years unsuccessfully trying to restore their image as the natural governing party. The party under Stéphane Dion and Michael Ignatieff has struggled to regroup and reunite. There is little evidence these efforts have been successful. Recurring public criticism of the leader from within, and especially from the Quebec wing of the party, has been reinforced by the party's ongoing financial and organizational woes, failure to recruit strong candidates, and unexpectedly poor showing in a series of by-elections. Like the Turner Liberals in 1984, today's Liberal caucus regularly appears to be marching to a different drummer. In several respects, the Liberal Party in 2010 appears less united than it was twenty-five years ago. Indeed, Canadians could be forgiven for thinking the 'new normal' for Liberals has become the legendary divisive and self-destructive behaviour of the old Progressive Conservative Party. This situation is all the more remarkable since the Harper Conservatives' hold on power is based on a slim minority, not the overwhelming majority of Brian Mulroney, and the Liberals' return to power is theoretically possible at any time.

How could this have happened to the once mighty Liberal Party? Conventional wisdom attributes these extraordinary developments to little more than the frustrated ambitions of one man, Paul Martin Jr. Convention also assumes the Liberals' internal party conflict originated only since 2000 or, at most, with Martin's defeat at the hands of Jean Chrétien in the 1990 leadership race. This interpretation is superficial and misleading, failing as it does to identify the important issues underpinning the conflict, and its much earlier origins.

The roots of the party's internecine warfare can be traced to John Turner's sharp differences of opinion with Pierre Trudeau, to Turner's eventual victory over Jean Chrétien in the 1984 Liberal leadership, and to the subsequent election of a Conservative government led by Brian Mulroney later that year. While personalities and ambition clearly played a significant role in the evolution of the party's internal conflict, starkly differing views on key policy issues have made it more than personal, more enduring, and much harder to resolve.

As this book demonstrates, Prime Minister Mulroney's introduction of the Meech Lake Accord triggered a chain of events that contributed directly to the party's current state of disunity, creating an entirely new and deep-rooted division among Liberals about the nature of Canadian federalism. Indeed, over the past twenty-five years the federalist cleavage has become a dominant if largely unrecognized characteristic of the Liberal Party, affecting both its leadership and its rank-and-file members. It is now arguably as important as the traditional left-right cleavage between 'social' and 'business' Liberals. For all intents and purposes the emergence of this new cross-cutting cleavage along the federalism axis uniquely defines the Liberals' history over the past twenty-five years, greatly increasing the challenge to party unity.

The new federalist cleavage unquestionably heightened the Chrétien-Martin leadership dispute. Supporters of John Turner – the party's original Meech Lake defender – formed the basis of Meech Lake proponent Paul Martin's early leadership campaign, just as it was Jean Chrétien's opposition to Meech Lake that ultimately secured his first-round victory in the race.

The ongoing connection between the Turner and Martin camps can be found in both the parliamentary and volunteer wings of the party. It was symbolized by John Turner's presence at Paul Martin's side at the November 2003 leadership convention and reinforced by Martin's highly controversial selection of former Turner enforcer Jean Lapierre as his Quebec lieutenant.

Both Turner and Martin also championed the modernization and 'democratization' of party operations, in sharp contrast to the more traditional top-down, laissez-faire views of Jean Chrétien. Significantly, this difference of opinion was also mirrored among their supporters and served to reinforce the conflict throughout two decades of debate on internal party reform.

Oddly, while the link between Trudeau and Chrétien supporters in the Liberal Party has been widely recognized, the close ties between supporters of John Turner and Paul Martin is not nearly as well-known outside the party. Yet, as this study reveals, their interrelationship constitutes an equally defining characteristic of the past two decades.

It is difficult to overstate the importance of the party's ongoing divisions and the damage caused by two decades of internecine warfare that has dominated the party's agenda. Moreover, the acceptance by many Liberals of the conventional explanation for their troubles has prevented them from correctly identifying and addressing the underlying causes. One of the most important consequences of the party's preoccupation with its internal schism has been its inability to renew its broad policy directions and organization. Another has been the profoundly negative impact on the party's traditional image of competence and the loss of its status as the party of national unity.

Finally, the inability of the party's leadership to overcome these divisions in the broader interests of the party suggests the discipline of power may be losing its relevance in a party that has become both more ideologically diverse and less accustomed to following the lead of its elites. Indeed, there is mounting evidence that these internal divisions are becoming intractable. Unresolved, they may well pose a more serious challenge to the Liberal Party's continued dominance of the Canadian political scene than any it has faced in the past.

1 Into the Wilderness

We knew then that there was more at stake than the survival of the party. We were really in a battle to preserve a world view – to keep alive a moderate, progressive voice in Canadian politics.

– Hon. Brian Tobin[1]

Within days of the September 1984 election that handed the Liberal Party its most humiliating defeat ever, the media began discussing the end of John Turner's leadership. Within weeks the speculation had turned to the possible demise of the party itself.

The Liberals had been reduced to 40 seats from 147. Incredibly, they held only ten seats more than the NDP. They barely retained a toehold in their longtime fortress of Quebec and were virtually wiped off the electoral map in western Canada. One analyst after another began to say publicly what many were thinking privately. Could this be the end of the 'natural governing party' that had dominated Canadian politics throughout the twentieth century? Had a realignment of popular support taken place, allowing the Conservatives to assume the reins of power for the foreseeable future? Would the Liberals be relegated to the ranks of third parties and regional rumps? Or might the party disappear entirely? As Brian Tobin later recalled, 'we all heard (NDP leader) Ed Broadbent declare the Liberal Party in Canada was about to disappear the way it had in Britain, that there was no place for a mushy middle any more, you were either on the left or the right and that was it.'[2]

It was in this context that a small group of the party's elite met in Ottawa shortly after the election to regroup. Fighting down panic, stunned and shell-shocked, the walking wounded of the disastrous Liberal campaign converged to devise an immediate plan for rebuilding the party. The sheer magnitude of their challenge was not lost on them. As one of the key players, Sudbury MP Doug Frith, ruefully recalled, 'We knew exactly what the task was.'[3] What they did not know was whether it could be achieved. With the party deeply in debt, lacking MPs with opposition experience, and severely constrained by involuntary reductions in staff and operating budgets, the task facing the Liberal Party appeared overwhelming.

When John Turner was selected to succeed Pierre Trudeau as the next party leader in June 1984, victory had once again seemed possible despite public opinion polls warning that voters could be ready for a change. Many of those gathering in Ottawa in the fall of 1984 were still asking themselves what had gone wrong. Others, only too well aware of the endless problems that plagued the campaign, were nevertheless shocked that this had happened to the Liberal Party. For all of them, the excitement and optimism of the leadership convention just a few months earlier now seemed a distant memory.

The June 1984 Leadership Convention

The race to succeed Pierre Trudeau began in earnest in February 1984, when he formally announced he would be stepping down as party leader. As in earlier campaigns, there was no lack of candidates. Unlike the previous two leadership contests, however, no 'outside' candidate emerged to throw his or her hat into the ring. Trudeau himself had come from outside the party establishment, a last-minute entry whose reluctance to seek the leadership has been well documented elsewhere.[4] So had Lester Pearson, a former bureaucrat who was finally persuaded by Louis St Laurent to leave the public service to become his minister of external affairs and shortly thereafter to run for the leadership. In one of the ironies of public life, both Pearson in 1958 and Trudeau ten years later had defeated the same 'inside' or establishment candidate, Paul Martin Senior.

By contrast, in 1984 the list of candidates for the Liberal leadership contained only one name outside the existing cabinet, and he was far from an outsider. John Turner was the complete 'party man,' a Young Liberal who had first entered politics in 1962. A losing candidate in the 1968 leadership race that selected Trudeau, he had served as Trudeau's finance minister until he left politics in 1975. Ostensibly his departure from government and public life was motivated by a desire to devote his attention to making money and raising his family in Toronto. Within Liberal circles, however, Turner's philosophical disagreement with Trudeau over the party's increasingly centre-left direction, lack of accommodation of 'business Liberals,' and strong federalist views was well known.

Despite this, Turner had been considered the heir apparent for more than a decade. Most believed his perceived 'star' quality would ensure another Liberal victory regardless of his differences with mainstream party thinking. He would be seen by Canadians as a fresh new face or, in fact, as an outsider. Turner himself was not so sure this was sufficient. When he first was approached by some party organizers to run for the leadership in 1979, during the brief Clark interregnum, he declined because he was convinced 'no one could turn this one around.'[5]

Turner hesitated again in 1984 while his closest supporters put together a 'Team Turner' group to test the waters. They included Bill Lee, a wealthy Toronto consultant who had dropped out of political life after the 1972 federal campaign, and John Swift, a well-regarded Vancouver lawyer and former ministerial assistant to Turner at Finance. Turner was finally persuaded by the team that he would win if he ran, but he needed to make a commitment to run in order for them to begin organizing. Finally he agreed to announce his candidacy on 16 March. In the meantime Lee recruited Stephen LeDrew, an executive with Manulife Insurance, as the campaign's tour director, and Heather Peterson, the wife of Toronto MP Jim Peterson, as campaign chair.

Although his decision to run for the leadership in 1984 was taken somewhat reluctantly, neither Turner nor his supporters thought the party was heading for certain defeat. His victory in the leadership, once he decided to run, seemed inevitable. From the beginning, however, Turner was a victim of overly high expectations. His almost legendary image as the charismatic, intelligent, and sophisticated pretender to the throne likely could not have remained intact throughout the leadership race under any circumstances. But his lengthy absence from the political arena made it all but certain he would disappoint. Any faults or hesitations would be highlighted. When coupled with his lack of experience and aptitude for television, which in his absence had become the primary medium for political communication, his air of invincibility began to crumble rapidly. On more than one occasion he was captured by the media looking more like a deer in the headlights than the next leader of the governing party.

These developments did not go unnoticed by his only serious rival for the leadership, Jean Chrétien. Trudeau's former justice minister had become a household name in Canada after his work on the 1982 constitutional amendment negotiations. He felt he could parlay that recognition into a successful bid for the leadership despite Turner's presumed lead. Nevertheless Chrétien originally hesitated to enter the race until Trudeau told the caucus the party's practice of alternating the leadership between English and French Canadians was not a hard-and-fast rule, as long as candidates were fluently bilingual. Trudeau had stated from the outset that he would follow the example of his predecessor, Lester Pearson, allowing the party to pick his successor without any intervention or indication of preference on his part. But his dislike of Turner was well known, and many assumed Chrétien was his personal choice. (At least two former ministers who were known to be supporting Turner have since confided that Trudeau approached them personally and asked them to 'think carefully' about their choice, although he did not suggest any alternative candidate.)

Much to his chagrin, Chrétien watched as most of the cabinet and caucus declared their support for Turner shortly after his 16 March announcement. Some feared their failure to jump on the bandwagon early in the race would affect their career paths. Others had specific reasons for not supporting Chrétien. Marc Lalonde, for example, later explained that he believed the alternating rule was still very important for the party, and it was clearly the turn of an anglophone.[6] In the end, only three cabinet ministers supported Chrétien – David Collenette, Charles Caccia, and Roméo LeBlanc.[7] None of his Quebec colleagues in cabinet supported him, an even more painful revelation. Chrétien was particularly wounded by the decision of André Ouellet to change sides and in the end support Turner. Two of the younger up-and-coming caucus members who signed on quickly for Turner, Doug Frith and Jean Lapierre, co-chaired the Youth for Turner campaign, which proved an important factor in his ultimate victory, while cabinet ministers such as David Smith and Ed Lumley organized provincial campaigns.

When Chrétien did decide to take the plunge, he told key supporters Turner was overrated. 'I *know* the man,' he said. As he later recounted in his memoirs, Turner's opening statement on 16 March convinced the staunch defender of the Trudeau vision that he was right. The conference had revealed a man nervous and ill at ease with the media, out of practice and out of touch. More important, it revealed Turner was 'vulnerable' in three areas Chrétien believed he could exploit during the campaign: 'he wanted nothing to do with Trudeau; he wanted to move the Liberal Party to the right; he wanted to woo the west by being soft on bilingualism.' Of these, Chrétien felt the third point was the most important, particularly in Quebec, where he was at the time running far behind Turner.[8] Trudeau's mistrust of Turner on the Quebec file was well known, and was epitomized during the FLQ crisis.

Although events later proved Chrétien right on all three counts, it was the third area that caused Turner the most difficulty during the campaign. In fact, the leadership race provided the first and most striking snapshot of the extent to which policies relating to federalism had come to be seen as more important to many Liberals than the traditional left-right struggle between 'social' and 'business' Liberals. Unfortunately for Chrétien, the campaign would also reveal that the desire to win at all costs was even more compelling.

Having barely concealed his disapproval of the Trudeau agenda in recent years, Turner believed he could offer the party electoral success by returning it to what he saw as its legitimate roots in the St Laurent era. With social programs already in place, he felt the emphasis needed to be returned to the economy. His speeches focused on ways to achieve international competitiveness, technological change, and economic growth. In one of his earliest interviews he even mused about the need to reduce the deficit by half, something no other candidate including Donald Johnston, another business Liberal, had raised.[9]

But Turner quickly learned that the party he left in 1975 had shifted along with the leader. The Trudeau vision of liberalism, and Canada, was now deeply entrenched in much of the caucus as well as the extra-parliamentary wing. Whenever Turner tried to distance himself from that vision, particularly on the issues of bilingualism and federalism, he immediately faced stiff resistance. Indeed, the party grassroots demonstrated repeatedly throughout the campaign that they were not at ease with much of Turner's policy direction. Instead, the delegates' enthusiasm was reserved primarily for the positions outlined by Jean Chrétien in the series of policy workshops leading up to the convention vote.

The extent to which Turner's right-wing policies were out of sync with many of his own supporters was well known. Yet Turner's apparent plan to shift the party to the right did not affect his support in cabinet and caucus, who were the automatic or ex officio delegates that made up one-third of all convention delegates. Indeed, among the early arrivals in the Turner camp were two of the most left-wing members of cabinet, Windsor area MP Herb Gray and Manitoba MP Lloyd Axworthy. Axworthy, for one, jokingly told several colleagues that Turner was 'more of a Tory than Brian Mulroney.'[10] Although Axworthy's support was explained by the fact he had once served as Turner's executive assistant, the rationale for Gray's decision remained a mystery for some time. It was only several years later that Senator Keith Davey recounted how he had decided to support Turner because he would win, and then recruited reluctant left-wing caucus members by convincing them they could keep Turner 'honest' on policy issues only if they had his gratitude. As Davey admitted in 1987, 'it was the worst political mistake I ever made in my life.'[11]

At the end of the day, however, the public opinion polls suggesting Turner could beat Mulroney were a key factor in the decisions of many in the caucus, despite their unease about Turner's policies. Even the campaign slogan emblazoned on the candidate's buttons – 'Win with Turner' – made this point unabashedly. As one party official said, 'two-thirds of Turner's support was based on his presumed electability, and only a third on his policy direction.'[12]

Yet, while the left-right split was apparently a joking matter, Turner's 'unorthodox' views on federalism – less well known to many in caucus and the party at the start of the campaign – proved to be a real concern. Nowhere was this disconnect more clearly demonstrated than on the Manitoba minority-language issue. Turner ran into trouble during the press conference announcing his intention to seek the leadership. When asked his views on an all-party parliamentary resolution promoting an agreement between the Manitoba government and the province's francophone minority, Turner appeared to waffle. Worse still, he seemed to suggest the protection of official language minorities was not a matter for federal leadership. 'On the Manitoba question,' he said, 'I support the spirit of the resolution, but I think that we have to recognize what is at stake here is a provincial initiative, and that a solution will have to be provincial ... I would also hope it would be resolved by the political process and not judicial review.' When he repeated this statement several times over the next few days on national television it became clear to many in the party that this was not a miscue.

The problem of Turner's ambivalence towards the Trudeau vision surfaced again on 11 April during a press scrum in Montreal when he replied to one reporter's question about Bill 101, Quebec's language charter. Asked in French if he approved of the bill's draconian restrictions on the use of English in the province, he replied 'en principe, oui.'

He later claimed he had been misinterpreted and his answer taken out of context – that he was making a distinction between rights and the provision of services – but in the end a full retreat to the existing party line was necessary to bring the matter to a close.

Certainly Turner could be seen as a victim of wishful thinking. Many supporters who considered him the party's best hope for victory against the Conservatives and their new leader, Brian Mulroney, simply refused to acknowledge that his position on as crucial an issue as federalism might not fit with the party's established views. Others believed the difference was more apparent than real. 'This was a leadership race. You have to make some effort to distinguish yourself from your opponents and your predecessor. It's normal. It doesn't mean a great deal,' one of Turner's cabinet supporters commented. Another supporter, Finance Minister Marc Lalonde, also indicated he was not concerned, primarily because he felt that 'the reality of governing' would automatically constrain some of Turner's initial inclinations. Perhaps more important, Lalonde said neither he nor anyone else in the Liberal Party expected the issue of the constitution to be raised again for at least a decade. 'We had just spent more than two years on that, and it was extremely intense. It seemed obvious that no one in their right mind would re-open the question.'[13]

Nevertheless, winning the leadership did prove to be more challenging for Turner than many of his supporters had first thought, particularly as his leadership campaign endured one miscue after another and revealed an organization that was badly lacking. According to party officials, Turner's victory was due principally to the support of the nearly 1,000 ex officio delegates, where he had led Chrétien by a three-to-one margin. Another key factor in his victory was the overwhelming support of the youth wing of the party, who had been captivated by his promise of 'no elites, no rainmakers' and a commitment to open up the party and the policy process to grassroots party members. Yet among ordinary riding delegates, who constituted roughly two-thirds of the total, the vote had been almost equally split.[14] Nevertheless John Turner's victory over Jean Chrétien was numerically convincing. With a lead of more than 500 votes after the first ballot, victory on the second ballot was virtually assured. Liberals in the end had shown they wanted to win above all else.

For the party that prided itself on its 'discipline of power' – its ability to close ranks behind the leader, put the party ahead of the individual, and above all never air its dirty laundry in public – there were few disquieting indications that all might not be well. No one seriously believed Trudeau's determinedly arm's-length handshake with the new leader, or party president Iona Campagnolo's 'first in our hearts' comment about the runner-up, were more than fleeting glimpses of personal pique. Once the leadership was decided, the task for all good Liberals was to close ranks behind the new leader as they had always done in the past. The task for the leader was also straightforward. It was up to John Turner to heal the divisions, put his stamp on the party, call an election, and win another term in office for the natural governing party.

Transition and the Turner Cabinet

John Turner was nothing if not a party man. Steeped in the traditions of the party, he knew that new leaders always accommodated their unsuccessful opponents in one way or another to ensure party unity. He himself had been made a cabinet minister by Trudeau after losing the 1968 leadership race to him. And so, shortly after the 16 June convention, he met for the first time with Jean Chrétien, the man who not only had finished a strong second but clearly continued to have a deep and loyal following within the party. Turner knew he needed to strike a deal with Chrétien before assuming office on 30 June in order to plan his cabinet.

Although their accounts of events over the next few weeks differ slightly, they concur on all important aspects. Turner offered Chrétien the position of deputy prime minister and any cabinet post of his choosing. Chrétien asked in addition to be Quebec lieutenant, for him the key political post, and also for ten of his supporters to be in Turner's cabinet. Turner delayed his decision for some time as he attempted to square the circle in terms of conflicting objectives. André Ouellet, his leading Quebec supporter, was expecting to be the Quebec lieutenant. Although Turner claimed he had not made specific promises, others who had supported him during the leadership were also expecting to be in his new cabinet. In fact, more people had ministerial ambitions than the total number in the old Trudeau cabinet. At the same time, Turner's managerial instincts led him to conclude the new cabinet should actually be much smaller. He had already agreed on this with his new principal secretary, John Swift, who had been persuaded to stay on in Ottawa. Instead of thirty-seven, they decided the new cabinet would be only twenty-seven to twenty-nine strong. It would also have many new faces to demonstrate Turner was putting his own stamp on the party.

This perceived need for the appearance of change, which Turner played up during the leadership race by reminding everyone he had been out of politics for nine years, was also motivated by the public opinion polls demonstrating some of the Liberal 'old guard' were a definite electoral liability. With that in mind, Turner accepted only three of Chrétien's ten nominees – Charles Caccia, John Roberts, and David Collenette – all of whom had been in Trudeau's cabinet. Chrétien himself was offered minister of external affairs. As for Quebec, Turner's solution was a hopelessly unworkable troika consisting of Ouellet, Chrétien, and Charles Lapointe, a Chrétien supporter. While neither Chrétien nor Turner was happy with the arrangement, they at least had reached an agreement that would allow the new leader to complete his cabinet appointments. However, Turner's difficulties did not end there. The concessions to Chrétien had limited his room to manoeuvre, but the new leader made matters worse by opting to keep several other Trudeau-era ministers as well. One very surprising appointment was Marc Lalonde in Finance. The former Trudeau finance minister had already announced he was not planning to run for re-election. He was also one of the most prominent of the old guard that Turner had promised to replace. But as Lalonde later recounted, he was asked to stay on precisely because he was not planning to run again, and also because of Turner's belief that he needed continuity in that important cabinet post, in the event he decided to wait until the fall or later to call an election.[15] As a result of these decisions, Turner found himself forced to disappoint loyal supporters, who were livid at failing to make the cut. These included Quebec MPs Pierre Deniger, Dennis Dawson, and Rémi Bujold, all of whom were long-standing Turner acolytes. In the end the new cabinet contained twenty-nine ministers but only five were newcomers. Two of these, MPs Doug Frith of Sudbury and Jean Lapierre of Montreal, were only added at the last minute at the insistence of John Payne and Bill Lee, who was furious with the list Turner showed him just days before the 30 June transition.[16]

This failure to reward some of his biggest supporters and his surprising decision to keep so many Trudeau ministers angered many of Turner's advisers. Some had agreed to work for him not only out of friendship but because of a genuine dislike for the Trudeau regime and policies. Although they constituted a small minority within the party, their convictions were strong and their dislike of the old guard ran deep. For them, Turner's promise that there would be 'no elites, no rainmakers' was far from idle campaign rhetoric. Meanwhile Tory leader Brian Mulroney was delighted with the composition of the new cabinet, sensing a partisan political advantage. As he remarked on 30 June, when Turner was sworn in at Rideau Hall as the twenty-third prime minister along with his new cabinet, 'What has happened is the old bunch went out one door and came right back in the other.'[17]

Turner's Problematic PMO

Yet for all Turner's problems in forming a cabinet, they paled in comparison with the political crisis he faced over the large number of patronage appointments planned by Pierre Trudeau before his departure. Here again, however, Turner added to his own difficulties. Accounts vary on details, but virtually everyone agrees Trudeau offered to make all of the appointments himself before departing. But Turner hesitated repeatedly to accept this offer, worried the departure of so many MPs would leave him with a minority government and might impair his ability to call an election when he chose. The strained relations between the two men were painfully evident in the way the issue was handled. Negotiations were carried out at arm's length through their intermediaries, John Swift and Tom Axworthy. Finally, after changing his mind several times, Turner decided to make the appointments himself after taking office, in order to guarantee there would be no constitutional problem. At this point Trudeau insisted on a signed letter from Turner promising to make the appointments before calling an election. During the election campaign that followed it became all too apparent that Turner's chosen approach was a political blunder. At the time, though, he was preoccupied on other issues that needed to be resolved before the 30 June transition, including the staffing of his office. The staff of the prime minister's office (PMO) are not public servants but political appointees. At the senior level they are also the personal appointments of the prime minister of the day, and are expected to change when he or she is replaced. As a result not only Tom Axworthy, Trudeau's principal secretary, but all the senior staff in the Trudeau PMO had left their offices in the Langevin Block after the leadership convention in anticipation of the changeover. However, the Turner team was determined to make a clean sweep. This resulted in the subsequent firing or voluntary departure of virtually everyone who was left, no matter how junior. This pattern was repeated at the party headquarters and marked the beginning of a new era in which, at the staff level, leadership victories would mean not only massive turnovers but the build-up of internal cliques with grudges, vested interests, and long memories.

As he later recounted, John Swift had thought replacements for PMO personnel would emerge out of the leadership campaign, but they did not. Instead, most of the senior staff from Turner's campaign had no interest in working in Ottawa once their candidate was elected, and Swift found himself with no staff to run either the government or the next election. Swift, an intellectual with a philosophical bent, was more at home in policy debates than in the backrooms of the party. He recognized they would need to locate some experienced campaign personnel but admitted he was unable to focus on the problem in depth while dealing with so many other transition issues.[18]

The magnitude of their problem only became evident on 30 June, when Bill Lee, whom Turner had finally persuaded to run the election campaign, visited the Liberal Party's national office at 102 Bank Street. Lee discovered a mere shell operation involving five or six employees and a photocopy machine. His immediate question was how to run an election campaign. A more deeply rooted question was how the Liberal Party had managed to coast to electoral victories for the last twenty years without any organization. A partial answer came from Tom Axworthy, who told Lee that he and his staff had been planning to run the election campaign out of the PMO as they had done in the past, assuming Trudeau had decided to stay and seek another term. As usual, they had compiled several massive binders assigning the responsibilities of various PMO staffers during the campaign. Unfortunately most of those staff were now gone, and there was no national party organization to pick up the pieces.

Timing of the Election Call

In parliamentary systems the timing of an election call has traditionally been the prerogative of the prime minister.[19] Typically, a wide variety of factors influence the decision. Consultations with cabinet ministers and caucus, discussions with campaign committee members about the state of readiness of the party organization, polling data on the party's level of support, and even the dates of important upcoming events can all play a part in determining the most advantageous timing of an election for the party in power.

As many of those present have since recounted, there was considerable enthusiasm for a summer election call within the cabinet and caucus. At the first meeting of the full cabinet in early July, only Jean Chrétien and Doug Frith counselled against dropping the writ so soon. Turner himself was initially ambivalent. On the one hand, as a deeply committed proponent of Parliament, he believed it was important to seek a mandate to govern. On the other hand, he worried it would be politically unwise to cancel a planned visit of the Queen in mid-July.

While these initial concerns were important, they were soon supplanted by others. Among the most important was a briefing Turner received from Finance Department officials. Although the economy at the time was reasonably buoyant, Turner later claimed the officials forecast a sizeable increase in the deficit in the second half of the year, which in his view would necessitate either program cuts or a tax increase. It would also lead to higher interest rates and unemployment levels. None of these was something he wanted to contemplate heading into an election in the fall, leading him to prefer an earlier vote.

Polling data were inconclusive, with some surveys giving the Liberals an eleven-point lead and others indicating the Tories were pulling even. Given the extensive media coverage of the party's leadership race, there was also reason to wonder whether the Liberal lead might be a temporary bounce that would quickly disappear once an election was called.

The one person who wanted to delay the election as long as possible was Bill Lee, the reluctant campaign director who was clearly aghast at the lack of organization, funding, and personnel. In a lengthy memo to the new PM in early July, Lee outlined at least eight reasons why the election call should not come before September and preferably November, although he was not opposed to a delay until the spring of 1985 if necessary. In addition to his concerns about soft polls and the negative impact of cancelling the Queen's visit, these reasons included: a lack of new or 'star' candidates (which the leader had been trying unsuccessfully to recruit) and the fact that very few candidates had been nominated; the lack of a platform; the lack of funds and the very poor state of organizational readiness of the party (to say nothing of the enormous head start of the other parties); the exhaustion of the leader and his leadership campaign team; and, lastly, the deep divisions within the party as a result of the leadership, which had yet to heal.[20]

Despite Lee's serious and ultimately well-founded concerns, Turner flew to London to arrange for a delay in the Queen's visit, returning on

8 July to meet with his inner circle and inform them of his decision to call the election not merely soon, but immediately.

The Campaign Organization

Conventional wisdom argues opposition parties do not win elections, governments lose them. If more proof of this axiom were needed, the 1984 federal election could be held up as a case in point. As *Globe and Mail* columnist Jeffrey Simpson wrote in his post-mortem on the election, 'Seldom if ever in Canadian political history has a major political party conducted a campaign of such sustained ineptitude.'[21]

The chaos began before the writ was dropped, when Turner backtracked on a commitment to Lee concerning the appointment of the three campaign co-chairs, positions traditionally drawn from senior caucus members or party officials. Lee had insisted on new faces and a west-east representation as well as gender balance. His choices – Manitoba Liberal Izzy Asper for the west, newly appointed cabinet minister Doug Frith for Ontario, and Lise St Martin Tremblay, vice-president of the Quebec wing of the party – were told of their roles several days before the announcement of the election call and had already informally begun to organize. With Turner's decision to drop the writ, they were expected to travel to Ottawa for a formal press conference with him on 9 July. However, Turner indicated to Lee on 8 July that he had already agreed to let Marc Lalonde organize Quebec as he had done in the past for Trudeau. This meant St Martin Tremblay was unceremoniously dumped. The Quebec change in turn forced Lee to replace Doug Frith with a woman, cabinet minister Judy Erola, at the eleventh hour. As Frith recounted afterwards, he was literally on his way to the press conference in Ottawa, having flown in from Sudbury, when Lee finally managed to reach him and tell him that he was no longer a co-chair.[22]

Then there were Lee's own controversial decisions. Among these was the change in party pollster from the long-serving Martin Goldfarb in Toronto to Angus Reid of Winnipeg. He also brought in former leadership campaign staff, including Stephen LeDrew to serve as Tour Director, despite the fact many Liberals felt Turner's leadership campaign had been successful in spite of its poor organization.

On the policy front Lee's decision to bypass the party policy director was equally surprising, particularly given the lack of material available from PMO. As co-chair Marc Lalonde later recalled, he was reduced to providing material on his own and distributing it widely to fill the void.[23] For his part John Swift was increasingly concerned that a 'counterbalance' was required in the PMO for the structures Lee was putting in place at the party office. He hired former party director Torrance Wylie to work in PMO and 'liaise' with Lee, and instructed LeDrew to report to Swift rather than Lee, actions which took Lee by surprise and led, inevitably, to misunderstandings and failed communications.

Most surprising of all to Lee and his small band of organizers was Turner's announcement he would not campaign nationally until August. It was the first of many poor political decisions that added to the disarray of the Liberal campaign. Having been out of public life for nine years, the new leader also needed to choose a riding and win a seat in Parliament for himself. Turner told Lee he was planning to run in Vancouver Quadra, where John Swift was president of the riding association. Yet for the first half of the election Turner devoted little time to this aspect of the campaign, mistakenly assuming Swift would somehow have matters in hand. Of course these decisions might have held less significance if the vaunted Liberal machine had been tuned and ready to go, but, as Lee had attempted to make clear to everyone, there was no machine at all.

The 1984 Election Campaign

In many respects the 1984 campaign was a watershed in Canadian politics. One of the most striking revelations concerned the legendary organizational prowess of the Liberal Party, which proved to be more myth than reality. As Lee had discovered earlier, this was partly due to the fact Tom Axworthy and other advisers had intended to run the national campaign from PMO if Trudeau remained as leader. This reliance on PMO, in turn, confirmed for Lee and other Turner supporters, as well as Turner himself, that they had been right all along in objecting to the limited role of the party's extra-parliamentary wing during the Trudeau years. For them, the exclusion of the party's national office from the platform process and other preparations for the election – to say nothing of the elected party officials – was simply unacceptable.

After the election Turner claimed that 'although he had realized the Liberal Party organization had been allowed to wither, he had never fully appreciated the extent of the atrophy.'[24] Yet it should hardly have come as a surprise. Pierre Trudeau had admitted from the beginning that he was not a party man. He knew few party activists and nothing of the financial and organizational side of the party's operations.

His interests in the political process lay elsewhere. Once in power he had introduced important changes to the Elections Act to limit campaign spending and ensure greater transparency and accountability in the funding of political parties. These efforts, along with changes to the nomination process and voting procedures, were designed to encourage the participatory democracy he considered so important. In the same vein he had attempted to broaden the party's base by promoting policy conferences and by establishing regional 'desks' in the PMO. Indeed, he spoke on more than one occasion of his desire to make the Liberal Party a 'mass party' full of diverse interests and dissidents.[25]

At the same time Trudeau had spent little time cultivating party activists or working with the elected leadership of the extra-parliamentary wing. Instead those functions were handled by advisers in his office and caucus, such as Jim Coutts, Keith Davey, and Marc Lalonde. For some Liberals this lack of interest in the party on the prime minister's part was made worse by the perceived authoritarian approach of these advisers, who over the years came to be known as the 'old guard' so despised by the Turner organizers.

Nevertheless the party had won four elections with Trudeau at the helm. Many reasons have been put forward for this stunning string of electoral successes, but a few are of particular relevance to the 1984 situation. First and foremost, the federal structure of the party meant that organizers at the provincial and constituency level, many of whom had been in place for twenty years, were well equipped to handle much of the campaign with minimal direction from the national level. This was particularly the case since, as the governing party, the bulk of the Liberal campaign would be spent defending the government's record rather than advancing an entirely new platform. Similarly Trudeau's position on important issues was already well known to Liberal candidates and in fact to the public. Trudeau himself was a highly popular leader for much of that time. In short, the prime minister carried the national campaign rather than the other way around.

Unfortunately for John Turner, virtually none of those factors was useful to him in the 1984 campaign. As media coverage during the election outlined in painful detail, his attempts to distance himself from the Trudeau era meant that he could not use the Trudeau legacy as his policy position. Yet his reappointment of so many Trudeau-era ministers and his difficulties with the patronage appointments meant he would also have trouble positioning himself as a new face and an outsider. Nor did he have a well-developed set of ideas from the leadership campaign which he easily could convert to a platform, and some of his most well-developed ideas were counterproductive for a Liberal victory. Most troubling of all was the fact that Turner himself remained an unknown quantity for most voters.

The Liberals' Technical Deficit

Another noteworthy aspect of the 1984 campaign was the degree of technological advantage held by the Conservatives, who were ahead of the Liberals in every respect. As Dalton Camp recounted, 'to step from the Liberals' headquarters to Norm's offices in Ottawa was to step from the horse-and-buggy age into a jet aircraft factory.'[26]

Campaign director Norm Atkins had made good use of the huge Conservative war chest, introducing a state-of-the-art computer system which allowed him to communicate policies or strategy to almost all of the riding associations across the country. The same computer system allowed him to raise funds or rally the troops by providing the wherewithal to create a national membership list.[27] Most important, it allowed for centralized control of the whole campaign.

Along with Atkins the most important person in the Conservatives' national campaign was pollster Allan Gregg of Decima Research. It was Gregg's interpretation of the data that was driving the material Atkins was putting on line. As Gregg later told one journalist, 'Norman relied very, very heavily on the numbers. At the risk of immodesty the research *was* the strategy.'[28] Also noteworthy is the fact that both Atkins and Gregg had been persona non grata in the party, in Atkins's case for decades. Nevertheless Mulroney overcame his personal credo of 'never forget, never forgive' in order to ensure the party had access to the most competent support it could attract.

Gregg's numbers showed the public was ready for change, but change in the *process* rather than the content of government. Less confrontation and more transparency, not new directions in policy, were what the Canadian electorate had in mind. More important, at the start of the campaign Gregg's numbers showed many Canadians were 'rooting' for John Turner as an ideal combination of change and continuity, largely because they did not 'trust' Brian Mulroney.[29]

In the Liberal camp, however, the public desire for change was being interpreted quite differently by Turner and his advisers, allowing Turner to follow his instincts and virtually disown the Trudeau legacy. Pollster Angus Reid's post-mortem concluded: 'In the early weeks of the election campaign the Liberal Party was "mis-positioned" because it appeared to have kept the management and changed the policy.'[30]

Apart from Marc Lalonde, who argued the Liberals could have won if they had run a different campaign, very few Liberals believed Turner could have beaten the sleek and sophisticated Tory machine or its sleek and wily leader. But almost everyone agreed the heir apparent to the Liberal throne was personally responsible for the magnitude of their defeat. Some blamed him for up to sixty seats.

The Liberal Meltdown

Even more serious was the fact that the Liberal campaign had managed to alienate almost every element of the coalition built by Trudeau, from women and francophones to low-income earners and immigrants. These voters, confused and worried, were beginning to look to the NDP to fill the void left by the disappearance of the Liberal Party they had known. At this point one of Turner's close friends who had been active in the Trudeau years as well, Senator Jerry Grafstein, wrote a confidential memo to the leader arguing that this strategy was a recipe for disaster. The memo, parts of which later appeared in *Maclean's*, warned Turner against sending the wrong signal to the various elements of the Trudeau coalition by moving to the right. But the memo reserved its harshest criticism for the leader's handling of Quebec and federalism, accusing him of being a 'flamethrower' for provincial rights. It concluded: '*Of more importance* to us both, the Liberal Party will pay a price if we allow our support to erode ... in Quebec. Quebec has stood by the Liberal Party because we stood by Quebec.' Grafstein concluded by warning Turner that Mulroney would 'step into Trudeau's shoes' if he were not careful.[31]

Grafstein's warning was prescient. Within the first week of the campaign the Liberals suffered a huge loss in support among the soft or 'leaning' voters, and their campaign went steadily downhill from there. With Brian Mulroney somehow appearing to be to the left of the Liberals, and taking a proactive position on language rights in Quebec which contrasted sharply with Turner's waffling, yet also playing on the sympathies of Quebec nationalists, the beginnings of a Conservative landslide could be detected in the polling data. As one caucus insider put it, 'we were in free fall at the end of the campaign' and 'if the election had gone on for another week we would have been wiped out entirely.'[32]

The halfway point in the campaign saw the Liberal organization come apart at the seams. Many members of Team Turner were not speaking to each other. By then there were literally two sets of advisers – one in PMO under Swift and one at the national headquarters under Lee – offering two sets of binders to the leader and two conflicting sets of advice on everything. There were even two pollsters. At the constituency level things were worse. In some ridings lawn signs had not yet been erected. Others had only just nominated candidates, and none of them had received material from the national headquarters. With their leader's personal popularity now in a nosedive, the earlier campaign decision to abandon the traditional party logo in favour of a personalized 'Turner-centred' logo meant some candidates were unwilling to use the material even when it did arrive. Many Liberal candidates who won their seats against the Conservative tidal wave later mentioned that they had refused to use the new signage. They included two of the most successful and politically astute campaigners the party had produced. 'I used my material from 1980,' said longtime Davenport MP Charles Caccia. Newcomer Don Boudria, a former Ontario MLA, agreed. 'The Turner signs were a big mistake and I knew it right away. They thought that would show change, but all it showed, in my view, was that we were lost.'[33]

This chaotic situation could not last. On 4 August Turner and Lee parted company, and the Trudeau campaign team of Keith Davey, Martin Goldfarb, Gordon Ashworth, and Tom Axworthy were back in control. The irony of the Turner campaign resorting to the Trudeau 'Old Guard' was not lost on anyone, but it did result in a somewhat more cohesive campaign in the few remaining weeks. Ads appeared stressing that 'Brian Mulroney is more interested in the free market than people.' Mulroney's extravagant campaign promises, which no one had bothered to cost, led Keith Davey to devise a strategy labelling him the '$20 million dollar man.' Turner switched from talking about the national debt to promising to introduce a youth training program and a tax on wealthy Canadians. In short, the campaign moved from Turner's business Liberal platform to one that reiterated the left-wing Liberal concerns with social policy, if not the Trudeau vision of federalism.

In the end it was too little and much too late. The Liberals were reduced to 40 seats on 4 September 1984, barely holding on to the title of Official Opposition as the NDP rebounded as Grafstein had predicted and took 30 seats. The Conservative landslide delivered 211 seats, the largest majority in Canadian history. In Quebec, where Marc Lalonde had run the show while André Ouellet went to the Los Angeles Summer Olympics and Jean Chrétien and his supporters were shut out of the action, the toll was unimaginable. The mighty Liberals – who had held all but one of the 75 seats at dissolution – were reduced to 17 seats. The Conservatives achieved a massive breakthrough and held the remaining 58. Turner himself was spared the ultimate humiliation when he managed to win in Vancouver Quadra by 3,000-odd votes.

John Turner's gracious speech conceding defeat was perhaps the most impressive part of the Liberal campaign. With the party in tatters and deeply in debt, no one could imagine how it could recover in only four years. As their winter of discontent began, some began to wonder if the natural governing party could ever do so.

2 Life in the Opposition, 1984–1987

We knew the only way we could survive was to pool our resources.
– Hon. Doug Frith[1]

The mood was ugly in the Liberal caucus after their party's stunning election defeat. Even staunch Turner supporters were angry with the leader, and their anger was visceral. Some blamed him for their lost colleagues. Others held him responsible for their straitened personal circumstances, reduced from cabinet ministers to opposition MPs. If there was one thing that saved John Turner it was the sheer magnitude of the Liberal loss, which essentially precluded any challenge to his leadership in the foreseeable future. If there was another, it was the degree to which the Liberal caucus was united in their dislike of Brian Mulroney. But Mulroney was not someone they had to work with or take orders from, and John Turner was.

The Liberal leader's own difficulties adjusting to life in the opposition, and to his fractious caucus, were covered extensively by journalists at the time,[2] but these accounts tended to be both superficial and personality-based. Little or no attention was paid then or since to the very real and practical problems faced by the Liberal caucus and party organization as they attempted to come to grips with their new and unexpected role in opposition. The caucus in 1984 was not only unequipped for their new role but hopelessly outnumbered. With only forty MPs, they encountered serious logistical problems simply fulfilling their obligations as the Official Opposition. Moreover, the Liberals' lack of resources and experience in opposition required significant changes to the way the caucus was organized and to the support structures designed to serve them, challenges that went largely unrecognized outside the party's inner circle.

To add to the Liberals' difficulties, nearly one-quarter of the thirty-nine Members of Parliament who had been elected along with Turner were newcomers. Among them were the trio of Ontario MPs who would come to be known as the Rat Pack – Sheila Copps, Don Boudria, and John Nunziata. In Quebec another new MP, Raymond Garneau, was a former banker and Quebec provincial cabinet minister who had been recruited as a star candidate. Expecting to be in Turner's cabinet, he instead found himself in opposition and facing considerable financial hardship.

Among the veteran MPs several had been good constituency representatives but, as backbenchers, had little experience in policy matters and even less as orators in Parliament. Only a few long-serving cabinet ministers – such as Jean Chrétien, Lloyd Axworthy, Charles Caccia, and Don Johnston – could be expected to provide leadership and the benefit of their knowledge of government. According to Doug Frith, 'Of the whole group of forty only fifteen at best could be counted upon to handle the load in Question Period or represent the Party at major events as a guest speaker.'[3] Quite apart from the lack of parliamentary experience of some of their new colleagues, senior Liberals realized they had a more serious problem: the party was deeply in debt. With public funding for the leader's office and the Caucus Research Bureau drastically reduced, the mere task of fulfilling their role as the Official Opposition in Parliament was daunting. At the same time, the technological and financial advantages of the Conservatives were clear following the campaign. The Liberals knew they needed to modernize party operations if they were to have any hope of fighting the next federal election on a level playing field.

In recognition of the strained relations between the caucus and their leader, a small group of senior Liberal MPs and senators met with Turner's chief of staff, John Swift, shortly after the election to plan a strategy for recovery and reconstruction. They laid out an ambitious plan for coordinating their efforts. As the group's informal chair, former Turner cabinet minister Doug Frith recalled: 'We knew the only way we could survive was to pool our resources.'[4]

In addition to Frith the group consisted of Windsor MP Herb Gray and senators Joyce Fairbairn and Allan MacEachen. Gray, a well-known member of the party's left wing who had been in and out of Trudeau's cabinet, had unexpectedly supported Turner in the early days of his candidacy. His reward, also unexpected, was to be named House leader by Turner, while Frith was picked to be the chair of caucus. Although an elected position, the support of the leader was usually required to be chair. In this case Joyce Fairbairn, the former Trudeau press secretary who knew most of the caucus well, shared Turner's view and urged Frith to take on the job in the name of caucus unity. Personable and capable, with exceptional interpersonal relations skills, Frith was possibly the only one who could have held the caucus together in the early years in opposition.

MacEachen meanwhile would serve as the Liberals' leader in the Senate, where he would prove invaluable as the institutional memory of the party, being one of the very few Liberal caucus members in either chamber with opposition experience. The advice of the wily MacEachen, who had served in many cabinet portfolios under Trudeau and Pearson, was an essential element of the Liberals' early strategy for survival. It was also MacEachen who made the crucial decision that the Liberals would maintain control of committees in the Senate. That decision was logically consistent with their majority status in the upper chamber, but not necessarily with traditional practice. As MacEachen's deputy house leader, Senator Royce Frith, later revealed, MacEachen's personality and credibility carried the day. 'Allan just told (Conservative senator and House leader) Bill Doody that's the way it would be and no one ever thought to question it.' Over the course of their time in opposition this decision would prove to be hugely important for the Liberals, who had so few other tools at their disposal.[5]

With virtually no hope of raising funds in the private sector after their disastrous defeat, the small planning group decided their first order of business was to determine what resources they actually had at their disposal and how best to utilize them. They began by concentrating on the parliamentary wing, which would be the most visible element of the party. There they could at least count on some predictable sources of funding and media coverage of their role as the Official Opposition during Question Period.

The Liberal Tactics Committee

For opposition parties, Question Period in the House of Commons is the only real opportunity to be seen by Canadians. It is perhaps not surprising, therefore, that opposition parties devote so much of their time and resources to this aspect of their work. Indeed, preparation for the daily Question Period is the single most demanding function of opposition MPs and their staff.

Many observers have criticized the way Question Period has evolved since the introduction of televised coverage in 1977. John Turner left politics in 1975. On his return in 1984 he was horrified to discover how the daily question-and-answer period had changed. Turner, who privately referred to it as 'bullshit theatre,' was never comfortable with the format during more than four years as opposition leader. The man the media dubbed 'the honourable school boy' clearly did not enjoy the cut and thrust of the daily confrontations. From his early use of cue cards to his frequent and well-known reluctance to go for the jugular, his performance in that political theatre, while sometimes inspired, was more often unconvincing.

To most Canadians it may seem the questions raised in the House of Commons are spontaneous. It may also seem that the MPs who pose questions are selected at random by the Speaker. Nothing could be further from the truth and the Liberals knew it, having been on the receiving end of well-orchestrated opposition attacks in Question Period over the years. All opposition parties have some type of formal procedure in place to ensure their one chance to attract public attention is as effective as possible. The Liberals put together their own plan immediately but were unprepared for the degree of discipline required to make the system work.

In theory their plan was simple. With the return of Parliament the primary function of House leader Herb Gray was to chair an early-morning meeting of senior Liberal caucus members. There they would determine what issues the Liberals would raise in Question Period that day and who would ask them. Once the decisions were taken, a list of approved Liberal participants would be provided to the Speaker, who would then follow the order of the list.

According to their original plan, membership in the Liberal Tactics Committee was to be deliberately confined to a few senior caucus members. Along with Jacques Guilbault, a long-serving Quebec MP who was appointed deputy House leader, the Tactics Committee consisted of the members of the original planning committee – Doug Frith, Joyce Fairbairn, and Allan MacEachen – as well as a select few former ministers including Jean Chrétien, Don Johnston, and Lloyd Axworthy. Caucus members were to submit questions to the committee in writing. The committee members would then select and prioritize questions, adding some of their own if necessary. But this plan to allocate the tactics of opposition politics to a few key players soon fell by the wayside.

There were a number of reasons why the plan failed. To begin with, not everyone was interested in participating in Question Period. One of the greatest shocks facing former cabinet ministers in the Liberal caucus was their inability to influence the policy agenda. For them, Question Period was something with which they were very familiar, but from the government side. They had spent years responding to opposition requests and had little interest in posing questions themselves, an exercise that seemed frustrating and pointless. For some of their colleagues, however, those who had toiled in obscurity as backbenchers or were newcomers to Parliament, the situation was quite different. These caucus members saw Question Period as an opportunity to assert themselves and become visible players, an opportunity that they seized readily.

The situation was exacerbated by the way the Tactics Committee functioned. First and foremost, there was the vetting system which former ministers and veteran MPs found humiliating. Submitting written questions was bad enough. Having passed the first hurdle and been selected for the Question Period line-up of the day, those fortunate MPs were required to attend a second meeting of the Tactics Committee several hours later. At this meeting they were expected to read their prepared question as well as their supplementals, which were then subjected to 'fine-tuning' by the committee members. Especially for those considered experts in their field, this second exercise was often seen as frustrating and sometimes hypocritical, pitting solid facts against media hype. Some, such as aboriginal affairs critic Keith Penner and environmental expert Charles Caccia, simply ceased to put forward any suggestions. Others sent their assistants to represent them, a practice the House leader opposed but was ultimately powerless to prevent. As one well-known and highly regarded caucus member recalled, the whole exercise came to be seen as the 'theatre of the absurd.'

Another serious problem was the rapid expansion of the committee's membership. It began with Quebec MPs, who felt Jean Chrétien did not represent the views of francophone Quebeckers. Reflecting the internal battles fought during the election campaign through the choice of provincial organizers, both André Ouellet and newcomer Raymond Garneau began attending the morning meetings. Additional MPs from Quebec, including Jean-Claude Malépart and Jean Lapierre, soon joined in as well. They were quickly followed by a number of Maritime MPs

– notably Brian Tobin of Newfoundland and Dave Dingwall of Nova Scotia – who felt the meetings were under-representing their region. In short order, as other caucus members realized the enormous power concentrated in the hands of Gray and the small cohort of advisers, they too began to attend the meetings without invitation.

Not surprisingly the operation of the Tactics Committee became increasingly chaotic and dysfunctional. Before long, the concept of a small planning group devising the tactics for the day was entirely lost, replaced by an unwieldy and often inexperienced collection of caucus members in which continuity was nearly impossible. The objective of the Tactics Committee had become short-term prominence, achieved through aggressive criticism of the government, rather than long-term reconstruction.

For their part, the Conservatives appeared to be having as much trouble adjusting to governing as the Liberals were to their new role in opposition. As the Mulroney government stumbled from one scandal to another, there were more and more opportunities for the opposition to exploit. The Tactics Committee achieved a certain number of successes in this regard, enough to convince the House leader that it would be possible to bring down the government. With each new scandal the regular members of the committee came to expect Herb Gray's solemn pronouncement that this time the government would fall if they could only keep up their concerted attack. But despite dedicated efforts to capitalize on such issues as the Oerlikon land scandal, the Quebec kickback scandal, and the Sinclair Stevens affair, the Mulroney government stubbornly clung to power with its huge majority intact.

Central to the daily Tactics discussion was an analysis of the media coverage the Liberals and their arch rivals the NDP had received the previous day. The clippings service provided by the Caucus Research Bureau soon became more important for its 'head count' – the list of media 'hits' Liberals had achieved – than for the identification of new and emerging issues. This print media coverage was supplemented by an oral briefing from Bureau researchers on the broadcast news coverage the previous evening. On those days when the NDP outscored the Liberals, committee members could be certain that recriminations would be the order of the day.

Compounding the problem was the leader's obvious distaste for Question Period. Turner did not attend the morning Tactics meetings despite the fact they were held in the boardroom of his suite of offices in the Centre Block. Instead Turner's legislative assistant, Scott Sheppard, and one of his policy advisers, Charles Bouchard, attended the daily Tactics meetings, although the two rarely spoke and only occasionally communicated the leader's view on a particular issue. Their role was to take note of the issues raised and report back on the topics selected. Unbelievably for some, the leader's own questions were identified by the committee as well. Turner himself frequently described this practice as part of his commitment to a democratic, egalitarian decision-making process. Certainly those who knew him well were not surprised. As one close friend stressed, 'John always prefers to compromise in order to achieve a consensus and avoid confrontation.' Some of his caucus, however, questioned whether this willingness to ask whatever questions the committee recommended did not demonstrate a lack of firm views of his own. Others took advantage of the situation, attempting to convince the leader in private conversations that he should take a different tack, or cover a different topic than the one proposed by the committee.

As Turner's principal secretary Doug Richardson later commented, the willingness to listen to all points of view and achieve a compromise whenever possible often led the leader to appear 'indecisive' and 'confused' on issues.[6] This image was reinforced by Turner's hard and fast rule of avoiding personal attacks in his questions. The rule stemmed partly from his belief in the importance of gentlemanly behaviour in the House of Commons, and partly from the fact that he was a personal friend of many of the Mulroney ministers – several of whom came from Toronto and almost all of whom were previously members of the Canadian business establishment. His approach did little to endear him to the more aggressive members of his caucus, whose response was often to push the limits further in their own questions.

However, for many caucus members the crucial problem with the Tactics Committee was not so much the determination to pursue short-term objectives, but the fact that this approach was not accompanied by an equal determination to provide a serious set of policy alternatives or outline a proactive Liberal agenda. This failure to address the positive aspects of Liberal policy was something the members of the original caucus planning committee and other senior caucus members viewed as a serious error in judgment on the part of the Tactics Committee. As Doug Frith later commented, 'when the 1988 election campaign faltered and it became clear our position on free trade alone was not enough to win, there was nothing else for voters to hang their hats on. In four years we had failed to tell them where we stood on other issues and you can't make up for that in a few weeks.'[7]

The House leader, by contrast, believed it was more important to keep the Liberals in the public eye by pursuing issues seen as 'newsworthy' by the media rather than selecting issues considered important by the caucus members. He frequently referred to the need to determine what the media would 'accept' as a subject worth covering. 'If a tree falls in the forest and no one hears,' Gray often intoned, would it matter to Canadians? It soon became apparent that any topic raised which did not immediately result in media coverage had little or no hope of returning to the Liberal line-up the following day.

This clear-cut difference of opinion on the role of the Official Opposition in Question Period – and indeed on the perceived role of the media in determining what were the important matters of public concern – was one that would continue to confound the Liberals throughout their first four years in opposition. Senior caucus members such as Chrétien and Johnston soon left the committee in disgust, never to return. Others, including Doug Frith, continued to press the House leader for action on several policy fronts. They suggested that weekly themes be adopted and that at least the first two or three Liberal speakers each day should concentrate on the chosen theme before others moved to the more ephemeral topics of the day. Despite their recommendations, the Liberals continued to focus largely on the immediate and the sensational. In an effort to provide the public with an alternative perspective, both the caucus executive and several former ministers turned their attention to other activities, several of which would provide a much-needed boost to caucus and party morale.

Caucus Policy Activities

Among the first and most prominent of these alternative activities were the Liberal responses to the Conservative budgets of 1985 and 1986. While the Tactics Committee was doing its part to demonstrate the Mulroney Conservatives could not be trusted, former senior Trudeau ministers Don Johnston and Lloyd Axworthy were spearheading efforts to draw attention to the serious fiscal and social consequences of many of the budget measures proposed by the government. Their inside knowledge and personal prominence, combined with extensive and well-prepared documentation from the newly strengthened Caucus Research Bureau, proved highly successful in attracting media attention to their cause.

The Liberals' budget offensive began shortly after the May 1985 budget was tabled. Journalists were provided with copies of the Bureau's budget briefing book prepared for caucus members. Persuaded of the accuracy of the material, many members of the media began utilizing the Liberals' statistics in their own analyses. The Liberals' strategy of cooperating with the media not only allowed them to communicate their policy concerns but initiated the process of rebuilding media and public trust in their fiscal competence. Perhaps more significant still, the briefing book also contained a section on 'the longer-term Liberal strategy' for deficit reduction and alternative measures to restore 'tax fairness and social policy balance,' which compensated to some extent for the immediacy of Question Period concerns.

In addition to their activities in Ottawa, Johnston and Axworthy took to the road with a Liberal 'Task Force' on the budget prepared by Conservative Finance Minister Michael Wilson. These efforts culminated in Ottawa with the holding of a two-day 'Liberal Forum on the Budget' in August 1985. Initiated by caucus members, the event was an effort to attract public attention to Liberal positions in advance of the return of Parliament in early September. The meetings were widely covered by the media and well attended by special interest groups and non-governmental organizations convinced the Wilson budget was unsound. Similar responses to successive Conservative budgets continued over the next three years.

On a number of other issues the Liberals took advantage of their ability to file minority reports when parliamentary committee reports were tabled. A prominent example was the Liberal Minority Report on Childcare tabled by caucus critic Lucie Pépin, a recognized expert in the field. The committee had been directed to examine various issues relating to childcare, but it became clear to Pépin that the Conservative majority on the committee was actually opposed to the concept of public childcare and would not be proposing any meaningful measures to increase either access or daycare spaces. Instead, the Conservative emphasis would favour tax reductions for stay-at-home parents and tax credits for parents to spend as they wished on 'childcare-related' services. Pépin's minority report, issued in March 1987 and widely covered by the media, outlined the problems with the Conservative approach and provided an alternative Liberal policy prescription that was well received by the various interest groups involved.

Last but hardly least, caucus members examined policy issues not assigned to parliamentary committees. Following a Special Caucus session held in Montebello in January 1985, the caucus was organized by the leader into broad policy committees on social, economic, and foreign policy as well as rural issues. Members were instructed to examine new and emerging issues in their areas. In a 21 January letter to each caucus member, Turner outlined 'the major policy areas we should study in the next six months.' He called for regular meetings of the policy committees, which he described as 'essential to anticipating issues in the House' and 'making the government accountable for its numerous promises.' In formulating their positions on issues, Turner urged his MPs to consult widely through public meetings, seminars, and targeted travel. Although not all members responded equally to this challenge, many took the task very seriously and several conducted public hearings on their issues in a similar fashion to the budget forum.

As part of the rebuilding plan, a significant number of senior Liberal MPs were also engaged in a well-organized effort to maintain caucus visibility within the party, and the party's visibility across the country. A Speakers' Bureau was established through the party's National Office to serve as the central coordinating point for the exercise. Its role was to take requests for Liberal speakers from Liberal party associations across the country and match those requests with caucus members willing and able to attend. The party had almost no travel budget, so MPs were obliged to use their own limited travel benefits and often were billeted in the homes of party faithful.

As chair of the Liberal caucus for the first two years in opposition, Doug Frith was among the most sought after of these speakers. He spent nearly every weekend on the road or in Toronto, where he was also assigned political responsibility for reorganizing the Greater Toronto Area as well as northern Ontario. In Quebec, Raymond Garneau and André Ouellet were assigned the reorganization task, and Garneau handled many of the speaking engagements along with Jean Lapierre, the chair of the Quebec caucus. In Western Canada Lloyd Axworthy was attempting to maintain the party's base in Manitoba through an ambitious set of speaking events.

Since the party held no seats in Saskatchewan, Alberta, or the BC interior, a system of twinning was introduced as a necessary part of the rebuilding process. In a 19 June 1987 letter to all caucus members, Turner outlined 'what I believe is one of the greatest challenges still facing our

Party, to become once again a truly national party.' Although he maintained there had been 'significant signs of improvement' across western Canada,' he also stressed that the 'biggest problem facing western Liberals today is organization.' Citing the deterioration in party organization at the riding level and the lack of finances which had prevented the use of field workers for several years, Turner proposed to reintroduce the formal concept of twinned ridings which had been used before 1984. MPs were to make at least two trips per year to the riding with which they were twinned, make calls to the local media outlining Liberal positions on relevant issues, and place local Liberals on their mailing lists. These trips were useful in terms of building bridges and in acquainting many of the newer caucus members with the issues in other parts of the country.

In all of these activities the Liberal caucus was assisted by its Research Bureau to an extent few would have thought possible given the extent of the cutbacks the Bureau had suffered. Researchers travelled with the various caucus task forces, provided support for parliamentary committee work, and, as the structures of their new life in opposition solidified, became the bedrock on which the caucus depended for its credibility. In ways that had never been considered when the party was in power, the Bureau also became the mainstay of the leader's policy initiatives, and eventually of the party platform.

The Pivotal Role of the Liberal Caucus Research Bureau

The party research bureaux were established by Pierre Trudeau as part of his plan to enhance political participation and broaden the base of policy input from all sources. But they were originally intended to provide independent research support only for the opposition parties. Ironically, the Liberal Caucus Research Bureau (LCRB) had been created as an afterthought in response to concerted pressure from Liberal backbenchers who argued they needed a separate research facility as much as opposition party MPs, since only cabinet ministers had access to the policy expertise of bureaucrats. Few could imagine in 1978 that Liberals might one day find themselves in opposition and dependent on this one source for *all* of their research support.

Unfortunately for the surviving Liberals in 1984, the Bureau was not well positioned to do so. In the years since the LCRB was established it had been utilized less for research or policy development and more for communications support and members' services. Since government departments and PMO were responsible for policy development, the capacity of the Bureau to conduct research or provide critical analysis had never been seriously tested. After the election of 1984, the return of Parliament found the Bureau's ranks decimated, much like the leader's office. A new team was needed to provide research and policy support if the Liberal caucus was to perform as a credible opposition. The restructuring and upgrading of the LCRB therefore became a top priority, and its evolution clearly reflected the various problems the caucus faced as they learned how to function as an opposition party.

The senior caucus planning group led by Doug Frith and John Swift actually began the rebuilding process in the fall of 1984 by identifying a number of 'core services' they expected the Research Bureau to provide for the parliamentary wing in opposition. At the same time, certain functions the Bureau had performed in the past were reassigned to the party's National Office, to the Office of the Leader of the Opposition (OLO), or to individual MPs' office staff.

Still other functions were eliminated entirely due to the lack of resources. For example, the four-person Caucus Communications Unit that had formerly prepared media documents for MPs was eliminated following heated debate within the planning group. As former cabinet minister Jean-Luc Pépin, head of the search committee, confided, his argument had won the day, supported by Frith and MacEachen. For the demoralized Liberals, credibility was crucial as they began their life in opposition. Without solid research the caucus would be flying blind and there would be nothing of value to communicate.[8]

A new LCRB director – a former senior public servant – was recruited in early 1985 and given carte blanche by the search committee to restructure the Bureau and hire new personnel. This remarkable lack of close supervision was perhaps one of the earliest and most obvious indications that even the senior Liberal caucus members were still preoccupied with the fallout from the election defeat.

Administrative reforms to enhance the professional image of the Bureau – long viewed as a sinecure for party faithful – were implemented immediately. A formal system of job classifications was put in place based on public service guidelines. Each research position was assigned broad areas of policy responsibility, while four senior officers were also assigned a regional caucus. In recognition of the central role played by the Tactics Committee in opposition strategy, two additional officers were assigned full-time to the daily Tactics meetings of the caucus to provide a rapid response team for Question Period. By the summer of 1985 the Bureau had been completely reorganized. Despite initial pressure to hire defeated caucus members and former ministerial staff, the hiring process was noteworthy for its lack of caucus intervention. The qualifications for Bureau research officers were actually upgraded. All of the new policy analysts possessed a Master's degree and several had experience working in government, credentials more valuable now that access to federal bureaucrats would be far more limited than when the party was in power. Although some research officers had been involved in partisan politics and were already party members, this was not a prerequisite for hiring. With the Liberals in public disgrace, only those sympathetic to the party were likely to consider working for the Bureau in any event. Some researchers chose to become card-carrying party members, while others never did. The emphasis on expertise proved itself in short order, however, delivering consistently reliable material in which the caucus – and the media on whom they now depended for their visibility with the public – quickly came to have confidence.

The Bureau's new 'core operations' identified by the planning committee included support for Question Period, regional caucuses, caucus policy committees, and for the Liberal members of parliamentary committees when contentious policy issues arose.[9] These functions alone were more than sufficient to occupy the Bureau's professional staff, originally consisting of only eight research officers in addition to the director. However, as time passed and caucus confidence in the Bureau increased, the demands placed on the small band of researchers grew exponentially.

One unexpected problem faced by the caucus in opposition involved the office staff of individual MPs. When the Liberals were in power with a large majority, many backbenchers had focused primarily on constituency matters and hired staff accordingly. In opposition, and with so few caucus members, it became necessary for almost all of the Liberal MPs to assume critics' roles. Several of the senior MPs were assigned more than one. The caucus planning group had expected individual MPs to use their office budgets to hire a staff member with the appropriate expertise to support them in their critic's responsibilities. In most cases this did not happen. Despite repeated urging, many MPs were reluctant to engage new personnel, largely because of loyalty to existing staff, whom they would be forced to let go to make room for such an expert, an expert who might not feel the same sense of loyalty toward the MP.

The result of the impasse was increased demand on Bureau personnel, who ended up working closely with many individual MPs on their critics' responsibilities. This also resulted in more administrative structures than might have been expected for such a small operation. Indeed, it soon became apparent that in opposition the coordination of activities and policy responses was crucial. It led, for example, to the creation of a number of special working groups such as the 'Steel Caucus' or the 'Rural Task Force,' in which relevant critics as well as those MPs whose ridings were most affected by an issue could participate to develop a common response. It also led the Bureau director to institute a weekly meeting of all MPs' assistants, held when the MPs were in regional caucuses on Wednesday morning. By chairing this session, the director coordinated the activities of research officers and assistants to further ensure a unified approach. The weekly meeting also provided an occasion for MPs' assistants to raise questions on policy or communicate with each other, and proved so successful that it continued after the party returned to power in 1993.

The need to coordinate activities also led to an unprecedented decision by the caucus executive. The Bureau director was invited to attend national caucus sessions, held immediately after the regional caucuses each Wednesday. National caucus meetings had traditionally been the sacrosanct preserve of members and senators only, and this decision to make an exception initially caused some concern.[10] However, the utility of the director's presence became apparent in short order and continued without opposition until 1990. This unusual privilege was also extended to regional caucuses, where the Bureau researcher assigned to each of the four caucuses was allowed to attend the weekly meetings.

A similar although less successful attempt at coordination between the parliamentary and extra-parliamentary wings involved weekly meetings of the LCRB director, the principal secretary of OLO, and the national director (later secretary general) of the party. One obvious reason for the lack of success was the absence of clear direction and, on occasion, conflicting directions, provided by their respective elected officials. Another was the ever-present problem of insufficient funding. Publicly funded party research bureaux could only use their budgets for staffing. Materials – ranging from computers to desks and paperclips – were government issue, provided through the House of Commons and the Department of Public Works. No funds were available for other operating costs, nor could the Bureau budget be used to support party functions. Instead, the party's national office, already strapped for cash, was required to pay for one-time or extraordinary expenses of the Bureau which the public funding would not cover.

A classic example of the lack of coordination between the two wings of the party, and the unexpected costs of life in the opposition, was provided by the controversy over the clippings service for the daily Tactics meeting. Until their relegation to the opposition, Liberal MPs had access to sophisticated wire services, as well as the Library of Parliament's daily *Quorum* package of politically relevant newspaper clippings. In opposition, the need for timely media input was deemed even more vital. However, the *Quorum* was of little use to the Tactics group, which met early each morning before the Library's package was issued. In addition, with prominent western and Atlantic MPs in the caucus, it was considered essential to broaden the base of clippings to include material from outside central Canada. As a result it was decided that the Research Bureau would create an independent clippings service expressly for the Tactics meeting.

Since this required independent subscriptions to newspapers flown in each day, as well as a small part-time staff of university students to peruse and prepare the clippings in the early hours, the expenses of the operation mounted. As an operational expense not covered by the Bureau's public budget, the costs of this exercise had to be picked up by the party. Yet, despite the perceived importance of this material to the caucus, the Bureau's subscriptions to various newspapers were suspended without warning on several occasions for non-payment of bills, to the consternation of MPs and staffers alike. Although a minor irritant, the problem was symptomatic of the party's dire financial straits, the different priorities of the extra-parliamentary wing, and the lack of communication between party officials and the caucus executive.

The most serious difficulty in coordinating the efforts of caucus support staff resulted from the conflict between competing claims on the Bureau's scarce personnel. As more demands were placed on Bureau researchers, it became apparent that priorities needed to be set. This led to a sustained battle between the caucus executive and the House leader over their own relative importance within the caucus hierarchy. In theory the Bureau was the responsibility of the caucus executive. The director reported to the caucus chair. But the demands of the House leader and various senior staff in the Office of the Leader of the Opposition constituted a significant element of the Bureau's workload. Underlying this conflict were substantive disagreements between the caucus executive, the House leader, and the Leader's Office over priorities and policy directions. With the House leader and most of the caucus executive coming from the 'social Liberal' end of the spectrum and the leader representing 'business' Liberals, this was perhaps not surprising.

In addition, it soon became apparent that many caucus members saw the NDP as a major threat to their own re-election, a factor which greatly influenced their approach to issues and tactics. The leader, meanwhile, was focusing his time and efforts on the Conservatives, whom he saw as the primary opponent *nationally*. On several occasions these disagreements emerged as full-blown policy dissent at the morning Tactics committee meetings. More often, however, difficulties arose because the leader was not present when the Tactics decisions were taken, resulting in contradictory statements from critics and the leader.

The Controversial Role of the OLO

Meanwhile, the staff of the Leader's Office came under severe criticism for their performance as well. In one respect this was to be expected. As one veteran backroom Liberal organizer succinctly noted, 'whenever people are unhappy with a leader, the first victims will always be their staff. It's easier to blame them for the failings of their boss.' Certainly this truism was recognized by Doug Richardson, the Saskatchewan lawyer and two-time Liberal candidate who served as Turner's principal secretary. Richardson often told the story of his encounter with Prime Minister Mulroney in the men's washroom of the Press Club, where his attempt to introduce himself was cut short by Mulroney's response that he knew exactly who Richardson was – 'the only man in Ottawa with worse press clippings than mine.'[11]

A former ministerial assistant to Marc Lalonde, Richardson was recruited by Turner on the recommendation of Lalonde and Keith Davey in the spring of 1985, as part of the exercise which had also recruited the new director of the Research Bureau. He had agreed to come to Ottawa to serve along with John Swift, the chief of staff, in organizing the leader's activities and liaising with the caucus and the party. When Swift left Ottawa and returned to Vancouver in the spring of 1986, Richardson assumed sole responsibility for the Office of the Leader of the Opposition. In short order, he became the focal point for caucus unhappiness with both the leader's frequent absences from Ottawa and his controversial positions when he was present. In many respects, the problems with Turner's OLO reflected the unique problems that plagued his leadership.

Among Richardson's first tasks was to recruit additional senior staff. In an effort to achieve party solidarity, Swift had already recruited Stuart Langford, a former Chrétien supporter, as Turner's executive assistant. Similarly, Brigitte Fortier, a supporter of John Roberts, had been hired as press secretary. With the western (David Miller, a Turner supporter) and Ontario (Sharon Scholar, a Roberts supporter) regional assistants also settled, one of the first and most pressing concerns for Richardson was the need to find a strong director of communications to improve the image of the leader and his caucus.

It was here that the most controversial of the OLO hiring decisions was made with the appointment of former Quebec journalist Michelle Tremblay, forcefully recommended for the post by André Ouellet. According to Richardson, Ouellet's rationale was that the leader needed someone unconnected to party history or leadership rivalries to rebuild the party's image, especially in Quebec. Although it was certainly true that Tremblay had little or no parliamentary or administrative experience, Richardson later learned the leader's new communications director was not without baggage. In Quebec circles, Tremblay was not only known as a strong nationalist but as a vehement critic of Jean Chrétien, and her appointment was viewed by Chrétien and his supporters as a direct slap in the face. This, Richardson later surmised, was why her appointment was also strongly supported by Raymond Garneau and Jean Lapierre. Certainly it would prove to be a mistake of major proportions when the constitutional issue arose, as Richardson himself later admitted.[12]

In the meantime, criticism of OLO operations tended to focus on the lack of communication between the leader and his caucus, and on the apparent lack of organizational coherence within the office. Many caucus and party members had no idea who was responsible for which functions in the office. After the professional operation of PMO under Trudeau, the OLO's vague structure and reporting relationships were cause for considerable concern among party veterans. 'It was never really clear who was speaking for the leader on any given issue,' one disgruntled senior caucus member recalled. 'Sometimes it seemed as if it depended on the topic, other times on who was closest to him personally.' One thing everyone agreed on was that it was important to be the last one to speak with him.

In addition to the organizational problems within the leader's office, there were constant reports of personality conflicts and bitter rivalries among staff members. Turnover in the OLO remained extremely high at all levels, adding fuel to the fire and creating even greater uncertainty for caucus and party officials attempting to maintain effective links with their leader. The departure of Stewart Langford, in particular, was seen as a clear indication that attempts to bridge the leadership gap had failed.[13]

The Leader's Rebuilding Efforts

Turner was spending far more time than his caucus travelling, involved in his own efforts to rebuild the party. Clearly uncomfortable with the role of opposition leader in the House of Commons, he also believed – unlike his House leader – that there was virtually no chance of making an impact, much less bringing down a government with the huge majority the Mulroney Conservatives had been handed in 1984. Convinced his presence in the House of Commons each day attacking Mulroney and his ministers was a pointless exercise, Turner spent nearly half his time in the first two years travelling across the country meeting grassroots Liberals. He, too, was aware of the enormity of the task which confronted the party and often told close confidants he considered it his obligation to soldier on in the face of adversity rather than return to the comforts of a law office in Toronto.

In a demonstration of character which even his harshest critics admired, Turner was determined to rebuild the party from the grassroots up, member by member and riding by riding. As he commented in early 1985, this would require 'a lot of travel, a lot of small towns, a lot of chicken dinners, a lot of therapy, a lot of morale boosting, a lot of emotional leadership and a lot of intellectual leadership.'[14] As a result, he spent much of his time attending Liberal events across the country.

One objective in rebuilding the party at the local and regional levels was to solidify the federal party's connections with the provincial Liberal parties – separate legal entities which did not necessarily lend support to their federal counterparts during federal elections. The federal Liberal Party in 1985 was very much in need of such support to provide on-the-ground assistance in the next federal election as it would have little 'machinery' of its own. Turner was convinced the key to success in the next election would lie in helping provincial parties to make electoral gains in areas where the federal party was weakest, such as western Canada, and to cement good relations with provincial counterparts in areas where they were in power, namely Ontario and Quebec. To that end, he assigned his Quebec lieutenant, Raymond Garneau, a former provincial cabinet minister, to liaise with the Bourassa government. Sheila Copps, a former Ontario MLA, was to be his link with the new Peterson government at Queen's Park.

A second objective was to strengthen the party's presence in western Canada and hopefully increase its support in the next election. For Turner, the west was as important as Quebec, and he agreed with those who felt the party had drifted badly from its status as a truly national party. Not surprisingly, some of his strongest supporters were in western Canada. He spent a disproportionate amount of his travel time meeting Liberals across the western provinces, repeatedly reminding them that he had chosen to run in Vancouver rather than Montreal or Toronto. This focus on the west was not shared by many in his caucus given their overwhelming representation from Ontario and the Atlantic, but it was remarkably well received by his new Quebec MPs, who toured with the leader on several occasions and participated actively in some of Turner's western initiatives.

While there were some who speculated Turner had a personal motive for his rebuilding efforts given that an automatic leadership review was scheduled for the fall of 1986, few could disagree with the positive results that emerged. Slowly but surely, Turner was rebuilding the trust of card-carrying Liberals and, at least to some extent, of Canadians. The *Globe and Mail* began the leader's public rehabilitation with an article that concluded 'five months after he led his party to one of the most humiliating defeats in Canadian history, the man who was one of the country's shortest reigning prime ministers is returning to the form he displayed before quitting the federal cabinet a decade ago.'[15] And in western Canada, one front-page newspaper article with the headline 'Turner Magic Restored?' speculated that 'a lot of Canadians are in for a big surprise' if they were to compare the Liberal leader in opposition to his performances during the election campaign.[16]

In addition to his work helping to rebuild the party organization from the ground up, Turner had one other major objective in the first two years in opposition, namely to promote policy renewal. He had attended the famous Kingston Conference when the Liberals were in opposition during the Diefenbaker/Pearson era and was convinced that opposition was the time for the party to renew itself through widespread consultation and exchange of views among the membership.

This drive for policy renewal began almost immediately. At a caucus retreat in Montebello in January 1985, Turner announced – in conjunction with party president Iona Campagnolo – 'a new process for the joint development of policy by the parliamentary and non-parliamentary wings of the party.' This attempt to bridge the gap between the two solitudes was a pointed statement by Turner about the way the volunteer side of the party had been excluded from policy development during the past twenty years, a criticism he had made repeatedly and with conviction during the leadership race. It was also a point on which the success of his leadership depended, since his victory had been achieved with the strong support of the youth wing of the party, for whom this involvement was crucial.

The January announcement was followed by a meeting of the party's National Executive in Scarborough in early February. Caucus policy committee chairs along with the caucus executive were invited to attend the meetings, as were members of the party's national policy committee. Ignoring entirely the party's lack of finances and organization, the announcement declared Turner's intention to 'decide on a plan of action for the development of policy for the rest of the eighties and nineties.'[17]

As a first step towards this objective, Turner convened a special policy caucus session in Memramcook, New Brunswick, in June 1986. Invited experts presented material to the caucus on Atlantic concerns, ranging from the future of regional development assistance and the role of crown corporations to fisheries policy and income security. The Memramcook exercise visibly energized many caucus members, who began to take policy development seriously and looked forward to other opportunities to participate. They did not have long to wait. Following on the Memramcook event an even more ambitious series of three Canada-wide conferences was unveiled by Turner with the intent of raising the party's policy profile in the lead-up to the anticipated 1988 election.

The Canada Conferences, or Kingston II

The Canada Conferences were organized on a much larger and more impressive scale than Kingston, with considerable resources and personnel devoted to their conception and execution. The conferences were seen by Turner as his personal project. He signed the letters of invitation to participants in which he once again stressed the importance of policy renewal for the party when in opposition. 'For generations' he wrote, 'the strength of the Liberal Party has been its ability to renew its people and ideas. In 1933, the Port Hope Conference ushered in an epoch of Liberalism that would see Canada through the great depression and into post-war prosperity. The Kingston Conference of 1960 introduced ideas and newcomers to the Party which would shape Canadian political life for a generation. The Canada Conference series follows in this tradition. The ideas we discuss here will guide Canada into the next century.'[18]

Turner kept in close contact with the conference organizers beginning with Senator Jack Austin, the man he appointed to chair the series. A former principal secretary to Trudeau, Jack Austin was widely known as an intellectual force within the party. He was also well connected in the business community and, since his appointment to the Senate representing British Columbia in 1975, had served in cabinet for a time as minister of state for social development. Turner, a former Rhodes scholar himself, could hardly have chosen a more impressive figure to chair the Canada Conferences.

Austin was quick to acquire the services of two key players to assist him, namely the director of the Liberal Caucus Research Bureau and the party's policy director, Mark Resnick. Against the odds, and with considerable help from Research Bureau staff as well as Austin's high-powered connections, the trio organized three highly successful and widely publicized events. The issues raised influenced not only the shape of the Liberal platform the following year, but many of the initiatives taken by the Liberal government after the party's return to power in 1993. As the list of participants demonstrates, the events also provided an opportunity for Turner to reach out to potential Liberal candidates and other high-profile individuals who later served the party in different capacities.

The first of the Canada Conferences, held in Montreal, 23–5 October 1987, saw academics, interest group leaders, and members of the business community come together with caucus members and the party's grassroots to discuss the theme 'Building the Canadian Economy: An Agenda for the 90's.' Five workshops held the first day of the conference were chaired by such well-known figures as Gordon Sharwood ('Entrepreneurship'), Manon Vennat ('Full Employment'), Dr Stuart Smith ('Education and Training'), Marie-Josée Drouin ('Sustainable Development'), and Rod Bryden ('Regional Equity'). Vennat went on to become the party's platform committee co-chair the following year, while Bryden later became president of the Ontario wing of the federal Liberal party. Even more significant was the choice of closing speaker for the event, none other than Paul Martin Jr. At the time, Martin was head of Canada Steamship Lines, but would soon become a candidate for the Liberal Party in the 1988 election. Martin's address concluded with the argument that 'it should be the goal of our party to deliver more than we can promise,'[19] a statement which would come back to haunt him years later.

The second Canada Conference took place in Halifax in December with the theme of 'Family and Social Values for a Maturing Nation.' Along with the requisite academics and senior spokespersons for national interest groups, the participants once again included several workshop chairs of note, including Maude Barlow (later an adviser to Turner on women's issues and a future Liberal candidate), Ron Duhamel (a professor at the University of Manitoba who became an MP and then a cabinet minister in the Chrétien government), Mary Schwass (an international consulting economist and wife of the Liberals' national policy chair Rodger Schwass), and Patrick Johnson (former head of the National Antipoverty Organization, future co-chair of the Liberal platform committee, and Liberal candidate).

The third and final conference in the series took place in Vancouver in February 1988. Under the broad rubric of 'Building the Canadian Nation: Sovereignty and Foreign Policy in the 1990's,' the conference addressed such issues as Arctic sovereignty, arms control and disarmament, global environmental management, cultural identity, Canada and the Pacific Rim, development aid, the world debt crisis, and international trade. Co-chairs of the conference were Maurice Strong and Nancy Morrison, and more than 150 academics, foreign policy activists, and international business experts participated.

Unfortunately for John Turner, whatever advantage this policy development work might have had in boosting his image was more than countered by frequent confrontations with his MPs in Ottawa. While Turner was focusing on the 'big picture' of party and policy renewal, there were seemingly endless problems confronting him on the parliamentary front. Part of the explanation for this confrontation lay in personality conflicts between Turner and many of the senior caucus members. Some cited the leader's inability to rein in individual MPs, his erratic management style, and his apparent disinterest in individual caucus members (demonstrated by their under-representation at the Canada Conferences) as factors contributing to an overall lack of morale in the caucus. There were two additional problems that few in the parliamentary wing seemed to recognize until much later. First, and most immediate, was the reality of life in the opposition. With another party in power setting the agenda, the bulk of the Liberals' policy statements were necessarily reactive. Convinced that simply criticizing the initiatives of the Mulroney Conservatives would lower them in the eyes of the media and hence the general public, the Liberals were in the unenviable position of having to find ways to constructively criticize and improve upon the initiatives of a duly elected majority government, however much they disagreed profoundly with the objectives.

The conflict between Turner and much of his caucus was also based on a more fundamental problem, namely, frequent contradictions between the leader's initial reaction on policy issues and those of his appointed caucus critics. At first, many MPs thought the problem could be solved by having Turner spend more time in Ottawa and communicating more effectively with his caucus. Eventually, however, they began to recognize that these contradictions reflected clear-cut policy differences rather than just weak leadership. Simply put, the party was beginning to pay the price for having selected a leader whose views were not in sync with much of the parliamentary wing and a sizeable chunk of the extra-parliamentary wing. John Turner wanted to talk about the economy and business competitiveness, and believed the party's future lay in western Canada. The caucus, on the other hand, wanted to talk about retraining programs, seniors' pensions, and pollution prevention, and believed their future depended on mending fences with immigrants, women, and low-income Canadians. As these conflicts became increasingly public, the image of a leader unable to keep his own caucus members in line reinforced the view of many Canadians that Turner simply was not leadership material. This perception would soon be reinforced by another serious policy challenge, this time on the national unity front.

Jean Chrétien's Resignation from Caucus

In many respects, Jean Chrétien's departure from the Liberal caucus was inevitable. Chrétien had been visibly unhappy with life in opposition from the beginning. As well, he had lost influence both in Quebec and in the national caucus. Although John Turner had offered him virtually any post he wanted after the leadership convention, this offer had not been repeated after the stunning election defeat, a point several of Chrétien's closest confidants were quick to note in interviews many years later. Clearly there was less for Turner to offer. The positions of deputy prime minister or minister of foreign affairs were no longer available. Chrétien *was* given the post of foreign affairs critic, which was the best available under the circumstances. But he did not have a political role to play in Quebec. For his part, Turner never appeared to lose his fear of Chrétien as a potential threat to his leadership. Having lost the election that he was expected to win, Turner came to realize many of the Trudeau old guard, and others in the party establishment who had supported him for the leadership, would have no reason to retain any personal loyalty to him. He became increasingly concerned about the upcoming leadership review scheduled for November 1986, and so did his advisers.

Chrétien soldiered on in the opposition ranks for more than eighteen months. In that time he wrote his memoirs and took a position with his old law firm to make ends meet. With the book finished, he became restless and began to question why he should stay on in public life. Several of his close friends and confidants recall lengthy discussions as to what his future plans should be and how much longer he should stay in caucus. One of his stated concerns was that, whenever he left, it would appear that he was unhappy with the leader. On the other hand, if he stayed his every move would be analysed for evidence of disloyalty.

Recognizing that their most prominent caucus member was unhappy and possibly considering leaving, a senior Turner official convinced the leader to invite Chrétien to have dinner with him. The two met on 4 February 1986 at the opposition leader's residence to discuss Chrétien's future in the party. The official believed Chrétien would finally be offered the post of Quebec lieutenant in order to keep him on side, but this was not to be. Instead, Turner dismissed that possibility early on and offered no other symbolic options. The two then discussed the upcoming meeting of the Quebec wing of the party. By all accounts, Chrétien had already asked his close supporter, Jacques Corriveau, not to run for the position of party president. Instead, he had suggested a former colleague of both men, former Trudeau minister Francis Fox, as a compromise candidate. When he left the dinner, Chrétien believed this proposition had been accepted. He learned the following day that Turner had actually asked Fox not to run. He also learned that his former assistant, Stuart Langford, had been dismissed from OLO having been accused of disloyalty.

Shortly thereafter, Chrétien decided to leave public life. On 27 February he met with Turner in his office to give him a handwritten letter of resignation. Accompanied by his executive assistant, Jean Carle, he was obliged to wait in the anteroom for some time before Turner made his way to his office from the national caucus meeting. With Carle in tears and Chrétien visibly upset, virtually everyone in the vicinity of the leader's inner sanctum realized a crisis was unfolding. Nevertheless, both Turner and Chrétien delivered gracious letters and complimentary remarks to the media. In the House of Commons, Turner referred to Chrétien as a 'great Canadian' who had an 'unparalleled' parliamentary career and 'deserves the gratitude of all his fellow Canadians.'[20]

But the leader's desire to forge his own path regarding Quebec soon became evident as well. At a press conference later the same day, Turner responded to one reporter's question about the party's prospects in Quebec without Chrétien by saying 'I think that we will continue to renew our forces and our ideas in Quebec. I think our Members and our associations will be even more determined. They know that to lose a Jean Chrétien is a serious matter and I think the Party, the members of the party, will tend to redouble their efforts.'[21]

Few could have predicted how the leader and his Quebec advisers would attempt to begin that rebuilding process, or with what disastrous effects, only a few weeks later. With the departure of the leading advocate of Trudeauvian federalism from the Liberal caucus – a bombshell in its own right – the occasion for Michelle Tremblay and Raymond Garneau to take advantage of the vacuum was soon presented.

The Origins of the Liberals' Constitutional Debacle

For Quebec nationalists, Brian Mulroney's 1984 election promise to bring Quebec into the constitutional fold by having the province sign on to the 1982 constitutional amendment was one of the most attractive aspects of his platform. When Robert Bourassa's Liberals defeated the separatist Parti Québécois government in late 1985 they wasted no time in taking advantage of this promise. By March 1986, the Bourassa government had produced a list of five issues it wanted to see addressed before it would agree to sign. As has been outlined elsewhere in detail, these concerns – which unfortunately were translated in English as 'demands' – were a bargaining position. Bourassa and his intergovernmental affairs minister Gil Rémillard hoped to have all the items on their shopping list resolved, but they hardly expected to impose specific solutions. As opinion polls at the time demonstrated so clearly, they were in no position to 'demand' anything of Mulroney, since neither Canadians nor Quebeckers in particular were interested in reopening the constitutional file.[22]

The federal Liberals, meanwhile, were in disarray after their stunning collapse in the province they had always counted on so heavily for their victories. Not only Chrétien but most of the high-profile Trudeau-era ministers were no longer in caucus, and several of the new Quebec MPs who replaced them had ties to the Bourassa government and the so-called soft nationalists, setting the stage for a new crisis in the parliamentary wing.

Although their views were in the minority within the caucus and the party, a small group of Quebec MPs including Raymond Garneau, André Ouellet, and Jean Lapierre was convinced that the only way to turn around Liberal fortunes in Quebec was to out-do Brian Mulroney by having Turner declare his acceptance of Bourassa's five points first. Garneau was viewed by many of his colleagues as naive and hopelessly provincialist, but well intentioned. The consensus on Ouellet and Lapierre was that they were uninterested in constitutional issues but highly skilled and opportunistic political strategists. All of them were committed to reversing the federal Liberals' fortunes in Quebec by demonstrating that Turner would be taking the party in a completely new, decentralist direction, because they believed it would return the party to power.

That the acceptance of the Quebec wish list would represent a new direction for the federal Liberal Party was never in question. Bourassa's five demands included the recognition of Quebec as a 'distinct society,' a new term for the 'special status' which Pierre Trudeau had rejected for twenty years. If the Quebec group's plan had been raised in advance in the Liberal caucus it would have been shot down in flames. As a result, they began working on a Liberal response to the five points in the spring of 1986 without consulting the caucus, including the executive or House leader. According to several accounts, not even Turner saw the response until the day it was announced.[23] Instead, Turner's communications director, Michelle Tremblay, functioned as the liaison with the Quebec MPs, increasingly implicated in the policy decisions and planning of strategy as well as the communications function.

Shepherded by Tremblay and Garneau to an editorial board at *Le Devoir* in Montreal on 12 June, Turner revealed the Liberals' new constitutional position, declaring, among other things, that he had no difficulty inserting in the preamble to the constitution a recognition of Quebec as a unique and distinct society. This was followed the next day by Turner's comment that there had been extensive consultations leading up to the announcement, something he apparently believed.

The decision to make this announcement in advance of the meeting of the Quebec wing of the federal party in St Hyacinthe meant that its contents became known to most Liberals – both rank-and-file members and the parliamentary wing – by reading the weekend newspapers. The Liberal delegates at St Hyacinthe were, therefore, the first to be able to voice their concerns about the party's new position. While it may have pleased Quebec nationalists, the text failed to find favour with the Quebec Liberals at the meeting, who promptly made several major changes to it before adopting it reluctantly as a resolution.

The reaction of the delegates was nothing compared with the reaction of the Liberal caucus in Ottawa the following Monday. Key senior Liberals such as Don Johnston – who now saw himself as the flag carrier for the Trudeau vision and the principal representative of the anglophone community in Quebec – were outraged. Not only did Johnston and many others disapprove of the package, but they were furious they had not been consulted. And, as caucus chair Doug Frith remarked at the time, 'you have to understand that there is nothing like the constitutional debate that stirs Liberals.'[24]

By Monday afternoon the OLO had retreated and issued a press release referring to the plan as a sort of trial balloon which the leader had 'floated' in Montreal. For the next several days both Turner and his caucus attempted to distance themselves from the Garneau/Tremblay/Ouellet text. When it became apparent from the huge number of phone calls bombarding the party's national office that ordinary Liberals were upset as well, Doug Richardson knew something more specific would be needed to calm the troubled waters, especially before the leadership review scheduled for the party's national convention in November.

A small, select committee, chaired by former Trudeau solicitor general Bob Kaplan and Quebec MP Lucie Pépin, was appointed by the leader to draft a compromise package that could be presented as the caucus resolution on the constitution at the convention. Members included the key spokespersons for the two opposing views, namely Don Johnston and Raymond Garneau, as well as Michelle Tremblay, party president Michel Robert, and the director of the LCRB. After many weeks of work, the original proposal was finally watered down to the point where both sides could live with it. The distinct society clause, for example, became a reference in the preamble to 'the distinctive character of Quebec as the principal but not the only source of the French language and culture in Canada,' along with recognition of 'the multicultural character' and 'aboriginal heritage.'[25] Few knew what the phrase meant, but at least it

was clear it would have no significant impact. Perhaps equally important, confidential delegations had been dispatched to consult with both
Bourassa and Trudeau to ensure there would be no outright rejection of
the proposal. Both had agreed to refrain from criticizing it.

At the November 1986 convention, the new and improved version
of the Liberal response to Bourassa's five points received much less
attention from either delegates or the media than had been feared. It
seemed that, after their initial concern over missteps by the leader, they
were satisfied that his extreme position had been disavowed. The party
had put to rest any differences of opinion on the constitutional front
by returning to the traditional approach and was once again united on
the national unity/federalism axis. The same could not be said of the
Liberal response to the Mulroney government's proposed free trade
agreement, which was bedevilling the party at the same time as the
constitutional issue.

Responding to the Free Trade Agreement

Like the constitutional issue, the debate over the Conservatives' free
trade proposal caused significant friction between John Turner and
his caucus. Brian Mulroney had dismissed free trade during the Tory
leadership race in 1983, saying 'Free trade affects Canadian sovereignty
and we will have none of it, not during leadership campaigns or any
other time,' only to reconsider the idea following his 1985 'Shamrock
Summit' with Ronald Reagan. This left both the Liberals and the Canadian public blind-sided and obliged to form an opinion on something that had not even been discussed during the election campaign.
This time the two former senior ministers who had joined forces to critique the Conservatives' budgets, Don Johnston and Lloyd Axworthy,
were on opposite sides of the debate. Axworthy, the trade critic, led the
charge for the social Liberal majority in caucus who objected to the deal
on various grounds, including its potentially negative consequences for
national unity and the welfare state. Johnston, the party's finance critic,
led the small minority of business Liberals in caucus who felt the effects of American protectionism could cripple the Canadian economy,
while the trade deal could enhance competitiveness and hence the standard of living for ordinary Canadians. In a classic demonstration of the
cross-cutting cleavages that were beginning to emerge because of the
constitutional issue, one of those who supported Johnston strongly in

his efforts to have the leader speak in favour of the free trade deal was none other than Raymond Garneau.

Caught between his natural philosophical inclination to support the concept of freer trade, his immediate concerns about this particular deal, and the clear political imperative not to take on most of his caucus again, Turner hesitated. The constitutional debacle, after all, still loomed large in everyone's mind. There was some uncertainty as to the Conservatives' ability to achieve an equitable deal with the Americans, but not enough to justify a direct challenge from the opposition leader. A special caucus meeting in January 1986 appeared to present a temporary solution to the situation. The Liberals returned to their mulitlateralist roots. They were in favour of freer trade, not just with the Americans, but with the whole world. And the mechanism they favoured to achieve this was international treaties negotiated at the GATT (General Agreement on Tariffs and Trade, later the World Trade Organization).

Turner responded to reporters' queries on the state of the free trade talks after a speech he gave to the Empire Club in Toronto in March 1986. Showing that he, at least, understood the problems were caused because the Liberals were not setting the agenda, he snapped 'We didn't start the talks. We didn't get us into this mess.' With the Liberals actually standing first in the polls by the spring of 1986 and the Conservatives plummeting in the wake of a never-ending string of scandals, the Liberals' political fortunes finally appeared to be on the rise. In this context, it seemed only prudent to avoid taking too strong a position on either side of this potentially divisive issue, especially in advance of the November leadership review.

Because Turner's OLO advisers were focused primarily on the leadership review throughout the first half of 1986, and then on the constitutional resolution, there was little time left for pursuing a consensus trade resolution as well. The result was a bizarre situation in which two conflicting resolutions were successfully passed at the convention, one promoted by Axworthy and the other by Johnston.

Nevertheless, having received 76.3 per cent of the delegates' support in the leadership review, Turner was now armed with a new source of authority. His response to the problem of the duelling resolutions was to downplay their importance, a move which may well have caused some concern among those Young Liberals who once again supported him because of his commitment to a more transparent, accountable party with a policy process flowing upwards from the rank-and-file party membership. Responding to a reporter's question about the policy resolutions, the leader declared that they were 'not strictly constitutionally binding' but 'generally persuasive' and would be 'taken into account' when formulating a party platform, thereby giving himself as much leeway as necessary to resolve the conflict at a later date.

The Cruise Missile Mini-Crisis

This was the same line he would have to use in light of two other contradictory resolutions passed at the convention, this time on the issue of cruise missile testing, which, once again, found Turner on the opposite side of the issue from most of his caucus. As he was already on record supporting the Trudeau government's decision to permit the testing in 1983, he would have had considerable difficulty explaining an about-face. Yet most of the caucus wanted to oppose the Americans' request to extend the five-year agreement, due to expire in 1988.

Interestingly, the opposition was led by Lloyd Axworthy, Charles Caccia, and Warren Allmand, all of whom had been in the Trudeau cabinet at the time of the previous decision. This suggested that the requirement of cabinet solidarity had concealed internal dissent then, but for Turner in opposition there were no similar parliamentary conventions to ensure caucus discipline. Moreover, out of power, it now appeared that at least half the caucus shared the three veterans' opposition to the testing.

In response to growing concerns in caucus and the OLO that the cruise missile issue could cause further problems just as the party was appearing unified, Turner took another tack, appointing his faithful supporter Doug Frith as defence critic. Along with Don Johnston, who was now to be the foreign affairs critic, and Senator Allan MacEachen, Frith was asked to chair a series of caucus policy committee meetings over the first two months of 1987 and to arrive at a new and comprehensive Liberal defence and foreign affairs policy for the north. The resulting compromise plan included a call for a 'weapons-free' Canadian Arctic and for a demilitarization of the entire circumpolar region, thereby neatly encompassing the issue of missile testing within a larger and more constructive policy objective.

The plan was supported by the vast majority of the caucus and the leader's policy adviser had been present at the meetings. As a result, Frith and Johnston confidently assumed they could refer to it when fielding media questions on the day the Mulroney government's intention to approve the American request was announced. However, the leader, who was absent from Ottawa at the time, responded to reporters' questions about the government's plan by appearing to contradict his two critics. He indicated the matter was still under consideration and no decision had been taken. The resulting internal furore in the Liberal caucus appeared, yet again, to be threatening Turner's leadership barely two months after his resounding win in November. More importantly, it also appeared to be threatening Liberal prospects for defeating the Conservatives in the next election. With less than two years to go until the expected election call, the party could not afford more public displays of dissent and confusion. In the end, this appeared to be the message most of the caucus accepted. Although some seats were empty on the Liberal side of the House of Commons for a vote on an NDP motion condemning the government's plan to approve the missile tests, only four Liberals ended up voting with the enemy and against their own party. Even Frith and Johnston, although humiliated by the leader's apparent disregard for their views and their careful work on the issue, ultimately voted with their party and their leader. As Frith later recalled, 'It's a tough choice but you have to remember that no one will remember your position on the issue. What they remember is whether you voted with your party or not.'[26]

And so, on two highly divisive issues along the left-right spectrum, the party managed to come together to salvage the situation and present a united front to the world. Unfortunately for Turner, this remaining vestige of the famous Liberal discipline of power would be tested even further in short order. Despite a degree of success adapting to life in the opposition and an enormous effort on the part of the extra-parliamentary wing to revitalize party organization and initiate the policy renewal process at the grassroots level, a constitutional storm was building on the horizon, a storm that would have significant repercussions for the Liberals in the months and years ahead.

3 Reconstructing the Party

Our job is to responsibly establish new institutional arrangements to enable the Liberal Party of Canada to meet the challenges of the 80's and a new generation of Liberalism.

– Hon. Iona Campagnolo[1]

The self-image of the Liberal Party was badly damaged by the 1984 electoral debacle. Apart from the fleeting 1979 defeat, which many viewed as an aberration, Liberals could not really remember a time when their party was not in power. The massive Mulroney majority was a sobering sign that the party could be on the outside looking in for a long time unless serious efforts were made to rebuild. With little relevant caucus experience to call on, the extra-parliamentary wing became the focal point of those efforts.

While John Turner and his small band of surviving MPs were finding their feet on the opposition benches in the House of Commons, party president Iona Campagnolo was surveying the ruins of the party organization and finances. These ruins were symbolized by the badly rundown office at 102 Bank Street, which stood in marked contrast to the well-provisioned, technically sophisticated Conservative operation. As Campagnolo stated in a presentation to the Reform Committee she had established in 1983, 'at the present time the diminishment of the party apparatus is readily apparent by the disgraceful ... situation of the offices in question.' Moreover, the 'impossible' financial situation led her to conclude 'the national office is now fiscally responsible but politically neutered.'[2]

The first party president to devote herself full-time to the job, Campagnolo – like her counterparts in the parliamentary wing – understood the severity of the crisis facing the party. She concluded that an immediate plan of action was necessary on the extra-parliamentary side as well, not only to rebuild the party but to bolster the spirits of rank-and-file members. It was these members, after all, who would play a crucial part in the reconstruction effort.

Campagnolo was in a difficult position. She had been elected president in 1982 and was therefore not the choice of the new leader. Although she and Turner knew each other, having served together in cabinet, the leader was ambivalent about her loyalty given her famous comment at the 1984 leadership convention about Jean Chrétien's pride of place in the hearts of delegates. Because Campagnolo was neither a senator nor independently wealthy, she demanded a salary, becoming the first party president to do so. With party finances in a precarious state, this unprecedented move further complicated her position.

In addition, conflict arose between the national office and the OLO over the salaries the party was subsidizing for several of Turner's top aides. This aid was considered necessary due to the severely reduced funds available to the Liberals from their parliamentary allowance. Turner supporters defended the expenses as unavoidable if the parliamentary wing was to appear professional. Doug Richardson noted his own salary was more than $45,000 less than he had earned as a lawyer in Saskatoon, even with the subsidy, a situation common to many of the senior staff in OLO.[3] On the other hand, similar sacrifices had been made by senior personnel in the Research Bureau, where no party subsidies were offered, and by Campagnolo herself, whose salary was also considerably less than that of senior OLO staff. For his part, John Swift pointed out that the Liberals' move from the PMO to OLO offices had not been accompanied by the transfer of their computers and other equipment as expected, so that 'we were starting from scratch' in terms of material management as well. The need to supplement OLO operations was a drain on the national office and its scant resources, and led to ongoing conflict.[4]

Nor was Campagnolo in control of the personnel at the party office. Among the first tasks of the leader was to appoint a national director, something traditionally done in consultation with the president. Demonstrating once again his commitment to the party's long-standing practice of reconciling opposing leadership camps, Turner took the advice of Keith Davey and Allan MacEachen and offered the position to David Collenette, the defeated Trudeau cabinet minister who had supported Chrétien. Campagnolo readily agreed with his decision once she was informed, recognizing the symbolic importance of Turner's gesture. The situation was made easier because of Collenette's previous experience as executive director of the party in Ontario. However, Collenette's equal status to Campagnolo as a former cabinet minister meant the president's authority was diluted.

The President, the National Director, and the National Office

Collenette maintains that the relationship among the three worked well.[5] He and Campagnolo arrived at a simple and workable division of labour which saw him administer the national party office while she travelled extensively, speaking to local riding associations, consulting with provincial executives, and attempting to rebuild the party machinery. She met with the leader as necessary while Collenette met weekly with Turner and members of the so-called Troika Committee – John Swift or Doug Richardson from the OLO and the director of the LCRB.

In later years, Collenette recalled that Turner's interest in party matters and his priorities for the party in opposition were clear from the beginning: 'to revive the local constituency associations, to revive the policy process, and to improve the party's image in western Canada.'[6] The perception of Turner as a concerned 'party man' continued to be held by many in the national executive over the next four years, including several who had supported him for the leadership on that basis. As former party treasurer and CFO Lloyd Posno recalled, 'Turner knew that he and the government couldn't exist without the party. Many members [of the caucus] have little or no allegiance to the party and don't understand that they are only where they are because of it.'[7]

Collenette also agreed with Campagnolo and Turner that it was imperative for the party to be visible, arguing that 'you need to spend to deliver results. People forget we actually made money on the 1986 convention.'[8] At the same time, the new secretary general admitted to being shocked by the state of the party's finances on his arrival in early 1985, a sentiment echoed by several other newly appointed or elected members of the party's financial oversight bodies. As one former member noted, 'It wasn't just the lack of money, although that was becoming quite serious. It was the lack of accountability. When I came in I discovered the party had no idea how many bank accounts they had.' Members of some bodies were elected, others were appointed by the leader, leading to different reporting relationships and obligations. The creation of the Federal Liberal Agency of Canada (FLAC) in 1975 further complicated the situation.

By 1984, the overall lack of coordination in the party's financial affairs was becoming a critical problem. Incredibly, revenue and expenditures were handled by different bodies with little formal communication between them. A discussion paper prepared by the Reform Committee pointed out this problem of a 'financial maze' was compounded by the federal structure of the party. Most of the party's revenue was raised at the constituency and provincial/regional level. This meant the national office and its operations were almost entirely dependent on the large corporate donations obtained through the Revenue Committee appointed by the leader. As a result, the national office had no predictable or stable source of income and its budget had to be negotiated every year.

To make matters worse, the party's overall revenue was declining. The same discussion paper noted that 'the Liberals now have the most anaemic fundraising campaigns of all three parties, the smallest number of donors, the most underfunded national headquarters and the only debt.' The debt was eliminated before the 1984 election campaign through a special arrangement negotiated by the party's finance chair, Senator Pietro Rizzuto, which saw individual riding associations contribute one-time special levies to the national level. But, as the committee concluded, 'while the party owes him a tremendous vote of thanks, the challenge now is to find routine ongoing means to avoid the problem in the future.'[9]

In this regard, the discussion paper conclusions were particularly salient. With the party now running a deficit *and* finding itself in opposition, the issue of falling revenues became far more significant, leading to a groundswell of support for streamlining the party's financial management structure. As a result, Turner established a Special Financial Review Committee almost immediately after the election. The committee reported its recommendations to the party's national executive in February 1985. Chief among the proposals was the creation of an overarching Financial Management Committee that would bring all of the key players together to 'prepare and implement long-range financial plans and operating budgets for all aspects of the national level of the party.'[10]

A second initiative taken by Turner on the financial front was the appointment of Senator Leo Kolber as his chief fundraiser. Turner had served on the boards of several large corporations with Kolber before returning to public life. Kolber, who was assisted by his senior aide, Herb Metcalfe, ended up playing much the same role as Pietro Rizzuto, repeatedly throwing the party financial lifelines which soon sank below the water under the weight of a crippling debt.

For his part, one of Collenette's first objectives was to evaluate the situation at 102 Bank Street and attempt to rebuild the national office despite the financial constraints. Within a relatively short period of time, several key personnel had left the office. In a similar fashion to the rebuilding at the Liberal Caucus Research Bureau a few blocks away, they were replaced by a group of young professionals. Among them were a new director of communications, Daniel Despins (who had been press secretary to Defence Minister Gilles Lamontagne during the Trudeau era) and a new director of policy development, Mark Resnick (who came to the party from his position as executive director of the Canada Israel Committee). With no political baggage from the leadership race, both Despins and Resnick were able to assume central roles quickly and enhanced the image of the national office.

Resnick in particular was given an intentionally broad mandate so as to underline the utility of the party office for the parliamentary wing. Cooperation between the party and parliamentary policy operations was without precedent. Caucus chair Doug Frith later recalled that this collaboration 'was one of the most successful and productive arrangements of the entire opposition operation.'[11]

Although Collenette handled the day-to-day operation of the national office, there were some areas where Campagnolo made it clear she had a specific rebuilding agenda in mind. Campagnolo also made a conscious decision to push ahead with two major projects despite their cost, convinced that the only way to build momentum and enthusiasm for the party was to generate activity. The first of these was an ambitious plan to acquire a permanent home for the party's national headquarters, to be owned by the party rather than remaining dependent on rental accommodation. In this the party had an advantage despite its lack of ready cash. The previous headquarters on Cooper Street had been located in one of two old houses owned by the party, a legacy from a party member. Although they were no longer useful, the land on which they stood was now worth a great deal. Consequently, they were sold to provide the capital for new permanent headquarters. Land was purchased nearby at 200 Laurier Avenue. Lengthy negotiations took place between the party and a local developer, Pat Gillan, who agreed to construct a building on the site. Two floors of the new six-storey building were to be owned by the party in a condominium-type arrangement in exchange for their provision of the land, and the building itself was to be called Liberal House. A highly successful campaign was launched to solicit funds from party members for interior design and furnishings, using the slogan 'Buy a Brick.' For a contribution of $250, each donor's name would be engraved on a wall of bricks in the lobby of the building. Within weeks of the launch, the available space had been committed. The culmination of these efforts was a modern and impressive suite of offices for the national party in a building within minutes of Parliament Hill.

As Campagnolo had hoped, the building project created a degree of anticipation and momentum which served to re-engage many of the rank-and-file of the party as well as the elites. On 26 November 1986, the official opening of the new national headquarters was held as part of the festivities surrounding the party's national biennial convention being held in the city at the same time. An overflow crowd assembled for the opening ceremony, at which both Campagnolo and Turner spoke. As Turner indicated at the time, the party appeared to be well on its way to recovery. 'We're rebuilding, and better than before,' he declared. 'The Liberal Party has always known how to learn from its setbacks.'[12]

The second project which Campagnolo personally oversaw was that of party reform, especially of the constitution. This was hardly surprising since she had been involved in several previous attempts to drag the party into the modern era while the Liberals were still in power. With the party's descent into opposition, the urgency of remaking the system provided very real incentive for meaningful change.

Start of a New Era

The defeat of the governing Liberals in 1984 marked the end of an era in more ways than one. The party that returned to power in 1993 bore little resemblance to the party that was brought to its knees less than a decade earlier. For that matter, Ottawa itself – both political and bureaucratic – changed forever during that time period as well. What John Swift described as 'the idyll of Camelot on the Rideau' was over even before the 1984 election, but few people knew it and even fewer realized how quickly and dramatically the system was changing.[13]

Party politics, like government, remained a gentleman's game in Canada long after the American system was overtaken by money, the media, and special interests. As Granatstein has outlined, Ottawa at the beginning of the Trudeau era was still a tranquil backwater, peopled by influential civil servants drawn largely from two or three ivy-league universities in central Canada. The relationship of these 'mandarins' with their political masters was based on mutual respect and personal trust.[14] The arrival of Pierre Trudeau saw the advent of a more technocratic and more representative bureaucracy, but also one which enhanced the pattern of bureaucratic influence and respect.[15] In this context, the extra-parliamentary wing of the party found itself playing even less of a role, in part because it lacked the credibility of a representative, professional organization. The Conservatives had spent the better part of a decade modernizing their operation before the 1984 election, but the Liberal machine had atrophied with the party in power, a phenomenon recognized by many Liberal Party activists but less appreciated by the long-serving elites.

As late as 1980 the Liberal Party still functioned more like a private club, run by a select few who were almost exclusively white and male. The total membership of the party was relatively small and extremely loyal. Everyone knew everyone. The same people had organized conventions and run elections for years. The even smaller party elite played a key role in determining the results of the infrequent leadership campaigns that served to renew the party's image. Senator Keith Davey maintained there were still only 250 'insiders' in the Liberal Party in 1979. And in 1984 this group – backroom organizers and ex officio delegates from the parliamentary wing – had anointed John Turner. But their grasp on the reins of power was already beginning to slacken by then, the result of changes which had their origins in the Liberals' 1979 defeat and unexpected return to power a few months later.[16]

Most Liberals had expected to use their time in opposition after the 1979 defeat to rebuild and renew the party. Many were frustrated by their inability to effect such change during what they considered to be an all-too-brief time in opposition. Undaunted, a small group of reform-minded Liberals continued to push for change over the next four years despite the party's return to power. The traditional tug of war between the parliamentary and extra-parliamentary wings of the party took on new dimensions in the fourth and final Trudeau mandate. The government's large majority allowed it to pursue an activist agenda that many of the reformers, coming from the business Liberal end of the spectrum, found disconcerting. In addition, that ambitious agenda precluded any serious attention being paid by the parliamentary elites to the state of the party apparatus. As a result, when John Turner launched his campaign for the leadership in February 1984, his call for greater democratization and modernization of the party touched a chord with the frustrated reformers, and especially with the Young Liberals among them.

By the time Turner took over the Liberal Party in June he inherited a party on the brink of crisis. Their electoral victory a few months later brought matters to a head. Reforms that some party activists believed should have occurred years earlier began to be adopted with surprising speed. Their implementation was accelerated by the new leader's tacit support, and by the fact that the extra-parliamentary wing now had the upper hand. Reforms were broad-ranging, affecting virtually every aspect of the party machinery from financial management and policy development to amendments to the party constitution regarding the composition of the executive, membership rules, the selection of convention delegates, and the operation of the national headquarters. To properly understand the motivation for these reforms and their significance for future conflict within the party, it is important to consider the traditional pattern of collapse and renewal that characterized the party's evolution, a pattern many believe was a crucial factor in its lengthy status as the natural governing party. It is also important to recognize the perennial themes underlying party reform in the modern era, such as the relationship between the federal structure of the party and the internal fiscal imbalance, the perennial conflict between the parliamentary and extra-parliamentary wings of the party, and the minimal role of the extra-parliamentary wing when the party is in power. Last but hardly least, an examination of the evolution of party reform issues reveals the long-standing involvement and complex interrelationships of many of the key players in recent leadership conflicts.

The Liberal Party's Cycle of Defeat and Renewal

The calls for change within the party after the Liberals' 1979 loss were, in themselves, nothing new. As Wearing and others have noted, the history of the Liberal Party has been characterized by a 'cyclical pattern of decay and renewal, the decay coming after a number of years in power and the renewal prompted by electoral defeat, either threatened or actual.'[17] Although infrequent, the party's brief periods in opposition were seen as essential to its continued dynamism and electoral success.

The changes brought about by these earlier reform efforts clearly demonstrated the problematic relationship between the two 'wings' of the party.[18] In 1964, at the first national assembly held after Pearson and the Liberals returned to power, a number of constitutional changes were approved. Some were specifically designed to remedy the perennial imbalance between the two wings. First and foremost, an amendment was adopted which provided for the national executive of the party to be elected by the membership, rather than appointed by the leader. Second, and equally significant, another amendment required the party to hold a national convention every two years. The adoption of future constitutional amendments would be determined by a vote of the delegates, who would be selected by their constituency membership.

After the 1964 assembly, prominent 'Cell 13' reformer Richard Stanbury – by now the national policy chair – was authorized to begin organizing the party's first full-blown national policy convention. The convention was held two years later, in 1966. With more than two thousand delegates, it was the first one ever that was not dominated by the parliamentary wing. One amendment adopted in 1966 was put forward by the president of the Liberal Youth wing, Montreal law student Michel Robert. This resolution, which called for a leadership review vote to be held at the first convention after every election, would only be adopted after considerable debate. The tone of the discussions was captured by one delegate who spoke in favour of the amendment when he declared, 'it is very easy for a party to have democracy when the Party is out of office. The real test of democracy in the Party is when the Party is in office.'[19]

In keeping with the thrust of these democratic reforms, in 1968 Richard Stanbury became the first president of the party not personally selected by the leader or his delegate. However, Stanbury later confided that he had realized his election would coincide with that of a new party leader, so he voluntarily approached each of the leadership hopefuls to ensure his candidacy would present no problems for them.[20] Although Pierre Trudeau did not know Stanbury personally, Wearing suggests that outgoing president John Nicol's support for Stanbury smoothed the way for him and ensured the new leader's acceptance of his candidacy.[21] Perhaps equally important, Stanbury, like his immediate predecessors Nicol and John Connolly, was already a senator and member of the Liberal caucus, thereby ensuring his role as president could serve to connect the parliamentary and extra-parliamentary wings.

Over the course of the next decade the party's national executive attempted to implement other Cell 13 recommendations to improve internal party communication and develop a greater national or pan-

Canadian presence. Remarkably, all of these objectives would still be priorities for John Turner and the decimated Liberal Party nearly two decades later.

The extra-parliamentary wing's role with respect to policy development when the party was in power was even less clearly defined or accepted. This situation had actually become worse over several decades of attempted party reform. As former Cell 13 activist and Trudeau adviser Jim Coutts later noted, political parties had historically served several purposes, and none more so than the Liberal Party. In Coutts's view, providing a source of input for regional grievances through the rank-and-file membership had been 'one of the keys to the party's continued success at managing regional cleavages and presenting itself as the party of national unity.' But the advent of new technologies of polling and mass communications had been 'eroding this traditional role of party members at the local level for some time.'[22]

The Impact of Trudeau's Participatory Democracy

When he assumed the leadership from Pearson in 1968 (having defeated, among others, leadership hopefuls John Turner and Paul Martin Sr.), Pierre Trudeau was largely uninterested in the details of the party's organization. Despite this he was directly responsible for some of the reforms which occurred during his first mandate, reforms which would have far-reaching consequences for the party after 1984. His motivation was the concept of 'participatory democracy' which he was promoting in society as a whole, beyond partisan considerations, but which he believed could have a potentially positive impact on political parties as well. In his various speeches during the 1968 leadership race and immediately after his election, Trudeau urged Liberals to 'exercise real, organic power and political action' in order to create a 'modern mass party.'[23]

Party president Richard Stanbury enthusiastically embraced the idea of greater participation within the party, albeit with the caveat that there was no real consensus on what this term might mean. From 1968 until 1971 the party and the government both struggled with the implementation of participatory democracy. Within the party many felt, as Cell 13 alumnus Keith Davey did, that the term 'participatory democracy' meant the same thing as 'the new politics.' For them, bringing in new blood, finding promising new candidates, and 'making the traditional party structures more responsive to local party elites throughout the country'[24] – especially in western Canada – were seen as the primary objectives.

The second and most fruitful aspect of Trudeau's vision of participatory democracy involved *broadening the base* of citizen participation in both government and political parties. It was this part of his project that would, in the end, be the most successful. It would also produce the most dramatic change to the way the Liberal Party operated. Over a remarkably short period of time, the country saw new Canadians from a wide range of ethnic origins begin to seek out opportunities to participate in the political process and to increase their representation in the various institutions of government, largely through their membership in the Liberal Party of Canada.

In 1974 Trudeau introduced a number of changes to the Elections Act, including the provision of tax deductions for political contributions, in an effort to encourage donations by ordinary Canadians and limit the importance of corporate funding. The legislation also imposed limits on campaign spending and provided rebates to all those candidates who received a minimum number of votes, in order to level the playing field for political parties.[25] Additionally, the changes were designed to encourage individuals from minority or marginalized groups to participate fully in the broader political process, including as candidates for public office.

Trudeau believed it was important for the Liberal Party to ensure its membership rules did not prevent new Canadians from participating, and in fact encouraged them to become active members of the Liberal Party. In 1973 the party created the Women's Liberal Commission and the Liberal Youth Commission to ensure the full participation of both those groups within the mainstream of party activities. Similar commissions followed for seniors and aboriginal peoples. Nevertheless the formal party organization and its traditional elites continued to suffer from a lack of attention from the parliamentary wing under Trudeau, which led to considerable unrest as his tenure as leader continued.

The Declining Role of the Extra-Parliamentary Wing under Trudeau

The decline of the volunteer wing whenever the party was in power is described by many Liberals as a phenomenon common to all democracies. Jim Coutts – Trudeau's principal secretary for most of that time – once mused, 'That is a general problem for all parties. How do you make a political party effectively part of an administration? The leadership is responsible to the party that brought it to power, but it has to avoid the favouritism of bringing in activists who weren't elected to run the country. So how does the political wing play a bigger role in articulating ideas and directions?'[26] Many grassroots Liberals and members of the party's extra-parliamentary elite believed they had even less influence under Trudeau after 1974.

One explanation for the party's lack of influence during Trudeau's mandate (an explanation offered by many of his supporters from the parliamentary wing) was that the party more or less *willingly* faded into the background from 1974 to 1979 because the vast majority of the rank-and-file membership was content with the policy direction Trudeau was taking. As former caucus chair and later senator Peter Stollery declared, for many Liberals 'Trudeau *was* the party.'[27] Nevertheless, a small but vocal minority opposed several of his more prominent policies. For them this policy conflict was compounded by the volunteer party's reluctance to assert itself. It was further exacerbated by the continued presence of Keith Davey (now ironically seen as part of the old guard rather than a reformer) as a key adviser to the prime minister, and by the growth in importance of the PMO under Jim Coutts.

One of the prominent Toronto Young Liberal reformers of the day, Alf Apps, specifically connected the two developments, noting that after 1974 'the party atrophied while all the talent was in PMO.'[28] His concern, however, was not shared by the majority of senior Liberals. 'It's inevitable, a matter of the political law of gravity,' former veteran Toronto MP and Trudeau-era minister Charles Caccia said. 'Of course everyone wants to be involved in government when the party is in power.'[29] As McCall Newman noted, other senior Liberals went further in their assessment of the problem. For them, some of those Young Turks were simply 'impatient for Trudeau to resign so that they could benefit from the circulation of elites that occurs when a new leader brings his own troupe into the party's power structure.'[30]

Reform Interrupted: The 1979 Defeat and the 1980 'Restoration'

Virtually all students of the Liberal Party agree that the 1979 defeat should have led to substantive party renewal, coming as it did after more than a decade in power and a declining sense of policy direction. Certainly some initial steps were taken to begin the process of consultation and renewal almost immediately after the party's loss to the Conservatives in May of that year. But the party's very brief stint in opposition, and the stunning return of Pierre Trudeau as leader and prime minister in early 1980, precluded any type of major party reform. Trudeau himself made it clear that he had his own policy agenda for his final term in office. Nor was he alone in this attitude. Marc Lalonde, his most trusted confidant and senior cabinet minister, later recounted, 'When we lost the election, I made up my mind as a result that if we ever got another kick at the can we were really going to kick it.'[31] Admitting that the final years of the last mandate had been ones in which the government had tended to 'compromise and react to events' rather than initiating policies, Lalonde concluded, 'we decided we were going to govern on the basis of what we believed. Then if we were defeated, we would know why.'[32]

Not everyone was pleased with these developments. Many in the national executive felt their constitutional authority had been ignored. Once having resigned, they believed the leader could not suddenly return to this position of his own volition. A leadership race was the only valid course of action, and they were in charge of that process. And yet the parliamentary wing had publicly declared their support for Trudeau shortly after the sudden election call which they themselves had orchestrated. Although the executive felt they had no real choice but to accept the decision of the caucus, they also were determined to exact a quid pro quo for their acceptance of this fait accompli. They presented a number of demands to the leader, including their input into the composition of the national campaign committee, but instead he accepted their request for a strategy committee and a national platform committee, with equal party representation among the members, a compromise solution promoted by Tom Axworthy. In the end, Trudeau's return was legitimized by the national executive when a motion urging him to resume the position of leader was introduced by one of the two party vice-presidents, Lorna Marsden. After the 'Restoration,' as it was referred to in the inner circles, Marsden would be able to parlay her crucial support for that vote into support within PMO for some of her policy initiatives.

The emerging signs of extra-parliamentary discontent following the 1979 defeat were temporarily silenced by the decisive victory of 1980, which returned Trudeau and the Liberals to power with a substantial majority. Nevertheless, Tom Axworthy was still committed to the concept of greater party participation. He attempted to further smooth ruffled feathers among what he referred to as the 'lay' members of the party by meeting with the party's platform representatives and incorporating much of the committee's unannounced policy recommendations into the 1980 Throne Speech.

At the same time, it was obvious the prime minister was reinvigorated and anxious to address his policy agenda. Axworthy saw the fourth mandate as a 'strategic prime ministership' in which Trudeau would focus on two or three personal priorities while a few key ministers led the charge on others. Foremost among Trudeau's priorities, of course, was the defeat of the separatists in the Quebec referendum. His subsequent announcement of a constitutional reform package (in which Jean Chrétien as justice minister served as his able second-in-command, liaising with his provincial counterparts) culminated in the 1982 patriation of the constitution with an amending formula and entrenchment of the Charter of Rights and Freedoms.

The degree of commitment and involvement Trudeau inspired among his caucus members on this constitutional exercise was, in the words of Montreal MP David Berger, 'remarkable and probably unprecedented. Everyone was caught up in the spirit of the thing and totally absorbed by it for nearly two years. Many of us felt it was a privilege just to sit in caucus on Wednesdays and hear the prime minister talk about it. You knew you were part of history in the making and you felt you were actually accomplishing something in Ottawa.'[33] The constitution exercise and the Charter itself were hugely popular in every region of the country, including Quebec.[34]

But the party's approval ratings began to decline dramatically as a global recession took hold and the highly progressive but politically unsaleable budget put forward by Allan MacEachen in 1983 (which he was soon forced to revise) was widely criticized. Ongoing conflicts with the premiers on other issues, from energy policy to fish to the funding of social programs, added to public discontent. Satisfied that national unity had been assured, Canadians turned their attention to other issues such as unemployment, high interest rates, and a faltering economy, and Liberal fortunes plunged as it became clear that they had few solutions to these problems. The ongoing concerns of some reform-minded Liberals began to be expressed in public forums, while all but the most sanguine of Trudeau's supporters began to consider the succession.

Another problem preoccupying the party's national executive was the lack of financial resources. Corporate fundraising, never the party's strong suit, especially since the advent of the Trudeau era, was falling further and further behind. Worse still, there had been little or no success in taking advantage of the reforms introduced by Trudeau in the 1974 Elections Act to make up the shortfall. The Liberals appeared unable to raise significant revenues from ordinary Canadians, something which both of the other major parties were now doing far better. While this was partly due to the fact that the other parties had national membership lists and the Liberals did not, the Conservatives had also mastered the intricacies of direct mail, while the New Democrats were increasing their funding from individuals as well as maintaining their strong support from unions. The Liberal Party's financial woes were becoming increasingly apparent to party activists as well and proved yet another source of widespread discontent.

Unrest and the 1982 Party Reforms

Even while the constitutional package was being crafted in the first two years of the restoration, a small group of Liberals, concerned about the government's direction on other policy issues, continued to meet outside of the party's formal organization. Frustrated with what they saw as a lack of options for meaningful input through the extra-parliamentary wing, they had already organized alternative policy meetings of like-minded Liberal reformers during the last Trudeau mandate, and they continued to do so more aggressively after the restoration. The Grindstone Group's chief architects were a former national director of the party, Blair Williams, and the party's communications director, Audrey Gill. Among its leading participants were future lynchpins of Paul Martin's leadership, such as the party's future financial officer and fundraiser, Mike Robinson, Ontario activists Alf Apps, Sean Moore, and Jim DeWilde, and Quebec MPs Dennis Dawson and Rémi Bujold, as well as Martin himself. In addition to their concerns with party reform, it is instructive to note that many of the Grindstone members were in the minority on both of the party's two policy axes: they were business liberals in an era of social liberalism and decentralists in an era of strong central federalism.

Things came to a head when Jim Coutts announced he would run for public office. Trudeau appointed him as the Liberal candidate in a Toronto-area by-election, bypassing the normal candidate selection process. The by-election had only become necessary because Trudeau had previously appointed the riding's incumbent MP and former national caucus chair, Peter Stollery, to the Senate. Accusations of PMO arrogance and isolation returned with a vengeance. It soon became apparent that public sentiment in the riding was overwhelmingly opposed to the unnecessary election. Historically, the party in power has always been vulnerable to by-election losses, but Coutts's stunning upset defeat by an obscure NDP candidate, Dan Heap, in one of the 'safest' Liberal ridings in the country still came as a shock. It convinced the group of young Liberal dissidents who had clustered around the Grindstone Group that the time had come for a more direct challenge to the prime minister and to the parliamentary wing, who in their view had become completely disconnected from the grassroots of the party.

One member of the disgruntled youth group, Alf Apps, later remarked 'the Coutts nomination fiasco was the catalyst' for their subsequent actions, even though 'the issue of party reform had been building for years.'[35] After the by-election defeat Apps wrote a scathing letter to Tom Axworthy in which he argued the party machinery was in a shambles, the leadership was 'anti-democratic,' and new blood was necessary if there were to be another Liberal government after the next election.[36]

As a direct result of the Apps controversy, policy took a back seat to proposed democratic reforms of the party structure at the 1982 biennial convention, which took place in the fall. The Liberal Youth Commission delegates were headed by Alf Apps and included future key Martin supporters David Herle and Terrie O'Leary. They delivered three priority resolutions – including an incendiary one known as Resolution 40. Alf Apps introduced Resolution 40 himself, taking pains in his remarks to distinguish between his ongoing support for the leader and his criticism of the 'backroom boys' around him. The resolution denounced the role of 'non-accountable, non-elected, members of the party [who] have direct informal roles in advising the government which totally bypass the democratically elected executive of the party.' Equating 'party reform' with 'party survival,' the resolution insisted 'the parliamentary wing must be more accountable to the rank and file.'[37]

To his dismay, many delegates on the convention floor heard Apps's positive remarks about Trudeau's leadership and mistakenly thought his intervention was in favour of the elite's resolution. Some took to chanting the leader's name, drowning out the proceedings. In the end, much to the chagrin of the Young Liberals, the resolution passed easily with the deliberate support of the party executive and the parliamentary wing. Years later, Apps admitted the Youth Commission had been 'snookered' by Marsden and what they perceived to be the party elites, who had 'essentially decided to adopt our recommendations as their own.' He also argued that the real purpose behind the resolution – namely democratic reform of the party and the provision of a 'counterweight' to PMO – had been 'usurped' by anti-Trudeau activists.[38] Certainly many pro-Trudeau participants at the time saw the resolution and its supporters as 'a stalking-horse for business Liberals who wanted to replace the interventionist Trudeau with the more amenable John Turner.'[39]

Iona Campagnolo's Election as Party President

In addition to their adoption of Resolution 40, the party elites also saw the potential benefits of providing the party with a more representative and progressive face. Largely through the efforts of Lorna Marsden and Marc Lalonde, popular former cabinet minister Iona Campagnolo was persuaded to run for the office of party president against the incumbent, Norman McLeod, who had served only two years. Another perceived benefit of Campagnolo's candidacy was her electoral base in western Canada, the region most in need of an enhanced party presence to restore electoral fortunes. With the election of the first woman president, Marsden's plan to work for change from within was at least partially vindicated.

Perhaps most importantly, Campagnolo was seen as a party activist herself. She soon demonstrated the accuracy of this view when she created a special President's Committee for the Reform of the Liberal Party of Canada in 1983. In her address to the committee at its inaugural meeting, the new president began by declaring 'Our job is to responsibly establish new institutional arrangements to enable the Liberal Party of Canada to meet the challenges of the 80's and a new generation of Liberalism.' For the most part this was taken to mean restructuring the party executive, financial arrangements, membership rules and processes for policy development; Campagnolo also stressed the need to provide more substantial assistance for the national headquarters. Echoing comments made nearly twenty years earlier by Richard Stanbury, Campagnolo lamented that 'there are lots of jobs the national office should be undertaking but cannot. There are lots of jobs the national office should be undertaking but which by default are being done by others. The jobs that the national office can and does undertake are now generally of low value and little importance to the welfare of the party.'[40]

The committee met again in September to consider the issues, which in large measure resembled the ones Keith Davey, Richard Stanbury, and the other earlier reform Liberals had been trying to resolve for more than a decade without success. The committee recognized this. 'In its structure and organizational assumptions,' they concluded, 'the Liberal Party continues to reflect a bygone era – Canada as it was, rather than Canada as it is today. These structures now need to be reformed in order to restore the Liberal Party's historic ability to lead in Canada's ongoing evolution.'[41]

However, events intervened to delay this reform process as well. By the end of February 1984 Prime Minister Trudeau had decided on the timing of his departure, and a leadership race was called for the first time in sixteen years. So it was that John Turner's leadership campaign pledge to bring about 'real' reform in the party found so much resonance with a group of Liberal dissidents who had been frustrated since 1974, as well as with the group of new Young Liberals, many of whom came from western Canada, who felt excluded by what they perceived to be the elitist nature of the party.

Although one of the last acts of the old guard was to deliver the leadership of the party to John Turner as their anointed heir, it was clear that the heir apparent had found an additional base of support within an element of the grassroots, a base quite different from the larger one which supported Jean Chrétien. In many important respects Turner's determination to ensure that these formerly marginalized supporters could play a greater role in party affairs, and that there would be 'no more rainmakers, no insiders,' would continue to be evident throughout his tenure as leader. But his ability to deliver on many of his leadership campaign pledges was severely constrained by the realities of life in the Official Opposition.

The committee created by Campagnolo to address the issues raised by Resolution 40 submitted its final report to her in August 1985. She then decided to organize a special constitutional convention of the party to be held in Halifax in November of that year, to provide a forum for party activists to discuss the recommendations in advance of the planned 1986 biennial convention.

The 1985 Halifax Reform Convention

In a final section of its report, the committee turned its attention once more to the issue of the relationship between the two wings of the party, stressing the importance of improving contacts and communications. 'Once the reconstruction process is complete,' the report concluded, 'the regular Party-parliamentary relationship is the key to long-term strength and survival.'[42] Within months the first opportunity for the two wings to come together was provided by the Halifax convention. At this event, members of the caucus and party activists explored the various options proposed by the Reform Committee in their final report, as well as proposed amendments that had been submitted by various riding associations, the two commissions, and the national caucus.

The first such party event to be held since the 1984 election defeat, the Halifax convention was unexpectedly well organized and well attended. As many participants indicated at the time, there was also a genuine interest in the subject matter. A vigorous debate ensued on several of the proposals, and notably those relating to membership rules, the selection of convention delegates, and the possibility of universal suffrage. Other major debates took place over the amendments put forward by the Youth Commission and, to a lesser extent, the Women's Commission. The youth amendments in particular were a harbinger of things to come. Like the women, they were intent on ensuring their role in the decision-making process, but they could not achieve their objectives by simply altering proposed amendments, as the women could by adding wording such as 'he *or she.*' Instead, the youth wing's approach was to insist on as broad as possible a definition of their membership category. They proposed amendments to extend the age limits, for example, and – most significantly for future developments – argued that not only university-based clubs but youth clubs at any other 'institution' should be accepted.

Despite some suspicion of the proposed amendments, which, it was pointed out by opponents, originated from a small but highly active group of riding associations in the west, the conference was judged a major success, boosting the morale of rank-and-file members and healing some of the internal divisions. Meanwhile behind the scenes, one brief incident revealed an internal caucus rift that had not yet healed. John Turner's keynote speech on Saturday evening was well received by the vast majority of participants, but not by the diehard supporters of Jean Chrétien. Many of them initially refused to join in the standing ovation. When caucus chair Doug Frith bounded on stage to stand beside Turner, all of the caucus members present began making their way to the platform as well, with the exception of Chrétien himself. Seated at a table with supporters from his riding, Turner's key leadership rival appeared taken aback by the move. Chrétien remained in his place long after the remainder of his colleagues had joined Frith, before finally acceding to the urging of those closest to him and making his way to the stage to take his place beside the leader. By the time the media were allowed into the room for the closing photo opportunity, they once again saw only a united caucus, overcoming personal differences in the interests of the party. These differences would not remain concealed for long, however, as the biennial national convention the following year would show.

The 1986 Leadership Review Vote and the Friends of John Turner

The first national convention after the 1984 election was a landmark event for the Liberal Party in many ways. Major changes to the party's organization and operations were being proposed through amendments to the party's constitution, and a number of highly divisive policy debates were scheduled to take place on issues ranging from free trade to the constitution of the country. These debates would take place simultaneously with the election of a new party president and national executive, positions whose importance had increased dramatically with the party's fall from power. Last, but hardly least, John Turner would have to face a leadership review vote, as mandated by the constitutional amendment introduced ten years earlier.

There was lively but coherent debate on a wide range of policy issues at the convention, but the free trade debate proved chaotic. Delegates ultimately approved two contradictory resolutions put forward by two opposing caucus members, Lloyd Axworthy and Don Johnston. The debate on Quebec and the constitution, by contrast, demonstrated conclusively the advantages of cooperation between the two wings of the party, as the jointly sponsored party/caucus resolution passed without difficulty and the Liberals appeared ready to face whatever the Conservative government of Brian Mulroney eventually produced in the way of a response to the Quebec government's demands.

Meanwhile the party's own constitutional reform process appeared to take a back seat to the issue of the leadership review, with many workshops poorly attended and a number of contradictory or ambiguous proposals approved. Nevertheless the concepts of a Platform Committee and a Financial Management Committee proposed by the President's Reform Committee were adopted. Also as recommended by the committee, and supported in Halifax, the number of ex officio delegates at national conventions was capped at 15 per cent of the total and the number of delegates per constituency was raised to twelve, with equal representation from the women's and youth commissions. These changes, though widely ignored by the media, would later prove extremely important.

When the Liberal Party adopted the concept of a leadership review vote, to be held at the first national convention after a federal election, there was little expectation that it would cause serious difficulty for the incumbent leader except on very rare occasions. For some, the 1984 electoral defeat was just such an occasion. Many rank-and-file Liberals argued John Turner could never have won an election so soon after the retirement of Trudeau and should be given another chance as Lester Pearson had. Others argued the 1984 defeat was exactly the type of scenario for which the provision had been adopted. As the party soon discovered, however, the nature of the review process was unclear, with key elements unspecified in the constitutional provisions. As a result, the review vote became a free-for-all that heightened the party's image of disorganization and set the combative ground rules for future leadership race campaigns.

Despite the resignation of Jean Chrétien from caucus in February of 1986, or perhaps because of it, speculation had quickly mounted at all levels in the Liberal Party apparatus about Turner's possible fate at the upcoming leadership review in November. Although Chrétien's resignation appeared to leave him free to manoeuvre, he gave no public indication that he was interested in challenging Turner. But Chrétien did campaign extensively for the Ontario provincial Liberals under David Peterson in the June 1985 election which saw them elected.

Still, there were many in the party who – while unhappy with Turner – did not want to return to the past by choosing Chrétien. Others felt the party's improving fortunes did not merit yet another disruption. With monthly public opinion polls consistently showing the Liberals in the lead over the hapless, scandal-ridden Mulroney Conservatives and the nondescript NDP, there was no obvious reason to rock the boat.[43] Several of Chrétien's closest aides and advisers had already reached that conclusion themselves. They advised Chrétien that the support was not there for him to mount a successful challenge. Others told him the time simply was not right. 'The party had no money. The organization was in a shambles. With Mulroney's huge majority, who would want to take over and lead the party in opposition for at least three years?' Sergio Marchi recalled.[44]

This did not stop a handful of Chrétien's supporters from beginning to work behind the scenes to organize for him.[45] As one key organizer, former Moncton MP Gary McCauley, explained, 'For us it wasn't simply that Turner lost the election. It was the *way* he lost it. He couldn't screw things up that badly and then expect us to let him have another go at it.'[46] McCauley was in a minority, but he was certainly not alone. Chrétien stalwart Henry Wright was busy attempting to organize support for Chrétien in Ontario, as was Jacques Corriveau in Quebec. The latter was all the more noteworthy since Corriveau at the time was serving as the vice-president of the Liberal Party's Quebec wing. In a seven-page text released at a press conference in Montreal on 20 September (copies of which were distributed in advance to all members of the Liberal caucus), Corriveau argued a leadership review vote would be a 'truly healthy rather than a divisive process' which would lend democratic legitimacy to the party's leader – whoever it might be – in the next election campaign. As the leader of the party in that future election, that individual would 'most likely become the next prime minister.' Admitting he 'would be less than frank if I did not tell you that I believe Jean Chrétien could lead us to victory and take office afterwards as the prime minister of a *strong, united and forward-looking nation,*' Corriveau nevertheless concluded 'I do not now automatically insist that we replace John Turner as leader ... I am simply suggesting that our troubled times demand a thorough, thoughtful, penetrating leadership review, to see if – as a united party – we have the leader we need to grapple with Canada's problems today.'[47]

Whatever his intentions, Corriveau's text was seen by Turner supporters as an open declaration of war. Their view was reinforced when George Young, a longtime Chrétien supporter who was serving as the president of the Ontario wing of the party, resigned from that position to actively organize for a leadership review. Years later, Young insisted that his decision stemmed from an 'anti-Turner' sentiment, rather than a pro-Chrétien one. 'I had tried to meet with the leader to tell him that he was in trouble, and to explain the issues, but no one was interested. I was tired of watching the incompetence and the indifference while others were working so hard. For many of us who supported the review it was primarily an anti-Turner sentiment, from which Chrétien happened to benefit.'[48] For Turner's supporters, however, the situation was seen as critical. 'We were under siege,' Turner's principal secretary, Doug Richardson, later recounted. 'They were on the attack.'[49]

Soon it was the turn of the review supporters to accuse the *Turner* organizers of open warfare. George Young, for example, believed he had reached an agreement with Turner's supporters, via Doug Richardson, to ensure a 'civil' process. Yet a few days after Young's meeting with Richardson, House leader Herb Gray issued a statement declaring the caucus was solidly behind Turner. Young stressed that Gray's statement was the direct cause of the subsequent media revelations of details such as the party's payments for the Turners' apartment in Toronto, a move which led to a series of increasingly nasty and personal attacks on both sides as the covert campaign operations continued. For his part Richardson later claimed Gray's statement was made without his knowledge, but he felt the retaliation through such personal revelations was 'completely out of line' regardless.

Afterwards, several Turner supporters were more sanguine about the real extent of the threat. Terry Popowich told one journalist: 'Whether it was a real threat or not at that point didn't matter. It was building momentum. People feed on that stuff and it catches on. The bandwagon looked like it was starting to move in the opposite direction.'[50] The consequences of this perceived or real challenge to Turner were huge, for the party and for the country. Nearly ten months of 1986 were devoted primarily to the leadership review by all sides in the debate. For Turner, this was seen as a life-or-death scenario. Virtually every senior staffer in OLO was assigned some task related to the leadership review. According to Richardson, he and Turner's key caucus supporters, led by André Ouellet and Senators David Smith and Al Graham, devoted nearly every Sunday from May until the convention to endless meetings in Richardson's office reviewing the situation and designing strategies to ensure victory. Although Richardson noted that Turner had told him 'at all times we were to avoid, wherever possible, a split in the party,' one memo from Richardson to the leader indicated he also had been instructed to 'move forward to protect your interests,' an exercise which would require not only time but personnel and money.[51]

The money required for the highly organized campaign to defend John Turner's leadership of the party came from a variety of sources, and it was substantial. Leo Kolber, the party's bagman and chair of the Revenue Committee, discovered to his chagrin that much of the funding for the newly minted 'Friends of Turner' campaign was being obtained from traditional party sources of revenue in the corporate world, leaving little or nothing for his ongoing efforts to reduce the party's ballooning debt. His discovery of the so-called 'Anderson Fund' was one of the reasons Kolber eventually refused to participate in a planned

photo opportunity at the convention, where he was supposed to deliver a symbolic cheque for more than $2 million to the leader.[52] As one
of the participants in the Friends later confided, 'We had more money
than we knew what to do with. Cash was coming in faster than we
could spend it.'

Meanwhile the personnel needed to defend Turner emerged in the
form of a new cadre of younger Liberals, most of them committed to
supporting the leader because they still viewed him as the man who
would 'open up' the party and get rid of the old guard (now defined as
the former reformers, Coutts, Davey, and Axworthy) once and for all.
Over the summer a number of Young Liberals were hired as part-time
staff in the OLO to work exclusively on the leadership review. Many of
them – such as David Herle, Terrie O'Leary, and Rick Mahoney – used
the tactics they learned in the 1986 battle to good advantage when organizing for Paul Martin Jr. four years later. Also engaged in this process
was an unknown aspiring pollster from Toronto, Michael Marzolini.
His task was to track delegate voting intentions.

The Young Liberals were led by a small group including Terry Popowich (a rising star in the Toronto Stock Exchange who later was obliged
to resign under a cloud), John Webster (a former law student and political junkie who had worked on Turner's 1984 leadership campaign
and the election campaigns of several Liberal MPs including Roy Maclaren), and Joe Volpe (a high-school vice-principal who was known
in Toronto as a master organizer in the ethnic communities). As one
of them later explained, at least for some of them the primary purpose
was the traditional one for backroom organizers in any party, namely to
acquire power within the party.[53]

Working under the direction of senior Turner advisers such as Senator David Smith, Stephen LeDrew (a future party president), and former party president Norman McLeod, they created a network which
came to be known as the Friends of John Turner. Popowich was the
most visible member of the group, devoting his time to strategies to
ensure the Metro Toronto ridings were solidly behind Turner. Webster
meanwhile became the de facto enforcer of the group. It was Webster
who devised the slogan 'Take No Prisoners!'

The Friends' slogan perfectly captured the tone and tenor of the leadership review process. Throughout the spring and summer additional
help was recruited by the Friends to take control of riding associations,
raise funds, and recruit heavily from the ethnic communities as well
as among the Young Liberals, whose role in turn would be greatly

enhanced under the proposed new party rules. In Quebec a similar scenario was unfolding. There it was organized primarily by Senator Pietro Rizzuto, the Quebec bagman, and Shefford MP Jean Lapierre, with considerable help from an up-and-coming Young Liberal aide to Rizzuto, Denis Coderre. In a brilliant tactical move, Doug Richardson convinced the party's national executive to subsidize the travel expenses of Young Liberal delegates – the group least likely to actually attend the convention if selected as delegates, because of a lack of funds – by increasing the fees for ordinary delegates. This was a precedent which would greatly benefit the Martin forces more than ten years later.

Despite the party's dire financial straits, both groups were able to raise considerable amounts of money for the review fight from sympathetic Liberals and, more significantly, from members of the business community who still saw Turner as their best hope among the Liberals. Not surprisingly, these same sources of funding had, by this time, abandoned all hope of the Conservatives winning re-election, given the Liberals' first-place standing in the polls and the Mulroney government's seemingly unending litany of scandals and ministerial resignations. But the most important benefits received by the Turner supporters were not financial. Instead, in what one senior Friends organizer later described as 'a gift from heaven' and George Young, by contrast, described as a 'fatal blow' to supporters of the leadership review, two of the most well-known members of the party elite's 'old guard' came out in favour of a leadership review. In October 1986 Senator Keith Davey published his memoirs, replete with negative comments about Turner's handling of the 1984 campaign and complimentary references to Jean Chrétien, whom he described as 'the most popular French Canadian in the Liberal Party.'[54] It was at the launch of his book in Montreal that Davey also commented on his 'huge' mistake in supporting Turner for the leadership in 1984.

Soon afterwards, in early November, former Quebec kingpin and Trudeau lieutenant Marc Lalonde – an early Turner supporter in 1984 – published an open letter to Turner in which he called for a review as well. Drafted by Lalonde with the help of Trudeau's former principal secretary, Tom Axworthy, and party bagman Leo Kolber's aide Herb Metcalfe, the letter was distributed to the parliamentary press gallery on 10 November. The following day Lalonde held a press conference in Montreal to elaborate on his concerns.

The letter itself required little elaboration. Ignoring entirely the 1984 campaign fiasco, it outlined three major areas in which he felt Turner was deficient, namely: fundraising, the party's standing in the polls, and its status with respect to the NDP. Taking a contrary position to the conventional wisdom, Lalonde argued the party's financial woes were the fault of an unpopular leader, not an unpopular party, and that Turner's personal expenses were unconscionable. 'A popular leader will not cost the party money. Popular leaders generate revenue,' he declared. Similarly, Lalonde disagreed with the view that the party was doing well because of its eight- to ten-point lead over the Conservatives and 38 per cent support in the polls. 'Logically, considering the Conservative record to date, we should be at 50 per cent,' he maintained. Finally, Lalonde pointed to the growing momentum of the NDP while the Liberals appeared stalled in popular support, and worried that the party might not even finish as the Official Opposition in the next election. 'I was afraid we were going to be wiped off the map,' he later confided.[55] While all of Lalonde's concerns would eventually prove to be well founded, they were dismissed out of hand at the time as overly pessimistic, even by many in the anti-Turner forces.

Meanwhile internal polling had suggested Turner would receive anywhere between 65 and 70 per cent of the delegates' support. The media had fixed on 67 per cent as a minimum, based on the perverse precedent set by Joe Clark and the Conservatives several years earlier. It was in this context that delegates began to arrive in Ottawa for the convention on Wednesday, 26 November. Meetings of the Young Liberals and the Women's Commission preceded the meetings of the full party in convention, and Turner was careful to attend both of those sessions to remind participants of his commitment to the party reform process. 'I have given this party back to you right across the country,' he told the Liberal youth; 'the clock will not be turned back.' He also used the occasion of several question-and-answer sessions to declare that the party's debt would be eliminated shortly after the convention had been put behind them.

Behind the scenes, however, considerable debate was taking place between the convention organizers and Turner's supporters, who by now were concerned about the allegiance of everyone outside of the leader's immediate circle. Chief among the convention organizers was David Collenette. As Collenette pointed out afterwards, he was 'put in an incredibly awkward position as secretary general.'[56] On the one hand all staff working for the party were supposed to be supporting the party leader as a matter of course. On the other hand, the constitution called for a leadership review and it was the job of the secretary general and his staff to organize it, as part of the convention. 'It caused a lot of hard feelings, because every time I would get in the way of something Popowich, Lapierre and that group wanted to do, I would be accused of being disloyal to Turner.' At the same time, 'I was bound and determined to run a fair convention for everyone, and I am satisfied that we did. What we had on our hands was a leadership convention without rules. At times it got pretty rough.'[57]

On one occasion this internal conflict spilled over into public view, when Jean Chrétien arrived at the convention to cast his ballot. Although accounts of the two men's supporters differ as to the agreement that had been reached, there was no dispute as to the end result. Chrétien's arrival with some of his key supporters provoked a chaotic melee among delegates. Collenette responded by calling the police to restore order. 'I was responsible for order,' he later said, 'and this was disorder.'[58] Although neither side was happy with the development, it was the Turner forces who found most fault with Collenette as a result.

A similar fate awaited caucus chair Doug Frith, who had been asked to co-chair the convention. In this role he would be the person to announce the results of the leadership review vote on the Sunday morning. A dispute had been ongoing for weeks in advance of the convention, with Turner's supporters arguing he should be informed of the results in advance, and in private. When this option was rejected by the organizers, the formerly warm relationship between Turner and Frith was irreparably damaged. The fact that Turner was not allowed to know the results in advance weighed heavily on the minds of several of his key strategists, who wanted to leave all options open in their planning of his response to the results. Frith later argued: 'I did the best I could. I arranged for John to see the results first, in his seat in the plenary, just before I announced them. But that wasn't good enough for his people, and they always blamed me for it.'[59] When Frith announced the results – a 76.5 per cent vote in favour of Turner – he paraphrased Campagnolo's remarks from two years earlier and declared 'I've been waiting a long time to say this to you, John. You're first in our hearts.'

Despite this declaration, Frith recalled that a 'lack of trust' permeated his relationship with Turner and his advisers in the succeeding months, part of the attitude of retaliation which saw Frith replaced as caucus chair and Herb Metcalfe and Leo Kolber resign from their fundraising posts shortly after, while David Collenette resigned as secretary general within the year. In Nova Scotia, party director Terry Mercer, who had spoken in favour of a leadership review on the convention floor, would soon be replaced as well.

On the floor of the convention, however, there was no visible evidence of the impending retribution, nor was there any real evidence of disgruntled supporters of review. Immediately after the results were known, a somewhat uncomfortable-looking Marc Lalonde and Keith Davey were shown wearing the ubiquitous Turner scarves that had been sported by his supporters among the delegates throughout the weekend. 'It's John's day,' Davey declared.[60] Once again it seemed the outward appearance of party unity was still considered essential by all good Liberals, whatever the personal cost.

Indeed, the delegates' overwhelming support at the convention was later used by Turner to defend himself and his leadership against several ensuing caucus 'coup' attempts. Ironically, some of those delegates – and especially some of the younger members of the Friends of Turner – would soon believe they had cause for concern about their decision to defend him. This was the case despite the fact Turner went further than any previous Liberal leader in according importance to the policy resolutions which had been passed at the convention. In an immediate post-convention interview he declared they 'are not strictly binding. But I consider them highly persuasive and they will form the general direction for the party going into the next election.'

Yet this was not enough for several of his younger organizers, some of whom later admitted to journalist Greg Weston that their displeasure with his lack of total commitment to a 'bottom-up' process was much less pressing than their dismay that they had not been given any positions of importance in the system in recognition of their efforts. 'There was an incredible resistance in the party establishment to this group of newcomers. It created all kinds of hassles and bad feelings.'[61] Worse still from their viewpoint, while they were being shut out of the action, 'Turner was delegating power to the same people who always had it – people like (senators) Mike Kirby, Jack Austin, that whole crowd.'[62] The accuracy of this interpretation was open to question, however. What took place may not have been an infusion of new blood from the younger members, but it was certainly a changing of the guard. Austin had in effect replaced Axworthy, Kirby had become the new Davey, and Ouellet replaced Lalonde. Shortly thereafter, Friends' organizer John Webster would be named the National Campaign director for the next election.

Senator Jack Austin argued the origins of the deep-seated resentment between the Turner and Chrétien camps that spilled into the open during the leadership review process lay with the original Turner/Trudeau confrontation. 'The cancer in the party actually stems from Turner's departure from the Trudeau cabinet,' Austin argued, and more specifically from the 1984 leadership in which Chrétien's people were seen as Trudeau acolytes. The unprecedented acts of aggression on both sides were deeply divisive and would cost the party dearly,' Austin maintained.[63] Certainly it can be argued that the clean sweep of personnel following the leadership review set a precedent that would be reinforced repeatedly over the next two decades, epitomized by the 'take no prisoners' mentality of Webster.

In the short term, however, the most significant fallout from the convention was the surprising lack of direction which seemed to permeate the caucus and the leader as they returned to their parliamentary duties. The drift which seemed to take hold of the Liberals, just when they were once again poised to win back the support of Canadians in the next election, would soon be swamped by a far more potent force. The hard-won appearance of unity, the party reforms, and the fresh start which Turner's renewed legitimacy seemed to offer were all abruptly and fatally derailed. The cause was not Turner's indecision and failure to seize the agenda, important as this would have been otherwise, but the announcement of the prime minister, Brian Mulroney, that he was organizing a meeting with the premiers at Meech Lake to discuss Quebec's conditions for signing on to the 1982 constitutional amendment.

4 The Meech Morass, 1987–1988

For the Liberal Party, Meech Lake is the issue that will not go away. Nor should it.

– Tom Axworthy[1]

When Brian Mulroney invited the premiers to Meech Lake to discuss the constitution one weekend in April 1987, he had no way of knowing the chain of events he had put in motion.

Mulroney's attempts to 'bring Quebec into the constitutional fold' and outdo his nemesis, Pierre Trudeau, have since been identified as one of the primary reasons for the collapse of the Progressive Conservative Party and the creation of two new regionally based political parties – the Reform Party and the Bloc Québécois – in its place.[2] The morphing of Reform into the Canadian Alliance party, and the subsequent 'merger' of the small Progressive Conservative rump with the Alliance to form a new Conservative Party in 2004, can be seen as the end result of this constitutional legacy, which has left members of the old Progressive Conservative Party as minority shareholders in the Reform-dominated Harper government. Canadians are well aware of the sad fate of the Progressive Conservative Party. They are less aware of the negative impact Mulroney's constitutional initiatives had on the Liberal Party. Disagreement over Meech Lake produced an entirely new cleavage within the party's ranks based on federalism, a cleavage that cut across the traditional left-right divide between social and business Liberals, and in many ways proved to be more intractable. This internal conflict led to an unprecedented public display of party disunity, and arguably cost the Liberals a return to power in 1988.

The Origins of the Federalist Cleavage

As with so many other difficulties the Liberals faced during their decade in opposition, the Meech Lake Accord emerged just as Canadians were beginning to take the party seriously again. Unlike other issues the party found problematic, however, this time the Liberals thought they had managed to get ahead of the curve. The parliamentary wing had regrouped after John Turner's hasty retreat from his initial reply to Robert Bourassa's five demands in June 1986. A successful caucus committee exercise resulted in a constitutional resolution sponsored by the caucus, approved by the national executive, and adopted unanimously at the party's national policy convention in November 1986. Unlike some other resolutions passed at the convention, the constitutional resolution was solidly supported by both the caucus and the party's rank-and-file membership. Armed with this consensus resolution, the Liberals believed they were ready to respond to anything Mulroney might put forward.

There are many reasons why this did not prove to be the case. The Liberals were caught off guard by Mulroney's initial announcement of an agreement. The agreement was only arrived at 'in principle.' With a two-month delay before an official text would be made available, it was difficult for anyone to either accept or criticize the deal in advance. For the federal Liberals, mindful of the need to regain lost ground in their former Quebec stronghold, the fact that the Bourassa government had apparently been successful in satisfying its five demands was also very important. Last, but hardly least, all ten premiers, including the Liberal premiers of Ontario and Quebec, had signed on to the deal, something the federal party could hardly ignore. Enthusiastic media coverage reinforced these concerns for many Liberals.[3] Nevertheless, when Brian Mulroney triumphantly announced that he and the premiers had broken the constitutional 'impasse' after their weekend retreat at Meech Lake, most Liberals automatically expected Mulroney's deal would be examined in light of their own convention resolution before the party took a formal position. The first and most immediate reason why this did not take place was that John Turner was in Montreal, not Ottawa, when the announcement was made. His Quebec lieutenant (Raymond Garneau, the former Bourassa cabinet minster) and communications director (Michelle Tremblay) expected Mulroney's two-day meeting with the premiers to end in failure, and recommended that Turner be in Montreal to take advantage of the situation. When the news broke the following morning that a deal had been reached, none of the senior OLO staff were with Turner in Montreal. Although Doug Richardson managed to reach Turner and speak with him briefly, he could not provide the in-depth analysis such an important development required. With Herb Gray and Scott Sheppard standing in his office advising him that the reaction of the MPs in the Tactics Committee was highly critical, Richardson recalls counselling Turner to say as little as possible. He recommended the leader point out at least two or three of the concerns that had already been raised by senior staff and caucus members, while trying to avoid the appearance of partisan or overly negative comments. According to Richardson, Turner concurred.[4]

In Montreal at a pre-scheduled news conference that morning, Turner initially stuck to the script. He briefly responded to questions on the deal, declaring only that it was an 'important day' for Quebec and the country. However, a few hours later, after he had driven to Ottawa with Garneau and Tremblay, Turner expanded his positive comments to the point where many in the caucus were extremely anxious. That afternoon, before Question Period, Turner even walked across the floor of the House of Commons to shake hands with Brian Mulroney, accompanied – or perhaps propelled – by Raymond Garneau. As Richardson later commented, Garneau's role in the Meech Lake exercise was 'pivotal, from beginning to end,' and the first day of the Liberal response made this clear.[5]

In his speech in the House of Commons that day, the prime minister indicated he would convene a first ministers' conference to 'seek a formal agreement.' From the background material released, it was already clear the premiers and the prime minister had gone far beyond the federal government's draft proposal prepared for the weekend meeting. Indeed, the accord appeared to go far beyond Quebec's original five demands. Several contentious provisions were singled out by constitutional experts. Chief among them was the fact that a 'distinct society' clause had not only been accepted, but would be located in the body of the text, not in the preamble as originally proposed by Bourassa. As such, it was unclear what the implications would be for the Charter of Rights and Freedoms. For each of Quebec's other demands the solution had been to arrive at a measure acceptable to Quebec and then extend it to all the provinces. The Cullen-Couture agreement on immigration, for example, would apply to all ten provinces. The appointment of all Supreme Court judges, not just those from Quebec, would be determined through provincial nominations. Opting-out provisions for national social programs, with compensation, would apply to all provinces as well. Meanwhile the concept of 'minimum national standards' was to be replaced with a vague requirement for programs to be 'consistent with national objectives.' Finally, the proposed amending formula gave not only Quebec but all provinces a veto, thereby introducing a unanimity requirement not found in any other federal amending formula. As many experts immediately pointed out, this made future constitutional reform – including reform of the Senate – extremely unlikely.

In short, the accord's contents were not merely additions to the 1982 constitutional amendment. Like the proposed free trade agreement and so many other policy initiatives of the Mulroney government, the accord represented a dramatic shift in policy direction. As one former Trudeau minister involved in the Liberal response to Meech Lake pointedly noted, the Mulroney government's constitutional proposal would prove so difficult for Liberals because its entire thrust was 'diametrically opposed to everything the Liberal Party had represented and worked for over the past twenty years.' Along with most members of the Liberal caucus, Bob Kaplan knew instinctively that the proposed accord was 'a terrible agreement that would be bad for the country.' Yet, as the Official Opposition, the Liberals felt they were 'painted into a corner' by the government.[6] If they were to have any political credibility, they believed their response would have to be more than an outright rejection of the deal. This already difficult situation was further complicated by Turner's initial response.

The Initial Liberal Response to Meech Lake

Responding to the prime minister's announcement in the House of Commons, John Turner first referred to the event as a 'happy day' and congratulated the prime minister and the premiers for their 'constructive' efforts. This alone suggested a greater degree of support for the accord than his initial comments in Montreal.

To the surprise of many Liberals, Turner did not refer to the Liberal Party resolution or compare its measures with those of the agreement in principle, as many expected he would. Nor did he reserve judgment, saying he wanted to see the final text before making a firm commitment. Instead, he argued that both the Liberals and NDP had contributed to the positive atmosphere in which the accord had been negotiated because they had indicated in advance their support for the inclusion of Quebec in the constitutional amendment process. In a cogent and revealing explanation for his contentious June 1986 declaration, Turner stated: 'I have always believed that it was essential to the future of our country that Quebec be a major and leading partner ... and a full-fledged participant in our evolution.' He then went on to mention the party's November 1986 convention resolution, but not in terms of its content. Instead, he offered up the resolution as evidence of the Liberal Party's helpfulness to the negotiation process. 'That is what has led the Liberal Party of Canada to adopt, at its convention last November,' he stated, 'a clear position on the place of Quebec within the constitutional agreement of 1982.'[7]

Having praised the intent of the Meech Lake agreement, Turner went on to raise a number of issues. 'We are concerned,' he said, 'about the limitations on the spending power. Do they preclude national programs?' Along the same lines he asked: 'How will the expansion of the opting out with compensation affect the quality of services and the uniformity of services in Canada? Who will decide national objectives?' Turning to the proposed amending formula, which required unanimity, he asked: 'Are we now in a constitutional straitjacket? Will we ever really see Senate reform?' And on the provision in Meech Lake declaring Quebec a 'distinct society,' the crucial point: 'Will it be in the preamble? Will it be in the body of the constitution? Do we know yet how widely it will influence the interpretation of the constitution?' Near the end of his speech Turner addressed the question of process. He took for granted the prime minister's obligation to bring the final text of the agreement before Parliament for approval. But two years' experience with the Mulroney government had taught Turner something about their lack of concern for parliamentary convention. And so he raised other questions for which the answers might have been considered self-evident a decade earlier, but were now far from certain. 'Will this Parliament have an opportunity to debate these issues before the final text is negotiated and signed?' he asked. And again, 'My question to the Prime Minister, which we will have to pursue over the forthcoming days is, will this Parliament have an opportunity for some input into the final text before it is finally signed?' Unfortunately for Turner and the Liberal Party, the answer to the last set of questions was an emphatic 'NO.'

For Canadians, and for the media who played a role in shaping their views, Turner's speech seemed rife with internal contradictions. On the one hand, the Liberal leader had congratulated the prime minister and the premiers. On the other, he had raised a number of serious concerns.

This struck many observers as another example of fence-sitting. Yet, for Turner, a product of the old school of parliamentary politics, there was nothing inconsistent about this approach. He genuinely believed in the objectives of the accord. And he genuinely believed it was the role of the Official Opposition to attempt to improve the agreement rather than simply denounce it. Brian Tobin, a well-known Chrétien supporter who was serving as chair of the national caucus at the time, recalled Turner saying that he knew the accord was not something Pierre Trudeau would have negotiated. Nevertheless, he considered the deal to be an important step forward and it would be 'unpatriotic' to 'play politics' with it. They would have to wait and see if it was something they could live with. 'That in my mind was the mark of a statesman,' Tobin later said. 'In the end, of course, he believed he could live with it, that it would be better to have this flawed document than none at all, while many of us disagreed.'[8] This nuanced approach was made explicit by Turner in an interview on 4 May. 'Of course we were glad that Quebec is finally into our constitutional family,' Turner replied, 'but we are concerned that the prime minister may have given away too much of the federal power in order to get it.'[9]

The Division Emerges

Tobin was correct in stating that most of the Liberal caucus did not share their leader's nuanced view. Before Turner spoke in the House on 1 May, he met with a delegation including Senator Michael Kirby, a key player in Trudeau's 1982 constitutional amendment, and Michel Robert, the new president of the Liberal Party. A prominent constitutional lawyer, Robert had coincidentally represented the Trudeau government's position on the constitutional accord in the 1981 Supreme Court reference. With the notable exception of Raymond Garneau, all of those present at the meeting spoke against the agreement, arguing that to reject Mulroney's particular deal did not mean the Liberal Party would be seen as rejecting Quebec's 'legitimate aspirations.' Garneau, on the other hand, was adamant. There would be no political fallout in Quebec if the party agreed with the deal, he insisted, and much could be lost by being the only party to oppose it. In the end it was Garneau's view that prevailed, and Garneau who walked with the Liberal leader to the House of Commons for the speech.

The following day, Turner appeared to recognize the seriousness of the brewing internal conflict. He convened a meeting of a dozen senior caucus members in his boardroom. The optics of the meeting were revealing. Former Trudeau ministers Don Johnston, Lloyd Axworthy, and Bob Kaplan sat at one end of the table while Raymond Garneau sat alone at the opposite end. Virtually everyone except Garneau spoke against the agreement. Don Johnston was emphatic about the potential damage the accord would do. In his view it was a 'complete disaster' which simply could not be improved by cosmetic changes. Furious, Garneau left the meeting before Turner concluded. For his part, the leader indicated he would make no further public comments until after the regular meeting of the national caucus the next morning.

The full extent of the problem emerged at the Quebec regional caucus meeting. Don Johnston's plea to reject the accord was dismissed out of hand by Raymond Garneau and also by André Ouellet and Jean Lapierre. Ouellet stunned some of his colleagues when he referred to the Trudeau vision as 'passé' and agreed with Garneau that 'all Quebeckers' supported the accord, the rejection of which would be political suicide. Johnston's retort that more than 800,000 English-speaking Quebeckers would be highly unlikely to support the deal led to an exchange of personal insults which culminated in Ouellet's use of the term 'Westmount Rhodesian' to describe Johnston.

In the national caucus meeting that followed immediately afterwards, the other shoe dropped. Veteran MPs such as Dave Dingwall, Russ MacLellan, Charles Caccia, Lloyd Axworthy, and others who had served with Trudeau, representing virtually every other part of the country, rose one after the other to denounce the agreement. Even more striking than the regional cross-section was the fact that the MPs who spoke against the accord came from both the social and business sides of the Liberals' left-right spectrum.

In almost every case the MPs who opposed the deal argued it was so seriously flawed that it could not be salvaged. Several also referred to a Research Bureau briefing note distributed to the caucus the previous day which had underlined the importance of the party's convention resolution. Charles Caccia cited a clause from the 'political considerations' section of the Bureau document that emphasized the resolution 'was the result of intense negotiation and debate and represented a delicate balance of interests, based on the willingness of those involved to compromise.' The briefing note cautioned: 'Any response to the current situation which appears to significantly deviate from this position could put that compromise in grave peril. Any area in which the Meech Lake agreement differs from the resolution, therefore, may have to be seriously questioned even if it is amenable to the Quebec government and/or all of the premiers.'[10] Other MPs and senators pointed out that the accord could be criticized for its numerous technical flaws, such as the absence of a deadlock-breaking mechanism in the Supreme Court appointments process, without raising the issue of opposing visions of federalism. They also argued it should be possible for Liberals to reject the deal without appearing overtly partisan, since increasing numbers of academics and constitutional experts were raising these same types of concerns. Despite these interventions, Turner once again urged caution. He concluded the meeting with a call to his caucus to reserve judgment until the final text of the accord was produced.

Whether this strategy would have worked or not quickly became academic. The prime minister scheduled a full debate on the Meech Lake Accord for the following Monday, 8 May, perhaps sensing that the disarray in the Liberal ranks could be exploited. The spectre of the imminent debate led Don Johnston to speak with several close friends and confidantes, including Pierre Trudeau. In the end, Johnston concluded that he must be free to speak on the accord *before* a final version was drafted if he was to have any impact. In his view, the writing was on the wall not only in terms of the final shape of the accord but also in terms of the likely final position of Turner. As a result, he resigned as external affairs critic in Turner's shadow cabinet. In a letter to the leader explaining his decision, Johnston wrote: 'I see long term consequences flowing from the Accord which could radically change the shape of the Canadian federation ... While my own views may not affect the outcome of the debate, I wish to put them forward to enable Canadians to assess what may be at stake if the Accord is implemented.'[11] That Johnston felt obliged to take this step, in spite of his thirty-year friendship with Turner and their common position at the 'business' end of the Liberals' left-right spectrum, spoke volumes about the importance the constitutional issue had taken on within the caucus.

Internal Opposition Grows

Driving the mistrust of Johnston and other senior caucus members was Turner's reluctance to state what he would do if the accord was not amended to reflect Liberal concerns. In the same 4 May interview, the Liberal leader repeatedly refused to be pinned down on that point, adding to the suspicion that he was attempting to please both sides in the debate. Asked whether, given his long list of concerns, 'you would be prepared to fight a deal if there aren't more specific provisions made to accommodate those concerns,' Turner replied: 'Well, the important issue is bringing Quebec into the unity of the country. We'll try to fight for as good a deal as we can get, but obviously it's up to the prime minister and the premiers to sign a final agreement.' Later in the interview he was asked again, 'so you'd be prepared to leave that up to them, and if the premiers seemed happy, then, Mr. Turner, you would not once it comes to the Commons, be prepared to get in the way of that process?' His reply was more convoluted than before. 'Well, we're going to try to improve the process, but as I've said, you know, anybody can get a deal if he gives too much away.' On a third and final try, the interviewer finally drew from Turner the crux of his assumptions, namely that 'what we'd like is for Parliament to take a look at the deal before it goes back to the premiers, rather than find that we get the signed, written document before us.'[12]

Turner persevered with his self-described approach of constructive criticism when formal debate on the Meech Lake Accord began in the House of Commons on 11 May. He noted the motion brought by the government asked the House to accept the statement of principles tabled by the prime minister the week before as a 'basis' for further discussion. 'In the absence of anything else,' Turner stated, 'we believe that the statement of principles is as good a place to start as any.' He went on to stress that he viewed the Meech Lake agreement as 'a general framework for discussion, not the final solution.' Then, returning to his theme of proper parliamentary process, Turner concluded: 'I also want to emphasize that we will insist upon full committee hearings on the final text which will be produced by the Government of Canada, and a full debate in this House when we see the final results, preferably before the issue goes to the Premiers. Parliament has a right to see this text in final form before it is again negotiated with the Premiers.'[13] His position was supported by the NDP leader, Ed Broadbent, who told journalists there was 'plenty of room for change' in the accord.

Turner was counting on the traditional respect for Parliament which had led, in 1981, to the various changes made by the Trudeau government to their original constitutional initiative in order to bring both opposition parties onside. What Turner did not count on was the single-minded intransigence of the prime minister, and his willingness – even on such a fundamental matter as the constitution – to flaunt parliamentary practice and convention. The first evidence of Mulroney's rigid stance came almost immediately, when he made it clear that Parliament would be seeing the final, legal version of the accord text only after it had been signed by the premiers in a few weeks. Turner had also underestimated the extent of the divisions within his own already fractured caucus. However, as former principal secretary Doug Richardson later admitted, one reason for Turner's failure to recognize the depth of caucus resistance to the accord was the tendency of the leader and his advisers to perceive any disagreement with his position as the product of divided leadership loyalties, even after the November 1986 convention had supposedly laid the matter to rest.[14] Sergio Marchi agreed. 'Opposition to the Meech deal was automatically equated by Turner's people with opposition to his leadership and support for Jean Chrétien. Just because I had supported Chrétien didn't mean I was "anti-Turner." On a personal level I felt for the guy. But Meech Lake ripped our caucus in two. I fundamentally disagreed with his vision of the country, and so did many others.'[15]

As a result of this defensive attitude on the part of the OLO, it would be some time before Turner and those around him realized that opposition to the accord transcended the traditional left-right party divisions and, equally important, leadership preference. Indeed, as the events of the next year would demonstrate, opposition to the accord came just as strenuously from some who had supported Turner or another Liberal leadership candidate in 1984.

First and foremost among those who had not supported Chrétien for the leadership was Turner's close friend Don Johnston, who had been a candidate himself. Along with another vocal Meech critic, John Nunziata, Johnston had strongly supported Turner in the 1986 leadership review. Even among Chrétien supporters the decision to speak out publicly in opposition to the accord was taken reluctantly. Both Charles Caccia and David Berger, for example, only publicly criticized the accord in late May, following Turner's speech. They were immediately fired from their critic's portfolios by Turner. Caccia insisted their decisions had been taken reluctantly, precisely because they did not want to appear to be criticizing the leader due to their earlier support for Chrétien. 'I thought you should fight from the inside and respect the rules of the game,' Caccia later commented. 'Going public was the last thing I wanted to do but I felt I had no choice.'[16]

Don Johnston took further action as well, but he kept his criticism within the caucus somewhat longer. On 28 May he circulated a memo to all Liberal MPs and senators enclosing a paper he had received from Stephen Scott, the renowned constitutional expert and law professor at

McGill University. Scott's brief, which later became public, described the Meech Lake Accord as a 'disaster' for Canadian federalism. After detailed analysis of the five provisions, Scott concluded the accord 'will give us weaker government (at the centre) and, I think, worse government and less just government ... Constitutional reform must promote, first and foremost, the fundamental rights and freedoms, and welfare, of citizens, ensuring effective government bounded by effective guarantees ... Instead Meech Lake indulges a barely-controlled provincial power lust and indeed explicitly sets the stage for more such meetings. It is a feeding frenzy upon federal powers.'[17]

Up to this point the leadership of the extra-parliamentary wing of the Liberal Party had also been careful to avoid public comment on the issue. Many caucus members had already received messages from Liberals across the country such as the one from the Prince George Liberal Riding Association which 'expressed extreme concern about the terms of the accord' and its 'long-term implications for Canada.' Failing to appreciate the limitations of the party's role in opposition, the association called on the caucus to delay its approval for at least a year while the deal could be examined in detail.[18]

The first formal sign of Liberal opposition to John Turner's constitutional position from outside the caucus came from the Young Liberals of Eastern Ontario, led by their president, Mark Marissen. In a press release dated 1 June, the youth group 'unanimously called upon Liberal Leader John Turner to oppose the Meech Lake Accord.' Citing the concerns raised by Pierre Trudeau as well as the November convention resolution, the group's resolution called for the leader and caucus to 'promote the vision of Liberal federalism so well articulated by the party for decades.'

This critique was soon followed by public comments from Jean Chrétien. Now in private legal practice in Ottawa and not bound by considerations of caucus solidarity, he nevertheless surprised many by speaking out against the party's position. He too was highly critical of the deal. In typical populist language, Chrétien warned that 'if Ottawa places too many limits on its power to redistribute wealth, what will happen is that the rich will have their money and the poor will not.'[19]

But the most serious blow to Turner's credibility on the constitutional file was delivered by Pierre Trudeau himself. Having retired from active politics three years earlier, Trudeau had been happily engaged in work and family, refraining from commenting on any issues including the free trade and cruise missile debates. His determination to remain out of the spotlight was so well known that reporters had actually stopped attempting to contact him for a response on any matter. It was a great shock, therefore, when Trudeau launched a scathing broadside against the accord in a letter to the editor published in Montreal and Toronto on 27 May. Trudeau later confided he had waited nearly four weeks before deciding to wade into the fray because he had hoped others would do so, and their objections would be sufficient to sway the federal government.[20]

Once he saw this would not happen, he still took pains to avoid criticizing Turner or the party. Trudeau's letter was directed at the prime minister, whom he referred to sarcastically as a 'magician' and a 'sly fox' for having 'forced' the premiers to accept a deal that would benefit them. 'In a single master stroke,' Trudeau wrote, 'this clever negotiator has thus managed to approve the call for special status (Lesage and Ryan), the call for Two Nations (Stanfield), the call for a Canadian Board of Directors (Blakeney and Faribault), and the call for a Community of Communities (Clark). He has not quite succeeded in achieving the separatist party's call for sovereignty-association, but he has put Canada on the fast track for getting there.'[21]

In the spirit of party unity, some caucus dissidents attempted to defend the beleaguered Liberal leader publicly by suggesting the two sides were not that far apart. Pointing to the various concerns Turner had raised in his speech, David Berger expressed the hope that Trudeau's intervention would 'turn the thing around.' Berger argued that Turner 'has not boxed himself in so completely that the caucus could not try to amend the Accord once a formal draft is presented to parliament.' Similarly, Toronto MP John Nunziata stressed that 'the caucus is in the midst of a very vigorous debate about the accord and I am sure we will come up with some amendments that will make the accord much better.'[22]

While the Liberals were dealing with the fallout from Trudeau's intervention, some *supporters* of the accord were inadvertently causing further damage to its credibility. Saskatchewan premier Grant Devine confirmed the critics' worst fears about the transfer of powers to the provinces when he told one journalist: 'The West made significant gains Thursday at the expense of federal powers.' Similarly, Robert Bourassa's intergovernmental affairs minister, Gil Rémillard, added fuel to the fire when he declared: 'Quebec will be able to use its new status as a distinct society in court to defend laws that might be seen as contravening the federal Charter of Rights and Freedoms.' Rémillard went on to speculate the clause might even provide ammunition for Quebec to expand its role on the international stage.[23] There were also unhelpful comments by politicians who had been excluded from the negotiations. Chief among them was Yukon territorial government leader Tony Penikett, who pointed out quite correctly that 'if this agreement is ratified (as is), any one province will have a veto over our constitutional future. One day some 100,000 people in PEI will decide if we are to join Confederation. This is completely unacceptable.'[24]

Liberal Disarray on the Langevin Accord

On 2 June, Brian Mulroney and the premiers met in the boardroom of the Langevin Block, across from Parliament Hill. The purpose of their second meeting was to approve the formal legal language of the agreement they had so quickly cobbled together four weeks earlier at Meech Lake. A private signing ceremony was to be followed shortly after by a public news conference. For Mulroney, this was a do-or-die session. After all, he had already taken credit for resolving the constitutional 'impasse' he blamed on Pierre Trudeau. For many of the premiers, however, the meeting was a chance to express their concerns after a four-week period of reflection. In fact, some of them were seriously reconsidering their position.

It soon became evident the meeting was not going as planned. The discussions carried on behind closed doors for a marathon nineteen hours, into the early morning of 3 June. Several reports of the discussion, including first-hand comments from some of the premiers, eventually trickled out. All of them mentioned the prime minister's obsession with Mr Trudeau, whom Mulroney described as 'thinking he is still running the country.' Joe Ghiz confided that all of them were becoming impatient with Mulroney's diatribe when finally Richard Hatfield exclaimed 'Will you forget about him?'[25] They eventually agreed to present a united front. When the text of the Langevin Accord was released, it hardly varied from the original Meech Lake document. Although Mulroney's self-congratulatory stance was criticized by some reporters, perhaps the worst faux pas of the press conference belonged to Gil Rémillard, who stood beside Robert Bourassa on the steps of the Convention Centre and boasted to waiting reporters: 'We got more than we asked for!'

For the Liberals, any hope the premiers would save the day was gone. Worse still, the prime minister referred to the Langevin Accord as a 'seamless web,' a catch phrase Mulroney used to reject calls for parliamentary committee hearings on the agreement. This was the Liberals' worst nightmare. Not only would they be forced to respond to a fait accompli signed by the premiers, but it appeared they would not even have an opportunity to examine the agreement in a parliamentary committee with expert witnesses.

Within the next week a flurry of activity took place within Liberal ranks, including a special two-day caucus meeting in which a number of MPs and senators expressed their opposition to the deal. Despite this, John Turner calmly announced at the end of the exhaustive session that he had decided to support the accord *even if amendments were not approved*. He also announced the creation of a Liberal Caucus Committee on the Constitution, to be chaired by Bob Kaplan, which was to work throughout the summer to develop a set of Liberal amendments. All caucus members were invited to submit suggested amendments to Kaplan's committee. In the absence of a parliamentary committee, these amendments were to be tabled in the House of Commons for a vote.

Then, on 4 June, the National Executive of the Liberal Party organized a conference call in which the concerns of the party's rank-and-file membership were outlined for the leader. This discussion led to a memo from the recently created Management Committee of the Party to the entire Liberal caucus, outlining serious concerns with the content of the agreement.[26] Still, the committee concluded: 'The position of the Leader to seek changes while, in the end, embracing the Accord, must be supported.' The memo called on the caucus 'to lead an inspiring debate in the House of Commons on the importance of the agreement, emphasizing the necessity for a full and meaningful discussion to deal with the flaws that are inescapable in a document so hastily prepared.' The Executive's political rationale for this position was very revealing. Referring to the fact that several provinces were planning to hold public hearings on the accord, and to the large number of special interest groups and experts who were beginning to speak out against various provisions of the deal, the memo stated: 'In the final analysis this is a movement and a debate which is going to happen anyway in some form. In some areas it is already happening. To not fully engage ourselves in this issue creates the likelihood that the "story" will be how the Liberal Party pulled back from the national debate.' The memo confirmed the view that the party executive, like the caucus, felt painted into a corner by the Mulroney government. 'By stating at the outset that our objective is not to undermine the Accord,' it continued, 'but rather to improve the document in the national interest, our credibility in seeking such changes is heightened. In management literature this is known as a win-win situation ... and is a well-known strategy frequently used in sophisticated business negotiations.' Then, demonstrating their concern for their political fortunes in Quebec, the memo concluded: 'We believe that the position announced by the Leader gives Liberals much room for a full and constructive role in the debate while reaffirming our embrace of Quebec. To reject the accord outright is to risk isolating our federalist colleagues in Quebec and to betray our historic role of finding common ground within which our nation can work as one.'

A second special caucus meeting was held on 10 June at which senior party strategists from across the country were invited to speak. There was also a presentation on internal Liberal polling results by Martin Goldfarb, which confirmed the bad news evident in a Gallup poll released the previous day. Although the Liberals retained the lead, their support had fallen from 42 per cent to 39 per cent among decided voters, while the NDP had risen from 30 to 35 per cent. Although some interpreted these numbers as a positive sign that the Liberals' dispute over Meech Lake had not helped the Conservatives, Goldfarb offered a different and more disturbing interpretation. Given the margin of error and the regional distribution of support, the Goldfarb projection was for a possible NDP minority government. According to several of the caucus participants, there was a concerted effort on the part of Turner-friendly party strategists and pollsters to emphasize that it was not the party's position on the issue(s), but *the division in caucus* that was negatively affecting their electoral chances. 'Their message was pretty clear,' one MP recalled. 'Either we get our act together or we lose the next election.' As if to reinforce that message, Liberal MP Brian Tobin raised the issue of Turner's leadership, even though no media questions had done so. Tobin declared Turner had 'shown remarkable patience, dignity, and poise. There is absolutely no question of his continued leadership. He will lead the party into the next election.'[27]

Despite this carefully orchestrated call for caucus unity, word leaked out of more opposition to the accord. Another opponent of Meech who had been an early and ardent Turner supporter, Senator Jerry Grafstein, was reported to have given one of the most heartfelt cris de coeur, concluding: 'If we support Meech Lake, where would we be? Where would we stand? We would be nothing!'[28] In the end, Turner was forced to admit at least ten of his thirty-nine MPs were opposed to his position on the accord and would not consider voting for it without changes. Sergio Marchi, the Toronto-area MP and Liberal critic for multiculturalism, took a different tack. He circulated material to various umbrella ethnic groups as well as the ethnic press attempting to mobilize their support for an amendment to the 'distinct society' clause which would include Canada's multicultural character. In doing so, Marchi indicated he was influenced first by Mr Trudeau, whose letter to the editor included the phrase, 'Those who fought for a single Canada, bilingual and multicultural, can say goodbye to their dream.' Marchi also referred to the November convention resolution, and used it as a source for his proposed amendment. In his conclusion, Marchi declared: 'Public debate and awareness of the Accord is just beginning.' Following along with the official party line, he stated: 'In the coming weeks and months, my Liberal caucus colleagues and I will be working in close partnership with Canadians from coast to coast towards the realization of this amendment.'[29]

The Liberals' Caucus Committee and the Special Joint Parliamentary Committee

Whether the Liberals' caucus exercise alone would have allowed Turner and the Liberal Party to move forward in a temporary truce is a moot point. Only a few days later Brian Mulroney was forced to yield to intense public pressure and announced the creation of a Special Joint Committee on the Proposed 1987 Constitutional Accord. It would hold five weeks of hearings in Ottawa over the summer, at which a number of expert witnesses and interest groups would testify. The Liberals were allocated four slots on the nineteen-member committee, demonstrating once again the impotence of their position in opposition. Turner then appointed senators Philippe Gigantes and Ray Perrault and MPs Bob Kaplan and André Ouellet (who were on the caucus committee as well) to represent the party.

Many Liberals did not have overly high expectations for the parliamentary committee exercise. André Ouellet later confided he saw the entire process as a public relations exercise and nothing more. Unlike the 1981 committee process (where the testimony of witnesses played a key role in the subsequent amendments to the Trudeau government's original draft), this time the prime minister had announced in advance that he would entertain no amendments of any kind. Afraid that the delicate balance he had succeeded in keeping alive at the Langevin Block would crumble the instant any changes were proposed, Mulroney made it clear the committee had no power. Flowing from his earlier 'seamless web' argument came his rather bizarre declaration that 'not one comma can be changed.'

There were two Liberal activities relating to Meech Lake that took place over the summer of 1987. On the one hand, Bob Kaplan chaired meetings of the internal caucus committee and took suggestions for amendments from his colleagues. John Nunziata sent a letter to the leader in which he stated: 'I sincerely believe the differences that exist in our caucus are not irreconcilable and that we can all move forward in a positive and constructive way.' He then offered seven possible amendments on the issues of multiculturalism, the distinct society clause, the amending formula, and appointments to the Supreme Court, which he felt 'may constitute common ground that can lead to a united approach to the constitutional accord by the Liberal caucus.'[30] Other caucus members soon took up the challenge and submitted recommendations as well, including Charles Caccia, Sergio Marchi, Keith Penner, David Berger, and David Dingwall. Almost all of them referred to the wording in the party's constitutional resolution when proposing alternative language or additional text.

Meanwhile Kaplan and Ouellet participated in the hearings of the joint parliamentary committee in which witnesses were overwhelmingly critical of the wording of the accord. More than 130 individuals made presentations, including former prime minister Trudeau. Not surprisingly, Trudeau's intervention received widespread media coverage. Canadians were once again made aware of his vigorous opposition to the accord, and especially his concern that the provisions on national social programs would lead to a 'chequerboard' Canada. Polls suggested that more and more Canadians shared his concerns, and, for a while, it looked as though it would be politically impossible for the Conservatives to move ahead without addressing the criticisms.

While these hearings were underway, John Turner took one last initiative to win over the dissenting members of his caucus and party. In a letter to all Liberals dated 22 July 1987, Turner clearly spelled out 'why I support the Accord.' He began by indirectly criticizing Pierre Trudeau, referring to the 'incomplete process' of 1981–2 and indicating that he agreed with Mulroney that 'the process needed to be completed, politically, emotionally and psychologically ... and we needed to do it in a united, non-partisan way.' Then the Liberal leader returned to his argument that the role of the opposition is limited and must not be obstructive. 'I was not at the table to make suggestions or improvements as the negotiations were underway,' he pointed out. 'In fact, I would have used the November resolution as the basis for the negotiations.' Finally he addressed the crux of the matter – his support for the accord even if unamended. In so doing, he clearly demonstrated his fundamental and deeply held difference of opinion with Trudeau over the party's approach to Canadian federalism, a difference already evident in the 1984 leadership race. 'In my judgement, the flaws in the agreement are not serious enough to override the necessity of having Quebec sign the Constitution ... Is the price too high? I don't believe it is,' he continued. Taking direct aim at Trudeau's claim that the highly controversial distinct society clause would have serious consequences for Charter rights, Turner said he believed 'it is a constitutional recognition of a basic fact. Quebec does have a distinct character.' He also dismissed his predecessor's concerns about the federal spending power, noting that the Meech provision only applied to shared-cost programs in areas of provincial jurisdiction and that no transfer of powers was contemplated. On the issue of future Senate reform and the unanimity clause in the proposed amending formula, a subject of keen personal interest, he continued to offer up the hope that changes would still be made. 'We will carefully examine the unanimity clause,' he declared, presumably referring to the parliamentary committee exercise, and then stated the obvious. 'We feel that the (existing) seven provinces/50% of the population formula would be more flexible.' Concluding his analysis, Turner declared: 'As the Prime Minister and the premiers have said, it is not perfect. It can be improved. We have been part of the process in bringing this agreement about, and we intend to be part of the process of seeking amendments.'

But Liberal members of the parliamentary committee were increasingly uncertain that such amendments were forthcoming. The prime minister was repeating his 'not one comma can be changed' dictum, causing a number of caucus members to repeat their objections to the accord. Meanwhile, despite the efforts of Raymond Garneau to persuade Quebec Liberals to stick by their leader, his attempt was undermined by Jean Lapierre, a former Turner supporter, who announced that he would support a call for a Liberal amendment to ensure that the Charter of Rights and Freedoms took precedence over the 'distinct society' clause. This very public crack in the wall of support from Quebec turned out to be one of the first signs of the impending leadership crisis.

The First Leadership Challenge

The first challenge to John Turner's leadership came on 25 August 1987.

Party president Michel Robert spoke to reporters after a Canadian Bar Association meeting where constitutional lawyers had examined the Meech Lake Accord. In an unprecedented public display of internal party conflict, Robert indicated 'there are caucus members who are questioning, more or less openly, Mr. Turner's leadership. And if measures are not taken within a certain number of weeks or months, there is a possibility of an open rebellion on this question.' Robert stressed that he himself was not challenging Turner. Rather, he was cautioning him to take action to correct a number of problems. 'I am expressing the opinion of all, or at least of an important number, of party members,' he said. Most telling was Robert's final warning. 'Do not forget that the party president is responsible for the continuity of the institution.'[31] Whether Robert was aware of a clandestine operation by caucus dissidents to bring about the leader's resignation remains unclear. The operation, though, was certainly real and potentially fatal to Turner's leadership. Organized by three former Turner supporters, it could not be attributed to the lingering leadership aspirations of Jean Chrétien, or to the emerging aspirations of Paul Martin Jr. It was, instead, an act of despair on the part of individuals who had not only committed their support to Turner during his leadership but had attempted to ride out their various policy disagreements with him, notably on Meech Lake. As one of the three later confided, they had simply given up. They were convinced nothing could 'heal' the party or the caucus except Turner's departure. At the same time, they were acutely aware of the fact that no formal mechanism existed in the party constitution to remove him, especially after his successful leadership review the previous fall.

By the end of August, the three had obtained signed letters requesting the leader's resignation from eight of their caucus colleagues. When Robert made his public statement, the so-called 'Group of Thirteen' were still waiting for two MPs to sign on to their putative revolt before taking the entire batch of letters to Turner. With no precedents or constitutional provisions to rely on, they simply assumed this would be sufficient, because the leader would be unable to refuse a request from one-third of his caucus. Robert's public statement occurred at the same time as the private caucus revolt and served as the catalyst for more public problems for Turner. Already concerned about the Liberal caucus disarray that was playing out in full public view, and the opinion polls showing the party again trailing the NDP, a group of one hundred senior Liberal Party strategists, executive members, and caucus representatives met on 29 August 1987 in Ottawa to discuss the deteriorating situation.

Among those present were Garneau and Lapierre, who in the end both agreed to a specific amendment to the 'distinct society' clause to ensure that there was no ambiguity about the Charter of Rights and Freedoms having precedence. Another participant confided that the very fact this matter was addressed at the meeting at the insistence of the extra-parliamentary wing spoke volumes about the degree to which the caucus conflict had come to dominate the thoughts of the entire party apparatus. Moreover, the fact that it was resolved in favour of the traditional party position demonstrated how entrenched the Trudeau vision had become. Interestingly, the lack of consensus on an alternative leader was equally revealing. Neither Chrétien nor Paul Martin Jr. – who attended the event and spoke strongly in defence of Turner – were considered credible alternatives at the time. Nor did most of those present believe the party could afford a leadership review barely a year before the next federal election. Although it was widely known that the meeting took place, the details did not become public at the time. Turner was able to diffuse media interest in the meeting by dismissing the event as a 'catharsis' for the party and for him. Alerted ahead of time to the existence of the letter, Turner and his advisers had time to prepare his defence and mount an offensive of their own. He argued that part of the problem stemmed from his own practice of 'opening up' the party. 'I am moving to establish an even wider advisory group for the leader and the party,' he stated, but 'there has never been a more open leadership.'[32]

On the evening of 2 September, House leader Herb Gray, along with the party's campaign co-chairs for the next federal election, senators Al Graham and Pietro Rizzuto, met with Turner at Stornoway. They presented him with a list of what were variously termed 'demands' or 'conditions for continued support of the Leader' which the Sunday exercise had produced. Although Turner once again played down the importance of this list in his comments to the press the following day, it was clear the meeting had been a difficult one. Keeping in mind that all three men had been appointed to their party positions by Turner himself, and that Rizzuto and Graham had played a key role in the Friends of Turner campaign less than a year earlier, the lengthy list of concerns they raised was particularly telling.

The next day the leader began his prepared statement by indicating he would 'seek the best replacements' for the staff vacancies. At the insistence of caucus leadership, a search committee headed by Herb Gray and including Turner supporters Gerry Schwartz and Rod Bryden was established to find just such replacements. Although Michael Robinson was initially proposed by many in the party to be the new principal secretary, in the end it was Peter Connolly, a former ministerial aide to Herb Gray, who was appointed. Another Gray protégé, Doug Kirkpatrick, was named as Connolly's assistant and Toronto journalist Ray Heard as communications director. However, it was John Webster of the Friends of Turner who was appointed the new campaign director for the upcoming federal election.

Turner devoted the remainder of his statement to an outline of the issues he had agreed to address in the very near future on an 'urgent' basis. After briefly noting the caucus would soon be announcing their specific positions on tax reform and the likely free trade agreement, Turner swiftly moved to discuss what he saw as the key policy problem for the Liberals, *the only one he addressed in detail.* 'The Meech Lake divisions in our party have caused us some difficulty and cost us some public support. We will have to work harder to advance the plan we were following,' he admitted. And, for the first time, Turner stressed that the caucus group was working on 'specific changes by way of specific amendments.'[33] In reality, the Kaplan committee had just put the final touches on their amendment package the previous evening, including the measure to ensure the supremacy of the Charter. The document was to be presented to caucus that morning in anticipation of its release a few days later.

The Special Joint Committee Report and the Liberal Amendments

When the Special Joint Committee tabled its report on 9 September 1987 it recommended no changes to the accord. The report outlined the large number of concerns raised by expert witnesses and then dismissed those concerns as premature or unfounded. On the question of national cost-shared programs, for example, the report concluded, 'We realize that proposed section 106A has the *potential* for creating elements of a chequerboard of social programs across Canada' but went on to say, 'We do not share the doom and gloom prophesies of the opponents of proposed section 106A.' The committee's report also stated bluntly: 'In our opinion, a chequerboard Canada, insofar as details of national shared-cost programs are concerned, can be countenanced.'[34] Similarly, having heard innumerable experts decry the provisions for appointment to the Supreme Court, especially the lack of a deadlock-breaking mechanism, the committee merely disagreed and concluded, 'we are of the view that the proposals ... are workable.'[35] When the members of the committee found themselves unable to reject critical testimony, as in the case of the exclusion of the two territories from the proposed Senate reform measures, or the concerns about English-language minority rights, their report merely called on the premiers and the federal government to move quickly to deal with these 'outstanding' issues in future negotiations.[36]

From the Liberals' point of view, their inability to bring about change through the committee was a major blow. The four Liberal members did not sign the report, a symbolic gesture that received little attention from the public or caucus ranks. Although the Liberal amendments were appended to their minority report, they were not widely reported. As a result, Turner was forced to 'officially' unveil the Liberal amendments package in an address to a meeting of the Women's Liberal Commission the next day. He assured his audience the amendments would be tabled in the House of Commons, thus forcing a vote in which his caucus would be unanimously supporting them.

The Liberal amendments were substantial, detailed, and technical. They affected virtually every measure in the accord. Unlike the NDP, which had issued only vague comments about possible future changes, the amendments were drafted in legal language and ready for inclusion in the body of the Langevin text. The response to the *content* of the Liberal proposals by most experts was generally very positive. As one remarked, if the Liberal amendments were accepted, the Langevin Accord would be 'stood on its head.'

Yet, to their dismay, the Liberals soon found that media and public response to the amendments was not nearly as enthusiastic given the widespread belief that their contents were irrelevant. The plan to introduce the amendments and then vote in favour of the accord even if they were not accepted was not seen as a clever or even a realistic response to their situation as an opposition party. The proposed amendments were viewed almost universally as hypocritical.

A *Toronto Star* editorial was among the first to deride the Liberals' 'continuing quest to have their cake and eat it too.' It argued that the Liberals could propose the amendments 'safe in the knowledge that [they] will be defeated by the overwhelming Progressive Conservative majority' and then, having voted for the accord, in the next election they would campaign on the amendments in Ontario while portraying themselves as supporters of the accord in Quebec. 'Schemes like this,' the editorial concluded, 'go a long way toward explaining why the federal Liberals are sinking in the polls.'[37] This same view was expressed more bluntly by Turner's old college friend and *Ottawa Citizen* columnist Marjorie Nichols, who pulled few punches when she referred to 'the cowardice and hypocrisy inherent in the Liberal Party's evolving two-nations policy on Meech Lake.' Nichols also pointed out the party's position was completely contrary to past Liberal policy. 'How ironic it all is. The Liberal Party now has a separatist policy to deal with the separatist Accord.' She went on to directly link the accord with Turner's leadership problems. 'John Turner's original support of the Meech Lake Accord,' she wrote, 'which in the view of most Liberals violated one of the fundamental tenets of true Liberalism, is the major cause of his current leadership problems.'[38] As the caucus spokesperson, Bob Kaplan encountered similar media scepticism that verged on hostility when he was interviewed by four national media personalities the day the amendments were unveiled by Turner. Alan Fryer of CTV News posed the key question at the beginning of the interview: 'A lot of people are asking themselves, with such fundamental differences, how can you turn around and say we're going to support it anyway?' Kaplan's response was instructive. First, he stated that Liberals believed the prime objective of bringing Quebec into the constitutional fold was sufficiently important for the accord to be accepted even if no amendments were made. Once again, the impotence of the Liberals' opposition status was raised as the determining factor. 'We'd like to see the Accord improved now, but this government doesn't care. They are saying take it or leave it. If that's the only alternative, if we can't get them to take amendments, we resolve the dilemma by moving ahead and maintaining our agenda, as Liberals.' Rejecting a suggestion by Marjorie Nichols that 'the Liberal Party is guaranteeing that there will not be amendments' by voting in favour of the accord, Kaplan reiterated: 'We are not the government. And we don't have enough members in the House for you to be able to say that by voting against it we could stop it.'

At the same time, Kaplan argued that the amendments were designed to strengthen the accord, not undermine it. These amendments would become part of the Liberal platform for the next election and, when they returned to power, the subject of negotiations in the next constitutional round. In response, Nichols declared: 'I'm incredulous that you could sit there and say this [package of amendments] doesn't undermine it ... The Liberal Party has proposed running a bulldozer through the entire Accord and you are trying to make the argument to us that you sincerely believe it would still be accepted by the First

Ministers?' Ed Stewart of Canadian Press picked up on this theme and asked 'what hope do you have' to implement the Liberal amendments in the future, given the unanimity clause for amendment in Meech, and given that 'no future Quebec government … in its right mind' would accept these amendments. All of the panellists raised the issue of the party's apparent rejection of the Trudeau vision. When Kaplan tried to ignore a direct question by Ed Stewart, moderator Pamela Wallin of CTV intervened: 'You were, as Ed pointed out, a Liberal cabinet minister under Pierre Trudeau. He spent his entire career dedicated to preventing Quebec from becoming a distinct society and now the Liberal Party is in favour of that.' Kaplan struggled on valiantly, arguing that the distinct society clause would have little 'legislative effect' and that court interpretations would eventually define its meaning. Fryer responded immediately. 'I get back to Mr Trudeau's argument before the committee, either a distinct society clause means something or it doesn't. If it doesn't, why put it in?'[39]

The Divisive Votes in the House of Commons and the Senate

The unveiling of the Liberal amendments did not end Turner's troubles with his caucus. It was true that all of his MPs said they would not vote against the amendments, but they were still badly divided over what to do when they were defeated. Up to one-third of his caucus was considering voting against the accord. By 26 September, seven Liberal MPs – Dave Dingwall, Don Johnston, Charles Caccia, Sergio Marchi, David Berger, John Nunziata, and Keith Penner – had declared publicly that they would vote against the unamended accord. Pouring salt on the wounds, Prime Minister Mulroney announced that debate on the accord would begin within days and stated: 'We believe that one cannot have it both ways. One has to be for or one has to be against. But one cannot be on both sides of a fundamental issue.'[40] In the end, despite Turner's earlier assurances, not all of his caucus supported even the party's amendments package. Three Liberal MPs – Don Johnston, Charles Caccia, and David Berger – abstained. On the final vote on the unamended accord, fully eleven of the forty Liberal MPs did not vote with their party.[41] This, of course, was in stark contrast to the public show of unity ultimately displayed over the cruise missile crisis and the trade agreement. The dissidents' reasons were diverse, but unrelated to the leadership issue. For some, the deciding factor was multicultural, aboriginal, and minority language rights, or objection to the diminished authority of central governments in establishing social programs. For others, including former Trudeau ministers Johnston and Caccia, it was the deeply held conviction that the entire package was so flawed and contrary to the Liberal vision of Canadian federalism that it could not be remedied 'by tinkering at the margins.'[42]

After the vote, the public focus of the debate moved to the Senate. There the Liberal senators formed the majority in the upper chamber and, thanks to the foresight of Allan MacEachen, still controlled the agenda. Many had already indicated they would not support the agreement if unamended. Independent Senator Michael Pitfield, a former Trudeau adviser, had gone further and publicly described the accord as 'a disaster, and an irreversible disaster ... offering a (future) separatist government in Quebec opportunities to do things subtly, gradually and under the table ... it invites separatism to develop in an insidious way.'[43]

In the mythology surrounding the ultimate defeat of the Meech Lake Accord, pride of place is given to the roles played by the Manitoba and Newfoundland legislatures. While it is certainly true that the refusal of Liberal MLA Elijah Harper to give unanimous consent for a vote in the Manitoba legislature was the final nail in the accord's coffin, the importance of the strategic 180-day delay of the accord in the Senate should not be overlooked. In fact, the six-month Senate hiatus was a crucial factor in the demise of Meech Lake. The Senate strategy was deliberate. Three key members of the caucus committee that drafted the Liberal amendments had proposed this option and the idea was well received by the Liberal senators. At a meeting chaired by MacEachen, a survey of individual senators confirmed widespread opposition to the accord. Beginning with Trudeau confidant Peter Stollery, the senators one by one outlined their concerns and argued it should be opposed as vigorously as possible. Particularly persuasive was the opposition of Senator Jean Lemoyne, a former Trudeau speechwriter whose views on Quebec issues were well regarded. Unlike Garneau, Lapierre, and Ouellet, Lemoyne made it clear he did not believe opposition to the accord would damage Liberal fortunes in Quebec, but he also indicated he would oppose the accord regardless.[44]

Over the next six months the Senate heard from a number of expert witnesses including former prime minister Trudeau. Trudeau's appearance before the Senate Committee of the Whole on 30 March 1988 received extensive media coverage. His detailed critique of the accord left little doubt about the depth of his opposition. 'In my view ... the proposed changes strike at what is, in a way, the very essence of the Canadian federation. They undermine the three fundamental components of any modern democratic state: executive power, legislative power, and the judiciary.'[45]

Trudeau went on to make concrete suggestions about the options available to senators if they were seriously opposed to the accord. Unwittingly echoing the thinking of the caucus strategists, he said: 'I suggest that the Senate pass amendments that will ensure the resolution is corrected so that it means what Senator Murray (the Conservatives' lead spokesperson) says it does mean, that "distinct society" has no effect on the Charter or the distribution of powers. That is the minimum amendment that you can make but there are many others ... I would be prepared to suggest to you.' Having outlined several possible changes, Trudeau concluded: 'the Senate can and must send an amended resolution back and ask the House of Commons to vote on that.'[46] The Senate followed through on Trudeau's advice, adopting the identical set of amendments introduced in the House of Commons. This procedure stipulated that the amended accord be returned to the House for a second vote, resulting in an overall delay of more than six months before it received parliamentary approval. This delay, in turn, allowed sceptical premiers to delay their own consideration of the deal, leaving less time for debate and passage in their legislatures.

More Liberal Conflicts

With Senate debates ongoing, there was more bad news for Turner's leadership. In January 1988, Don Johnston declared publicly that he was so dismayed by the party's position that he was leaving the Liberal caucus to sit as an Independent Liberal. The suggestion for this label came from none other than Allan MacEachen, whom Johnston had consulted, and was approved by the Speaker. Referring to his decision years later, Johnston lamented the fact that Meech Lake had come between him and Turner and 'poisoned a relationship dating back to 1958.' He also specifically noted it was because of Meech Lake that he had chosen to 'step out' of caucus. By contrast, although he subsequently voted in favour of the FTA – despite his party's position opposing the agreement – he made it clear he would not have felt obliged to leave the Liberal caucus in order to do so.[47] Johnston would go on to publish a book with Trudeau about the Meech Lake Accord, entitled *With a Bang, Not a Whimper: Pierre Trudeau Speaks Out*. In his introduction he warned: 'If you believe in One Canada, a strong federal government and the individual rights and liberties you now enjoy, you owe it to yourself' to reject the Meech Lake Accord.[48]

Unrest was also apparent in the Atlantic provinces. Frank McKenna, a constitutional lawyer and newly elected leader of the provincial Liberals in New Brunswick, tabled his own 'companion document' of amendments. In Nova Scotia, Liberal opposition leader Vince Maclean voiced his opposition to the accord, as did Clyde Wells in Newfoundland. Wells, another constitutional lawyer, had actually campaigned against the accord in the provincial election and now as premier he threatened to rescind the province's agreement if changes were not made. Further west in Manitoba, Liberal opposition leader Sharon Carstairs challenged her Conservative counterpart, stating that the 'noble purpose of achieving Quebec's signature on the Constitution was achieved by dealing off Federal powers ... The deal was accomplished by granting important powers to every province ... Canada is more than the sum of its parts. The national will must always be stronger than the regional will if the federation is to survive.'[49]

In short, the leadership of the federal Liberal Party was finding itself increasingly isolated from provincial Liberals as well. Worse, a national poll of Liberals by the Gallup organization indicated that more than two-thirds of the party's rank-and-file members were unhappy with the party's position and with Turner's leadership. In this atmosphere, a rogue poll on 25 March 1988 showing the Liberals in third place with the electorate caused predictable caucus hysteria. Although it was discredited almost immediately by a second national poll placing the Liberals once again in first place by a slim margin, the panic remained below the surface.

The Second Caucus Revolt and Leadership Challenge

Driven partly by the erratic polling results and the ongoing financial plight of the party, and even more by serious policy difference with the leader on Meech Lake, the thirteen disgruntled caucus members who had signed letters calling for the leader's resignation in the summer of 1987 returned to the charge. Using the same 'cell' strategy they had used before, a few key players collected signatures and gave them to the principal organizer to place in a safety deposit box. Once again, only one person would know the names of all the signatories. This strategy, designed to protect individuals should the revolt fail, actually proved to be the downfall of the second caucus revolt.

Within a few days the rebellious MPs had secured enough additional signatures to pass the 50 per cent mark – twenty-two votes of non-confidence in a caucus of thirty-eight. With twenty-two letters in his possession demanding Turner resign and call a leadership convention, Senator Pietro Rizzuto – the former leader of the Friends of Turner and his chief fundraiser in Quebec – met with the leader on the evening of 25 April 1988. As several of them later confided, there was a general assumption that such an overwhelming number of rebel MPs would leave the leader with no choice but to resign. As a result, they had made no contingency plans. When the leader's advisers encouraged him to simply ignore the calls for his resignation, the rebels were stunned. Worse still, instead of the secret coup they had expected, their actions were reported to the media by one of Turner's own aides, who also threatened to release the letters and list of conspirators. This threat successfully routed the dissidents and left Rizzuto, nonplussed, holding the bag. It also left the Liberal Party looking more divided than ever, only months away from the next election. In the national caucus the following morning a number of the signatories, including novice Quebec MPs Sheila Finestone and Lucie Pépin, went to the microphone to explain their actions and withdraw their opposition to Turner's leadership, *but not to the accord*. Some who had been expected to speak in favour of the leader, and notably Senator MacEachen, did not do so. Predictably, Raymond Garneau spoke eloquently in the leader's defence, outlining the sacrifices he had made to keep the Liberal Party viable in Quebec. At the same time Garneau argued forcefully in favour of the accord for political reasons, warning that opposition to Meech Lake 'could finish us with the Quebec electorate for the foreseeable future.' André Ouellet, whose actual role in the coup attempt remained unclear and who fortuitously had been in Paris when the letters were delivered, spoke at great length. When he concluded, no one was any the wiser about his position on Turner's leadership, but it *was* clear that he, too, believed it was politically imperative to support the accord. One of the conspirators later concluded: 'It may well be that those who originally supported Jean Chrétien for the leadership were more inclined to dislike Turner. Certainly for some of them the constitutional issue provided the opportunity to speak out against him and justify their opposition.' However, in his view, 'the debate in our caucus that day decisively demonstrated that the opposition to Turner's constitutional position was fundamental and for the most part unrelated to the leadership issue.'

It was already apparent that the opponents of Meech Lake and of

Turner's leadership came from both ends of the Liberals' ideological spectrum. One prominent business Liberal who had not given up the fight against Meech was Don Johnston. In late April 1988 he was still busy lining up support among dissident Liberal MPs for alternative amendments to the government's package that would 'bring us back to the November '86 resolution.'[50] But at the 26 April caucus meeting it also became clear that the *supporters* of Meech Lake represented both sides of the Liberals' traditional left-right cleavage as well. They ranged from Warren Allmand and Jean-Claude Malépart at one end to Raymond Garneau and Bob Kaplan on the other. House leader Herb Gray's impassioned plea for the caucus to keep in mind that 'this is only the constitution, free trade is forever,' summed up the significant support behind Turner on Meech Lake from such left-wing Liberals as Gray, Lloyd Axworthy, and Sheila Copps. Yet Raymond Garneau, the most ardent supporter of Meech Lake, was a business Liberal who became livid at the prospect of the caucus opposing the free trade agreement.

The landmark caucus session actually adjourned for Question Period and returned to debate into the night. Tempers flared and voices were raised. More than one verbal altercation continued in the corridor outside the caucus meeting room where Turner's chief aide, Peter Connolly, was stationed. 'This is your doing,' one irate conspirator shouted, referring to the press leak which had scuttled the coup. In the end, however, it was clear the leader was not planning to leave. Most of the caucus finally decided it was too close to an election to make any further attempt to dislodge him. Moving on was essential, especially considering that the free trade issue was one on which the Liberals could unite and stand a real chance of winning an election. Despite the apparent calm after the storm, however, there was continued evidence that no quarter would be given on Meech Lake no matter how secure Turner's leadership appeared to be. In one of the clearest *public* indications that opposition to the leader's position on the accord was separate from the Turner-Chrétien leadership issue, Turner's own election readiness chair and strategy committee chair, Senator Michael Kirby, penned a lengthy article opposing the accord barely a week before the scheduled leader's debates that would precede the second vote in the House of Commons. Seeking to deflect criticism from the Liberals' schism, Kirby first reiterated the simple but essential point that the accord was the result of the Mulroney government's negotiations, not the Liberals'. Kirby, who had been a key player in the 1981 constitutional amendment process, described the two competing visions of federalism demonstrated by the accord and the Trudeau government's Constitution Act, 1981 which entrenched the Charter of Rights and Freedoms.

The Conservatives' accord, Kirby argued, reinforced the concept of Canadian federalism as a type of 'provincial compact' in which 'the rights or powers of provincial governments are more important than the rights of individuals.' This vision was 'precisely the opposite' of the Trudeau vision in which the rights of individual Canadian citizens are paramount. Kirby went on to note the consistency of Conservative views over time, citing those of Robert Stanfield and Joe Clark at the federal level and several provincial premiers, including Brian Peckford and Peter Lougheed, who clearly stated: 'We view Confederation as a compact.' Kirby concluded: 'It is therefore completely misleading to suggest, as Conservative spokesmen do, that the Meech Lake Accord is a natural sequel to the 1981 constitutional agreement. In fact, it reflects exactly the opposite vision of Canada.'[51] Kirby's effort to shift the focus to the Conservatives was unsuccessful in terms of the media, but it did provide a line of argument for other opponents of Meech Lake to pursue without further damaging the leader. For many Liberals the option of saying nothing did not exist, but for the majority of loyal Liberals who wanted to avoid conflict, especially so close to a probable election call, this alternative was most expedient. As Kirby once again underlined after the 1988 election, the divisions were based on the difficult if not impossible position in which the Conservatives had placed the Liberals:

> What you had was two goals that Liberals had long aspired to. One of them was to get Quebec to sign the constitution, something that Trudeau and everybody else had wanted. The other was to maintain the vision of federalism and the role of the federal government that Trudeau had. In order to get Quebec to sign the constitution, you had to abandon significant tenets of the Trudeau vision of Canada. The reasons for the deep divisions within our party ultimately came down to whether or not you thought the price paid to get Quebec to sign was justified.[52]

The Second Vote in the House of Commons

The final round of parliamentary debate on the accord began on 14 June 1988. The Senate had adopted the Liberal amendments and sent the accord back to the House, where the changes would either be rejected again or adopted. This second vote would be final. The accord would not return to the Senate, which had the power to delay but not to veto legislation approved by the House.

The debate opened with speeches by all three party leaders. Each expressed concerns about the consequences of failing to adopt the accord. A somewhat chastened prime minister spoke of the importance of accepting the deal even though it might be less than perfect. 'Let us not make the perfect the enemy of the good,' Mulroney urged. 'Surely we have a much better chance to improve our constitution with Quebec as a full participant at the constitutional table.' Likewise NDP leader Ed Broadbent argued: 'We must respond by saying "oui" to Quebec. Should we fail to grasp the significance of the moment, future generations will live to regret it.' And John Turner, consistent with his position throughout the debate, insisted that 'Quebec's absence from the constitutional table impedes any future constitutional development. Those who oppose Meech Lake fail to take that into account.' He maintained the party's amendments could be accepted without destroying the agreement, but he nevertheless stated: 'I do not believe the Accord is the straitjacket its detractors make it out to be.'[53]

Demonstrating the ongoing division in Liberal ranks, only fourteen of Turner's thirty-eight caucus members were in the House of Commons when he spoke. In the week between the leaders' speeches and the actual vote, several Liberal MPs indicated they would oppose the accord again. In a new twist, Toronto MP and Immigration critic Sergio Marchi, who had voted against the accord the previous October, indicated he would abstain on the second vote 'to make a statement on behalf of the party that there's a healing process there.'[54] But in addition to the previous eleven Liberal dissidents, some new voices were added to the opposition. Former caucus chair and Turner supporter Doug Frith, who had voted in favour of the accord in October, now indicated he would abstain on this second vote, suggesting the full extent of the opposition to the accord previously had been muted by concerns about caucus solidarity.

This suspicion proved well founded. On 22 June, a total of fifteen Liberal MPs did not support the accord. Five of the original eleven MPs opposed to the deal – Berger, Caccia, Finestone, Johnston, and Penner – voted against it again. Both Marchi and Frith abstained, and eight other MPs did not show up for the vote. As one MP confided: 'Liberals wanted to avoid a public confrontation with Turner because an election (was) imminent and the party did not want to appear divided.' Nevertheless, the message was clear. As one reporter noted: 'Even though party ranks closed publicly after the failed caucus revolt last month, opposition to the accord remains strong in the party's rank and file.'[55] Just how strong this opposition really was became clear over the next two years. Another federal election and a leadership contest drove the two competing visions further apart. As Trudeau's former principal secretary, Tom Axworthy, wrote: 'For the Liberal Party, Meech Lake is the issue that will not go away, nor should it.'[56]

5 The Fight of His Life: The 1988 Election

We built a country east and west and north. We built it on an infrastructure that deliberately resisted the continental pressure of the United States. With one stroke of a pen you've reversed that.

– Rt Hon. John Turner (leaders' debate, 1988 election)

Although few would remember it later, there was a point during the 1988 election campaign when the Liberal Party was leading in the polls and poised to regain power. In view of the Liberals' many widely publicized policy disputes and attempted coups, it was a stunning repudiation of Prime Minister Brian Mulroney and his Conservative government. The electorate was not enthusiastic about the Liberals, but they were deeply unhappy with the government. It was a striking development, especially given the unprecedented majority Mulroney had won in 1984. For a short time, it looked as if the Liberal Party would be handing the Conservatives a repeat of the 1963 Diefenbaker defeat, and the Conservatives knew it.

There is no single explanation for the Liberals' brief flirtation with victory. Apart from the government's unpopularity, there were several other factors prompting voters to give the Liberals serious consideration. To begin with, there was grudging respect for the leader, who had persevered through four turbulent years with some grace and much determination. There was a comprehensive and well-prepared Liberal platform – the first real Red Book. Then there was John Turner's brilliant performance during the leaders' debates, which allowed him to claim a decisive victory, and an exceptional ad campaign which heightened the party's visibility. The ads captured the imagination of millions of Canadians and temporarily stunned the Conservatives. And, finally, the Liberals were on the right side of public opinion on the free trade debate, the dominant issue of the campaign.

But there were as many reasons why a Liberal victory was not likely, many of them more compelling. First and foremost, their fractious past caught up with the caucus and thwarted the Liberals' efforts to present themselves as a government-in-waiting. Incredible as it may seem in light of their historic reputation for party unity, infighting actually continued during the campaign and added further fuel to the fire. Meanwhile the platform and policy work, excellent in conception, was sometimes flawed in execution. Even more important, the party had little in the way of an on-the-ground organization. Particularly galling was the decision of Robert Bourassa (whom Turner had courted so assiduously by defending Meech Lake in the face of all opposition) to throw his organizational support behind Brian Mulroney on account of the Free Trade Agreement (FTA). Last, but hardly least, when the election became almost a single-issue campaign and the Conservatives appeared to be in real difficulty, the business community united to defend the FTA. Using third-party advertising they overpowered all opposition while the Liberals stood by helplessly, lacking the financial resources to fight back in the final weeks of the campaign.

Despite the end result, the party that flirted with oblivion in 1984 made a remarkable comeback in the 1988 election. With few resources and limited personnel, the Liberals demonstrated a high level of preparedness and professionalism. This was due in large part to the efforts of the group that gathered in the wake of 1984 to initiate the rebuilding process. Their work was evident in every aspect of the operation, from logistics and policy development to support for candidates and the leader's tour. As one analyst noted, 'even after the campaign was over, candidates and organizers agreed that the party had never been readier, even when the Liberals were in government and could control the timing of the election.'[1]

Moreover, John Turner's performance in the 1988 campaign was stellar. That he rose to the occasion despite a painful back injury, to say nothing of a bizarre series of unexpected setbacks caused by his own campaign personnel, heightened the nature of this accomplishment. Unfortunately, the Liberals' troubles during the 1988 election came primarily from internal strife and from events beyond their control. The situation was exacerbated by damaging and arguably biased media coverage, the ethics of which would be debated in journalism classes for years to come. At one point the party was in danger of being replaced as the Official Opposition. Yet the Liberals eventually rebounded to finish with twice the number of seats they had taken in 1984. There were problems to be sure, but the transition was impossible to ignore. They may not have returned to power, but only four years after their ignominious 1984 defeat the 1988 campaign demonstrated the Liberal Party was in no danger of disappearing from Canada's political scene.

The Strategy Committee and the Senate's Free Trade Gambit

One of the reasons the Liberals were so well prepared for the 1988 election was because they had to be. Their lack of resources had been a serious constraint throughout the previous four years, but the rebuilding campaign had begun almost immediately despite this. A key to their election readiness was the Strategy Committee, which began its work shortly after the November 1986 convention. The committee was chaired by Senator Michael Kirby, the former Privy Council bureaucrat and Trudeau adviser whose reputation for Machiavellian manoeuvres was well established. In addition to the two national campaign co-chairs, other members of the Strategy Committee included House leader Herb Gray, Senate opposition leader Allan MacEachen, senators Jack Austin and Joyce Fairbairn, OLO chief of staff Peter Connolly, caucus chair Brian Tobin, party president Michel Robert, and the director of the Liberal Caucus Research Bureau. Gerry Schwartz, the party's chief fundraiser, was also expected to participate by giving updates on the financial situation, but was rarely able to attend.

The Strategy Committee was responsible for planning the leader's tour, the approval of the ad campaign, and the publication of the platform document, all of which were to be ready by the time the prime minister dropped the writ. In reality, they were ready ahead of time. Partly because they were ready, and partly because they were worried about the impact of the Free Trade Agreement should it be passed before an election call, the Strategy Committee supported going to the polls over the issue. This move had three advantages: it would effectively give the Liberals control of the timing of an election, it would marginalize the NDP, and, most important, it would prevent Turner from having to discuss his opposition to the deal and how he would quash it if elected.

The Conservatives, it turns out, were also agonizing over the question of timing, although their internal debate was motivated by different concerns.[2] Poor showings in pre-election polls and the fear that they might slide even further made an earlier election attractive. As well, their traditional four-year term of office was nearly up. At the same time, however, the Tories worried an election would not leave enough time to recall Parliament and pass the trade legislation before 31 December 1988 as stipulated in the agreement.

The problem was solved for them when Turner and the Liberals seized control of the agenda. For Turner, Liberal opposition to the trade deal was a certainty as soon as the actual agreement was released in October 1987. It confirmed his worst fears about the Mulroney government's ineptitude in negotiations and failure to understand Canadian culture. Those present in Turner's office at the time recall him reading through the massive agreement and, without a moment's hesitation, announcing as he put it down that it would mean 'the end of Canada as we know it.' Privately, he confided that he had suspected as much when the chief Canadian negotiator, Simon Reisman, whom he knew from his days as finance minister, first walked away from the deal. As a result, Turner raised the possibility of using the Liberal majority in the Senate to stop the trade deal. There were two ways to do this. The first was to ask the Senate to block the deal, as it had done with Meech Lake, and wait for the deadline to pass. Turner disapproved of this option, arguing that it did not get at the fundamental problem with free trade, the government's complete lack of a mandate to sign such a deal. Instead, he preferred the second option, which was to use the Senate as the means of forcing an election. The Liberal leadership in the Senate could publicly state that they would not pass the bill until an election was called. If the Conservatives called the election and won, the Liberals would promise to pass the bill in plenty of time for the government to meet the 31 December deadline. If the Liberals won, Turner would not have to tear up the deal as it would not have been implemented.

Turner's idea was put to the Strategy Committee in late May 1988. In a memo responding to the leader's suggestion, Kirby outlined the potential advantages and problems the Committee anticipated with each of the two options, indicating they also were in favour of the second approach. The memo recommended that the leader make an announcement before Labour Day, noting he could argue 'in view of the fact that the prime minister stated in 1983 that he was opposed to free trade, that the government did not mention free trade in the 1984 election platform, that free trade will have a dramatic and irreversible impact on Canada and Canadian society, and that a clear majority of Canadians want an election on free trade before it becomes law, you have instructed the Liberal-dominated Senate to ensure that the bill is not passed until an election is held.'[3] The memo also stressed that such a strategy would allow Turner to defend Canadian sovereignty and unite the Liberal Party behind a strong national vision shared by members at both caucus and grassroots levels.

John Turner announced his decision to delay passage of the FTA at a special caucus meeting on 20 July 1988. Using the message he had fine-tuned over the past several months, he declared: 'Brian Mulroney wants to be governor of the 51st state and I want to be Prime Minister of Canada.' According to caucus chair Brian Tobin, support for the plan in national caucus that day was virtually unanimous, and the mood was 'buoyant and enthusiastic.'[4] An Angus Reid poll barely a week later found that six in ten Canadians supported Turner's position. The poll suggested that, if an election was held, the Conservatives and the Liberals would each receive roughly 40 per cent of the vote, with the NDP far behind at 20 per cent.

With the memory of the Meech Lake divisions still hanging over the caucus, the appeal of such a forceful and clear-cut position on the part of the leader was self-evident. The lead caucus critics on the file, Lloyd Axworthy and Herb Gray, were quickly supported by colleagues from both ends of the Liberals' left-right spectrum, all of whom were anxious to demonstrate party unity in the run-up to the election. Even business Liberals in the caucus who supported the trade deal, such as Raymond Garneau, felt they were in no position to protest since they had so recently won the hard-fought battle for the constitutional position of the party. Thus on the key left-right policy issue to emerge during their four years in opposition, internal discipline and outward solidarity reigned. Allan MacEachen – whose historic decision to retain control of committees was once again proving to have been both prescient and crucial to the Liberal strategy – would have no difficulty ensuring that the Liberal Senate caucus was on side with the proposal.

Virtually the only Liberal to publicly oppose Turner's move was, technically, no longer a Liberal. Independent Liberal Don Johnston now found himself on the wrong side of the two major issues of the day. He had been a staunch opponent of Meech Lake, and his equally strong support for the trade deal had been almost forgotten by others, but certainly not by Johnston. With Turner's irrevocable decision to oppose the deal, Johnston announced in July that he would not be seeking re-

election, a move which touched off a nomination battle in his traditionally safe Liberal seat of Westmount.

Behind the scenes, former Quebec MP and Turner supporter Pierre
Deniger shared Johnston's view that the party's position was the wrong
one. Deniger, who had recently won the Liberal nomination in his old
riding, quietly told colleagues at the Brewers' Association of Canada
that Turner's decision would likely cost him the election.[5] This was an
accurate perception of the political situation in Quebec, where Premier
Bourassa had already been making it abundantly clear he would not
be assisting the federal Liberals through his provincial machine. This
came as no surprise to many of the Trudeau-era veterans in Ottawa
who had dealt with the premier in the past. Nevertheless Turner felt his
support for the Meech Lake Accord deserved Bourassa's appreciation.
At a minimum he expected that the premier would remain neutral. But
when the Liberal leader travelled to Quebec City in mid-August to meet
Bourassa, his hopes were dashed. At the press conference following
their meeting, Bourassa stressed his appreciation for Turner's support
on Meech Lake, but remained studiously quiet as Turner explained his
position on free trade. In the French-language press, Bourassa was seen
as condescending to Turner, with headlines such as 'Bourassa se moque
encore de Turner.'[6] A few days later, Bourassa and Brian Mulroney appeared together and demonstrated the close relationship Turner had
not achieved. One reporter described Mulroney as looking like 'the cat
that had swallowed the canary.'[7]

Meanwhile the high-profile vacancy in Westmount served to shine
a spotlight on the continued difficulty the party was having with its
candidate selection process, even in opposition. This problem was destined to plague it throughout the next twenty years, despite several
attempts to redress the root causes, and would ultimately lead to the
adoption of significant constitutional reforms at the party's 2006 leadership convention.

Selecting the Liberal Team: Nomination Woes

Just as his determination to 'democratize' the Liberal Party by allowing others to participate in policy formulation had led to accusations
that John Turner did not have a firm set of convictions, so his decision *not* to interfere in the candidate selection process for the next election reinforced the widespread view that he was weak and indecisive.
Somewhat perversely, the man who was elected leader because he had

promised to 'open up' the party and ensure there were 'no backroom boys, no elites, no rainmakers' was frequently criticized in the run-up to the 1988 election because he refused to block certain individuals or impose 'star' candidates on unwilling local riding associations.

The Liberal Party had long had difficulties with candidate nominations in ridings where the party was expected to win. The safer the seat, the more likely the contest would be long, drawn out, and expensive. The stakes were high because whoever succeeded in winning the nomination was virtually assured of becoming the next MP. And since the Liberal Party had historically been the governing party, it naturally had the greatest number of 'safe' seats likely to be contested. More recently, the 'safe seat' contests had been further complicated by two new factors.

First, the participatory democracy efforts of Pierre Trudeau had produced a growing desire on the part of various ethnic groups to become more deeply involved in the political process. Mobilized as members and/or delegates during the 1984 leadership race, and the 1986 leadership review exercise, many of these groups decided it was now time to become major players themselves, representing their communities as members of Parliament. From the Portuguese, Macedonian, and Italian communities of central Canada to the Sikh and Chinese communities in British Columbia, their involvement in Liberal Party riding associations was becoming a major factor in candidate selection, just as it had earlier been a force in delegate selection for the 1986 leadership review convention. And it was the Liberal Party to which these new Canadians overwhelmingly turned when they decided to run for public office, due to its historic openness towards immigrants as well as its long record of electoral success.

A second new factor was the more problematic phenomenon of 'instant Liberal' candidates who came from the ranks of single-issue interest groups, and most notably from the anti-abortion movement. When a Supreme Court ruling struck down the existing abortion law, the Mulroney government's failure to introduce new legislation before the end of its first mandate had once again placed the issue on the political agenda. As a result, a variety of right-to-life groups became active in nomination races across the country. They vowed to try to capture the nomination of whichever political party was most likely to win in a particular riding. Their stated goal was to elect as many pro-life MPs as possible in order to influence the new bill whenever it would finally be introduced in the House of Commons.[8]

These two developments meant Liberal nominations were targeted more than ever. Historically the NDP and the Conservatives had not faced the same challenges to their candidate selection process, precisely because their nominated candidates were not likely to win in the general election that followed. As well, most sizeable ethnic groups were located in urban ridings, which had traditionally been Liberal strongholds. Even the right-to-life movement was less likely to target the Tories and the NDP, partly because the NDP would never allow them to be candidates and partly because in many Tory-held ridings, especially in western Canada, the sitting MP was already a pro-life advocate.

In an effort to counterbalance these developments, Turner encouraged high-profile Liberals to stand for office. Shortly after the 1986 convention he placed Paul Martin Jr. – a likely candidate himself – in charge of candidate recruitment for the next election. Although Martin travelled extensively across the country in search of 'star' candidates, he met with little success. As Martin and Turner soon learned, the risk of winning a seat and ending up on the opposition benches – as happened to Raymond Garneau – was something most star candidates were loath to contemplate. And while the Liberals were doing better in the polls, their victory was far from certain.

An additional problem arose when several long-serving and popular MPs announced they would not be running again. Although several declined to comment or cited 'personal reasons' as their primary motivation, it was well known within the party's inner circles that most were opting not to run because of their disagreement with the leader over the Meech Lake Accord and other related issues. Doug Frith, one of the most high-profile MPs who decided not to seek re-election, recalled: 'It was a real concern at the time. Looking back, though, I think it was even more serious than we realized, because it had lasting consequences. Basically we lost the apprenticeship of the party, the next generation of leaders.'[9]

The attrition problem was compounded by the leader's decision not to protect his caucus members from nomination challenges. Both the Liberals and Conservatives had traditionally protected their sitting MPs from internal party challenges. There was a simple reason for this. Potential candidates were already wary of devoting considerable time, money, and effort to a nomination race in which the outcome was uncertain. Those who *did* agree to run were prepared to risk defeat at the hands of the electorate, but not to members of the same party. How, they asked, could MPs be expected to devote all their energies in Ottawa when fellow party members were busy preparing to challenge them for the nomination before the next election? For them, the importance of guaranteeing the safety of sitting members was self-evident.

At the other extreme were those party members who had argued for years that it was important to be able to replace an MP who was not perceived to be doing a good job. Although they believed this would not occur very often, the self-styled Liberal democrats concluded it was important to let the local party members have the final say. In the end Turner agreed with them and decided to break with tradition. However, it should also be noted that his genuine belief in the need to democratize the party was reinforced by his personal concern that his own leadership would once again be diminished if he were to be caught up in individual nomination battles which his preferred candidates eventually lost.

At the time no one realized these new factors would lead to so many nomination battles or such bitterly fought ones. In this respect, as in so many others, Turner's leadership coincided with a period of major change in the way political parties operated, and in the people who participated in them. Under the party's new rules of the game, the clash of old and new Liberal Party members in safe urban ridings, such as Toronto and Vancouver, produced many public relations disasters for the party. One, in Mississauga East, saw future Martin cabinet minister Albina Guarnieri unexpectedly win the nomination, prompting long-time Liberal activist Roberta Need to state publicly: 'I want nothing more to do with the Liberal Party of Canada or its candidates.'[10] Across Toronto a number of similar ethnically driven battles took place, resulting in the nominations of future Martin cabinet ministers Joe Volpe and Tony Ianno. In both cases sitting Liberal MPs – Roland de Corneille and Aideen Nicholson – were unceremoniously dumped, to the dismay of other veteran MPs in the Liberal caucus.

Turner remained unapologetic, saying he believed the contests were an example of the democratic process at work and the 'revitalization' of the Liberal Party. Michael Kirby expressed the same opinion in comments as a panellist on CTV's *Canada AM*. 'I think it is good for the political process in general,' he declared, 'and frankly I don't think it's a phenomenon that is going to be unique to the Liberal Party. In the years to come I hope the Conservatives and NDP will be facing the same problem because it is good for Canada and good for new Canadians if everyone participates in the political process.'[11]

Privately, the leader expressed his disappointment when Patrick Johnson was defeated for the nomination in Scarborough West by right-to-life candidate Tom Wappel. Johnson, the highly regarded social policy expert who had served as director of the National Anti-Poverty Organization and was Turner's platform co-chair, had spent ten months assiduously collecting the support of longtime Liberals in the riding, only to be trounced at the nomination meeting by Wappel's massive influx of 'instant Liberals' from the anti-abortion movement.

As Johnson recalled: 'We knew there was something wrong when we were canvassing door-to-door among existing Liberal members and none of them had been approached by Wappel's team, even though he had declared he was running against me.'[12] It finally became apparent that Wappel was deliberately ignoring the longtime Liberals. Having struck a deal with Campaign Life, he was recruiting new party members from the pro-life group. He was also working in close cooperation with members of the Catholic Church in the riding. At the nomination meeting in September 1988 Johnson recalled delivering his speech to an audience in which six priests in full clerical garb occupied the front row. When the time came for the party members to cast their ballots, Johnson watched in dismay as many of his supporters, evidently intimidated by the presence of their parish priests, quietly melted away without voting. It was a defeat for which Johnson and his organizers (most of whom would become important members of the Martin leadership drive) were unprepared but from which they learned a lot about this new political phenomenon.

The Liberals' difficulties with the leader's new laissez-faire approach were also exacerbated by the electoral redistribution which occurred in the middle of the election preparations.[13] In Ottawa, for example, another of Turner's few star candidates – feminist activist and author Maude Barlow – had been duly elected in a nomination contest before the new riding boundaries came into effect. Although the boundaries did not change significantly, it was deemed necessary by the party to have a second nomination meeting, a nomination which Barlow lost to Chrétien supporter Mac Harb, an Ottawa alderman. More than one potential candidate, discouraged by these incidents, took themselves out of the running altogether, by which time it was too late to recruit a credible replacement.

In Quebec a different situation unfolded despite the best efforts of Raymond Garneau to implement the leader's new approach. While he may have been the Quebec lieutenant, Garneau was not in charge of the Quebec wing of the party, which was determined to reserve certain safe seats for star candidates. One such star was party president Michel

Robert, who deliberated for a long time about which riding to run in before finally deciding he would not run at all. During this time several other potential candidates had been actively discouraged from seeking the nomination in these ridings by the party executive. Some of these frustrated would-be candidates complained publicly, leaving Canadians with the clear impression that the Liberal nomination rules in Quebec were different from the rest of the country. In the end, the attempt to open up the party to broader participation and a more 'democratic' nomination process had the obverse effect on public perception.

Overcoming the Party's Financial Crisis

While the parliamentary wing was planning the content of the upcoming Liberal campaign, the extra-parliamentary wing was grappling with a crippling lack of resources. The party's financial situation had deteriorated dramatically between the 1984 federal election and the election of Michel Robert as party president in 1986. 'The party had no debt in 1984 when John Turner took over,' Robert recalled. 'It rose to $3.2 million after the election and had hit $6 million when I took over.'[14] The shortfall was partly due to the abject failure of early direct mail efforts, but also to the steep decline in traditional corporate donations. While some argued that historically this was to be expected when the party was in opposition, others (such as Marc Lalonde) believed the leader himself was a large part of the problem.[15]

Still others pointed to the expenditures of the National Office. Not everyone agreed with the arguments put forward by Collenette and Campagnolo about the necessity of maintaining a certain level of spending to ensure the party's ongoing visibility and retention of its membership. One executive member stressed that Campagnolo had been 'assiduous' in minimizing her own expenses and recognized that the office had tried to cut back on operating costs. But, he complained, these measures were hardly sufficient given the party's dire situation. 'No one seemed to realize the magnitude of our problem. All of the special events and activities were simply unaffordable. I couldn't believe 200 Laurier was still spending money like water, long after it had run out.'[16]

Both Robert and party treasurer Lloyd Posno admitted the party had difficulty simply meeting the payroll many times in 1986–7. Posno remembered one occasion when 'I was forced to rush home from the cottage and fly to Ottawa with Gerry (Schwartz) to try and avert a major crisis with our suppliers, many of whom had been threatening to cut us off for some time. Each month it was a case of deciding which bills to pay and putting others off as long as we could.'[17] Frequently payment was delayed longest for those bills relating to the activities of the leader's office and the Research Bureau, raising the level of mistrust between the two wings of the party.

As party president, Michel Robert worked hard to improve the revenue situation. He introduced an expanded series of leader's dinners held annually in major urban centres across the country with Turner as the keynote speaker. According to Robert, by 1988 these events had become 'the single most important source of revenue for the national party.'[18] A second principal source of revenue was the Laurier Club, a select group of party members who contributed at least $1,000 to the party annually. Laurier Club meetings were held across the country as well, with members invited to attend cocktail parties or receptions attended by the leader and some of the key caucus members from the region.

Despite the increased fundraising efforts and the imposition of further spending constraints on the national office in 1987, the party's debt was rapidly becoming unmanageable. Revenues from the leaders' dinners and the Laurier Club were not only the most important source of revenue, they were practically the *only* sources of funding the party could count on. By 1987, Robert said, the Liberal Party was for all intents and purposes 'insolvent.' Some believed it was only a matter of time before the party was obliged to close down its national office. 'Legally we could not go bankrupt because we were not incorporated. Only the FLAC could be sued in that sense. But yes, we were essentially bankrupt.'[19]

With the Royal Bank in Toronto as the sole holder of the Liberal Party's debt, Robert also admitted that the bank's president, Allan Taylor, had become 'increasingly nervous' about the extent of their commitment. As a result, one of Robert's most important contributions in the run-up to the 1988 election was to arrange for the party's debt to be shared with another lender. Although the Royal Bank remained the principal debt holder (at $4 million), the Banque National du Canada (BNC) agreed to take on the remaining $2 million of party debt, and both banks agreed to extend the party a line of credit. This proved to be but a temporary solution, however. The situation continued to deteriorate. By late 1987 there was a serious concern that the party would not be able to finance a *national* election campaign. At one point speculation turned to the possibility of a campaign without a leader's tour, a scenario in which the possibility of the party winning, or even holding on to the title of Official Opposition, would be all but impossible.

By early 1988 even the party's line of credit had been exhausted. Michael Robinson (who had been appointed the CFO by Turner in the wake of the August 1987 crisis management meeting in Ottawa) was obliged to renegotiate the agreement with the Royal Bank to spread the debt among a larger consortium, thereby obtaining sufficient funds through lines of credit to support the party's efforts through the election period.

Robert's other major effort on the financial front was to negotiate special arrangements with various provincial wings of the party, whose financial status was somewhat better. It was to these provincial wings that individual Liberal candidates remitted a portion of their election rebates. In the interests of the national campaign, an agreement was reached for a one-time transfer of these rebates to the national level, to contribute to the debt reduction and election campaign efforts. As a result of all of these extraordinary measures the Liberal Party was finally prepared financially for the 1988 election, albeit at a much reduced level than it had been accustomed to in the past.

Sadly, Michel Robert – who had originally sought the post of president because of his interest in policy development – spent most of the first two years of his presidency dealing with the party's financial crisis. When not occupied on that issue he had been heavily involved in the internal Meech Lake debate, attempting to play a positive role while asserting the importance of the extra-parliamentary wing. Neither function had endeared him to the leader. Since he was the first party president elected without any input from the leader, and was an 'outsider' who had never been part of the parliamentary wing, he was already at a considerable disadvantage in pursuing these roles.

There were other sources of conflict as well, including Robert's appointment of Marie-Andrée Bastien as secretary general in 1987. The rocky working relationship between Bastien and national campaign director John Webster, a Turner appointee, represented a broader conflict between the two wings of the party as the 1988 election drew near.

Drafting the Liberal Platform

The concept of political parties producing a written, detailed policy document had been virtually unknown in modern elections in Canada.

Instead, Canadian voters evaluated political parties based on a combination of three factors: leadership, local candidates, and general party philosophy.[20] In Canada the relative importance of the three factors varied over time, but the concept of 'general party philosophy' was traditionally the most significant until the Trudeau era, when leadership became the most important. This trend appeared to be continuing under Brian Mulroney.[21] The Liberal strategists in 1988 were convinced Turner's low rating on leadership was likely to improve during the campaign. His strengthened communications skills and grasp of the issues were still largely unknown to the electorate, a situation he could capitalize on. At the same time, the campaign team was convinced it would take more than improved leadership ratings to win the election and, with a strong set of policy positions in place that would appeal to the Canadian liberal majority, the advantages of a written list of commitments seemed obvious.

Once again it was the LCRB to whom they turned for assistance. The role of the Research Bureau had already expanded dramatically to fill the void left by reduced funding. With a federal election approaching, the bureau's role was once again enlarged, this time to include many functions related to the party's extra-parliamentary wing. Most important, the director of the bureau was asked to serve as the secretary of the Platform Committee, and the bureau's research officers prepared all of the platform planks. Nevertheless, several platform committee members stressed that this work was always done under the overall direction of the platform committee.

Indeed, virtually everyone agreed this was a platform that emerged from the ground up. According to the party's national policy chair, Rodger Schwass, the linkages between party resolutions at the 1986 convention, the recommendations of the various Canada Conferences, and the deliberations of the platform committee itself were linear and direct. Schwass also stressed that the party's 1986 convention resolutions were the product of a lengthy consultation and policy development process. In the end, Schwass noted, 'over 300 resolutions were brought to the national policy convention, with over 70 high priority resolutions.'[22] By the time platform committee co-chairs Patrick Johnson and Manon Vennat formally submitted their recommendations to the leader, it was reasonable to conclude, as the party's director of policy development Mark Resnick did, that this had been 'one of the most open, responsive and responsible platform development exercises in the history of the Liberal Party.'[23]

This process was part of Turner's commitment to open up the party and was one of his most successful initiatives. It began in the summer of 1987. As the Canada Conferences came to an end, Turner approached two individuals who had been involved in the conferences to lead the platform exercise. Patrick Johnson, the former director of the National Anti-Poverty Organization, had been a participant in the second conference. He recalled that his invitation to become a platform co-chair followed a meeting with Turner in Halifax, arranged to discuss issues such as the guaranteed annual income and income security measures generally. Turner asked him to take on the platform assignment to provide a social-Liberal counterbalance to the business-Liberal-oriented co-chair, Manon Vennat. A well-known Montreal management consultant, Vennat came to the leader's attention when she participated in the first Canada Conference. Johnson was not a card-carrying party member at the time of his appointment but accepted the offer because he believed his input would make a difference. 'What Turner was trying to do was to involve people who had not been active party members, but who were liberals as well as policy experts in various fields, in order to broaden the base and revitalize the party, similar to the thinking behind the Kingston conference years earlier.'[24]

Not all members of the extra-parliamentary wing were supportive of the decision to expand participation in the platform process. Sean Moore, the party's communications chair at the time and therefore a member of the national executive, argued there was no need for a separate platform committee when the constitution of the party had already created a duly elected national policy committee, of which Roger Schwass was the chair. Other members of the executive agreed, suggesting their support for Turner had been diminished by this decision to consult 'outsiders' rather than turn to the party executive. However, most of the executive, and especially Schwass himself, did not share this view. Years later he reaffirmed his belief that the 1988 process had been 'extremely respectful of the party' and 'the most productive and successful' one in which he had ever participated.[25]

The effort to broaden the party's base resulted in an unwieldy organization. The full platform committee consisted of over forty members, including some ex officio representatives of the party, caucus, and campaign organization. There were members of the strategy committee, fundraisers, caucus members, and members of the various Liberal commissions. Virtually all of the membership of the party's national policy committee was included, and this was to be the core source of policy development. Among the lengthy list of names were a large number who would later become prominent in the Martin leadership campaigns, such as Heather Reisman, Gerry Godsoe, Senator Jack Austin, Charles Kelly, Dennis Dawson, Peter Nicholson, and Jack Graham.

Although the entire platform group met twice in Ottawa, the party's ever-present financial constraints prevented any further meetings of the whole committee. Instead, a steering committee consisting of Johnson and Vennat, vice-chair Gerry Godsoe, and national policy chair Rodger Schwass worked closely with Mark Resnick and the LCRB director on a platform outline that would encompass the thrust of important party resolutions and recommendations from the Canada Conferences. At one point the Research Bureau staff actually produced a cross-referenced chart demonstrating the source of the various platform planks and their linkages with other policy documents.

The two co-chairs signed off on the platform document and forwarded it to the leader with a covering letter on 4 May 1988, noting once again the inclusiveness of the process and the positive consensus about the contents. The document then went to the Strategy Committee, chaired by Senator Michael Kirby, where it was reviewed, approved, and broken down into thirty-nine specific platform planks. Next Kirby and the bureau director met with the leader to obtain final approval. The only real change made to the content of the document at this stage was the *addition* of a platform plank at the suggestion of Kirby, who felt 'there should be an even 40 planks. Who wants to try and sell a platform at the door or write ads about the Liberals' 39-point plan?' The party's proposal on the Free Trade Agreement was only a single point, the third item in the forty-point plan.

The Release of the First Red Book

The result of these efforts was the Liberals' first real Red Book. It represented an important innovation in Canadian politics and was the precursor of the more substantial one which would prove to be a key factor in the Liberals' successful 1993 campaign.

The platform contents were forwarded to the Red Leaf advertising team to be formatted and prepared for general distribution. Under the subheading 'What a Liberal Government Will Do for You,' the bright red pamphlet contained 'highlights of the platform of the Liberal Party in the coming election.' It stressed that 'further details on each plank will be released as the campaign progresses.' This was the compromise

the Strategy Committee had agreed upon, allowing the leader to release the platform in advance while still keeping the detailed explanation of each plank confidential until after the writ was dropped. (It was
also the compromise reached with the party's financial officers, who
informed the committee the party could not afford to mass distribute a
more substantial document.)

Long before the writ was dropped, a brochure was distributed to
candidates for use in door-to-door campaigning. Media kits containing
the additional background material for each plank were ready for distribution on the leader's tour. With the help of Dr David Husband, an
economist and former Bank of Canada official, and Mike McCracken,
president and CEO of Infometrica, the planks had also been costed. A
summary sheet was prepared which detailed the total cost of the Liberal commitments and the proposed sources of income to pay for it,
although these costing details were not included in the original media
kits. Finally, a schedule of the policy announcements was agreed upon
and drawn up by the Strategy Committee. The housing plank would
be released in Toronto on Day 3 of the campaign, for example, and the
childcare plank in Montreal on Day 4. This system allowed for advance
planning and preparation since it could be applied regardless of when
the election was actually called.

The decision to release the platform *before* the election was called was
suggested by the Strategy Committee, the rationale being that such a
move would show a party organized, competent, and ready to govern. The idea was much debated at the Strategy Committee beforehand.
Some of Turner's advisers, such as Doug Kirkpatrick, were convinced
that other policy issues should be left until the leader had demonstrated
his mastery of the trade file. In a memo to Peter Connolly, Kirkpatrick
argued that trade was clearly the leader's strength and should be emphasized at the beginning of the campaign. Several key members of the
committee, including Herb Gray and Al Graham, supported the idea of
opening up a broader policy front but argued an early release was too
great a risk, fearing the Conservatives would have time to respond and
criticize each plank. Others, such as Kirby and Robert, insisted it was a
risk worth taking. The leader's personal popularity was still trailing far
behind the other two party leaders. The temporary boost in the polls
from the free trade manoeuvre had long since worn off and, it was clear,
would not translate into broader support. Most committee members
believed additional policy positions would bolster the party's chances,
and eventually the leader agreed.

The Liberal platform was unveiled on 28 September at a special caucus meeting in Ottawa attended by nominated candidates. The special caucus event also marked the release of the party's campaign slogan: 'This is more than an election, it's your future.' The theme was prominently displayed on the cover of the Red Book and deliberately intended to reflect several possible meanings related to free trade, social programs, and the Mulroney government's untrustworthiness.

The platform was a public relations success. Behind the scenes, two other documents were also well received. Because the Liberals were now in opposition they produced additional material that would not have been necessary if the party had been in power. The first was a Policy Handbook, prepared and distributed by the Research Bureau to the caucus in late June, and to nominated candidates as they were selected. As the covering memo indicated, the handbook was intended to 'reflect the Liberal positions which have already been taken, largely in response to government initiatives.'[26] This was necessary for several reasons, the most important being that there were only thirty-nine sitting MPs, some of whom were not running again, and the party would have a very large number of new candidates across the country. Few could be expected to know the party's detailed position on every issue, and it would be potentially embarrassing to the party and the national campaign if these novices were to advocate an opposing position through ignorance.

The third major campaign document prepared by the LCRB was a compendium of the Mulroney government's actions over the past four years. *Broken Promises: The Tory Legacy* was made public and distributed to the caucus on 15 July 1988. John Turner used the occasion to remind Canadians about the Conservative record on policy and on political scandals. 'Canadians are rightly asking why they should trust the government now,' he said. 'They see words like economic renewal coming from the same Government which has dramatically cut its aid to the regions of the country and abandoned farmers, fishermen, and miners. They see words like "social justice" coming from the same government that has drastically cut social programs when it once called them a sacred trust.'[27]

The party's national office prepared its own Candidates' Handbook, providing information on technical issues that candidates were likely to confront during the campaign. The result of the lengthy process begun by David Collenette to rebuild party personnel and modernize the production of election materials, it too was widely praised by Liberal insiders. This candidates' handbook, entitled *Ready, Set, Go*, provided another campaign slogan for the party and the leader. When the writ was finally dropped, John Turner announced: 'The Liberal Party is ready, our people are in place, we're set to go.'[28]

The Election Call

In the end, Prime Minister Mulroney decided to take a chance. Rather than wait and pass the FTA first, he called the election on 1 October 1988, just two days after the release of the Liberal platform. A week earlier, Mulroney had told his caucus he was sure they would win, first because John Turner was so far behind him in public opinion polls on leadership and, second, apart from trade the Liberals had nothing else in their policy arsenal.[29] Although the Liberals' subsequent release of their forty-point plan must have given him pause, Mulroney proceeded with his game plan, based once again on Allan Gregg's polling and earlier prediction that Liberal support would crumble over the summer.

On 1 October Mulroney asked the governor general to dissolve Parliament and call an election. 'We are at a point where the differences in our political parties require the judgement and the decisions of Canadians,' he said. Sticking to this script, he declared: 'The key question for the electorate will be who best can manage change in the years ahead … We intend to run on our record of the past' to demonstrate that the Conservative Party was best able to manage change.[30] After reading his prepared text, Mulroney agreed to take questions from the media, something he had not done since the resignation of former minister André Bissonnette nearly a year before. It was not an auspicious start. Several reporters asked him about free trade and the public's apparent concerns with the deal while others focused on the scandals that had plagued his administration over the past four years. After the CBC's Wendy Mesley asked him whether he thought he was still popular with the electorate, his responses became shorter and more acerbic with each question.

By contrast, John Turner's opening statement attracted sympathetic media coverage. 'For two months,' he declared, 'I've been waiting for the Prime Minister to let the people decide. Today he finally agreed.' Turner went on to outline what he considered the two major issues of the campaign. The first was 'an independent and sovereign Canada, which has never been so threatened as it is now by the Mulroney trade deal.' The second was 'fairness, particularly for low and middle-income

Canadians who have been hit by Tory tax increases over the past four years.' Sounding like a social Liberal, he concluded 'this campaign is about equality for women, it is about rights for our minorities, secure pensions for our grandparents, it is about decent, high-quality child care for our children, it's about preserving our environment, and it's about creating opportunities in all parts of the country.'[31]

When he turned to the topic of the FTA, Turner's emotional commitment to Canada and his belief that the proposed trade deal would be bad for the country came through clearly. He described the deal as one which would 'fundamentally alter our way of life, our way of doing things ... it endangers our social programs, our regional development programs ... and denies us the right as Canadians to choose an independent future.'[32]

The Liberal Election Organization

By early 1987 John Turner had put most of his election campaign team in place. He had named senators Al Graham of Nova Scotia, the former party president, and Pietro Rizzuto, the former Quebec head of the Friends of Turner, as his two national campaign co-chairs. All of the provincial chairs were in place, as was the national campaign director, John Webster. Several of these early appointments were rescinded after the second caucus revolt in April 1988 in which Rizzuto played a pivotal role as messenger. Eventually André Ouellet was named the new national co-chair to replace Rizzuto, a somewhat perplexing move given his own involvement in the coup attempts. Similar changes were imposed upon the Ontario and Quebec provincial chairs, Doug Frith and Jean Lapierre, who, rightly or wrongly, were believed to have been disloyal in light of events leading up to the April coup attempt. For a second time, Frith learned from a reporter rather than Turner that he would be replaced, this time by none other than former party president Norman McLeod, while former Quebec MP Rémi Bujold replaced Lapierre.

During the election period, the Liberals' Strategy Committee and other aspects of election readiness came together to form the National Campaign Committee under the nominal direction of campaign co-chairs Ouellet and Graham. This body included not only the core strategy committee members but also provincial campaign chairs and other regional representatives. Peter Connolly and Joyce Fairbairn, representing the leader's tour, were generally in attendance, as were Ouellet or Graham.

The day-to-day operations of the campaign, however, were the responsibility of the national campaign director, John Webster. The young Toronto party activist and fervent Turner supporter had been selected to perform this task after the unexpected departure of the highly regarded former Turner staffer, Sharon Scholar. No one questioned his dedication or determination, but his ability to perform under pressure was untested. His reputation for ruthlessness and single-mindedness had been forged during his time as co-organizer of the Friends of Turner, but some were anxious about his judgment and lack of experience.

During the campaign, Webster chaired a daily meeting at the Liberals' headquarters, a somewhat modified version of the Strategy Committee. Members included senators Michael Kirby and Joyce Fairbairn, party officials Mark Resnick and Sheila Gervais, Turner's communications adviser Ray Heard, and special policy adviser Bob Jackson, as well as the director of the Research Bureau. A representative of the leader's tour was generally in attendance as well. Strangely, for a meeting meant to evaluate party performance and ensure the campaign was on track, party pollster Martin Goldfarb was never in attendance. Results were delivered in summary by Kirby, but neither the numbers nor the questions were ever seen by the members. The entire polling question was to be of crucial importance to the Liberal team.

Once the writ was dropped the party's headquarters became 'election central,' and the entire staff of 200 Laurier became fully occupied with the campaign. Among the most significant tasks was the need to respond to calls from candidates, many of whom were new nominees without much experience. To make matters worse, many experienced Liberal campaign workers who had supported the party during the Trudeau years were not participating in the campaign because of disagreements with the Turner wing of the party or, most frequently, disenchantment over the party's position on Meech Lake. Consequently, the role of the national headquarters was crucial. As one senior Liberal staffer later stated, the party was the 'lifeline' for candidates from BC to Newfoundland, who inevitably found the technical and legal issues of fundraising, campaigning, and organizing more complicated than they had anticipated.

While the national party office advised candidates on technical and legal issues, the Liberal Research Bureau assisted candidates with questions about the party platform and on issues of a purely local nature. These latter requests were handled in consultation with the party's national office, where policy director Mark Resnick was in charge of the local issues component of the campaign. Throughout the campaign the research staff of the bureau manned the candidates' policy hotline for more than fourteen hours per day, handling some 1,236 calls in total. The bureau also served as a resource for the leader's tour and the Campaign Committee, preparing background material on subjects not included in the platform.

The Unflappable Leader's Tour

The leader's tour was the most visible and arguably the most important aspect of the Liberals' campaign. In light of their disastrous 1984 campaign, the Liberals needed to prove that they could run an efficient tour, and Turner needed to show Canadians how much he had improved. Although the Liberals were successful on both counts, it was not enough to overcome the unexpected problems that emerged over the course of the seven-week campaign.

Like everything else about the 1988 campaign, the Liberals were indeed in far better shape than in 1984. They had sufficient resources for a well-managed campaign, if not a deluxe version. They also benefited from the fact that Turner, as a former prime minister, could travel anywhere on the two major airlines of the day for free. This allowed him to make additional tour stops without the campaign plane. Most important, they had a competent team and a tour strategy that had been planned far in advance. There had even been time to 'test drive' several of the proposed tour venues and events.

Doug Kirkpatrick of the OLO served as tour director. He had extensive organizational experience and was widely viewed as the primary reason for the unqualified success of the tour. Senator Joyce Fairbairn was another valuable presence, described by one senior member as 'an important calming influence' on virtually everyone, including Turner. Wagonmaster Andy Shaw, recruited from outside the party ranks for his organizational expertise, also proved to be an extremely valuable member of the team, ensuring that the entire operation ran as smoothly as possible.

Careful financial planning for the election ensured that the resources that were available were focused to provide maximum benefit. The tour had the standard plane and bus rental arrangements of modern federal elections, as well as new technology such as a fax system, mobile phones, and state-of-the-art facilities for the media to produce and distribute their stories electronically from the tour. Compared with the 1984 effort, the 1988 leader's tour, in Michael Kirby's words, had moved 'from the stone age to the space age.'[33]

Launching the Policy Announcements: The Childcare Debacle

Months of hard work and advance planning appeared to be paying off when the leader went to Toronto to make the first of the scheduled policy announcements on 4 October. The fourth plank in the Red Book platform, 'affordable housing' was specifically geared to lower- and middle-income Canadians in urban areas like Toronto, where a housing crisis was looming. The background material provided to the media outlined the provisions of the plan in considerable detail, and the leader responded to additional questions with an air of comfortable ease. The event was not only a success but a revelation to the journalists accompanying the leader's tour, many of whom had taken to joking that two days in a row without a Liberal crisis would be a miracle.[34]

In contrast, the Liberals' childcare announcement in Montreal on 5 October was an unmitigated disaster. That this occurred despite careful research, consultation, and preparation of a model childcare plan frustrated those who had worked on the plank for months. The party's critic, Quebec MP Lucie Pépin, had already introduced many elements of the proposal in her minority report to a parliamentary committee nearly two years earlier. The details had been worked out with her participation, and the Strategy Committee had arranged for Pépin to be present at the policy announcement, joining the leader's tour at a childcare facility in Montreal. Despite these well-laid plans, it soon became apparent that neither the critic nor the leader was able to answer reporters' questions about the timing and number of spaces to be created, or how the proposed tax provisions would work. Turner appeared shocked by his critic's inability to explain the plan, but worse was yet to come.

A second line of questioning focused on the total cost of the plank, an unexpected development given the lack of media interest in previous elections. Rather than take their questions under advisement and agree to provide the relevant details shortly, speechwriter David Lockhart was dispatched to 'clarify' the party's position on the spot. When his efforts proved ineffective, Peter Connolly decided to enter the fray. His response not only contradicted the leader on the total price tag, but disagreed with Pépin on the number of spaces. Despite the accompanying background material which provided these details, Connolly was quoted as stating: 'no small child shall go in need of daycare.'[35] Raymond Garneau disagreed with both Turner (who fixed the total cost at $4 billion) and Connolly (who mused that it could cost up to $8 billion) by putting the figure much lower.

This display of confusion was a serious blow to the Liberals' credibility. One article the following day demonstrated the extent of the problem when it declared: 'One of the bright spots of the Liberal election platform, a national day care policy, turned into a publicity nightmare for party leader John Turner, who could not explain how it would work or what it would cost.'[36] After three days of debate on the plane and on the ground about the best way to respond, Patrick Johnson was asked to provide a detailed briefing to the media after consulting with the relevant bureau researchers. In doing so, he essentially ignored the incorrect information provided by the various interveners at the fateful press conference. Although the crisis certainly cost the party, this resolution went some distance towards limiting the damage, and the fact that it occurred early in the campaign allowed the party to regroup and rebound.

Equally fortunate for the Liberals, the Conservatives were having difficulties of their own in the early days of the campaign. First the chair of their Finance Committee, Ontario MP Don Blenkarn, admitted that the Tories' proposed future tax reforms would not be revenue-neutral as Finance Minister Michael Wilson had suggested. This provided ammunition for the Liberals, whose tax reform plank – titled 'no more tax grab on the middle class' – enumerated the many 'unfair' tax measures already introduced by the Mulroney government.

But it was the Conservatives' minister of state for housing, John McDermid, who inadvertently demonstrated the importance of the Liberals' platform by responding to it. Declaring that his government had no intention of matching the Liberal housing plank, McDermid went on to say that there was little need for social housing assistance because the homeless were largely in that situation by choice. Turner and his candidates wasted little time describing McDermid as 'the minister of homelessness,' but the broader point about the significance of the Liberal platform had also been made.

During the next two weeks, successful announcements were made on the environment and acid rain in Quebec, regional development in New Brunswick, support for seniors in Winnipeg, small business policies in Edmonton, and foreign policy in Vancouver. In each case, detailed background documents were provided to the media, and the presence of the respective Liberal critics at the events proved more than sufficient to overcome earlier concerns about the depth and accuracy of the Liberal platform.

More Campaign Difficulties

Unfortunately, the Liberals' policy message was consistently overshadowed by other events that received much more media attention. As Mike Kirby noted in one memo to senior campaign personnel, 'the TV clips being used of Turner are generally unfavourable, even at events which have gone well.' At the Liberals' Confederation Dinner fundraiser in Toronto on 12 October, for example, a masterful speech by Turner was reduced to a short clip in which he was seen to mispronounce 'birth right' as 'birth rate.'

Compounding Turner's problems was the state of his health. An avid tennis player and generally very fit for his age, he had suffered a sports-related back injury at the beginning of the campaign. In considerable pain but persevering with the tour's vigorous campaign schedule despite his doctors' recommendation, Turner soon developed a slight limp which further hindered his image and provided the media with endless photo opportunities. A disturbing example of the fifth estate's negative mindset occurred early in the campaign when one reporter was overheard telling his cameraman to 'get the limp' as Turner and his wife walked back to the campaign plane after the Toronto event.[37]

Coverage of the regional development announcement provided another striking example of negative media attention. In addition to the leader and the caucus critic, the announcement in Fredericton was attended by the two Liberal premiers – Joe Ghiz of PEI and Frank McKenna of New Brunswick – along with Nova Scotia Liberal leader Vince McLean and Newfoundland Liberal leader Clyde Wells. All of them said positive things about the regional development proposal, as did a number of local officials. Yet, despite their enthusiastic response to this plank, the media focused on the differences of opinion between Turner and three of the Atlantic Liberals on Meech Lake. This focus was particularly unexpected given that Meech Lake had not been an issue in the campaign to date, and indeed never became one. Polls showed the public was far more interested in tax reform and free trade, childcare and the environment.

Michael Kirby's analysis of the second week of the campaign concluded there was 'a consistent pattern: Turner turned in one good performance after another only to be buried by events beyond his control.'[38] The result was that the Liberals appeared to be in free fall after the first week, actually running third in several polls behind the NDP.

Another event beyond Turner's control was the publication of a book by former Trudeau principal secretary Tom Axworthy and the Liberals' own pollster, Martin Goldfarb. *Marching to a Different Drummer* had been written more than a year before its publication. Its authors protested they had no control over the timing of its release, but the book could hardly have emerged at a worse time for the Liberal leader or the party. Much of the book's contents served to differentiate the Liberal and Conservative parties by analysing their underlying values and beliefs. As such, it should actually have been a useful tool for the Liberals during the campaign, highlighting as it did the considerable distance between the two parties. It was also helpful in demonstrating that Mulroney's major initiatives – the FTA and the tax reform proposals – were entirely consistent with the Conservatives' anti-government and pro-market philosophy. The problem arose with the authors' discussion of Mulroney's Meech Lake initiative, which they saw as demonstrating the Conservatives' decentralist view of federalism. 'The Meech Lake Accord strikes at the heart of Liberal belief,' they argued. Echoing the views of Mike Kirby in his letter to the editor the previous year, they stressed that 'Brian Mulroney moved in tandem with his party's deepest beliefs in forging a deal with the provinces.' However, the authors did not stop there. They went on to conclude that 'John Turner's endorsement of the pact repudiated his party's intrinsic heritage. Liberals would not have negotiated the Meech Lake pact.'[39] Perhaps understandably, the media focused on the book's one-paragraph reference to Meech Lake to the exclusion of almost everything else, reminding voters once again of internal party dissent.

Another unexpected problem for the Liberals was the abortion issue. As the date for the leaders' debates drew closer, those who would be coaching Turner began identifying issues that might be raised by his opponents and drawing up possible options for him to consider as a response. Research Bureau staff were asked to provide background material on these contentious issues, abortion being one of them.

Turner had already responded to a question at a town hall meeting, stating that he personally supported a woman's right to choose and affirming that individual MPs should be allowed a free vote on matters of conscience. He had not addressed the issue since and would not do so unless forced. However, the team working on debate preparation suggested that he announce a new Liberal policy on abortion if he felt he was losing the debate. Their memo containing this recommendation, and a specific proposal based on the position paper put forward earlier by the Canadian Medical Association (CMA), was faxed to the campaign plane for consideration.

Separately, the weekly meeting of the full campaign committee on 15 October also discussed the possibility of taking a position on the issue. After heated discussion the majority concluded that an announcement should be made and that it should be made *before* the debates to solidify Liberal support among women and as a means of anticipating the issue. Although timing and specific details were not settled upon, the committee generally agreed to support the position of the Canadian Law Reform Commission.

The following Monday, the major news story concerning the Liberals was not about the excellent presentation and reception of their environmental platform in Quebec City, but rather about the party's relegation to third place in the most recent opinion polls and the fact that John Turner was about to announce a new party position on abortion based on the CMA recommendations. The abortion revelation was allegedly based on an interview with Peter Connolly in Quebec City on Sunday, 16 October. Although he vehemently denied having stated that this would be the party's position, Connolly did admit he had outlined possible party options to a *Toronto Star* reporter in an informal conversation. Not only had there been no media preparation and no press conference scheduled, the actual position of the leader had not yet been decided upon. Perhaps most egregious was the fact such a controversial decision ended up being communicated to the party's candidates and campaign workers by the media rather than the campaign hierarchy in Ottawa.

Predictably, the result was widespread outrage and mass confusion in the ranks. The Research Bureau hotline and the national office were flooded with calls. Senior Liberal MPs from predominantly Roman Catholic ridings, and notably Herb Gray, expressed shock and dismay at the idea that the party would even consider taking a position on the issue during an election campaign. In the end, the campaign committee decided it was no longer feasible for the leader to announce any position on abortion. Put another way, they concluded that the reversal of their earlier decision to do so, while it would attract some media criticism, would be far less controversial than a plan to continue with their originally proposed course of action. Either way, it was clear to the media and to senior strategists that this was a major and potentially irreversible slip-up.

The costing issue proved to be a perennial source of difficulty. Some committee members were strongly in favour of releasing the costing document as soon as possible. Others, including Webster and Kirby, were opposed, arguing that it could become yet another target for the Conservatives and for the media. The decision was repeatedly put off, mainly because Kirby reported that Goldfarb's polling data did not show costing to be a major problem for the Liberals, despite the fact Liberal candidates were finding the opposite to be true in their door-to-door canvassing. Kirby himself later described the Liberals' failure to release the full costing document sooner as 'the big mistake' made by strategists during the campaign. In his view, the delay had two significant effects on the Liberal campaign: first, it allowed the Conservatives to continue to portray Turner and his party as incompetent, and, second, it prevented the Liberals from criticizing the Conservatives' tax reform plans as they could not show how they would fund their own election promises without similar tax changes.[40] By the time Turner finally released the document at the beginning of the sixth week of the campaign, the damage had been done.

As if these problems were not enough, Turner was faced with a bizarre suggestion by several of his senior advisers and caucus members, namely that he step down as leader in the middle of the election campaign. This unprecedented development naturally strained relations between the leader's tour and the rest of the campaign operation and dealt an irrevocable blow to the public perception of the Liberals.

The Final Coup Attempt

Much has been written about the events of 19 October 1988 that came to be described by the CBC as another leadership coup attempt, and by many Liberal insiders as the 'night of the long knives.' At the time of the news story, virtually everyone who was alleged to be involved took great pains to deny the media accusations categorically. With no smoking gun, indeed with no hard evidence of any kind, the decision by Peter Mansbridge and the CBC to describe a number of disparate incidents as a concerted plot to remove John Turner as leader of the Liberal Party in the middle of the election campaign provoked much critical comment within the industry and among objective observers.[41]

Inside the party the conflicting explanations of events did little to shed light on the matter. Given the degree of mistrust between the various players, and especially between the leader's tour and the ground campaign, this is perhaps not surprising. Nevertheless, the preponderance of facts suggest that the Liberal Party had lost its vaunted discipline, along with its reputation as the natural governing party. As one observer later concluded: 'The main problem is that Liberals don't know how to lose.' Faced with the prospect of not only losing the 1988 election but quite possibly finishing in third place, panic evidently set in. Coupled with the fact that they had planned so carefully for this election and done so much better in organizing and preparing for it, that fate seemed even more offensive. There is considerable evidence to suggest that at least three groups of individuals expressed some concern about the leader, but much of this information was not available to the media at the time.

Of the three groups, the least significant was probably the small band of caucus members, including Herb Gray, Lloyd Axworthy, Raymond Garneau, and Bob Kaplan, who interrupted their individual campaigns and travelled to Ottawa. Although there were widespread reports that the purpose of their visit was to request the leader to step aside, all of them insisted their concerns were primarily about the operation of the campaign. 'We were far more unhappy with Connolly and Kirby,' Kaplan confided later. 'The abortion position was the last straw. We thought they had lost it and we wanted to talk to them in person to make sure they understood what we were up against. This kind of nonsense had to stop.'[42] None of the MPs involved ever admitted that they threatened to withdraw their nominations, and all denied they had raised the issue of Turner stepping aside.

The second alleged rebel group was an inner circle of the campaign committee itself, variously described as including Mike Kirby, John Webster, André Ouellet, and Al Graham, as well as chief financial officer Mike Robinson. As Kirby himself noted in his account of the event, no one disputed the fact that the group had written a memo to the leader on 14 October outlining the state of the campaign. The memo highlighted the fact that internal polling clearly showed the party's policies had been a major asset to the campaign, despite the various missteps. The most significant problem was the leader's image. While the memo recognized this came in part from the controversial media images of Turner limping, it could not be discounted. 'Three quarters of this week's sample in Montreal and Toronto say that [you] are losing momentum. Since leadership is the single most important motivator of voting behaviour, the data suggests that we may not have bottomed out.'[43] Although Kirby later admitted there had been some discussion about what should be done in the event the leader became too ill to continue, or decided to step aside, neither of these two considerations was included in the memo itself.

It was apparent that the earlier coup attempts had an impact on the thinking of many Liberals. Quite simply, internal dissent had become not only commonplace but acceptable. After two unsuccessful attempts to replace the leader, the previously unthinkable concept of forcibly replacing a Liberal leader began to seem less offensive to some in the party. Even many of those who opposed the idea of a coup tended to reject it as politically suicidal rather than morally unacceptable. Jean Chrétien's departure from the caucus may have helped to bring about this change in perspective, but the deep divisions caused by Turner's position on Meech Lake had unquestionably been the main catalyst.

It also became apparent that some discussion about the possibility of Turner stepping down had actually been going on for weeks, if not from the very beginning of the campaign. Doug Kirkpatrick recalled numerous conversations among small groups of organizers at the Confederation Dinner, more than ten days before the CBC bombshell, that ended abruptly as he approached. He also recalled a 'Kafka-esque scenario' in which he tried to reach any one of four key members of the campaign committee – Kirby, Ouellet, Graham, or Webster – to verify the committee's instructions for the coming week and the 'line of the day,' only to be told by each of their secretaries that all of the individuals were unavailable. When he eventually located Webster by cellphone, it was apparent the national director was in André Ouellet's parliamentary office along with Graham and Kirby, rather than at 200 Laurier. The four of them were holding what Webster hastily described as a 'core committee' meeting.[44] A fifth participant at this meeting, Mike Robinson, has since maintained he was invited without being told the reason for the meeting. He also categorically denied that either he or Graham had been in favour of replacing the leader. In fact, Robinson asserted that it was his and Graham's categorical rejection of the idea of Turner's removal that forced the other participants to rethink their approach. 'It was almost surreal,' Robinson recalled. 'I couldn't believe they were even contemplating such a crazy idea. And if they succeeded, on what possible basis could they select another individual to lead them in the middle of the campaign? Simply because he finished second in a leadership race years earlier? The whole thing was bizarre.'[45]

The third and most explicit admission came from Doug Kirkpatrick years later. He recounted how a letter to the leader and the committee memo were delivered personally by André Ouellet to Stornoway the same night as the meeting in his office had taken place. According to Kirkpatrick, he and Turner had just arrived at the leader's residence shortly before. Ouellet gave Kirkpatrick a package and specifically told him some members of the campaign organization felt Turner should resign for the good of the party.[46] Kirkpatrick's claim was supported by Peter Connolly, who later said the request for Turner to step down was repeated by Ouellet in a brief private meeting with Connolly the following day at the weekly campaign committee meeting. In this instance, although Ouellet did not directly claim to be speaking for the entire committee, Connolly was left with the clear impression that this was the case.[47] Moreover, according to Doug Kirkpatrick, Ouellet said he was prepared to call all of the party's nominated candidates to Ottawa within forty-eight hours to make an announcement that Jean Chrétien would be taking over the leadership of the party. Connolly later revealed he had called Turner to pass on this message, and Turner had immediately rejected the suggestion as 'crazy.'[48] For them, the matter was closed. There was therefore no reason, Kirkpatrick noted, to assume any of these conversations would become a matter of public knowledge.

Jean Chrétien confirmed he had been approached by several Quebec candidates and provincial party organizers who wanted him to assume the leadership of the party, but he, too, had rejected the suggestion out of hand.[49] Shortly afterwards a furious Raymond Garneau called a press conference to deny persistent rumours that *he too* had been part of the plot, declaring: 'If there is one Liberal who has been loyal to John Turner it is surely me!' This led one of the party's Quebec candidates to complain that Garneau would remain loyal to Turner even if it meant the party took no seats at all in the province. With the party's internal polls showing they could end up with only four or five seats, this was not out of the question.

It is impossible to overestimate the importance of the Mansbridge 'attempted coup' report. It destroyed trust within the campaign committee and between the committee and the leader's tour. Indeed, the revelations led some members of the campaign committee to conclude there were actually two committees, with the smaller 'core committee' operating separate from the whole. One member later described the scene at 200 Laurier on the night the story broke: 'Several of us were sitting in John's (Webster) office watching the nightly news coverage as usual when all of a sudden here are the faces of several people sitting in the room flashing across the TV screen in front of us. Outside on the street CBC cameras are panning our building, aimed up at the room we're in, and this is also appearing on the screen in front of us. It was like being in a parallel universe. After that everyone began to look at everyone else in a different light.'[50]

Publicly, the impact of this extraordinary development would come home to roost in the last weeks of the campaign. Bob Kaplan later described the fallout as 'simply devastating.' His colleague Charles Caccia, who had represented the Toronto riding of Davenport for twenty-five years, recalled: 'On the doorstep in the riding I had many people say to me that they didn't like the internal fighting in the party, that it wasn't the Liberal way. I can't ever remember that type of comment in any other election before or after.'[51]

The opposition parties were, quite simply, incredulous. Mulroney himself was reportedly ecstatic but also disbelieving about the self-inflicted chaos in the Liberal camp. Allan Gregg thought they might have to turn more of their attention to the NDP if the Liberals continued to implode. Conservative strategist Hugh Segal confessed he did not know what to make of it. 'It didn't make sense. It was the very opposite of the discipline of power. Even the Conservatives, known for their infighting when the party's fortunes were low, had never been through anything quite so messy during an election.'[52]

The CBC's coverage of the story was roundly criticized by many journalists at the time, and continues to be a source of discussion in academic circles. While some print media compounded the problem by reproducing and even expanding on the CBC story, the *Toronto Star* actually denied the story and then published a lengthy editorial denouncing the CBC. But the damage was done. At the time, journalist William Johnson described the reporting as 'television at its most impressionistic, least precise and most irresponsible.'[53] Liberal media adviser Pat Gossage later told a group of journalists he viewed the CBC's story as 'the most flagrant political intervention by a major news organization in a national campaign in the modern life of Canada.'[54]

John Turner soldiered on. Looking more like Don Quixote with every passing day, the leader's efforts to focus public attention on the Liberal platform were taking on heroic proportions. Indeed, Hugh Segal believed 'the events surrounding Turner had become so chaotic and so depressing' that he feared 'they threatened to transform (Turner's) image from that of an incompetent leader of a disorganized rabble into that of a sympathetic, tragic figure' who might soon be the recipient of a considerable public sympathy vote.[55]

In the end the revelations of internal dissent forced all concerned to work together as best they could. This was particularly important because of the impending leaders' debates. Equally important was the fact that if Turner participated in the debates, it would be too late to replace him with someone else even if the alleged conspirators wanted to. Under the Elections Act the deadline for nominating candidates would have passed.

The Leaders' Debates: Turner's Revenge

In light of these problems, John Turner's performance in the nationally televised leaders' debates was all the more remarkable. At a time in which the debates were becoming more and more important given increased media attention, the leader knew this was his chance to sway public opinion and turn the campaign around. His decisive win not only represented a personal victory of enormous magnitude but proved to be the high point of the Liberal campaign.

The 1984 debates of four years earlier were noteworthy for Brian Mulroney's attacks on John Turner, especially on the patronage issue, and for Turner's feeble responses. But Turner's fate – and that of the party – had arguably been sealed before that debate took place, and Mulroney's comments simply reinforced the Liberals' disastrous showing. In 1988 the Liberals had nothing to lose going into the debates. They were in third place in the public opinion polls and senior strategists believed they might sink still further. As Ray Heard, Turner's communications adviser, put it, by the fourth week of the campaign the Liberals were in such distress that for them 'the debate [was] the single most important event in the campaign.'[56]

To prepare for the event, the Liberals arranged for mock debates in a rented television studio. Staff played the roles of Mulroney and Broadbent, posing difficult questions and throwing as many unexpected challenges at the leader as possible. A second dry run was held over the weekend in French. These practice sessions paid off and have since become standard practice for all of the parties in preparing for televised debates. In addition, Turner used the massive briefing book prepared by the Research Bureau to fine-tune his arguments. For the Liberals, the perception that John Turner had won, or at least held his own in the debates, was essential if they were to have any hope of finishing in second place and retaining their status as the Official Opposition.

Turner rose to the occasion. In the French-language debate on Monday, 24 October, he impressed everyone with the calibre of his interventions in French and with the aggressive approach he took from the very beginning, particularly on the issue of patronage. Having lost the 1984 election on this issue, Turner was anxious to remind all Canadians (and especially Quebeckers) that Mulroney had engaged in what Turner described as a veritable orgy of patronage for the past four years, far exceeding anything the Liberals had managed. He also drew attention to the various scandals that had plagued Mulroney's government, many of which had involved his Quebec ministers and caucus. Although much of the media coverage of the event hesitated to declare an outright 'winner,' the influential daily *Le Devoir* proclaimed Turner the victor the following morning. In virtually all other media coverage of the debate, Turner and Mulroney were considered to have fought to a draw while NDP leader Ed Broadbent had been sidelined.

The French-language debate went much better than many observers expected, and far exceeded Liberal hopes, but the English-language debate was an explosive event which changed the course of the campaign. The performance of the leaders in the first two hours of the three-hour event was relatively evenly matched. No one expected the outbursts that began almost immediately at the start of the third hour when moderator Pamela Wallin returned to the issue of free trade. In the course of the next half-hour, Turner and Mulroney engaged in an increasingly vocal and emotional debate over the FTA. Turner outlined in some detail his reasons for opposing the deal and then concluded his intervention by saying: 'I happen to believe you sold us out as a country ... Once a country opens itself up to a subsidy war with the United States, then the ability of that country to ... remain as an independent nation is gone forever, and that is the issue of this election.'[57] When Mulroney responded by protesting his patriotism – 'I believe that in my own modest way I am nation-building, because I believe this deal benefits Canada and I love Canada' – Turner delivered the clearly heart-felt coup de grace: 'We built a country east and west and north. We built it on an infrastructure that deliberately resisted the continental pressure of the United States. For 120 years we have done it. With one stroke of a pen you've reversed that, thrown us into the north-south influence of the United States and will reduce us, I am sure, to a colony of the United States, because when the economic levers go the political independence is sure to follow.' Mulroney, clearly nonplussed, was reduced to describing his prized deal as 'a commercial document that is cancellable on six months notice,' a line on which the Liberals quickly seized to suggest Mulroney was as prepared to tear up the deal as Turner.

The next morning the verdict was in. Both the national media and the general public declared Turner the winner. An instant CTV poll showed 59 per cent of viewers considered Turner to be the winner of the English-language debate, compared with 16 per cent for Mulroney and 11 per cent for Broadbent. By Wednesday morning a Gallup poll found some 72 per cent believed Turner had won. By Sunday, Turner's debate victory had translated into electoral movement. Two public opinion polls actually placed the Liberals in first place, ahead of the Conservatives, with others declaring that the race was neck and neck.

Turner's solid victories in the English- and French-language debates resulted in an immediate turnaround in Liberal fortunes. In addition to single-handedly pulling the party back from the brink of oblivion and giving them a second chance, Turner's performance on 24 and 25 October came close to transforming the 1988 election into something rarely seen in Canada, a single-issue campaign. Although there were other factors involved in the voters' eventual decision, the Mulroney government's Free Trade Agreement had suddenly, by dint of Turner's performance in the debates alone, become the single most important issue of the campaign and, for most of the next three weeks, the *only* issue of the campaign. Suddenly the Conservatives were on the defensive, scrambling to replace their totally forgettable 'managing change' theme with one which focused on defending the FTA.

The Liberal's Ad Campaign and the Post-Debate Strategy

No one was more surprised than the senior Liberal strategists to find they had a potential victory on their hands. Campaign workers and grassroots party members were re-energized by Turner's performance, and the questions on the minds of the campaign committee the next morning were very different from the ones they had been considering a week earlier. The first and most obvious was whether they could maintain the momentum. The second was how to prevent any further miscues from damaging their fragile hold on first place in the remaining three weeks of the campaign. There was little agreement on the first two questions, but there was a unanimous feeling that one of their best remaining weapons was about to be unleashed.

The Liberals' ad campaign was to prove invaluable. As in previous elections, the ads had been in the hands of a group of advertising executives with long-standing ties to the Liberal Party, a practice that had become part of the tradition of Canadian elections for all the major parties. In the case of the Liberals, these agencies were Vickers & Benson and MacLaren. The director of the Liberal ad campaign traditionally known as Red Leaf was a vice-president of Quaker Oats, David Morton. Like many of the senior campaign personnel, Morton volunteered both his time and considerable expertise for this effort despite the party's gloomy prospects at the beginning of the campaign. The ad campaign also benefited from the screening of proposed material in focus groups organized by Goldfarb and Kirby.

Given the growing importance of television in election campaigns, the percentage of their overall budget that each party would spend on advertising had been growing as well. By 1988 the Liberals allocated $3 million, or more than one-third of their total allowable expenses, to advertising. In the case of English-language ads, this proved to be money well spent. Although the French-language ads were judged acceptable they were less successful, largely because the designers had so little to work with. Because the Quebec government and the vast majority of Quebeckers supported the FTA, this could not be the primary focus. This left the Liberals' French-language ads to highlight issues such as the environment and the Tory scandals.

The English-language ads were considered by many experts to be the best the Liberals had ever produced. Michael Kirby was effusive in his praise. 'Despite the makeshift nature of a temporary election organization like Red Leaf,' Kirby said, 'it ran very smoothly, free of tension, and with an incredible sense of commitment to the Liberal cause. The result was a tribute to Morton's extraordinary leadership skills.'[58]

The first set of Liberal ads aired on Sunday, 23 October, the day before the first of the two leaders' debates. They attracted immediate attention, focusing as they did on the FTA. The first showed a map of Canada and someone presumed to be an American trade negotiator erasing the 49th parallel while a voice-over praised the deal before concluding: 'There's just one line that's getting in the way' of an agreement. In the second ad, the Liberals contrasted a shot of Brian Mulroney before the 1984 election declaring 'free trade, we'll have none of it' with one during his speech in 1987 supporting the FTA. In this case, the voice-over warned voters: 'Say one thing, mean another. Don't let Mulroney deceive you again.' Both ads concluded with the Liberals' slogan: 'This is more than an election. It's your future.'

A second string of Liberal ads featured Turner talking about various planks of the Liberal platform. Two, on affordable housing and pay equity, were considered to be exceptionally effective. According to Kirby, one particularly striking feature of the focus group response was how favourably impressed they were by Turner himself, thereby reinforcing the argument that the leader could actually be an asset during the campaign.

A final set of ads focused on the Conservatives' tax reform plans. These ads were expected to open up a second front for the Liberals after the trade issue had taken hold. One was aired almost immediately after the debates and came to be considered another classic. It showed the prime minister in his office kicking a football on which the words 'middle class' were written.

But the success of the Liberals' ad campaign served to highlight once again the disadvantages of being out of power. It also drew attention to some unexpected problems with the election legislation which had been reformed by Pierre Trudeau in 1974 in an effort to level the playing field for political parties during federal elections. Although the maximum limit on allowable election expenditures was now the same for each party, the way those funds could be spent was not. In the case of television advertising, the ability of the parties to communicate with the public was dependent not on money alone but also on their standing in the House of Commons – that is, on their showing in the previous election. The legislation required Canadian broadcasters to offer the parties a total of 10 hours of advertising time, divided between 3.5 hours of free time and 6.5 hours of paid time. In 1988, the percentage of that time offered to each party was heavily skewed in favour of the Conservatives because of their unprecedented majority in 1984. While they would be allowed nearly 200 minutes of paid advertising time, the Liberals would have only 90 minutes and the NDP just under 70, with fringe parties dividing up the remaining crumbs. Thus the decisions the Liberal strategists made on which ads to air and for how long were crucial, as they could not release all of them and be effective. Moreover, these decisions would need to be based on accurate polling data. As a result, the Liberals decided to increase the frequency and coverage of their own polling, despite the drain this placed on their limited coffers.

Meanwhile the strategists at 200 Laurier began once again to consider whether they should stop making platform announcements. This was partly to ensure their advertising message on free trade was complemented by their second front criticizing the Tories' tax reform plans, and partly to make certain they gave the Conservatives no new ammunition to attack them. In the first few days after the debates, John Turner announced the Atlantic Accord and platform proposals for part-time workers and pay equity. All were well received. But some of the committee members, and notably Kirby, continued to be nervous about each announcement, fearful there could be another childcare crisis looming. A total of twenty-three of the forty planks were released before it was decided there would be no more announcements. Instead, the committee agreed that each of Turner's scheduled speeches in the last three weeks would adopt the same formula: a critique of the FTA; another critique on tax reform; and a third and final section in which one or two of the most popular planks that had already been released would be highlighted.

While this may have seemed a sensible strategy in theory, in practice it backfired. First of all, the lack of confidence which Turner now inevitably had in his senior strategists after the CBC debacle meant he was loath to take their advice about the tax reform issue. As he later recounted, he was convinced the trade issue was *the* issue of the campaign. It was also the issue with which he felt most comfortable. In light of the leaders' debates, it was certainly the issue the media were pursuing almost single-mindedly. The end result was that, whatever prepared text Turner was given, he tended to stray from it to embroider his anti-FTA theme. Even if he held religiously to the script, the media questions after the speech concentrated on free trade whether he had mentioned it or not. And his answers to the questions on free trade, as the strategists soon learned, became the news coverage of the day for the Liberals for the rest of the campaign, no matter what else they attempted to highlight.

Unfortunately, this resulted in a one-note samba for the Liberals in the last three weeks of the campaign. Although it appeared their position on free trade was bolstering their support in the polls, that support was tenuous. When the Conservatives realized the extent of their difficulties, they began to fight back in defence of the trade agreement with all the fire power at their disposal, and the Liberals were in no position to respond or to diversify their appeal.

Bombing the Bridge: The Conservatives Fight Back and Corporate Canada Weighs In

In an election campaign filled with memorable comments, Conservative pollster Allan Gregg contributed another when he described the Conservative response to the Liberals' electoral surge in military terms. 'What we had to do was bomb the bridge,' Gregg declared, 'and that is precisely what we proceeded to do.'[59] The 'bridge' in question was John Turner. According to Gregg, Turner served as the bridge between growing public fear of the Free Trade Agreement and support for the Liberal Party. By destroying the bridge – Turner's credibility – that link with party support would be severed.

The Conservatives began to bomb the bridge from both ends at once. On the one hand, they went on the offensive to support the FTA. Not only did the prime minister himself begin to deliver fiery speeches defending the deal, but numerous cabinet ministers and prominent Canadians were conscripted in the war for the hearts and minds of voters.

Even in their defence of the deal, however, the Conservatives were assiduous in attacking Turner's credibility at the same time. These personal attacks represented a distinct departure from the 'high road' Mulroney had originally intended to follow, and, more important, they signalled the beginnings of an American-style approach to election campaigns in which personalities and individual attacks figured prominently. Mulroney referred to Turner's stated concerns about the FTA as 'deceitful' and 'ingenuous.' Conservative Finance Minister Michael Wilson, a normally urbane and restrained partisan, delivered a speech in Toronto within days of the debates in which he accused Turner of lying.[60] The Tories' speeches were accompanied by a campaign document printed and distributed to some 800,000 households across the country within little more than a week of the debates, demonstrating once again the deep pockets and efficiency of the Conservative campaign organization. Entitled 'Ten Big Lies,' the pamphlet outlined arguments used by critics of the deal and rebutted each one.

As Mulroney continued his scheduled campaign tour across the country he added a new 'myth a day' line into virtually all of his speeches and public appearances. The 'myth' of the free trade deal's implications for the environment was addressed in Winnipeg, while its alleged impact on pensions was discussed in Edmonton and its supposed negative consequences for cultural industries in Vancouver. To wrap up his speeches, Mulroney asked audiences whom they preferred, 'Brian the Builder' or 'John the Ripper.'

A variety of well-known Canadians who supported the deal were also brought to the media's attention by the Tories. Among the most prominent was former Supreme Court justice Emmett Hall of Saskatchewan who had chaired the royal commission on health care in the 1960s and was viewed by many as the father of medicare. Hall's statement that he did not believe the FTA would affect the Canadian health care system was persuasive and reassuring to many voters. While both the Liberals and the NDP attempted to counter Hall's remarks and those of other famous Canadians by pointing out that these individuals, while justifiably admired, were not trade negotiators or experts on the political process, their rearguard efforts had little effect.

Shortly thereafter a new wave of aggressive Conservative television advertisements was released. They too were more critical and personality-based. Acknowledging the success of the Liberals' free trade ads, one of the new spots actually portrayed the Conservatives redrawing the border line between Canada and the United States. But the new Conservative ads were not the only addition to what had become, for all intents and purposes, a one-issue campaign. Much of the Canadian business community began to organize and pool resources for a 'YES' campaign, as if the election were in fact a referendum on free trade. Headed by Tom d'Aquino of the Business Council on National Issues (BCNI), the YES group produced television and print media advertising of their own. According to one inside observer, the business community's 'muted verbal support' quickly became 'a vocal and far-reaching campaign in support of free trade' in which 'considerable' sums of money were spent on print media ads and 'numerous targeted letters bearing the same message were delivered to employees within their companies.'[61]

In this respect, the 1988 election assumed a new dimension. Although the Elections Act was clear on the spending limits placed on political parties, it was silent on 'third parties' – that is, groups or individuals unconnected to a particular political party who wanted to promote or criticize a specific issue. The drafters of the act had assumed few if any such third parties would be interested or wealthy enough to intervene. That assumption was proven wrong in short order, as the YES side spent more money on advertising than the Liberals and NDP combined. Moreover, the act made it possible for the Conservatives to separate this expenditure from their own election spending. The other unstated assumption of the Elections Act was that such advertising would be highly unlikely to make a difference. Here again the role of the business community in the free trade debate proved this assumption wrong. As one study for the Lortie Commission on Electoral Reform concluded several years later, the impact of the business community's additional third-party advertising in favour of the FTA was indeed significant.[62]

Of course the fact that two of the three major parties, the Liberals and the NDP, opposed the FTA also worked to the Conservatives' advantage. The NO vote was split, while the YES vote could only go to the Tories. Nevertheless, the lack of a level playing field was clearly exposed by the meagre funds raised by the NO group, which sprang up in the last weeks of the campaign, and by the Liberals' own inability to fund further ads to rebut Conservative arguments.

Instead, in one of the many ironies of the campaign, the same Liberal strategists who had earlier considered replacing him were now planning to make use of several clips from John Turner's performance during the leaders' debates to use up their remaining allocated ad time. They assumed they 'owned' the leader's performance and it would be theirs to use as they saw fit, but the networks refused to release the tapes, claiming it would be an infringement of their proprietary rights. The Liberals, nonplussed, spent several futile days attempting to negotiate a compromise. On 7 November they launched a lawsuit, although a preliminary court decision was not handed down until six days later, leaving little time to prepare an ad to run over the weekend before the networks launched an appeal.

Meanwhile, at the other end of Allan Gregg's bridge, the Conservatives were equally engaged in dropping incendiary bombs to destroy the credibility of not only John Turner but much of the Liberal caucus and campaign team. The potential composition of a Liberal cabinet was fodder for endless Conservative speculation. Michael Wilson mused about the possibility of Liberal Rat Pack veteran John Nunziata becoming finance minister. Others raised the spectre of Sheila Copps becoming defence minister or Brian Tobin the minister of international trade. After four years of Rat Pack antics and caucus disarray, the Liberals had little to offer as a rebuttal. These attacks on the Liberal caucus, which Conservative pollsters immediately perceived were having an effect, received unexpected support from the media when columnist Jeffrey Simpson wrote an article about the Liberal candidates across the country, describing them as 'the weakest in this century.' Written while the Liberals were still ahead in the polls, Simpson speculated: 'If John

Turner should win, his cabinet would surely be the shallowest in the history of Canada.'[63]

By 10 November, slightly more than two weeks after the leaders' debates and with two weeks still to go in the campaign, Gregg's polling showed the two-pronged attack had worked. 'Our post-debate slump has been arrested,' he wrote in a memo to Mulroney, and 'Liberal support has peaked, while the NDP are heading for a distant third-place finish.'[64]

In the last two weeks of the campaign the Conservatives employed a technique of 'saturation bombing' in which – due to their greater air time and financial resources – they were able to blanket Ontario with more campaign ads than the two opposition parties combined. According to one analyst within the Tory ranks, the effect was dramatic. 'Within the last four days of the campaign,' he wrote, 'an Ontario loss was turned into a province-wide electoral plurality.'[65]

In the last week of the campaign, having run out of money and alternatives, the Liberals could only watch as their numbers continued to fall. Michael Kirby later confided he believed the final results would have been worse if the campaign had lasted another few days. With no more funds to spend on advertising, they could not have launched an equally negative personal ad campaign even if they had wanted to.

End of a Dream

On 21 November 1988, the massive Conservative majority Brian Mulroney had obtained in 1984 was significantly reduced. The Conservatives fell from 211 to 169 seats, and from an unprecedented 50 per cent of the popular vote to 43 per cent. Nevertheless, Mulroney delivered a second majority government for his party, and this was more than most Conservatives could have hoped for. At the same time, more Canadians voted against the Conservatives than supported them. Moreover, political scientist Jon Pammett has argued that leadership was important only in a negative sense. Voters were not happy with Mulroney, but the Liberals did not present a convincing alternative as a government-in-waiting under John Turner, and so electors were obliged to choose the best of what they considered to be a bad bunch.[66]

The Liberals, meanwhile, improved their standing considerably despite the many contretemps of the election campaign. Their total representation in the House of Commons more than doubled, from 40 seats to 83. This was cold comfort for John Turner. At 32 per cent, their share of the popular vote was only 4 per cent higher than their 28 per cent showing in 1984 and represented their second-lowest result since 1945. Regionally as well as nationally, they were still in great difficulty. While they had gone from 5 to 20 seats in Atlantic Canada at the expense of the Conservatives, this was almost a given after four years of Mulroney's cutbacks and widespread reversal of popular Liberal policies in the region. In Ontario, where Premier David Peterson had supported Turner throughout the campaign, only 29 additional seats went to the Liberals, moving them from 14 to 43. The Conservative juggernaut took 46 seats in the province. And in the west, where Turner had devoted so much time and effort, the party barely moved at all – from 4 seats to 5 – and only held the one seat in BC which the leader represented.

If the west was a disappointment, Quebec was a disaster. The party actually lost seats in the province, falling from 17 seats to 12. In short, the party that under Pierre Trudeau's last term had held all but one seat in Quebec had actually fared worse in 1988 than in 1984. The strategy of supporting Meech Lake had been an unmitigated disaster, compounded by premier Robert Bourassa's thinly disguised support for the Conservatives because of the FTA.

For John Turner, the writing was on the wall. Although the election results allowed him to claim victory and leave with his head held high, especially in light of the friendly fire that had plagued him throughout the campaign, it was clear to everyone that he would not be given a third chance.

6 Transition: Chrétien Takes the Helm, 1989–1992

Meech was the alpha and the omega of the leadership race.
– Martin adviser Mark Resnick[1]

John Turner doubled the Liberal Party's representation in the House of Commons, but he did not win, something every Liberal leader is expected to do. Having failed twice to return the party to power, he knew his days were numbered. At the same time he had earned the right to a dignified exit, especially after delivering more than could reasonably have been expected in the circumstances. Despite the past actions of some in the caucus, Sergio Marchi maintained: 'Most Liberals simply weren't accustomed to forcing anyone to leave. We knew he knew he would have to go, and we were willing to wait for him to pick the time and place.'[2] And, although the party's election expenses were covered, its overall financial situation was still bleak, another good reason to delay an expensive leadership convention.

For many of the eighty-three Liberal MPs arriving in Ottawa, the shock of finding themselves on the backbenches – whether once again or for the first time – was another reason to delay the transition. The newcomers needed to learn the ropes. Many had expected to find themselves on the winning side and were now disillusioned. This was particularly serious since there were even more first-time MPs than in 1984. Despite the dismal showing in Quebec, the novice Paul Martin Jr. was elected, while many former MPs who had tried for a comeback were not. In Ontario, with thirty additional seats, more than half the Liberal MPs were newcomers. Some, such as Tom Wappel, won in spite of their connections to a single-issue interest group and lack of history in the party. Others had decided to enter politics primarily because of John Turner, only to find he was on the way out. That group included the winners of many ethnic nomination wars, such as Joe Volpe, Tony Ianno, and Albina Guarnieri from Toronto, and Stan Keyes and Tony Valeri from Hamilton, all of whom would go on to be strong supporters of Paul Martin. Even in Atlantic Canada and the west, where the number of new Liberal seats was much lower, there was a preponderance of first-time MPs. From Admiral Fred Mifflin in Newfoundland (one of Turner's few vaunted star candidates) and Doug Young in New Brunswick, to Ron Duhamel, David Walker, and John Harvard in Manitoba, the Liberal caucus had more than its share of rookies.

For many of the returning MPs there was excitement in the air. This was not 1984, after all. The party was on the rebound and the Conservatives were no longer invincible. However, most of the veterans from the Liberals' pre-1984 governing era were gone. This meant that the class of 1984, including the Rat Pack, were now among the most senior caucus members. Such a curious combination of excitement, inexperience, and disappointment was bound to create another fractious caucus.

In early 1989, the entire Liberal caucus met in Newfoundland, home of caucus chair Brian Tobin, for a special retreat before the return of Parliament. Tobin assumed the position from Marcel Prud'homme in early 1988 and was involved in the election strategy. A skilled communicator, Tobin was able to put the best possible spin on difficult caucus positions in the months leading up to the election. After the defeat, however, Tobin had no detailed plan going into the special caucus. The sheer magnitude of the 1984 defeat had prompted the caucus leadership to act quickly in order to save the party from disaster, but no such imperative loomed in 1988. Instead, much of the time at the Newfoundland special caucus was devoted to internal bickering, recriminations, finger pointing, and especially the failure of the Quebec wing to deliver new seats and hold on to existing ones. Further time and effort were spent criticizing party officials and national office and parliamentary staff, many of whom were to be replaced anyway. The reality of a caucus twice the size of the previous one meant that there would be considerably more financial support available for staffing the Research Bureau. However, the bureau director's planning memo to the chair warned of ongoing problems with the funding of non-salary aspects of the bureau's operations, since the party's financial situation remained dire. 'The Party has once again begun to talk of eliminating our support in the next fiscal year as a cost-cutting measure,' the memo stated, and 'despite any increase from the House, we are still entirely dependent on the party for our operational expenses ... As you know, that means many of the services we provide to caucus would have to be curtailed or eliminated.'[3] If there was one issue on which caucus was united, it was that the party's financial problems would have to be addressed as an immediate priority.

Election Post-mortem

Meanwhile, the party executive conducted its own post-mortem on the defeat. On 6 March 1989 the two co-chairs, Al Graham and André Ouellet, held a day-long meeting of the national campaign committee in Ottawa. Reports were presented by each of the provincial and territorial chairs, whose comments bore little resemblance to those after the 1984 debacle. Virtually all of them praised the leader's tour, which was variously described as a 'first class operation' and 'an unqualified success.'[4] Similar praise was offered up for the platform, and for the policy assistance provided to candidates. The Nova Scotia report stressed that 'the substance of the platform that was released was excellent' while also noting 'our total lack of success in explaining how the platform would be financed ... undermined our credibility.'[5] Even the Quebec report summed up the technical and policy sides of the campaign in glowing terms. 'In four elections as a candidate,' chair Rémi Bujold wrote, 'I have never received as much support from the party, either in terms of policy content or campaign organization, and our advertising campaign was the envy of our opponents, except with respect to frequency.'[6]

The Quebec report went on to emphasize that it was a lack of funds that had prevented Liberals from responding adequately to Conservative attacks in the last two weeks of the campaign. The Newfoundland report expressed concern that 'the party appeared to run out of funds and was unable to meet the media campaigns of the PC and NDP in the final weeks of the campaign ... This may have been the cause of our slipping more than any other single event.'[7]

Lack of funding was referenced in the Ontario report as well but was superseded by another, more serious, concern, that of candidate nominations. Citing 'a divisive nomination process which left some successful candidates with few experienced workers,' the report concluded that 'the nomination process requires immediate attention.'[8] Problems with ethnic and single-issue groups were also considered part of the reason why 'although we gained 29 seats, we honestly expected to do much better.' Interestingly, the BC report also expressed concern with the Ontario nomination difficulties, concluding that 'press coverage of nominations in Quebec was (even more) damaging to the credibility of the party and to the claim of the leader to have democratized the party.'[9] The members of the national campaign committee presented reports in their respective areas of responsibility – Senator Mike Kirby on the Strategy Committee, Doug Kirkpatrick on the leader's tour, David Morton on the advertising campaign, Michael Robinson on finance, Allan Lutfy on legal issues, Ray Heard on communications, and the director of the Caucus Research Bureau on platform and policy. Several raised the issue of finances once again, this time making the connection with the issue of third-party financing. Red Leaf president David Morton concluded: 'Certainly even without the pressures of third party advertising in the last election our expenditures would have been far less than the Tories, but we would have been far more competitive without the $2–3 million that the third party advertising put into the marketplace over the last ten days of the campaign.'[10]

Morton also raised the issue of regional allocation of the media buy, highlighting another of the party's problems caused by the lack of funds. 'While I recognize that this is a very tough subject,' he wrote, 'the fact remains that in trying to win an election, we ought to be placing our media dollars where they will get the most bang for the buck. In the last election we spent a great deal of money in markets where we knew we probably couldn't win any seats ... I recognize the importance of keeping up appearances but in this case, spending money to keep up appearances may well have cost us seats.'[11]

The report of the Strategy Committee chair, Mike Kirby, addressed primarily the polling and costing issues. It reiterated his earlier admission that the failure to release the costing sooner had been a major error. He too stressed that funding was a limiting factor, particularly with respect to the lack of adequate polling data. Similar comments were made by the director of the Caucus Research Bureau before reporting on the platform and the policy hotline. Turning specifically to the concept of the Red Book, the director's report noted that candidates viewed it as an 'important and highly successful element' of the campaign. The report argued that 'the unusual one-issue nature of the campaign suggests that such a document would be even more useful and better utilized in more "normal" future elections.' Acknowledging that 'a less detailed and more limited set of announcements' might be in order for the next campaign as 'the party's credibility on policy matters would likely be greater and there would be less to prove,' the director still insisted that 'this concept bears repeating.'[12]

Only one of the reports touched on the thorny issue of party unity and the travails of the leader. After a thorough review of technical successes and minor difficulties connected with the leader's tour, Doug Kirkpatrick concluded his report with a blunt message. 'This campaign was without a doubt the strangest that I or any members of this committee have or are likely to participate in,' Kirkpatrick declared, and 'the struggles of the last four years both internally and externally were truly reflected in that 61-day period.' He closed with an appeal for unity: 'The external forces that impacted on this campaign and on the party over the last four years have been outside our control. The internal ones have been fully within our control as a Party. I hope that we can use the next four years to show Canadians we are capable and deserving of their trust.'[13]

Turner's Departure as Leader

Having met briefly in early December to ensure passage of the FTA, the thirty-fourth Parliament began in earnest in the early spring of 1989. John Turner spent the next few months looking more self-assured and authoritative than ever before. His performance in the House of Commons was polished and convincing. Many of his backbenchers remarked that he appeared to be hitting his stride. Sergio Marchi, for one, recalled that 'he was finally in the groove, showing us the leader he could have been' and the media concurred.[14] Some believed it might be in the party's interest for Turner to stay on until at least 1991, allowing the new leader to use the publicity generated by a leadership contest to follow through to an election campaign in 1992.

Turner's confidence began to worry some Chrétien supporters outside the caucus, who feared he might become sufficiently 'rehabilitated' that he would stay on as leader for several years. Within caucus, a small minority of Chrétien supporters began to disrupt weekly caucus meetings. During one notorious debate on the handling of the GST, an exasperated Turner declared: 'as long as I'm leader that's how we'll do it,' to which a chorus of disgruntled voices could be heard responding that it would not be for long. Yet despite the impatience of some, when Turner finally announced that he would step down as leader the following year, many Liberals were of two minds about his departure. He had become the leader many expected he would all along, but unfortunately it was too late to make a difference.

Turner's departure, like his acknowledgment of defeat in two federal elections, was gracious. He told his caucus pointedly that he would never embarrass the party by accepting a patronage appointment from Brian Mulroney – unlike the NDP's Ed Broadbent, who had announced his departure from Parliament and almost immediately accepted an appointment from the prime minister. Given Turner's uncertain future on Bay Street after his opposition to the FTA, this was particularly noteworthy.

In his letter to party president Michel Robert, Turner indicated his intention to resign sometime later and suggested a leadership convention be held the following summer in order to give the party time to arrange both the organization and financing of the convention. His choice of words was not accidental, since an 'intention' to resign did not represent an actual resignation. According to the Liberal Party constitution, the party executive had to schedule a convention within twelve months from the date of a leader's resignation or death. By referring to his 'intention' to resign, Turner kept that one-year clock from ticking.

It did not escape the attention of Chrétien supporters that the lengthy interim allowed sufficient time for a real leadership race to emerge, but there was little publicly expressed discontent. One reason why there was no real opposition to Turner's suggested timetable was, of course, financial. Another was the fact that Turner supporters continued to control most of the party apparatus. Although he had long been at odds with many in his caucus and the grassroots over his deviation from Trudeauvian federalism, there were enough of his supporters left in the key party executive posts to ensure that his wishes were respected. Many Chrétien supporters speculated that Turner's intention was to ensure as many candidates as possible entered the race to oppose Jean Chrétien. Journalist Susan Delacourt noted: 'Strategically Chrétien's gambit to take the race from outside had earned him the heir-apparent status, but on this issue (party organization) he was now at a disadvantage.'[15]

Some of the participants in the party's national executive meeting of 15 June 1989 began to describe themselves as part of a Turner/Martin coalition, leaving the clear impression that not only Turner but most of his supporters were hoping a long leadership race would benefit their preferred candidate, Paul Martin Jr. Delacourt described participants leaving the meeting to speak with journalists and inform them that 'the Turner/Martin forces had prevailed' and 'a long leadership race was in the works.'[16] At the end of the meeting, party president Michel Robert announced that the convention would be held on 23 June 1990. This would make the leadership race the longest in Liberal history. The announcement contained another surprise. The convention would be held in Calgary, only the second time a Liberal convention had ever been held outside of Ottawa, the first having been in Winnipeg in 1980. Apparently unintentionally, the date chosen for the event coincided with the deadline for ratification of the Meech Lake Accord, which gave the convention another surreal twist.

Though he would stay on as Liberal leader until the convention, Turner arranged for Herb Gray, who would not be a candidate for the leadership, to become acting leader of the Official Opposition in the House of Commons. By doing so, Turner hoped to avoid any potential controversy or accusations of bias in the House given the presence of four potential leadership candidates in his caucus.

The Leadership Race Begins

Candidates began coming forward as soon as Turner made his announcement. Nearly all of them were drawn from the ranks of the caucus as in years past, but the similarities between this and previous leadership races ended there. Jean Chrétien was the only candidate with cabinet experience as opposed to Trudeau's nine cabinet opponents in 1968 and the seven cabinet colleagues who challenged Turner in 1984. Three caucus candidates were not only rookies but had little chance of winning. To the surprise of many, the field included Sheila Copps and John Nunziata of the Rat Pack, along with the even more surprising Tom Wappel, who had only recently been elected for the first time and who had no base within the Liberal Party. Equally surprising was the absence of Lloyd Axworthy, who indicated that financial support was not available to him, a fact he attributed to his strong opposition to the FTA.

The fourth caucus candidate was, of course, Paul Martin Jr., another newly elected MP with little political expertise or experience, although that did not appear to hinder his chances within the party. Speculating on the reasons for this, some have cited his reputation as the new heir apparent, while others referred to his family connections. Interestingly, Jean Chrétien, whom Martin consulted about running as an MP in 1988, *did* feel that Martin was presumptuous in putting himself forward.

Nevertheless, as an MP and finance critic, Martin had as high a profile with the public as any of the other caucus members in early 1989.

Jean Chrétien, by contrast, did not need to raise his profile. Even though he had been out of active political life for nearly five years, his name was still a household word. This was due in large part to his role in the Trudeau cabinet during the constitutional amendment process, but it was reinforced by the publication of his autobiography in 1985. However, his widespread public recognition did not necessarily translate into popularity among the Liberal rank and file, many of whom began to worry that, like Turner, he might be out of touch after his time in the private sector. This fear of the 'Turner syndrome' was something other candidates would attempt to capitalize on during the race, referring to Chrétien as 'yesterday's man' whenever possible.

The departure of Clifford Lincoln, a former Quebec environment minister, only two months after declaring his candidacy in early 1990 left only the veteran Chrétien, an outsider, and four rookie caucus members as possible leaders of the Liberal Party. This also left Sheila Copps – the first female candidate for the party leadership – as the sole spokesperson for left-wing or 'social' Liberals, a distinct change from previous campaigns. Both Martin and Nunziata were viewed as business Liberals, while Chrétien was viewed as the ultimate pragmatic centrist. Wappel was considered something of a wild card.

Nevertheless there was the potential for a genuine race. Both Martin and Chrétien had substantial teams from the beginning. Chrétien's team consisted mostly of those who had worked for him in his earlier 1984 run, and Martin's was made up largely of former Turner supporters from the same race. Both men were considered to have a solid chance, although Chrétien was seen as the frontrunner. Despite the fact that Copps entered the race somewhat late, many thought her potential to attract the women's vote, and her widespread popularity in Quebec, could help her to come up the middle on a second or third ballot. Meanwhile both Nunziata and Wappel were depending on large numbers of single-issue interest groups, including ethnic communities and especially the anti-abortion movement. By the end of the race in Calgary, it was apparent that these groups were another new aspect of the Liberal leadership process. Following from the nomination battles in 1988, the Liberal Party's 1990 leadership race was heavily influenced by a delegate selection process which now included aggressive membership recruitment from such groups, many of whom also constituted large blocks of 'instant Liberals,' an unexpected consequence of the party's drive towards greater democratization.

The Chrétien and Martin Teams

For Jean Chrétien, there was little need to 'assemble' a team for the leadership race. Almost all of his key supporters from the 1984 campaign were still planning to work for him this time, despite the fact most had been engaged elsewhere for the past six years. There were long-standing loyalists such as Henry Wright, George Young, Patrick Lavelle, Isabelle Finnerty, Penny and David Collenette in Ontario. In Quebec John Rae, Eddie Goldenberg, Jacques Corriveau, Michel Veillette, and Pierre Bussières had been with Chrétien since the beginning, as had Ross Fitzpatrick in British Columbia and former New Brunswick MP Gary McCauley in the Atlantic. Several had been active during the leadership review of 1986, and most had maintained their personal ties to Chrétien despite distance and work-related demands.

Within the caucus there were also longtime supporters such as David Dingwall, Sergio Marchi, Brian Tobin, Charles Caccia, and Alfonso Gagliano, as well as more recent converts such as Dennis Mills and Jim Karygiannis. But more of Chrétien's caucus strength was in the Senate, where, incidentally, opposition to Meech Lake on the part of the Trudeau-era appointees was unanimous. Several of his key organizers came from the Senate, including Quebec senator Pietro Rizzuto, the former Quebec kingpin of the Friends of Turner. Senators Roméo LeBlanc of New Brunswick and George Furey from Newfoundland also worked to organize delegate support in their regions.

Paul Martin's leadership team was also ready to do battle even before the date was announced, but for different reasons. As Brian Tobin later observed: 'They brought Paul to the party, not the other way around.' After Turner's leadership failed, the same group 'went looking for another horse to saddle up, and Martin was available. They gave him a ready-made team.'[17] They also groomed him for the run at public office. As journalist John Gray recounted in painful detail, Martin required extensive training in public speaking and media relations before his supporters felt he was ready to reach for the brass ring. Even his longtime supporter Mike Robinson later recalled, Martin had 'none of the skills that seem instinctive with most politicians.'[18]

All of Martin's original supporters had been involved in the party since their teens, and several of them had been close friends for years before they began working on Martin's leadership race. Terrie O'Leary first met Martin in 1982 when, as director of the Ontario party's youth wing, she travelled to Montreal with fellow youth party activists Alf Apps and Peter Donolo to invite him to speak at a national convention of Young Liberals. David Herle, a Saskatchewan native, convinced Martin to speak at a similar gathering in that province in 1985 and shortly thereafter moved to Montreal to work for Martin at Canada Steamship Lines (CSL).

Another member of this group was Rick Mahoney, a young Toronto lawyer who met both Herle and O'Leary in 1982 and worked with them on the 1984 leadership campaign of John Roberts after Martin decided not to run. When Roberts dropped out of the race after the first ballot and threw his support to Chrétien, Mahoney and Herle conspicuously moved to the Turner camp, although O'Leary did follow her candidate to the Chrétien section of the stands.

Mahoney, Herle, and O'Leary were joined by Dennis Dawson, a former Quebec City MP defeated in the 1984 rout, who had also gone to work for Martin at CSL in 1985. Dawson and Herle spent considerable time working on Martin's candidacy over and above their paid duties at CSL. Specifically they worked to build bridges between Martin and the Quebec provincial Liberal Party (described by one observer as 'already a very different creature from its federal counterpart and much more Quebec-nationalist leaning')[19] and the struggling Liberals in Saskatchewan, who were led by a new young leader, Ralph Goodale. Martin himself spent considerable time and funds in both provinces and developed an extensive network of acquaintances who would serve as key regional supporters in 1990.

Adding to the interrelationship between the Turner and Martin camps was the presence of Heather Reisman and Gerry Schwartz among his Toronto supporters and fundraisers. Another was the fact that Dennis Dawson, like Herle and O'Leary, had been heavily involved in the Friends of Turner movement, working to ensure Turner's continued support in the 1986 leadership review. This was also true of Mahoney in his capacity as national president of the Young Liberals. By 1987, when Martin was asked by Turner to head a candidate recruitment committee, virtually all of these young Liberals were working for their future leadership candidate in one way or another, and the eventual 1990 leadership race simply solidified their various roles. David Herle was named national campaign director and Mahoney travelled with the candidate. Terrie O'Leary, meanwhile, left a job in finance in Toronto to become the campaign's director of organization, the counterpart of Penny Collenette in the Chrétien camp.With the actual race underway, other Turner supporters were added to the Martin campaign team. They included the party's former policy director, Mark Resnick, former lobbyist Mike Robinson (Turner's choice for the party's chief financial officer), and, after considerable urging by Robinson, Turner's former campaign director John Webster, who organized Toronto for Martin. Resnick served as policy director for the Martin campaign, aided by other former Turner policy advisers such as Jim deWilde and John Duffy. Another young Toronto lawyer who had supported Turner and knew Mahoney well, Tim Murphy, took a leave of absence from his law firm to become the Martin team's Ontario chair. Yet another former party official during the Turner era, Daniel Despins, became Martin's communications adviser along with lobbyist Jaimie Deacie of Association House (where Mahoney would later practise). Turner's former Atlantic desk officer in the OLO, Kaz Flynn, helped to organize the Atlantic provinces for him.

Together this group formed the core of Martin's leadership bids for nearly two decades and were charter members of what came to be known as the Board.

One of the most striking similarities among the Turner/Martin supporters was their dislike of Pierre Trudeau, something which put them outside the mainstream of the party and much of the country. Another similarity was their shared emphasis on economic policy and lack of interest in constitutional matters, as well as their keen commitment to party reform and democratization. Like Stephen LeDrew, Tim Murphy later stressed that he became active in the party because he was unhappy with the economic policies of Pierre Trudeau and the 'elitism' of the party. 'I was fed up with the economic mismanagement and the Trudeau-dominant party which focused on form – the constitution – not substance,' he later recounted. The connection between Turner and Martin, to them, was clear. Martin was Turner's obvious successor as part of the new guard 'and Jean Chrétien was part of the same old tired way of thinking.'[20]

Another common feature of many of Martin's supporters was their western or rural roots, again an unusual characteristic among members of the Liberal Party. Both Mike Robinson and Ruth Thorkelson came originally from Alberta, David Herle from Saskatchewan, while Terrie O'Leary and Scott Reid both stressed their rural Ontario origins in heavily Conservative regions of the province. As more key supporters signed on to the Martin team over the next several years, both of these demographic patterns would be strongly reinforced.

By contrast, Martin's caucus support was actually quite minimal, especially given his close ties to Turner. While the Chrétien MPs remained committed to their original choice from 1984, many of the other MPs were committed to other candidates. The most significant support for Martin came from Quebec MP Jean Lapierre, a Turner backer and fierce supporter of Meech Lake, who became campaign co-chair. Ironically, Martin's other national co-chair was former party president Iona Campagnolo, whom Turner had mistrusted as a closet Chrétien supporter. In the Senate, meanwhile, Martin's support for Meech Lake meant that he could count on almost no votes from the second chamber.

The New Tactics of Delegate Selection

As had been the case in 1984, Chrétien could not expect to win the leadership on the basis of the parliamentary wing or ex officio delegates. Many years of experience within the party had taught him and his organizers the importance of delegate selection and the now pivotal role of local organizers in getting out the vote for delegate selection meetings. With the rapidly decreasing role of the party elite in predetermining the leadership outcome, these functions were now far more important than support from the caucus or a few backroom boys. Although one of the aspirants for the mantle of Keith Davey, short-lived Turner minister David Smith, had actually told several of Martin's supporters that 'it's Jean's turn,' the phrase carried little weight. In the new world of delegate selection battles, Smith's contribution to Chrétien's leadership success would be measured by his ability to deliver delegates' votes.

Martin's supporters knew this as well. But they had much less experience in organizing at the riding level, especially since the opening up of the party to minority groups and, inadvertently, to single-issue groups. Indeed, one other striking difference between the Chrétien and Martin supporters was that Chrétien's team were older and more experienced. They came from across the country and included many francophones and visible minorities. By contrast, Martin's team was much younger, were predominantly anglophone, and could count few members of minority groups among their inner circle.

As the candidates began to assemble their teams, several additional differences emerged between this race and those that preceded it.

First and foremost was the way in which the various teams attempted to influence the delegate selection process for the convention. Each of the leadership camps established a team to recruit delegates, 'the only activity that really matters,' as one Martin supporter ruefully noted afterwards.

In Toronto, Chrétien organizers Sergio Marchi and Jim Karygiannis made extensive use of their contacts in the Sikh and Macedonian communities. Similarly, Terry Mercer, who was responsible for the western half of the city and was the first to use seven-day-a-week phone banks, employed individuals with the appropriate language skills to recruit new members from the Ukrainian, Polish, and Lithuanian communities. In Parkdale High Park, Mercer's efforts meant Martin supporter Jesse Flis became the first MP to be unable to deliver his riding's delegates to his preferred leadership candidate. Similar and highly controversial tactics were used with equal success by the Chrétien forces in British Columbia, primarily in the Sikh community.

The Martin team was far less successful. After a series of initial victories in February 1990 in Martin's home base in southwestern Ontario and in eastern Ontario, the momentum stalled. Chrétien took Toronto and most of northern Ontario, while Sheila Copps's supporters were elected as delegates in the Hamilton area, resulting in a close three-way race for delegates from the province. In the rest of the country, however, it was a different story. Chrétien delegates were overwhelmingly elected in the west, Atlantic Canada, and Quebec. Despite Dennis Dawson's efforts to recruit soft nationalists, both Lawrence Cannon and Marc-Yvan Côté decided to support Sheila Copps. As a result, the small pro-Meech Liberal vote in Quebec was split with the Martin forces to a degree they had not imagined possible, while Chrétien took the vast majority of delegates. Even in Saskatchewan, where Chrétien was not a factor and the Martin team worked long and hard, they fumbled the ball and lost many delegates to right-to-life groups.

Overall the Martin team's failure to adequately respond to the new reality of recruiting from ethno-cultural communities was a significant issue, one which they themselves later admitted. But, to some, organizational problems were not the decisive factor. 'They were on the wrong side of the key issue of the day. Liberals didn't support Meech, period. We wouldn't have been nearly so successful with some of those ethnic groups if they didn't already have the idea that Meech was bad for Canada. Most of them thought Trudeau was a god, and if he didn't like it, neither did they.'[21]

By April of 1990, delegate selection was complete and it was obvious that Chrétien had amassed an unassailable lead with more than 1,500 delegates committed. Martin was a distant second at 500 and Copps an even more distant third with barely 150. None of the other candidates had even 100 committed delegates. Despite this result, Martin supporters continued to hope that delegates' votes could be influenced at the convention itself or during the remaining policy forums, which had already begun in January.

At this point, despite the tensions inevitably produced during a lengthy leadership race, most participants agreed the situation was still under control and comparable to other campaigns. Longtime party activist and Copps's campaign chair Joe Thornley underlined this point, stressing there had always been a common understanding among senior representatives of leadership candidates that, at the end of the day, one of those candidates would become leader of the Liberal Party and 'no one wanted to kneecap the leader.'[22] There was traditionally a high degree of civility and professionalism among the various backroom organizers as well as the candidates, precisely because the prevailing view was that 'we were all in it together, we were all Liberals and the real enemy was outside the tent.' However, at the last of the policy debates this tradition, like so many others, was undermined.

The Liberal Leadership Forums

By September 1989 the party not only had settled on a date for the leadership convention but had instituted a series of six regional policy forums leading up to it, events known collectively as the Liberal Leadership Forums. As the last party convention had been in 1986, it had been four years since the party had come together to discuss policy, a hiatus that troubled both the party executive and grassroots members. As party president Michel Robert later explained, the leadership forums were as much an attempt to redress this unusually long delay in the party's policy renewal process as they were a vehicle to probe the positions of the candidates.[23]

Unlike the situation in 1984, when policy 'sessions' were held during the convention itself, these forums were to be full-scale events held across the country over a period of several months. All leadership candidates were expected to participate. Each event would involve a series of policy workshops in the morning and an all-candidates' debate in the afternoon. The forums would be attended by grassroots Liberals from the region, many of whom would also be delegates to the convention. As a result, the potential for the forums to influence the direction of the policy debate among leadership candidates, and perhaps even the course of the leadership race itself, was considerable.

The director of the Caucus Research Bureau was appointed secretary general of the leadership forums and tasked with developing six major policy themes for the forums in consultation with the National Policy Committee, as well as preparing a comprehensive policy primer for distribution to all participants. The importance attached to these leadership forums was further highlighted by caucus chair Brian Tobin, who said they would be 'the centrepiece of the leadership process between now and next June … the focus of policy development for the party and crucial in providing the general public with a positive image of the Liberal Party in the interim.'[24]

The six leadership forums were held between January and June of 1990. Beginning in Toronto on 28 January, they were followed by Yellowknife in February, Vancouver in March, Winnipeg in April, Halifax at the end of the same month, and Montreal in early June. Attendance figures demonstrated the success of these events and the extent of grassroots interest in policy issues. From a high of 2,500 in Montreal, participation ranged from 1,200 in Toronto and Vancouver to 900 in Winnipeg and Halifax, and a remarkable 500 in Yellowknife. As forum co-chairs Mary Clancy and Senator Serge Joyal wrote in the preface to the forum policy primer distributed to participants in advance, 'the forums are evidence of the continuing commitment of the Party to involve the grassroots membership in policy development.' In keeping with Turner's views on transparency and accountability, the chairs also stressed that 'a formal record of the forum activities will be compiled and a report on these deliberations will be presented in Calgary.'

At each forum, six workshops were held in the morning based on the six policy areas, one of which was national unity. The primer provided to participants contained 'a brief overview of some of the current issues' in each policy area, along with 'relevant party resolutions from the 1986 convention, the 40 planks of the Liberal platform in the 1988 general election and, where relevant, post-1988 caucus positions or statements by the leader.'[25]

The morning workshops produced priority questions on each of the six topics, which were put to the leadership candidates in the afternoon debate session. The debates themselves consisted of opening and closing statements by each candidate, the debate section moderated by a neutral individual selected for the task, and a question-and-answer period with the audience in which the priority questions were posed. The priority questions varied significantly from region to region. More attention was paid to regional development as the economic policy issue in the Atlantic, for example, or to transportation on the prairies and aboriginal issues in BC. On the national unity issue, by contrast, every workshop except the one in Toronto produced a priority question on the Meech Lake Accord and the role of the federal government. All of the Meech priority questions focused on two points: where the candidates stood on 'maintaining a strong national government versus decentralizing powers to provincial governments' and 'what position they would take on June 24th if Meech Lake failed.' This was hardly surprising since, as Tom Axworthy had predicted, Meech Lake had not ceased to be an issue for the Liberals even though it had been approved by Parliament.

The forums unfolded without incident, with many participants and observers viewing them as a template for future leadership contests. In her closing remarks in Whitehorse, Mary Clancy declared: 'these events have more than proven their worth' and 'will no doubt become a standard part of the leadership selection process.'

The Meech Lake Factor

Throughout the lengthy leadership race 'the Meech Lake issue had been percolating' within the party and the general public, as one senior organizer in the Martin camp put it. When asked to recall the most important event of the leadership race, Mark Resnick declared without hesitation: 'Meech was the alpha and the omega.'[26] The problem was simple; the deal was not yet a fait accompli as expected. It had been adopted by the federal Parliament in early 1988, but the accord still required approval by all provincial legislatures before the deadline of 23 June 1990, the very day of the Liberal leadership convention. Yet Prime Minister Mulroney's continued intransigence concerning possible amendments to the deal, coupled with a change in government in three of the provinces, created something of an impasse. This presented a kind of crisis for the Liberals. Having attempted to put the issue behind them, leadership candidates were now forced to address the possibility that the accord, once considered a sure thing, could fail.

A prime reason for its potential failure was the opposition of provincial Liberal governments in two provinces. In New Brunswick, Premier

Frank McKenna's new Liberal government served notice shortly after their election in 1987 that they were interested in reopening the deal to obtain significant modifications. McKenna, whose opposition to the deal had been clearly stated during his time as leader of the Official Opposition, was a lawyer who often told acquaintances he had won a gold medal in constitutional law during his university studies. More recently he had won all fifty-eight seats in the provincial legislature, and most observers expected his concerns to be dealt with promptly given his strong bargaining position. That did not prove to be the case. Instead, as his intergovernmental affairs minister noted in the fall of 1988, 'One month after we took power we told federal officials that they had to take our objections seriously. But their minds were closed, and so were the doors for improving the Accord.'[27]

A similar situation was unfolding in Newfoundland, where Liberal Clyde Wells had been elected. An even more adamant opponent of the deal, the new premier – also an expert in constitutional law – threatened to rescind his province's earlier support for the deal. Yet, as Wells complained in the fall of 1989, neither Mulroney nor his federal intergovernmental affairs minister, Senator Lowell Murray, had made any attempt to speak with him let alone address his concerns.

Both New Brunswick and Manitoba established legislative committees to examine the accord. The Manitoba committee report was issued on 23 October 1989 and dealt a serious blow to Mulroney's hopes for the accord's adoption. Among its long list of concerns was the 'distinct society' provision, an element considered fundamental by Mulroney and Quebec Premier Bourassa. The New Brunswick report, although containing a similar list of concerns, struck a more conciliatory tone. It proposed the adoption of a 'parallel accord' to redress that province's issues, thereby allowing the original deal to pass unamended. Premier Wells's lengthy set of objections was contained in a letter sent to the prime minister on 18 October 1989, to which he received no reply. Instead, the federal government's approach seemed to be to wait and see, although Lowell Murray suggested publicly that the deal might be discussed at a federal-provincial first ministers' conference already planned for 9 November.

One Liberal who was not prepared to wait and see was former prime minister Trudeau. At a book launch in Montreal for his collected commentaries on the accord, *Trudeau Parle*, Trudeau publicly deplored the lack of criticism coming from other Liberals and particularly francophone Quebeckers, leading many to speculate he was prompting Jean

Chrétien to speak out. 'I was hoping some of the people who were around when we were in office would get up and lead the campaign against Meech Lake,' Trudeau told reporters at the book launch. 'Nobody is showing Quebeckers the other view of Canada.'[28]

Among Liberal leadership candidates, that was certainly true. Paul Martin and Sheila Copps were fervent supporters of Meech Lake while John Nunziata and Tom Wappel, who opposed it, were unknown in Quebec and in any event were attempting to build leadership support based on their opposition to abortion, support for party reforms, and a right-of-centre economic agenda. As the frontrunner in the recently declared leadership race, Jean Chrétien was conspicuous by his silence. Some grassroots Liberals were anxious about whether he would maintain his opposition in the face of growing pressure from Mulroney and Bourassa, both of whom were now warning the deal's failure would mean political disaster for Canada.

Paul Martin made Meech Lake a central focus of his leadership bid. When he announced his candidacy on 17 January 1990 in Montreal, he drew a line in the sand between himself and Chrétien. 'Let us be clear,' he said. 'First and foremost, I unconditionally support the Meech Lake Accord, with or without a parallel accord.' Many in the Martin camp attacked Chrétien for his perceived opposition to the deal. 'Meech was a fundamental divide,' Mike Robinson later declared. 'Most of us genuinely believed if we lost Meech we would lose the country.'[29] Martin's campaign co-chair and former Turner supporter, MP Jean Lapierre, told reporters: 'We are all waiting to see if Mr. Chrétien will continue to insist that *Meech Lake* will destroy the country.'[30]

They did not have to wait much longer. In early January, Jean Chrétien delivered a major speech at the University of Ottawa. Entitled 'A Challenge of Leadership,' the speech covered a wide range of issues but focused on constitutional issues and Meech Lake in particular, with a full two-thirds of the text devoted to the accord. As the only serious leadership candidate opposed to Meech Lake, and as a Quebec Liberal, Chrétien found himself in a difficult position. On the one hand, he needed to retain the strong support of the Trudeau Liberals in the party to win the leadership. On the other hand, he did not want to alienate those Quebeckers, whether Liberals or not, who were inclined to support the deal. His speech was a model of political acuity, demonstrating his commitment to the Trudeau vision while sounding a conciliatory note to supporters of the accord by offering a solution to the impasse.

Chrétien began his analysis with blunt criticism of Mulroney, who he argued had 'repudiated the historic nation-building role exercised by his predecessors from Macdonald to Trudeau.' The speech was actually vetted by Trudeau and, not surprisingly, echoed much of the former PM's thinking on the nature of Canadian federalism. 'The national government,' Chrétien insisted, 'must seek cooperation with the provinces. But it is the national government which must speak for Canada ... A strong national government has always been necessary to meet the great challenges of the day for the benefit of all parts of the country. A strong national government is more than ever necessary to meet the global challenges of the 1990's.'[31]

Chrétien went on to criticize the process Mulroney had employed to develop and promote the Meech Lake Accord, contrasting it with the open, consultative process used by the Trudeau government to achieve the 1982 constitutional amendment and Charter of Rights. 'The result of [Mulroney's] refusal to listen to the public debate,' Chrétien argued, 'has been that the political debate is polarized. Those who support the current text are deemed to be pro-Quebec. Those who want it modified are deemed to be anti-Quebec. This is unfair; it is wrong; it is dangerous.'[32] He then outlined a number of modifications to the accord which he felt would make it acceptable while still achieving the objectives of the Quebec government's original five points. These changes reflected the amendments proposed by the Liberals in Parliament the previous year.

Chrétien concluded his speech with a call for a return to the negotiating table and for an end to the escalating discourse of political crisis. 'We should be careful not to exaggerate the importance of the current difficulties,' he cautioned.

> Quebec's ability to grow, develop and address its concerns has not been impaired by the absence of the Meech Lake Accord. The new Quebec has flourished and prospered within Canadian federalism without Meech Lake ... If Meech Lake is not ratified there will be new negotiations ... To escalate the debate by characterizing it as 'all or nothing' and raise the spectre of dire consequences only serves to increase the risks ... What is required is a new negotiation over whatever time it takes – without artificial deadlines and the pressures such deadlines impose – which will lead to a revised, improved and amended Accord.[33]

The speech solidified Chrétien's position with Trudeau Liberals before the race had even begun. Contrasted with the enthusiastic support for the deal professed by both Martin and Copps, it left much of the party with no other choice than to turn to Chrétien. The fact that the constitutional issue trumped the left-right issue was reinforced by the reluctant support Chrétien received from many social Liberals as well as those who should have been the natural constituency of other candidates, such as Sheila Copps. Like many Liberal women, Maria Minna (a leading feminist activist in Toronto and future MP) opposed the accord for many reasons but primarily because of its perceived threat to the equality-rights section of the Charter, for which many feminists had fought long and hard. In the end, Minna declared her support for Jean Chrétien rather than the first female candidate for the leadership. Asked why she would not be supporting Copps, Minna simply said: 'I don't understand Sheila's avid support of the Accord.'[34]

Yet neither Martin nor Copps wavered in their support of the deal, evidently believing it was possible to win the leadership regardless. This was primarily because they saw themselves as being on the side of the majority. Both believed it was Chrétien who represented the minority view and that that view was outdated, a perspective apparent in interviews and in their comments during the forum debates. In one notable exchange, Copps declared: 'We Liberals embraced change when we repatriated our constitution after 115 years and we Liberals must now embrace the challenge of renewed federalism that recognizes all parts of Canada as crucial to our survival as a nation.'[35] Martin's arguments were similar, but more directly critical of the Trudeau approach. In a statement titled 'Nationalism without Walls,' he argued that 'the reflexive responses of the 1970's' such as 'tough-guy federalism will not work.' Instead, the way to 'bring down the walls' between the centre and the regions was Meech Lake. 'The first step is the establishment of a constitutional accord that brings Quebec into the Canadian family,' he declared. 'In this way we will be able to balance the unique needs of Quebec with a new commitment to bringing regional voices into national institutions.'[36]

Virtually all of Chrétien's advisers and campaign workers opposed the deal, but not all of Martin's strategists were on side in supporting it. Although years later, several key strategists would speak passionately about it, at the time it was clear that few of Martin's close advisers considered Meech Lake *the* crucial issue, and some, such as Terrie O'Leary and Michelle Cadario, were almost indifferent about it. O'Leary commented: 'To the extent I thought about it, I just wanted it to be settled. I felt this whole constitutional debate was preventing us from getting on with the work that needed to be done on the economy,'[37] a statement remarkably reminiscent of Tim Murphy and Stephen LeDrew's comments about Pierre Trudeau's 1980 initiative.

Meech and the Leadership Debates: A New Dynamic

The internal debate over Meech Lake came to a head in Montreal at the final leadership forum. By then the Martin forces knew they could not win unless they were able to force a second ballot. They had already lost the delegate selection battles in Ontario, BC, and Saskatchewan, and were trailing badly in Quebec. Although there were several heated exchanges at the previous leadership events, there were no untoward incidents, so no one was prepared for what ensued in Montreal.

Having actively recruited delegates in Quebec via new Liberal youth groups, the Martin forces had a large contingent of young pro-Meech supporters in the audience. Martin himself decided to pursue the constitutional division aggressively, hoping to acquire more support in Quebec by taking a strong stand on the issue. He went on the attack almost immediately. 'Answer the question,' he urged Chrétien. 'What is your bottom line on Meech Lake?' Chrétien, clearly unhappy with the turn of events, outlined the stand he had taken in January – the accord as written was fatally flawed but could be salvaged if a number of amendments were made. The Martin youth group in the audience began to yell 'Yes or No' and 'Le Flip, Le Flop,' drowning out Chrétien's answer. Martin followed his initial parry with a warning: 'Those who reject the new Quebec will transform nationalists into separatists.'

Sheila Copps intervened, telling Chrétien that he did not understand Quebec and was 'gambling dangerously with the survival of Canada.' When Chrétien, struggling to be heard, finally managed to communicate that 'if the Charter is not protected it's NO!' the youth group began chanting 'Vendu' and 'Judas' while he sat motionless and outwardly calm. Those who knew him well, however, were aware of is true feelings. Afterwards he told reporters, 'I don't attack anyone personally in the campaign. It's the tradition in the party and there are some who didn't follow it today.' Chrétien adviser Eddie Goldenberg's response was more direct. He described Martin's tactics as crossing a line in politics, an act which 'makes it very hard to bring people together afterwards, a fundamental mistake for any group and especially for a loser.'[38]

Party president Michel Robert was of the same view. Visibly upset, he spent much of the debate lambasting Martin organizers for what he viewed as an unacceptable and organized insurrection on his watch. However, Martin's candidate liaison, Mark Resnick, insisted at the time and afterwards that the event was unscripted, at least by senior Martin organizers. Resnick believed the youth delegates acted on their own, reflecting a genuine anger within the Quebec wing of the party over Chrétien's position.[39] One of Chrétien's closest advisers disagreed, insisting that many if not most of the young Liberals were actually from Ontario because they could not pronounce 'vendu' correctly. Another claimed 'it was Daniel Dezainde [later head of the party's Quebec wing under Martin and executive assistant to a minister in Martin's cabinet] who set it up, one of Martin's youth organizers. Our Quebec people knew it. And in the end it led to a thirteen-year war.'

What was certain was that, as the leadership race drew to an end, the constitutional issue was of such overriding importance that Martin and Chrétien – the only ones who could realistically win the leadership – were the only real options for both supporters and opponents of the deal. As one Chrétien delegate complained afterward: 'I didn't even like the guy, I thought he was too far to the right, but what can you do? The alternatives were worse. He was the only one opposed to Meech Lake and that's the only issue that counted for Liberals then. We have to be able to trust our leader to do the right thing on the constitution or where would be? Look at what happened with Turner! For the rest we just had to wait and see.'

This sentiment was echoed by many in the final weeks leading up to the convention. Two weeks before his date with destiny in Calgary, Chrétien was taken by surprise when Brian Mulroney suddenly announced he had reached a compromise agreement with the premiers. Immediately the whole issue took on added urgency. A team authorized by Chrétien had been negotiating secretly in Montreal with Stanley Hartt, Mulroney's point man on the issue, and an agreement seemed close. However, Robert Bourassa's last-minute rejection of a proposed addendum, and Mulroney's precipitous press conference at the conclusion of the negotiations with the premiers where he announced, 'I decided to roll the dice,' infuriated not only Chrétien and his supporters but most Canadians. Any hope of the deal being supported by the Liberal leadership hopeful was ended.

Worse still, the media's sighting of Goldenberg and another occasional Chrétien adviser, lawyer Eric Maldorf, at the meeting led to increased speculation about the role Chrétien was actually playing in the negotiations. For the Chrétien team, the issue became whether to sign on to the revised agreement – and hopefully end the controversy – or not. There was considerable infighting among Chrétien's advisers. Some, like Goldenberg, argued the new agreement was close enough to Chrétien's position to be accepted. Others, such as Ontario organizer Patrick Lavelle, insisted it would be political suicide to appear to agree with Mulroney or, more importantly, Paul Martin.

In the end it was Chrétien's former mentor, Mitchell Sharp, who advised the politically expedient path of saying nothing. There were, after all, still a number of hurdles for Mulroney and the premiers to overcome. In Manitoba, a native Cree MLA named Elijah Harper was threatening to hold up the proceedings on technical grounds to protest the lack of provisions guaranteeing aboriginal rights. Newfoundland Premier Clyde Wells introduced a motion in March to revoke the province's agreement to Meech, and a vote was still scheduled for only days before the 23 June deadline. The accord and the more recent agreement could come undone without Chrétien having to say a word.

Instead of speaking out, he spent the days before the convention at his cottage in Quebec, avoiding reporters and leaving more than a few of his supporters nonplussed. Once again, fears arose as to whether he was the man to take up Trudeau's mantle. On the Martin side, there was considerable optimism. In his silence, Chrétien began to look vulnerable. Not only was he seen to be avoiding the issue, Martin organizers were convinced this would result in delegate defections from his camp to theirs. Martin campaign manager Mike Robinson told reporters that 'the country is going through a trauma. That means there is more fluidity now than at any time in the leadership race. We think now this will be a multi-ballot contest where anyone can win.'[40] Martin told the same reporters on his arrival in Calgary: 'I said a month ago we needed to switch about 300 delegates to push this thing into a second ballot and to win it. As a result of all these occurrences over Meech Lake in the past two weeks, we've now got those 300 delegates.'[41]

The Landmark Calgary Convention

Besides the selection of a new leader, other important, even groundbreaking, things happened at the Liberal convention in Calgary. As outgoing party president Michel Robert noted in his welcoming address, the changes to the Liberal Party's constitution made in 1986 meant there would be up to 5,200 delegates (as compared with the 3,400 maximum eligible in 1984), and fully half of them would be women. He also reminded delegates the changes meant 'we have significantly reduced the number of ex officio delegates,' a move designed to 'give the grassroots more of an opportunity to participate in this important democratic exercise.' The creation of women's and youth commissions, the expansion of the aboriginal committee, and the changes to delegate selection rules also meant 'the Convention [saw] participation of more delegates from diverse ethnic and cultural backgrounds.' In addition, the convention included a Judy LaMarsh brunch, the first convention fundraiser to assist the LaMarsh fund created in 1984 under the auspices of Iona Campagnolo to support Liberal women candidates in federal elections.

On the financial side, Robert informed delegates that the party's debt had been significantly reduced to $3.5 million in the past year and would likely be down to $2 million by the end of 1990. This was largely the result of cutting costs, suggesting that the party still had a long way to go on the fundraising side. With luck, the debt would be eliminated by the end of 1991, although Robert acknowledged it would leave the party with little in the way of reserves to fight the expected 1992 election. Finally, the outgoing president recognized 'the present system for choosing our leader has caused extensive debate within the party and the media' and 'our constitution obviously has weaknesses, as shown by the difficulties experienced in the control over the delegate selection process.'[42]

The convention was not simply a leadership convention but one at which both policy resolutions and proposed amendments to the party constitution were to be debated. These constitutional amendments were the result of renewed pressure from party militants, who organized conferences and issued memos in an effort to press particular issues such as party membership, leadership selection, and candidate nominations in the lead-up to the convention. These recommendations from party dissidents and activists influenced, to some degree, the agenda in Calgary, although issues specifically related to the leadership were clearly the order of the day.

A memo circulated by Sean Moore to the national executive in advance of the convention stressed the importance of particular issues. 'The current system is bad politics,' Moore lamented. 'At its best, it encourages "machine politics" by forcing leadership candidates to focus on organizational logistics … at the expense of policy. At its worst, it promotes the practice of "instant Liberals" we have seen in recent years.'[43] A formal discussion paper prepared for delegates focused on two key issues: membership rules and the federal nature of the party. Noting that 'hotly contested nomination meetings in recent years have, in many parts of the country, become controversial and increasingly embarrassing for the Party,' the document concluded that 'the current practice of the individual who is most able to sign up new members in a short period of time, generally winning a nomination, is fraught with problems.' It also posed a number of questions concerning the direction of reform:

> Is it truly democratic for a large number of people to join a party for only one very specific purpose? Should more emphasis be placed on the member who has a proven commitment to the party? In a perfect world, a candidate would be chosen on the basis of ideas, ideology, societal representativeness and organization, not purely organization.[44]

Interestingly, while dissidents such as the Grindstone activists and the formal party document agreed on the nature of the problems, they differed on solutions. Where the authors of the party primer preferred to focus on limiting membership (by such measures as constituency residency requirements, minimum age, and minimum length of time as a member before voting rights accrued, etc.) as the best means of preventing abuses during delegate selection and candidate nominations, the activists favoured universal suffrage. 'The best response,' Moore's group argued, 'is to broaden the party's base, rather than to curtail anyone's ability to join the Liberal Party.'[45] Generally speaking, groups such as Moore's included former Turner supporters (Rosemary McCarney, Lloyd Posno, Rodger Schwass, Ross Milne), while the formal party position was the preferred option for Chrétien's people.

The policy workshops and constitutional reform sessions of the party were held over several days during the convention. In the case of the constitutional sessions, there was very little interest and the meetings were poorly attended. What's more, it became clear that many of the amendments were not understood except by constitutional experts or the drafters themselves. In the end, the debates were almost as chaotic as the free trade policy furore at the 1986 convention and were terminated prematurely due to a lack of participation.

Some constitutional amendments were adopted which – without the approval of others that had been submitted as part of a package – left the party with a system that was patently impractical. As Moore later agreed, this dual system was 'ludicrous. They failed to complete the re-form process.'[46] As a result, a motion was passed calling for the creation of yet another reform commission to examine the measures adopted by the convention and make recommendations to reconcile the various inconsistencies. In addition, some clearly regressive amendments were adopted. As the party's director of operations at the time noted, many of the changes adopted in 1990 actually undid reforms introduced in 1985 and 1986. 'The most significant amendments adopted … related to re-instating the *ex officio* delegate status of unelected national executive members and the creation of and provision of delegates to a new Aboriginal Commission.'[47]

Few of the candidates for party office referred to any of these developments except to recognize them in passing. The increase in number and type of delegates in particular was seen by the majority of candidates as a positive move that furthered the objectives of opening up and democratizing the party. One of the very few to take exception was John Roberts, the former Trudeau minister and Liberal leadership candidate from 1984 who was running for the party presidency. Roberts, considered the frontrunner for the position going into the convention,[48] was clearly unhappy with the nomination problems of 1988 and the delegate selection debacles which had occurred in the run-up to the Calgary convention. Although he supported the spirit of the changes, he also believed new rules were required to ensure those objectives were met with fewer unintended consequences. Roberts's platform included a commitment to push for a constitutional amendment requiring Liberals to be party members for at least one year before being considered eligible to vote for delegate selection or candidate nominations. He also called for more stringent limitations on spending for leadership campaigns. Perhaps most important, he addressed the issue of the federal structure of the party, calling for reforms such as a national membership list and a system of provincial presidents who, along with the president, would make up the national executive.

Roberts's major challenge came from another former Trudeau cabinet minister, Don Johnston. Having retired from politics two years earlier, Johnston was now back working in the same law office as Pierre Trudeau. As he later recalled, he had no intention of running for the position until he was approached by several former colleagues (including Gerry Regan, Gil Molgat, and LPCO president Rod Bryden) looking to replace a former mayor of Ottawa who had abruptly pulled out of the race. As he had an agenda of his own, Johnston decided to accept their offer. His platform focused on what he saw as the party's dire financial straits and on the need to retire the debt as well as modernize fundraising methods to increase revenue before the next federal election. Johnston pledged to eliminate the debt as scheduled and to continue the tradition of the presidency as an unpaid position, something Roberts did not do.

It is worth noting that, despite the party's dire straits, the leadership candidates had no difficulty raising funds, a point raised by several members of the executive who felt spending limits should be imposed. Indeed, this was the first leadership contest in which the funds raised by the various contenders exceeded those raised by the party in a federal election campaign. According to journalist John Gray, the 1990 Liberal leadership race was the most expensive in Canadian history. Chrétien's campaign cost $2.44 million, Martin's cost $2.37 million, and Sheila Copps spent a mere $800,000.[49]

It was also the first convention in which the party 'establishment,' so influential in 1984, was virtually invisible. Certainly the Chrétien team had learned their lesson from 1984. They relied on themselves and the new party rules rather than support from the establishment. Delegates were the key. As the delegate selection battle was won, the only remaining challenge was to make sure they voted. This was true for the other camps as well. Considerable time and money were expended by both Chrétien and Martin organizers to ensure their troops were happily occupied and prevented from straying. On the Martin side, chief strategist David Herle, known to insiders as The Enforcer, was determined to take as many votes as possible even though he knew his candidate's cause was lost. As one participant observed, 'Herle ... kept pushing for every last vote, and every last elbow in the ribs, whether or not the ribs belonged to a fellow Liberal, because in politics there are no Marquis of Queensbury rules.'[50] Many Chrétien delegates were actually sequestered in Banff until their presence at the convention was required. On the convention floor, the various organizers for the major camps were more active than ever before, coordinated and precise in their operation.

In addition, the Chrétien camp had decided on a slate of candidates for the various party offices. With the exception of the presidency – left open as either Roberts or Johnston would do from their perspective – one candidate for each post was identified as the 'Chrétien' choice, a move which caught many other candidates by surprise. Several did not see themselves as part of any slate or as supporting any particular leadership candidate and objected to being 'claimed' in such a way.

Others such as vice-presidential candidate Colin Macdonald of Calgary expressed surprise at finding himself on the Chrétien slate but did not complain as the support gave a boost to his campaign. In the end, Macdonald, a former aide to Allan MacEachen, won the contest against Elvio del Zotto, a candidate closely associated with the Turner/Martin camp.

Meech Lake at the Convention

All of these developments, however, were overshadowed by the national unity drama unfolding alongside the convention and the leadership race. Technically the convention began on Thursday, 21 June. However, the Women's Liberal Commission and the Liberal Youth Commission scheduled meetings on the Tuesday and Wednesday leading up to the full event, and their meetings included leadership candidates' debates. As Jean Chrétien quickly discovered, Meech Lake was not going to go away. Along with Brian Mulroney and Ontario Premier David Peterson, both Copps and Martin went to Newfoundland, the province singled out as the most likely stumbling block for the accord, to attempt to influence the vote.

When the issue arose during the youth commission debate, both Copps and Martin accused Chrétien of abrogating his responsibility as a potential Liberal leader and prime minister by failing to take a stand or tell Canadians his views on the revised deal. A visibly nervous Chrétien confirmed that he had spoken two months earlier to Wells, McKenna, and aboriginal leaders to see if a satisfactory agreement could be reached. However, he also claimed that Brian Mulroney's pressure tactics and insistence on sticking with the 23 June date had put an end to those behind-the-scenes diplomatic efforts, which he described as 'more responsible' than the 'grandstanding' of some of the accord's supporters. Pressed repeatedly by Martin to say whether he would support or reject the compromise agreement, Chrétien demurred. 'I don't want to pour oil on the fire. I'd like these people [Manitobans and Newfoundlanders] to make up their own minds.'[51]

The following day Brian Mulroney addressed the Newfoundland legislature. The same day Gary Filmon finally introduced the accord in the Manitoba legislature and former prime minister Pierre Trudeau arrived in Calgary for the convention. When asked by reporters at the airport about his views on the amended 9 June deal, Trudeau replied: 'I said three years ago that Meech Lake was a bad deal for Canada and a bad deal for Quebec. Nothing in the June 9 deal changes that. It's a bad deal and it shouldn't be passed.'[52]

That same evening John Turner gave a farewell address to the delegates. Reflecting on the extraordinary situation in which they found themselves, he used the occasion to make a plea for national unity. He also roundly criticized the prime minister for his handling of the Meech Lake process, which he described as 'demeaning, degrading and divisive.' After reiterating his support for the accord, Turner indirectly criticized Jean Chrétien's failure to state his position on the amended constitutional package when he noted that 'I never hesitated to speak out on the issues of the day, even to my own political cost.' Asked in a press scrum before his speech whether he had any comments to make about Chrétien's loyalty during his time as leader, Turner replied that he expected 'that's one of the elements and facts that will be on people's minds as they cast their ballots.'[53] Although Turner was officially neutral during the race, it was almost universally believed that he, like most of his staff and friends, supported Paul Martin.

The surrealistic quality of the Liberal convention continued on Friday. Pierre Trudeau signed copies of his newly released book *Towards a Just Society* at an officially sponsored party event. His presence drew more of the party faithful than most of the policy sessions. Lines of delegates trailed around the corner and out of the building, waiting for him to autograph their copies. Coupled with the arrival of Frank McKenna at the convention, almost all of the key Liberal players in the Meech Lake drama had converged on the convention, creating a tense atmosphere in which delegates were more often heard debating the merits of the accord than the various leadership candidates. As well as president Michel Robert, both Don Johnston and John Roberts, the two leading contenders for the party presidency, were known opponents of Meech Lake, although Johnston had been far more active on the file. Sharon Carstairs and Clyde Wells arrived the next day, completing the circle of famous Meech opponents.

During the day on Friday, more delegates were glued to their television sets than the convention proceedings, which included the speeches of the four candidates for the presidency of the party. Like large numbers of Canadians across the country, most Liberal delegates in Calgary watched the demise of the Meech Lake Accord on national television. First Senator Lowell Murray appeared in a special televised address stating that, if the Newfoundland legislature passed the revised deal, he would go to the Supreme Court to attempt to obtain an extension of the 23 June deadline in order to allow Manitoba enough time to approve the accord. Shortly afterwards, MLA Elijah Harper refused once again to give unanimous consent to extend the sitting of the Manitoba legislature, which then adjourned without passing the accord. In Newfoundland, Clyde Wells announced that, as a result of the developments in Manitoba, he would not hold the vote. In Quebec, Premier Bourassa's intergovernmental affairs minister, Gil Rémillard, angrily declared that Quebec had 'had enough' and there would be no extension of the deadline. Later in the afternoon, Murray took to the airwaves once more to declare that Meech Lake was, in fact, dead.

It was in this subdued context that the leadership candidates delivered their final addresses to the convention on Friday evening. Both Tom Wappel and John Nunziata criticized the prime minister's handling of the accord process. Sheila Copps never referred to the accord, although in French she spoke of the importance of Quebec in defining Canada. However, after urging delegates to choose 'freshness and vigour' over the 'status quo,' she called for a 'healing process' within the country and within the party to 'take us to 24 Sussex Drive.' Paul Martin also avoided direct references to Meech Lake, speaking instead of his determination to 'build a new coalition.' In a pointed reference to his chief opponent, he declared: 'Some leaders say we must return to history, but I say there is no turning back.' Martin was the only one of the candidates to refer to the party itself, pledging to continue the work of John Turner.

By contrast, Jean Chrétien tackled the failure of the Meech Lake Accord head on. In a straightforward speech, the Liberal frontrunner said: 'The Canadian people are watching us tonight because they are hungry for leadership they can trust. Canada needs a healer and Brian Mulroney is no healer.' Chrétien returned to his analogy of a car rocking in the snow, and stressed that the failure of Meech 'will not be the end of the world. Afterwards Quebec will still have the same powers it has today.' Arguing that Canada had always come through adversity strengthened and renewed, Chrétien called on Liberals to support him as the man to deliver national unity. 'We have work to do,' he declared repeatedly. 'We will unite this party and we will build back this country.'

His national unity message was crucial to the overwhelming support Chrétien received the next day. In a stunning blow to the Martin forces, Chrétien took the leadership on the first ballot, with 57 per cent of the delegate support and 2,652 votes. Martin finished a distant second, with only 1,176 votes, and Copps ended up a poor third with 499.

The Chrétien slate won a clean sweep of the party offices as well. Don Johnston, the first and most vigorous Liberal opponent of Meech Lake, came in from the cold to become party president. His surprise defeat of John Roberts was attributed by many insiders to his focus on the debt, now considered to be the most serious impediment to Liberal chances in the next federal election. However, many Martin supporters, especially from Quebec, believed his strong opposition to Meech Lake had also been a significant factor. Years later Johnston recalled Trudeau saying that 'obviously the party agreed with your positions.' He himself felt he did not 'return to the fold' but rather 'the fold and I were always on the same wave length.'[54]

The Divisive Victory

After his victory was announced Jean Chrétien made a tour of the convention hall to thank his supporters and greet well-wishers. With the television cameras still rolling he was seen embracing Clyde Wells, the man many Meech supporters considered the architect of the accord's defeat. Both Chrétien and his aides later explained the reason for the friendly exchange was to thank Wells for his support in bringing Newfoundland delegates to the Chrétien camp, but supporters of Meech believed otherwise. Martin supporters in particular were livid that an opponent of Meech had won the leadership of the party so handily. Among them was Liza Frulla, a Quebec provincial Liberal who many years later would become a cabinet minister in Paul Martin's government. 'We were extremely disappointed,' she said of Chrétien's win. 'Furious. Furious. And the hug he gave to Clyde Wells the same night – this was a symbol. A terrible symbol!'[55] Similar concerns were expressed by Francis Fox, a former Liberal cabinet minister who was not only a Martin supporter but the president of the federal party in Quebec. Fox, who more than a decade later would become Martin's principal secretary, said he believed Chrétien would not be able to 'have the same [Trudeau federalist] position 10 months down the road' because 'Quebeckers are looking for a new federalist vision.'[56]

Frulla's comments were hardly the most extreme. Quebec MP Gilles Rocheleau resigned from the Liberal caucus the next day and announced he would sit as an Independent, accusing Chrétien of 'betraying his home province by opposing Meech and secretly plotting against former leader John Turner.' Martin's Quebec campaign chair and former 'Friends of Turner' organizer, MP Jean Lapierre, donned a black armband to mark the death of Meech Lake, as did most of the other Martin supporters. Almost immediately after Chrétien's victory was announced he was seen on national television tearing up his Liberal membership card. 'I would not want to have an association for one minute with that individual who is now the shame of most Quebeckers,' the impetuous MP declared. Lapierre (who years later would become Martin's Quebec lieutenant and cabinet minister) promptly left the Liberal Party as well. But in his case it was to sit with Brian Mulroney's former minister, Lucien Bouchard, as an Independent.[57] Shortly thereafter the two men co-founded the Bloc Québécois and Lapierre sat as a Bloc MP for several years.

What was particularly striking about the Martin camp's reaction to Chrétien's victory was that the most negative responses came from Martin's Quebec supporters even though Martin failed to win delegates in the province. David Herle's assumption that Martin's support for Meech Lake would make him the logical choice of the grassroots membership had been proven wrong. Instead, Chrétien organizer Senator Pietro Rizzuto delivered the 800 Quebec votes he had promised. Fifteen years later, senior Martin adviser Mark Resnick admitted: 'Why Paul Martin, whose views were generally considered to be far more sympathetic to the aspirations of Quebecers than those of Chrétien, was not able to win delegate support in that province is a question which many Martin supporters asked themselves in the wake of that bitter defeat and, indeed, continue to ask themselves to this day.'[58]

Many Martinites believed the answer was rooted in the party's long-standing way of doing business in the province, including the close relationships that had been developed over time and the elitist nature of the organization. A newcomer such as Martin simply could not 'break in' to the old boy system. Liberals opposed to Meech Lake tended to take a different view. Most believed Martin's failure to make inroads in Quebec was precisely *because* of his views on federalism and Quebec, which were well known but not shared by most grassroots Liberals in that province. His views, the Trudeau Liberals maintained, were only popular with the small provincial Liberal elite who, like Bourassa, were also nationalists. In short, it could be argued the Martin forces learned the wrong lesson from their defeat in 1990, a problem which would colour their actions for years to come.

Meanwhile Jean Chrétien's troubles on the constitutional front were far from over. With many disgruntled Martin volunteers vowing not to work for him in the next election, and with Prime Minister

Mulroney vowing that he would launch another constitutional initiative to replace Meech Lake, it was obvious the issue was not dead. That night, at a small private gathering in a luxurious condominium high above downtown Calgary, former prime minister Trudeau found himself among old friends and confidants. Responding to a question from longtime Liberal and Winnipeg media baron Izzy Asper, Trudeau uncharacteristically offered his views on the new Liberal leader. As he confided to the small group around him, he was worried about Jean Chrétien's depth of understanding and commitment to the federalist cause. But, he said, there should be no real problem because Chrétien would surround himself with the right people, as he had done as a cabinet minister. Trudeau recalled that before accepting any new portfolio, Chrétien would ask for time to think about the matter and then come back to him, accepting the post on the condition that he be given a particular individual as his deputy. That individual would invariably be the one considered by his peers the best person to deal with the issues at hand. Trudeau confidently assumed some of the people in the room that night would become part of the new Chrétien PMO, an assumption that would quickly prove unfounded.[59]

Jean Chrétien Takes the Helm

In his acceptance speech at the convention Jean Chrétien described Martin and Copps as 'two superb candidates.' When Paul Martin spoke, he demonstrated equal grace and civility in defeat, telling reporters 'Jean and I are good friends. I can work with Jean.' However, he also took the unusual step of stressing the constitutional divide once again, saying 'I'm sure we will be able to work out our differences of vision.' Then he addressed his supporters directly, declaring 'We have built a new coalition for this party. We have formed friendships, and let me tell you we have formed friendships that are going to last the rest of our lives.'

Immediately after the convention Jean Chrétien followed the long-standing tradition for new leaders. First he met privately with his leadership opponents. Then he met with his entire caucus the next day in Calgary. There he began by trying to downplay his opposition to Meech Lake. He told the caucus he had been 'trapped' and found himself in 'one hell of a situation' after the deal he had attempted to broker fell apart due to Mulroney's pressure tactics and Bourassa's intransigence. Liberals should not be blamed for the death of Meech, he said, since it was Mulroney's project and Mulroney had killed it. Quebeckers would soon see that the Liberal Party, the traditional party of national unity, would ultimately be the one to arrive at a solution to the impasse. The emphasis on Quebec continued with caucus interventions. Senator Pietro Rizzuto, for example, stressed the need to rebuild the party in Quebec and enhance the visibility of the leadership if they were to win seats in the province, first in the upcoming by-elections and then in the next federal election.

Stung by the charge of 'vendu' and media hostility in his home province, Chrétien assured his caucus that he planned to make a major effort to restore his status there in the lead-up to the election, which everyone thought would come sooner rather than later as a result of the Meech failure. Then he specifically referred to Copps and Martin and said he would need their help. He invited them to campaign with him in Quebec over the next six months and asked Martin to take charge of the by-election campaign in Laurier-Ste Marie, the riding left vacant with the passing of Liberal MP Jean-Claude Malépart.

Chrétien's senior organizers engaged in similar peacemaking activities with their counterparts in the Martin and Copps camps. Chrétien adviser Eddie Goldenberg commented, 'Our view is we got 57% of the vote and the only way we can have a successful party is to have 100% of the party with us.'[60] Chrétien would do what was necessary to keep the party together in order to win. As one of his friends declared later, 'he knows you don't have to like someone to work with them. This isn't personal, it's business, the party's business.'

It was an approach that worked well for the most part. Copps's campaign manager, Joe Thornley, declared: 'they are doing a very good job. It's being done very quietly and that's the way it should be done.' He also noted that 'Sheila has indicated to Jean Chrétien that she'll do her best to help him become Prime Minister.' Mike Robinson, Martin's campaign chief, agreed 'there has been a reaching out.' However, in another demonstration of the importance of the constitutional cleavage for the party, he also stated: 'this time is not like other leaderships ... There is the constitutional question and the ability of Mr. Chrétien to forge a position the other candidates and their supporters can live with. That will be the litmus test.'[61]

Not everyone would benefit from Chrétien's conciliatory attitude. There were a number of individuals, such as André Ouellet and Ed Lumley, whom Chrétien believed had let him down in the previous leadership campaign, and others whom he did not trust. As one of his longtime friends confided, 'The loss in 84 was devastating for him, and it left psychological scars.' Others described the new leader as 'less open ... a more defensive and cagey politician.'[62] Simply put, those associated with John Turner, the man whom Chrétien saw as unnecessarily having dragged the party down and left it in chaos, could expect little sympathy. However, some Turner supporters who also had important connections to the Martin camp benefited from the leader's conviction that he needed to ensure the support of leadership opponents. Martin, like Copps, could identify advisers he wanted to see 'rewarded' by being kept on in the system in some capacity. But for those perceived Turnerites who had no such association, the normal rules of reconciliation did not apply regardless of their competence or previous contributions to the party, a precedent that would not serve Chrétien or the party well in the long run.

Chrétien wasted little time in assembling his team in the office of the leader of the opposition. Unlike Turner, Chrétien did not lack candidates. Apart from John Rae and David Zussman, most of Chrétien's supporters saw themselves as prospective employees in the leader's office. In fact, there were more candidates than could reasonably be accommodated, even with the greatly increased funding for the OLO that came with the doubling of his caucus numbers. Also unlike Turner, Chrétien did not feel obliged to find positions in his own office for key staff members of his leadership opponents. Instead, Chrétien used his new position to reward loyalty and to put together a team he knew and trusted. Longtime aide Eddie Goldenberg, who had been with Chrétien since his days as minister of justice, was made chief of staff. Jean Carle, another former staffer who had actually lived with the Chrétiens and was seen by many as a surrogate son, became his executive assistant. Another longtime Chrétien supporter and former editor of the *Toronto Star*, George Radwanski, was hired as his speech writer, and lawyer Warren Kinsella, Chrétien's staunch defender, as Ontario regional adviser.

Changes were also made in critics' portfolios and in the senior leadership of the parliamentary wing. Paul Martin asked for and promptly received the environment portfolio. Sheila Copps was given her first choice as well. And, to ensure caucus solidarity on the right-left spectrum, Chrétien appointed Roy MacLaren, a well-known business Liberal, as his trade critic, balancing that with the appointment of Lloyd Axworthy, the social Liberal who continued to support Turner largely on the basis of his opposition to the FTA, as his foreign affairs critic. Chrétien supporters were placed in key roles in the caucus leadership as well. Sergio Marchi became chair of the Liberal caucus, Alfonso Gagliano was made the whip, and David Dingwall was appointed House leader. Ironically, those MPs hoping for a respite from the Tactics Committee regimen were astonished to see Dingwall take charge and make the operation more efficient but also more demanding. Stopwatch in hand, with an actual bench from the House of Commons placed in the boardroom of the opposition leader's office for them to stand behind as they practised their questions, the Liberal MPs soon realized the new leadership meant business.

The new leader also made it clear he wanted to take control of the party apparatus immediately. Hence the Chrétien slate at the Calgary convention, which ensured he would have that control. His lack of regard for many of the people in the old party executive was apparent immediately. Seeing them not as elected representatives on the extra-parliamentary side but as Turner/Martin partisans, Chrétien made it clear that he had little use for them. Outgoing national policy chair Rodger Schwass, the mild-mannered academic who had laboured for so long and contributed so much to the 1988 platform, recalled going to the first meeting of the new national executive in Calgary along with Red Williams, the Saskatchewan policy chair, and several other members of the outgoing national policy committee. They assumed there would need to be a transition briefing to bring the new executive up to date on the post-election policy process to date. Their arrival, however, was greeted with hostility. Schwass recalled: 'Chrétien simply looked up and told us to get out.' Years later Schwass commented: 'On reflection, after the stress of the leadership battle with Paul Martin, his reaction was actually quite understandable, as we very well *had* been Martin and Turner loyalists, but somehow we had not thought of ourselves as the enemy until then.'[63]

Certainly Chrétien wasted no time appointing people he knew and trusted to key unelected positions throughout the party machinery. But this was not just a matter of trust. As one former national director of the party noted, 'in Chrétien's case this was partly because he thought many of these people were incompetent as well. He just couldn't understand how the party was in such a mess financially or so disorganized. I don't think he realized the extent of the problem they had faced since 1984. He left too soon [in February 1986] to see much of that.' The appointment of Leo Kolber, former bagman for John Turner, to help raise money and the return of Lloyd Posno both reinforced the argument that Chrétien simply wanted the best people for the job.

With media scrutiny still focused on the party's problems with nomi-nations and delegate selection, Chrétien acted quickly, creating a Re-form Commission to try and resolve these challenges. Heavily slanted in favour of reformers, the commission included an entirely new cast of characters. As one member, former Copps chair Joe Thornley, noted: 'It was also a determined effort to reach out to the supporters of defeated leadership contenders and offer them a meaningful role in the party.'[64] With Senator Lorna Marsden and the president of the party's Quebec wing, Pierre Dalphond, serving as co-chairs, other members included former Turner/Martin and Copps supporters such as Rémi Bujold, Zoe Rideout, Gerry Robinson, Barbara Nault, and Jack Graham.

One thing Chrétien took his time about was his return to the House of Commons. Brian Mulroney immediately challenged the new Liberal leader to run in one of the two by-elections scheduled for August, but Chrétien indicated he was in no hurry. Instead, he said publicly that he planned to set his own agenda. 'No one will tell me what to do.' He announced he would spend 'the next six months concentrating on fundraising, appointing a transition team and healing the wounds in the party after the leadership race.'[65]

The logic of Chrétien's plan was inescapable, but the reality of poli-tics intervened. Nearly half of his caucus did not know him, as they had only been elected in 1988 after his departure from the House. Many of them, like many ordinary Canadians, wanted to know whether he still had his political instincts. He spent most of the summer out of the public eye, failing to comment on the Oka crisis, the possible inclusion of Mexico in the FTA, or the government's proposed Goods and Servic-es Tax. Lucien Bouchard and Jean Lapierre announced the creation of the Bloc Québécois in July, and in August, after nearly seventy years of Liberal domination, the party lost the Laurier-Ste Marie by-election to the upstart Bloc. Yet Chrétien remained what journalist Geoffrey Stevens famously termed 'the invisible man.'[66]

Finally in early September Chrétien gave his first press conference since Calgary. In response to a question about the Oka crisis, Chrétien actually prefaced his remarks with the bizarre statement: 'I'm not a lawyer.' Having practised law in Quebec before entering politics and during his time out of office, this remark left journalists nonplussed and many in the party anxious. As Sergio Marchi later recalled: 'First we had Turner come back rusty, and he was finally back in the groove by the time he left. Now here was Chrétien and he was looking pretty rusty as well. You couldn't blame some of them for worrying, especially if they had never seen him at his best, as we [his key supporters] had in the past.'[67]

His erratic performance took its toll. By the fall of 1990, only months after his election as leader of the party, the Liberals had fallen more than 10 per cent in the polls despite the Mulroney government's rock-bottom numbers. With the Conservatives at 18 per cent many Liberals were stunned to find their party with only a slim lead. At 39 per cent, their support was barely ahead of the NDP at 33 per cent, far less than was required to win power, to say nothing of a majority government. A delegation led by House Leader Herb Gray finally convinced Chrétien that he would have to change his plans and run for office sooner rather than later. With the voluntary resignation of Chrétien loyalist and New Brunswick MP Fernand Robichaud, Chrétien had a tailor-made seat available in a by-election to be held on 12 December.[68] Despite this, there was actually concern that he might not win. His early showing as leader was so shaky, his connections to the riding so tenuous, that George Radwanski was sent to the riding the day before the vote with two texts, one in case of a victory and one in the event of a defeat. In the end Chrétien won the riding handily, but his troubles were far from over.

Leadership Woes

Jean Chrétien, like John Turner before him, did not like the role of leader of the Official Opposition. He was uncomfortable with the rhetoric and the hyperbole of Question Period, a problem made more significant by the presence of so many MPs in his caucus who had spent four years perfecting the technique. Although less obsessed with media coverage, they still had not managed to go beyond criticism and demands for resignations. It began to seem as if the Liberals truly did not know how to function as an effective opposition.

The problem was compounded by the policy issues the party was constantly facing. Simply put, they were not Liberal choices or even, in many cases, Liberal issues. Turner had been forced to confront the FTA and Meech Lake. Chrétien was faced with the GST. Urged by his caucus to declare that he would 'scrap' the GST, he reluctantly agreed and, still unelected himself, he announced in the fall of 1990 that the unelected and Liberal-dominated Senate would oppose the legislation. But this was not the FTA, and he could hardly argue the GST would be delayed only until another election. The legitimacy of the procedure was called into question by many observers, while Liberals questioned the political wisdom. Mulroney did not wait and see what would happen. First he filled the fifteen existing vacancies in the Senate. Since this was still not enough to overcome the Liberal majority, he invoked an obscure clause in the constitution that allowed him to appoint an additional eight new senators, all Conservative, thus creating a Conservative majority in the Senate to pass the bill.

Despite valiant efforts by the Liberal leadership in the Senate, the bill passed in early December. Their tactics may have been unpopular, but luckily for the Liberals the GST was even more disliked by average Canadians. According to confidential polling data presented by Mike Kirby to the Senate leadership, more than 75 per cent of Canadians were actively hostile to the new tax.[69] In the end the Liberals would benefit from this hostility.

During his first year as leader Jean Chrétien appeared ill at ease in almost any public event, not simply Question Period. His use of a teleprompter, so reminiscent of Turner's initial reliance on cue cards, added to his evident difficulty. After one disastrous event, Eddie Goldenberg was overheard shouting at George Radwanski: 'Could you possibly have put any more difficult words in that #**%! speech if you tried?!'

Initially Goldenberg believed the solution was to create more tightly scripted events and to work on Chrétien's presentation and appearance. From dental work to English lessons, he was subjected to an intensive 'makeover.' In another strikingly familiar scenario for those who had lived through the Turner era, everyone from Andre Morrow and Gabor Apor to Brian Tobin were called in to help with the leader's 'image problem.' After several months observing his plight from afar, some of Chrétien's closest and oldest confidants, including Henry Wright, Ron Irwin, George Young, and Isabelle Finnerty requested a meeting to discuss his 'disastrous' performance. As George Young later recounted, 'He told us they spent a whole morning learning how to say "the." We told him we had not worked to get him elected so that we could watch him deliver Radwanski's speeches. He needed to be himself. That's what got him elected.'[70] Chrétien received similar advice from Brian Tobin, who by now had assumed the almost full-time role of communications adviser. Like many other politicians who had tried to change their style, Chrétien was clearly more confident – and therefore most effective – when he was himself. No amount of image makeover was going to make a difference. Dispensing with the teleprompter, the elocution lessons, and the assiduously prepared texts would prove to be the first step on the road to recovery.

Still, Chrétien's return to the House of Commons in December was dogged by a number of unfortunate events in his personal life. First, a tumour was removed from his lung, leading many to speculate on the overall state of his health. Not long after, Chrétien and his wife endured a difficult family crisis involving their son Michel, who faced criminal proceedings. Intensely private, the Liberal leader did not discuss these difficulties with his advisers or the media. Whether these events contributed significantly to his problems as leader is a moot point. What quickly became evident after his return to the House was that the new leader, a seasoned political veteran, was unsure of himself on policy matters. His first year saw him lurch from one public relations disaster to another. His response to the Mulroney government's participation in the U.S.-led invasion of Iraq to defend Kuwait was contradictory at best. His initial approach of urging caution and defining a unique Canadian policy was well received, but it quickly degenerated into a confused muddle. In the end he appeared to recommend accompanying the Americans to Iraq but withdrawing immediately if hostilities ensued, a position Mulroney and the media ridiculed mercilessly.

This policy debacle was followed by several others. The worst involved his handling of a hypothetical question on the possibility of future constitutional reform, posed at a press conference in Quebec City where he was trying to repair his and the party's fortunes. Apparently believing that a referendum would have to be held to confirm any negotiated deal – a referendum in which the rest of Canada might conceivably approve a deal while Quebeckers might not – Chrétien declared it was technically possible for a new deal to be accepted without Quebec's consent. This perceived misstep was quickly pounced on by Quebec nationalists. Premier Robert Bourassa, for example, referred to Chrétien's statement as 'political stupidity,' a damaging enough assessment but a predictable one. More surprising were the opening comments of Paul Martin during a special caucus held in the spring of 1991. In a highly revealing demonstration of the genuine division between the two men on the federalism axis, Martin left no doubt as to what he thought about Chrétien's leadership on the national unity file. 'There is a vacuum in Quebec right now,' he declared, 'and we are not filling it.' Like many other caucus interventions, this one was promptly reported to the media, forcing Chrétien to respond. 'We have a party position,' he declared, and it 'will remain the same until I change it.'[71]

There were successes, though, one being the Bélanger-Campeau Commission, established by Robert Bourassa to examine possible constitutional reforms after the failure of Meech Lake. Chrétien's detailed forty-page document echoed the views of Trudeau but added some innovative solutions of his own, including the election and increased regional representation of the Senate, the identification of a number of 'common values' such as bilingualism, multiculturalism, and the protection of human rights, and clarification of Canadian federalism to dispel separatist 'myths.' The document went on to outline minimum conditions and possible options Chrétien would endorse in a future constitutional reform package and emphasized his opposition to an asymmetrical model of federalism. A key point, which he emphasized repeatedly, was his opposition to an overtly asymmetrical model of federalism. As he pointedly noted, apart from considerations of efficiency and harmonization, 'an asymmetrical model would appear to *weaken* Quebec's influence in federal institutions, since Quebec MPs could not be viewed as full participants.'[72]

However, Chrétien's presentation was not widely reported in Quebec. Many in the media were hostile to the new Liberal leader. Well-known writers such as Alain Dubuc and Lise Bissonnette, for example, criticized his fractured French, lack of presence, and likely embarrassment to Canada on the world stage.[73] Equally worrying for Chrétien and his advisers was the fact that both the Copps and Martin camps had not yet dismantled their leadership teams. The once-united natural governing party had fallen into such a mental state of siege that, as one astute observer noted, they were still 'at the ready, should a Chrétien collapse or a caucus coup precipitate another leadership campaign.'[74] Even the *Toronto Star*, a traditional bastion of Liberal support, reported that 'Liberal strategists hope Chrétien will quit.'[75]

The leader was saved by a number of factors which came together at the end of his *annus horribilis*. Among the most important was the forgiving nature of his caucus. Unlike John Turner, who inherited a large component of hostile Trudeau/Chrétien MPs in 1984, Jean Chrétien's caucus consisted of many of his own supporters. They were hardly going to disown the man they had just made leader six months earlier. It also consisted of a large number of MPs who, whether they had supported Turner or not, had lived through the devastating chaos of the 1984–8 period. Most believed the chaos was instrumental in denying them a return to power in the last election and were keen to avoid any signs of internecine warfare.

Another important factor in Jean Chrétien's rehabilitation was the personnel changes he made in his own office. Chrétien did not make the mistake of allowing a bad situation to deteriorate further. And unlike Brian Mulroney he did not take long to recognize that to 'dance with the ones that brung you' does not always work. As he told one of his closest confidants in early 1991, he was concerned from the beginning that some of his initial appointments were a mistake. Yet he felt he had little choice. How could he not reward some of his most faithful supporters? But the past eight months were much worse than expected, and the time spent recovering in Florida from his operation allowed him to put things in perspective.

On his return changes were made quickly. Several OLO officials left in short order, including speechwriter George Radwanski and press secretary Eleanor McMahon. Most important for Chrétien, and most difficult, was his decision to replace Eddie Goldenberg as chief of staff. After nearly a year of institutionalized chaos, Chrétien's long-serving minion, whose lack of people skills was well known, managed to alienate many of Chrétien's closest confidants in caucus. He was summarily replaced by the stately and diplomatic Jean Pelletier, a former mayor of Quebec City, who was known as a consummate manager and a natural fixer. Order was imposed in the OLO. Caucus now had someone with the ear of the leader to confide in. The leader had an adviser of maturity whose judgment on the Quebec file he trusted. Pelletier in effect became the deputy minister Chrétien had always relied on in his ministerial assignments.

Both Pelletier and Chrétien felt it was imperative to locate a more senior person with an equally deft touch to handle the national media. The man selected for the task was Peter Donolo, another former Quebecker who once campaigned for Pierre Trudeau in Montreal's Mount Royal riding and served as the president of the Ontario Young Liberals in the early 1980s. Donolo was a longtime Liberal but had no real connection with the Chrétien camp. After several years in the ad industry, he was working as press secretary to Toronto mayor Art Eggleton when he was approached by Goldenberg to consider taking on the assignment of director of communications in the OLO. Donolo's genial, self-effacing style and ability to handle the press soon made him a crucial player in the repositioning of the Chrétien Liberal opposition. And, although not a member of Chrétien's inner circle, he clearly shared the leader's views on the most important issues. Discussing the constitutional divide in the party more than a decade later, Donolo indicated: 'The pro-Meech people are 20 per cent of the party, a distinct minority.' As he saw it, his job was to help the party recover from the 1990 leadership race, 'the most destructive leadership campaign that a party had experienced in Canada.'[76] It was a job he plunged into with relish.

Meanwhile Goldenberg, who considered leaving the OLO after his demotion, decided to stay on in the position of senior policy adviser. In addition, he assumed de facto responsibility for the Caucus Research Bureau, which subsequently operated as an appendage of OLO. The bureau had been struggling under the direction of an interim director hastily appointed with the departure of his predecessor the year before to manage the leadership forums. He was soon replaced by an old friend of Goldenberg's from Montreal, Chaviva Hosek, a former president of the National Action Committee on the Status of Women. She too arrived in 1991, in time to help with the platform development process Goldenberg would ultimately supervise.

Within months the OLO was completely revamped. From a chaotic group of Chrétien supporters right or wrong, the OLO became an ef-- ficient and professional operation that arguably served as the focal point for Chrétien's ultimate play to take over not only the party but the country.

Strengthening the Party Machinery

While the leadership of the parliamentary wing was putting its house in order, the Liberal Party's extra-parliamentary wing under the presidency of Don Johnston was doing the same. On the one hand, the Reform Commission dealing with the fallout from the 1990 constitutional amendments was working to provide alternatives for adoption at the next convention in 1992. On the other hand, Don Johnston was hard at work trying to improve the party's financial situation.

Building on the initiatives of Michel Robert, Johnston spent tireless months touring the country and raising money to eliminate the party's debt. This was no mean feat, with the party still more than $2 million in debt and more money needed for the upcoming election campaign. By the time the election materialized in 1993, the national office was operating without a deficit and a sizeable campaign war chest had been accumulated. Despite the enhanced fundraising efforts, though, it took the sale of the second floor of the building on Laurier Avenue to bring this situation about.

The party's dream of a permanent national headquarters, launched with such fanfare in 1986, ran into financial and legal difficulties almost immediately. To begin with, there was an ongoing question regarding the party's ownership status; the paperwork relating to the complicated real estate deal was criticized by one former FLAC member as 'inexplicably vague and inconclusive.' There were also increasing condominium fees and other operating costs that proved impossible to sustain. The sale of the second floor, which the party never used, was seen not only as a means of achieving a much-needed infusion of cash in the short term, but as a more realistic option in terms of the long-term plans for the national headquarters.

To prepare for the election campaign Johnston hired Penny Collen-ette, a longtime Chrétien loyalist and former Ontario party staffer who had recently completed her law degree, to serve as the newly created director of legal affairs for the party. In Johnston's view, this position was made necessary by the many recent changes to the electoral laws. Collenette was dispatched to brief provincial chairs, local associations, and various other Liberal groups in the regions on the implications of the new legislation for the party, and also to liaise with the Chief Electoral Officer.

Meanwhile, plans for the upcoming election continued. In a clear-cut demonstration of Chrétien's ability to put the party ahead of personal issues when necessary, he appointed André Ouellet as a campaign co-chair. Ouellet attended weekly meetings with Johnston and other key party officials to discuss strategy and campaign planning. But increasing tension between Ouellet and the party's director of operations and acting national director, Sheila Gervais, led to growing concerns about the viability of the election team. In the end, Gervais left for a position in the private sector and Penny Collenette was asked by Chrétien to fill the void.[77] With the party's organizational plan taking shape, Chrétien turned his attention to his policy agenda. He did not intend to rely on one or two issues, but rather on a general set of principles and values as outlined in a document that became the centrepiece of the campaign, the Red Book.

The Aylmer Conference and the Making of the Liberal Platform

Although the party may have been ready for the next election financially and technically, it was still up to Chrétien and his team to construct an alternative policy agenda Canadians would find appealing. Without this, the Liberal Party could not hope to return to power. As political scientist Jon Pammett demonstrated, the importance of leadership for Canadian voters declined after the departure of Pierre Trudeau. Instead, and despite the Liberals' own emphasis on the leadership issue under Turner, by 1990 the most important factor in determining voter intent was once again the broadly based concept of 'the party as a whole.'[78]

This, of course, was a problem for Chrétien in several respects. He inherited a party that was now split on both the traditional business-social Liberal axis (over the FTA) and on the newer constitutional axis (over Meech Lake). As the meeting of policy-minded Liberals organized by the Grindstone group in Montebello in 1989 demonstrated, the 1988 election did nothing to alter this situation. Meech Lake was front and centre at Montebello once again. Meech opponent and Liberal MP David Berger wasted no time tackling the issue head on. 'Clearly we are not the government. But when Canadians need the leadership of the Liberal Party, when they need to be reassured about our basic values, our caucus has let them down by condoning a vision of Canada which is destructive and divisive by supporting the Meech Lake agreement,' he stated.[79]

Adding to this dilemma was the very real problem that Chrétien himself was not seen as a 'policy man.' His former executive assistant and one of his closest policy advisers, David Zussman, once commented: 'With Chrétien, it was all about values.' The details of various policy options were not of interest to him, but their intent was. Zussman referred to this as 'value-based pragmatism.'[80] His critics referred to it as a lack of ideas or vision.

Eddie Goldenberg's understanding of Chrétien's mindset and his awareness of the policy vacuum is what led to the Aylmer Conference. Held in November 1991, the conference was meant to give Canadians a taste of Liberal thinking on particular policies as well as to position the party as issue-oriented. Unlike the Canada Conferences, Aylmer did not involve the party's national policy committee or indeed any of the party executive except in a belated and peripheral fashion. Consistent with Chrétien's more independent-minded view of the party's extra-parliamentary wing, it was Goldenberg and Zussman who initially determined the topics to be discussed, selected all of the speakers, and organized the various panels. Research Bureau personnel functioned as rapporteurs, while staff from the party's national office organized the conference logistics.

First and foremost, the conference was intended to emphasize policy areas in which Liberals were considered weak. It was also intended to help resolve the split within the party on the left-right spectrum concerning free trade.[81] This split was not as great as it might have first appeared, however, and certainly not as serious as the constitutional divide. Turner argued against the FTA because he believed it was a bad deal, not because he was opposed to free trade per se. Traditionally the Liberal Party favoured the elimination of tariffs. Chrétien too believed the Mulroney FTA was not a good deal, but primarily because it focused only on the United States, while Liberals were inclined to prefer a multilateral approach to trade through the WTO. Yet Turner and Axworthy also stressed the importance of the multilateral approach, as had the party resolution on trade in 1986.

At the conference the economic theme concentrated on the impact of globalization and the need for economic reform to ensure Canada's continued productivity and high standard of living. Among the speakers were Canadian-born international trade adviser Ken Courtis and Bank of Nova Scotia vice-president Peter Nicholson. Both conveyed the same underlying message – that globalization was inevitable and national economies in the West would have to adapt to maintain their competitive edge. Ken Courtis argued 'the key issue Canadian political parties face in the 1990's is how to reconcile the new international realities that we cannot avoid with the values and objectives that are fundamental to us as a society.'[82] Peter Nicholson was less sanguine: 'Today, like it or not, the world is in the thrall of global market forces that cannot be defied by a relatively small, trade-dependent and massively indebted country like Canada. We have nowhere to hide.'[83]

The leader's attempt to minimize internal conflict while moving the party to accept change on the economic front was encapsulated in his closing remarks. 'Protectionism is not left-wing or right-wing,' he said. 'It is simply passé. Globalization is not left-wing or right-wing. It is simply a fact of life.' Not everyone agreed with the new theology. Lloyd Axworthy was heard to protest loudly that 'globalization' was simply a new phrase to justify implementing a right-wing social agenda. Roy MacLaren was heard to crow 'Lloyd Axworthy, eat your heart out.' On the whole, however, the party and the media were impressed with the effort the Liberals made and the issues they addressed. Social Liberals took comfort in another of Chrétien's statements, namely that 'in a world of profound economic and political change, Canada must consolidate its social programs while adapting to radically different economic programs.' He added, 'I believe that Canada's competitive advantage will be found in investing in human capital and in maintaining universal public medicare, safe cities and access to quality education.'[84]

Afterwards, in a move to reinforce Chrétien's image as a man with ideas, the proceedings of the Aylmer Conference were published in book form in early 1992. The book was 'edited' by Chrétien himself. Even the title – *Finding Common Ground* – was chosen to reflect a specific objective. The text contained a foreword by the Liberal leader in which he declared that a key role of an opposition party is not simply to oppose but to 'propose constructive alternatives and to develop a platform which at the appropriate time is put forward to the people.' Aylmer was to be the springboard for the platform process. The leader concluded: 'I am certain that the presentations put forward in this book will help the Liberal Party to develop a program for the 1990's in keeping with the fundamental values and principles it has stood for over the years.'[85]

From Bottom Up to Top Down

The Aylmer Conference was considered by some to be a 'seminal event' in the history of the Liberal Party. Henceforth, the Liberal platform was prepared in a top-down fashion reminiscent of the Trudeau years, rather than the ambitious and expensive approach symbolized by the Canada Conferences. Party officials, including Mark Resnick's replacement, Mary Ann Veit, were dispatched to consult with the former bureau director who supervised the 1988 process. They returned to emphasize the crucial supporting role of the Research Bureau, but ignored the direction and input which came from the platform committee and party resolutions. As one of the bureau's senior researchers involved in both exercises later confided: 'There was absolutely no similarity between the two.'

Most surprising about this development was that the party membership, which less than a decade earlier had declared itself intent on democratizing party operations, made virtually no comment on this return to closed doors. Moreover, conventional wisdom that the extraparliamentary wing was stronger when the party was out of power did not apply in this case. With only eighty-three seats and a shaky image in public opinion, Chrétien nevertheless succeeded in returning the platform exercise to the leader's office. There were clearly advantages to this situation. The platform could be developed by a small group of individuals (whom the leader trusted) rather than a large committee which would inevitably produce too much and in some cases even contradictory material. There was also no need to justify particular planks in terms of their relationship to party resolutions or past policy. And if successful, the product could be seen as putting the leader's personal stamp on the party, as Trudeau had done.

A second anomaly in the 1993 platform process went equally unremarked, namely the widespread perception that Paul Martin and Chaviva Hosek 'wrote' the platform. This in itself was a stark admission of a top-down process. At the same time, it was essentially a public relations myth as the 1993 platform was essentially written by Research Bureau officers as it had been in 1988. However, in 1988 the public attribution of authorship was given to a party platform committee which had, in fact, directed and supervised the exercise. In 1993, authorship was publicly attributed to two platform co-chairs alone, and more extraordinarily, those chairs were not members of the party executive but a caucus member and a senior staffer. Paul Martin – who had asked to be involved in the platform development process – was appointed by Chrétien primarily to ensure the ongoing support of his former leadership opponent, although Martin also consulted widely with his caucus colleagues, a process which endeared him to many of them and, as Donolo later noted, kept many MPs occupied. Martin's official co-author, Chaviva Hosek, the new director of the Research Bureau, was seen as someone who would lend public credibility to the exercise by virtue of her social activism, counterbalancing Martin's business credentials.

Given Chrétien's insistence that 'I'm the leader. I make the decisions,' it was hardly surprising that the platform exercise was very much a top-down one. Martin and Hosek went across the country to 'consult widely' with civil society, experts, and selected grassroots members of the party while bureau researchers prepared the actual documents that Hosek and Martin reviewed. But, after the co-chair's input – which according to Hosek included considerable disagreement between the two ('I want a divorce from him and we're not even married')[86] – they were all submitted to Eddie Goldenberg for approval. Frequently they were returned for rewriting or with major modifications made by Goldenberg himself, reflecting his understanding of Chrétien's objectives.[87] On certain issues the leader directly intervened, such as a commitment on deficit reduction that Martin wanted included but that Chrétien ultimately rejected out of fear it would be too disruptive. Chrétien was inclined to balance the urgency of deficit reduction with the need to reduce unemployment and, ultimately, demonstrate that government could still be a force for good. He was also constrained by his desire to ensure that any promises made would be kept. As a result, Martin's plan for a specific target number was replaced with a pledge to move to a deficit that would represent 3 per cent of GDP by the third year of a Liberal mandate, an approach borrowed from the European Union's plan for monetary union.

Once the material received Goldenberg and Chrétien's approval, it was forwarded to Toronto to be edited and 'massaged' by Martin supporter John Duffy, a move many saw as an effort to placate Martin by allowing him to reward a loyalist. However, much of Duffy's work, which contained what one senior LCRB researcher referred to as 'several flagrant attempts to change the direction or intent of platform planks,' was subsequently and quietly undone by Research Bureau officers or Goldenberg.

There were unquestionably benefits to this top-down platform process. Not only were far fewer people involved in the platform's creation, making for a more coherent approach, but, even more important, there was more money and expertise available to develop this second Red Book. This allowed for a more comprehensive set of explanations with expanded documentation. With the disastrous 1988 childcare announcement presumably uppermost in their minds, the 1993 drafters also ensured the last two pages of their platform document contained a detailed explanation of the costing and revenue sources to pay for the various planks. This material was developed by Patrick Grady, a former Finance bureaucrat and business partner of Dr David Husband, the man who costed the 1988 platform and one-time director of the LCRB.

At the end of the day, the product of this internal effort proved a brilliant success. Entitled 'Creating Opportunity: The Liberal Plan for Canada,' the bright red pamphlet was a larger and more refined version of the original 1988 document. Instead of numbered planks, it contained five major themes under the headings of Jobs, Growth, Change, Health, and Independence. Under each theme a number of commitments were made with the preface 'A Liberal government will.' They totalled twenty-seven in all, considerably less than the forty planks of the 1988 version. The broadly distributed document was on larger pages than the 1988 version, and as a result, though still only ten pages long, was able to communicate far more information. Sidebars contained facts and figures to bolster the arguments used in the main text. Even more detail was provided in the special 112-page version compiled for Liberal candidates and the media. In the 1988 campaign this detailed supporting material was included only in the background documents for the media, not in a second book.[88]

A message from Chrétien at the end of the short document emphasized yet again that he and his party had alternative ideas to propose to Canadians, not merely criticism of the current government. 'We in the Liberal Party want to bring those priorities to Ottawa,' he wrote, 'and we have the plan to do it.' Chrétien's message also stressed fiscal prudence. 'It is a balanced, realistic plan, with concrete goals, not empty promises. It is an economically responsible plan that will actually reduce the deficit.'

The Liberal platform played a crucial role in Jean Chrétien's overwhelming 1993 victory. And with success came another popular myth, namely that this platform was an entirely new innovation – the first, rather than the second, Red Book. Yet as Stephen Clarkson observed, even the content of the 1993 Red Book closely resembled the 1988 version. It also reflected many of the themes that were promoted 'in the 1960's and 70's by the Pearson/Trudeau party in its more generous moments.'[89] Years later a resigned Turner supporter pointed out the obvious. 'They won. We lost.'

The Second Constitutional Crisis

One of the subjects which the Aylmer Conference and the platform deliberately ignored was the constitution. As the Spicer Commission demonstrated, Canadians did not want to discuss the matter further. However, under Premier Robert Bourassa a parallel consultation process took place in Quebec. In late 1990, the premier established a Liberal Party committee on the constitution, apparently believing it was politically necessary to respond to the growing separatist rhetoric in that province. The Allaire Committee produced an unexpectedly aggressive report in January 1991. Not happy with that response, Bourassa then created an all-party public inquiry, the Bélanger-Campeau Commission, which tabled its own, more moderate report at the end of March 1991. However, this second report contained an unexpected recommendation as well. It called for a provincial referendum on sovereignty if the federal government did not come forward with an acceptable replacement package for Meech Lake within a year. Bourassa decided he could not ignore the thrust of the recommendations. In another ill-advised decision, he announced he would table referendum legislation that would trigger a vote by 26 October 1992 if the federal government did not respond.

This move sparked an equally alarmist response in Ottawa, where Prime Minister Mulroney declared he was creating an extraordinary 'national unity' cabinet which, despite the name, simply involved a shuffle and the announcement that former prime minister Joe Clark would become the minister for intergovernmental affairs and chief negotiator for the government. In May 1991, the Throne Speech announced a 'national reconciliation' agenda that proposed developing a new constitutional reform package and, if necessary, legislation for conducting a national referendum.

By the fall of 1991 a draft proposal for constitutional reform was tabled in the House of Commons. An all-party special joint committee (Beaudoin-Dobbie) was established to tour the country to consult. In the end the Liberals tabled a series of amendments to the government's proposed package, some of which were accepted. When the committee finally tabled its report in February 1992, it was with all party approval. It was also at this point that Brian Mulroney, sensing a successful resolution to the constitutional impasse was possible, indicated there would be no federal election in 1992. The election would not be held until 1993, an unusual move that would extend the government's mandate to the constitutional maximum of five years.

With some of their amendments accepted and all-party agreement reached on the Beaudoin-Dobbie report, many Liberals felt free to criticize the government's proposed referendum legislation, and it provoked vigorous internal debates. On 20 May André Ouellet, their point man on the referendum legislation, outlined some twelve specific proposals for change to the draft legislation in a presentation to national caucus. A heated discussion ensued, in which many intervenors stressed the importance of not appearing to block the process. Others urged caution in supporting it, lest they appear to be co-opted by the government. Rookie Manitoba MP John Harvard made an impassioned intervention in which he first argued that it was essential to insist on a double majority for a referendum vote to be successful. Then he recommended communicating this position to Canadians, 'telling them how strongly we feel about it.' He also argued 'we should be ready to vote against the bill and we should not let the Tories spook us.' Herb Gray expressed concerns about the financing provisions and donations from foreign companies, while Sheila Copps and Brian Tobin worried that financing both sides of the debate could produce a situation in which federal money appeared to be funding separatists.

In all cases the concern with the bill's substance was accompanied by a concern about their party's prospects in the next election. Several MPs feared they would be 'sidelined' by the NDP if they did not oppose specific provisions of the legislation. But in his closing remarks to the caucus Jean Chrétien emphasized that Liberals not only proposed the idea of a referendum in 1980, but he personally forced Joe Clark to come through with legislation at this time. As a result they could hardly oppose it now, although they could try to make improvements. In addition, he said, it would be far better for the people to decide the fate of Mulroney's constitutional proposal than the politicians. 'We will set a precedent,' he said. 'The constitution will be in the hands of the people and not of the premiers.'

When Conservative House leader Harvie Andre tabled Bill C-81 in the House four days later, his choice of words betrayed the government's own discomfort with the legislation, which was strongly opposed by the Conservatives' Quebec caucus. He stressed: 'This legislation is a precautionary measure. No more and no less. This legislation would enable the federal government to hold a referendum on Canada's future should such a step be required.'[90] Even more revealing was the absence of detail about the nature of the question or the definition of a victory. During debate on the bill Liberal House leader and Chrétien supporter David Dingwall raised numerous objections to the legislation, as did fellow MPs Sergio Marchi and Charles Caccia. The government rejected many of the changes they proposed, but some were accepted.

Up to this point it appeared the Mulroney government had learned a lesson from its failure to consult or modify its position during the Meech Lake process. It had set up a committee, listened to the concerns of opposition parties, and made changes to its proposal. Then in March 1992 the process moved to the next stage, namely negotiations with the premiers. Incredibly, this again was a closed-door operation like Meech Lake. It was here that things once again began to fall apart as the government lost sight of the need for compromise and consultation in its desire to achieve a deal. There were two pressing reasons for haste. The first was the Quebec government's fast-approaching referendum deadline of 26 October. The second was Premier Bourassa's refusal to attend the negotiations between Mulroney and the nine other premiers until they agreed on a deal to offer him. This absurd situation resulted in another series of last-ditch efforts throughout the summer which culminated in a tentative deal. Bourassa then 'consented' to attend sessions, which led to an eleventh-hour agreement signed with Meech-like fervour in Charlottetown on 28 August 1992.[91]

For the Liberals this was a worst-case scenario. Having supported the government's efforts on Beaudoin-Dobbie and the referendum legislation, they now found themselves forced to approve or reject a deal which bore little or no resemblance to Beaudoin-Dobbie. Instead, as had been the case with Meech Lake, Mulroney ended up agreeing to numerous peripheral but significant requests by premiers in order to forge a unanimous agreement. This time, however, the sheer magnitude of the deal was astonishing. Nearly one-third of the constitution would be impacted by the proposed changes, including everything from Senate reform and eliminating the federal disallowance power to a new amending formula, a revised version of the distinct society clause, and changes to provincial representation in the House of Commons. Everyone familiar with the Meech Lake provisions could see that only marginal improvements had been made to the most offensive sections of that earlier deal while a number of new problems were contained in this deal. Simply put, it was 'Meech Plus' in more ways than one. Despite the cosmetic changes, most critics believed the accord would lead to an even more decentralized federation in which national minimum standards for social programs would quickly disappear. It would also call into question the authority of the Charter by virtue of the new and improved distinct society clause.

The Charlottetown Accord and the Referendum Conundrum

Nonplussed, the Liberal caucus met in Ottawa on 8 September to discuss the deal and plan their strategy before the return of Parliament the following day. Several MPs, primarily Chrétien supporters, raised serious concerns. They also noted a legal document was not yet available. With the federal referendum vote scheduled for 26 October in order to mesh with the Quebec referendum date, barely six weeks were available for debate and for Canadians to make up their minds. Senator Allan MacEachen reported that there were 'deep divisions' within the Liberal Senate caucus. He urged caution, saying 'there must be room for legitimate dissent.'

History repeated itself with the leader's remarks at the end of the session. Jean Chrétien, like John Turner, began by noting 'if we had been the government we would not have (made) this deal.' Then he suggested the real question to be asked in the referendum was whether Canadians wanted this deal or to lose Quebec. Most important, he underlined, was the absolute necessity of keeping any divisions within the caucus and not in the public eye. Not only the future of the country but of the Liberal Party was at stake, he said.

The following day a debate began in the House on the proposed referendum question, which the government had hastily drawn up. It read *'Do you agree that the constitution of Canada should be renewed on the basis of the agreement reached on August 28, 1992? Yes or No?'* The official spokespersons for the three parties devoted little time to the question, and instead focused on the merits of the accord. The only Liberal to speak against the question was the former Trudeau minister and Chrétien supporter Charles Caccia, who raised a number of technical points about the referendum question before zeroing in on the key flaw in the process used by the government to achieve the agreement, namely that it had only consulted widely *before* arriving at the deal. Now that the Charlottetown Accord had been agreed to, the prime minister had returned to his old ways. There would be no public hearings or consultations, and very probably no legal text in time to be analysed before the referendum vote. Instead, Brian Mulroney had 'rolled the dice' one more time and accused anyone who disagreed with him of being 'an enemy of Canada.'[92]

Despite this, Chrétien apparently believed there was little choice but to support the accord. On 16 September he told his caucus he believed the deal must pass to save the country. In addition he argued that much in the accord was similar to what he had suggested in his submission to the Bélanger-Campeau Commission. He reiterated that the deal was now in the hands of the people and they would decide. He also indicated a number of senior Tories had told him they believed the referendum might fail. Asked in a caucus meeting on 30 September about Mr Trudeau's public opposition to the accord (Trudeau wrote an article opposing the deal in *Maclean's* magazine), Chrétien replied that as a minister he had always supported the prime minister in the past, but 'that was then and this is now.' Now he was leader, and he was going to make his own decisions. Nevertheless, no doubt recognizing the weight of Trudeau's opinion within the party, he urged everyone to respect Trudeau's position and refrain from criticizing it.

Finally, and most revealing about his determination to form a government, Chrétien concluded 'I can run the country with this constitution next year when I am Prime Minister.' In short, Chrétien took much the same tack that John Turner had taken with Meech Lake. But his justification was different. He did not believe in the underlying principles of the deal, including more decentralization. In fact, he disliked the Charlottetown Accord on several levels, but he felt that the failure of Meech Lake and Mulroney's mishandling of the whole issue left him with little choice but to acquiesce for the future of the country. Perhaps most important, he believed the referendum made the situation entirely different from the one faced by Turner on Meech Lake since it gave the last word to Canadians.

Politically, Chrétien also felt his tacit support for the deal might help to revive the Liberal's electoral fortunes in Quebec. This last point was crucial to Liberal thinking at the time and heavily influenced him in light of his own self-doubts after the defeat of Meech Lake made him a figure of widespread scorn in the province. In virtually every one of their special summer meetings the Liberal caucus was given presentations by their election readiness group, including Gordon Ashworth and the interim national director, Sheila Gervais. Although by now it was known the federal election would be delayed until 1993, everyone was geared up for the next vote and sensed that the Conservatives were on borrowed time. Almost as many caucus interventions concerning the Charlottetown Accord focused on its possible impact on Liberal electoral fortunes as on the contents of the deal. Senator Pietro Rizzuto made this point graphically at the 16 September caucus when he asserted, without evidence, that '60 per cent in Quebec are getting ready to vote YES and also to vote Liberal. Various polls show that 90 per cent of Liberals across Canada are planning to vote YES. We should keep these numbers in mind.'[93]

Nevertheless there were many MPs and senators who were uncomfortable with the deal and said so within the confines of caucus. Most were Chrétien supporters, and virtually all of them had opposed Meech Lake. In an ironic twist, this was one of the factors which saved Jean Chrétien from a repetition of John Turner's fate. Chrétien's own supporters would ultimately follow his lead despite their misgivings, particularly after the disastrous caucus split on Meech Lake. And Paul Martin's supporters – both those who had been in caucus under Turner and supported Meech Lake and those new MPs who had arrived in Ottawa in 1988 as Turner acolytes – actually *supported* the deal wholeheartedly. Another huge advantage for Chrétien was that he did not have to maintain caucus unity over a long period of time while debate raged in the House of Commons. Once the referendum question was adopted on 10 September, Brian Mulroney peremptorily adjourned Parliament until after the 26 October referendum vote. Last, but hardly least, Chrétien threatened any MP who publicly opposed the deal with expulsion from the Liberal caucus, a move Turner had never seriously considered.

In the end, most caucus members were simply unwilling to engage in a highly public battle as they had done on Meech Lake. Many also believed the stakes were higher this time and the future of the country might actually be at stake due to Mulroney's mismanagement of the file. The rift between the two groups of MPs in the caucus remained and even deepened, but this time they were not made public. Some Liberal MPs worked hard to secure a YES vote. Many more remained on the sidelines, and some, such as Charles Caccia, skirted Chrétien's directive by holding 'information sessions' in their ridings which patently favoured the NO side. Others, such as Sheila Finestone, were even more overt in their opposition to the deal, but no action was taken against them.

Although Chrétien agreed to speak in favour of the Charlottetown Accord at a few public events, he was rarely called on. He became the invisible party leader in the campaign Brian Mulroney called a 'crusade' to 'save' Canada.[94] While the other party leaders as well as all of the provincial premiers and the heads of most important national interest groups were campaigning vocally for a win, Chrétien was conspicuous by his absence.

This proved a clever political strategy. Over the course of the next several weeks it became clear the Tories were fumbling the ball and Brian Mulroney was making the situation worse by the minute. In one truly appalling display, Mulroney ripped up a copy of the Charter of Rights at a rally in Sherbrooke, arguing it would be worthless if the accord failed. Shortly thereafter pollster Angus Reid reported his most recent survey found the prime minister 'has emerged as the second most important figure nationally, but he has done so by unintentionally helping the NO side.'[95] As Reid also noted, by far the most influential figure in the campaign was Pierre Trudeau, who delivered the fatal blow to the accord when he spoke out at the famous 'Maison Eggroll' dinner in Montreal on 1 October. With few notes and an understated, almost academic delivery, he gave a virtuoso performance dissecting and ridiculing the deal's many provisions. Although it was only one intervention, delivered entirely in French, it was widely reported in virtually all English-language newspapers the next day. Within days public opinion polls showed a dramatic decline in support for the accord across the country. When the results of the referendum came in the night of 26 October, Canadians had delivered a resounding NO to the accord. Jeffrey Simpson's column the next day succinctly concluded 'The Trudeau Vision Triumphed.'[96]

Yet none of this damaged Chrétien or the Liberals. Both the accord and the referendum were seen as Mulroney initiatives just as Chrétien predicted. What also became crystal clear after the vote was that Brian Mulroney was finished as leader of the Conservative Party. Before a federal election could be held, the Conservatives would have to hold a leadership convention of their own. Even then, it looked like they were hopelessly out of the running. The Liberals, it seemed, were about to come in from the cold.

7 Return to Power: The 1993 Election

> The Liberals are back in power, with a majority government, as they have been for most of this century.
>
> – Political scientist Jon Pammett[1]

The Charlottetown Accord may have delayed the election but it could not prevent the inevitable. In fact the referendum defeat ensured Brian Mulroney would step aside as leader of the Conservative Party. Despite the problems Jean Chrétien was having as leader of the Official Opposition, the Conservatives remained mired at an all-time low in public opinion and Mulroney himself was deeply unpopular.

The country was in a deep-seated depression. Not only had the accord been roundly rejected by voters, but much of Mulroney's inflammatory rhetoric had been dismissed as the boy who cried wolf once too often. To top it all off, the economy was faltering. Unemployment was rampant, ensuring that job creation would be an essential issue in the upcoming election. The Conservatives had promised jobs in 1984 and failed to deliver. They had also promised to deal with the deficit, but ended up increasing it during their time in office. With Canadians profoundly discontented and his party badly divided, Mulroney had no choice but to put in motion the plans for a leadership convention. The party's eventual choice of Kim Campbell, a rookie cabinet minister from British Columbia, appeared at first blush to be inspired. She was a fresh face with little attachment to the Mulroney era, a potential symbol of a new start. As a westerner, many Conservatives thought she would overcome the threat posed by the upstart Reform Party. Many also thought that, as the first female prime minister, Campbell might win votes away from the Liberal Party. Campbell was a generation younger than her Liberal counterpart, and Conservative organizers hoped she would be able to capitalize on Chrétien's negative image as 'yesterday's man.'

Kim Campbell's political fortunes rose dramatically in a short time. She appeared decisive and forward-looking. Her promise to 'do politics differently' appealed to voters. Opinion polls showed Campbell running well ahead of her party, and then the party itself began to creep back up, hovering around 31 per cent at the start of the campaign while the Liberals remained stalled at 37 per cent. Some Liberal insiders worried the election was no longer a sure thing. As Peter Donolo later recounted: 'Some of my colleagues began to ask themselves whether we were in a contest with the new Trudeau and our man was Robert Stanfield.'[2] Chrétien himself remained self-conscious and tentative. Although he had abandoned the teleprompter he was still hounded by the Quebec press for his unsophisticated French and in the English press for his mangled verbiage.

A small group of Liberal MPs – most of whom were known Martin supporters – became sufficiently anxious that they aired their concerns publicly, leading Chrétien to step up plans for a pre-election tour, which he hoped would enhance his image as a vigorous and forward-looking leader. It was an image the party tried to emphasize, releasing photos of Chrétien playing sports and dressed in a more casual manner than that normally expected of politicians, hoping to appeal to ordinary Canadians.

After the demise of the Charlottetown Accord, Chrétien began to gather steam in the House of Commons as well as with the public. With the caucus and the party now focusing exclusively on the upcoming election, the plan to concentrate on the Mulroney government's disastrous economic record began to pay off. Chrétien's confidence also grew as the people who had been with him during the leadership race began to master their roles in the party organization. It was clear to everyone, not just the leader, that the party's election machinery was in a high state of readiness.

The Liberal Election Organization

In selecting his national campaign co-chairs, Chrétien demonstrated his ability to put aside personal feelings. Despite her yeoman's service during the Turner years, Senator Joyce Fairbairn was named campaign co-chair, reprising her 1984 role as lead spokesperson on the campaign plane. Joining her was André Ouellet, a man with whom Chrétien had barely spoken since 1984. Chrétien knew he needed to take seats in Quebec if he was to win a majority. Ouellet's combination of competence and ruthlessness was exactly what he needed in Quebec, where his image had been damaged by the Meech debacle.

With one exception, the provincial campaign chairs were all strong Chrétien loyalists, from George Furey in Newfoundland and Willie Moore in Nova Scotia to Pat Gleeson in Alberta and Ross Fitzpatrick in BC. The exception was Ontario, where David Collenette convinced Chrétien to use the services of David Smith, the short-lived former Turner minister who, like Ouellet, had cultivated contacts in the Chrétien camp as well.

The most important volunteer job in the election campaign fell to someone who did not like titles, but whose authority everyone recognized. John Rae, Chrétien's first ministerial assistant and closest non-political adviser, took a leave of absence from his private-sector job and returned to the fray once more to assume a unique position in the campaign structure, a position described as national campaign coordinator. Whatever the title, Rae would come to be seen as the man in charge of the 1993 campaign as well as every subsequent election while Jean Chrétien was party leader.

At party headquarters, National Director Penny Collenette was joined by a former colleague at the Ontario party office, Gordon Ashworth, whom Chrétien appointed as national campaign director. Ashworth had filled the same post in the 1979 and 1980 Trudeau campaigns and reprised the role in the latter part of the 1984 campaign after the return of Keith Davey. He worked closely with John Rae, to whom he essentially reported and spoke with at least twice a day. As he later admitted, the 1993 campaign was particularly challenging because 'there was either no or very little organization on the ground. I spent most of 1991 travelling across the country attempting to establish an organization in each of the regions and provinces.'[3]

While Ashworth chaired the election readiness sessions in the boardroom of 200 Laurier, Collenette was fully occupied with candidate recruitment issues. She later recalled that one of her most significant challenges was ensuring all 295 Liberal candidates were duly registered with the chief electoral officer. This supposedly simple task proved highly stressful when she learned, less than a week before the deadline, that more than forty candidates were not properly registered. In addition to the paperwork of the election campaign, Collenete's staff continued the tradition of a party-based election hotline for candidates and worked closely with the Research Bureau staff, who manned the policy hotline.

One new feature of the 1993 Liberal campaign was the 'Task Force,' a concept borrowed directly from the Clinton Democratic campaign run by the legendary James Carville. In Ottawa, the Liberals' team was run by Senator Roméo LeBlanc, a former Trudeau press secretary and long-time Chrétien loyalist who would eventually become governor general. Working with him were a number of very junior but enthusiastic Liberal staffers from ministers' and MPs' offices, including Bruce Hartley of Herb Gray's office, Randy McCauley from Senator Michael Kirby's office, Marc Laframboise of the LCRB, and Warren Kinsella from OLO. The plan was to have a 'rapid response' team that would follow the actions of the other parties and devise critical lines or responses to highlight opposition gaffes. As Warren Kinsella later commented, these became so frequent that staff members were obliged to develop a short-hand signal system to communicate which of the many faux pas were sufficiently serious to warrant a response from the Liberal leader.

Eddie Goldenberg and Peter Donolo were along to provide policy and communications advice while Kevin Shea served as Chrétien's speechwriter. Another significant position was held by Martin supporter Terrie O'Leary, who served as wagonmaster on the campaign plane. Once again the tour was extremely well organized. But with considerably more funding than 1988, the leader's tour was able to cover more of the country more often. In the final weeks, it was even possible to return to areas where it was considered necessary to shore up support, a luxury not possible in the previous election, when the party was struggling to avoid further debt.

Selecting the Liberal Team: Chrétien's Dilemma

Jean Chrétien made it clear from the beginning that he did not want a repeat of the nomination scandals that plagued the Turner Liberals. As one who had not embraced the democratization of the party, it came as no surprise that Chrétien intended to take control of candidate recruitment as well. Yet many in the party were shocked that the leader was making a concerted effort to impose his will.

The work of the Reform Commission appointed by Chrétien eventually tabled one hundred proposed amendments for consideration at the 1992 biennial convention, the last one before the next federal election. Unlike 1990, when the constitutional session had failed to attract a quorum, the debate in 1992 on many of the amendments was intense. The Commission members were not expecting the degree of opposition they met with at the convention, especially regarding leadership races.[4] However, another group led by longtime members from Ontario, including constitutional expert Jack Siegel, proved equally determined to implement the procedural formula they had adopted in Ontario. Debate carried on for so long that the session was forced to rush through a number of votes in order to complete its work before the end of the time allocated. As a result, conflicting resolutions were once again adopted.

By contrast, there was no confusion about candidate selection. In an obvious effort to ensure ultimate control by the leader as the best way to avoid another media circus, 'the party chose to move virtually the entire setting of parameters for, and administration of, nominations from the constitution to the "rules" which would be developed under the auspices of national and provincial/territorial campaign committees, headed by individuals appointed by the Leader.'[5]

Chrétien also pushed for and succeeded in obtaining what essentially constituted *authority for the leader to nominate candidates*. In the past, a Liberal leader in rare cases could refuse to sign a candidate's nomination papers *after the fact* (that is, after someone the leader deemed inappropriate had been nominated). As a result of the 1992 rule, Chrétien obtained the right to inform riding associations in advance, through the National Campaign Committee, that he personally would be appointing a candidate. According to Jack Siegel, 'the intent to use [the new rule] to permit appointments was well recognized by one and all.' It was also not precedent-setting. The Quebec wing of the party had adopted the rule several years earlier, a point Gordon Ashworth made at an Ontario campaign meeting. Siegel himself was among those supporting the additional rule at the 1992 convention, as was MP Brian Tobin.[6]

Among the most vocal opponents of the proposed rule at the convention was former Trudeau-era minister John Munro. Like his former colleague and presidential candidate John Roberts, Munro had been actively discouraged by the OLO from putting forward his candidacy in his old riding. He was instrumental in forming a protest group called 'Liberals for Democracy' which attracted a number of pro-democracy caucus members including John Nunziata. Another opponent was well-known Toronto-area organizer Styli Pappas, who distributed leaflets at the convention decrying the proposal as a 'power grab' by the leadership. Several delegates recalled Brian Tobin following along after Pappas and collecting up his leaflets, telling them to 'ignore that guy who gave these out.'

There were three stated reasons for the introduction of the new rule. The first was to curtail the number of messy nomination battles. By appointing someone in 'vulnerable' ridings the leader could preclude the possibility of ethnic or single issue groups such as the anti-abortion movement taking control of an association and then obtaining the nomination. As national director Gordon Ashworth later commented, it was frequently not necessary to actually use the provision, since the fact of its existence was often sufficient to deter certain individuals from putting their name forward.[7]

The second reason for the new rule was also the principal reason why many within the party supported it. The leader's new authority could be used as a form of affirmative action, to promote the greater participation of women, ethnic groups, and other minorities. Given the Liberal tradition of protecting sitting MPs, it would normally be extremely difficult to increase the representation of such groups when the party was in power. However, with only eighty-three held ridings, the next election provided an obvious opportunity for the party – and the leader – to make a difference. This action was seen as increasingly important because nomination contests, especially in ridings likely to be won by the party, were becoming more expensive than the election campaigns that followed.

Like the other mainstream parties, the Liberals had established a special fund to provide financial support for Liberal women candidates (the Judy LaMarsh Fund), but this fund could not be used for nomination battles. The result was that many women and representatives of ethnic groups were effectively prevented from seeking a nomination due to lack of resources. In preparation for the 1993 campaign, therefore, a group of Liberal women chaired by Sheila Copps launched the 'Judy Campaign' to recruit women candidates. As one of the key participants, Isabelle Metcalfe, later recalled, it was an innovation firmly supported by the leader and one that produced results. 'We had more women candidates and more women MPs as a result, than we would ever have had otherwise,' she stated, 'and Mr. Chrétien was very, very supportive of our efforts.'[8]

Ironically this second purpose was the one most vigorously opposed by some other members of the party, who argued that if a political party was not democratic how could one expect citizens to believe the rest of the system was. It was a classic conflict of interest between those who wanted to democratize the party – to increase its bottom-up decision making – and those who wanted to enhance participation – to broaden its base and increase representativeness.

A third rationale for the new rule was to allow the leader to appoint 'star' candidates. Here again, however, the pro-democracy forces argued a top-down appointments process would be not only offensive but counterproductive, citing the Coutts fiasco. Chrétien argued he needed highly qualified candidates to demonstrate he had cabinet material, something Turner had lacked, and without the ability to appoint this would not happen. Desirable candidates simply would not agree to stand for the party if they were obliged to go through a messy and controversial nomination process, the result of which was uncertain.

Appointing candidates in selected ridings, he argued, would overcome all three problems. As Jean Chrétien told his caucus on 28 October 1992, if he did not intervene then few women would win Liberal nominations anywhere in the country. He also informed them that some MPs who were not seeking re-election, such as Bob Kaplan, had already authorized him to use their ridings for these purposes. In addition, some Liberal riding association executives had approached the party about the possibility of using this provision, as they anticipated a difficult nomination situation or had no particular candidate in mind.

In the end Chrétien used the provision to appoint fourteen candidates in 1993, nine of whom were women, including Jean Augustine in Toronto.[9] As Equal Voice chair Rosemary Speirs pointed out, had the Liberal leader not intervened in 1993 there would have been no Liberal women candidates in the entire metro Toronto region. There were also several high-profile candidates appointed, including Doug Peters, Art Eggleton, Marcel Masse, Allan Rock, and Bob Blair. Almost all of the leader's appointees won their riding and many quickly were taken into the cabinet. After the 1993 election the women's Liberal caucus was the largest in history, with thirty-six MPs representing 20 per cent of the total.[10]

Nevertheless many grassroots party members were unhappy with the new rule. Familiar arguments about the need for riding-level autonomy were raised, as well as new concerns about the danger of the leader appointing friends and supporters. Ontario MP Don Boudria, who would later become a minister in Chrétien's cabinet, was one of those who felt the intent of the rule had not been to include such appointments. 'The need to ensure the Leader had the tools to override single issue candidates and narrow interests in favour of the broader viewpoint was clear,' Boudria argued. 'But after that it was the thin edge of the wedge. Yes, there were nine women appointed in 1984, but there were also five men. Do we overlook them just because of the women?'[11]

The case of Marcel Masse in particular caused concern for many of the pro-democracy members, since his appointment was only obtained after the leader cancelled a scheduled nomination meeting at which another candidate would have been acclaimed. Chrétien argued that Masse, having been persuaded to run for the Liberals and already having resigned from his job as the head of the public service, could not be allowed to lose a nomination race.

Meanwhile, ordinary Canadians were inclined to perceive the leader's interventions as unnecessary and undemocratic. This was particularly frustrating for senior Liberal organizers, who had seen the public's equally negative reaction to the Turner era's many brutal nomination battles. They knew, as Brian Mulroney himself once said, that 'no one will vote for a party that can't run itself.' In short, it appeared the party would be criticized whichever route it decided to take, and Chrétien did not hesitate to make the appointments. As he told Hec Cloutier, a party activist in Renfrew who wanted to challenge the sitting Liberal MP, Len Hopkins, it might be possible for Cloutier to win but he would not have the chance to prove it. 'I am the boss. I have the right to make this decision. I have an agenda for the country. I want to be Prime Minister and do great things, and I've got to put people in place who I know can win.' Hopkins had won eight times for the party, and Chrétien was not about to let him lose in a nomination battle that might cost the party the seat. Period.[12]

Resentment about appointments was arguably greatest in western Canada, where the Liberals were also weakest. At least one female candidate actually insisted she *not* be appointed because it would ruin whatever chance she had of winning the riding. Yet hard-fought contests between two potential candidates also caused more difficulties for the party, in some cases because of the extended Chrétien-Martin battle. One memorable contest occurred in Regina, where Chrétien supporter and well-known local lawyer Tony Merchant, the expected winner, was narrowly defeated by Martin supporter Ralph Goodale in a marathon match orchestrated by none other than David Herle, Goodale's campaign manager.

In the end the use of appointments to recruit high-level candidates worked. As one reporter noted, the Liberal team in 1993 was light years ahead of the 1988 crop.[13] With the Red Book completed, the election machine in place, and a good field of candidates nominated, Jean Chrétien was ready to face Kim Campbell and take the Liberal Party back to power. He was a 'man with a plan' and a team that was ready to govern.

Election 93

When the Conservatives finally dropped the writ in September 1993, Jean Chrétien, like John Turner in 1988, had one major challenge. His party was ahead of the Conservatives but his personal popularity trailed the other party leaders, and he had to devote all of his efforts to restoring his credibility with Canadian voters. Unlike Turner, though, Chrétien had three crucial advantages. First, he was an experienced and skilful campaigner. Second, there was overwhelming public antipathy towards the Conservatives, as opposed to the interest in a fresh-faced Brian Mulroney in 1984. Third, there was the disastrous campaign run by the inexperienced and strong-willed Campbell.

Little of this was apparent at the beginning of the campaign, however. A mild form of 'Campbellmania' swept the country throughout the summer and the new Conservative leader had considerable success in distancing herself from the Mulroney record. Her campaign pledge to 'do politics differently' appealed to voters. Her challenge was to demonstrate during the campaign that there was substance behind the charming exterior.

In Chrétien's case, the challenge involved demonstrating, first, that he too had substance, and secondly that he was not 'yesterday's man' but was capable of taking over from Mulroney and running the country. Although the Liberals had been well ahead in the polls for more than two years, Campbell's unexpected popularity narrowed the gap somewhat. At the start of the campaign it was likely the Liberals would eke out a minority, but far from clear they could obtain a majority. With both the Reform Party and the new Bloc Québécois threatening to siphon votes from the mainstream parties, many pundits began predicting a 'pizza parliament' in which there would be no clear winner. This initially would prove helpful to the Liberals in western Canada, where many voters were so concerned about the Bloc Québécois becoming the Official Opposition that they felt obliged to vote Liberal to ensure a strong majority government to deal with that threat. However, this concern was counterbalanced by the hostility directed towards Mulroney and the Conservatives, primarily over the Charlottetown Accord, which was driving many traditional Conservative voters in the west into the arms of the Reform Party. Recognizing this trend, Chrétien made one of the most unusual campaign commitments of modern times, namely *that he would not reopen the constitutional debate during his time in office.*

The extreme loathing and anger focused on the Conservatives was readily apparent in Ontario. Many veteran Liberal candidates recalled this animosity as the most striking aspect of the campaign. According to David Collenette, 'the level of fury directed at the Conservatives and especially at Mulroney was unlike anything I'd seen before. This really was a case of them wanting to "throw the bums out" at all costs.'[14] Toronto MP Dennis Mills concurred, recalling that in Toronto it was a 'love-in' for most of the Liberal candidates. His colleague Charles Caccia, a successful veteran of ten election campaigns, agreed: 'In 1980 under Trudeau we were greeted almost as an army of liberation and the only time I experienced anything like that again was in 1993. We were greeted with open arms on the doorsteps.'[15] While this was helpful to the Liberals it was not sufficient to ensure their majority, especially since the NDP could still split the anti-Tory vote in other parts of Ontario as well as the west. With their problems in Quebec, the Liberals hoped to make inroads in the west but they needed to take most of the Atlantic and Ontario seats as well.

In the first few weeks of the campaign, Campbell helped the Liberals' cause considerably. The Conservatives were deeply unpopular across the country, and even her own party did not expect her to win the election. But even more damaging to her chances was a series of political blunders that gave Chrétien an opening. First, she told reporters at the start of the campaign that there would be no real improvement in the unemployment situation for several years. Then she informed them that an election was no time to discuss important policy issues, as they were too complex to be examined rationally in the heat of a campaign. Shortly thereafter she declared that she had no idea what the actual size of the federal deficit was, since the books had not been closed on the fiscal year and in any event it was beyond her knowledge as a former minister of justice.[16]

Chrétien was quick to seize on all of these missteps. First and foremost, he began to define the key issue of the election campaign as 'jobs, jobs, jobs.' With the help of his invaluable prop, the Red Book, he emphasized the Liberal program to create jobs 'immediately, not in ten years.' The infrastructure program became one of the most well-known planks in the book. Second, he began to mock the Conservatives, who literally had no new policies to announce, having hinged their campaign on Campbell's personal popularity.[17] The Liberals, by contrast, released their entire Red Book on 18 September, just days after the start of the campaign. Despite the fact this move duplicated the strategy of the Turner Liberals four years earlier, the Tories were apparently taken by surprise.[18]

The Red Book as Campaign Bible

The launch of the Red Book was a major coup. A cross-Canada conference call was held with all of the Liberal candidates and media present. This was followed by Paul Martin's appearance on a CBC Town Hall debate on 20 September where he explained the plan's monetary assumptions. His arguments faithfully followed those laid out over the past several years by the Liberals' new Toronto-area star candidate, Doug Peters. Peters's argument was simple and persuasive: the Conservatives were wrong to think that reducing inflation alone was sufficient to eliminate the federal deficit. Nor were tax increases a solution to the problem. On the contrary, Martin and the Liberals argued that eliminating the deficit would require a combination of policies to reduce unemployment, lower interest rates, and promote economic growth through increased productivity.

The Liberals' strategy to re-establish voters' faith in their economic competence was an immediate success. It also contributed greatly to the popularity of the Red Book, whose promises both the media and the public now felt could be taken seriously. Soon Chrétien was speaking at ever-larger rallies, clutching his Red Book as Peter Donolo had advised. It became the leader's and all Liberal candidates' bible for the campaign. Bob Kaplan recalled people coming up to him on the street and asking him for a copy. ('I couldn't get enough of them. Everyone wanted their own. I had never seen anything like it.')[19] As National Director Gordon Ashworth later pointed out, the advantage of the Red Book for Chrétien was that 'it was both sword and shield. They could not claim he had no policy, but it also allowed him to move on to key issues without having to spend a great deal of time on it.'[20] Proof of the impact of the Red Book was that the Conservatives, the Reform Party, the Bloc, and the NDP all scrambled to assemble their own platforms and to disseminate them in a similar fashion.

The second prong of the Liberals' campaign strategy was to attack the record of the Conservatives and of Brian Mulroney in particular. Long before Campbell was selected as the new Tory leader Chrétien had told his closest advisers that he would be fighting the election against Mulroney, whomever the Conservatives chose. This strategy proved very successful. Public opinion polls continued to show massive discontent with the Mulroney government's overall record of patronage and corruption, quite apart from their unpopular policies. To this end, Chrétien constantly emphasized the Liberals would represent a return to honesty, integrity, and ethical government. With his unblemished thirty-year record of serving in public office, this too was a strength which Chrétien could highlight, in defiance of the 'yesterday's man' theme. The Red Book also played to this strength, promising the creation of a parliamentary ethics commissioner and a more open, consultative policy process giving more power to backbench MPs.

The Leaders' Debates

At the mid-point in the campaign the Tories were down to 23 per cent in the polls and falling. Yet the numbers still indicated only a minority Liberal government. Many voters were still undecided while others were siding with another party. However, both Donolo and Joyce Fairbairn felt the Liberals had the momentum and could win a majority if their leader could survive the debates on 3 and 4 October. These would be quite different from 1988. There would be five leaders involved instead of three. With Mulroney and Broadbent gone, Chrétien and Campbell would be facing off as unknown quantities. From the point of view of his advisers, Chrétien was facing not only Campbell, whom everyone agreed was articulate, but Lucien Bouchard, the fiery and popular new leader of the Bloc Québécois whose French was impeccable and whom the chattering classes in Quebec found much more socially acceptable. This exchange would be equally important, since if the Liberals were to win a majority they would have to regain ground in Quebec. Then there was the wild card, Reform leader Preston Manning. During the French debates he would simply read a prepared text, but in the English debates he would be a full participant.

For this reason it was decided to extend the English format by thirty minutes and to allow a short section at the end for questions from the audience. Each party appointed an official agent to participate in negotiations about how the debates would be formatted, illustrating just how important this aspect of the election campaign had become. Significantly, Mike Robinson, the former chair of Paul Martin's leadership campaign, was chosen as the Liberal party's official agent.

While Jean Chrétien practised in a studio with advisers posing as the other leaders, Kim Campbell committed another rookie mistake, refusing to follow the advice of her communications advisers and adopt the debate preparation technique that had served John Turner so well in 1988. Campbell insisted on sitting around a table discussing issues with her team of advisers.[21] The result was predictable. Campbell appeared uncomfortable with the format. Overly aggressive in some cases, at other times she failed to answer direct questions and sounded tentative. No knockout punches were delivered by anyone, but Campbell fared badly by comparison with Chrétien and Bouchard, and actually was rated fourth by the live audience.

Jean Chrétien, on the other hand, performed better than expected. He held his own with Bouchard in French, at one point delivering the classic line 'I'm a proud Quebecker, a proud francophone and a proud Canadian.' In English, the debates provided the opportunity for him to appear statesmanlike and confident, although the less-disciplined proceedings occasionally forced him to participate in strident free-for-alls if he wanted to make a point. This debate also allowed him to reiterate his commitment not to reopen the constitutional file during his time in office, a commitment that struck a responsive chord with many voters. Although no clear winner emerged in either debate, for Chrétien the fact he emerged unscathed was enough.[22]

In the second half of the campaign it became increasingly obvious that another new factor had arisen in the election, namely the regionalization of the political party system. This was an emerging phenomenon in the previous election and crystallized in 1993 with the strong performances of the Bloc and Reform parties. As a result, the Liberals were obliged to face off against different political parties as their chief opponent in different parts of the country – the Conservatives in Atlantic Canada and Ontario, the Bloc in Quebec, and the NDP and Reform Party in the west.

The Regional Campaigns

This development was more significant for the leader's tour, since his comments in one part of the country could be reproduced within minutes across the nation. At the local level it was somewhat less of a problem, primarily thanks to the Red Book. Local Liberal candidates could choose to highlight different planks of the platform to suit local and regional priorities. In Atlantic Canada and Ontario, this was a routine directive from provincial campaign headquarters. However, the tendency of many first-time Liberal candidates to invent party policy on the fly or to alter policies to suit local peculiarities was a major problem in this election. Independent thinking by individual candidates is always a potential problem for any party, but the Liberals' lengthy tenure in government had made this less of a concern before 1984. Sitting MPs typically have a better understanding of party policy and of the importance of solidarity. In 1988, although most of the Liberal candidates were newcomers, the dominance of the free trade debate had overshadowed most other issues, while the internal conflict at national headquarters had overshadowed any media interest in the contrary positions of individual candidates.

In 1993 the situation was quite different, particularly in western Canada. The Liberals' lack of sitting MPs in the region, coupled with the widely anticipated success of the party in BC and Saskatchewan as demonstrated by their frontrunner status in the polls, attracted a strong group of candidates. But few had legislative experience. A 'Candidate College' held in August in Kelowna demonstrated the extent of the problem, as many candidates who rose to speak during briefing sessions did so primarily to disagree with party policy. Their primary concern was that the official party position on an issue would be fatal to their electoral chances. Senator Joyce Fairbairn and BC campaign chair Ross Fitzpatrick told a number of anxious candidates from the Vancouver area that there were many party policies that would appeal to their constituencies and urged them to keep in mind that few voters would reject a party on the basis of one issue. Yet high-profile candidates such as Ted McWhinney and Hedy Fry continued to express their unhappiness with certain party positions, and many of the less prominent candidates clearly shared their views.

Since BC was one area where the Liberals had high expectations of increasing their representation, this mini-revolt was seen as a potentially serious problem. In several unheld ridings, internal party polls were 'highly encouraging' and several Liberal candidates were perceived to be 'frontrunners or on an equal footing with their Reform Party opponents.'[23] The problem was partially solved for them by the media, who arranged a series of debates with one representative from each party. Since the campaign chair was responsible for choosing the Liberal participant, the party could at least be certain the views expressed on the province-wide broadcasts would reflect party policy. In addition both Chrétien and Paul Martin made landmark trips to the province during the campaign to promote local candidates and helpful party policy. In Quebec, meanwhile, public opinion polls continued to suggest the newly formed Bloc would win many of the seats in rural and francophone areas, while the Liberals would likely pick up seats in the urban core on the island of Montreal. This split between francophone and anglophone Quebeckers was of serious concern to the Liberals as well, but the extent of the problem would not be apparent until election day.

The Tory Ad Debacle

In the face of emerging regionalization and competition from the Reform Party, the NDP, and the Bloc for second place, the Conservatives decided that a revised version of the 1988 'bomb the bridges' approach was in order. Their initial ads were notable failures. Many featured Campbell speaking about issues followed by a voice-over stating 'It's time.' Virtually no one knew what this meant. Chrétien took advantage of the ambiguous message to argue 'It's time for a change. It's time for a Liberal government.' Party pollster Allan Gregg concluded that a new series of attack ads were overdue. Focus groups had demonstrated that much of the Liberal support was 'soft' primarily because of uncertainty about Chrétien himself.

Unfortunately, the method the Conservatives chose to destroy the credibility of the new Liberal leader backfired. Taking a page from the Quebec elites who felt Chrétien's lack of sophistication and minimal speaking skills would prove embarrassing on the world stage, the ad featured a picture of Chrétien's face and voice-overs asking whether this was the face of a prime minister, or whether Canadians would be embarrassed to have this man as their leader. The problem was that outside Quebec, no one knew the arguments of Alain Dubuc and Lise Bissonnette. Instead, to most Canadians the ad appeared to be ridiculing Chrétien's physical appearance rather than his character (a childhood illness had left one side of his face partially paralysed, something the photo appeared to accentuate). Gordon Ashworth recalled being in Toronto with Kevin Shea when they first saw the ads, and neither one connected them with the comments of Quebec columnists. 'We were stunned at first,' Ashworth said, 'and then we started to discuss how we could bring this to the media's attention without appearing to be too aggressive. In the end we didn't need to worry. Everyone had the same reaction.'[24]

Canadians were almost universally appalled by what they perceived to be the ad's message, a message Gregg and other Tory advisers immediately declared was unintentional. Pandemonium reigned in the Campbell camp. Former minister Sinclair Stevens wrote a public apology to Jean Chrétien. He threatened to withdraw as a Conservative candidate if the ad was not pulled, as did Public Security Minister Doug Lewis, who actually issued a press release to that effect. The *Globe and Mail* editorial the following day described the ad as 'the most bone-headed act of the election campaign' and concluded 'in thirty seconds of symbolism the Conservatives seemed to confirm what disaffected voters have been telling anyone who will listen for weeks: politicians have no scruples. Politicians will say anything to get elected.'[25]

Chrétien was quick to seize on this development and turn it to his advantage. The next day on national television he declared: 'God gave me a physical defect and I've accepted that since I was a kid.' The March of Dimes called the Tories' national headquarters to protest. Kim Campbell, who had not actually seen the ad, immediately ordered it withdrawn, but the damage was done.

One perverse result of the Conservative collapse was the widespread perception that the Liberals would form a majority government. Almost immediately in western Canada, and particularly in BC, a perceptible shift in voting intentions took place. Those electors who had been planning to vote Liberal to ensure a strong majority government and thwart the Bloc no longer needed to do so. As a result, they were free to channel their anger with the Conservatives elsewhere, and most chose the new Reform Party as their medium. Many hoped that by doing so they would be able to deny the Bloc official opposition status, conferring it on Reform instead. The result for the Liberals was that once again they took no seats in BC outside the urban core.

The Making of the 1993 Liberal Majority

As many students of Canadian elections have concluded, there were two essential issues in the 1993 election campaign. The public's visceral dissatisfaction with the Mulroney Conservatives was caused by their disastrous economic policies, but also by their failed efforts at constitutional reform. Frizzell, Pammett, and Westell's election analysis concludes: 'The single most important factor in the election, without doubt, was the state of the economy.' But the authors also immediately note: 'A second major factor undermining the Conservative government was the failure of its constitutional initiatives, which had enormous and un-forseen consequences in federal politics.'[26]

The Chrétien Liberals were successful in obtaining one of the largest majorities in Canadian history because they addressed both of these issues. First, they managed to convince voters that they could put the country's economic house in order and that they could do so while pre-serving most of the social safety net and creating jobs. Second, they offered constitutional peace after nearly a decade of upheaval under the Conservatives. The promise of no new constitutional initiatives appealed to a broadly based constituency for whom a repeat of Brian Mulroney's 'brink of disaster' scenarios was to be avoided at all costs. While the importance of the first point is unassailable, it should be un-derlined that the Liberals, of all parties, needed to demonstrate their ability to handle the national unity file if they were to be successful. Just as voters had lost faith in the Liberals' ability to manage the country's finances, so the events of the previous nine years had gone a consider-able distance towards destroying the Liberals' reputation as the party of national unity. Although the promise of doing nothing in terms of constitutional reform might have seemed only marginally noteworthy, it was in fact of huge importance in reassuring Canadians on this sec-ond front. As political scientist Jon Pammett demonstrated, more than 50 per cent of Canadian voters identified the Liberal Party as the 'party closest to you' on the national unity issue in 1993. The next largest block of voters chose 'None,' while Reform finished a distant third at 13 per cent and the Bloc at 11 per cent.[27]

It is in this context that the results of the election must be considered. Some analysts concluded that the Liberals' return to power was, if not to be expected, then at least nothing out of the ordinary. 'The Liber-als are back in power, with a majority government, as they have been for most of this century.'[28] While technically correct, this assessment understates the magnitude of the Liberal Party's and Jean Chrétien's accomplishment. With 41 per cent of the popular vote, the Liberals took 177 seats. This was more than Brian Mulroney in 1988 (169 seats) or Pierre Trudeau in 1980 (147). It was also more than four times the number of seats the Liberals managed to retain in 1984 and more than double their representation after 1988. While their situation in Quebec increased only marginally, from 12 to 19 seats, they swept the Atlantic provinces and took all but two ridings in Ontario.

Put simply, in less than ten years the Liberals had come back from the brink. Facing oblivion after the 1984 election, with few resources and the threat of bankruptcy looming large, they had returned to power in 1993 despite the many systemic barriers they faced in the parliamentary system and in electoral legislation, to say nothing of the internal caucus feuding and lengthy leadership battle. While the solid campaign performance of Jean Chrétien, the huge success of the Red Book, and the solidarity of the Liberal caucus in the face of the Charlottetown Accord crisis all contributed enormously to this turnaround, it must also be recognized that this victory was built on the solid foundation laid through the efforts of many other members of the Liberal Party, from both the parliamentary and extra-parliamentary wings, since the day of their initial defeat in 1984. As Senator Al Graham, a former party president and national campaign co-chair commented, 'a party is made up of volunteers. Those of us in parliament need them to get us here. If we lose them, we can't carry on.'

In Rodger Schwass's view, there was a tendency on the part of the media, and of the public to 'take the Liberals' return to their "rightful" place in government for granted,' a situation which, in hindsight, would prove unhealthy for the system as a whole. Bob Kaplan, a key player in the opposition caucus dramas, agreed with this assessment. He suggested this 'somewhat blasé' public attitude after the 1993 election victory reflected a 'lack of appreciation of the degree to which the party had been decimated in 1984' and allowed the system to continue without modifications for another ten years.[29]

This was particularly relevant since the magnitude of the Liberal victory owed much to the regionalization phenomenon described earlier. Ironically, the party's nearest rival was the Bloc Québécois. With only 13.5 per cent of the popular vote and a mere 54 seats, all in Quebec, the Bloc had nevertheless become the Official Opposition, as many feared. The Reform Party, however, was close behind with 18.5 per cent of the vote and 52 seats, only one of which was east of Manitoba.

Another major development of the 1993 election was, as a consequence, the total collapse of the Conservative Party. It is here that the 'enormous and unforseen consequences' referred to by Frizzell came into play. Canada's only other truly national political party, and the only other party capable of forming a government, for all intents and purposes had been destroyed. It was reduced to only two seats and was going to lose its status as a political party. Kim Campbell lost her own seat in Vancouver and resigned as leader shortly thereafter. The Tories were decimated despite receiving 16 per cent of the popular vote primarily because of the pan-Canadian nature of their support as opposed to the regionally concentrated support of the Bloc and Reform. And, as many voting analyses demonstrated, the support for the Bloc and Reform parties came almost entirely from former Conservatives. The 'winning coalition' which Brian Mulroney built in 1984 to form a government had proven, in the final analysis, to be a Trojan Horse. Another striking reality of the new regionalization phenomenon was stressed by University of Quebec professor Pierre Drouilly, namely that for the first time since Confederation the Liberal Party of Canada had managed to win a majority government without the support of Quebec.[30] Although both the Liberals' share of the popular vote and the number of seats increased, the Bloc retained a clear majority status in the province. This situation led to speculation that the Liberals could retain power for the foreseeable future, since no other federal party would be in a position to recoup the Bloc votes.

The Liberals began to realize they could potentially stay in power indefinitely. They held a sixty-seat lead over the total combined opposition parties. Since the NDP and Conservatives were fragmented, the new Liberal government's only opposition came from two 'fringe' parties in what was now a five-party system. As Allan Frizzell's analysis of the 1993 election concluded, 'if there is no comeback by the Conservatives, and no breakthrough by Reform, the Liberals will be left as the only national party in Canada. Under this possibility, the party may establish itself in a hegemonic governmental position well into the next century.'[31]

Equally significant, the opposition benches in the House of Commons would now be dominated for the next four years by two opposition parties which were regionally based and whose main concerns did not reflect the views of most Canadians. With the Bloc focused exclusively on Quebec independence and the Reform Party more concerned with the return of the death penalty, 'family values,' and the abolition of the Official Languages Act, the Liberals would be left alone on centre stage. With the traditional left-right axis of Canadian politics suddenly rendered less meaningful, the real possibility of the Liberal Party expanding the definition of the 'moderate middle' loomed large as well. With the socialists and traditional conservatives severely weakened, the Liberal Party could, if it chose, move to occupy positions on the right or left of its traditional domain, at least in the short term.

This new set of political realities was not lost on Jean Chrétien and his closest advisers after their stunning 26 October victory. But there was a downside to the unexpected disappearance of their traditional opposition, one that would only become apparent as the Liberals attempted to implement their agenda. As political scientist Ken Carty would later argue,[32] the election represented a transition in Canadian politics from the 'third'-party system which had existed since the 1960s to a new, 'fourth'-party system in which regional interests would predominate and all national parties – but especially the Liberals – would be forced to attempt to reconstruct a pan-Canadian support base.

8 Return to Governing: A Tale of Two Crises

This country has the right to political stability, and as prime minister of Canada I will make sure that we have political stability in this land. That is my duty. That is my constitutional responsibility.

– Jean Chrétien[1]

By the time Jean Chrétien became prime minister in 1993 he had been active in federal politics for thirty years. No other PM came close to matching the depth and breadth of his experience before taking office. During his seventeen years in cabinet he held seven portfolios, including Indian Affairs, Treasury Board, National Revenue, Industry, Finance, Energy, and Justice. He was the youngest cabinet minister in the twentieth century when Pearson appointed him in 1967. His single most influential mentor was his former boss at Finance, Mitchell Sharp, whom he had served as parliamentary secretary, but his formative years were spent as a cabinet minister in the Trudeau era in which he became the first francophone finance minister.

Experience had given Chrétien an in-depth knowledge of government and the policy process. As well, his long tenure in cabinet covered periods of economic growth and recession, heightening his appreciation for the impact of government programs on the lives of ordinary Canadians and the difficult decisions politicians sometimes had to make. The Liberals' lengthy period in power also gave him a firm grasp of the machinery of government and a positive image of federal public servants. Conversely, as a minister, Chrétien had disliked the complexity of the Trudeau cabinet committee system. He also viewed the growing number of central agencies – with their superbureaucrats – as an affront to ministerial authority.[2]

Equally important, Chrétien had never forgotten the time Pierre Trudeau returned to Canada from a G7 meeting and announced a detailed fiscal policy shift without consulting him first despite the fact that he was finance minister ('I was made to look like a fool').[3] Advised by many to resign, Chrétien ultimately stayed on but took the lesson to heart. Now that he was in charge, he would not only reward his leadership rivals, he would allow his ministers to make their own decisions without intervening.

Finally, Chrétien worried about growing public cynicism in response to the Mulroney government and set out to present both himself and his government as the exact opposite of the Conservative administration. As the head of Chrétien's transition team told an audience at Queen's University, the new Liberal prime minister believed he would have 'little time to prove his worth and his worthiness before the electorate wrote him off as one more "all talk and no walk" politician.'[4] Chrétien was determined to set an early example of prudence and self-discipline in government. He began by eliminating the pomp and circumstance of the Mulroney Conservatives, dispensing with Mulroney's Cadillac in favour of a Chevrolet. His would be a frugal 'no-frills' government. Chrétien believed the excesses of the Mulroney era were not limited to podiums, limousines, or an office for Mulroney's wife in the Langevin Block. The Liberal leader was shocked to learn how the Conservatives politicized the public service and, at the same time, added many layers of political advisers in ministers' offices to shield cabinet ministers from the advice of their professional staff. He was determined to return power to the ministers in line departments and to their bureaucrats.

All these factors influenced Chrétien's decisions about the composition and size of his cabinet, the structure of his government, and how he would implement his agenda.

The Role of Chrétien's Transition Team

As virtually everyone who knew him could attest, Chrétien was a pragmatist, not a philosopher like Trudeau. Intelligent and astute, he was nevertheless not an intellectual. Quick to grasp the essence of an issue, he would rarely spend time on the details. His briefing notes were point form with concise options to choose from. He valued expert advice. To be successful as prime minister, however, would require all this and more. In addition to expertise he would need individuals in his office and in cabinet who had experience and good political judgment.

At the same time, Chrétien's view of the prime minister as 'boss' meant that his ministers exercised considerable authority on their own. He did not want to interfere in ministers' areas of responsibility or master their files. As he told those who were new to the cabinet table at the first meeting of his government, they should only be talking to him if they needed help or got into trouble. John Manley, one of the new ministers, commented that the prime minister's lengthy experience in various cabinet posts meant 'he was always calm and in control. I think he thought he had seen it all, and for all we knew he had.'[5] His colleague Brian Tobin agreed: 'He just sat back and watched. He wasn't a micro manager. The trick was to realize that he had given you authority and it was up to you to use it ... He couldn't stand to have people coming to ask him for permission every two minutes.'[6]

Not that the new prime minister didn't have an agenda. His objectives were, in fact, crystal clear. He was intent on bringing the country out of its negative reverie and rebuilding public confidence. In Calgary in 1990, Chrétien told reporters: 'leadership is to make people feel good about themselves and challenge them.' More specifically, David Zussman said Chrétien 'saw a more targeted government – one that did not do everything. But he saw government playing a huge role on the social side. To be responsible for the less fortunate was very much a large part of his thinking.' Particularly significant was Zussman's revelation that he himself was in favour of greater decentralization while Chrétien was not. 'Definitely I think he's a centralizer. He sees a very vigorous role for the federal government. He wants the feds to have a physical presence as well as a fiscal one.'[7]

It would be the task of Chrétien's transition team to help him decide how to achieve his objectives. This team had been working for nearly a year before the election to hammer out the details of the machinery of government. Headed by Zussman, a management professor at the University of Ottawa and one-time executive assistant to Chrétien, they laboured in anonymity. Zussman regularly consulted Chrétien to resolve various issues raised in their discussion papers and recalled that the exercise forced the PM to address issues early and develop a point of view. 'In hindsight,' Zussman said, 'we were really engaged in a sort of training exercise, preparing him to be the prime minister.' Issues such as the size and structure of cabinet, the organization of cabinet committees, and the operation of the PMO were all discussed. According to Zussman, once engaged on the subject the Liberal leader had little difficulty deciding what he wanted and what processes would best suit his management style. One cause for concern was the large number of Conservative advisers who sought refuge within the ranks of the public service in the last days of the Mulroney era. A provision had existed for many years allowing longtime political advisers to apply for public service positions. The provision was considered reasonable given the lack of job security of the political posts, the age and experience of most of the ministerial staff, and the valuable departmental knowledge they gained over time in a minister's office. But the Mulroney Conservatives had abused the system. From the beginning, individuals with very little relevant background or experience had been hired in cabinet ministers' offices. The size of those offices, in turn, had become as overblown as the PMO.[8] Near the end of the Mulroney mandate, people with very short tours of duty in ministers' offices were being parachuted into senior departmental positions at a dizzying rate.

The problem was compounded by the fact that Mulroney demonstrated little regard for the public service, promising during the 1984 election that he would hand many bureaucrats 'a pink slip and running shoes.'[9] As a result, many career public servants, perceived as being too close to the Liberals, were dismissed. The Conservatives' decisions to dismiss well-regarded senior bureaucrats such as Ian Stewart and Ed Clarke did not sit well with other public servants or with the Liberals during their time in opposition. Yet nine years later several of Mulroney's closest advisers had managed to position *themselves* within the bureaucracy at very senior levels. Most were not career bureaucrats but partisan advisers hired by Mulroney. Could they be trusted to provide impartial advice to the new Liberal government or would they use their new-found positions of influence to derail the Liberal agenda?

It was a classic dilemma. If the Liberals actively purged these Conservatives from the public service they would be seen as no different than Mulroney. If they did nothing, they risked being seen as weak. A lengthy internal debate ensued in which Zussman argued that the political costs of trying to remove these Conservative staff members would be too great. Gordon Ashworth, speaking from a more partisan and party perspective, argued that a signal would have to be sent to other parties that this type of interference was not acceptable, and to the public servants that they would be protected. In the end, Zussman's argument won but Chrétien was sure to note, in his first meeting with all deputy ministers, that he expected their full support.

In addition to the transition team's discussion papers, Zussman tried to create a more broadly based and innovative consultation process for Chrétien. At one point he arranged for four outside experts – former Economic Council of Canada Chair Judith Maxwell, professor Donald Savoie, Public Policy Forum director Sheldon Ehrenworth, and Dan Gagnier, a former PCO official who had worked with Chrétien on intergovernmental affairs and was now a private-sector executive – to have dinner at the opposition leader's house to discuss his overall priorities for government. Several left frustrated. Instead of addressing new and emerging issues that required the government's attention, Chrétien spoke about his core values. When pressed on the priorities of his first mandate, he answered immediately that he had three: to keep Canada independent from the United States, to keep the IMF from intervening in Canada's economy, and to ensure national unity. These broad objectives, they feared, were simply not focused enough to provide sufficient direction. Equally worrisome, in their view, was that he did not seem concerned with the fiscal dilemma they all believed would prevent him from implementing whatever agenda items he eventually decided upon.[10]

As the memoirs of one of Chrétien's senior policy advisers, diplomat James Bartleman, demonstrate, these fears were largely unfounded. At his first meeting with Chrétien in early 1994, Bartleman recalled Chrétien stressing that 'the greatest and most immediate threats facing Canada as the millennium came to a close were economic and psychological.' The prime minister cited the lengthy and deep recession, record unemployment, and a jobless recovery, concluding that 'the state of the economy is the most pressing problem.' However, Chrétien's initial solution to these economic difficulties was based on promoting economic growth and international trade rather than making cuts to government programs, just as part of his solution to the psychological malaise of the nation was grounded in a restoration of the country's status in international affairs as opposed to further constitutional reform. His strategic objectives, according to Bartleman, were straightforward. 'He would stimulate export-led growth, reverse the decline in our international position, and establish better-balanced ties with the United States.' He would also 'take full advantage of our membership in the G7 to influence global macroeconomic policies to Canada's benefit, consolidate bilateral ties of privilege with the big countries, work hard to have Canada emerge as the leader of the so-called middle powers, and embrace rather than shy away from globalization.'[11] In short, the transition exercise served to crystallize Chrétien's thinking on a range of important issues and also renewed his confidence after his shaky start as Liberal leader.

The Making of the Chrétien Cabinet

One of the most important decisions Chrétien faced on assuming office was how to organize his cabinet. Even before the election he had decided the actual number of ministers would be reduced to twenty-three from forty during the Mulroney years. Given the long-established tradition of ensuring regional representation and gender and linguistic balance in appointments, cabinet selection was not an easy task. With only twenty-three slots it would be even more difficult.

An added problem for Chrétien was the slim representation the party had garnered in the west, and especially in BC. With provincial expectations of cabinet representation running high, but few MPs of cabinet calibre, it was important to ensure inexperienced newcomers appointed for regional considerations were not given posts beyond their abilities.

Another consideration for Chrétien was the need to balance rewards for loyalists with consolation prizes for leadership opponents. His first cabinet was a masterpiece of compromise, consolation, and accommodation. It began with the appointment of his closest leadership rival, Paul Martin, to the powerful Finance portfolio. Although the two disliked each other, Chrétien was intent on demonstrating that he could work with his former opponent. As he told one journalist: 'For me, it was essential that you turn the page. If you don't do that, you don't have a party.'[12] Martin originally asked for the Industry portfolio, leading Chrétien to offer the Finance position to John Manley. However, Martin's many business interests and the prospect of endless conflicts as a result of them precluded him from the Industry file. At the same time, Martin's connections in the business community made his credibility in the Finance portfolio much more likely than Manley's. Ironically, Martin resisted the Finance appointment for some time, believing the Industry portfolio would be of much greater interest. He was finally persuaded to take on the Finance assignment by a number of colleagues and confidants including David Smith (a former aide to Martin's father) and Ed Lumley (a former minister and friend from Windsor) after which Manley – a former head of the Ottawa Board of Trade – took on the Industry file.[13]

This prolonged deliberation on Martin's cabinet appointment demonstrated how important Chrétien believed it was to accommodate his former leadership rival. Other potential cabinet appointees would not be given time to consider, refuse, or 'bargain' about their appointments, but Chrétien and his advisers waited patiently for Martin. In the end, Martin's position as finance minister proved the making of his political career.

Chrétien also rewarded Sheila Copps despite her third-place finish and aggressive attacks during the leadership debates. In addition to assigning her the Environment portfolio, Chrétien made her deputy prime minister, a largely symbolic post but one which would allow her to respond in his absence in Question Period and to represent him at state functions abroad. She was also assigned the chairmanship of the cabinet committee on social policy, a position of considerable importance.

As a longtime party man, Chrétien knew his next task was to balance the social and business Liberals in the cabinet. With left-leaning veterans Lloyd Axworthy in Human Resource Development and Herb Gray as solicitor general to balance off Roy MacLaren in the Trade portfolio and Martin in Finance, the composition of his cabinet was meant to send a clear signal that the government would pursue both fiscal prudence and social responsibility. New cabinet ministers who had been 'star' candidates were similarly balanced. Allan Rock was appointed to Justice and Art Eggleton to Treasury Board, while Marcel Masse was named minister for intergovernmental relations. Among his own loyal supporters Chrétien appointed David Collenette to Defence, Ron Irwin to Indian and Northern Affairs, Sergio Marchi to Immigration, David Dingwall to Public Works, and Brian Tobin to Fisheries. Charles Caccia was offered a minister of state post but declined, preferring to chair the House committee on the environment.

Regionally, Chrétien's problems focused on Quebec and British Columbia. With Jean Pelletier and most of his other Quebec cabinet hopefuls defeated, he had little to choose from. He recognized that, despite the popularity of the Bloc, Liberal representation had improved in Quebec and that this was largely due to the organizational efforts of André Ouellet. Having made his peace with Ouellet for the campaign, Chrétien offered him Foreign Affairs. One of the few successful new party candidates, Michel Dupuy, a former Canadian ambassador to France, was given the Heritage portfolio.

In western Canada the Liberals' problems were equally severe. In Alberta Anne McClellan barely won her seat and her appointment as the new energy minister was literally delayed until the eve of the swearing-in ceremony at Rideau Hall on 4 November when word arrived that the obligatory recount confirmed her victory. Although only one Liberal was elected in Saskatchewan, it was an efficacious choice for Chrétien – Ralph Goodale was a veteran who could easily assume responsibility for the Agriculture and Wheat Board files.

The most difficult decisions were in British Columbia. Here again the likely cabinet hopefuls had been defeated. Although there were six Liberals elected, none had the background or experience to make them strong candidates. Yet it was in that province that the Liberals saw their strongest showing west of Ontario. Worse still, there were public expectations of multiple cabinet appointments. As a result, Chrétien and his advisers adopted a practice which Joe Clark had attempted more than a decade earlier with little success. They created a number of junior ministers. While not part of the cabinet, these ministers of state had the title and many of the symbolic perks. This allowed Chrétien to appoint veteran David Anderson of Victoria as the only full cabinet minister (in the National Revenue portfolio) while making Raymond Chan and Hedy Fry ministers of state. For public relations purposes, the Liberals could claim there were three BC ministers, or half of the province's elected MPs.

Despite ensuring regional representation, the lack of strong ministerial bench strength in some regions meant there was much less emphasis on the concept of political 'regional ministers' in the Chrétien cabinet. In some areas (Alberta and BC, for example) Chrétien actually divided responsibility between two individuals. As Lloyd Axworthy, the epitome of a regional political minister in his home province of Manitoba, would later argue: 'the absence of strong regional ministers was a key political mistake' of Chrétien's era.[14]

Finally, Chrétien made a significant change to the cabinet committee system, which served as the policy refinement process for new initiatives before they reached full cabinet. Given his dislike of the overly complex cabinet committee system he experienced during the Trudeau years, the number of policy committees was reduced to only two – the Cabinet Committee on Social Union (CCSU), first chaired by Sheila Copps, and the Cabinet Committee on Economic Union (CCEU), chaired by André Ouellet. When necessary, ad hoc cabinet committees were established to deal with additional and/or unexpected issues. The first of these occurred shortly after the Liberals took office when the severity of the fiscal crisis led to the creation of the ad hoc Committee on Program Review chaired by Marcel Masse.

The Chrétien PMO and the Caucus Research Bureau

The organization of Chrétien's PMO was almost as important as the composition of his cabinet. He did not plan to have a huge partisan operation such as Mulroney had created. Nor did he intend to change many of the people who were already in place from the OLO, but he did have some specific innovations in mind.

The key player in Chrétien's PMO was Jean Pelletier. Having lost his bid to enter Parliament as an MP, Pelletier agreed to return to Ottawa and run the operation he had already put in place. As chief of staff his role continued to be one of competent manager and fixer, ensuring the smooth operation of the whole team, although in power there were additional responsibilities. Pelletier was seen as a consummate professional who ran PMO firmly but gently. Meetings each morning began on time and finished promptly. Everyone knew their place and their assignments. Civility was an essential aspect of the organizational culture. Relations between the PMO and the PCO were excellent, further contributing to the efficiency of the government and the prime minister's ability to focus on important issues.

Peter Donolo remained as director of communications, assisted by Patrick Parisot as press secretary. Donolo's excellent rapport with the national press gallery also contributed to the success of the Chrétien PMO, particularly during the difficult first mandate when cost-cutting and a national referendum campaign were the order of the day. Similarly Jean Carle remained as director of operations, although this would soon prove to be a more problematic appointment. Eddie Goldenberg continued on as senior policy adviser, and Chaviva Hosek was brought in from the Research Bureau to assist him and given the title of director of policy and planning. She in turn recruited two of her former Research Bureau officers – Alfred McLeod (on social policy) and Stephanie Cairns (on the environment) along with Marjorie Loveys (on economic issues).

The role of Hosek's policy group was to staff the two cabinet committees, liaise with the respective PCO and departmental officials, and troubleshoot on upcoming legislation or other policy proposals. As Marjorie Loveys recalled, 'our primary role was to facilitate compromise on policy issues where there was interdepartmental conflict, or where there were conflicting views on the best way to implement election commitments.' Several years later Loveys, the only member of the policy shop to remain for the entire Chrétien era, concluded: 'In all the time I watched what came and went in the CCSU, I would be hard-pressed to identify more than one or two issues on which the prime minister ever intervened.'[15]

Chrétien maintained the tradition of regional desks introduced by Trudeau and followed by Turner. This worked well in the Atlantic (Dominic LeBlanc) and in Ontario (Warren Kinsella), but the west proved much more difficult as there were considerably different concerns across the provinces. Although the original function of regional desks had been to alert politicians to emerging political issues, in some cases the western desk took on a primarily service function under Chrétien, organizing prime ministerial trips and arranging events at which he could meet loyal Liberals. The position was filled initially with Albertans, including David Hastings and Raj Chahal, but their time was divided with other duties. An additional BC desk was created and staffed by Randy Pettipas.

Chrétien also made two significant appointments that would affect the course of his mandate. The first was a director of appointments. For this position Chrétien chose one of his earliest supporters, Penny Collenette. Collenette was initially surprised at the offer, having assumed her colleague Gordon Ashworth would have priority to round out the PMO team. As she later recalled, it was not a position she would have chosen, but 'you don't say no to the prime minister.'[16]

Collenette's concern initially proved well founded. The only PMO staffer to report directly to the prime minister instead of to Jean Pelletier, she had a loney task. The need for confidentiality was imperative. At the same time, her role in setting up a professional, competence-based appointments process, complete with job descriptions and advertisements in the Canada Gazette, did not endear her to some Chrétien supporters who assumed positions would be provided as a reward for loyal service. Her task also made her unpopular with certain ministers when she did not recommend their original choices for some appointments to the prime minister. Still, Collenette stressed that many ministers were committed to the new, less partisan approach to appointments, viewing it as a welcome change from Brian Mulroney.

Despite occasional opposition to Collenette's recommendations, Chrétien proved consistently supportive even though some of the pressure came from his close friends and colleagues. His objective was not simply to establish a more professional, merit-based system. He was soon convinced by Collenette of the need to improve representation in senior appointments. Under Chrétien a record number of women and minorities were appointed. In one of his last addresses to national caucus before the 1997 election he devoted considerable time to the role Collenette had played in establishing the Liberal government's reputation for integrity and for keeping its commitments. 'Because of her we won't be having patronage as an issue in the upcoming election,' he told his caucus to roars of approval and much applause. As one of her former PMO colleagues later added, 'It wasn't just the number of excellent appointments she made – it was the number of bad ones she prevented.'

The second unexpected Chrétien appointment to PMO was that of a foreign policy adviser to be seconded from the public service. Jim Bartleman, a thirty-year veteran who had served as Canada's ambassador in several countries, was chosen on the recommendation of Chrétien's nephew, Raymond Chrétien, a career foreign service officer. As Bartleman recounted, Chrétien believed he needed a counterweight to the information he received from PCO and Foreign Affairs, 'an independent player in decision-making, offering personal views at all times on foreign policy and crisis management situations.'[17] Equally important, given the increasing importance of Canada's trade and diplomatic relations in an era of globalization, the prime minister felt he needed someone to be with him on all of his missions abroad and when hosting foreign dignitaries in Canada, a requirement his G8 counterparts had long ago adopted. Because of the Bartleman appointment, the policy unit in Chrétien's PMO never handled either foreign policy or defence issues, nor were such issues discussed in cabinet committee.

Bartleman remained in the PMO for the entire first mandate, working closely with Pelletier, Goldenberg, and Donolo, and was the one senior PMO staffer to accompany the prime minister on all foreign trips. His subsequent account of this period, and in particular of the organizational relationships between the prime minister and his ministers of foreign affairs, international trade, and defence, is particularly instructive.[18] In concrete terms the first mandate saw the introduction of the high-profile Team Canada trade missions, four of which were conducted between 1994 and 1997, and the memorable Halifax G7 Summit in 1995.

A third change of some importance was the closer relationship between the Liberal Caucus Research Bureau and the PMO. Although the Bureau's budget increased considerably due to the much greater level of party representation in the House of Commons, the status and independence of the Bureau were somewhat reduced. To begin with, the reporting relationship between the director and other sectors of the Liberal organization changed. Goldenberg and Hosek were frequently involved in Bureau assignments and the Bureau director would meet regularly with them. Candidates for research officer positions were often referred to the director by Goldenberg, who also provided requests and instructions directly to Bureau staff on occasion. More significant still was the fact that the Bureau director no longer attended the weekly national caucus meetings. Nor did his researchers attend the regional caucuses. Instead, the executive assistant to the regional minister attended. Similarly, the director now had virtually no contact with either the PMO chief of staff or the party's national director, as the troika function was taken over once again by the principal secretary.

Nevertheless Dan McCarthy, Hosek's successor as director and a highly regarded senior researcher who had been part of the Bureau's original opposition research team, retained essentially the same structure and organization of the Bureau. He also continued to maintain the high professional standards that had been set since 1985. As he later recounted, it was his intention to maintain the Bureau's policy capabilities as much as possible in order to avoid a repeat of the 1984 debacle that he had witnessed first-hand. It was, after all, inevitable that the party would once again find itself in opposition at some point in the future.[19]

The Bureau's policy work with the Liberal caucus continued to be substantial both for caucus policy committees and parliamentary committees. 'We worked hard in those years to help equalize the policy playing field for backbenchers and committee chairs in assessing government policies,' McCarthy recalled. Citing the work of his research officers with such prominent committee chairs as Reg Alcock, the Liberal caucus social policy chair who took on Human Resources Minister Lloyd Axworthy over proposed changes to employment insurance, and Charles Caccia, the House of Commons Environment Committee chair who took on several environment ministers over environmental protection, species at risk, and climate change legislation, McCarthy also stressed that both chairs maintained excellent communications with the ministers and their staff, keeping them informed of committee developments. 'Because we did not ambush our own government,' McCarthy said, 'we had the full support of PMO in this regard. For all the criticism they took for heavy-handedness from caucus, there was a genuine respect for the caucus role and backbenchers who did their homework.'[20] One significant structural change within the LCRB was the addition of several communications officers and the provision of additional media services for caucus members. The re-creation of a communications unit, which had been abolished out of necessity in 1984, came as little surprise. Liberal MPs, now backbenchers on the government side, did not need Bureau support in parliamentary committees and task forces, but their profile in their respective ridings was an ongoing concern. Weekly columns, newsletters, and other material for the use of MPs, as well as 'Talking Points' on some government initiatives, were to become mainstays of the material prepared by the Bureau's communications unit, using material provided by the research officers.

The Western Communications Project

One noteworthy addition was the experimental Western Communications Project, funded jointly by the Bureau with the western caucus. Part of the plan to improve visibility and election readiness in western Canada, the project stemmed from the long-standing concern that the federal government's efforts to inform citizens about its programs and services were limited and largely unsuccessful. As well, the lack of western caucus members necessitated an alternative early-warning system for new and emerging issues in the region. And, given the party's non-existent organization in the mostly rural ridings of the region, the recruitment of local Liberals to participate in the Communications Project would hopefully provide a base on which to build for the next federal campaign. With the PMO downsized, the regional desk and correspondence capacities of the Chrétien PMO paled in comparison with that of the Trudeau era, to say nothing of the Mulroney years. In some respects, therefore, this project was also intended to perform functions previously carried out by a regional desk officer.

At one of the first meetings of the group, Ralph Goodale stressed that far less effort had been expended on communications in the west than Quebec despite the widespread misconceptions and ignorance fuelling western alienation. He argued that the federal government should utilize weekly community papers, which had not been done in the past due to reluctance to purchase advertising space in regionally based media. Anne McClellan stressed the importance of the project in helping to identify issues of concern to western Canadians. Among the most active caucus members in the development of the project, she consulted regularly with the project coordinator and put considerable emphasis on the need to develop a western policy agenda reflecting demographic realities such as the growing urban aboriginal population.

The project began with considerable enthusiasm and caucus support in mid-1995. A large network of Liberal volunteers was quickly organized across the region, and within months their input revealed several emerging western concerns, including possible conflict between the Pacific salmon fishery and Fisheries Minister Fred Mifflin's conservation plan, widespread resistance to the government's gun control legislation in Saskatchewan, and growing public unease over the 'faint hope' clause in Alberta and BC. Another important role played by the local Liberals was to submit letters to the editor and/or columns provided by the coordinator to their weekly media outlets. This function was considered particularly successful in addressing erroneous or misleading commentary by opposition politicians and local editorial staff. A progress report submitted in September 1996 referred to the 'growing enthusiasm of local Liberals for what they perceive to be the meaningful role they have been asked to play in this project' and 'their increasing willingness to recruit additional volunteers.'[21]

But the initial success of the project was not enough to save it. It was terminated in late 1996, a victim of the fiscal constraints brought on by program review. Originally a one-year pilot project, its continued operation was dependent on ongoing funding from a dedicated source. With departmental budgets slashed, no one minister felt able to support the project as a priority. The consequences of this failure to pursue the western initiative would eventually come to light in the 1997 election. The national campaign, unaware of the project or its recommendations, was unprepared to address the issues that had been identified as problematic for the party in the region. Worse still, most of the project volunteers failed to materialize as campaign workers, having been unceremoniously dismissed a year earlier. Most infuriating for western Liberal candidates, the Conservatives rather than the Reform Party (or even the NDP) were incorrectly identified in the party's campaign advertising – prepared in central Canada – as the Liberals' main opponent. Unfortunately for the party, this pattern of good intentions about the west, followed by rapidly fading interest in light of more pressing priorities, would be repeated by both the parliamentary and extra-parliamentary wings several times in the next decade.

The National Party Organization in Power

After consultation with party president Don Johnston, Jean Chrétien appointed one of his earliest and closest supporters to the position of national director in 1984, replacing Penny Collenette. George Young was a lifelong party activist and former president of the Ontario wing of the party. He had resigned from that position to organize the anti-Turner forces for the 1986 review convention. In Young, Chrétien secured someone intimately familiar with the internal workings of the party and its membership. He was also a close confidant of the prime minister with guaranteed access.

On taking up the post, Young asked the PM what his personal objectives were for his mandate. Chrétien's immediate response was 'that he wanted to be remembered as a great prime minister and a great leader of the party, but the second was more important.' Bearing in mind the state of the party under Trudeau, Chrétien made it clear to Young that he wanted to be kept abreast of party issues and developments. His lack of enthusiasm for the 'democratization' of the party should not be interpreted as lack of interest in party business.[22]

On the contrary, Chrétien's interest in party issues resulted in Young becoming the first national director to be invited to daily meetings at the PMO. Although he did not attend regularly, Young noted that he did do so on numerous occasions when issues warranted. He also stressed that Chrétien's commitment to his role as leader of the party was 'remarkably well maintained' for at least the first mandate.

At the same time, Young noted the leader's interest in party matters was not shared by many senior PMO officials, most of whom had little or no previous involvement with the party. This division between party and government focus within the PMO was confirmed by David Zussman, who said that policy advisers such as Goldenberg and Hosek were 'more interested in the application of ideas than the management of election campaigns.' In his view the only individual in the first Chrétien PMO able to cross the divide between policy and operations was Peter Donolo, and it was Donolo who was most often in contact with Young.[23]

During his four-year term in charge of the national party office, Young oversaw a number of significant changes. First and foremost, he proposed leaving the site at 200 Laurier and purchasing an entire building to provide a permanent headquarters for the party. However, with the party's deficit still close to $6 million, his arguments failed to persuade either Chrétien or Johnston. Instead, the party offices moved into rental accommodations at 81 Metcalfe Street, not far from the Laurier address, a move that put an end to discussions of a permanent party headquarters and disappointed many advocates and donors who had been fighting for one since the Turner era.

Among George Young's personal innovations was the re-introduction of a newsletter from the national headquarters to all party members, something that had been discontinued for more than a decade. As he later recounted: 'I felt it was time we gave the grassroots members something back for a change. We always ask them for money or to work on campaigns, but what do they get for their membership fees? We needed to make sure they felt included between elections.'[24] The *Liberal Times* provided an opportunity for a message from the leader as well as the national director, and several articles discussing recent policy initiatives. It was distributed free of charge and met with instant approval from party members. Young also hired a specialist in fundraising, Terry Mercer, to attempt to increase revenues and counter the effects of the expenditure-reduction exercise being promoted by Johnston at the national office. Mercer, director of the party's Nova Scotia wing a decade before, had since moved to Toronto and become an expert in the field of corporate contributions for charitable organizations. Young originally envisaged Mercer focusing on a direct mail operation, the vehicle still seen by many in the party as the one which would increase revenues and finally put the Liberals on a financial par with the Conservatives. Having failed to implement the recommendations of the president's 1985 Reform Committee concerning revenue, and still encountering financial difficulties despite the return to power, the party saw this as a clear priority. However, as both Young and Mercer later admitted, the project met with limited success. Instead, Mercer emphasized the Laurier Club, the leader's dinners, and corporate campaigns as essential sources of additional revenue.

As a result of the difficulties with direct mail, and despite the more limited appeal of political parties to the general public, Mercer experimented with freestanding inserts in newspapers – another first for the party – with 'respectable' results. 'We needed to emphasize specific policy positions to get a response. The so-called "fish wars" was our first big hit. Our costs were half of our revenue,' he indicated, 'so there was a 100 per cent return. That's not bad. By contrast direct mail accounted for 5 per cent of our revenue and we could maybe have raised that to 7 or 8 per cent at best, with a great deal of effort.'[25]

The Party's Ongoing Financial Problems

Although sufficient funds had been raised for the election campaign, the party's long-term debt was not yet eliminated. Spending two to three days per week in Ottawa and many more on the road as a speaker at Liberal events, Don Johnston found his presidency was as demanding as that of his predecessor, Michel Robert. Johnston met on a regular basis with Chrétien, primarily to discuss the financial state of affairs of the party, but also to review policy options and personnel decisions. Several party insiders underlined that this was unusual. The two men had been cabinet colleagues and had known each other for more than two decades, so their relationship was built on mutual respect and shared experience. 'The two operated in separate spheres and rarely interfered in each other's activities, but remained in close communication,' George Young recalled, noting that both men 'understood government and what was needed to return the party to power.' Similarly, although not a caucus member, Johnston was widely known to most of the MPs and senators, another benefit of his 'inside' experience.[26]

Johnston stated: 'My overriding objective was to get Jean Chrétien and the Liberals elected. That we achieved. However, the supportive objectives to accomplish that were getting the party out of debt, making appropriate financial arrangements with a bank consortium to eliminate dependence on one bank in particular, and ... getting the fundraising mechanisms efficient and effective.'[27] Fundraising certainly improved during Johnston's tenure, but his contributions to restructuring the party's debt and distributing the revenue are seen by party elites as his most significant achievements. 'We could not have carried on without the new arrangement with the banks,' Johnston's immediate successor Dan Hays concluded. 'It was essential to our rebuilding efforts.'[28] To that end, Johnston met with a number of the participating bank presidents and convinced them to further divide the party's debt among them. At the same time he succeeded in reducing the interest rates being charged, a feat of considerable importance given the party's still substantial debt.

Another challenge was to distribute the revenue the party received in a manner that was seen as fair and equitable by the provincial wings. This too had been raised during the 1983–5 Reform Committee's deliberations but remained unresolved. Johnston devoted considerable time and energy to meetings with the provincial presidents. These negotiations resulted in the so-called 'Johnston formula,' a landmark agreement that provided certainty as well as an agreed-upon rationale for the distribution of revenue to various levels and regions. As Terry Mercer later noted: 'It worked extremely well in BC, Alberta, and Saskatchewan ... especially because money was given to "non-held" ridings.' It was less important in Ontario, 'where the amount of money involved was simply too little to matter.' Mercer also admitted that in the Atlantic provinces, where the federal wing of the party was still unified with the provincial party, it caused some particular difficulties. In Quebec 'it was crucial. They were always trying to strike separate deals, and the formula was a saving grace.'[29]

Johnston served two terms as president before stepping down in 1994 to run for the position of president of the Organization for Economic Co-operation and Development (OECD). With considerable lobbying on his behalf from the Canadian government, prompted in no small measure by Jean Chrétien's gratitude for the efforts Johnston made as party president, he was successful. In June 1994 Johnston became the first Canadian, and indeed the first non-European, to be appointed to the post.

New President, Same Problems

Johnston's departure led to a race for party president at the 1994 convention. With no leadership issue to complicate the selection, the campaign was both uneventful and straightforward. Once again the overarching concern was the party's need for financial stability. Many also felt it was time for a westerner to take the reins of the national party given the weak representation in caucus from the region. In the end, the contest became an exclusively western one, with Alberta Senator Dan Hays vying for the presidency against another Albertan.

Hays later confided that he had considered running for the position in 1990 but instead served as co-chair of the 1990 Leadership Expenses Committee. Convinced by another longtime Liberal from western Canada, John Essican, to throw his hat in the ring in 1994, he was successful on the very first ballot. Hays's reasons for running were as clearly spelled out as those of Johnston. Describing Johnston's primary objective as 'survival,' Hays saw his own tenure being driven by the twin themes of 'financial consolidation' and 'expanding the party's base.' To that end, he introduced another first for the party, serving simultaneously as chair of the party's Fundraising Committee. As he later recalled: 'We were extremely successful in achieving my first objective.

The debt was eliminated by 1996, a year ahead of my own expectations, and we went into the 1997 election with a seven-figure surplus.' In fact, Hays believed the early election call demonstrated that the parliamentary wing and the leader could now operate in confidence, without regard for their financial plight.[30]

With the Liberals' return to fiscal health, Hays instituted a new organizational feature to further the party's electoral development work. 'Before 1997 there was a trade-off between debt reduction and the elimination of regional organization. We didn't have much to begin with, but we had to let it go. In retrospect I sometimes wonder if we should have tried to keep some of it and reduce the deficit more slowly.' After the 1997 election, with the surplus still intact, Hays promoted the concept of paid, full-time organizers in provinces with largely non-held ridings, which of course meant the west. He also encouraged the provincial wings to do the same. In reality the party's major efforts were focused on British Columbia, Alberta, and Saskatchewan, although Manitoba and Quebec were also entitled to support based on the formula worked out by Hays with his counterparts.

The individuals hired by the party were natives of the region and longtime party workers familiar with the system. 'We had some first-rate people. I thought it was self-evident why we needed to start building our support right away after the election. You can't wait until the next one is due to start doing that kind of spade work. We needed to build up the membership, identify potential workers, and develop a network. Unfortunately the program met with a lot of resistance from the provincial wings, especially in Alberta. They didn't like the idea of someone from the "national" party coming into "their" province.'[31] In the end the party's plan, which had been given an initial two-year mandate, suffered the same fate as the parliamentary wing's Western Communications Project. It was abruptly dismantled, and, although some of the original organizers became assistants to senators in Ottawa, most local personnel simply disappeared from the party's radar.

Since Hays was better integrated with the parliamentary wing than most of his predecessors, he was able to bring party issues to the attention of the leader. He emphasized that Chrétien always expressed interest in the well-being of the party and took steps to ensure ongoing communications. He arranged for Hays to attend the conclusion of every cabinet retreat and make a presentation outlining the party's major issues and concerns, another first for the party. According to Hays, Chrétien regularly attended meetings of the party executive and answered questions, something Turner had not done. But, as Hays also noted, Chrétien 'appreciated the importance of the party but he didn't understand the nuts and bolts of its operation.'

Meanwhile Hays's interest in policy development as a means of broadening the party's base in western Canada was heightened by his tenure first as the chair of standing Senate committees on Agriculture and Forestry, and then of Energy, the Environment, and Natural Resources. 'I was very much interested in helping to improve Liberal Party fortunes in the west, and Alberta especially, and I thought that, given my experience, I could make a real contribution in that regard. Unfortunately, I was much less successful in making progress on this front.' This was not surprising given the two major challenges the Chrétien government faced in its first mandate. 'What with the fiscal crisis and the national unity crisis, obviously the focus was on national issues. The importance of regional policy initiatives designed for Alberta paled in comparison.'[32]

It is interesting to note that this lack of policy influence was ongoing despite the fact that Hays was a senator and his election symbolized a return to the pattern of selecting 'insider' presidents. As Hays himself noted, he could attend caucus and was privy to policy decisions in a way that no president from outside the parliamentary wing, including Johnston, could be. Hays was not a close confidant of the prime minister, but he emphasized that this had no impact on the professional relationship between the two. 'Our relationship was always cordial. We met when necessary,' he said, 'and certainly I could see him when I wanted to, probably once per month. There was hardly any need to meet on a more regular basis given that I was in caucus.'[33] By the same token, Hays was aware of the priorities Chrétien had set for his first term, and this awareness allowed him to be philosophical about his lack of success on the western initiative.

Chrétien's Policy Agenda

Jean Chrétien's policy agenda was set out in the Red Book and prioritized with the help of the transition team before he took office. As such he hit the ground running. David Zussman recalled that the Red Book played a key role in the thinking of senior bureaucrats as well as Liberal ministers throughout the first mandate. Outgoing prime minister Kim Campbell had agreed to let Zussman meet with Privy Council officials before the formal transition took place, and he had arrived for a meeting with PCO Clerk Glen Shortliffe to discover the commitments of the Red Book already organized on a spreadsheet in front of him. Over the next few years Zussman would often meet senior bureaucrats, who gleefully reported to him how many promises had been checked off at that point and which ones were in train.

The contents of the Red Book reflected Chrétien's activist view of government. At the same time, Chrétien the cautious pragmatist wanted to implement those planks carefully, avoiding trouble and maintaining the party's image for competence as well as integrity. Infrastructure would be funded to create jobs, but the money would come from reallocating existing program expenditures. A national childcare plan would be developed when the country's finances permitted. The GST would be eliminated, but replaced with a more efficient harmonized tax that would provide equivalent revenue.

Part of Chrétien's caution was driven by his vast experience in government. In his first address to the Liberal caucus on 1 December, he specifically noted that there would always be unanticipated events the government would have to deal with, some of which would delay or even alter platform commitments. He cited the Conservatives' Pearson Airport contract as a classic example of this. It was not in the Red Book. Cancelling it would be expensive and siphon funds from other projects. But it was unavoidable if they were to live up to the expectations of honesty and integrity in government. Chrétien also stressed the need to recognize that politics is the art of the possible. 'Clinton gave us two out of three,' he said, referring to the American president's agreement to establish sidebar agencies on the environment and labour relations as part of the NAFTA accord. A further letter of intent had also been extracted assuring the Canadian government that the Americans had no intention of using the agreement to divert water. This, said Chrétien, should be presented as a major concession and an example of the way in which people of goodwill can resolve issues.

At the national caucus on 14 December Chrétien again tackled the problem of the government's agenda and the huge deficit and debt. 'Young men in red suspenders,' he warned, could create serious problems for the country and its currency if productivity and job creation were not dramatically improved. It was the role of government to promote these objectives. 'We need to tackle the problems of small business,' he said. 'We need to talk about jobs. We have to avoid falling in to the Tory trap on the deficit. We are no worse than the Europeans. It is an international problem and we will solve it through trade and job creation ... We have managed to improve the deal on NAFTA, and GATT will prevail in any event ... We have to be cheerful and maintain our course. It will not be easy but we have no choice.' While Chrétien recognized the importance of the deficit, these comments made it clear he still believed his agenda could be maintained as well. Job creation and economic growth could go a long way towards achieving the 3 per cent objective. Certainly he was intent on fulfilling the Red Book promises, not only because of their merits but also to show that his government kept its commitments. At the first cabinet meeting, Chrétien made this point exceedingly clear to his ministers. Their marching orders included identifying which of the planks fell within their jurisdiction and then setting about to implement them as quickly as possible.

Implementing the Red Book

The implementation of their election platform after the 1993 election began well for the Liberals, who enjoyed a definite honeymoon effect in their first few months in office. As Environics pollster Donna Dasko remarked: 'People get up in the morning and the first thing they see isn't a picture of Brian Mulroney.'[34] There was also a positive response to the introduction of their first platform planks, and especially to the popular municipal infrastructure program which was seen as the Liberals' primary vehicle for immediate job creation.

In a move reminiscent of Lester Pearson's 'sixty days of decision,' Jean Chrétien was determined to demonstrate his government was working hard and moving fast to implement their agenda. In another first for a Liberal government, the Chrétien Liberals reinforced the importance of the Red Book by issuing 'report cards' on their progress on several occasions during their first mandate. According to Liberal Party pollster Michael Marzolini, this innovation was not only popular but politically important. Some Liberal insiders believed it was in fact *essential* given the emphasis placed on their commitments during the campaign. Peter Donolo noted 'the feeling within PMO from the beginning was that the Red Book could be a double-edged sword.' Not only did they believe the commitments would have to be kept, but they assumed (in the end correctly) that both the opposition parties and the media would track their progress and trumpet any failures or policy reversals. 'The idea of the first report card was to get the Liberal message of accomplishments out ahead of time.'[35]

The first of these report cards, *Creating Opportunity: The First One*

Hundred Days, was described as a 'report on the achievements of the Liberal Government' and was released on 13 February 1994 to widespread and generally favourable coverage. As one opposition MP later commented, 'It almost doesn't matter what they've actually done, any more than it mattered what they promised in the first place. It's the *idea* of the promises that everyone likes.' The report's introduction reiterated Chrétien's broad objectives, namely 'restoring Canadians' confidence in themselves, their government, and their future.' A checklist of actions taken to achieve those objectives was arranged under the headings of 'Economic Growth and Jobs,' 'Securing Our Markets,' 'A Social Security System to Meet Canada's Needs,' and 'Giving Government Back to the People.' The document referred to concrete measures such as the launch of the National Infrastructure Works program, the cancellation of the Pearson Airport deal and the helicopter deal. But it also contained more general references to 'reducing the size of cabinet and cutting PMO and ministerial staff,' implementing an 'appointments process based on merit and expertise,' 'achieving major improvements in NAFTA,' 'opening up' the budget process, and 'beginning the process of replacing the GST.'

This first report was a slim, two-page pamphlet prepared for widespread distribution. It was followed on 8 July by a more comprehensive report prepared by the Caucus Research Bureau for Liberal MPs. This second report card, titled *Promises Made, Promises Kept: The First Eight Months of Liberal Government*, provided more detailed information on virtually all of the Red Book commitments which had been addressed to that point, or some 48 of the 197 official commitments. These included such measures as the creation of a commissioner of the environment and sustainable development, and an ethics commissioner.

After one year in power Jean Chrétien had reason to be optimistic. His government had kept many of its campaign promises and was working on others. The Liberals were further ahead in the polls and the prime minister's personal approval ratings were in the stratosphere, hovering between 60 and 70 per cent. Yet barely a year after taking power, both the sheer magnitude of the federal fiscal crisis and an entirely unexpected national unity crisis would seriously curtail the remainder of the Liberals' Red Book agenda. More would be accomplished, but far less than their initial progress suggested. The importance of the 'unanticipated event' referred to by Chrétien in the first caucus, and so often identified in public policy literature, was about to be demonstrated in spades.[36] Even more significant, the difference in the way the Liberals reacted to these two crises foreshadowed the problems to come on the federalism axis.

The Fiscal Crisis

Only a few months after taking office, the Liberals were forced to come to grips with the fiscal legacy of the Mulroney government. Despite the Liberals' initial concerns that they would not be taken seriously as managers of the public accounts, Paul Martin's first budget (in February 1994) was well received and stuck to the Red Book commitment to reduce the deficit to 3 per cent of GNP within three years. Moreover, Bank of Canada Governor John Crow had been replaced by the more moderate Gordon Thiessen a month earlier without visible backlash from the international money markets, something the Liberals also feared.

The budget contained a number of positive innovations which would become permanent features of federal budgets in the future. First, given the wide discrepancies between the optimistic economic forecasts of Mulroney's ministers of finance – Michael Wilson and Don Mazankowski – and the grim reality of their ever-burgeoning deficits, Martin insisted the economic assumptions on which *his* budget was based should err on the side of caution. Second, he was determined to allocate a reserve amount as a 'contingency fund' for further fiscal prudence. Last, Martin personally introduced the concept of a two-year rolling deficit projection rather than the traditional five-year term. As he told an audience of American bankers in 1995, he saw the conventional approach as a 'political never-never land' in which 'elections intervene before the magic date arrives. Political accountability is lost and the bureaucracy can safely put off the day when they really have to buckle down and find the savings. The result, as we saw in Canada during at least the last 10 years, is a progression of missed targets, looming fiscal crises, and growing public cynicism.'[37]

But the 1994 budget was not without controversy. On the one hand, it introduced significant cuts to departments such as Defence, resulting in the politically difficult closure of bases and the Collège Militaire St Jean in Quebec. On the other hand, some economists, especially those involved in international finance, shared the view of the Finance Department's deputy minister, David Dodge, that the cuts and restraint did not go far enough, a view shared by editorial writers at the *Globe and Mail*, who attacked the budget, and Martin, for weeks on end. The criticism resulted in an explosive editorial board meeting in which Martin and lead critic Andrew Coyne exchanged angry insults before Martin walked out.

With the Mulroney government's legacy of a $42 billion annual deficit and a $550 billion debt, the critics were convinced that only aggressive action could restore fiscal health. Neither Dodge nor the majority of his staff believed the existing cuts plus economic growth could achieve even the 3 per cent target the Liberals advocated. More important, they did not see that target as meaningful. Dodge argued the demographics of increasing numbers of seniors and Aboriginal Canadians would soon require increased social spending, outstripping what he saw as the meagre spending reductions the Liberals planned.[38]

But Martin himself was not yet persuaded of the necessity for further action, and certainly the prime minister was not. In an interview in Edmonton a month after the budget was tabled, Chrétien thought he was *supporting* his finance minister when he asserted that there would be no further cuts. 'To go to our goal of 3 per cent of GNP,' he told radio talk show host Ron Collister, 'all the cuts have been announced in the budget. There will not be a new round.'[39] One month later the bottom fell out of the Liberals' budget assumptions. Interest rates began to climb dramatically as a result of actions taken in the United States. Almost overnight, the 3 per cent goal which Martin had seen as easily achievable was beginning to look almost impossible if nothing further was done. Over the course of the summer he wrestled with various options. He was heavily influenced by Dodge, who had an agenda ready and waiting. Dodge believed he could convince his latest minister to accept his advice if the situation deteriorated further because he knew how important the Red Book commitments were to the prime minister. Martin himself often dismissed the Red Book out of hand whenever one of its commitments – such as the elimination of the GST – caused further problems on the deficit front. One senior official told journalists one of the minister's most common phrases was 'Don't tell me about the Red Book, I wrote the damn thing and I know that a lot of it is crap.'[40]

Martin eventually decided to bring in an outside adviser to counterbalance departmental input, conscious that some of his colleagues were concerned about Finance Department advice. His choice, bank vice-president Peter Nicholson, was someone he had known for years. A fellow Grindstone participant and former member of John Turner's King Edward Group, Nicholson had been a keynote speaker at the Aylmer conference at Martin's suggestion. But Nicholson's views mirrored those of the Finance officials, who were happily prepared to work with him as a result. Nicholson also agreed with the extensive reductions to the government's expenditures recommended by Dodge – especially on social programs – although he also supported a stronger effort to increase productivity.[41] It was Nicholson who supported the cuts to pensions which Chrétien would later reject, and Nicholson whom Martin would ask to make the case to the prime minister, unsuccessfully as it turned out.

Paul Martin's conversion to the Finance Department's cause was complete by the fall of 1994, but he still had his work cut out for him. He needed to bring the prime minister, his cabinet colleagues, and the Canadian people on side if he hoped to succeed in imposing the harsh medicine he now believed would be necessary. Internal polling results indicated a serious lack of financial literacy on the part of most Canadians. As a result, he began making speeches across the country outlining the difficult fiscal situation, a delicate balancing act in view of the potential impact of his remarks on international financial markets. This communications effort, which his successor John Manley described as Martin's most important contribution to the deficit reduction exercise, set the stage for the severe cutbacks to come. His commitment to eliminate the deficit 'come hell or high water' and his warning that 'tough medicine' would be necessary to do so soon became household phrases.[42]

Martin also used the Finance Committee, chaired by his close friend and former college roommate Jim Peterson, to gain public acceptance for his goals. For the first time, the committee toured the country and consulted Canadians in advance of the budget. Martin himself would begin the process by testifying before the committee in Ottawa, laying out the dilemma he believed he faced. In addition, the Finance Department released a series of trial balloons to gauge public reaction to possible measures. By the time the budget was eventually tabled, there would be very little to surprise the business community or the media.

Meanwhile, within cabinet Martin was fortunate on two fronts. First, in light of the interest rate crisis, the prime minister reluctantly concluded that drastic measures – including a freeze on all government spending – were necessary. He had been continuously supportive of his finance minister, ever mindful of his own embarrassment at the hands of Trudeau, and was not prepared to withdraw that support despite the difficult conditions. One famous exchange in cabinet epitomized Chrétien's unwavering support and was widely discussed by several of the participants, all of whom left the Langevin Block severely chastened. After Martin announced that no new funds would be available due to the freeze, several ministers attempted to make the case for particular projects as exceptions. The first one to do so was chastised by Chrétien, who asked whether the minister had not heard what the finance minister said. 'There will be no new money,' the prime minister repeated. When a second minister later broached a similar project, Chrétien snapped 'Didn't you hear what *I* just said?'[43]

Less well known and rarely acknowledged by anyone, Martin's second advantage was the presence in cabinet of Marcel Masse, the former secretary of the Privy Council. Masse shared Martin's view of the seriousness of the fiscal situation. Based on his extensive experience in the public service he also concluded that across-the-board cuts were counterproductive and ineffective. What was necessary, he was convinced, was a review of all of the discretionary programs to determine which ones no longer served a useful purpose. He believed the savings would be substantial and funds would thereby be freed up to accomplish the government's new objectives. Although there is some debate as to who first proposed the arrangement, the preparations for the 1995 budget were seen as a team effort when Masse assumed responsibility for the highly unpopular cabinet exercise known officially as 'program review' and unofficially as the 'Star Chamber.' Cabinet colleagues such as John Manley later described Masse's role in the entire deficit reduction exercise as 'absolutely crucial' and 'largely unrecognized.'[44] A former cabinet colleague and Martin supporter concurred. 'Without Masse, Paul would have been nowhere. Yet he gets almost none of the credit.'

Jean Chrétien's own involvement in this exercise was less direct, but nevertheless equally crucial. First, he gave Masse his unqualified support, just as he had done with Martin. As Eddie Goldenberg later confirmed, Chrétien was obsessed with the importance of a united front. Despite considerable pressure from various quarters, he refused to make concessions even though his own inclination was to exempt various social programs and activities. 'If I change anything, everything will unravel,' he said repeatedly.[45] Second, in what one former cabinet colleague described as a 'brilliant political move,' Chrétien ensured Martin and Masse that they had to achieve consensus on the cuts with other members of the Program Review Committee before the duo could move ahead with their plans. Chrétien personally selected the members with care. His appointees included some of his most left-wing and politically astute ministers, including Brian Tobin, Sheila Copps, Sergio

Marchi, and Herb Gray. As virtually everyone involved later agreed, it was the reluctant acceptance of the need for deficit reduction by these social Liberals which ultimately secured the cabinet solidarity necessary to impose the cuts.

The fruits of the Program Review Committee's labours represented nothing less than the most draconian spending cuts in federal history. Individual ministers were given huge expenditure reduction targets for their departments to meet. More than $25 billion in cuts to programs worth less than $60 billion in total were to be achieved in three years. Thousands of public servants would lose their jobs. The cuts affected everything from the CBC, Petro Canada, and regional development programs to women's shelters and employment insurance benefits, all areas of traditional Liberal support. Cuts of 50–60 per cent were not uncommon. Ministers were given their bottom line and sent away to determine how to accomplish it. They then brought their proposals before the committee for approval. The debates were long, difficult, and often frustrating. Many ministers were sent back to reconsider their plans. Even after the social Liberals on the committee became convinced of the necessity of budget cuts, it was inconceivable to many of them that so many valuable programs would have to be sacrificed. Marcel Masse's idea of eliminating only those programs that were no longer relevant had long since been abandoned, as it soon became apparent that this approach would not deliver sufficient savings. As Sheila Copps recalled, at one point Masse declared the exercise was no longer about selecting what were the Liberal programs, but deciding which were the *most* Liberal.[46]

The degree of cabinet solidarity required for the exercise to succeed was almost unprecedented. One senior cabinet minister of the day later insisted that 'nothing since the cruise missile test crisis' of 1981 had strained '[his] ability to respect that principle. It was touch and go whether I would stay on.' One reason this solidarity was possible, of course, was successful communication between Martin and Masse. Virtually everyone stayed 'on message,' marking a dramatic return to the Liberal tradition of party unity. This demonstration of the discipline of power also provided a stark contrast to the failed efforts of the Mulroney Conservatives on the same file. As former immigration minister Sergio Marchi commented,

> the whole thing hinged on the fact there were no exceptions. I tried to get an exception for the settlement programs, which were the only thing we

could cut in terms of discretionary finances in the department, and they turned me down. I had to go back with a different plan, and that was when we brought up the idea of landing fees. It was the only way to save the settlement programs. I had to put up with comparisons with the head tax. You have no idea what it was like. But I still believe it was the lesser of two evils. There couldn't be any exceptions or it wouldn't have worked. We could all see that.[47]

His views were supported by Don Boudria, another social Liberal and former cabinet minister involved in the exercise, who declared later: 'We were all in it together. And we knew we would be a lot *less* Liberal if we hadn't done this.'[48]

Yet, as both Marchi and Copps noted at the time and afterwards, it was not the line departments themselves but the Finance Department that fixed the size of the cuts for each department. While there was general agreement within the cabinet that across-the-board cuts were usually unjust and often counterproductive, and also that targeting some programs more than others was better public policy, it was still unclear to many social liberals why Finance officials should be in charge of determining the relative value of the various departments.

They were not alone. One explosive outburst by the generally mild-mannered Ralph Goodale, a business Liberal, was widely reported and served to illustrate the level of ministerial angst. 'What gives you the right to act as judges on what generations of other people have created?' he thundered. 'How come you think you know what is right and what is wrong? What is in the national interest or not? The future of thousands of people is going to be decided right here ... From what divine right do you derive the power to decide that fifty of my scientists will be without work tomorrow?'[49]

Three years later, with the deficit eliminated and replaced by surpluses, several of the social Liberals in cabinet continued to wonder whether it had been necessary to cut as deeply and as quickly as Martin and Dodge had advocated. They also expressed concern that the cuts were somehow attributed to them individually as ministers, while the return to a surplus was described as the result of Martin's efforts alone.[50]

Ironically, another cabinet minister who resisted the cuts was John Manley, the industry minister who would later become finance minister after Martin's 2002 resignation. A business Liberal who appreciated the importance of deficit reduction, Manley nevertheless argued his department was unfairly singled out for excessive cuts and that it was the programs in his department – including research and development, technology transfer, and scientific support programs – that were essential if the economy was to grow and facilitate the 3 per cent target for deficit reduction. Years later, Manley said he simply could not believe 'landmark programs' such as the Defence Industry Procurement Program (DIPP) were going to be axed. 'I thought they were joking,' he said, recalling a meeting with Masse and Dodge where he was told his department would suffer a 50 per cent reduction. 'Of the fifty-four programs in our department, we had to totally eliminate forty-five to make our target.'[51]

Manley acknowledged some of the most egregious cuts were only temporary. The DIPP, for example, was replaced in large measure the following year by the 'Technology Partnerships' program, primarily as a result of his personal interventions with the prime minister. In the end, Manley concluded the cuts, while 'extremely painful,' did produce a positive benefit. 'The overall outcome was better government.'[52]

In addition to the savings achieved by expenditure cuts within the federal government, a second prong of the deficit reduction strategy was a lengthy freeze on public service salaries. This was largely symbolic since the freeze would have little impact on the government's ability to achieve its deficit reduction objective. It *would* prove highly unpopular and destroy much of the positive goodwill of the public service that had greeted Liberals on their return only a short while earlier. Yet both of these measures taken together were still not sufficient to eliminate the deficit. As a result, David Dodge argued that the only sufficiently large expenditure reductions would have to come from the federal transfers to individuals and provinces for the programs of the social safety net, and Paul Martin concurred.

This third prong of the plan was most contentious. Keeping in mind the Red Book commitment to improve relations with the provinces after the Mulroney government's unilateral changes had incensed the premiers, the handling of any such cuts would be a difficult political exercise. Ultimately Martin managed to minimize provincial objections by agreeing to give the premiers two other items that had long been on their wish list. The first was a promise of certainty in this funding, an issue which had arisen when the Mulroney government arbitrarily made changes to its funding formula without advance warning and in the middle of multi-year funding agreements. Martin told the premiers they would never receive less than the amount of his first round of transfers, and afterwards they could count absolutely on the consistent increases outlined in the budget.

The second concession was a change in the delivery of federal funding, giving the premiers more discretion in how the transfer payments were spent. Although it may have seemed a technicality, this change would soon have major implications for the delivery of social programs, and for the national unity file. The change saw federal transfers for three specific programs – post-secondary education, welfare, and health care – replaced with a lump sum the provinces could divide up as they saw fit. This new single block of funding – called the Canada Health and Social Transfer (CHST) – became the focal point for debate over the future of Canada's social union. Even more directly, it would be used as a weapon by the separatists in the second sovereignty referendum that was about to unfold.

This second change caused serious concern in the PMO. Although Chrétien did not intervene at the time, his misgivings eventually led him to reject the finance minister's plans for a further reduction in social program funding, this time through Old Age Security (OAS). The plan to reduce or eliminate payments for 'rich' seniors had been proposed by David Dodge years earlier. Michael Wilson attempted to implement it, only to have Brian Mulroney intervene and cancel the plan after the Conservatives were subjected to vitriolic public criticism. Martin bought into the Dodge plan as well and, as Sheila Copps later recounted in her memoirs, raised it enthusiastically within cabinet only to meet with considerable resistance.[53] But Martin did not give up. Instead, he pursued the idea with a vengeance. Even his own advisers began to worry that he was creating a public relations nightmare for the government. On this issue, Jean Chrétien for once refused to give his finance minister permission to move ahead with his plans, pointing out that it had not been approved by the Masse committee.

As several independent accounts of the ensuing conflict make clear, Martin's persistence caused a near-rupture in the Chrétien-Martin relationship, which until then had been professionally cordial if not warm. 'Martin had been told "no" by the prime minister three times and still he persisted ... his insubordination was unprecedented. It got to the point where [Chrétien] had to draw a line in the sand and say "I'm the prime minister and you're the finance minister and I'm saying no."'[54] In the end Eddie Goldenberg and David Dodge agreed Martin could refer in the next budget to a potential review of the pension system by the year 1997, thus saving face. Not surprisingly, future meetings between Martin and Chrétien on budget measures did not take place until Goldenberg and Dodge or their envoys met in advance to hammer out the details.

What is most significant about this conflict is the reason Chrétien gave for rejecting Martin's proposal. Like many of his social liberal ministers, Chrétien was unhappy with the cuts to social programs, but he accepted them as a necessary evil. His rejection of the proposed pension cuts was not motivated by this concern alone, however, but by his centralist vision of federalism and concern about the decentralist implications of Martin's plan. As he stated on several occasions and communicated to Martin through Eddie Goldenberg, his principal concern was the impact the cuts would have in Quebec, particularly in light of the probable upcoming referendum.[55]

The 1995 Referendum and the National Unity Crisis

One thing Jean Chrétien did not expect to face in his first mandate was another national unity crisis. Promising Canadians he would not reopen the constitutional file, he saw the whole issue of Quebec's special status fade from public interest. Moreover, by 1994 Robert Bourassa had been replaced as Liberal leader and premier by Daniel Johnson, someone with whom Chrétien felt much more comfortable. Chrétien's mistrust of Bourassa stemmed from episodes such as the premier's unexpected reversal and rejection of the Victoria Charter in 1971, his controversial handling of the War Measures crisis, and his dismissive treatment of John Turner during the Meech Lake debacle. He was also convinced 'Bourassa's degree of commitment to federalism depended on the size of the latest equalization cheque.'[56] Under Johnson, a nationalist but a less 'devious' one than Bourassa, there were skirmishes on manpower training and the closing of the Collège Militaire St Jean, but Chrétien knew it was unlikely the federal Liberals would find a more committed federalist in charge of the provincial Liberals.

This did not help Johnson in the provincial election in the fall of 1994. The Quebec Liberals were widely expected to lose to the Parti Québécois, and a key reason was Robert Bourassa's handling of the Charlottetown Accord. He had adopted the same alarmist tone as Brian Mulroney, creating a crisis mentality by demanding Meech-plus or more during the Charlottetown round to assuage Quebeckers' 'humiliation.' Despite being burdened with this legacy, Johnson fought a strong campaign and lost a close race to the PQ and its leader, Jacques

Parizeau. The popular vote was almost identical (44.7 per cent to 44.4 per cent) but this translated into a considerable difference in seats. The PQ now held 77 seats in the legislature while the Liberals had only 47.

By late 1994 everyone knew it was only a matter of time before a province-wide referendum on Quebec separation was held. A former provincial finance minister under René Lévesque, Parizeau had resigned a decade earlier over Lévesque's 'soft' position on sovereignty. Parizeau was well known for his hardline position that there should be another referendum as soon as possible. It was also well known that he favoured a short, simple question on separation, nothing like the ambiguous one put forward by Lévesque a decade earlier.

Yet public opinion polls repeatedly demonstrated the separatists had no hope of winning. Consequently the Liberals viewed the election of the PQ as an opportunity to crush the separatist movement once and for all. To lose once, as Lévesque had done in 1980, and still speak of another try might be acceptable. But to lose twice, as the PQ was certain to do if they launched another referendum in the near future, would be fatal. Parizeau's determination to call the referendum on principle was seen by the federal Liberals as sheer folly, but also as an ideal opportunity to demonstrate the merits of Canada – and the futility of the separatist option – to Quebeckers.

For much the same reason, Jean Chrétien enjoyed taking on the Bloc Québécois in the House of Commons. Chrétien's conviction that a separatist victory was impossible led him to ridicule the more fanatical Bloc MPs as well as Bouchard himself, especially since the Bloc leader at various times had said he believed an independent Quebec could continue to use Canadian currency and passports. When Bouchard openly referred to himself as a separatist in the spring of 1994 on a visit to Washington, DC, Chrétien saw the admission as a huge political mistake. As he told his caucus shortly afterwards, 'we have them cornered.' On 18 September 1994, barely a week after the PQ election victory, Chrétien gave a speech to the Chamber of Commerce in Quebec City in which he explained how he planned to handle the situation. He intended to focus on providing 'good government,' raising Canada's profile in the world, and putting the country's fiscal house in order as the best way to secure Quebeckers' commitment to Canada. Echoing Trudeau's long-standing argument that Quebec did not need special status, Chrétien declared Quebeckers would choose to stay in Canada without any special incentives because they knew it was their best option.

Despite this confidence, however, Chrétien chose to appoint Roméo

LeBlanc, an Acadian, to the position of governor general in February of 1995. The prime minister was well known in bureaucratic and political circles for his fear of 'closet separatists.' He frequently appointed francophones from outside Quebec when it was the turn of a French-speaking appointee if he was not satisfied with the list of eligible Quebeckers. Choosing LeBlanc, who was also a longtime Chrétien supporter, was the safer bet given the potential role the incumbent could play in case of a turn for the worse in the unity crisis.

Behind the scenes the Chrétien team was also monitoring the situation and organizing federal participation, limited as it might be. Chrétien established a special unit within the PCO to coordinate these activities, headed by foreign service officer Howard Balloch. Although this 'strategic planning unit' resembled the one established by Trudeau in 1980, it lacked the high-profile names and talent of the earlier group. Nevertheless the creation of the unit signalled the Chrétien government's recognition of the separatist reality and their determination to put the national unity question behind them once and for all.

It is therefore incorrect to suggest the federal Liberals were unprepared for the Quebec referendum of 1995. They knew well in advance that it would materialize and had planned their response. Moreover, shortly after Daniel Johnson was defeated both he and his officials began meeting regularly in Montreal with federal advisers such as Goldenberg, John Rae, and Montreal lawyer Eric Maldoff to discuss the general strategy they would follow in the expected referendum campaign.

The Quebec referendum legislation provided for YES and NO campaigns, and the federal Liberals knew that Johnson, as the leader of the official opposition and the provincial federalist forces, would automatically be the official leader of the NO campaign. The real question was what role, if any, the federal Liberals and Chrétien himself would play in such a campaign. Though more of a federalist than Bourassa, Johnson still represented a particular nationalist perspective that mistrusted the federal Liberals. A more serious problem was that Johnson's referendum co-chair was none other than Liza Frulla, the former Bourassa minister who had bitterly attacked Chrétien's role in the failure of Meech Lake after his victory in Calgary. Frulla made it clear to the federal team that his participation would not be welcome. The last thing they needed, she insisted, was someone who would remind Quebeckers of the 'scare tactics' used by the federal Liberals in 1980 when Chrétien had played a prominent role as Trudeau's minister of justice.[57]

Negotiations were conducted between the federal team and two representatives of the provincial NO side organizers, Pierre Anctil (Johnson's chief of staff) and John Parisella (Bourassa's former adviser). Despite their reputation for professionalism, Anctil and Parisella were viewed with scepticism by many of the federalist organizers due to the nationalist perspective they shared with their political masters. True to form, they quickly demonstrated they were anxious to head off any aggressive participation by a federal Liberal Party they viewed as being almost entirely composed of Trudeau sympathizers.

The two groups eventually settled on a federal strategy which Chrétien outlined several times for his caucus. They would divide the campaign into two periods. In the first half, the federalist forces would focus on the economic advantages of federalism. In the second half, they would speak about the benefits of belonging to Canada. Chrétien would deliver three speeches in Quebec during the campaign, and there would be a major federalist rally near the end. Paul Martin as the senior Quebec Liberal in cabinet and also as the finance minister was asked to give two speeches as well.

The federal negotiators, and especially Chrétien, were unhappy that provincial forces wanted as little interference from outsiders as possible, but Jean Chrétien's image problem in Quebec – and the consistent predictions of a large NO vote – led them to conclude there was no point in arguing and risking alienating the provincial leadership. Most polls predicted a margin of victory for the NO side equal to or greater than the 60 per cent of 1980. Regardless, some of the federal ministers and staff found their treatment both astonishing and humiliating. Lucienne Robillard had served as a minister in Bourassa's cabinet and was initially expected to liaise with the provincial group. Despite her provincial credentials, however, she was virtually ignored by Johnson's team. Jean Pelletier, a former mayor of Quebec City, voiced the frustration many of the federal organizers felt when he confided: 'It's difficult for any Quebecker who is at the federal level to be seen as a stranger in his own province ... Even the federal Liberals from Quebec were not welcomed by other provincial Liberals, which I think is nuts ... So this was disturbing and certainly unpleasant.'[58]

Only the Liberals' Quebec cabinet ministers and MPs were expected to play a role in the campaign, much to the chagrin of various Chrétien loyalists from outside the province such as Brian Tobin and Sergio Marchi, to say nothing of Sheila Copps. Copps, the deputy prime minister, was also the only fluently bilingual, high-profile federal Liberal cabinet minister outside the province who actually had positive ratings in Quebec. As she later recounted, she was 'floored' to learn her services would not be required. 'We were frozen out,' she recalled. 'We were kept away from the greatest debate in Canadian history because the provincial Liberals, led by Daniel Johnson, insisted on running the show. "Keep out," they told us. "Leave it to us."'[59] At one point Copps did venture into Quebec and incurred the wrath of Pierre Anctil. According to Copps, he insisted this was a matter to be decided 'within the family,' not by outsiders, and that 'he did not care what the outcome of the race was, win or lose, as long as the difference between the YES and the NO was not too great.'[60]

Some Quebeckers were urged to keep a low profile as well, including Brian Mulroney. Another prominent Quebecker whom the provincial NO forces specifically asked to refrain from public comment was former prime minister Pierre Trudeau. Trudeau's close friend and confidant Don Johnston later described this exclusion as 'an insane decision that almost cost us the country.'[61] Trudeau's absence from the debate was widely noted and unsettling for many Canadians who were unaware of the reason for his silence. Meanwhile in Ottawa, Chrétien and his ministers encountered an unprecedented situation. The prominence of the Bloc Québécois in Parliament gave the provincial separatists a natural ally in the nation's capital, able to reinforce their message daily on national television. Although Parizeau and Bouchard disliked each other, their officials worked together closely to ensure the separatist message was consistent. One aspect of that message was criticism of the government for its reductions to social programs. Bouchard frequently referred to Chrétien as 'the assassin of Meech Lake,' but now he, along with Parizeau, hammered home an additional message. Chrétien was the public face of a federal government 'which had run up a $550 billion national debt and brought in a draconian budget that slashed social programs.'[62]

But the Bloc was only half of the problem. The other major party in the House of Commons was the Reform Party led by Preston Manning. The significance of having to deal with not one but two regional parties became obvious shortly after the unofficial referendum campaign began. Manning promptly served notice that Chrétien could not count on the Reform Party to support his centralist position on federalism, any more than he could count on the Bloc. Having come to Ottawa on a wave of protest and western alienation, the Reformers, too, were in favour of a far more decentralized federation. They frequently made common cause with the Bloc, much to Chrétien's chagrin. Now, in the fight for Canada, he discovered the federal government for the first time could not count on the support that Pierre Trudeau had received from the Conservatives and the NDP. (Later it came to light that Manning approached the American ambassador to Canada to discuss potential scenarios in the event of a YES vote, a revelation that shocked Ottawa veterans.)

Manning's insistence that Chrétien address the validity of a YES vote infuriated the Liberal leader. The prime minister responded that a recent ruling by the Quebec Superior Court specifically found that the Quebec government had no constitutional authority to declare independence in the wake of a YES vote, as Jacques Parizeau planned to do. 'The prime minister has a constitution to abide by,' Chrétien replied at one point. 'And there is no mechanism in the constitution permitting the separation of any part of the Canadian territory.'[63] Chrétien also refused to be pinned down on the percentage required for the vote to be viewed as successful. Although he would not provide any specifics, he made several comments that demonstrated his thinking on the issue. Most noteworthy was his reply that 'you need 66 per cent to dismantle a fishing camp!'

Unfortunately, Lucienne Robillard had already mused publicly that the federal government would recognize a 50 per cent plus one referendum result, forcing Chrétien to clarify the government's position more than once. This small public display of dissension in the federal Liberal ranks was indicative of the more substantial behind-the-scenes disagreement between Chrétien and several of his Quebec ministers, most of whom had not been in politics during the Trudeau era and many of whom, like Robillard, had first been involved in Quebec provincial politics. As John Manley and Sheila Copps both noted later, the prevailing view among those Quebec ministers was that the referendum result would have to be respected no matter what. To take any other stance, they believed, would lead to negative electoral consequences for the federal Liberals in Quebec and very possibly to violence. As John Manley later recalled: 'The concept of the federal government taking a hard line in the event of a negative referendum result (that is, a YES vote), even if it was by the smallest of margins, was simply unthinkable to them. Masse had a fit at the thought of it. Most of us didn't bother to argue because we thought a NO vote was in the bag.'[64]

The official referendum campaign did not begin until 2 October, but both sides had been unofficially campaigning since early September, when debate began in the Quebec National Assembly. On the day of the official launch, various opinion polls showed the federal side with a substantial lead, varying between 55 to 45 and 48 to 41. At the weekly caucus meeting on 4 October Chrétien said he recognized some of his troops were frustrated at their lack of input, but he assured them 'the situation is evolving absolutely beautifully.' He would speak on Friday in Shawinigan. The strategy would be to 'call them separatists, not make any constitutional offers and tell them what Canada is all about.'

Chrétien noted pointedly in his caucus address that the provincial Liberals and NO organizers had not used the term 'separatist.' Nor did they want to use national symbols such as the Canadian dollar or flag in their campaign. Clearly of two minds about the wisdom of their approach, he nevertheless remained confident based on the reports he was receiving from his advisers, who in turn were relying largely on their provincial counterparts. Certainly there was every indication that the YES side was in complete disarray. Looking dispirited, Jacques Parizeau participated in fewer events than expected and the Johnson organizers reported grassroots separatists working for the YES side had virtually given up.

Chrétien's first speech on 6 October was quite successful. An early speech by Paul Martin on the economic consequences of separation and the potential difficulties Quebec could encounter in obtaining a NAFTA-type agreement with the Americans was also well received. Certainly it seemed the momentum was in favour of the NO forces.

The Turning Point in the Crisis

The decisive moment in the campaign was the 8 October announcement that Jacques Parizeau was stepping aside in favour of Lucien Bouchard. The formal explanation, that Bouchard would be named chief negotiator in the event of a YES vote, was a patently face-saving gesture. It was widely understood that Parizeau handed over the campaign in desperation. Bouchard, in turn, insisted on the right to change the referendum question as a pre-condition for assuming control. As a result, in mid-campaign the question facing Quebec voters would now be an ambiguous and convoluted one asking them whether they favoured sovereignty-association, not separation. Shortly thereafter the referendum dynamics changed dramatically. As John Manley later put it, 'Bouchard nearly won the referendum single-handedly.'[65]

On 19 October Chrétien and his team received the first worrisome polling results. Several members of his cabinet had already expressed serious concerns, but two weeks before the end of the campaign they continued to receive favourable reports from their chief organizer on the ground, public works minister Alfonso Gagliano, and from Johnson's two provincial liaisons. Sheila Copps complained that everything was 'just tickety boo' according to the provincial people, 'even as we could see that the wheels were coming off.' David Collenette concurred: 'There was an almost surreal sense that everything would work out in the end. We should all just be calm.'[66] Finally, sensing danger, they urged Chrétien to intervene.

Indeed, Bouchard was dispensing flagrant misinformation and equally outrageous but reassuring guarantees to Quebeckers that little would change under an independent Quebec. The popularity of his cause increased dramatically in a short period of time. From a deficit of more than twelve percentage points, the YES side was almost even with the NO forces by 22 October. Even Bouchard's most objectionable pronouncements (such as describing Quebeckers as 'one of the white races that has the least children')[67] drew little or no criticism.

The federal NO organizers were caught flat-footed. Jean Pelletier later remarked, 'Who could possibly have expected them to change leaders in the middle of the campaign?'[68] Don Boudria, one of the few MPs from outside Quebec who had been permitted to work on the campaign because his eastern Ontario riding was next door to Johnson's, confided: 'We didn't think it would make a difference. We thought changing leaders would be like shuffling the deck chairs on the *Titanic*, because everyone knew they were in trouble.'[69] As Boudria commented years later, the real question was *when* the change in YES leadership started to appear in polling results. '*When* the provincial NO organizers knew our side was losing is something nobody seems to know. If it was only a day or two before they told us, it probably made no difference, but if they knew for longer than that, obviously it would have made a big difference to us.'[70]

Ignorant of the sea change taking place, the federal leadership followed their original game plan. Martin and Chrétien delivered their second speeches in the province on 17 and 18 October respectively. Chrétien's speech focused in equal measure on the benefits of Canada and the deceptive nature of Bouchard's arguments. Martin's talk underlined the economic issues once again. He referred to the potential loss of 1 million jobs and more than 80 per cent of the province's exports. Its negative message completely overshadowed any possible impact the prime minister's more positive speech might have had. Although Martin would later claim his speech had been widely vetted and was not inaccurate, it was described by several of his colleagues as 'a fiasco.'

The perception in the Quebec media that Martin had greatly exaggerated the economic consequences of separation was immediate and visceral. Jacques Parizeau issued a scathing response in which he pointed out that Quebec had only 3.2 million jobs to begin with. The old fears of a repeat of the 'economic blackmail' approach used in 1980 re-emerged and many Quebeckers lost interest in the substantive arguments of the debate.

In the long run, Martin's misstep was not surprising to many of his colleagues. As one well-known reporter commented: 'On other issues Martin came across as smooth and sophisticated. When he opened his mouth on Quebec, he seemed accident prone.' The incident also reinforced Jean Chrétien's existing opinion that Martin 'could not be trusted' on the national unity file, because he was 'soft on nationalists' and 'too eager to grant concessions to the provinces.'[71]

From then until the end of the campaign the two sides were locked in an emotional struggle for the hearts of Quebeckers. Focus groups confirmed that most voters believed they could keep their Canadian passports and currency after a YES vote, and some even assumed they would be better off financially because they would pay only one level of tax. The NO side realized it was in serious difficulty.

Another headache for the federalists came when the newly elected president of France, Jacques Chirac, announced his government would recognize a YES vote. As a Gaullist, Chirac was following in the tradition begun with his predecessor's 'Vive le Québec libre' comment during an official visit to Canada in 1967. But he was also responding to ongoing lobbying by Quebec separatists, who had courted the French assiduously for more than twenty years. With Bloc MPs such as Francine Lalonde, the party's foreign affairs critic, taking advantage of every opportunity to participate in Canadian delegations to Europe to promote the separatist cause, the result was hardly surprising. It was, nevertheless, a perfectly timed blow to the federalist cause.

Also disturbing to the federalists was the increasingly prevalent public belief, promoted by Bouchard, that Quebeckers could choose sovereignty-association with impunity since the rest of Canada would simply acquiesce. The federal side argued this was incorrect. Chrétien referred often to the Quebec court decision, and there had been other attempts by the federalists to demonstrate this was hardly a reasonable assumption. But the fear of appearing to blackmail voters prevented them from adopting more aggressive counter-arguments at the time. Nevertheless the defence minister at the time, David Collenette, later confided there had been contingency plans involving the army protecting federal buildings in the province and removing F-18s, and the use of force had not been ruled out.[72]

Most troubling were the revelations that Bouchard's arguments about the social safety net had made an impact. Many Quebeckers now believed the costs of separation would no longer be as great because their social benefits had already been substantially reduced by the federal government. The loss of their health care overage, unemployment insurance or welfare payments, or even future pension benefits simply did not appear to be as significant a cost.

It was in this context that Jean Chrétien and his closest advisers began to consider promising Quebeckers some movement on the more traditional nationalists' demands, something he had categorically refused to do until then. In the end his hand was forced by comments made by his putative ally, Daniel Johnson, on 21 October. Speaking to reporters after a rally, Johnson said he would 'welcome' a commitment by the prime minister to introduce a constitutional amendment recognizing Quebec's distinct society. When Chrétien was reached in New York, in meetings at the United Nations, he did not know about Johnson's comments and indicated he had no intention of doing any such thing. By Sunday, Quebec newspapers were highlighting the apparent rift in the NO side with headlines such as 'Chrétien dit non a Johnson.'[73]

By now the NO forces were the ones in complete disarray. Chrétien's last two appearances of the campaign were tinged with desperation. At a meeting of federal NO volunteers in Montreal on 24 October, Chrétien said, 'I don't want to be the last prime minister of Canada.' The day before his scheduled television address on 26 October, he broke down during a national caucus meeting. The shock waves reverberated through the Liberal caucus, and many MPs and senators were seen leaving the meeting in obvious distress. Then in the televised statement, and again at his last scheduled speech of the campaign on 27 October in Verdun, Chrétien did the previously unthinkable. He committed himself to some type of recognition of Quebec as a distinct society, to the provision of a veto for Quebec over future constitutional change ('Any changes in constitutional jurisdiction for Quebec will be made only with the consent of

Quebeckers'), and to the transfer of manpower training programs to the provincial government as Johnson had long requested.

Meanwhile some of Chrétien's strongest supporters, led by Fisheries Minister Brian Tobin, were organizing a massive rally in downtown Montreal to be held on 27 October. Its purpose was to demonstrate to Quebeckers that the rest of Canada did not want them to vote YES. While the provincial organizers were opposed to the move, they were unable to prevent the event from taking place and decided to manage it as best they could. Most of the outside participants were accommodated, but Sheila Copps, who had asked to speak at the event, was refused. She left in a fury while Liza Frulla delivered the final address. 'We act as though the province is already separate and then we wonder why people want to separate,' Copps stormed. She later claimed that invitations for federal Liberal speakers had been 'flooding in' to NO headquarters from groups and municipalities across the province, but they were routinely rejected because the provincial Liberals did not want 'outside' participation.[74]

In Ottawa, John Manley and Anne McClellan met informally with Justice Minister Allan Rock on Sunday evening to discuss possible legal measures the federal government could take immediately in the event of a YES vote, such as a reference to the Supreme Court. 'We knew that legally the referendum was a consultation only and had no significance,' Manley later recounted. 'But we felt the events of the campaign, and especially the change in leadership and of the question, meant that there would need to be some sort of formal ruling on the validity of the results.'[75] Others, including Brian Tobin, spent the evening discussing more practical implications of a possible loss, including the difficulties of having a prime minister from Quebec attempting to negotiate with that province. Regardless of who was leader, however, Tobin and David Collenette at one point speculated that 'some new structure might have to emerge and some new coalition.'[76]

Chrétien rejected the notion of either resigning, as Pierre Trudeau had threatened to do in 1980, or of forming a coalition, in the event of a YES vote. His position was strengthened by the publication of a nationwide public opinion poll in October which showed some 81 per cent of Canadians expected him to remain prime minister after a YES vote. Chrétien later declared, 'I was the prime minister and I would have remained prime minister as long as I had the confidence of the House. And I'm sure that in a crisis I would have kept the confidence of the House.'[77]

Aftermath of the National Unity Crisis: Chrétien's Ten-Point Plan

In the end the NO side won by the slimmest of margins. Chrétien delivered a nationwide address underlining the need for cooperation and conciliation, and emphasizing non-constitutional issues. 'I ask the premier of Quebec to work with the government of Canada to respond to the real and pressing needs of Quebeckers.' In Montreal, shortly before Chrétien's speech, Premier Jacques Parizeau commented that 'money and the ethnic vote' were responsible for the defeat of the separatist forces, a remark quickly denounced by most other Quebec politicians but not by Lucien Bouchard. Parizeau also announced his impending resignation and was soon replaced as premier by Bouchard.

While the YES forces lost again, Jean Chrétien and the federal Liberals were blamed for the close call which many felt had been unnecessary. As Chrétien remarked to Eddie Goldenberg: 'I prefer the speech I just gave to the other one you gave me today.' Both Goldenberg and Peter Donolo later recalled that Chrétien also indicated he would never have entered into negotiations to break up Canada on the basis of the ambiguous question that had just been posed in the referendum. The same night he also told Goldenberg: 'I will never allow Canada to be put through a trauma like this again,' and began almost immediately to plan the Liberal response.[78] The next night in Toronto at a party fundraiser Chrétien repeated this commitment. 'This country has the right to political stability,' he declared. 'And as prime minister of Canada I will make sure that we have political stability in this land. That is my duty. That is my constitutional responsibility.'[79]

Fault for the near disaster was distributed widely, but several key advisers concurred on two points. 'We were repeatedly told we should play by the rules of the day,' Jean Pelletier later confided. 'In retrospect we should not have played by the rules of the day.'[80] Similarly, Peter Donolo, largely sidelined during the campaign, confirmed that many of Chrétien's closest advisers believed he should have trusted his instincts and intervened aggressively to defend the Trudeau vision of federalism rather than relying so heavily on economic arguments geared to the Bourassa vision of 'federalisme rentable.' Chrétien himself remained bitter about the role played by the provincial Liberals, whom he felt had betrayed him.

The event dealt a devastating blow to Chrétien's confidence. According to David Zussman, the crisis caused him to lose his focus for several weeks, after which he spent the rest of his first mandate single-mindedly implementing the commitments he had made in the last few days of the campaign and addressing what he considered to be the root causes of the near disaster.[81] Among those causes were the failure to defend federalism against the false or misleading accusations of the separatists; the failure to communicate the significant role of the federal government in Quebeckers' lives; the lack of a clear referendum procedure and acceptable question; and the need to re-establish the federal presence in social programs.

Although it may not have been obvious to Canadians at the time, many of the most noteworthy initiatives in the remainder of his first mandate were in some way connected to this issue, as were several in his two succeeding terms. As Chrétien himself later stated, in his view 'the single most important priority of every prime minister since 1867 has been to preserve the unity of the country.' The threat of another referendum loomed large in Chrétien's mind. His concern was fuelled by Bouchard's greater popularity and also by the new premier's subsequent pledge to hold another referendum whenever the 'winning conditions' appeared to be present. 'For the next eight years, the unity of Canada was my number one priority as prime minister,' he declared in his public statement to the Gomery Inquiry. 'It was never an issue of party, it was always an issue of country. I was determined that there would be no winning conditions for the proponents of separation.'[82]

Chrétien's defence of the sponsorship program at the heart of the Gomery Inquiry specifically noted that the program 'was only one part of a comprehensive strategy ... It was not created in a vacuum and cannot be understood in isolation.' At least ten specific measures were taken by the Liberal government in the aftermath of the referendum to promote national unity, of which the sponsorship program was neither the most important nor the most costly. The first two measures were taken by December of 1995. Earlier, Ontario Premier Mike Harris made it clear he would not agree to a constitutional amendment to achieve either the veto Chrétien had promised Quebec or some recognition of its 'distinctive' society. The prime minister felt it was essential to do something as a goodwill gesture and so he introduced a resolution in Parliament on the 'distinctiveness' of Quebec society. He also introduced a resolution which committed the federal government to seek Quebec's approval as well as that of the three other regions originally defined in the 1971 Victoria Charter amending formula before proceeding on any future reforms. The move was not without controversy. Ironically it was the west that objected, reinforcing the Liberals' problems there. After considerable protest by representatives from BC, including a personal intervention by Senator Ross Fitzpatrick, Chrétien reluctantly agreed to a change. The amending formula was altered to include British Columbia as a fifth Pacific region and the resolution was passed. In light of Harris's intransigence and as a follow-up to the first federal initiative, the nine provincial premiers negotiated their own text of an agreement acknowledging the distinctive nature of Quebec. These negotiations finally culminated, at Chrétien's urging, in the adoption of what was dubbed the Calgary Declaration. However, their willingness to do so came with a price tag. The quid pro quo for their symbolic gesture was the federal government's agreement to meet with the premiers to address the issue of funding and standards for national social programs under the overarching concept of a 'social union.'

A third initiative of Chrétien's post-referendum national unity strategy was the recruitment of additional francophone Quebeckers into his government who supported the Trudeauvian approach to Canadian federalism. Chrétien believed he needed to develop his front bench strength. He was unhappy with the shallow pool of talent from which he could draw in his caucus, and deeply conscious of the fact that several of his existing Quebec ministers not only shared the provincial nationalist perspective but apparently failed to see how far the tide had turned during the referendum campaign. He sought out strong, credible federalist voices from Quebec to come to Ottawa and become the face of the federal government in that province, conveying the federal message and challenging separatist propaganda on an ongoing basis.

David Zussman recalled being contacted by Chrétien one day in early January 1996 for his opinion of Stéphane Dion and Pierre Pettigrew. The following day he learned Chrétien had decided to appoint them directly into his cabinet. Dion, a political scientist and university professor in Montreal, was well known as an articulate opponent of separatism. Pettigrew, who was also seen as a federalist, was well connected to the Montreal business community. As a former EA to Allan MacEachen, he was already familiar with the machinery of government in Ottawa. Similar considerations motivated Chrétien's decision to replace foreign affairs minister André Ouellet as his Quebec lieutenant and chief organizer by appointing him to a patronage position at Canada Post. Declaring that he was intent on bringing 'new blood' into the federal Liberal Party in Quebec, Chrétien authorized another Quebec minister, well-known organizer and longtime loyalist Alfonso Gagliano, to begin the process of reversing the party's fortunes in the province. The vacant

Foreign Affairs portfolio was quickly filled by Lloyd Axworthy, a move which would prove fortuitous for Chrétien's nation-building agenda.

The fourth initiative, which came to be known as 'Plan B,' was unveiled in short order. Newly appointed Intergovernmental Affairs Minister Stéphane Dion began a dedicated campaign to 'set the record straight' in light of PQ propaganda and frequent misstatements by Lucien Bouchard, now the Quebec premier. His public letter-writing duel with the premier, his frequent statements and appearances in the Quebec media, and his determination to ensure a more acceptable, legally binding process in the event of any future referenda were all part of Chrétien's determination to demonstrate a more hard-line approach to separatism.

In a speech in Vancouver, Chrétien raised his fifth point, partition, an issue that had been raised by anglophone and aboriginal Quebeckers, and notably spokespersons for Alliance Quebec, during the referendum campaign. 'If Canada is divisible,' he said, 'then Quebec is as well.'[83] This argument had been raised in reference to parts of the province such as West Quebec, the island of Montreal, and the northern part of the province. The separatists had difficulty refuting this argument, particularly since well-known Bloc MP and former Montreal law professor Daniel Turp had written an article years earlier supporting the legality of partition. As Peter Donolo later recounted, there was immediate public resonance with the idea, and 'in retrospect we should have pursued it more aggressively at the time.'[84]

A sixth measure taken by the government in 1996 was the decision to pursue a reference to the Supreme Court on the legality of Quebec's unilateral separation. That decision was strongly promoted by Stéphane Dion, who told his cabinet colleagues he believed the Court's eventual ruling would demonstrate to Quebeckers how difficult separation actually would be and how the separatists were misleading them. As Chrétien later recounted in his public statement to the Gomery Inquiry, PMO officials worked closely with the Justice Department to complete the draft text of the reference. It contained three fundamental questions which were designed to prove that a separatist government could not legally invoke a unilateral declaration of independence, that even a clear referendum result could only be used to initiate negotiations, and that the rest of Canada would have to be involved in any such negotiations, not simply the federal government. On the assumption of favourable rulings by the Court on these questions, the February 1996 Throne Speech also anticipated what would eventually become the Clarity Act of 1998. Should another referendum be held in Quebec, the Throne Speech promised, the federal government 'will exercise its responsibility to ensure the debate is conducted with all the facts on the table, that the rules of the process are fair, that the consequences are clear, and that all Canadians will have their say in the future of the country.'

Not surprisingly, this renewed federal firmness, so reminiscent of former prime minister Trudeau, was publicly rejected by Quebec provincial Liberals, including Frulla and Johnson. It was also cause for considerable debate and disagreement within the Liberal cabinet and caucus. As several former ministers recalled, the split in cabinet was between those Trudeau disciples who favoured the more hard-line approach and those Martin supporters who became known as the 'appeasers.' It was not simply along regional lines, with Quebeckers lined up against the rest of the cabinet. Instead, Quebec newcomers Dion and Pettigrew were in favour of the approach, and some anglophone cabinet ministers from outside the province were opposed. Along with Paul Martin, whose unhappiness with the tougher stance was well known, two other opponents were Martin supporters from western Canada, Anne McClellan and Ralph Goodale. Within caucus, the distinction between Martin and Chrétien supporters was even more apparent.

Another immediate initiative of the Chrétien government was the creation of an ad hoc cabinet committee on national unity, chaired by Marcel Masse. The committee reported in early 1996, recommending a number of measures, one of which was heightened federal visibility in Quebec. All of them were unanimously adopted at a special cabinet meeting on 1–2 February 1996. Both the creation of a National Unity Information Office to be located within Canadian Heritage, and the development of the sponsorship program within the Public Works Department (the seventh and eighth points in the government's response plan) were a direct result of this committee's recommendations. However, a suggestion to highlight the irregularities in the referendum vote-counting procedures, as a rationale for future federal intervention, was definitely *not* acted upon. One cabinet minister present at the meeting recalled Masse 'hitting the roof' at the mere suggestion Quebec was not capable of conducting its own electoral process.

An improved position internationally was a ninth aspect of the plan. For example, less than a year later the federal government responded aggressively when the Bouchard government unexpectedly arranged to host an international meeting in Quebec City. Organized by the speaker of the Quebec National Assembly, the Conference of Parliamentarians of the Americas provided an opportunity for Bouchard to deliver a vitriolic speech promoting Quebec independence. Its impact, however, was minimal, because Chrétien himself delivered a major address after Bouchard, correcting what he perceived to be the many misleading or incorrect claims made by the premier.

According to Don Boudria, the minister responsible for international cooperation at the time, the separatists 'tried to snooker us' with their planning of the conference but 'we weren't going to be caught with our pants down again.'[85]

In the same vein, one behind-the-scenes initiative that would prove highly successful was the assignment Chrétien gave his closest adviser, Jean Pelletier. Although Pelletier was known as a skilled administrative fixer in Ottawa, he had been a well-regarded mayor of Quebec City for many years before Chrétien approached him to join the PMO. During that time, he had become a close friend of his counterpart in Paris, Jacques Chirac. With Chirac's rise to the presidency and unfortunate intervention in the referendum, Chrétien saw an opportunity to take advantage of Pelletier's relationship to attempt to repair the damage done by separatist lobbying in France. According to several insider accounts, Pelletier travelled several times to France to meet with Chirac and explain the Canadian position in detail. Pelletier's successful efforts, along with Chrétien's appointment of his nephew, career public servant Raymond Chrétien, as ambassador to France in 2000, are considered by insiders to have been the key to dramatically improved Canada-France relations. Eddie Goldenberg later noted that Chirac actually referred to 'the essential role that a united Canada plays as model for the world' at a dinner he hosted for the retiring Chrétien in 2003.[86]

A tenth and final federal government effort in response to the referendum was the popular one-year program introduced by Sheila Copps in 1996 (after her move to the Heritage portfolio) to distribute Canadian flags to ordinary Canadians. Copps, once a strong defender of Meech Lake, later confided that she changed her mind soon after. 'Once we formed the government and I became a minister, I soon learned how important it is to have national programs, and how much damage Meech Lake and Charlottetown would have done.'[87] After the referendum crisis, her perception of the importance of the federal role was heightened, but she worried that individual Canadians were not sufficiently knowledgeable or engaged. In the end the flag program exceeded expectations and provided more than a million flags to households across the country.

Copps, who later said, 'It came as no surprise to me that I was viciously attacked by the separatists for the program,' also indicated her most significant regret of the referendum campaign was that 'we never spoke with pride about our country, our flag, our diversity, we merely made the economic case for Canada.' Like Chrétien, she felt the lack of effective communications was a major problem. 'It was a propaganda war and we were losing it ... Every instrument in the hands of the [separatist] Quebec government ... was devoted to subtly and not-so-subtly promoting the idea of a sovereign nation in partnership with Canada. The propaganda in those days was so successful that to fly a Quebec flag was strong, a Canadian flag was silly.' Years later, Copps continued to defend the program, noting in 2005 that 'nearly ten years after the program ended, I still receive letters from people thanking me for the flag.' Copps also argued the program 'provided a change in our culture' by encouraging Canadians to become more visibly patriotic. 'I see more flags now on July 1st than ever before,' she noted, 'and I'm told the run on flag poles each year is greater than the previous one, even in Quebec.'[88]

An underlying and lasting effect of the referendum crisis was the fact that virtually all policy issues considered by the Chrétien government, and especially by the prime minister, were now coloured by their implications for Quebec. As Herb Gray said, the prime minister's 'biggest theme' was a united country, and 'he would talk of how important it was for him to leave office with the situation calm in Quebec.' This point of view was echoed by Art Eggleton, an eight-year cabinet veteran who told journalist Lawrence Martin, 'in every cabinet meeting I was in there was nothing more important than the political situation in Quebec. Nothing close.'[89]

Moving On: Return to a Liberal Agenda

The fiscal crisis and the national unity crisis came to be seen as intertwined by the Chrétien Liberals. One of the most significant recommendations of the Masse committee was to pursue a 'good government agenda which includes fiscal responsibility,' something the committee considered 'essential to achieving the objective of defeating separatism.' According to Chrétien, 'our whole economic strategy over the next several years to put the books of the nation in order was also an integral element of our national unity agenda.'[90]

The February 1997 budget, which predicted a dramatic decrease in the deficit for the coming fiscal year and a balanced budget by 1998–9, provided a number of indications of the ways in which the Liberals were thinking of developing social policy in the near future. The effectiveness of the separatists' arguments about federal cuts to social programs had not been forgotten. In addition to confronting new realities such as growing child poverty and declining funding for post-secondary education, research, and development, proposals such as the National Child Benefit, increased financial assistance for student loans, and the creation of the Canada Foundation for Innovation were designed to increase the presence of the federal government in citizens' lives and to provide positive incentives for Quebec and the other provinces to work together cooperatively.

With the deficit all but eliminated and the broad outlines of the Liberals' proposed deficit-elimination dividend sketched out, Chrétien decided the time had come for a renewed mandate, after which he hoped to begin to implement his 'real' Liberal agenda, an agenda that would not only remind Canadians of the values they shared but give Quebeckers additional reasons to choose Canada over separation.

9 Return to Liberalism: The Clarity Act and the Deficit Dividend

The genius of the act was the name. How could you oppose clarity? Were you going to argue in favour of obfuscation?

– Liberal MP Paul DeVillers[1]

With the fiscal crisis all but eliminated by the February 1997 budget, the Chrétien Liberals could point to a major success story during their first mandate, quite apart from the implementation of many Red Book initiatives. As for the national unity crisis, most felt it had been firmly addressed by the prime minister's ten-point plan. Support for separatism in Quebec was already beginning to recede. The Liberals' opposition was still fragmented. The Bloc Québécois was clearly limited to its regional base and reeling from the loss of Lucien Bouchard. Outside of Quebec, Preston Manning's Reform Party was locked in a divisive battle for the Right with the remaining Conservatives under their new leader, Jean Charest.

In short, there was no alternative government-in-waiting and the Liberals knew it. But they also knew this was largely due to the presence of Reform, which had siphoned off the traditional Conservative vote in the west. Having lost much of their own traditional base in Quebec to the Bloc, the Liberals could only count on re-election with a majority if the right-wing vote in the rest of the country remained divided. It was hardly surprising, then, that in his closing remarks to caucus on several occasions during 1996 and 1997, Jean Chrétien referred to the importance of Manning and cautioned his MPs not to forget 'we need this guy.'

It was not surprising, considering these many factors, that public opinion polls showed the party on the verge of winning another substantial majority. Yet despite months of deliberation about the timing and focus of the next federal election, the Liberals failed to capitalize on these advantages when they finally took the plunge. Instead, from the moment the writ was dropped they were reduced to playing a game of catch-up with the opposition parties.

The unexpected difficulties of the Liberals in the 1997 election led to a much closer than anticipated result, although the election itself was almost a non-event. Certainly few Canadians could identify many issues that arose during the campaign. Fully 29 per cent of those surveyed in one national poll indicated there were *no* important election issues.[2] As political analyst Christopher Dornan concluded, the election 'was a dutifully tolerated annoyance' which evoked irritation and little interest.[3] The lack of interest in the election campaign also meant fewer Canadians voted. One senior Liberal later described it as 'the election that never was.'

In the end Jean Chrétien's margin of victory was drastically reduced. Most analysts agreed that no mandate was given to the Liberals for specific policy initiatives as a result of their eventual victory.[4] Nevertheless the party retained its majority. The two major opposition parties – the Reform Party and the Bloc Québécois – simply traded places, while the Conservatives and NDP remained on the distant backbenches. At first glance the election seemed inconsequential.

Notwithstanding their inauspicious performance during the 1997 campaign, the Chrétien Liberals went on to implement a number of major changes to social policy as well as introducing more initiatives on the national unity file. Interestingly, the prime minister who was known to favour political caution and an incremental approach to governing presided over a series of dramatic policy developments whose potential impact was largely unrecognized at the time. As he told his caucus shortly after the election, the deficit battle had been won, the 'tough days' of spending cuts were over, and it was time to return to 'real' Liberal policies.

The Timing of the 1997 Election

When Jean Chrétien went to Rideau Hall to ask the governor general to dissolve Parliament and call an election in the spring of 1997, only three and one half years after the party returned to power, it was a move he had been anticipating for nearly a year. The Liberals' standing in Ontario was higher than ever, leading him to conclude another majority was in the cards. Much of the 1993 Red Book had been implemented and the deficit commitment had been met ahead of schedule. Perhaps most importantly, it seemed to Chrétien that it made no difference whether the election was held in the spring or fall of 1997. Everyone knew there would be an election at the end of the government's four-year term. House leader Don Boudria recalled: 'By the time I was appointed to cabinet in 1996 we were already talking about an election next year.'[5]

Following on the example of the one-hundred-day report card, the Liberal government's accomplishments were spelled out again in the fall of 1996 in a party publication entitled *A Record of Achievement: A Report on the Liberal Government's First 36 Months in Office*. The unique nature of their 1993 Red Book was underlined once more in Jean Chrétien's introduction. 'Three years ago,' he wrote, 'the Liberal Party did something no national political party has ever done before in Canada: we laid out the most comprehensive, detailed plan for governing ever put to Canadians in a general election.' Furthermore, he noted, 'we told Canadians at the time that a Liberal government would be held accountable for our Red Book commitments. We meant it then, and we mean it today.' By giving a 'full accounting' of the status of their commitments, Chrétien said, the party was once again 'breaking new ground.'[6]

The Liberals repeated their earlier approach of anticipating criticism, producing this final report card on their 1993 election commitments to coincide with the party's biennial policy convention in 1996, well in advance of an election call. The layout of the document was virtually identical to the original Red Book, its text organized in the same fashion and cross-referenced to the original promises to make comparison easier. The report claimed some 78 per cent of the Red Book promises – or 153 of 197 – had been implemented. A further 12 per cent, or 24 commitments, were described as 'still in progress' and a small minority (1.5 per cent) 'have been implemented but, because of fiscal constraints, at funding levels less than 75 per cent of what was promised.' While the text painted the Liberal achievements in the best possible light, few critics emerged to quibble over the party's interpretation. Once again, it appeared the very fact of having published such a report card was considered a major coup. However, Brian Tobin, who as a former caucus chair had been in charge of the Caucus Research Bureau, also noted that the credibility of the Liberal team that produced the report card was well established by then with the parliamentary press corps. Bureau director Dan McCarthy concurred: 'We were all waiting for the inevitable fault-finding, and we couldn't believe it when almost nothing happened. The media pretty much took our numbers at face value.' What was more, not only the media but grassroots Liberals and the general public wanted to obtain copies. 'We never anticipated such a demand,' McCarthy said. 'Of course we thought it was important in preparing for the election, but no one predicted *how* important.'[7]

The press commentary ranged from the simple ('He has done what he said he'd do')[8] to the enthusiastic praise offered in one editorial: 'The Liberals are sketching out a vision of a future Canada that will still be prosperous, still be able to offer a fine array of social programs, where children can indeed expect to live better than their parents.'[9] Even in Quebec there was more than grudging recognition of the Liberal record, as Chrétien pointedly noted in a caucus meeting shortly before the election call. 'All in all, it is an excellent track record,' reported *La Presse*, 'one that reflects Mr Chrétien's political qualities, his sense of balance and his ability to choose capable people.'[10]

Given his initial resistance to the deficit reduction exercise and the pain it caused, Chrétien believed this accomplishment should be highlighted. As the *Liberal Report*'s economic section emphasized, the original promise to reduce the $42 billion annual deficit left by the Mulroney Conservatives to 3 per cent of GDP within three years had not only been met but exceeded. This success, the document claimed, 'has resulted in increased investment and strength in the Canadian economy.'[11] Subsequently, the budget brought down by Paul Martin in February 1997 projected a deficit of less than $17 billion, or 2 per cent of GDP, and most observers expected it to be much less. The prospect of a balanced budget, or even a surplus, was clearly within reach. One academic review concluded the government's handling of the deficit was 'impressive by international as well as Canadian standards.'[12] The OECD recognized the Liberals' efforts as well, predicting Canada would have the highest economic growth of all member countries in 1997. This accomplishment alone, Chrétien believed, would be sufficient for the public to reward his government with a second majority.

Despite this, Chrétien's advisers, cabinet, and caucus went through nearly six months of divisive debate on the timing of the election call. Most were opposed to an early election. George Young later confided that a disagreement with the leader about the timing of the election call led him to resign as national director. According to Young, the party machinery was not yet in place to ensure a smooth campaign, and the political situation was still in flux. 'Yes, we had reduced the deficit and inflation was low, but incomes were not going up and unemployment was sitting almost exactly where it was when we took office.'[13] The jobless rate was 10.4 per cent in 1994 and had only fallen slightly, to 9.5 per cent, by the time of the election call. Youth unemployment had actually risen dramatically, and this so-called 'jobless' recovery would become an important issue in the next Chrétien mandate. Other concerns expressed by cabinet ministers included the fallout from the cuts to Employment Insurance, especially in Atlantic Canada and Quebec, the failure to resolve the GST conundrum, and the possible backlash from the referendum in Quebec.

The Liberals' unease was heightened by pollster Michael Marzolini's report at a special caucus meeting in Quebec City in January 1997. His findings showed the Liberals' deficit-reduction exercise was seen by many Canadians as having led to a significant reduction in services. He also found decreased enthusiasm for the party among many of its core supporters. Women, immigrants, and low-income voters affected by the cuts were now placing themselves in the undecided category or drifting towards the NDP. According to Marzolini, this 'soft' Liberal support was not yet captured by the national media polls, which continued to show the party with a solid majority. The pollster also cautioned that the party's relatively high level of support in BC was very soft and would not likely translate into more seats as some were hoping.

Although one senior caucus member joked that 'caucus is *never* ready to go, unless it's been five years and they have no choice,' the voices of many MPs opposed to an early election call were raised at every opportunity during the first months of 1997. Several shared the perennial concern that, while the party might not be in trouble, they could have difficulty in their individual ridings. This time, however, many also recalled the fate of Ontario Premier David Peterson, who called an election after only three years in power and lost to the NDP under Bob Rae. Toronto MPs with ridings vulnerable to the NDP, such as Dennis Mills and Tom Wappel, were particularly vocal about this possibility.

But the so-called 'Peterson effect' was dismissed by Chrétien and some of his closest advisers as the result of the former premier's ardent support for the Meech Lake Accord. The Chrétien team saw little similarity between that situation and the one in which they now found themselves. Peter Donolo remembered thinking, 'We had Ontario pretty much sewed up, especially because of Harris.' The Liberals were riding high in the polls with no real opposition and a legitimate record of accomplishments. The now smoothly functioning party machinery had geared up for a campaign. Materials were ready and nomination meetings were being scheduled in non-held ridings. Gordon Ashworth and John Rae once again agreed to serve as the national campaign directors, while Terry Mercer would remain the party's national director.

Behind the scenes, though, there were signs of internal conflict within the party. At David Collenette's suggestion, former Turner minister and Martin confidant David Smith, now a senator, was appointed campaign co-chair by Chrétien along with his Quebec senate colleague, Céline Hervieux-Payette. But unlike 1993, when several key Martin supporters were asked to participate in the campaign and agreed to do so, this time most declined. David Herle indicated he would not have time to do any polling for the party. Terrie O'Leary said she would be travelling throughout the campaign with Martin and could not be on the campaign bus to look after communications again. Michael Robinson demurred when asked to handle negotiations on the leaders' debates. Among the few Martin supporters who worked during the campaign were three junior staff in the war room, namely Karl Littler, Ruth Thorkelson, and Scott Reid. Their decision to join other members of the Martin camp on election night, rather than celebrating with everyone else at the World Exchange Plaza, was later described by Peter Donolo as 'sending all the wrong messages' and increasing the level of tension between the two groups.[14]

In the end both Chrétien's belief that his government's record – especially on deficit reduction – would sustain him through an election campaign, and his assumption that an early election call would not cause any problems, would prove far too optimistic. One critic later described the Liberals' original election strategy as 'planning some sort of ticker-tape parade to celebrate the beating back of the deficit,'[15] a strategy that would soon have to be revised in the face of public apathy.

Signs of voter discontent emerged even before the writ was dropped. The trouble started when the Red River overflowed its banks and created a crisis in Manitoba just days before Chrétien planned to call the election. As David Zussman later confirmed, the wheels were already in motion and the leader believed it was virtually impossible to delay the election. Don Boudria agreed, saying 'an election is like a train that starts leaving the station on its own, and then you just have to jump on board.'[16]

As a public relations gesture, Chrétien travelled to Manitoba, ostensibly to see the degree of disruption for himself. The visit backfired, however, when an onsite volunteer handed him a sandbag and Chrétien was heard to ask: 'What do you want me to do with it?' before throwing the bag on a dyke and leaving. With concerns mounting that the Liberals could lose every seat in the province as a result of the fiasco, it fell to the chief electoral officer to tour the region and determine whether it was necessary to delay the election call. His finding that only minor accommodations were required, to provide alternative voting locations for displaced electors, was a godsend for the leader and the party. Chrétien proceeded to chair one more session of cabinet on 27 April, after which he adjourned to visit the governor general and put the election campaign in motion.

Chrétien's miscalculation on the timing of the election was the first significant development of the campaign. Even without the Manitoba crisis, the general public did not expect the election call to come so soon. Not since Laurier in 1911 had a prime minister with a majority government called an election as early as Chrétien proposed to do. His attempt to describe the 2 June 1997 election date as being 'in the fourth year' of his mandate during the media scrum at Rideau Hall was unsuccessful. Several journalists pointed out he would have had to wait until November to argue that he had served four years.

The timing issue would not have been so important if the Liberal leader had been prepared to answer media questions about his reasons for calling the election. In what one Liberal insider described afterwards as a 'complete mystery,' Chrétien seemed wholly unprepared to explain the rationale for his decision. Communications director Peter Donolo later confirmed that the prime minister was indeed unprepared. 'He felt it was obvious why the election was being called, and simply did not expect questions on that point.'[17] In a series of increasingly vague answers to reporters' queries, Chrétien mentioned at various points that there had been four budgets, that the deficit reduction battle had been successful, that he felt he needed a new mandate to continue in the same policy direction, and lastly, the fact that opposition parties were anticipating an election. Chrétien's shaky performance on the first day of the campaign eliminated much of the advantage normally enjoyed by a governing party in determining the date of an election call and framing the election debate, thereby allowing the opposition parties – and especially the Reform Party – to fill the vacuum and define the campaign issues themselves.

The 1997 Red Book and Internal Divisions

The most important reason for Jean Chrétien's inability to define either the purpose or the major issues of the election was the lack of consensus on these matters within the Liberal ranks. These divisions came to a head in the preparation of the election platform and delayed the election call more than once. They reflected not only the long-standing divisions between business and social Liberals but also the more recently formed cleavage between Chrétien/Trudeau federalists and the Turner/Martin decentralists.

The platform development process followed an outwardly similar path to that of 1993. The platform co-chairs – party president Dan Hays and cabinet minister Lucienne Robillard instead of Martin and Hosek – travelled across the country consulting Liberals. There was also a Liberal Party policy convention in 1996. Yet once again the platform was developed primarily in the PMO, with strong input from Chrétien confidants outside the system.

Despite this top-down process, with little or no party consultation, there was infighting among the few key players involved on both the fiscal and national unity files. In the first instance, the social Liberals in cabinet and caucus – Chrétien's bedrock supporters – wanted to introduce three or four major new national projects that would capture the public's imagination and provide a 'vision' for the country. This group included several senior cabinet ministers and MPs from the Trudeau era, as well as newcomer John Godfrey of Toronto, who was promoting a children's agenda. Apart from the predictable childcare, pharmacare, and homecare plans, there were calls for such diverse master projects as a high-speed rail system, a national university, and a national broadband network. Arrayed against them were the business Liberals led by Martin who were horrified at the thought that the deficit-reduction exercise might have been for nothing and feared the branding of their government as 'tax and spend' Liberals.

Among the PMO and outside advisers this division pitted David Zussman and Chaviva Hosek against pragmatists such as Eddie Goldenberg and John Rae. The latters' concerns about promising too much and failing to deliver were influenced by their difficulties with the GST and childcare promises in their first mandate. The two sides in the debate mirrored Chrétien's own indecision. On the one hand, his reluctance to fight the deficit through the reduction of social programs, and desire to return to his social Liberal roots, led him to support the idea of a renewed investment in the welfare state. On the other hand, the Liberal leader's natural inclination to govern cautiously and preside over incremental change caused him to shy away from grand national projects.

Attempting to square the circle, the drafters of the Liberals' second Red Book, *Opportunity for All: The Liberal Plan for the Future of Canada*, produced an uninspired and confusing document. Countless rewrites resulted in a text which lacked the clarity and conviction of the 1993 version. Outwardly it appeared to be an exact copy of the original, filled with data, quotations, and rhetoric, and complete with a costing section at the end. There were six chapters devoted to economic, social, and cultural policy as well as the environment, foreign policy, and an industrial strategy. However, in addition to the six chapters there were an equal number of new sections inexplicably entitled 'portfolios' for which no rationale was given. Much of the material was a reworked justification of the government's actions over the past three and a half years, and some sections revisited promises originally outlined in 1993. Other text closely resembled the 1996 report card. Major commitments were few and far between. There were almost no surprises and, despite its title, little to inspire a vision.

One area in which the platform made some specific commitments was justice and public safety. Unfortunately the key pledge proved controversial. During their first term the Liberals had felt obliged to respond to the Reform Party's focus on violent crime and young offenders, and the Red Book continued that trend. For the most part the solutions identified in the six-page 'Safe Communities' section reflected a classic Liberal approach, stressing crime prevention and 'the underlying factors that lead to criminal behaviour.' Some targeted organized crime while others focused on the root causes of family violence. One of the few 'tough' measures was the gun control legislation which had already been tabled in Parliament. Although its origins lay in the École Polytechnique massacre of 1989, some Liberal strategists assumed the legislation would appeal to western voters as well, since Reformers had placed such a heavy emphasis on a 'law and order' agenda. As a result, the measure was given considerable prominence in the Red Book, which declared 'effective gun control is central to the Liberal government's strategy to reduce and prevent violent crime.'[18]

The assumption made by the Liberal campaign strategists proved to be wrong. The debate in Parliament over the gun control legislation mirrored the debate in the country, pitting cities against rural areas.

With much of the west still largely rural, opposition to gun control legislation played a key role in the defeat of all Saskatchewan Liberals except Ralph Goodale in the 1997 election. Moreover, the Liberals' failure
to respond to other emerging 'western' justice issues identified by the
defunct Western Communications Project, such as the faint-hope clause
and parole provisions, led to more losses and close calls in Alberta and
British Columbia.

Other platform commitments represented only small incremental
steps, building on initiatives first outlined in 1993. Nevertheless, there
were three highly significant developments in the 1997 Red Book. First,
Liberal organizers believed it was essential to have a written platform
document, so much so that possible election dates came and went as
debate raged over its actual contents. Second, with surplus budgets
projected for the future, the Red Book laid out a formula for handling
that surplus, just as it had done for the deficit four years earlier. This
formula – later a major source of division between social and business
Liberals – proposed allocating 50 per cent of the surplus in a given fiscal
year to new program spending. The other 50 per cent would be divided
equally between debt reduction and lower taxes. This 50/50 formula,
a Chrétien initiative, was intended to satisfy all sides of the internal
party debate and to ensure fiscal rectitude, a major source of concern
for western Canadians.

The third, and perhaps most important, feature of the new Red Book
had to do with national unity. Given the significance of the 1995 referendum and its fallout, an entire chapter, the first in the book, was devoted to it. The challenge was to persuade the public that the Liberals
had the situation in hand without making national unity a campaign issue. With the Reform Party and the Bloc exacerbating regional tensions,
the Liberal organizers felt, as one insider later confided, that 'there was
simply no percentage in having the matter come up at all.' By addressing it head on and getting it out of the way in their platform, they believed they could spend the election focusing on their own economic
and social policy issues.

As a result of internal divisions over federalism, however, the national unity chapter promised very little apart from a vague commitment to
create an 'international forum of federations.' The chapter reflected the
conflicting views of the Liberals' decentralist 'appeasers' led by Martin, and the strong central federalism of 'Plan B' proponents who took
their lead from Trudeau. On the one hand the document referred to
the ultimate goal of a constitutional amendment to formalize the gov-

ernment's earlier parliamentary resolution on the veto. On the other hand it stressed the need to 'ensure that any future debate that puts into question the continuing existence of unity of Canada will be character- ized by clarity and frankness,' promising to enact specific legislation once the Supreme Court had ruled on the federal reference. Apart from foreshadowing the Clarity Act, the chapter focused primarily on what the government had already done. Reflecting the ambivalence of the cabinet and the caucus, it concluded with the promise that 'a new Lib- eral government will continue meeting the needs of the people of this country by governing in a way that benefits all regions and all parts of Canada.'[19]

Fortunately for the Liberals, the discipline of power prevailed throughout the deliberations on the platform. The internal differences of opinion, while significant, remained out of the public eye. Once the text of the platform was finally approved, Jean Chrétien felt confident call- ing the election. The release of the Red Book was expected to provide a major boost early in the campaign, after which the Liberals would cruise to a second majority. This plan fell apart almost immediately as a series of extraordinary events conspired to undermine the Liberal agenda.

The Liberals' Campaign Setbacks

After the election call the weather in Manitoba continued to dominate the news. Western discontent increased when some Reform candidates suggested the Liberal government would not have called the election if the flooding had occurred in Quebec. Public discontent grew with the revelation that the chief electoral officer had failed to take into account the time difference in Saskatchewan.

The day after the writ was dropped, the Liberals tried to focus atten- tion on their planned campaign message – that they were 'securing the country's future' by the sacrifices made to reduce the deficit. Now that those sacrifices were almost over, they argued, Canadians would begin seeing the results. This was a difficult message to communicate given the internal party divisions. At a press conference in Halifax, the party announced some $6 billion in additional funding for health care over five years, but many in the media described it as 'too little too late,' focusing instead on the cost of such a move.[20] Furthermore, it was obvi- ous the event had been staged to showcase star candidates like David Dingwall, whose seat was threatened by the backlash from Liberal cuts to EI and other social programs.

The media's attention did come around to the Liberal platform although not for the reasons they hoped. In one of the more bizarre twists in electoral theatre, the Red Book fell into the hands of Reform leader Preston Manning, who wasted no time dissecting the Liberal commitments at a special press conference. Describing their platform as a return to tax-and-spend liberalism – the very thing that Martin, Manley, and their business Liberal colleagues feared – Manning's 'Goodbye Red Book, hello chequebook' line received widespread coverage. It seemed that, once again, the opposition was setting the agenda.

The next day, in Saskatoon, Chrétien attempted to regain control. Flanked by a number of well-known business Liberals, including Martin supporter Ralph Goodale, he formally released Red Book II. It was not a success. The media focused on the Reform Party's criticisms rather than the contents, and Manning's coup cast a chill over the Liberals' planned future campaign announcements. Afraid to highlight further spending on social programs, and unable to identify an alternative agenda, the Liberals drifted. The Red Book and its commitments were rarely referred to again during the campaign.

In addition, the Liberals attempted to isolate their leader from further public relations problems by keeping him out of sight. Senior cabinet ministers were dispatched to various events in his place and media requests were declined, even as the opposition leaders eagerly accepted. The national advertising campaign was also uninspired. Virtually all of the ads featured Chrétien speaking vaguely about building a strong country and a strong economy. Uncannily reminiscent of the disastrous 'the land is strong' theme of the 1972 Trudeau campaign, Chrétien was seen declaring, 'This country is much stronger than it was a few years ago' and 'people are starting to dream again.' One of his few specific references to a political opponent was not to the Reform Party or its platform but to the Conservatives' proposed tax cuts, suggesting Liberal strategists believed the Conservatives were the real opposition, a mistake that dogged the rest of the campaign and especially frustrated candidates in the west. Several Liberal insiders attributed the mistake to Chrétien's preoccupation with Quebec. With Jean Charest now leading the Tories, the presence of a fellow Quebecker and federalist presented a considerable challenge to ensuring success in the province and diverted much of the leader's attention.

As if that were not enough, an unexpected ruling by the Alberta Court of Appeal further reduced the Liberals' advertising advantage. As the party with the most seats, they were legally entitled to more time than their political opponents – roughly 120 minutes compared with only 50 for the Reform Party, 40 for the Bloc, 35 for the Conservatives, and 25 for the NDP. However, the court's ruling removed the upper limit. Any party that was willing to spend more money could have an increased amount of air time. The problem was that the other parties had no chance of winning nationwide support. Because they were regionally based, both Reform and the Bloc could devote all of their resources to regionally based, much cheaper advertising. They could also afford to produce ads they knew would not be seen in the rest of the country. The Conservatives and the NDP naturally wanted to run national campaigns, but their scarce resources forced them to recognize that there were parts of the country in which they had little or no chance of taking seats.

Only the Liberals were obliged to run a truly national advertising campaign as a result of this regionalization of the party system. Apart from the much greater cost, the content of their ads inevitably caused dissent within their own ranks as regional organizers clamoured for more regionally sensitive material. Campaign director Gordon Ashworth maintained a firm commitment to the pan-Canadian approach to Liberal television ads, arguing that radio was the medium in which provincial or local issues could be addressed. In the end his solution was accepted by everyone, with one notable exception. Despite their emphasis on a national approach to campaign ads, the Liberals had always had an entirely separate advertising campaign in Quebec. Although they introduced a Red Leaf type structure for the Quebec campaign as opposed to relying on individual firms, the fact remained that the duplication of efforts resulted in yet higher costs for the Liberal campaign.

Luckily for the Liberals, the other parties were encountering their own difficulties. The Bloc, now under the direction of Gilles Duceppe, faced a significant challenge from Jean Charest's Conservatives, who stood at 25 per cent in the polls at the start of the campaign. Duceppe's hapless adventures in a cheese factory, and lost on a bus in rural Quebec, accentuated the party's problems. But Charest was hardly in a better position. Outside of Quebec his preference for the 'appeaser' approach to national unity and flat rejection of Plan B did not sit well with most voters. Equally problematic, his platform had been developed by supporters of Mike Harris. Far to the right of traditional Progressive Conservative positions, it served to alienate potential supporters in Ontario and Quebec but did little to return western voters to the Conservative fold.

While Reform scored an initial victory with its criticism of the Liberal platform, the party lacked policies that appealed to central Canada and would allow it to break out of its western regional base. Reform had already been undercut by the Liberals on its principal issue – deficit reduction – and tried to raise the bar to include elimination of the national debt, an idea few Canadians understood or supported, rather than promising to reduce or eliminate the unpopular GST as expected. Reform's emphasis on crime and immigration issues also alienated voters in Ontario and Quebec.

Still, the Liberals faced significant challenges. Their principal problem was that deficit reduction was considered a positive accomplishment by most voters, but was not seen as an important election issue because the work was already done. Instead, a mix of other concerns with a decidedly regional flavour – unemployment, social programs, and the future of Quebec – occupied the minds of voters. Ominously, none of these issues ranked as highly as the option of 'none' selected by one in three respondents.[21] The Liberal campaign strategy was therefore undermined on two fronts. They could not win broad support based on their successful record of deficit reduction, and many items on their proactive platform program were disliked in western Canada where they hoped to pick up seats.

Worse still, Liberal strategists worried about the surging strength of Jean Charest and the Conservatives in Quebec. Ads were put together featuring Paul Martin as the finance minister, disputing the Conservative platform, and concluding 'the numbers just don't add up.' Martin, who, like John Turner before him, did not enjoy the trust of his prime minister on matters relating to Quebec, became a valuable asset in the province as the party tried to shore up its existing support by stressing its economic record. But the lack of a proactive agenda continued to cause problems for Liberals across the country. Whether they would have returned to the Red Book promises and adopted a more aggressive strategy in promoting their social policy planks became a moot point when the national unity card was placed on the table.

The National Unity Issue Resurfaces

Although the Liberals experienced misfortune in the early part of the campaign, they were able to capitalize on a number of unanticipated events that befell their opponents, several having to do with the national unity debate. The first of these events was the publication of a book by former Quebec premier Jacques Parizeau. Reports of its alleged contents in the Quebec City daily *Le Soleil* rocked the campaign and the country. The official position of the separatists in the 1995 referendum campaign had been that they would first seek to negotiate a better deal for Quebec within the federation before considering any move towards separation. But Parizeau's book revealed that he had planned to move unilaterally to take Quebec out of Confederation after a YES vote of 50 per cent plus one. Hasty denials by both Duceppe and the new premier, Lucien Bouchard, did little to assuage the fears of soft nationalists in Quebec or voters in the rest of Canada. While Jean Chrétien could scarcely believe his good luck, his initial comments were understated. He simply pointed out that Duceppe and Bouchard could hardly disclaim all knowledge of their former colleague's plans, and went on to outline his government's own plan to introduce legislation defining the rules of the game in the event of another referendum.

The Parizeau revelations came just days before the nationally televised leaders' debates at which national unity, predictably, was a major issue. This suited the Reform Party, which supported Plan B and depended on western voter support, but caused difficulties for the Liberals, who would have to develop a position that remained faithful to Plan B and their proposed legislation while not appearing too rigid and inflexible in Quebec. Chrétien's greatest fear was that he would be obliged to define what constituted a referendum victory, the very question Manning had attempted to pursue in the House of Commons during the referendum campaign. In one of the most unusual developments of any election, that very question had just been put to the Liberal leader when debate moderator Claire Lamarche collapsed and was taken away in an ambulance, bringing the debate to a sudden end without Chrétien having to respond.

But the die was cast. The national unity issue came to dominate the remainder of the 1997 election campaign. For the Liberals this proved to be an invaluable development. Countless opinion polls demonstrated they were still the party of choice on the national unity issue, viewed outside Quebec as the party best able to 'deal with Quebec.' Their advantage had shrunk due to their perceived mishandling of the 1995 referendum and the robust defence of Plan B by the Reform Party. However, as political scientist Jon Pammett noted, the support for Reform's national unity position served primarily to reinforce that party's existing hold on voters in western Canada and may actually have decreased their potential support in Ontario.[22]

Certainly the Liberals profited from Reform's decision to aggressively pursue the Quebec card. In a move that was reminiscent of the disastrous 1993 Conservative ad mocking Jean Chrétien's facial appearance, the Reform Party released an attack ad on national unity that appeared to criticize the leaders of other parties because they were francophone Quebeckers. 'Isn't it time for a leader who is not from Quebec?' the ad asked, underscored by images of Chrétien, Duceppe, Bouchard, and Charest. Incredibly, this ad was not introduced in desperation, as was the case with the Conservatives in 1993. Instead it was a deliberate attempt by the Reform Party to solidify its western support, something which most analyses of the 1997 election agree it accomplished. Some argue it may have even secured Reform the position of Official Opposition in place of the Bloc.[23]

For their part, internal polling made the Liberals increasingly worried that they would be reduced to a minority government. From a high of 48 per cent when the writ was dropped, they had fallen to 38 per cent. Media reports discussed the possibility of a minority as well, prompting Chrétien to appeal to voters even more strongly to ensure a majority. While this appeal did not work in the west, where both the unity issue as well as the gun control issue played into Reform's hands, it did have an impact in central Canada. Not only did the negative Reform ad solidify support among traditional Liberals there, but in the last weeks of the campaign there is evidence to suggest that many of those who were considering other options were motivated to vote for the natural governing party to ensure that the Liberals had a majority government to deal with the unity issue.[24]

Another unusual aspect of the campaign was the battle taking place in Chrétien's own riding of St Maurice, a battle focused almost exclusively on the national unity issue. Although Chrétien had little difficulty winning the riding in the 1993 election against an obscure Bloc candidate, the situation was much different in 1997. To begin with, the riding had voted in favour of separation in the 1995 referendum by a margin of 56 to 44. From Chrétien's perspective the already humiliating possibility of a sitting prime minister losing his seat was made worse by the unthinkable prospect of losing to a separatist, a distinct possibility in 1997. His Bloc opponent was Yves Duhaime, a fellow lawyer who was well regarded in the area. The two knew and disliked each other, with Duhaime coming from the francophone elite which had savaged Chrétien ever since his entry into politics. For most of the campaign Chrétien actually avoided the riding, assuming that his role as prime minister would serve him in good stead.

When Chrétien finally appeared in his riding, he was accompanied by almost all of the Liberal candidates from the province. His speech took direct aim at the national unity issue, and the political rhetoric of Lucien Bouchard in particular. Mocking Bouchard's ongoing description of Quebeckers as 'humiliated,' Chrétien assured the crowd, 'Me, I don't feel humiliated.' Pointing to his Quebec candidates lined up on the stage behind him, he continued, 'We don't feel humiliated when we know for the last thirty years the prime minister of Canada has come from Quebec!' On the eve of the election, Chrétien attended a final rally in the riding. With a row of Canadian flags prominent in the background, he concluded the Liberal campaign with the words 'Vive le Canada, merci beaucoup!'

The Election Results and Caucus Post-mortem

In the end the Liberals won a second, albeit reduced, majority. This alone, as Jean Chrétien reminded his caucus in their first meeting after the election on 10 June, was quite an accomplishment. Despite the fact that the Liberals had been in power for most of the century, it was the first time since Louis St Laurent in 1953 that the party had won back-to-back majorities. The party also elected MPs in every region of the country and finished second in 104 of the 146 ridings it lost. Thanks to Chrétien's aggressive use of affirmative action, the party not only nominated a record number of women candidates (84) but elected 37 of them. Chrétien won his riding by a comfortable margin and most of his cabinet team were also returned. The Reform Party failed to achieve the breakthrough it desperately wanted in Ontario, and the Bloc lost its momentum along with 10 of its 54 seats in Quebec.

But there were also some setbacks. To begin with, Atlantic Canada massively rejected the Liberals in favour of red Tories and the NDP. Cabinet ministers David Dingwall and Doug Young were defeated along with several other long-serving Liberal MPs. The party's representation fell from 34 to 11 seats in the region. Wiped out in Nova Scotia, the Liberals lost half their seats in New Brunswick and Newfoundland as well. Only in Prince Edward Island did they manage to avoid the groundswell of opposition they had rightly feared.

On the prairies, the Liberals fell from 21 to 9 seats. In BC, where campaign organizers had such high hopes, they only managed to hold on to the 6 seats they had won in 1993. Worse, the party did not even finish second in many ridings across the region. Perhaps most significant, for the second time the Liberal Party won a majority government without the support of Quebec, a point Jean Chrétien's critics were quick to make. Although representation was marginally increased in the province – from 19 to 26 seats – it was clear the new stronghold of the party was Ontario and not Quebec. Liberals now held 101 of 103 seats there, nearly enough to form a government.

The regionalization of Canadian politics seemed to solidify in 1997 with the success of the Reform Party in western Canada and the Bloc in Quebec.[25] Reform increased its hold on the west and formed the Official Opposition. With the Conservatives taking the bulk of their seats in the Atlantic, and winning 5 more from the Bloc in Quebec, it seemed the schism within the Canadian Right was deepening. This fragmentation aided the Liberals in the election, but it would continue to cause problems for them and the country in the coming mandate.

Although the Reform Party and the Bloc merely traded places, it was significant that both the NDP (with 21 seats) and the Conservatives (with 22 seats) made enough of a comeback to qualify for official party status, thereby complicating matters in the House of Commons. All things considered, the election settled very little. As Jon Pammett concluded, although they had wrestled the fiscal crisis to the ground and delivered competent, scandal-free government during their first mandate, the Chrétien Liberals seemed stalled in a 'holding pattern' after the 1997 election.[26]

It was in this context that the Liberal caucus as well as defeated MPs, key Liberal organizers, and advisers met in Ottawa on 10 June to discuss the election results. Several cabinet ministers, notably the business Liberals led by Martin, Masse, and Manley, argued that the party's problems had been exacerbated by the health care funding announcement in Halifax, which gained them nothing but ridicule during the election and would hamper them fiscally following their victory. A number of social Liberals, including Sheila Copps and David Dingwall, argued that the real problem was an ambiguous campaign in which the party had tried to run from both the right and the left. 'You know what Keith Davey used to say,' Sheila Copps told her colleagues. 'We win when we run from the left and govern from the centre.' Copps and several like-minded senior Liberals argued that the party lost ground because it stood for nothing. 'We should have gone for the national projects,' another left-wing MP declared. 'They wanted something positive to identify us with, something to look forward to, so they could see the sacrifices were worth it. We were simply far too cautious. You can't win a hockey game by trying to hold on to a one-goal lead.'

Their views were subsequently reinforced by academic analyses of the 1997 campaign, which demonstrated that the Liberals had indeed made crucial errors in defining their issues. With the deficit eliminated, voters were looking to the Liberals to reassert their traditional values and outline a socially progressive vision for the future, as well as a strong role for the national government. Had the national unity issue not surfaced despite the Liberals' original intentions to ignore it, they would likely have done much worse.

The defeated Liberal MPs from western Canada focused on what they considered to be the party's disastrous campaign strategy in that region. Edmonton MP Judy Bethel complained that the party had actually started out with ads attacking the Conservatives, prompting her to call headquarters and explain that the Conservatives were out of the running in the west and Reform was the real opposition. Her views were echoed by her former colleagues Morris Bodnar and Georgette Sheridan from Saskatoon. Bodnar pointed out that in Saskatchewan, despite several good initiatives by the federal government since 1993, nothing could overcome the resentment caused by the gun control legislation. Worse still, since even the NDP was against it, people didn't have to vote for Reform to send a message. In Manitoba the flooding crisis had abated but the party had lost half of its twelve seats despite the efforts of provincial kingpin Lloyd Axworthy and his protégé, Reg Alcock. Among the defeated were Jon Gerrard, former secretary of state for science and technology. Gerrard expressed dismay at the lack of positive policy announcements, a view shared by Peter Donolo, who admitted 'it wasn't a disastrous campaign but it wasn't an inspired campaign.'[27]

As a result of these concerns, a deliberate attempt was made to recruit more western Liberals to the centre. For example, when the highly regarded Dan McCarthy resigned as director of the Liberal Research Bureau in 1998, he was replaced with Jonathan Murphy, a social activist and defeated Liberal candidate from Edmonton. The regional desks in PMO were strengthened with the addition of both a BC (Randy Pettipas) and Alberta (Raj Chahal) officer, whose role was now to be more content-oriented rather than simply acting as advance men for prime ministerial tours. Western regional ministers were also given more resources and personnel for their regional offices.

Another result was the swift action taken by Chrétien and his team to introduce a 'real' Liberal agenda. While it was true the Red Book had been largely ignored during the campaign, it did not take long for many of the platform planks to be implemented once the Liberals recalled Parliament. Most cabinet ministers were eager to determine which existing programs should benefit from the country's return to fiscal health, but others urged caution, stressing that the election campaign had demonstrated the importance of appearing fiscally prudent. At one of the first cabinet meetings after the election, Jean Chrétien specifically noted it had been *his* idea to place the new 50/50 formula in the Red Book. His views were reflected in the Speech from the Throne in late September, which emphasized the 'balanced' approach that had become Chrétien's trademark:

> The Government has regained the ability to address priorities of Canadians while living within its means. It is now in the position to make strategic investments in our children and our youth, our health, our communities, and our knowledge and creativity while continuing to improve the nation's finances. The Government is committed to following this balanced approach of social investment and prudent financial management as it leads Canada toward renewed and lasting economic health and increased social cohesion.[28]

At the same time, the importance of the national unity file remained top of mind for Chrétien and his advisers. In a key section of the Throne Speech entitled 'Building a Stronger Canada,' the government pledged to introduce legislation that would bring 'frankness and clarity to any debate that puts in question the future existence or unity of Canada.' It also pledged to introduce a resolution adopting the Calgary Declaration and committed the government to a new style of 'collaborative' federalism, working in partnership with the provinces to promote 'social union.' Unlike many Throne Speech promises, all of these measures were implemented within the next two years.

The National Unity File and Plan B Continued

The dust had barely settled after the 1997 election when Intergovernmental Affairs Minister Stéphane Dion resumed his letter-writing campaign against the separatists. In a letter to Premier Bouchard dated 11 August, Dion made three points: first, that any attempt to unilaterally secede from the federation would potentially lead to anarchy; second, that the boundaries of an independent Quebec were debatable (the so-called 'partition' argument); and, third, that any future referendum must produce 'substantial consensus' (far more than 50 per cent plus one) in order to be considered successful. Interestingly, it was Deputy Premier Bernard Landry, a well-known hardline separatist, who replied on behalf of Bouchard on 13 August. Landry rejected outright the notion of partition and the need for more than a bare majority. He also pointed out that the separatist government had committed to negotiations with Ottawa rather than a unilateral declaration. Dion wasted little time following up on Landry's response. His second letter, dated 27 August, stated flatly that Quebec's borders would be up for debate in any negotiations and also that the federal government would never agree to the separation of the province without the consent of all of Canada. This tense exchange culminated on 28 August with Landry's declaration that the PQ government was more preoccupied with the province's fiscal situation and job creation than it was with constitutional matters.

Only two days later a public opinion poll found support for sovereignty had dropped to its lowest level since the 1995 referendum. Buoyed by this progress, the Chrétien Liberals continued their offensive. On 16 September, the prime minister announced he would introduce a resolution in Parliament supporting the Calgary Declaration once formally adopted by the provincial premiers. (Avoiding the controversial 'distinct society' terminology, the final text of the Declaration recognized the 'unique character of Quebec society' as well as 'the equality of citizens and provinces.') Although Premier Bouchard immediately issued a statement rejecting the declaration as meaningless, an Angus Reid poll two weeks later demonstrated that a majority of Canadians – including Quebeckers – supported the declaration, despite believing it would have no impact on the separatists' agenda.

November and December 1997 were marked by a flurry of court decisions and related announcements by various ministers. First, Quebec's intergovernmental affairs minister, Jacques Brossard, insisted that 'no parts of Quebec would remain within Canada after a separation vote.'[29] Shortly thereafter, the Bouchard government requested that the federal government agree to a bilateral constitutional amendment, a move designed to transform the province's school system from a religious to a linguistically based one. It was a popular decision in the province given that it would reduce costs and balance the provincial budget, but it also allowed the federal government to demonstrate that 'federalism works,' a point made repeatedly by Jean Chrétien in cabinet and caucus.

In February 1998, the federal government's 1996 Supreme Court reference was finally heard by the court. While the court was deliberating, Stéphane Dion and Marcel Masse held a press conference to announce that they would participate aggressively in any debate in a future referendum, regardless of the provisions of the Quebec referendum legislation prohibiting outside interventions. Although it would be several months before the court's final decision would be rendered, it was widely expected the result would favour the federal position. Premier Bouchard, apparently fearing such a ruling, declared that he would call a provincial election if the court found that unilateral action on Quebec's part was unconstitutional, a somewhat perplexing move in view of his deputy's assurances to Stéphane Dion only a month before.

The persistent federal offensive was rewarded. On 2 April 1998, an Ekos poll found support for sovereignty had fallen to 31 per cent. Nearly two-thirds of Quebeckers were against another referendum in the foreseeable future. These findings undoubtedly influenced Lucien Bouchard, who announced two days later that he would not hold a referendum if Quebeckers did not want one.

It was about this time that Daniel Johnson resigned as Liberal leader, paving the way for federal Conservative Jean Charest to take over as leader of the provincial Liberals. It was a controversial move which many saw as part of a federal Liberal plan to undermine Bouchard. However, several of the key federal Liberal players denied any role in the unexpected change in provincial leadership. In the end, Charest's move to the provincial Liberals did not produce the desired result. When the Supreme Court ruled in late August 1998 that Quebec did not have the right to secede unilaterally, Lucien Bouchard called the provincial election he had threatened. Campaigning against Ottawa rather than his provincial counterparts, Bouchard once again drew a connection between social policy and the national unity file. Early in the election he announced that, if re-elected, he would inject an additional $1.2 billion into health care in the province to compensate for what he termed federal cutbacks.

The election settled little. On 30 November 1998 Bouchard and the Parti Québécois were returned to power with another majority government and an almost identical number of seats. The PQ's share of the popular vote was actually less than that of Charest and the provincial Liberals, ensuring ongoing conflict with the federal government. For Jean Chrétien, however, Bouchard's victory meant that the national unity battle would continue to be a priority throughout the rest of his second mandate.

The Fiscal Dividend Debate and the New Federal Unilateralism

When Jean Chrétien entered the caucus room for the first time following the federal election, he was greeted with the traditional standing ovation accorded a victorious Liberal leader. When he told his caucus that the 'tough days' of program cuts were over there were more cheers and another, far more enthusiastic, standing ovation. But the return to 'real' Liberal policies would not be as easy or speedy as many in the room might have imagined. Both the aftermath of the national unity crisis, and the ongoing role of Paul Martin as the minister of finance would have significant consequences for the Liberals' policy agenda over the next few years. One observant Chrétien supporter noted that 'not everyone was cheering and not everyone looked all that comfortable at the thought of a whole slew of new program spending.'

Unlike most of the activities related to the national unity file, social policy involved the budgetary process. As a result, it directly involved the minister of finance and other business Liberals who had not been involved in the Quebec dossier. Paul Martin's deeply ingrained commitment to fiscal prudence was now juxtaposed with the pent-up desires of social Liberals to use the surplus to finance new social initiatives. As Sergio Marchi recalled, 'there was definitely a feeling that our time had come. We needed to demonstrate that we had only done some of the things we did over the last few years because we had no choice.'[30] David Collenette agreed: 'Everyone understood this was payback time for the cuts. The only question was where to start.'[31] Chrétien himself spoke more than once about the political difficulties a prime minister faces in making everybody happy when dividing a surplus. That was why he had insisted on the 50–25–25 formula in Red Book II, he said, and he planned to stick to it. It soon became apparent, however, that some key players in the Finance Department and Paul Martin himself were not enthusiastic about that formula.

Years later Peter Donolo stated that 'Mr Chrétien should have moved Paul Martin out of the Finance portfolio in 1998.' Donolo made the suggestion at the time. 'I thought it would be good for Martin as well as Mr Chrétien,' Donolo said. 'Martin had never been responsible for programs in a line department. And I thought he would become restless in Finance now that his role as deficit-fighter was over. He was someone who needed a challenge.'[32] One of Martin's closest advisers, David Herle, later agreed that Martin was bored in Finance after 1997, but went further, concluding: 'Paul would have been restless in any department after that election,' as the government seemed to him to have 'gone into neutral' with no challenging agenda.[33] (In fact, with the deficit dragon slain, Martin began looking for ways to make an impact on the international stage, successfully spearheading the creation of the G-20 and a G8 initiative to provide massive debt relief to underdeveloped countries.)

Donolo also felt it would be politically advantageous for Chrétien to move Martin to another portfolio, since it would likely 'take the shine' off Martin's popularity once his performance in a program department was evaluated. Last, but hardly least, Donolo believed Martin's continued presence in Finance would make it harder for Chrétien to move on his social policy agenda. Several of Martin's former cabinet colleagues shared this concern. One of them complained, 'He talked a lot about his father's role in creating social programs, but then he always seemed to have other priorities that needed to be dealt with first. He felt bad about not being able to do more, but it didn't change his mind.'

Interestingly, these views about Martin's place on the Liberals' philosophical spectrum run counter to the impression that the two men had few if any philosophical differences, a popular belief later on when Martin challenged Chrétien for the leadership. Yet the different priorities of Chrétien and Martin on the allocation of the fiscal dividend could be seen almost immediately following the 1997 election. In early September, Chrétien personally announced a special $90 million program to counter youth unemployment. Only two days later, Paul Martin launched another public relations campaign, stressing fiscal prudence over social spending. This time his mission was to convince Canadians of the need to reform the Canada Pension Plan and increase premiums.

Chrétien was inclined to emphasize spending on social programs over tax cuts or debt reduction, and he was intent on using the federal surplus to make such investments in order to secure national unity. No sooner had Lucien Bouchard announced a comprehensive provincial childcare policy in late June, for example, than the federal government responded with its own plan. Human Resources Minister Pierre Pettigrew promptly announced the federal government's 'Children's Agenda' would be unveiled before Christmas. In the meantime, the Speech from the Throne committed the government to an expenditure of $850 million through the newly created Child Tax Benefit.

When Paul Martin issued an economic statement in mid-October – concluding that the federal deficit for the previous fiscal year would be far less than expected and a surplus likely imminent – the social Liberals were ecstatic. At Chrétien's direction an exercise began in which all ministers were to consult with their departments and propose a wish list for cabinet to determine priorities. But this 'program review in reverse,' as it came to be known internally, was precisely the type of development Martin felt he must guard against. Speaking to the House of Commons Finance Committee at the beginning of the pre-budget consultations in November, he argued there could only be very small fiscal dividends in the next two or three years of surplus. Tax cuts and certainly any large spending increases would have to wait. Unfortunately for Martin, an Ekos public opinion poll in early November 1997 demonstrated that Canadians disagreed, favouring immediate spending on employment, child poverty, and health care.

The February 1998 budget consequently contained a number of provisions for health care and education, and was actually referred to as the 'Education Budget.' It also contained the first of what would soon be many unilateral initiatives by the federal government in the area of social policy, namely the Millennium Scholarship Foundation. This fund, promoted by Chrétien personally, was also significant because it would not be enacted until the year 2000 despite the fact that the funds were allocated in the 1998–9 budget. This technique allowed the federal government to spend revenue before the end of the fiscal year, thereby preventing it from being considered part of the surplus which would have been used to pay down the debt. But it was the unilateral nature of the fund which caused concern among provincial premiers, prompting them to resume negotiations with the federal government on the social union proposal that had been part of their agenda since 1995, their quid pro quo for supporting the Calgary Declaration.

In February 1999 the Social Union Framework Agreement (SUFA) was signed with considerable fanfare in Ottawa. It was based on the idea of 'collaborative' federalism promoted enthusiastically by the premiers. Supporters, including federal Intergovernmental Affairs Minister Stéphane Dion, believed it would usher in a new era of federal-provincial harmony based on an agreement among equals. As Dion said, 'the Canadian federation is evolving towards greater cooperation and consensus-building ... rather than towards extensive centralization in favour of the federal government or extensive decentralization in favour of provincial governments.'[34] Dion also emphasized that the premiers had signed the agreement, which expressly recognized the federal government's legitimate role in social policy.

For opponents, however, the decentralist thrust of the deal was ominous. That the federal government would not be able to pursue any new social programs without the consent of a majority of the provinces was seen as a serious setback. In addition, despite repeated federal attempts to circumvent provincial proposals permitting opting out, some of those measures remained. Equally important, much remained to be clarified concerning the provinces' obligation to account for their expenditure of federal transfers, a provision that federal negotiators had insisted upon. Yet the Quebec government refused to sign on to the agreement and Premier Bouchard actually attacked it as a centralizing move by Ottawa, even as he was prepared to accept federal funding flowing from it.[35]

For a while optimists believed this new approach to the funding of social policy would provide a third way for intergovernmental relations. If Dion was right, the centralist-decentralist constitutional cleavage within the Liberal Party would become unimportant as well. But it soon became apparent that the collaboration envisaged by the supporters of the SUFA was more myth than reality. Several provinces – notably those with right-of-centre governments such as Ontario and Alberta – almost immediately reneged on aspects of the deal. They regularly failed to commit the matching funds required under agreements subsequently negotiated on childcare, social housing, and welfare, and most did not follow through on their commitment to voluntarily account for spending. In some areas, money allocated for programs was not spent at all. As Ottawa continued to accumulate sizeable annual surpluses, it was unable to convince the premiers to support even such initiatives as homecare or pharmacare, which the Liberals tried to define as part of the existing medicare program, rather than new social spending.[36]

Stéphane Dion may have been an enthusiastic supporter of the collaborative federalism model, but the same could not be said for Jean Chrétien and the Trudeau federalists. As political scientist Jane Jenson and others have noted, it was with considerable reluctance that Chrétien entered into the negotiations in the first place, the result of his bureaucrats' agreement in exchange for provincial support on the national unity file and his lack of other options in the immediate post-referendum, deficit-reduction era.[37] With both the deficit and the referendum behind them, the Chrétien Liberals were not prepared to wait for changes in the governments of various provinces to pursue their activist social policy agenda, particularly as the separatists in Quebec had not signed on to the agreement.[38] In short order SUFA became largely irrelevant. The premiers were sidelined as well, as Chrétien simply chose not to convene first ministers' meetings.

Instead, the Chrétien Liberals adopted a new unilateral approach for pursuing their social policy agenda, developing niche programs in as many areas as possible. In addition to the original Millennium Scholarships, measures such as the Canada Foundation for Innovation, the Canada Research Chairs, the Registered Education Savings Plan and the Education Assistance Grant, the Medical Equipment Fund, Genome Canada, and the Canadian Institute for Health Research were introduced. Both Chrétien and Martin developed policy agendas during this time period; Martin's focused on research and education while Chrétien's favoured health care, social housing, and childcare. One of the advantages of this unilaeral approach, from Chrétien's perspective, was that it highlighted the presence of the federal government in the lives of citizens. By introducing programs which funded individuals or institutions directly, the value of the federal government's social policy dollars was, in his view, greatly enhanced.

But there was also a downside to this approach. Many of the provinces proceeded to implement social policy change unilaterally as well, leading to a sort of 'dual unilateralism' that was often counterproductive. The exception was Quebec. Although the province implemented many programs independently, they were almost always intended to pursue the same objectives as the federal Liberals. Childcare, pharmacare, and even dental programs were put in place, and full use was made of federal funding in the area of social housing. Several other provinces, by contrast, either failed to act or implemented changes which effectively cancelled out the benefits of the federal measures. In Ontario, for example, the advantages of the Child Tax Credit were largely eliminated by the Harris government's countermeasures.[39]

These regressive developments, in turn, spurred the Chrétien government to adopt further unilateral measures to compensate for the negative impact of those provincial decisions. In some cases the federal moves were also an effort to compensate for the unintended consequences of the government's conversion to the CHST. With no control over the provincial allocation of resources among the three policy fields, the federal government could only indirectly supplement the victims of decreased welfare and post-secondary education funding by provinces whose priority had become the funding of health care. Over time, the implications of this shift for the welfare state and for national unity would become a growing concern for Chrétien. It would also lead to additional friction between Martin and Chrétien, as Martin continued to maintain that the CHST worked well while Chrétien wanted to re-structure the federal transfers to regain control of the agenda.

Even in the area of foreign policy the question of national unity was never far from Chrétien's mind, as James Bartleman's account of the PM's trade missions and APEC initiatives demonstrated. This was most evident in a unique initiative launched in 1999. The idea of creating an international body devoted to the study of federalism was mentioned briefly in Red Book II, but Dion had been promoting it for some time. The plan was to stress the importance of federalism in countering ethnic nationalism, an argument so often made by Trudeau when dealing with Quebec separatists.[40] Following on the favourable Supreme Court deci-sion rejecting unilateral action by Quebec, and in light of the re-election of the PQ, Dion convinced Chrétien that the time had come to launch a public relations counter-offensive against the separatists on their own territory. The result was the Forum of Federations, an international in-stitution to promote research and information exchange among federal countries, whose head office would be located in Canada.

The Forum's first public event was an international conference on federalism held at Mt Tremblant, Quebec, in November 1999. Delegates from more than twenty countries attended, as well as academics and practitioners from Canada. Many of the foreign participants stressed Canada's importance as a role model for other plural societies. A keynote speech by American president Bill Clinton reinforced their comments, providing a masterful dissertation on the advantages of federalism. Clinton's not-too-subtle subtext – a spirited defence of Canadian na-tional unity and rejection of the Quebec separatists' claims – delighted his Canadian hosts. It responded point by point to earlier allegations made by Lucien Bouchard in a lengthy unscheduled monologue the night before, and those which emerged during a heated exchange the previous day between Stéphane Dion and his provincial counterpart, Joseph Facal. As the American ambassador to Canada, Gordon Giffin, later recounted, 'Bouchard was shaken by [Clinton's] speech. You could tell he was visibly shaken. Clinton had just sucked all the oxygen out of [their efforts at] the conference.'[41]

Still, the overtly aggressive behaviour of the separatists, coupled with the $250,000 propaganda offensive Bouchard's government had launched in the spring to persuade Quebeckers that the federal government's February budget was 'anti-Quebec,' convinced Chrétien that he needed to follow through on his plan to introduce legislation defining the parameters of any future referendum.

The Clarity Bill: Chrétien's Ultimate Response

The seeds of the Clarity Bill were sewn on the eve of the 1995 referendum when Liberals began contemplating possible steps in the event of a YES vote. Jean Chrétien, for his part, felt action was required even after the NO side won. According to Eddie Goldenberg, Chrétien actually considered a response to the vague referendum question and the threats of unilateral action as he was returning from his televised address after the federal victory. 'In the car that night he said to me "I will never allow Canada to be put through a trauma like this again."'[42]

Certainly the 1996 federal reference to the Supreme Court was intended to lay the groundwork for such legislation. But when the court finally delivered its favourable verdict in August 1998, Chrétien hesitated. Separatist propaganda seemed to have slackened, support for sovereignty was falling dramatically, and the PQ had not received as many votes as the Liberals in the last provincial election. What would be the point of stirring up controversy when things were relatively calm?

Moreover, because of the SUFA negotiations, it appeared an administrative alternative to constitutional reform had been found that might restore intergovernmental harmony. Although Premier Bouchard did not sign the SUFA, he was prepared to take the money, just as he had been prepared to ask the federal government for a constitutional amendment to implement his public school reforms. Many people urged Chrétien to put his idea aside and let sleeping dogs lie. They included several senior cabinet ministers and MPs as well as members of his inner circle such as Goldenberg.

Despite their urging, Chrétien persisted in the preparation of draft legislation. As he told the national caucus on 20 September 1999, he had the responsibility 'as prime minister, not as leader of the party' to ensure Canada remained united. 'We may not need the bill now,' he said. 'My preferred choice is to do nothing. But one day there will be another referendum. When? When they feel good and we are in trouble!' That was not the time, Chrétien said, to think about putting such federal legislation in place. His longtime colleague Charles Caccia agreed, telling him that day in caucus that the dogs were only sleeping, not dead.

Eventually the separatists' ad campaign attacking the federal budget, coupled with their behaviour at the Tremblant conference, convinced Chrétien that something had to be done. Once his mind was made up, he acted with lightning speed. The draft legislation for the Clarity Act was revised, finalized, and brought to cabinet by Chrétien himself. Unlike the fiscal crisis, the prime minister's handling of the national unity crisis did not involve lengthy cabinet consultations and consensus-building. He spent little or no time attempting to bring everyone on-side. Convinced this would be a pointless exercise, he relied instead on the principle of cabinet solidarity. In an extraordinary move which revealed not only his determination to proceed quickly, but his deep-seated distrust of the political judgment of some of his cabinet ministers about Quebec, he announced there would be no cabinet debate on the legislation except for any proposed technical amendments. He planned to have Stéphane Dion table the bill before Christmas. As David Collen-ette and John Manley both recalled later, there was some unease around the cabinet table, particularly among the Quebec ministers, but very little was said.[43]

The only real debate within the parliamentary wing took place in na-tional caucus. Once again the battle lines were drawn between appeas-ers and hardliners who, for the most part, were Martin and Chrétien supporters, respectively. With the addition of several new Liberal MPs after the 1997 election, supporters of the Trudeau vision, although still a majority in caucus, were less dominant. Attrition removed some of the oldest and most committed Trudeauvian federalists. Some of the new MPs were not so much ardent decentralists as they were simply una-ware of the background to the federal conflict and easily influenced by senior colleagues. Among this group, the desire to let sleeping dogs lie was very high, and concerns about upsetting Quebec Liberals as well as soft nationalists dominated their thoughts. But there were also several new MPs who were committed Trudeau federalists, and they quickly joined forces with the veteran MPs and senators on the Plan B side of the debate. For this new generation of Trudeau Liberals, the Clarity Act was not only necessary in light of recent events, but a politically astute move to make. As Paul DeVillers said, 'the genius of the act was the name. How could you oppose clarity? Were you going to argue in fa-vour of obfuscation?'[44]

One of the most telling developments was the number of MPs who wanted to know what Trudeau himself thought of the plan. Several asked the question outright. Others, old friends and colleagues of Trudeau, spoke with him directly. In the end Chrétien informed his caucus that he too had spoken with Trudeau. After some initial hesitation, the former prime minister gave his approval for the plan. He concluded that the situation called for some type of action in light of the fallout from Brian Mulroney's failed attempts at constitutional reform and the recent referendum imbroglio. For a large number of caucus members, Trudeau's approval constituted a sort of papal dispensation for the plan. For those who opposed the Clarity Act, Chrétien had produced a winning card they could not trump.

Paul Martin was not happy with the proposal, and although he did not voice his opposition directly, his bizarre reaction to media queries on the issue spoke louder than words. Although he would later argue that his reluctance to say anything publicly stemmed from Chrétien's injunction that only he or Stéphane Dion would speak about the bill, Eddie Goldenberg scornfully rejected that excuse. He noted in one interview that the prime minister's injunction not to discuss the bill's contents did not prevent any minister from expressing his support for the legislation. 'He wasn't told to run up the stairs when asked whether he supported the bill,' Goldenberg said. 'It doesn't mean that you are not allowed to say you support a bill when you are asked.'[45]

In an uncanny repetition of the Meech Lake debate, many of those who opposed the legislation argued it would harm the Liberal Party's electoral chances in Quebec. According to some of his closest confidants, Paul Martin shared this concern. He also harboured a deep-rooted reluctance to take a hard line against the nationalists. Several MPs who were known to be part of Martin's inner circle spoke out against the legislation in caucus, and this was seen by most of their colleagues as an indication of Martin's thinking. Even more revealing were the clandestine visits to Liberal MPs in Ottawa by Martin's longtime supporter, Dennis Dawson. The intense briefings about the 'misguided' approach of Dion's bill were widely known in Liberal circles at the time, and Dawson too was taken as a surrogate messenger for Martin himself.[46]

For several days Martin avoided public commentary on the bill, leading national media outlets to pursue him even more aggressively, sensing conflict in the air. Even Lucien Bouchard broached the issue of Martin's questionable support. 'What does Paul Martin think?' he asked in an interview several days after the government's intentions were made known.[47] In the end Martin could not avoid the issue. His official comment on the bill before it was tabled was a lukewarm, clearly reluctant endorsement. 'On questions of national unity the prime minister speaks for Cabinet,' Martin said. 'He speaks for all of Cabinet and I am a member of that Cabinet.' Pushed to say more as he left the House of Commons, he concluded somewhat lamely that 'I think matters ought to be clarified.'[48]

The Clarity Act became the focal point of debate at a convention of the Liberal Party's Quebec wing later that month. At the suggestion of Brian Tobin and Françoise Ducros, the Chrétien team were successful in launching the debate about the bill on their own terms. A resolution was tabled supporting the bill. A strenuous debate ensued on the floor of the convention between Ducros and Dennis Dawson, the former Turner adviser who had supported both Meech Lake and Charlottetown. Dawson described the bill as unnecessary provocation while Ducros argued it was essential as a demonstration of the strong leadership necessary to curb nationalist ambitions. The resolution passed easily, providing Chrétien with another weapon in his public relations arsenal.

Lucien Bouchard remained curiously silent after his initial outburst when he learned of Chrétien's plans in the fall of 1999. Instead it was the Quebec Liberals, led by Jean Charest, who opposed the Clarity Act most vigorously. One of the most strident was none other than Liza Frulla. 'We were sure that he had made a mistake,' Frulla later told journalist Lawrence Martin, 'and that here again they [the federal Liberals] were scaring people and starting a battle, and we wondered "Oh my God, what is he doing?" There I have to admit we made a mistake,' Frulla reluctantly concluded.[49]

Chrétien's instincts on Quebec did not let him down on this occasion. Not only was the proposed legislation widely supported in the rest of Canada, but a raft of public opinion polls indicated it was met with overwhelming approval in his home province as well. Paul Martin recognized this fact in a year-end interview. 'In terms of saying that in any referendum the question has to be clear, as well as the results, is one that has been very well received by Québécois.'[50] By the time the bill was debated in the House of Commons in January 2000 the finance minister's support for the legislation had become 'unequivocal.'

Shortly after the Clarity Act was passed by the House of Commons in February 2000, a Leger and Leger poll found that the federalists enjoyed a fifteen-point lead over the sovereignists. Chrétien subsequently referred to it as one of his three most significant accomplishments. In fact, with the deficit eliminated and the threat of separation severely reduced, it appeared to many observers that the passage of the bill gave Chrétien an ideal opportunity to step down as leader of the Liberal Party, a move that Martin supporters most certainly would have welcomed. Some of Chrétien's own long-serving supporters began considering their own departure from the political arena, assuming their leader would do the same.

The Changing of the Guard

By 1997 Jean Chrétien had lost several of his key supporters in cabinet. Brian Tobin left in 1996 to assume the premiership of Newfoundland, Indian Affairs Minister Ron Irwin decided not to run, David Dingwall was defeated in the 1997 election, and International Trade Minister Sergio Marchi left for personal reasons. In 1999 Chrétien also suffered a strategic loss when Lloyd Axworthy – not a Chrétien loyalist but an important member of the social liberal wing and a strong cabinet minister – announced that he would not be seeking re-election in order to take a position in academia. Soon other loyalists such as Alfonso Gagliano and David Collenette began musing about the possibility of their departure from politics as well.

Chrétien's cabinet losses were accompanied by an increasingly serious turnover in his own office, which had been exceptionally stable in the first mandate and regarded as one of the keys to the smooth operation of his government. Penny Collenette was the first to leave the PMO after the 1997 election, to be replaced as director of appointments by Percy Downe, a former adviser to several Atlantic ministers with solid party credentials. Peter Donolo was next, citing his eight years in the OLO/PMO and the need for a change. He was replaced as communications director by Françoise Ducros, a somewhat controversial appointment given that her strong suit was policy rather than communications. In short order her combative handling of the national media and relations between the PMO and the Martin camp came in for significant criticism.

Donolo's departure was followed in 2000 by that of chief of staff Jean Pelletier for similar reasons as Donolo. His replacement was Percy Downe, whom many believed lacked the degree of seniority and self-confidence Pelletier and Donolo brought to their roles. The declining authority of the Chrétien PMO, coupled with its newly aggressive stance towards the outside world and especially the Martin camp, soon led Martin adviser David Herle to declare that there was a 'lack of adult supervision' in the office. At the same time, observers noted a major departure from the Martin office, Terrie O'Leary, who went to Washington to take up an appointment at the World Bank. Ms O'Leary was widely regarded as the one individual who could work closely with Martin and yet retain good relations with those in the Chrétien organization. Her long-standing friendship with Peter Donolo and her ability to compromise were frequently cited by Liberal insiders as key elements in the successful working relationship Chrétien and Martin had developed.[51]

The many departures of senior PMO staff hampered Chrétien's ability to stay in touch with his caucus and his supporters in the party, to say nothing of public opinion. As Sergio Marchi later noted, 'as prime minister you are automatically isolated in a bubble. You have so many responsibilities and so little time. The relationships that precede you taking power are always more able to influence you. You trust them more. When those people are gone the bubble gets bigger.'[52]

Chrétien also faced unexpected challenges in the selection of caucus chairs. Although chairs were elected by caucus members, it was traditional for the leader to make his preference known, especially for the position of national chair, and that individual would normally be the person chosen. Among other things, the national chair's role was to meet regularly with the leader to convey caucus concerns. A cordial if not intimate relationship was necessary if the position was to function well.[53] As one former chair, Paul DeVillers, described it, the role of chair was something like a shop steward. In addition to the regular weekly sessions with the leader after meeting with the four regional chairs, the national caucus chair would often need to take the initiative to alert the leader to emerging issues on short notice. As a prime example, DeVillers recalled the time he called Chrétien in Florida during the Christmas recess. 'I had received thirteen angry calls from MPs in the space of a few hours, shortly after [industry minister] John Manley announced that aid package for the Ottawa Senators,' DeVillers said, noting that within hours of his call Chrétien personally ordered the plan scrubbed.[54]

Sergio Marchi filled the role of shop steward for Chrétien when the Liberals were still in opposition after 1990, and Chrétien protégée Jane Stewart occupied the position in the early years of the first mandate. However, Stewart was succeeded in 1995 by Joe Fontana, a known Martin supporter, the first sign that Chrétien's hold over the caucus was slipping. This was particularly evident since Fontana's opponent for the position, Saskatchewan MP Georgette Sheridan, was widely seen as

Chrétien's choice even though she vigorously denied it. When Fontana decided to seek an unprecedented third year as chair he was challenged by two perceived Chrétien supporters, DeVillers and Bernard Patry, who split the vote, thus allowing Fontana to win again.

Many MPs have since stressed that until then the Chrétien-Martin split was not sufficiently important to prevent them from voting for their preferred candidate. But in January 1999, when Fontana finally stepped down, the schism between the prime minister and Martin was coming close to open warfare. DeVillers's second campaign to become caucus chair was successful, this time against Martin choice Nick Discepola of Montreal, but the campaign was corrosive. Aggressive tactics, threats, and recriminations were the order of the day among supporters on both sides, as many in the Martin camp took DeVillers's candidacy as a signal of Chrétien's determination to reassert his authority.

Chrétien also moved to minimize his problems with the party's national office. After the departure of George Young in 1997, Chrétien selected longtime supporter Terry Mercer, the fundraising director originally recruited by George Young, to replace him. Party president Dan Hays noted that, although he was technically asked for his approval of this choice, 'you don't really say no to the leader, and certainly not one who has just delivered a second majority government.'[55] However, Hays also stressed that he had no problems with the appointment and worked well with Mercer during his remaining time as president.

Mercer immediately began to attend the daily PMO staff meetings chaired by Jean Pelletier in which his predecessor, although invited, had only participated on an as-needed basis. This situation, accepted as routine practice by Hays – who was already a member of the caucus – became a bone of contention under the next party president, Stephen LeDrew, who was an outsider unable to attend caucus meetings. This conflict was nevertheless unexpected, as Mercer had run LeDrew's campaign to become president of the Ontario wing of the party only a few years earlier.

Early in his tenure, Mercer focused on two key party issues, namely the continued development of a national membership list and the strengthening of grassroots ties. He attempted to address both problems in part by expanding the scope and distribution of the *Liberal Times* newsletter. As someone only too familiar with the fundraising difficulties of the national office, Mercer viewed the need for a membership list as crucial. He struck a deal with the provincial wings in the four western provinces and then with most of the others. The *Liberal*

Times would be distributed at no charge to party members across the country in exchange for mailing lists provided by the provincial executives that would, in fact, constitute membership lists.

Soon after, at a national caucus winter retreat in Collingwood, Ontario, Mercer went a step further. He distributed disks with lists of donors known to the national headquarters, organized by riding, to MPs. Since donors were not necessarily party members, a list of donors to the party in each riding would be an invaluable tool not just for the national headquarters but for each riding association. The move was designed to convince MPs that the national office was sincere in its efforts to limit 'double-dipping' and also that it was possible to coordinate fundraising activities at that level. Although not everyone bought into the project, Mercer maintained that considerable progress was made.

On the policy front, the departure of Chaviva Hosek as director of policy for the PMO in 2000 was followed by the recruitment of one of her former research officers at the LCRB, Paul Genest. But Genest, who had left the Bureau some years earlier to work in the federal government, came to PMO with little relevant experience in terms of the policy development work that had been done for the 1997 Red Book and 2000 Red Pamphlet. As a newcomer to PMO he initially wielded less power and, perhaps more significantly, owed his appointment largely to his acquaintance with Eddie Goldenberg. Goldenberg, in turn, assumed an even larger role in policymaking. In the final eighteen months of the Chrétien mandate, however, Genest's policy work and knowledge of government proved crucial to the implementation of Chrétien's 'legacy' legislation.

Unfortunately the departure of Dan McCarthy and his replacement as LCRB director by Jonathan Murphy in 1998 was more problematic and led to further changes in the structure of the Bureau. Greater emphasis was placed on communications and less on research as the Bureau struggled to maintain its relevance when the party was in power. Over the next two years a high turnover of research officers also ensued, creating a significant morale problem and undermining institutional memory. Moreover, a number of the new researchers lacked the academic credentials established as minimum criteria after the 1984 election, since greater emphasis was placed on communications skills and political experience. These problems became obvious in the lead-up to the next election, even with the PMO's decreased expectations for the Bureau's role in platform development.

Another significant departure was that of the Clerk of the Privy

Council, Jocelyne Bourgogne, the most senior bureaucrat in Ottawa and someone whose interactions with PMO were of necessity both frequent and detailed. Don Boudria was one of many who regarded Bourgogne's departure as yet another indication that the prime minister would soon be leaving himself. Others placed a different interpretation on her leaving. A holdover from the Mulroney era, she had imposed the draconian cuts on the public service deemed necessary to accomplish program review. Many Liberal ministers saw her as a drawback in terms of their planned prosperity agenda and the good relations with the bureaucracy so essential for its implementation. Chrétien's decision to replace her in 1999 with Mel Cappe, a former deputy minister at HRDC and the Environment, was seen by some as a positive move indicating a commitment by the PM to stay on and help take advantage of the fiscal dividend.

To Leave or Not to Leave?

At the Liberal Party's biennial convention in 1998, Jean Chrétien received the support of over 90 per cent of the delegates in the obligatory leadership review vote following the 1997 election. At the time, he declared that this show of support gave him a mandate to fight the next election, although several of his close confidants have since voiced the belief that Chrétien never intended to fight a third election campaign. George Young, for example, stressed how strongly Chrétien felt about ensuring a smooth succession, particularly in light of the problems that Trudeau's departure had caused for the party. 'He always saw himself as the leader of the party as well as the prime minister. He believed he had an obligation to make sure the party was in better shape when he left than when he took over.'[56] Young's successor as national director, Terry Mercer, concurred. 'I have no doubt he was planning to leave in 2000 or 2001 to ensure a timely transition,' Mercer later said. 'If nature had been left to take its course, that is exactly what would have happened.'[57]

Chrétien's director of appointments, Percy Downe recalled being so certain of a 2000 or 2001 departure that he sold his house in Ottawa and was planning to move back to the Maritimes in time for the new school year when Chrétien called to ask him to fill the role of chief of staff.[58] Allan Rock, who approached Chrétien about seeking the leadership after his departure, was also under the impression that this was the timeline.[59]

The departure scenario was altered by two very significant events. The first was the emergence, in full public view, of the split between Chrétien and Martin. The second was the unexpected emergence of a new leader of the Alliance Party who appeared to be more of a political threat than the departing Preston Manning. Of course the schism between Chrétien and Martin had always existed but, in the interests of the party and the country, the two men had managed to overcome their differences or, at a minimum, keep them under wraps. As noted earlier, this truce was accomplished largely through the use of intermediaries such as Donolo, Goldenberg, and O'Leary, and their leaving in the past year made this accommodation much more difficult. But Chrétien himself indicated repeatedly to his supporters that he felt it was still important to maintain the relationship with Martin and ensure his opponent's continued presence in the cabinet for the good of the party. Before their departures, Marchi and the others disagreed. They argued it was time for Martin to move on, either to another post or to the private sector. Further, they argued Chrétien needed to broaden the base of the party and warned that he was letting certain aspects of the party operation slip. In the words of Sergio Marchi, 'He just became complacent.'[60]

According to Terry Mercer, the high level of support for Chrétien at the 1998 leadership review was not difficult to achieve, but 'we took nothing for granted. It was the result of an organized effort on the part of the prime minister's supporters across the country to ensure that he had the highest possible vote of confidence.' Mercer also admitted that the vote count from the ridings – necessary under the new (and contradictory) constitutional rules in addition to the convention delegates' vote count – became a bone of contention because of the way it was handled. In some respects it was reminiscent of the difficulties faced by David Collenette during John Turner's 1986 leadership review vote.

As national director, Mercer was automatically the national returning officer as well, responsible for the ballot count. 'This was the first time it had been done,' Mercer recalled. 'There were no procedures spelled out. In my view the process was certainly fair and equitable. Ballots were sent to the ridings and returned in double envelopes. We kept them all in a conspicuous pile, waiting to open them at the same time as the convention vote.' However, given his close ties to the Chrétien camp, Mercer's role was already suspect in the eyes of Martin supporters. That national directors were traditionally appointed by the leader created a perpetual problem. In his case, Mercer took what he thought were appropriate precautions. He arranged for his executive assistant and an outside lawyer to supervise the ballot count with him. But 'in retrospect I can see that I probably should have had someone else there in the room as well. I just didn't realize how extreme the distrust was.'[61] Several Martin advisers later agreed. One senior spokesperson said pointedly, 'How could they possibly expect us to sit back and let Mercer, who admits he actually worked to get out the pro-Chrétien vote, turn around and count the ballots?'[62]

'It was not long after the '98 convention,' Mercer recalled, 'that we began to see the first evidence the Martin camp had no intention of letting nature take its course, and this began to cause problems throughout the system.' Until then, the animosity between Chrétien and Martin advisers (more significant than that between the two principals, as Martin himself acknowledged)[63] had been well concealed. However, with the arrival of Ducros in PMO and the growing impatience of Reid, Littler, and Thorkelson in Martin's office, such conflicts became an obvious, very visible problem.

The ongoing presence of a very large cadre of Martin supporters in the private sector in Ottawa – primarily as government lobbyists – created growing unease in PMO and cabinet. Indeed, Martin's original leadership team from 1990 had remained virtually intact for more than a decade, an extraordinary development. This remarkable cohesion was achieved partly through Martin's ability to provide employment for several of the key organizers through his various business holdings. A more significant means of keeping advisers together in Ottawa was the creation of the Earnscliffe Strategy Group in January 1994 following a merger with Anderson Research. The chief executive of the new lobbying and public research firm was a former Tory adviser, Harry Near, but most of the other senior members of the new entity were well-known Martin supporters, including his former campaign chair, Michael Robinson, and David Herle, his closest confidant. Robinson was in charge of the lobbying section and Herle was tasked with the research side of the organization, with a 'Chinese wall' dividing the two, as both men emphasized on numerous occasions.

Although some controversy had developed around the awarding of contracts to Earnscliffe by the Finance Department,[64] it had been considered a minor irritant by Chrétien's advisers with the important exception of Warren Kinsella. A former ministerial aide who had worked briefly in the Chrétien PMO, Kinsella had vigorously pursued the Earnscliffe issue as a potential political problem while working there and earlier as an EA to cabinet minister David Dingwall. Kinsella was frequently described by some senior members of the PMO as 'paranoid' on the subject of Martin and his people. But, by 1998, growing public revelations about the Earnscliffe operation and its ties to the minister were increasingly viewed by the rest of the Chrétien camp as a political problem. For his part, Martin was incensed by any criticism of the organization. 'If I've been a reasonably successful Finance Minister, it's because of them. They ... participated in those massive fights. They're every bit as responsible for the government's success.'[65]

At party headquarters, the replacement of Senator Dan Hays as president by Stephen LeDrew – a Toronto lawyer and formerly tour director for John Turner in 1984 – was considered something of a shock, especially given the extent of his triumph over Newfoundland MP Brenda Hicks, Chrétien's presumed choice. Nevertheless, in the context of the Chrétien-Martin axis, LeDrew was seen as impartial. LeDrew himself later acknowledged that Chrétien always demonstrated a commendable interest in party affairs. Like Senator Leo Kolber, LeDrew also stressed that Chrétien was prepared to participate in a great number of party-related activities in order to raise funds or to consolidate support. At the same time, he recalled that the leader was 'scrupulous' about having the party pay for clearly partisan activities.

Above all, LeDrew expected to enhance the party's influence with the parliamentary wing now that the financial status of the party was on an even keel. 'Robert's was a survival presidency where they were paying things off with credit cards to stay afloat,' he declared. 'DJ's presidency was about financial recovery, and Dan Hays was primarily a fundraiser.'[66] Referring to the 'parliamentary vortex' that typically developed when the party was in power, LeDrew made it clear that he intended to pursue what he described as a 'renewal agenda.'

This ambitious agenda quickly foundered on the rocks of political exigency and lack of connections. As Terry Mercer later recalled, the election of LeDrew coincided with the leadership review vote, leaving many in the Martin camp unhappy about Mercer's role as national director. This was mirrored by LeDrew's increasing unhappiness with Mercer as a result of his close ties with the PMO, which LeDrew did not share. Mercer's attendance at the PMO daily senior staff meetings soon became a significant bone of contention. LeDrew did not have weekly meetings with the leader. Although both sides later agreed the president could obtain a meeting whenever he requested one, they were infrequent. As a result, he expected to be briefed on the substance of the PMO meetings, but Mercer insisted he could only reveal those items related to the party, not the government, or he would be barred by Jean Pelletier from attending in future.

At first, Mercer attempted to serve as a bridge, arranging a lunch between LeDrew and Pelletier to resolve the issue. The meeting was unsuccessful. Subsequently, while Mercer viewed LeDrew's concerns as 'unreasonable' and 'unprecedented,' LeDrew believed Mercer's refusal to brief the president 'made my situation almost untenable' and 'bordered on treasonous.' LeDrew later claimed Mercer told him: 'I don't work for the party, I work for Jean Chrétien,' a statement LeDrew said was viewed with concern by other members of the national executive as well.[67] The tension between the two men also led to problems highlighting party concerns with caucus and cabinet ministers, leaving LeDrew frustrated and impatient with the lack of action on a number of policy files despite the elimination of the deficit.

The Martin Team's Action Plan

The impatience of the Martin organizers grew after the 1997 election. As one Chrétien supporter later said, 'Somehow there was this attitude on their part that Martin would obviously be next, and the only question was when.' In an interview with journalist John Gray, even one of Martin's oldest friends agreed 'there was a sense of entitlement, almost a sense of divine right' in Martin's leadership aspirations. 'There seems to have been always the sense that this was his due, that the longer the other guy held office, the more Paul was being cheated.' Perhaps more importantly, the friend said 'there's a certain group around Paul that always questioned Chrétien's legitimacy … even though his authority within the party and his mandate with the electorate were pretty robust.'[68]

By 1999 their impatience had translated into significant activity. With Chrétien's tacit admission to Allan Rock that he would be leaving before a third term, the Martin team sprang into action. John Webster, Martin's Ontario organizer in 1990, had always advocated keeping the Martin team together based on his disastrous experience with the dismantled Turner organization in 1984. Now he returned to play a key role in organizing Martin's support within the party. This time he was aided by a new full-time campaign worker, Michele Cadario, who was on his payroll at Maple Trust.

As part of the overall effort, one of Martin's most enthusiastic young supporters, Karl Littler, prepared a discussion paper outlining the many rule changes to the party's constitution since 1990 concerning the leadership. As noted earlier, the party's concerns about single-issue interest groups taking over local riding associations had come to the fore in the late 1980s. Many changes had been introduced to thwart that possibility, in addition to the leader's newly acquired ability to block the nominations of undesirable candidates. Among the most important were the changes which gave the party executives – local and provincial presidents and officers – control over the membership forms needed to recruit new members. The changes led Littler to conclude that these forms were the key to any attempt to win a future leadership race because the winner would be determined by a new system of delegate selection by party members. If someone could control the distribution of membership forms, they could effectively hamper the efforts of opponents to recruit new members and, hence, to win delegates.

In the past, delegates to a leadership convention were selected on the basis of which candidate they supported. If a majority in a riding was in favour of a particular candidate, then all of the delegates from that riding would be voting for that candidate at the convention. Fifty-five per cent of the riding membership could secure 100 per cent of the delegates for a particular candidate. A riding could be described as being a 'Chrétien' or 'Turner' riding. A more proportional type of representation was put in place under the new system. In general, if 40 per cent of the members in a riding voted for a particular candidate, then that candidate would have 40 per cent of the delegates but his opponent(s) would also send delegates from that riding. There were additional complexities. For example, the votes of the women's and youth commission members were separated out, so that if a candidate did not have a youth or women's delegate specifically listed on the ballot they could not send a delegate, even if they received the most votes. By contrast, they would be assigned delegates even if only a handful of women or youth commission members voted. Last, but hardly least, the votes in each riding would now be counted as part of a two-stage selection process. The successful leadership candidate would have to win both the riding-level vote and the convention vote.

For Karl Littler, the possibilities of utilizing this new system to Paul Martin's advantage appeared endless. He concluded that the first move should be to take control of as many local riding associations and provincial executives as possible in order to gain control of the distribution of membership forms. Then it would be necessary to recruit youth and women members for these ridings and to establish as many Liberal women's clubs and university clubs as possible. Throughout 1998 and 1999, John Webster and Michele Cadario did just that. By September of 1999 the Martin forces had taken control of the Ontario wing of the party and were about to do so in several other provinces.

An inside perspective on this process was outlined by Martin's former Ontario leadership chair and eventual chief of staff in PMO, Tim Murphy. Murphy stressed that calling it the 'takeover' of local executives was 'a misnomer.' He insisted it would be more accurate to say that 'the main characteristic of the party under Chrétien was decay.' Referring especially to western Canada, Murphy said, 'We had to build a new party, there was nothing to take over in most cases.'[69]

Murphy's view was shared by Martin's top BC organizer, Mark Marissen, who had been involved in provincial politics since moving to the province from Ottawa several years earlier. Marissen was married to a provincial Liberal MLA, Christy Clark, who later became a minister and eventually deputy premier in the Campbell government, thereby increasing Marissen's own visibility and influence. According to Marissen, his initial efforts to develop a stronger federal party presence in BC were not related to the leadership struggle or events elsewhere. 'This was an independent BC movement ... I was still a Chrétien supporter in 1998,' he insisted. He maintained his efforts 'were an attempt to make the party organization stronger' and more importantly were 'motivated by a desire to increase the influence of the province on the national party. I thought we needed to change the culture of the party, from one of "access to the leader" to one of "organizational clout" in order to increase BC's clout in the country,' Marissen said. 'At the time we were victims of the party's success nationally. There simply was no incentive for them to make the provincial wing stronger.' According to Marissen, when he and his group succeeded in building up the BC wing, 'we were seen by the Chrétien camp as "enemies of the state." And so we became what they thought we already were – Martin supporters. After that, things just escalated.'[70]

Many disagreed with this explanation. A very different perspective on Marissen's actions was offered by Chrétien's close friend and one-time BC organizer, Senator Ross Fitzpatrick, who was frequently the focus of public criticism by Marissen and his group. Fitzpatrick pointed out that he had been elected president of the BC wing of the party in 1991 when the Liberals were still in opposition. 'It was hardly a position of prestige at the time as the party had neither money nor organization,' he recalled. Although he served as Chrétien's 1993 BC campaign chair, Fitzpatrick resigned as election readiness chair for personal reasons by 1995 and others chaired the 1997 and 2000 BC campaigns. 'I was in no position to prevent or promote access to the leader, whatever that might have meant,' he concluded.[71] Others involved in the dispute noted that Steven Kukuchka, not Mark Marissen, had been appointed executive director for the 1997 campaign by Chrétien, and that Marissen's activities to recruit new members and take control of riding associations began soon after, not in late 1998 as claimed. Little of this dispute was public knowledge. It occurred largely below the radar screen of the national media but did not escape the attention of Chrétien's inner circle, who unsuccessfully urged him to take countermeasures before it was too late. Sergio Marchi, for one, 'told the boss that he was letting things slide. I urged him to let us organize and run slates for delegates before this started, but he wasn't very concerned. Others were telling him the same thing. I think he just never believed anyone would try to do such a thing [push out a sitting prime minister] and he probably didn't realize how the new rules would allow it to happen.' Brian Tobin agreed: 'I think he really didn't know what was going on. Of course one reason was that Eddie always told him not to worry, not to pay attention to what some of us were saying to him.'[72] Goldenberg, Tobin pointedly stated, knew nothing about the party.

When the extent of the conflict between Martin and Chrétien became a matter of public knowledge, the situation – and Chrétien's perspective – changed dramatically. As Jean Pelletier confided, faced with public exposure of an apparent plot to force him out, Chrétien felt he had no choice but to stay. Apart from his own natural inclination to stand and fight, he felt a dangerous precedent would be set if he were to be pushed aside. Unlike the Conservatives, there was no precedent for a Liberal leader to be removed against his will, and certainly not a successful one. Chrétien reminded his advisers that even after he lost the election of 1911, Wilfrid Laurier stayed on as leader for several more years. The long-serving Mackenzie King, Chrétien declared, actually lost an election and survived minorities as well as the loss of government through the King-Byng affair, but remained virtually unopposed throughout six terms of office. And while Lester Pearson won two elections, he delivered only minorities. In the end, all of these leaders established their own timetables for departure, as Pierre Trudeau had done twice. Even John Turner had chosen the date of his departure after losing a second election in a row. Certainly they had all been mindful of the fact that losses would not be tolerated by the party forever, but

Chrétien was hardly in the same position. He had delivered two majority governments and was described by the CBC's Peter Mansbridge as 'one of the country's most popular politicians ever' on the very eve of the infamous Constellation Hotel debacle in March 2000. Surely he could expect a grateful party to allow him to choose the timing of his departure.

Caucus Dissent Escalates

Intimations of the conflict between Chrétien and Martin actually began in 1998. Backbenchers whose chances for promotion in the Chrétien government seemed slim to non-existent (virtually all of them were Martin supporters) began to publicly air their grievances, and Chrétien strategists fought back. In one account of this extraordinary conflict, journalist Susan Delacourt attributes the so-called 'newspaper wars' between the two Liberal camps to the emergence of the new national daily owned by Conrad Black. She describes the growing conflict between reporters of the upstart *National Post* and the suddenly threatened *Globe and Mail*, in which a new atmosphere of desperate competition led to 'a rush to publish any and all tips or leaked information. It became far easier for backbench MPs and strategists to plant their stories in the national press, sometimes just for mischief and sometimes to send a message to their enemies.'[73]

The situation escalated in 1999, when several of Martin's supporters began challenging cabinet ministers in parliamentary committees. In the Transport Committee chaired by Comuzzi, for example, Transport Minister David Collenette encountered fierce resistance to his plans to salvage Canadian Airlines and possibly arrange a merger with Air Canada, resistance that came largely from Liberal backbenchers rather than the opposition.

The Liberal MPs involved described their resistance as an effort to exercise some discretion rather than simply toeing the government line at all times. Critics saw it as the discontented flexing their muscles. Either way, it represented the first public concerns about the increasingly impotent role of backbenchers that Paul Martin would soon term the 'democratic deficit.' This phenomenon was also highlighted by political scientist Donald Savoie in his study of prime ministerial power.[74] At the same time, several veteran MPs disagreed with this terminology. Former cabinet minister Charles Caccia objected strongly to the term and wrote a lengthy rebuttal against it. 'Individual MPs are already in the position to make a difference and to participate in many ways in the policy process,' he wrote. 'This is not to suggest that there is no need for rules and procedures to be updated. But it is unfortunate that the legitimate desire for improvements to the legislative process has been subsumed with such inflammatory discourse about a democratic deficit, leading many Canadians to further question the credibility of one of the finest parliamentary systems.'[75]

Other caucus members felt the dissidents' rationale was 'a thinly disguised excuse for causing trouble and getting some publicity.' Some of Chrétien's staunch supporters attributed the resistance to the single-minded ambitions of the backbenchers and to the overarching leadership ambitions of Martin.

Chrétien dismissed such concerns. He pointed to the elevation of longtime Martin supporter Jim Peterson as minister of state for financial institutions, and the appointment of Martin loyalist Maurizio Bevilacqua as the new Finance Committee chair, as evidence that Martin supporters were not being excluded. Interestingly, while Peterson's appointment was actually encouraged by Martin, with whom he would work, the subsequent appointment of Bevilacqua to the junior ministry was viewed by Martin and his supporters as a selling out that would cost the former Martin confidant a cabinet appointment when Martin finally became prime minister.[76]

According to a number of Chrétien supporters, there was at least one other reason for caucus dissatisfaction. They pointed to Paul Martin's tendency to avoid making difficult decisions, a tendency which even some of his supporters recognized.[77] In Percy Downe's view, this often led to an 'unfortunate' situation in which 'many caucus members (who were advocating specific measures for inclusion in the budget) would be left with the impression that Mr Martin supported their request and it was Mr Chrétien who opposed it. Then they would come to see me and, when I would ask him about their proposal, he would know nothing about it.'[78] Several Chrétien supporters in cabinet confided that they often felt *they* were the ones receiving the short end of the stick in Martin's budget allocations, a perception shared by many senior bureaucrats. According to Martin biographer John Gray, one veteran mandarin confided that he believed 'everything divides in that government into who you supported in 1990. You can look at any single issue, any decision in budget of who got the money. Martin will deny that ... and everybody else will deny it, but I can tell you there's a 95 per cent correlation ... I don't care what the idea is, you tell me who's supporting it and I'll tell you whether it will go through or not.'[79]

The problem of caucus unrest came to a head when Chrétien supporter Carolyn Parrish publicly accused some of her fellow MPs of
disloyalty. In reply, several members of the self-described 'spaghetti
caucus' led by Joe Fontana asked to see Chrétien to assure him that
their actions were not motivated by Martin's leadership ambitions.
Chrétien's response, according to several accounts of the meeting, was
dismissive. After noting that all of the supplicants were Martin supporters, he outlined the various appointments they had received from
him during his term in office and then pointed out that Comuzzi had
actually declined the offer of a parliamentary secretaryship.

The problems Chrétien and his cabinet encountered with disgruntled
backbenchers bore considerable resemblance to those faced by Brian
Mulroney when he was handed a second majority government. In
Mulroney's case the majority was overwhelming, and he lacked a sufficient number of posts with which to reward those not in the cabinet.
In Chrétien's case the majority was not that large, but by 1999 virtually
everyone had been given a chance to perform as a parliamentary secretary, and there were fewer parliamentary committees to be chaired than
had been the case during Mulroney's time. As well, with no credible
challenge to government policies, due to the divided and marginalized
nature of the opposition parties, a new phenomenon was emerging
whereby the only 'real' opposition to the government came from within
its own caucus, as policy-minded Liberal MPs filled the void.

Chrétien's situation differed from Mulroney's in two important ways.
First, on policy, the discontented backbenchers came almost entirely
from the business Liberal end of the spectrum, meaning that their objections to government policy proposals in the era of the fiscal dividend
were increasingly out of step with their own government. Worse still
from Chrétien's perspective, almost all of them shared Martin's preference for Plan A and the accommodation of soft nationalists and had
expressed the most concerns about the Clarity Bill. Second, in practical
terms many of the MPs within the Martin camp were simply not considered cabinet material by the Chrétien team, and correctly believed
that after six years their chances of ever being promoted to that level
were virtually non-existent. But unlike the Mulroney backbenchers in
that situation, the Martinites had an option. They could aspire to higher
things under an alternative leader.

This hope was shaken when Françoise Ducros described the January
2000 cabinet shuffle as a deliberate attempt to send a message to the
Martin camp that the prime minister would be staying on as leader.
It was, in her words, 'a shot across the bow.' Shortly thereafter came a

public revelation by the CBC that a group of some twenty-five known Martin supporters in caucus had attended a meeting at the Constellation Hotel in Toronto chaired by Martin's former executive assistant, Richard Mahoney, with Martin advisers such as Webster, Herle, Cadario, and Littler also in attendance. The marriage of convenience between the two men soon foundered. The meeting also foreshadowed the unusual and uneasy relationship between Martin's advisers and Martin's supporters in the caucus. When criticism of the meeting turned to ridicule of Martin's advisers, Martin's defence of them proved prophetic, demonstrating a loyalty that would cause him considerable difficulty once in power. 'First of all, I owe them a lot,' he declared. 'Second, they're friends. And third, whatever the hell they did they ... did for me.'[80]

As numerous accounts have since chronicled, the ill-fated meeting at the Constellation Hotel was a poorly planned and executed event. Tim Murphy later conceded that there were two key problems. 'It was done in secret and, when it was discovered, it was not handled well.'[81] Perhaps equally important, the purpose of the meeting seemed unclear even to the organizers. Worried by Ducros's implied threat that Chrétien would be staying on, one group of Martin supporters decided to circulate the rumour that the finance minister would resign shortly, just as Turner had done under Trudeau. This caused considerable consternation among the Martin MPs, several of whom saw this as the loss of not only a potential party leader but their potential cabinet appointments. Attempts by another group of advisers to play down these concerns and calm the MPs down were partly behind the decision to invite the MPs to Toronto. Another apparent reason was to highlight Martin's appeal to the general public, demonstrated by David Herle's presentation of polling results. Yet some who attended the meeting cautioned that no overt action should be taken until Chrétien made his intentions clear. According to one participant, MP Walt Lastewka advised all of those present to avoid criticizing the prime minister, and another MP, Carolyn Bennett, argued that they should make sure the convention was a positive event for the leader because he 'wouldn't react well if cornered.'[82]

Years later, Martin confidant Mike Robinson, who had not been involved in the meeting, agreed with this assessment. 'If I had known about it I would have told them not to do it. I never advocated any attempt to force his hand. I believed it would lead to him deciding to stay.'[83] Not surprisingly, many caucus participants came away from the meeting perplexed as to why it had ever been called. When they learned of the CBC interpretation, that the meeting was evidence of a plot to re-move the leader, some of the participants were quick to describe it as harmless and, in hindsight, an error in judgment. Others, however, felt it was time to put their concerns on record. MP Stan Keyes willingly told reporters that his constituents were saying 'You know what, Jean? Maybe you should step aside … You're at the crescendo of your career. Pass the torch.'[84] He was echoed by MPs Diane Marleau and Ovid Jackson as well as attendees John Harvard, Paul Bonwick, and Joe Fontana, who told reporters: 'If Chrétien decides to go we'll understand.'[85]

For Chrétien, the problem was one of a perceived public challenge to his authority, whether that was the original intent of the meeting or not. As Peter Donolo later recounted, the escalation of the 'crisis' surrounding that meeting was nevertheless something that he 'would have handled differently. Once you confront them publicly, you can't back down. It's like confronting a spouse about their infidelity.'[86] Certainly Françoise Ducros did not hesitate to confront the Martin supporters publicly. Nor did the media, who pursued Martin at length for a comment on the purpose of the meeting. Seen once again fleeing from journalists, this time down an escalator, Martin was described by almost everyone who saw the news clip as looking decidedly guilty. One person who saw the clip was Aline Chrétien. According to an adviser who was with the Chrétiens when the news story appeared on television, Mme Chrétien immediately turned to her husband and said 'Four more years!'

With the 2000 biennial party convention scheduled to take place only two days later, the Constellation Hotel debacle caused both sides to sit back and carefully plan their strategy. For Martin and some of his most senior advisers it was a lose-lose situation. If they were to challenge the leader at the convention (which was not, in any event, one at which there would be a leadership review vote) they would appear disloyal. If they did nothing, they would be resigned to fighting a third election with Chrétien as leader, and Martin (already 61) would be a senior citizen before he would be in a position to lead the party himself. Underlying these calculations, as Mike Robinson later indicated, was a significant concern about the policy direction of the party. The dramatically increased expenditures on existing and new social programs, for example, were seen as exorbitant and harmful to the government's ability to fund the productivity agenda Martin favoured.

At the convention, it soon became apparent that Martin's forces were chastened. A 'down tools' order had been given, as Tim Murphy later put it. Brought into line once again by the discipline of power and the traditions of the 'natural governing party,' they were out to make amends. Some MPs tried to calm the troubled waters by speaking with reporters and assuring them the coup attempt was all a huge misunderstanding. Martin himself gave several interviews in which he made it clear he was not planning to resign and intended to run in the next election, whenever it was called. When Chrétien entered the convention hall, strategically placed groups of Young Liberals immediately began chanting 'Four more years!'

In his address to the convention, Chrétien laid the groundwork for the next campaign. The Liberal Party was the champion of public health care, the originator of the Canada Health Act, and would defend this birthright of Canadians against all assaults from the far right. His motivation was the metamorphosis of the Reform Party into the Canadian Alliance, the second development that derailed Chrétien's departure plans. The publicity given to the Right during its recent meetings to bring about the name change provided an ideal opportunity for Chrétien to emphasize the Liberals' fiscal dividend agenda and highlight plans to pursue new social programs which the Reform/Alliance party steadfastly opposed. It also provided him with a theme to once again unite the majority of grassroots Liberals, and especially the Liberal youth, behind his leadership.[87]

Shortly thereafter the new Alliance Party chose Alberta cabinet minister Stockwell Day as its new leader. Although Day initially appeared photogenic and forward-looking, an examination of his record in Alberta suggested otherwise. Yet for a short time the novelty of Day, in contrast to his well-known and widely ridiculed predecessor, Preston Manning, produced polling data which implied the Liberals might be in for a contest in the next federal election.

10 Implosion: The Third Chrétien Mandate

Jean Chrétien stands astride the Canadian political scene without much effective opposition at the federal level.

– Political scientist G. Bruce Doern[1]

Many Martin confidants still believe Jean Chrétien's snap election call in late October 2000 was motivated by his desire to stave off further caucus unrest or leadership challenges.[2] Chrétien insiders disagree. They argue it was the prime minister's perception of the Alliance Party as a potential threat that ultimately led him to pull the plug barely three and half years into his second mandate. Polls taken after Stockwell Day's election as Alliance leader showed the party enjoying its highest approval ratings ever, hovering near 30 per cent. But despite this improvement, Liberal support remained near 50 per cent. This was an unheard-of feat for a party approaching the end of its second term in power, and one not expected to continue the following year when an economic downturn was forecast.[3]

The decision was certainly Chrétien's alone. Once again many in his caucus, including some of his own supporters, were nervous about the idea of returning to the electorate before their mandate had expired. Liberal Party president Stephen LeDrew entered the fray as well, calling a senior PMO official to urge the prime minister to delay dropping the writ because he could not possibly win another majority.[4] Even members of the election readiness committee believed Chrétien should wait.

Those who opposed an early election call also pointed to the recent passing of former prime minister Pierre Trudeau on 28 September. With extensive media coverage of the state funeral and retrospectives on his life and legacy, many backbenchers feared an election call would be seen as opportunistic. In the end it was Stockwell Day who was seen to take advantage of the situation, declaring before a group of parliamentary press gallery reporters that 'many of [Trudeau's] values are values I happen to endorse as well.' He was later forced to clarify that he was referring to 'personal' values such as 'courage, and standing in the face of opposition,' but many Canadians concluded 'Day's comments had been primarily designed to ensure his name would be linked with that of Trudeau on the evening news.'[5]

According to several members of his inner circle, three points made up Jean Chrétien's mind. First was the government's high approval rating, bolstered by a healthy economy and the widespread perception of the Liberals as fixers. This alone was a significant difference from 1997, when the elimination of the deficit had yet to translate into job creation or economic prosperity. Second was the release of the Alliance platform on 5 October 2000, which reinforced Chrétien's belief that Stockwell Day was as extreme as Preston Manning and gave the Liberals the chance to counter the most politically attractive elements (such as a reduction in personal income tax and a substantial payment on the national debt) early on. The third factor was the opposition leader's direct challenge on 19 October during Question Period.

Priming the Big Red Machine

Virtually all expert observers agreed with Pammett and Dornan's assessment that 'the personal decision of Prime Minister Jean Chrétien to call an election in the fall of 2000 rather than the spring of 2001 appears in retrospect to have been a masterstroke of political strategy.'[6] Although the election was called with little warning, the party was prepared. Chrétien had already taken steps on the policy front and in candidate recruitment to reinforce the party's pan-Canadian appeal. He had also introduced measures to increase Liberal support in areas where they had proven weak in 1997 such as Atlantic Canada.

With John Rae and Gordon Ashworth reprising their roles as national campaign coordinator and national director for the third time, a seasoned campaign team was at the helm. Indeed, by now the competence of the Liberals' campaign was taken for granted. Gordon Ashworth noted that, having started preparations in late 1999, there was little sense of surprise on the part of the senior election personnel when the writ was dropped. 'We had our organization in place across the country as well. Sure, there were a few holes to fill, but by and large it was the same team as last time, and required nothing like the effort we had to make in 1993.'[7]

One striking difference was to be found in the war room, where former PMO staffer and diehard Martin opponent Warren Kinsella was back in action along with lead writer Ken Polk, a longtime Chrétien aide, and John Milloy. Perhaps not surprisingly, there were no Martin staffers in the war room this time around. In fact, no Martin personnel were to be found anywhere in the campaign organization with the exception of Mike Robinson who again negotiated the leaders' debates and served as a liaison between the campaign committee and Martin. Chrétien organizers attributed their absence to the unwillingness of Martin's team. Martin staffers insisted that PMO failed to reach out and invite them to participate. At the same time, many key Martin personnel argued they made a major contribution by working with Martin on a parallel campaign. Michelle Cadario stressed this point: 'Once the writ was dropped, there was no question of leadership issues. We all worked very, very hard to make sure that a Liberal government was elected.'[8] Certainly Martin attended numerous events for fellow candidates across the country, albeit almost exclusively for known Martin supporters, and Francie Ducros invited Martin to represent the prime minister on several occasions over the course of the campaign.

On the policy front, Chrétien's government had been working hard for years to prove that the deficit resulted in social policy gains and economic prosperity. Now, in the run-up to the election, additional measures were introduced to underscore the government's return to liberalism. On 11 September, Chrétien signed a Health Accord with the provinces which provided an additional $23.4 billion over five years. The deal was sealed with the help of Newfoundland Premier Brian Tobin and Saskatchewan Premier Roy Romanow.[9] On a more pragmatic note, the 18 October mini-budget addressed regional policy concerns by reinstating EI benefits for seasonal workers in the Atlantic.

Chrétien had also spent considerable time in the months before the election call recruiting new candidates, especially in Atlantic Canada and the west. He convinced Brian Tobin to leave his sinecure as premier of Newfoundland and return to national politics, this time as the powerful industry minister. He also won over well-known Nova Scotia cabinet minister Bernie Boudreau. His attempt to recruit former New Brunswick premier Frank McKenna, however, fell on deaf ears. A similar effort in western Canada saw the Liberals attract Stephen Owen, a well-regarded former provincial ombudsman, to run in British Columbia. In Saskatchewan, NDP MP Rick Laliberte defected to the Liberals to run for them in the upcoming election. But Chrétien's concerted efforts to entice his old friend Roy Romanow to run for the Liberals ultimately failed.

In addition to his concern about regional representation, Chrétien worried about the growing imbalance in cabinet between social Liberals (badly outnumbered with the departure of Lloyd Axworthy) and business Liberals. From this perspective, the PM's efforts to recruit Brian Tobin were especially significant seeing as he provided a solution to both the regional and philosophical imbalance. Tobin also provided Chrétien with another potential leadership candidate to prevent Paul Martin from becoming leader by acclamation, a point several of Chrétien's advisers were quick to note. 'He believed he had a responsibility to ensure he left the party in good hands,' George Young maintained, 'and for that there needed to be a race. He didn't want to see a repeat of the Turner coronation.'[10] Martin and his advisers were quick to note this reality as well.

The most significant change in the selection process was Chrétien's decreased emphasis on women and visible minorities. His appointments concentrated on star candidates such as John McCallum, a bank vice-president, and Allan Tonks, former mayor of York and Metro Toronto Chair. The Judy Campaign, as veteran Liberal organizer Isabelle Metcalfe lamented, 'simply never got off the ground in 2000' either in terms of candidate recruitment or in terms of fundraising for existing women candidates.[11] One disappointed observer ascribed this decline to the perceived importance of the Alliance Party as the main opposition to the Liberals and the near-disappearance of the NDP as a threat. 'Where the NDP had pushed for the nomination of more women, Reform – after 1993 the dominant force in opposition to the Liberals nationally – targeted the Liberals for criticism as "undemocratic" because leader Jean Chrétien appointed women to certain ridings over the objection of local riding associations.'[12]

The 2000 Platform: The Red Pamphlet

Another area in which the party backed away from earlier efforts was the platform. Despite predictions by several academics that the 1993 Red Book had changed the nature of all parties' campaign promises,[13] the Liberals' 2000 platform could best be described as a Red Pamphlet. Only thirty-one pages in length, it was disparaged by critics as a rehash of the October mini-budget and the health accord. There were several reasons for the lack of new substantive commitments, including the lengthy record to defend and the lack of preparation time to assemble proposals. Still, as senior PMO adviser Marjorie Loveys pointed out, there had been work going on in preparation for the platform on a nearly continuous basis. 'We had much less time to draft a text,' she agreed, 'but we knew what we wanted to have included.' Loveys noted that several items included in the 2000 Liberal platform were put there primarily because the drafters had been unable to convince the bureaucracy to proceed with them over the past several years. 'We believed there would be a better chance of having them implemented if they were part of the now-famous Red Books to which the bureaucracy had definitely paid attention,' she conceded. For the mandarins, at least, 'the Red Books were gospel.'[14]

Despite its brevity, the 2000 Red Book was long on rhetoric. A reworking of the health care accord and budget commitments on taxation were accompanied by 'new' commitments to build a 'smart economy,' to ensure 'healthy citizens in a healthy environment,' and to promote Canadian culture and values at home and abroad. One of the most important commitments in the economic section was to 'make high-speed broadband internet access available to residents and businesses in all communities in Canada by 2004.' Another was to introduce a 'registered individual learning account' to enable workers to save for their own retraining. Throughout the campaign, in all of his speeches, these were the only commitments specifically mentioned by Chrétien,[15] a fact that would come back to haunt him.

Another reason for the brevity of the Liberals' 2000 platform was the lack of consensus between the Chrétien and Martin camps. Goldenberg and Hosek tried to engage Martin directly in the 2000 platform exercise, but he declined.[16] There was also less input from the party executive and the grassroots. 'The exercise was not party-driven,' one senior PMO spokesperson said bluntly. Interestingly, the takeover of much of the national executive by Martin supporters, and the disenchantment with party president Stephen LeDrew, led the official to suggest this was at least partly due to the PMO's lack of confidence in the extra-parliamentary wing. Instead, *Opportunity for All: The Liberal Plan for the Future of Canada* was prepared after cursory consultations with cabinet ministers, caucus, and a few outside party experts.

Another problem with preparing the Red Book so quickly was the lack of access to the bureaucracy, as Marjorie Loveys noted. 'Long before an election is called the public service shuts down. They won't talk to you or provide detailed information on anything they think might be part of a campaign. They're scrupulous about that, and rightly so. But this idea that being the government is a big advantage in terms of access to information is only right if there is a lot of time to plan ahead.' For the Liberals in 2000, the major problem was the cost of their promises. The Martin team claimed the PMO drafters were uninterested in costing, but PMO participants maintained it was simply a lack of bureaucratic input. Another recalled: 'We had to get the LCRB people working on it. And I think Karl Littler [then Martin's assistant at Finance] helped out as well.' 'It certainly isn't true that we would have released it without a costing section.'[17] In the end, the lack of costing information was a major reason for the delay in launching the platform.

The Liberals' ad campaign, by contrast, was ready to go and sharply focused on what, for the electorate, were the key issues. They knew Canadians were satisfied with the Liberal government's record but were increasingly worried about the apparent decline in party unity and constant infighting. Voters wanted to be reassured about the Chrétien/Martin alliance. Even though there was a growing sentiment that it was time for Chrétien to retire, he continued to lead in the opinion polls. Voters were also uneasy about the new Alliance leader, something the Liberals could exploit to their advantage.

Chastened by the embarrassing plot revelations earlier in the year, Paul Martin was determined to reinvent himself as a loyal Liberal soldier. He spent the summer considering whether to retire from politics – urged to do so by his closest advisers, David Herle and Terrie O'Leary – but decided to remain as a show of solidarity with his caucus followers.[18] In early October he spent a day with Chrétien at the prime minister's official country residence at Harrington Lake, filming a series of campaign ads showing the two men cheerfully walking and talking together in a flower-filled field. As one observer concluded, even at this late date in their deteriorating relationship, 'they performed as good friends for the sake of those who would vote for this government as long as it was a joint Chrétien-Martin exercise. As soon as the cameras stopped rolling, they retreated behind the walls of stiff civility that now characterized their face-to-face dealings.'[19] The ad's message was clear. Not only were Liberals united, but the country was in good hands. As the campaign unfolded, it became evident this was a message Canadians were once again prepared to accept.

The 'Liberal Values' Campaign

When Jean Chrétien asked the governor general to dissolve Parliament on 22 October, he did not make the same mistake as in 1997. He knew why he was calling the election and he was prepared to tell anyone who asked. 'It is an opportunity for Canadians to choose between different visions and different values. This election offers two very different visions of Canada, two crystal-clear alternatives.' It was a theme outlined by Brian Tobin when he announced his decision to leave Newfoundland and return to Ottawa shortly before. 'Canada is more than a Monopoly board,' he declared. 'The Alliance Party and all that it stands for is the single most compelling reason that I have accepted the prime minister's request to consider a return to national politics ... The coming election should be about how we continue to build the country, not divide it.'[20]

The most significant aspect of the Liberals' campaign plan was not their attack on Alliance values but rather their relentless promotion of Liberal values, reinforcing the idea that they were synonymous with Canadian values. Coincidentally, the emphasis on pan-Canadian values was seen by Chrétien as an important mechanism for reinforcing national unity, especially in the face of growing regionalization in federal politics. The introduction to the Red Pamphlet, signed by Chrétien, was explicit on this point. 'In an era of globalization, Canada needs a vision for the future that recognizes a national perspective and the aspirations of all Canadians. Our vision sees Canadian society as more than a collection of competing interests.' In a veiled reference to the Alliance, it continued: 'We see Canadians not only as taxpayers but as citizens with obligations to one another.' And, most telling, 'Our vision sees a strong national government as essential to serving the broader public interest.'[21] Even their critics recognized 'the Liberals' success in turning the campaign into a question of values helped them avoid taking a stand on potentially divisive issues, and so present themselves as the most "national" of the parties.'[22] The Alliance knew what the Liberals were doing but were helpless to counteract it.

In view of this strategy, it is hardly surprising the Liberals released a series of campaign ads defending social programs, especially health care, from the 'threat' of the Alliance. Day tried hard to deflect certain accusations but was constantly undermined by his own colleagues. Alliance MP Keith Martin's stance in favour of 'profit-driven health care' was regularly highlighted by Liberal spokespersons and the media. Martin's position might have been dismissed as simply one individual deviating from party policy until the Alliance national campaign co-chair, Jason Kenney, made a similar point on CBC Newsworld's *Counter Spin*. Asked to repeat and clarify his remarks by the program's host, Avi Lewis, Kenney confirmed that he believed in a universal public health care system and 'in allowing some people some choices.'[23] While Day tried to distance himself from such comments, Kenney's position was supported by Alliance MP Val Meredith and Day's own national campaign director, Rod Love, who argued that the country already had a two-tier system.

Jean Chrétien took advantage of the confusion as he had years earlier when neophyte Conservative leader Kim Campbell slipped up. 'Never, never, never will we let the Alliance destroy health care,' he thundered. The Alliance Party's ongoing image problem finally led to Day's hand-printed sign declaring 'No Two-Tier Health Care' during the leaders' debates two weeks later. By then Day had several other fires to fight. In fact, Liberal strategists started to worry that Alliance support might collapse altogether, allowing Joe Clark and the Conservatives to take seats away from the Liberals in Atlantic Canada and Ontario.

By and large, both Chrétien and the media ignored the Liberal platform soon after its release and presentation two weeks into the campaign. As David Collenette reflected, 'It almost didn't matter what was in the Red Book at that point. We had established a reputation and people just wanted to be reassured that we had another plan for the next four years. I don't think anybody ever asked me anything about the details during the whole campaign.'[24]

The Leaders' Debates and the Alliance Tailspin

The leaders' debates were scheduled earlier than usual in the 2000 campaign. The Liberals knew going in that Chrétien would be attacked from all sides. With Day's support plummeting it was clear the debates would be an essential element of the Alliance leader's survival strategy, and he was expected to go on the offensive. This was indeed Day's plan, but his lack of fluency in French prevented him from participating aggressively in the first debate. His card trick early in the English debate marginalized him even further. Joe Clark's jibe that Day 'looked like a talk show host' was particularly telling. Clark himself was considered by most observers to have been the winner of the second debate. But with little popular support and even less organization backing him, there was no possibility of Clark and the Conservatives doing more than holding the government accountable, a point he actually made near the end of the debate in conceding the Liberals would win again and the Alliance would be the Official Opposition.[25]

There were some minor public relations successes for the Alliance in the remaining weeks of the campaign, but they were few and far between. With their support slipping, Alliance strategists convinced Day to give up his 'agenda of respect' and attack Chrétien more directly. They also convinced Day to return to standard Alliance themes like law and order, immigration, and aboriginal policy. Although this may have shored up their support among their traditional voters, it continued to reinforce the Liberals' argument that the Alliance was too extreme. The leak of a confidential Alliance document which raised the issue of abortion deepened public suspicion of a hidden agenda.

True to form, Jean Chrétien seized the opportunity in a speech to a women's group in Laval, Quebec. 'We have social peace on the question of abortion,' he said. 'Canadians do not want a party that threatens a woman's right to choose.' Stockwell Day attempted to blame the document on junior party researchers and insisted, 'Abortion is not even in the platform. It's been discussed but it's not in the platform.' Yet the platform did contain a commitment to allow virtually any subject to be raised and put on the national agenda through the referendum provision. One journalist complained, 'What was one to believe? The party's document said one thing. The party's Leader claimed another. Could anyone be blamed for wondering if the dreaded hidden agenda was at play here?'[26]

The *National Post* attempted to downgrade Alliance failings, reporting dubious interpretations of polling results and characterizing Chrétien as an aging warhorse. But the voting public wasn't buying it.[27] National polling numbers showed that the Alliance was fading fast, reduced to their core support in the west. Still, there were some concerns in the Liberal camp that their own numbers were beginning to drop, and it was unclear how much damage this might do in the Atlantic or Ontario. They were still ahead of their opponents by a comfortable margin, but the Conservatives, not the Alliance, were in second place, and there was the possibility of a better Conservative result cutting into a Liberal majority. At one point Chrétien seemed to be unnerved by the constant references to his decreased popularity and the increasingly personal attacks of his opponents. He began to muse publicly that 'history shows that the best governments are those with the best teams.' Even more revealing was his statement that 'in the third year, or something like that, I will decide whether I want to [run again or retire]' but 'at this moment I intend to serve out the mandate I'm seeking from the people of Canada.'[28]

Despite these problems, the final days of the campaign were essentially a gift to the Liberals. Recalling the disastrous role played by the Mansbridge 'exposé' during the 1988 campaign, one war room participant declared, 'Maybe [the media] were compensating us for that. Who knows? The fact is, we hardly needed to do anything. We just sat back and watched [the Alliance] self-destruct.' Ridicule from popular personalities like Rick Mercer and a damaging CBC documentary highlighting Day's religious beliefs and faith in creationism cemented public antipathy towards the opposition leader. As one national columnist put it, 'the transformation from Stock to Laughingstock was complete.'[29]

The Third Liberal Majority: Quebec Returns to the Fold

'We won, we won big,' Jean Chrétien declared the morning after the 27 November election. The Liberals obtained an extraordinary third straight majority government. Only two other Liberal prime ministers, Mackenzie King and Wilfrid Laurier, had matched this achievement. Not only was the Liberals' overall majority increased from 155 to 173 seats, the party's performance in every region of the country met or exceeded expectations. They regained seven seats in Atlantic Canada, captured the lone Conservative seat in Ontario, and increased their overall representation in the west by one seat. Most important, they increased their representation in Quebec by eleven seats, returning to a level last seen in 1980. The magnitude of the Liberal victory stunned their opponents and led many observers to conclude that the party's dominance was likely to continue for the foreseeable future. Political scientist Bruce Doern declared, 'Jean Chrétien stands astride the Canadian political scene without much effective opposition at the federal level.' For Doern, one of the key questions after the election was 'the extent to which a one-party state is congealing at the federal level.'[30]

The victory was a personal one for Chrétien, something he underlined in his press conference the next day. Since Peter Mansbridge had said that 'no one has more at stake than Jean Chrétien' because 'it was his decision and his decision alone to call the election,'[31] Chrétien was now prepared to take the credit. Repudiating the 'naysayers' in his own caucus who had objected to his election call, he said, 'It is amazing – some who were the most worried, you know, got their majority increased.' Asked by reporters about his future plans he replied, 'I intend to serve out my term.' In a conciliatory gesture to Paul Martin, he added that, in four years, his primary challenger for the leadership 'will still be younger than a number of past prime ministers' and 'is a great asset to the party and he should stay. I told him that.'[32]

The 2000 election cemented the marginalization of the Reform/ Alliance party as a regional, protest-based party with no potential to expand its base. Despite the party's change of name, a charismatic new leader, and increased spending on virtually all aspects of their campaign, they had little to show for their efforts, particularly in the Ontario heartland they had so assiduously courted. With a mere 6 per cent increase in popular support and six additional seats, the Alliance may have remained the Official Opposition but Stockwell Day's time as leader was clearly near the end.

Election results were described by one analyst as 'good news for the Liberals and bad news for everyone else,' particularly the Bloc Québécois. Despite a solid campaign and a good performance from leader Gilles Duceppe, they were reduced to the same number of seats as the Liberals, who had increased their Quebec caucus to 37 or half of the provinces' MPs. The Bloc declined even though the PQ electoral machine and the personal support of Premier Lucien Bouchard were behind them. For Jean Chrétien, his party's resurgence in Quebec was the most important aspect of the victory, a clear vindication of his ten-point plan and recent decision to introduce the bill setting rules for future referenda. The icing on the cake was the unexpected resignation of Bouchard only months later, when the separatist leader announced that he did not believe the 'winning conditions' he had declared necessary for holding another referendum would occur any time in the foreseeable future.

With the delivery of a third straight majority government, Jean Chrétien returned to Ottawa 'virtually impregnable.'[33] Rejuvenated and confident that the government's fiscal situation was stable, he hit the ground running, determined to implement the remainder of his agenda. First, he replaced the Clerk of the Privy Council with a veteran public servant known for his expertise in social policy, Alex Himmelfarb. This appointment sent a message to the public service and the Liberal caucus that social Liberals would become the driving force of the third mandate.

The Legacy Agenda

With the departure of Jean Pelletier and Chaviva Hosek, virtually no one from Chrétien's original office staff remained. Rather than reach out to new blood, the PM turned to familiar faces like Percy Downe, his director of appointments, who took over from Pelletier, and Paul Genest, a former LCRB researcher and ministerial aide, who became the PMO policy director. Many saw this reliance on existing personnel as a sign that Chrétien was considering his own departure.

Similarly, when Jonathan Murphy's troubled tenure at the Research Bureau ended, the position of director was filled by Craig Ryan, a highly regarded policy adviser to several federal ministers. Under his tutelage, the Bureau enthusiastically took on several new functions, including initiating policy debate through the publication of a series of 'Issues and Ideas' documents for caucus on new and emerging issues. In addition to providing materials for individual MPs, there were special publications on such topics as aboriginal peoples and youth. Bureau researchers would do considerable work for the special caucus task forces as well. 'There was some sense that we were approaching the end of an era, but I was determined that we not become passive. The caucus was preoccupied with other matters and we were under-utilized to some extent, but there were areas in which I felt we still had a significant role to play. Certainly we worked well with the policy team in PMO, and the "centre" as a whole was solid. They were competent and professional; we always knew what they were trying to do and why,' Ryan recalled.[34]

In constructing his cabinet, Chrétien finally took Peter Donolo's advice and offered Paul Martin another post, minister of foreign affairs. Martin's role in Finance was already considerably diminished with the end of the deficit-reduction battle by 1998. It would now be further reduced as the prime minister asserted his personal priorities in what would likely be his final term in office. Martin refused the new appointment and did not ask for a different portfolio. Several Chrétien supporters noted that no other cabinet minister would have been allowed the option of refusing a 'transfer' and still remain in the cabinet. Martin's supporters, by contrast, insisted the Foreign Affairs offer was designed to remove Martin from any position of importance in cabinet and indeed from the country. As events would soon demonstrate, they could hardly have been more mistaken. Martin stayed put and John Manley moved from Industry to Foreign Affairs, while Brian Tobin, once more an MP, took over the Industry portfolio he had specifically requested.

Soon after the cabinet was constituted, the Throne Speech of 30 January 2001 reiterated the Liberals' platform commitments in key areas such as the broadband network, the lifelong learning account, and the national strategy on organized crime and drugs. In short order most of these measures were implemented, suggesting Chrétien's renewed determination to take advantage of this unexpected third term for as long as possible, similar to Pierre Trudeau's approach after his 1980 resurrection.

Following rapidly on the Speech, Environment Minister David Anderson tabled a bill to protect species at risk, while his colleague, Justice Minister Anne McClellan, introduced legislation on organized crime. This was followed in May by her announcement of a new community-based crime-prevention strategy for which $145 million in new funding was to be allocated. Also in June, Anderson unveiled Canada's Climate Change Action Plan, a package of forty-five measures negotiated with the provinces over many months, designed to meet the requirements of the Kyoto Accord that Canada had accepted in principal the previous year. Among the most prominent measures were major funding for research to develop fuel efficient vehicles, promote urban public transit, upgrade Via Rail, and reduce air-based pollution.

Even more ambitiously, Chrétien launched the first major public service reform in over thirty years. As a follow-up to the health accord signed the previous fall, he appointed Roy Romanow to chair a Commission on the Future of Health Care in Canada. Continuing the pattern of high-profile affirmative action appointments he had begun with Adrienne Clarkson's nomination as governor general in 1999, Chrétien appointed the first female Commissioner of Official Languages, Dyan Adam, the first female chief justice of the Supreme Court, Beverley McLachlin, and the first female auditor general, Sheila Fraser.

Chrétien also launched a number of special caucus task forces. In an effort to placate disgruntled Martin supporters, he tapped several of them to chair these task forces. Ontario MP Judy Sgro headed the Prime Minister's Special Task Force on Urban Issues, Albina Guarnieri was appointed to examine the gun registry, Ontario MP Bob Speller was assigned an agriculture task force, and Manitoba MP Reg Alcock was named chair of the Special Task Force on Parliamentary Reform.

In a similar vein, Chrétien turned his attention (belatedly, in the opinion of some) to the issue of western alienation and the party's ever-decreasing support in the region outside of the large urban areas. First, he appointed Manitoba MP and Martin supporter John Harvard to chair the Prime Minister's Special Task Force on the Four Western Provinces. Although the Liberals managed to increase their representation in the region by one seat, the results in the west were the one aspect of the 2000 campaign which party and caucus members alike viewed with disappointment. Once again they took seats only in the major urban centres, losing virtually all of the rural seats across the region to the Alliance. Not only had the party failed to make inroads despite the improved economic situation and strong cabinet representation from the region, but the Liberals' argument that the Alliance did not represent Canadian values appeared to have fallen on deaf ears.

Chrétien's efforts with respect to the west did not stop with the task force, however. Two new positions for western desk officers were created in the PMO, and the three western 'regional' ministers – Ralph Goodale, Anne McClellan, and David Anderson – were given increased budgets. Special national caucus meetings were also held in western venues over the summer of 2001. Intergovernmental Affairs Minister Stéphane Dion paid several visits to the region and delivered a major policy address in Saskatchewan.[35] Chrétien spent more time in the region as well, making a number of key announcements personally, accompanied by local Liberal senators or other prominent Liberals from the area. The government's focus on the knowledge-based economy, as outlined in the 2000 platform, was reinforced in the region with federal infrastructure funding going to support major research projects such as the Synchotron Light Project in Saskatoon, the Genome Canada facilities in Alberta, and technology transfer projects such as the Ballard hydrogen fuel cell in Vancouver.

Nevertheless the attention paid by Chrétien to western issues was described by one provincial party president as 'too little, way too late.' A prominent Martin supporter, the president also argued that if Martin were leader of the party the Liberals' western support would increase dramatically. 'He's very well-liked out here, and he understands the problems business faces in the resource-based industries.' Political scientist Alan Tupper offered a different critique, arguing that the policies promoted by Chrétien after the 2000 election were focused primarily on the urban centres, where the party was already successful, thereby reinforcing the urban-rural divide.[36] His views were echoed by none other than Brian Tobin, who argued that the broadband initiative was precisely the type of project Liberals should have supported in western Canada because it would connect isolated rural communities to the new economy. Coincidentally, that proposal was later rejected by Paul Martin as impractical and unaffordable.[37]

Meanwhile the traditional economic update offered by the finance minister in May 2001 confirmed the economic slowdown Chrétien had feared when deciding the timing of the election call. But it also demonstrated the solid fiscal base of the federal government. As Paul Martin stated in his presentation to the House of Commons, 'what is clear is that all of the available facts and figures show that, albeit at a slower pace than last year, the longest Canadian economic expansion since the 1960s – some 22 quarters of growth – is continuing.'[38] And this was the case, he noted, despite the cost of the health accord and the income tax cuts promised the previous fall as part of the election platform.

The stage was set for further social policy measures to be implemented in quick succession, along with additional funding for infrastructure and environmental projects that had been languishing on Chrétien's to-do list. It was at this point, however, that the proverbial unanticipated event occurred, temporarily altering the course and timing of his agenda. It was an event that had vast implications for the party and led to the ultimate split between the Chrétien and Martin camps.

The Impact of the National Security Crisis

The 11 September terrorist attacks on the World Trade Center caused the Canadian government to turn most of its attention to national defence and security issues. From new security measures for air transport to increased immigration screening to increased funding for the Canadian Security Intelligence Service (CSIS), the government's plan of action following 9/11 was substantial.

The need to reassure Canadians of their own safety drove the Liberals into uncharted waters. Not since the invocation of the War Measures Act in 1970 had a federal government been confronted with such a perceived threat to the state and its citizens. The government's across-the-board response was criticized by some civil rights experts. Despite arguments favouring the legislation put forward by Justice Minister Anne McClellan and Liberal MP Irwin Cottler, the constraints on individual liberties appeared excessive to many rights activists. In the end, the government was forced to accept several amendments, including a sunset clause for some of the most contentious aspects. The legislation also caused difficulties for the Liberal Party with its traditional immigrant and visible minority support base. Fallout from the new legislation and other security measures opened a wedge between the party and some of its most loyal constituencies, a rift which Stephen Harper would not only recognize but attempt – with some success – to exploit for electoral purposes in the not too distant future.

But it was two administrative changes adopted on Chrétien's personal instruction that proved most significant for his future and that of the party. First, he asked his new principal secretary, Percy Downe, to alert cabinet ministers to the fact that the PM would be the only one to speak for the government in the first few crucial days. For senior bureaucrats, such a move was merely standard procedure. 'There has to be one spokesperson for the nation and that happens to be the prime minister,' Downe maintained. But, as Susan Delacourt revealed in her account of the Martin camp's leadership drive, the finance minister felt he had been singled out. 'I should have been encouraged to tell the Canadian financial area that things are okay, and then basically tell the world on behalf of the G7 that everything's okay. But I was told: "Paul Martin, you can't speak." I was stunned.'[39]

Second, Chrétien directed that, in future, all ministers were required to provide the PMO/PCO secretariat with advance notice of their travel plans. This was deemed necessary given the difficulties the government encountered in the immediate aftermath of the attacks when several key ministers were either away from Ottawa or unreachable, and decisions had to be made in their absence. As David Collenette, for one, recalled, 'I had to make many decisions almost immediately. Do we close the border? Do we shut down all air traffic? Can we accommodate all of the flights already in the air that are in or headed for the U.S.? I made those decisions largely on my own. There wasn't much time to consult, and very few people to consult with.'[40] While many ministers were unhappy with the new procedure, Downe argued this too was standard procedure. 'We tried to accommodate everyone as much as possible. I even had a chart made up to show who had been refused or allowed to travel and when, so we could be sure everyone was getting treated fairly.'[41] Despite this rationale, the application of the new travel regime further irked Paul Martin.

Martin had little to do for the next several months. He was basically invisible while several of his colleagues acquired a much higher public profile. The transportation and justice ministers spoke often on security-related issues. Martin's potential leadership challenger Brian Tobin captured headlines with his organization of a massive memorial service for the 9/11 victims on the grounds of Parliament Hill. Martin's supporters watched with increasing concern as another probable leadership contender, John Manley – now the foreign affairs minister – gained new-found prominence and respect for his numerous public interventions after the tragedy. In a matter of weeks, media accounts began to speak of Manley, not the finance minister, as the second most influential person in Ottawa. For Martin supporters, this was seen as a deliberate attempt to 'minimize Paul now that he had done the heavy lifting on the deficit.'[42] The PMO perspective, as expressed by Francie Ducros, was quite different. Noting that in the past there had been many foreign affairs ministers who had been the key member of cabinet, she concluded, 'It isn't always the finance minister. It's the lieutenant you need at the time.'[43]

When Paul Martin did emerge, it was to table a budget in December 2001 which included massive expenditures for security-related issues. Here again Martin and his supporters felt he had been treated differently. He was obliged to obtain Chrétien's consent to table a budget in December, since it was not expected until late February. But Martin argued it was essential to bring down a budget early. 'It was very clear that the country required a confidence measure,' he told journalist Susan Delacourt. 'It was manifestly evident to me and everyone else who could add two and two … that I had to do this confidence budget. And then, amazingly, the PMO opposed it.'[44] For their part, both Chrétien and Manley expressed concern at Martin's haste, fearing that it would result in poorly thought-out measures or exclude important options. In the end, Chrétien agreed to Martin's proposal.[45]

On 10 December, the Liberals announced a $6.5 billion package 'to build greater personal and economic security for Canadians by keeping Canadians safe and terrorists out.' Despite these large and unanticipated expenditures, the funds to finance the tax cuts and the health accord announced in February 2001 were still accounted for. A number of other measures promised in the 2000 election campaign (relating to the environment, infrastructure renewal, and research) were also contained in the budget. Taken together, they demonstrated the soundness of the government's fiscal position even in the face of the costly security demands.

Political Setbacks and the Underground Leadership Race

One glaring omission in Martin's budget was funding for the party's crucial campaign pledge to develop a national broadband network. The commitment was clearly spelled out in the election platform and had been repeatedly singled out by the prime minister. Given his experience as fisheries minister during the cod wars, new federal Industry Minister Brian Tobin expected the prime minister's support on the initiative he described as 'the most important way to achieve equality of opportunity for those on the wrong side of the digital divide.' In advance of the December budget, Tobin publicly lauded the measure as 'both socially progressive and economically essential if the country is to remain competitive in the post-industrial knowledge-based economy of the future.'[46]

Despite such enthusiasm, the broadband initiative was still controversial. It would require $1 billion in federal funding to complete, a figure that raised economists' eyebrows instantly. The fact that Tobin, a leadership candidate, was so strongly behind it led to considerable scepticism in the Martin camp as well. Tobin insisted later that he had requested only $100 million, or 10 per cent of the expected cost, as a compromise in order to launch the project in the coming fiscal year. He also noted that he spoke to the prime minister 'in the days leading up to the budget to ensure this compromise' and that '[Chrétien] made it clear to me that the broadband item would be in the budget, no ifs, ands, or buts.'[47]

When funding for the project was not included in the budget, Tobin was 'floored.' The 2001 budget declared only that the government would 'work with Canadian industry, the provinces, communities and the public on private sector solutions to further broadband Internet coverage in Canada, particularly for rural and remote areas. More planning is required to properly achieve the Government's commitment, particularly given rapidly changing technology; as a consequence, the Government will shift its target to the end of 2005.'[48]

When he asked the prime minister what had happened, Tobin recalled Chrétien saying 'his instructions had not been followed.'[49] The official position of the Finance Department, as communicated by bureaucrats, was that the project was not viable. But Tobin believed other actors, including Eddie Goldenberg, played a role in the decision as well, a fact later confirmed by Goldenberg himself, who stressed the importance Chrétien placed on maintaining a united front with his finance minister. 'No matter how much he might have wanted to help Tobin, the institutional relationship between a finance minister and a prime minister, especially at budget time, was far more important to Chrétien than internal Liberal Party politics.'[50] Certainly the project was widely perceived as falling victim to the increasing tension over the expected leadership race. As political scientist Richard Schultz concluded, 'Martin did not want to support a high-level program that was so closely associated with his rival, especially one that would be popular with a potential source of major leadership campaign donations.'[51]

Tobin would not be around to confirm his suspicions. Chastened by the experience and wary of Martin's increasing control of the party executive, he abandoned his plans for a leadership bid, resigned, and returned to Newfoundland once again. His departure forced the prime minister to shuffle his cabinet in early January 2002 before the return of Parliament after the Christmas recess. Chrétien seized the opportunity to tackle the problem of Martin's increasing impatience. After several years languishing on the backbenches, Toronto MP Bill Graham was finally appointed to cabinet. Although the fact that he represented a Toronto riding was the main cause of Graham's long wait, his ascent to cabinet was seen by many as an effort to appease the Martin forces since Graham was a longtime friend and former classmate of Martin.

More surprising was Chrétien's choice of Maurizio Bevilacqua as the junior minister responsible for science and technology. Bevilacqua was associated with the Martin agitators and was present at the infamous Constellation Hotel meeting. One cabinet minister close to Chrétien later admitted he had 'suggested the idea to the prime minister as a way to sow dissension in the ranks.' Key Martin advisers admitted Bevilacqua was frozen out of Martin's first cabinet 'as payback.'

The shuffle also saw Justice Minister Anne McClellan move to the Health portfolio and the appointment of Quebec MP Martin Cauchon to Justice. Allan Rock, a possible leadership contender, moved from Health to take on the newly vacant Industry file.

It was in the midst of these transitions that Chrétien told Rock and Sheila Copps, the two likely contenders, that they could begin discreetly organizing for an eventual leadership race. This tacit acceptance of an informal start to a leadership race would have serious consequences for Chrétien in less than six months, producing a breakdown in cabinet discipline reminiscent of Lester Pearson's unruly final months in power.

Meanwhile the Alliance Party selected a new leader of its own. Former Reform MP and National Citizens' Coalition president Stephen Harper won a decisive victory over Stockwell Day, who had decided to run to succeed himself. Shortly thereafter, Chrétien called by-elections in several ridings to deal with vacancies. Harper, unopposed by the Liberals in Preston Manning's former riding in Calgary, easily won a seat in Parliament. With Harper's victory on 13 May 2002, Chrétien, savouring the moment and his own seemingly secure situation, welcomed Harper back to the House of Commons, noting that he had seen six leaders of the Reform, Alliance, and Progressive Conservative parties come and go during his time as prime minister.

Other by-election results proved more problematic for Chrétien. Looking for fresh cabinet material in Newfoundland and Quebec, Chrétien had appointed two sitting MPs – George Baker and Raymond Lavigne – to the Senate and sent his former Quebec lieutenant and public works minister, Alfonso Gagliano, to Denmark as Canada's ambassador. He had also 'retired' long-serving deputy prime minister Herb Gray in order to promote John Manley, a move for which the prime minister was criticized.

It was to be expected that the party would lose some seats in the traditional by-election backlash, but the losses were more than most analysts expected. John Efford (a hugely popular Newfoundland politician) replaced Brian Tobin, but Chrétien's choice of Barton Tulk to replace George Baker in Newfoundland did not succeed; nor did the Liberal candidates selected to replace Gray and Gagliano. At the time, the only other positive note appeared to be the success of former Bourassa minister Liza Frulla. The significance of Chrétien accepting Frulla as a candidate can hardly be over-emphasized given her many negative public comments about him in the past. With key losses looming large, both Efford and Frulla were quickly appointed to the cabinet.

Implementing the Legacy Agenda

Despite the setback to his policy agenda and succession plans, it is important to note that Chrétien merely delayed on the remainder of his legacy initiatives. They were not abandoned. As PMO policy analyst Marjorie Loveys confirmed, work continued throughout the fall and winter on a number of projects viewed as central to the Liberal agenda. 'We could walk and chew gum at the same time. Other people were working on the 9/11 files, and we continued to do our work on social policy and the environment,' she recalled.[52] Chrétien's policy director in PMO, Paul Genest, concurred. 'We just kept our heads down and beavered away at the files we were assigned. Most of the foreign affairs and security issues never affected our shop anyway. He made it clear to us he intended to proceed as planned.'[53]

But Chrétien's primary focus was not on security. Former advisers noted that Chrétien had been concerned for some time about Canada's declining contribution to the area of development aid, a situation aggravated by the funding cuts brought about as part of the deficit-reduction exercise of his own government. Here again, Chrétien's determination to maintain solidarity with his finance minister masked considerable personal unease. As Eddie Goldenberg recalled, Chrétien's support for a major increase in development aid fell on deaf ears with his finance minister, who once argued that the Third World conditions of aboriginal peoples in Canada meant any available funding should be spent on them as a priority and considered as development assistance.[54]

With a surplus in hand, Chrétien was determined to burnish the country's image on the international stage. When the Organization for African Unity (OAU) adopted a new plan for African development (NEPAD) in July 2001, Chrétien took advantage of Canada's upcoming chairmanship of the G8 to promote the plan.[55] Identifying Africa as one of Canada's three priorities for the G8 summit, Chrétien would invite African leaders instrumental in drafting the NEPAD plan to attend the actual summit, which he would chair in Kananaskis, Alberta, in late June.

While Chrétien spent considerable time abroad on the African initiative and on preparations for the G8 summit, the underground leadership race at home was deteriorating rapidly. The situation would ultimately force Chrétien to confront Paul Martin in an open acknowledgment of their differences.

Implosion: The Collapse of Internal Party Unity

The breakdown within Liberal ranks, evident shortly before the 2000 election, had only temporarily abated. Despite Chrétien's 'invincibility,' by early 2001 many of the advisers and MPs who supported Paul Martin were working hard to take control of the caucus executive and the machinery of the party. As David Herle told many of his colleagues, if Chrétien could change his mind once and run for a third term, he could just as easily do it again, and they were not prepared to let that happen. Most party dissidents had come to see Jean Chrétien as an albatross around the party's neck. They were certain his leadership had prevented them from obtaining an even bigger majority against an inept opposition in the recent election and that it would destroy them in the next.[56]

The dust had barely settled on the 2000 election when some Martin supporters turned their attention to the leadership review that would automatically take place at the next biennial convention. They believed this event would put pressure on Chrétien to declare his intentions. Either he would be forced to call out his troops to organize and ensure he received a significant majority vote, or he would choose to avoid the vote by announcing instead that he would resign. Since the last party convention was held in 1998, many argued that the next convention should take place as early as possible, no later than the spring of 2002.

Despite his past record of calling conventions quickly after an election, Chrétien wanted the next convention delayed as long as possible. His reasoning was straightforward. He wanted to serve as much of his final term as possible without becoming a lame duck. His third back-to-back majority, he believed, entitled him to leave at his leisure. He knew as well that once his departure date was announced, his ability to control the troops and ensure his policy objectives were accomplished would be jeopardized. He had seen the situation deteriorate under both Pearson and Trudeau and wanted to avoid such chaotic infighting around his own departure.

When the party's national executive met in early January 2001 to discuss the next biennial convention, the two sides squared off. The long-standing conflict between parliamentary and extra-parliamentary priorities and the role of the party's constitution versus the priorities of the leadership were once again graphically highlighted. As party president Stephen LeDrew later recounted, the Chrétien supporters on the executive first argued the review vote should be seen as a 'report card' on the leader's record rather than a verdict on his future. When this approach was flatly rejected, they insisted the convention be delayed until late 2002 at a minimum. LeDrew himself supported this position in the beginning, arguing that the leader had earned the right to determine the timing of his departure. 'I wasn't on anybody's side. I just wanted to prevent an open rupture between the two camps. The *party* wasn't split, it was the organizers and strategists. They were like the Hatfields and the McCoys.'[57]

But important changes had taken place in the interim. Karl Littler's plan produced results across the board, and far more than half of the national executive were now Martin supporters. Some insisted that the need for an early convention was purely a matter of principle and had nothing to do with their support for Martin. Typical of this group was Mario Cuconato, a former Young Liberal whose views were shaped by the Resolution 40 era of the early 1980s and who had since become a ministerial aide on Parliament Hill. Arguing that the schism between elected and grassroots members had once again grown too wide, he put forward a motion calling for an early spring convention. 'All the party has is the Constitution and conventions, and if we don't honour those we are basically dismissing the Liberal party grassroots,'[58] he said. Members of the caucus executive were present at the meeting because of their status as automatic members of the national executive, thereby reinforcing Martin's dominance. At one point Ontario caucus chair Brenda Chamberlain, a prominent Martin supporter, produced a pile of letters from local riding executives arguing for an early convention and, in some cases, for an imminent departure of the current leader.

Several participants have since described the meeting as a pivotal one in which 'the gloves came off.' Worse still, the media learned about the meeting and reported it in detail. Whether this public revelation caused the eventual compromise or whether, as others have speculated, it was Paul Martin's strong desire to avoid appearing disloyal in light of the Constellation Hotel fiasco, Martin's supporters backed down. In the end, however, it was not the national executive that determined the outcome. Flying in the face of formal party rules, the final decision was reached by 'negotiators' for the two sides – Martin's former ministerial aide, Richard Mahoney, and Chrétien's national campaign chair, Senator David Smith. After much dickering, the two ultimately agreed the convention would be held in February 2003.

On the face of it, the compromise seemed to give Chrétien considerable breathing space, but it was clear to some supporters that the prime minister had much less time than he thought. According to new constitutional rules, delegate selection would begin in the late summer of 2002, only eighteen months away. And, thanks to the two sets of conflicting rules adopted in 1992, it was possible the riding-level vote, set for November 2002, could determine the outcome long before the convention. To the frustration of some, Chrétien did not believe he could lose such a vote.

The Caucus Revolt

There had already been indications that a loss at the riding level was a real possibility. In caucus, discontent quickly resurfaced. No one reminded MPs of the disaster that ensued when John Turner was challenged from within – an argument that had worked well with the Martin supporters for nearly a decade, because so many of them had been Turner supporters. Instead, there was a sense that this was an entirely different situation. Convinced that Canadians were yearning for a new Liberal leader, many believed the party was secure in power and could afford to push harder for the leader's departure. This was obvious to Chrétien's supporters as well. With Brenda Chamberlain's 'insubordination' in calling for an early convention, several senior PMO advisers decided it was time to rein in the discontent before it spun out of control. In the elections for the caucus executive, Chamberlain and several of her colleagues who were known Martin supporters found themselves out of a job, having lost key caucus posts to Chrétien organizers intent on teaching them a lesson. Similarly, the position of national caucus chair went once again to Paul DeVillers, the second time that Martin supporter Nick Discepola had been defeated.

But this too was a temporary victory for the prime minister. Over the course of the next year, as Chrétien busied himself with matters of state and foreign affairs, Martin supporters stepped up their calls for the PM's resignation. Angry confrontations in the weekly caucus meetings started to appear in major newspapers, prompting Chrétien's advisers to impose stronger measures to ensure confidentiality. In the caucus elections in February 2002, the Martin supporters, who had been planning their strategy for months, regained control of several regional caucuses. Much to the consternation of Chrétien, the most important position, that of national caucus chair, went to a staunch Martin supporter when the non-Martin vote split between two other candidates. The new chair was none other than Hamilton MP Stan Keyes, who had already asked for Chrétien's resignation publicly. 'I think it was one of the few times I have ever seen him at a loss for words,' one of Chrétien's oldest friends and colleagues recalled. 'He knew what it meant, and he was stunned.' In much the same way that they had taken control of the party hierarchy, the determined group of Martin organizers achieved even greater influence in caucus. Now all that was left was to exercise that influence.

As caucus chair, Keyes assumed an unprecedented role in the media by claiming to speak for the national caucus on a range of issues, a claim that outraged Chrétien supporters. 'The caucus chair is supposed to represent the consensus of caucus, not express his own views,' one angry Chrétien senator charged, 'and this Chair is certainly not representing *my* views.' In a strongly worded letter to Keyes, MP Charles Caccia called for his resignation. At the very least, Caccia wrote, 'you should stop using your privileged position as chair of national caucus to communicate your views to the national press.'[59] Outgoing caucus chair Paul DeVillers added, 'the role of the chair is to speak to journalists to clarify issues or mistakes they may have made, not to contribute personal views or reveal what went on in caucus.'[60] Keyes disagreed. He argued it was his job to speak on behalf of the caucus not only to the prime minister but to the media, and that he was reflecting the majority viewpoint. Behind the scenes, confrontations between the Martin and Chrétien staffs escalated, as did public suspicion of an imbalance in government. As Percy Downe recalled, the perception was well founded. 'There was no question that the constant arguing with the Martin people disrupted the operations and took our focus away from governing.'[61]

Chrétien vs. Martin: 'Quebec is why Jean won't go'

Two administrative decisions in February 2002 led to direct confrontations between Martin and Chrétien. Once again, disagreement centred on their differing views of federalism. Although the clashes received little media coverage, they were symptomatic of the deep-seated federalist cleavage that continued to divide the party. The first conflict surfaced when Statistics Canada announced a change to its technical calculations concerning property values in Quebec, a change that would perversely affect equalization payments. The new methodology would have resulted in a shortfall of $1 billion for the Quebec treasury in that same fiscal year. As finance minister, Martin was furious that he had not been notified in advance. Did Statistics Canada officials not realize the consequences of a $1 billion cut in funding for any provincial government, let alone the separatist government of Quebec? At a hastily called meeting of senior Finance officials to assess the implications, Martin was reported to have left the discussions repeatedly to confer directly with his Quebec counterpart, PQ Finance Minister Pauline Marois. In the end, Martin decided that the current system would remain in place for a year while a more detailed study of the consequences could be carried out.

Martin made his decision public on 28 February 2002 in response to an opposition question in the House of Commons. Instead of announcing that the changes would be put on hold, he indicated they would be suspended *only for Quebec* since there would be negative consequences for that province. More than a few of his colleagues were astonished to hear him continue: 'At the same time we are going to implement the positive consequences of that change for those provinces concerned until such time as a final decision comes down.'[62]

Chrétien was disturbed by the approach of his finance minister, which surprised Martin, who saw the decision as his alone. For Chrétien, the political ramifications of the decision, especially for federal relations with Quebec, were of such importance that they required his personal imprimatur. Once again, in Chrétien's view, Martin demonstrated either a shaky grasp of or a disregard for the underlying principles of the traditional Liberal approach to federalism which valued pan-Canadian solutions, harmonization, and minimum national standards, and avoided ad hoc or asymmetrical policy treatment as much as possible.

Lysiane Gagnon was one of the few journalists to recognize the significant difference of opinion between the two men on the federalism axis. She concluded in an article soon after Martin's announcement that 'Quebec is why Jean won't go.' Arguing that Chrétien 'will be able to boast that he saved national unity,' Gagnon maintained he would 'fight to the death against anyone he thinks might destroy what he believes he has built.' Correctly noting that Chrétien believed Paul Martin 'is another Brian Mulroney – someone who would reopen the Pandora's box by giving in to the nationalists' demands for some kind of special status,' Gagnon concluded, 'Chrétien is convinced Martin won't be able to resist the push for decentralization coming from his friends in the Quebec Liberal Party and the various conservative provincial governments.'[63]

The second disagreement between the two men stemmed from another bureaucratic error. Revenue Canada officials admitted the federal government had 'overpaid' four provinces due to 'a flaw in their tax collection agreements.' The provinces had apparently received more than $3.38 billion to which they were not entitled. Martin was in favour of writing off the entire amount, while Chrétien was determined to recover the funds. Eddie Goldenberg recalled: 'If an error had been made the other way, he didn't think the provinces would all send cheques to Ottawa. And he didn't like the precedent' it would set.[64]

Because of the implications for other federal transfer payments, Chrétien asked John Manley to chair a small ad hoc committee to determine how to handle the matter. Though he was aware the matter was one for the Revenue Department and not Finance, Martin was nevertheless perturbed. Manley's committee decided to recover a portion of the funds as a compromise – $90 million from Manitoba and $1.3 billion from Ontario. In addition, it was decided that the money returned to Ottawa would be used as a special payment on the debt as a conciliatory gesture.

More Party Problems

By now Chrétien and his advisers were involved in an ongoing struggle with the national executive over the party's organization and the underground leadership race. When Brian Tobin met with Chrétien in January 2002 to tender his resignation, he explained how the party hierarchy had been 'captured' by Martin sympathizers and told Chrétien that it was virtually impossible for anyone else to mount a successful campaign.[65]

A key problem was the limited access to membership forms. If workers for potential candidates could not obtain large numbers of membership forms, they could not hope to recruit new members and win the battle that now, with the changes to the constitution, would be fought at the riding level. Once Martin supporters took over in a province, they introduced a number of rule changes that thwarted these efforts. In Ontario, for example, a rule was passed limiting organizers to one form at a time. The form would have to be signed and returned along with the membership fees for a new member before another form could be obtained. The BC executive imposed similar limitations.

By the spring of 2002, Chrétien took a number of steps to try to resolve the problem before the remaining leadership hopefuls dropped out of the race in dismay. But efforts at negotiating a deal with Martin supporters were unsuccessful. The so-called 'hawks' among Martin's advisers – Karl Littler and David Herle, for example – were now firmly in charge and in no mood to make further concessions. Chrétien planned to attend the national executive meeting and urge them to loosen the restrictions in the interests of party unity but was aggressively discouraged by president Stephen LeDrew, who argued it would be seen as 'another attempt at intimidation' by the leader.[66]

A deal brokered by Eddie Goldenberg and Martin's chief of staff, Tim Murphy, appeared to break the deadlock. They decided that five memberships would be distributed at once. It was a modest improvement, but still it was rejected at the national executive meeting. After much debate the agreement was adopted but only as a 'recommendation' to the Ontario wing. Almost immediately a modification was introduced at the riding level that called for the names of the five new members to be provided before the forms were released, a condition that practically nullified the compromise.

For Allan Rock, arguably Martin's most serious leadership threat, this was the final straw. 'I think this decision not only tears up the party executive's compromise last week, but it's also an attempt to undermine the prime minister and anyone who would like to succeed him. Worst of all, it strikes a blow at the heart of the Liberal Party ... In my mind there is no doubt which group of people are behind this and what they are doing is sacrificing the democratic nature of our party on the altar of their own ambitions.'[67]

A number of public revelations concerning the fundraising activities of the Martin camp fuelled Chrétien's discontent. The unprecedented extent of Martin's fundraising activity had already been highlighted when a Martin campaign donation from former Alberta treasurer Jim Dinning was inadvertently sent to the party's national office in Ottawa rather than to Martin campaign headquarters. (Dinning's accompanying invoice indicated only that the contribution was for 'Project 2000,' but his personal covering letter stated: 'I can only hope that Mr. Martin ... might be able to inject a sense of urgency, passion, and priority into the affairs of our nation. Soon.')[68] Further complicating matters was the fact that the $25,000 cheque had originally been sent to Martin's Calgary fundraiser, Jim Palmer, who at the time was doing work for the Department of Finance. Alliance MP James Rajotte raised the issue of Martin's fundraising practices in the House of Commons during Question Period on 22 April 2002. Rajotte claimed the lack of guidelines for cabinet ministers about such practices contributed to the increased public perception that Canadian politicians were 'highly or somewhat corrupt.'[69] Moreover, Chrétien's ethics commissioner had prepared a set of ministerial guidelines and forwarded them to the prime minister the week before, but he had yet to consider them when Rajotte raised the matter in the House. Despite Chrétien's argument that the Alliance had not agreed to disclose the fundraising sources of its own candidates, the damage was done.

With the loss of the traditional Liberal safe seats in the May 2002 by-elections, Martin supporters in caucus became even more concerned about the party's electoral fortunes. Many of them represented swing ridings where the combined Alliance/Progressive Conservative vote would have been sufficient to defeat them. Several began to speak about the need for Chrétien to retire sooner rather than later. Former LCRB director Jonathan Murphy added fuel to the fire when he published a lengthy opinion piece arguing the 'growing malaise permeating both the caucus and the party apparatus ... can only be cured by Jean Chrétien's retirement.'[70] In the words of former caucus chair Paul DeVillers, Murphy's article touched off 'a firestorm' in caucus and among senior staff of the two 'combatants.'[71]

The Final Rupture

It was in this atmosphere of distrust and confrontation that the final act in the Martin/Chrétien tragedy unfolded. It began with the report tabled by MP Judy Sgro and her Task Force on Urban Issues. The differing reactions of Martin and Chrétien underlined their fundamental disagreement about federalism. Martin was supportive of the report, and went even further. In response to growing media interest in the 'cities issue,' he called for a 'new deal' for cities in which 'all options are on the table' and argued, 'we need to work with them directly' to address crucial challenges. Chrétien was reluctant to comment on the report. When pressed, he replied that, while he was in favour of providing assistance to cities through the kind of infrastructure and social housing programs he had negotiated with the provinces, 'We [the federal government] don't deal directly with the cities. They are under provincial responsibility. We are not in a position to give them more power. They are the creation of the provinces.'[72]

Perhaps influenced by a number of his more recently acquired advisers such as Brian Guest, a former aide to Ottawa's mayor, Martin and his senior staff had already positioned the cities agenda as a major part of his future platform. This was more than a little ironic given his federal plan for cities would directly invade provincial territory. But Martin seemed unconcerned with the apparent contradiction. In fact, he planned a major speech on the subject at the annual meeting of the Canadian Federation of Municipalities, an important venue as many of his cabinet colleagues, including other leadership contenders, were invited to speak as well.

Martin's speech was the cause of considerable concern in PMO. His use of the term 'new deal' for cities had been a bone of contention for some time. Both Paul Genest and Eddie Goldenberg had spoken with Tim Murphy to see whether another phrase could be used that would not imply direct federal involvement. 'We had never had speeches vetted like this before. You either have control of your own agenda or what's the point? Other ministers were speaking at the convention and they weren't having their every word examined.'[73] By now, however, Downe and Goldenberg were indeed reviewing the speeches of all of the ministers because, as Downe later explained, 'with things the way they were, we wanted them all to sing from the same hymn book. Copps's speech was alright but I remember we asked Rock to make several changes too.'[74] Unfortunately the PMO's new approach did not appear to have been communicated to Martin and his advisers, who continued to believe he was receiving special attention.

Another reason for Chrétien's increasingly hands-on approach was the steady string of mini-scandals involving cabinet ministers that appeared throughout April and May 2002. Worse still, certain advertising contracts in the Public Works Department caught the eye of the auditor general, leading to an investigation in which several embarrassing revelations came to light, including department officials' failure to locate a report prepared by an ad agency in Quebec for which the government had paid $500,000. On 9 May, the auditor general issued a special report in which she recommended the RCMP investigate contracts totalling some $1.6 million to the agency in question.

Chrétien was quick to respond. Speaking from Spain where he was attending the annual Canada-European Union Summit, he told reporters he was fully supportive of the referral to the RCMP, saying, 'If anyone has done something wrong, then of course they will have to face justice.'[75] At the same time he denied that these revelations implied his government was guilty of corruption. Having run a scandal-free administration for nearly a decade, he was unprepared for the spate of conflict-of-interest charges that suddenly caught up some of his most loyal supporters in cabinet.

In the end he felt obliged to dismiss Defence Minister Art Eggleton (who had awarded a departmental contract to an ex-girlfriend) and to demote Public Works Minister Don Boudria (who had vacationed at the lodge of an ad executive, even though he had paid for the use of the accommodation). The position at Public Works was taken over by Ralph Goodale, who immediately suspended the entire sponsorship program and instituted a review of the rules and procedures for awarding advertising contracts.

Frustrated by these distractions, Chrétien decided to take action. On 23 May, he announced an eight-point 'Ethics Package' in the House of Commons. It included a code of conduct and guidelines for cabinet ministers, revised rules for governmental dealings with corporations, and a commitment to table legislation on the financing of political parties and candidates. In his speech, he denied there had been deliberate ethics violations and denounced many of his critics for their hyperbole. 'I am humble enough to admit that mistakes have been made and to correct them,' he said, 'But I ask of everyone – opposition, government, and the media – let us tone down our rhetoric. Let us acknowledge our differences but respect our motives.'[76]

Two other Chrétien supporters and key Quebec organizers, Justice Minister Martin Cauchon and Amateur Sport and Fitness Minister Denis Coderre were also being targeted by the opposition. A remarkable string of media stories claimed to reveal new information about their friendship with various Quebec businessmen. However, the earlier firings and other measures appeared to have cleared the air. Assuming the situation was under control, Chrétien left for a brief meeting of NATO leaders in Italy in late May. During his absence, a number of incidents raised suspicions that the underground leadership race was responsible for at least some of these problems and perhaps all of them. Reports of comments made by caucus chair Stan Keyes and his close friend, London MP Joe Fontana, at a union dinner in Ottawa fanned the flames of internal conflict. Fontana was alleged to have claimed that both Cauchon and Coderre would have to resign as well, and 'Chrétien's going to go down too.'[77] Also during Chrétien's absence, a controversial fundraising letter distributed by the Friends of John Manley was made public in which contributions of $25,000 were suggested and donors were advised to attempt to deduct the contributions as business expenses.

Percy Downe stressed that the negative fallout from these developments was cumulative. 'It wasn't any one thing; this had been building for months. By the time Mr Chrétien came back to Ottawa and heard about the Keyes thing from Minister Coderre, he had had enough. He believed these stories were being leaked to the media by some Liberals to discredit him, and he couldn't understand how anyone in the same party could do this.'[78] At the very least, Chrétien believed Martin could not control his supporters. Several of the Martin advisers, however, attributed many of the leaks to the PMO itself, and specifically to Francie Ducros. One senior cabinet minister and longtime Chrétien organizer admitted later that he had reached a point that spring where he no longer cared who was responsible: 'This was bad for all of us and for the party. It had to stop.'[79]

Exit Martin

According to several of those present, the result was a stormy cabinet meeting on 30 May, the day after Chrétien's return. The Liberal leader declared he would be serving his full four-year term, evidently thinking this would put an end to the problem. He then ordered a halt to all leadership campaigning, stating that anyone who wanted to continue should resign from cabinet. This message came as a shock to all the leadership hopefuls, but it was Martin who was most affected because he had many full-time campaign workers on his payroll. This announcement alone might well have prompted Martin to leave cabinet. As Mike Robinson later commented, 'the machinery was in motion and it was virtually impossible to stop.'[80] Tim Murphy concurred: 'We couldn't ask our people to down tools a second time.'[81]

What is more, Chrétien introduced new conflict-of-interest guidelines whereby ministers would have to disclose all financial contributions, including those already received. Martin's campaign contributions were already in the millions of dollars, and he believed many of his major donors would not want to be identified. Questioned about his possible departure from cabinet, Martin said: 'Some time ago, the prime minister stated that it was fine for people to organize for the leadership. In fact, he encouraged some candidates to present their candidature. Now it would appear that he has changed his mind. That's his prerogative. I just really don't know how this is going to work ... Let me just say that I'm obviously going to have to reflect on my options.'[82]

The situation was complicated by the fact that Percy Downe who, as the PM's chief of staff, attended all cabinet meetings, had learned the same morning that Martin was scheduled to speak at a fundraiser in Toronto the next evening. Martin's event would conflict directly with a speech the prime minister was scheduled to give at the same time in the same city. The finance minister's earlier speech to the Federation of Municipalities in Hamilton was duly reported on the travel plan filed by his office with the PMO as per the post 9/11 procedures, but the subsequent fundraiser in Toronto was not. David Collenette, Chrétien's political minister for Toronto and the person who told Downe about the scheduling conflict, later noted, 'I didn't care about Paul's fundraiser, I cared about the optics of the thing. I just thought we could do without more stories about the internal conflict. The last thing we needed was the media reading something into these two events.'[83]

Unfortunately for all concerned, the measures taken to try to 'remedy' the situation only made matters worse. When Tim Murphy refused to agree to Downe's request to have Martin cancel his speech, a number of party 'fixers' were called into action. Senator David Smith called Murphy to suggest not only that Martin cancel his own event, but that he attend Chrétien's event instead and introduce the prime minister. At one point during the day of his visit to Toronto, Chrétien gave a press conference in which he declared his plans to face the leadership review at the February convention. 'You know me, for thirty-nine years I never ran away from a fight, so I'm not about to start at my age.'[84]

For several members of Martin's entourage, this was interpreted as a declaration that Chrétien might indeed run for a fourth term of office. Covered extensively in the media, the press conference was seen as a defining moment for Martinites. Martin would either have to refuse the prime minister's requests or give in and fold his tent for good. Speaking to Martin, Tim Murphy argued that deferring to Chrétien's 'demands' would amount to 'giving up the opportunity to control your future.' At the same time, there was a real concern that leaving cabinet would mark the end of Martin's leadership chances. 'Walking away was a big risk,' Murphy believed, 'especially since he could easily be seen as leaving his supporters in the lurch.'[85]

In the end, Martin delivered the municipalities speech with more than a dozen direct references to a 'new deal' for cities. He then attended the fundraising event in Toronto which had been scheduled months earlier. At a press conference afterwards, he indicated that he was 'considering his options' but did not explicitly state that he would resign. Instead he stressed that 'we are now at a point where we have some very, very important decisions to make, as a government and as a country. And I must say, given the events of the last couple of days, that I have to reflect now on my capacity as a member of the government to have an impact on those decisions, matters that I feel very strongly about.'[86]

Negotiations and manoeuvres by the two sides continued and were duly reported in journalist Susan Delacourt's narrative of Martin's drive to the leadership.[87] Reconciliation, it seemed, was now impossible. Whether Martin was fired, as his people claimed, or he resigned, as the Chrétien forces stated, is a moot point, although there is little debate about the facts. Martin refused to commit himself on his future intentions for more than forty-eight hours, having retreated to his country estate. By Sunday evening, both Chrétien and John Manley decided they had no choice but to replace him if he had not made up his mind by the next morning, since the opening of the money markets could result in chaos if the lead news story indicated the finance minister's fate was still up in the air. As John Manley recalled, 'What could we do? When a minister of finance says he is considering his options, I'd say that was a resignation, plain and simple.'[88] Manley also noted that the finance minister's office had been cleaned out on the Sunday evening, suggesting he was not expected to return. Tim Murphy did not deny those actions, or even that they suggested Martin's departure was imminent. Instead he argued that '[Chrétien and his advisers] changed the conditions of employment. They intervened in budget matters and demonstrated repeatedly that the minister had lost the prime minister's confidence. That means he was fired.'[89]

When Martin finally spoke with Chrétien on Monday morning, he told the prime minister he needed more time. Chrétien then instructed Eddie Goldenberg to read Martin the text of a draft letter which was shortly released to the media. Martin refused to co-sign the letter as Goldenberg suggested, and instead released his own account of events shortly thereafter. Chrétien's letter thanked Martin profusely for his contribution as finance minister and as part of his government. But it continued, 'unfortunately, matters unrelated to governing have gotten in the way of our working together on government policy. As such, we both understand, with real regret, that it is in the best interest of the government and the country that you step down from the cabinet.'[90] Martin's statement, by contrast, emphasized the differences of opinion between the two men on policy matters and the prime minister's lack of confidence in his finance minister, making no reference to matters unrelated to government such as the leadership. 'For a long time the natural tensions between my views and those of the prime minister were well within the manageable range in a healthy working relationship,' he declared. 'Unfortunately, in recent months ... that working relationship has deteriorated. It was therefore threatening to impede our focus on the very important choices that confront us as a nation.'[91] With that, the remarkable partnership ended badly for the two men and for the party. They would not speak to each other again except when forced to in social situations.

Civil War

The open warfare, unprecedented in the history of the modern Liberal Party of Canada, continued over the summer. Chrétien supporters such as David Collenette told friends that 'Martin is finished.' He assumed Martin's star would fall to earth now that he was no longer in the cabinet. This was soon proven wrong. A similar assumption on the part of several pollsters was equally unfounded. Ekos pollster Frank Graves, for example, concluded less than a week after Martin's departure from cabinet that 'Mr. Martin's popularity does not appear to have dislodged the prime minister and, in the absence of further difficulties, his popularity may wane ... as public interest in the issue declines.'[92]

What few people understood at the time was the extent to which the dynamics within the Liberal Party had changed. This was largely the result of the constitutional rule changes that had allowed Martin's organizers to rebuild and take control of much of the extra-parliamentary wing, but it was also due to the new willingness of a growing number of caucus members to challenge the leader publicly, even at the perceived expense of party unity. As Jim Coutts pointed out, the leader of the Liberal Party now had fewer tools at his disposal to prevent such developments.

As a result of these new realities, Martin's advisers redoubled their efforts to ensure that Chrétien would be obliged to leave before the February 2003 convention to avoid embarrassment or be defeated in the leadership review vote. At one point Chrétien's natural resources minister, Herb Dhaliwal, became sufficiently upset about the activities of Martin's supporters in BC that he called on the president of the provincial wing, Bill Cunningham, to step down. Cunningham was a strong Martin supporter who had been elected as part of Karl Littler's takeover strategy. He defended the active organizing being done by riding associations to ensure that delegates to the next convention would endorse a leadership review. Cunningham rejected Dhaliwal's criticism and insisted his 'only objective is to increase the party's ability to win seats in BC ... I think we should leave it in the hands of the party.'[93]

Furious, Dhaliwal declared publicly that 'no prime minister should be confronted with this type of problem ... I think there's going to be a backlash against those Liberals who are trying to divide the party and trying to push the prime minister out ... Canadians don't like to see these divisions.' When a poll found nearly two-thirds of the province's riding associations were planning to send delegates to the convention to vote against Chrétien, Dhaliwal warned: 'If they decide to push someone out, it will be pretty difficult for them to look themselves in the mirror and say "We pushed out someone who devoted his life to the party and the country."'[94]

Within caucus, the number of MPs prepared to speak out publicly for attribution was also growing. One person prepared to speak on the record was Quebec MP Liza Frulla. In an interview with a Montreal radio station, Frulla declared there would be 'general relief' within the Liberal Party if Chrétien were to 'wake up and step down as leader.'[95] Another outspoken critic was Brenda Chamberlain, who sold eight hundred new memberships in her riding since Martin's departure from cabinet in early June to people intent on ensuring a vote for review at the convention. 'We've just never had anything like it,' she told one reporter. 'People stopping me on the street, people stopping me at yard sales, it doesn't matter where I go, we're selling lots of memberships.'[96]

There were still a substantial number of Chrétien supporters in caucus. Twenty-five of the forty-nine MPs who responded to an internal survey said they would vote against a leadership review in February. Many believed the Martin supporters constituted barely half of all the MPs and virtually none of the senators. In one of the last national caucus meetings before the summer recess, one veteran MP angrily warned that 'if it is OK to attack the PM in the media today, the precedent is set for doing the same in the future.'[97] Not all of Chrétien's defenders were members of the old guard or longtime colleagues. One relative newcomer, Ontario MP John Finlay, suggested the activities of the Martin organizers were actually hurting the party's electoral chances. 'There's really very little support for what Mr Martin is attempting to do, or what he appears to be attempting to do,' Finlay said. 'The attitude in my riding is not as pro-Martin as it once was.'[98] His views were echoed by a number of academic experts. Daniel Weinstock of the Université de Montréal pointed to the example of British cabinet minister Michael Heseltine, the man who successfully unseated Margaret Thatcher as leader of the Conservative party but failed to replace her. 'By the end, everybody was so fed up with the bloodiness of the conflict,' Weinstock noted, 'that the party faithful started looking for a way out. If the fight gets too bloody, both the combatants get sullied by it.'[99]

Martin himself was well aware of the Heseltine debacle. According to Tim Murphy, Martin voiced his concern at becoming 'another Heseltine.'[100] Certainly Martin did not want to be seen as disloyal. As he crossed the country meeting with supporters, he insisted he was not campaigning to replace Chrétien but only 'speaking with Canadians' and 'discussing important issues facing the country.' After one event, he told reporters, 'We're here to discuss ideas. We're here to discuss

Co-chairs Doug Frith and Lise Thibault with John Turner, celebrating his successful leadership review vote at the party's 1986 convention. All photos are © Jean-Marc Carisse / www.carisse.org.

MPs Doug Frith and Raymond Garneau (back to camera) and party president Michel Robert with opposition leader John Turner at a tense national caucus debate on the Meech Lake Accord.

Liberal leader John Turner, the author, and MP André Ouellet, campaign co-chair, unveil the party's platform in national caucus, 28 June 1988, Senator Jacques Hébert looking on.

Former prime minister Pierre Trudeau, Liberal leader-elect Jean Chrétien, and second-place finisher Paul Martin at the 1990 Liberal leadership convention in Calgary.

Pierre Trudeau at the 1990 Liberal leadership convention. Newfoundland Premier Clyde Wells is in front and to the right of Trudeau. Trudeau adviser Tom Axworthy and Liberal senators Allan MacEachen (to Trudeau's right) and John Stewart (beside MacEachen) look on.

Pierre Trudeau denouncing the Charlottetown Accord at a *Cité libre* dinner at La Maison Eggroll in Montreal. The author, MP Charles Caccia, André Breton, and Senator Anne Cools look on from the head table.

Liberal leader Jean Chrétien looks on as platform co-chair Paul Martin launches the party's Red Book in 1993.

Jean Chrétien campaigning with the Red Book during the 1993 federal election.

Prime Minister Chrétien and Finance Minister Paul Martin discuss the 1996 deficit-reduction budget.

Finance Minister Paul Martin delivering the budget, 28 February 2000.

Prime Minister Chrétien speaking at a NO rally in Montreal during the 1995 Quebec referendum campaign.

Prime Minister Chrétien conferring with Quebec Liberal leader Daniel Johnson, federal Conservative leader Jean Charest, and former Robert Bourassa adviser John Parisella (back to camera) during the 1995 referendum.

Prime Minister Paul Martin speaks at the 2005 Liberal policy convention with Quebec lieutenant Jean Lapierre and MP Eleni Bakopanos looking on.

Former prime minister Chrétien testifying at the Gomery Inquiry.

John Turner and Paul Martin embrace at the 2003 Liberal leadership convention in Toronto.

Jean Chrétien and Pierre Trudeau chat at a National Library and Archives Canada ceremony in Ottawa in 1994. Former prime ministers Joe Clark, John Turner, and Kim Campbell are in the background.

where the country should go next, what the government should do next, and what challenges we face.'[101]

Martin was not only discussing ideas (some of them quite controversial such as the notion of a 'democratic deficit' in Parliament), he was meeting with a wide range of ethnic groups as well. Chrétien's advisers saw this as an attempt to recruit more new members in favour of a February leadership vote. Not to be outdone, Jean Chrétien launched a tour of western Canada in late July, meeting with members of the same communities and making a number of specific announcements, including the funding for the Chinatown Millennium Gate in Vancouver and the opening of a Canadian immigration office in the Punjab.

Chrétien Fights Back

By now Chrétien's organizers were all telling him the same thing – his chances of winning a leadership review vote in February were slim. 'It was simply too late,' Sergio Marchi said. 'By the time he called on us to see what could be done, we had no way to overcome the head start Martin had on the ground. He was in control of practically the whole executive of the party.'[102] This meant it was virtually impossible for Chrétien's supporters to obtain membership forms and sell new memberships, preventing them from attempting a comeback. If Chrétien supporters were unable to recruit new members, they could not hope to win the vote for the selection of delegates to the convention, a vote which would take place in November 2002.

In BC, this situation produced a particularly dramatic conflict. The rules introduced by the provincial executive stated that 'Members of Parliament, riding association presidents and riding membership chairmen (could) have up to 100 membership forms at a time,' but 'ordinary' party members could only have five forms. With Martin forces controlling at least twenty-five of the thirty-four ridings in the province, the reason for this approach was obvious, and, with the party holding almost no seats in the province, the inclusion of MPs in the first group was gratuitous. One of Chrétien's strongest supporters in caucus and his longtime provincial campaign chair, Senator Ross Fitzpatrick, protested that senators should be included in that first category as well. He was rebuffed by provincial president Bill Cunningham as well as Martin's BC organizer, Mark Marissen. Cunningham again stressed that Martin supporters were only in executive posts because they had been elected, and therefore had the support of the grassroots. In addition, he argued that 'the only way Liberals can build support is on the back of Paul Martin.'[103] Incensed, Fitzpatrick and another BC senator supporting Chrétien, Mobina Jaffer, launched a lawsuit against the party and its rules.

This example of highly public infighting produced a considerable amount of sympathy for Chrétien, but little positive support for the party. Marissen himself later admitted that, while the original purpose of the rule changes was to ensure a more equitable and tamper-proof membership system, it 'spun out of control' during the leadership review and the decision to exclude senators was 'spite, pure and simple.'[104] As one editorial concluded, 'It is simply wrong to have one set of rules for one's contender's supporters and another set of rules for everyone else. If Mr. Martin is to avoid further dividing the party and tarnishing his own reputation as a straight shooter, he should instruct his troops to allow his opponent, Mr. Chrétien, a fair chance to compete.'[105]

Chrétien explained his predicament. 'I did not have to run against myself. So the organization and who is president in what riding, it was my last preoccupation. As long as they were Liberals I was happy.'[106] Privately he admitted to several of his close advisers that he realized he had made a mistake in not paying enough attention. At the same time he was both surprised and hurt that this would be necessary.

As an alternative to the now hopeless membership drive, some of Chrétien's supporters attempted to launch an 'air war' or communications campaign. With some 55 per cent of the public believing Martin had been fired, and more than 70 per cent thinking he had been treated badly, it was clear that Chrétien's image was in difficulty. Peter Donolo and John Rae were called upon to launch a rehabilitation campaign for the Liberal leader. Both referred to the party traditions of respect for the leader and internal unity. In one interview, Rae specifically stressed that 'the party has a winning tradition of loyalty, respect, unity and support for the leader. This leader has secured three majority governments ... We have a review process and we will be working to ensure that winning tradition of the party is maintained.'[107] Other Chrétien spokespersons repeatedly told the press Martin was receiving a 'free ride' on key issues, such as same-sex marriage, while arguing the prime minister was accessible and his challenger was not.

These comments brought on a heated set of rebuttals from Martin supporters. 'There were all those people back in 1999 saying if we gave him a really good score [in the last leadership review] – wink, wink, nudge, nudge – then he wouldn't run again. [Now] he uses the 90 per cent to say he can run forever. It's spun as a loyalty thing by people who know better.'[108] MP Andrew Telegdi agreed: 'Voting for leadership review now does not make people bad Liberals.'[109] Another Martin supporter, Tony Ianno, added, 'I think we have finally come to a head, I think it's unavoidable, considering Mr. Martin is the best Finance Minister this country has ever had, including Jean Chrétien.'[110] In response to the Chrétien communications offensive, Martin's supporters actually established a 'war room' in Ottawa designed to 'respond quickly to the almost daily charges being brought against the former finance minister by the prime minister's loyalists.'[111]

Many Liberals who knew both men well were not surprised that the alliance of convenience had finally broken down. As Sergio Marchi observed, 'the *real* story is how long they were able to make it work.'[112] His former colleague Doug Frith concurred, adding that the differences between Martin and Chrétien reminded him of those between Turner and Chrétien.[113] Despite this, no one directly involved on either side would agree that the events unfolding were similar to those that took place during John Turner's leadership.

For the Chrétien supporters, who were now the ones being challenged, the differences between the two situations were obvious. Turner had lost, and lost badly, not once but twice. Their man had won three elections. Moreover, Turner was on the wrong side of the federalism divide, having supported Meech Lake. Even so, they argued, they did not challenge Turner the way Chrétien was being so openly challenged now by Martin's forces. They believed the Martin people were endangering the reputation of the party with their actions. George Young insisted, 'we would *never* have risked destroying the party just to make Chrétien leader.'[114] In retrospect, Percy Downe concluded it had indeed been an error for Chrétien to assume the party was in good hands. 'Our mistake was in not putting someone up for the presidency back in 1998,' he argued. In Downe's view, 'LeDrew wasn't so much biased as inept and weak, and the party needed a strong president more than ever at that time.'[115]

On the Martin side there was an equal and opposite reaction. Many of his followers were former Turner supporters who remembered only too well the difficult times in opposition. They too maintained that the current situation was completely different. They had pulled together and closed ranks behind Chrétien, even though they had not supported him for the leadership. They had stayed with him for three elections. Now he was being unreasonable, putting his own wishes ahead of the best interests of the party. In short, Martin's supporters believed their actions would save, not destroy, the party.

Neither side appeared to recognize that Canadians disapproved of the behaviour of both groups. One poll reported a large majority of Canadians felt the Chrétien-Martin battle was 'childish.'[116] Party pollster Michael Marzolini confirmed that the battle was 'tarnishing the Liberal brand.' In an article for the *Liberal Times*, he reported Canadians 'are fascinated by the historical relevance of what is taking place, and by their opportunity to "peak behind the curtains."' At the same time he warned that 'they are also wishing the issue would go away, and that the government would get back on course.'[117]

Desperate Measures

Public opinion was reinforced by two other developments. The first concerned Paul Martin's response to the fundraising rules for cabinet ministers. When the rules were announced in early July 2003, Martin was faced with a difficult choice. Although he was no longer a minister, the rules were retroactive and affected the funds raised while he was in cabinet. But Martin was loath to reveal the names of his financial backers, most of whom came from Bay Street or the energy sector in Alberta and did not want to be identified. He claimed he was unaware of the individual contributors and that supporter Gerry Schwartz and his national director, John Webster, took care of the details through the blind trust known as Project 2000.

Martin initially argued it was unfair to change the rules of the game after the fact, an argument that would likely have been accepted by most Canadians. But the statement he issued explaining his decision to ignore the new rules suggested a more serious concern. 'Many people harbour fears that disclosure of their names at this time, and in the current political climate, will put them at a disadvantage – particularly concerning their relationship with the federal government.'[118] Almost immediately the new finance minister, John Manley, forcefully rejected that idea. By the same reasoning, Manley said, financial contributors to opposition parties would also be at risk of some type of retribution by the government of the day. 'If he doesn't want to disclose because he doesn't think it's fair to the people who contributed … that's one rationale. But to suggest that there could be some type of action taken against them … I think it's ridiculous, quite frankly.'[119]

This was followed by revelations of Jean Chrétien's increasingly desperate efforts to stem the tide of MPs willing to publicly challenge his leadership. First a letter was sent to all MPs asking for their policy input, a move ridiculed by Martin supporters as too little, too late. As Toronto MP Albina Guarnieri put it, 'It's refreshing that he has suddenly discovered our worth – at least until February.' Another fellow Toronto MP, Joe Volpe, was even more severe. 'How long can you play someone for a fool?' he demanded. 'This concept of loyalty and dignity cuts both ways.'[120] To make matters worse, an article in the *Hill Times* listed caucus members who were willing to be identified as supporting or opposing a leadership review, and PMO officials frantically began contacting dissenters to attempt to change their minds, a move that quickly became public knowledge.

In addition, as the special summer caucus in Chicoutimi drew closer, a letter described as a 'pledge of support' for Chrétien's leadership was prepared. All caucus members who were considered uncommitted received calls from the PMO requesting their signature. It was seen as an act of desperation by most and was spectacularly unsuccessful. Even some Chrétien supporters objected to what they saw as heavy-handed tactics. The list would eventually be distributed at the start of the Chicoutimi meeting with some seventy-nine names attached, but several of those on the list denied having been consulted, discrediting the entire exercise.

A third effort called on all senators to sign a letter which declared, 'Our prime minister has served and is serving Canada and our party well. He heads a third consecutive majority government which has brought successive budget surpluses for the first time in fifty years.' The letter concluded, 'We are proud to serve under his leadership and will cast our votes for him in November 2002 and February 2003. We urge all party members to join us.' As one senior Liberal organizer in the Senate commented, 'I find this completely insulting … It's a very, very stupid thing to do, because if we all don't sign it's going to hurt the prime minister, not help him.'[121] In the end, the effort was scrapped.

A fourth initiative met with the same fate. In this case, Chrétien personally requested help from some of his oldest supporters and former cabinet colleagues, urging them to release a statement of support signed by privy councillors. This letter, which never became public, was to be presented at the Chicoutimi caucus as well. It read in part, 'The fact that we have not publicly repudiated our leaders, but have accommodated an orderly transition from one leader to the next, has been an important factor in our success as a party. We are therefore profoundly concerned to see a process developing within our party which has the potential not only to split the party but, more importantly, to undermine Canadian democracy.'

The first time Chrétien spoke publicly about the internal party conflict was during a stop on his Ontario summer tour. At a science fair in Toronto featuring astronomy projects, he joked, 'I remember in 1993 that we had a star all summer, that we later called a shooting star. She had a summer job. It was Kim Campbell.' For his part, Martin could not resist responding. 'It's been a long time since he's called me a star, shooting or otherwise.' Shortly after, it became clear to Chrétien that his efforts would not succeed. Faced with the unprecedented organizational and caucus challenges to his leadership, he realized he could not brazen out a leadership review. As Percy Downe said later, 'I think he had made up his mind at least a week before Chicoutimi. I did one day of the Ontario tour with him and I felt then that he had decided to announce his departure.'[122]

By now few Liberals remained uninvolved in the conflict. Even Chrétien's mentor Mitchell Sharp felt obliged to intervene at this point, volunteering comments for the media about what Chrétien should do, and making it clear that he was concerned about the state of the party. Telling reporters he believed there was virtually no chance Chrétien would want to run for a fourth term, Sharp concluded: 'I would have thought what he would like is to complete his work ... and then leave in a graceful way ... with the thanks of the people for making all the efforts he's made.'[123] It was a sentiment that irked some Martin supporters, who saw Sharp as the architect of the 'long goodbye' that caused them so much angst.

Dethroning the Leader

In the final week before Chicoutimi, Chrétien received more discouraging news from Peter Donolo and David Smith. He also received an unexpected visit from Stephen LeDrew, who claimed he was trying to prevent a leadership vote that would be both divisive and unnecessary. 'I told him my purpose in avoiding the vote was to ensure he would not be humiliated – I didn't think he'd even get 20 per cent – and not to be painted into a corner. I wanted to let him have an exit with some dignity. All he had to do was say he was going.'[124] Nevertheless, LeDrew left the meeting uncertain as to what the leader would do in Chicoutimi, as were Martin's advisers. Tim Murphy insisted, 'We only wanted him to give us a date and say for sure he was leaving. We didn't want to appear that we were pushing. I'm not sure what would have happened if he had decided to stay and fight. And we did think he might still do that.'[125]

The first day of the two-day special caucus in Chicoutimi unfolded in an atmosphere of considerable tension and anticipation. Chrétien delivered a lengthy 'agenda' speech that Eddie Goldenberg had written for him, in which he outlined the ambitious number of items still on his to-do list, primarily in the areas of social policy and the environment. He also categorically rejected the proposals Martin had been making about the 'democratic deficit.' He argued the removal of some 'essential' governmental controls over caucus members in a parliamentary system would lead to the Americanization of Canadian politics, in which individual MPs would be captured by lobby groups and money would become far more important in determining policy. Then he pointedly noted that his agenda 'cannot be put in place overnight. It will take some time, and possibly two budgets ... to set the legislative and fiscal framework.'[126]

Chrétien's closest advisers were told of his decision to announce his departure only after he delivered his agenda speech. As a result, many Martin MPs were still calling for his resignation the following morning. The only MP to publicly oppose them was Paul DeVillers, the former caucus chair. In a strongly worded statement to CTV's Mike Duffy, DeVillers said he believed the entire debate had been harmful to all concerned and concluded, 'In the Liberal Party, we do not depose our leaders.'[127]

Many in caucus made it clear that they would fight for Chrétien when the subject arose. But the debate never took place. Shortly after 1 p.m., Chrétien unexpectedly held a press conference outside the caucus room and made his dramatic announcement that he would be stepping down as leader of the Liberal Party in February 2004. Noting that both the Conservatives and the NDP would have chosen new leaders at that point, he referred to the dual role he played as leader and prime minister, and described himself as a guardian of the party. He also made reference to the lengthy internecine warfare and the damage it had done, and concluded with a rationale for his choice of departure date:

> For forty years the Liberal Party has been like a family to me. Its best interests are bred in my bones. I have reflected on the best way to bring back unity. To end the fighting. To resume interrupted friendships. I have also

thought about how much time it will take to finish the job we were elected to do. To complete the agenda for governing I set out last night ... I have taken into account my duty to protect for my successors the integrity of the office. An office that is non-negotiable. Here is my conclusion: I will not run again. I will fulfil my mandate and focus entirely on governing from now until February 2004. At which time my work will be done and my successor will be chosen. This will be after three of the opposition parties have chosen new leaders, so Liberals will know who they are facing. And it will be early enough to give a new prime minister all the necessary flexibility to choose the date of the next election. Everything we have achieved as a government we have achieved because of the unity of our caucus ... I thank you from the bottom of my heart ... I will need all of you to complete our work over the next eighteen months. And then, at the age of seventy, I will look back with great satisfaction secure in the knowledge that the future of Canada is unlimited.[128]

Paul Martin was given a note earlier by a Chrétien aide. The note simply said 'I am making this statement to help heal divisions within the Liberal party.' After Chrétien's statement, Martin and his aides, stunned by the announcement, disappeared for nearly four hours. During that time several angry Chrétien supporters, and a furious Maurizio Bevilacqua, denounced the Martin supporters for having caused what they saw as a serious breach in party discipline that would come back to haunt them.

When Martin finally emerged to speak with an increasingly impatient group of reporters, it was to read a short prepared text. 'I can tell you that none of us in government would have enjoyed the success we did without his support, his leadership,' he read. 'Jean Chrétien is a man who has shown courage all his life. He is a man for whom I have the highest respect.'[129] With that brief comment Martin left without taking any questions, and the future of the party was sealed. A Liberal leader and sitting prime minister had been deposed and a leadership race was underway.

Several of Martin's advisers later stressed there was little debate about the timing of Chrétien's departure at that point. According to Tim Murphy, they were prepared to live with the February 2004 date he had chosen, even though they had expected a convention in spring 2003. 'We weren't going to go to the wall over a few more months,' he insisted.[130] But small groups of Martin MPs, obviously unhappy with what they would soon refer to as 'the long goodbye,' almost immediately began discussing what could be done to remove Chrétien from office sooner. One Chrétien supporter later insisted, 'they were more worried about having to wait for their cabinet posts than anything else.' But, as the next eighteen months would demonstrate, they might also have been worried about the policy agenda Chrétien had just laid out for them, an agenda many of them opposed.

Chrétien's Legacy Agenda Resumed

After his decision was made, many of those closest to Chrétien said he appeared serene and purposeful. He referred to himself as 'liberated.' Senior adviser Paul Genest confided that initially 'we didn't know if his eighteen month scenario would fly. When it did, most of us felt a sense of exhilaration. We knew we were going to get things done.' Moreover, Genest noted, 'it wasn't that he suddenly started to think about leaving a legacy, as many of his critics have suggested. We had been working on these plans all along. Most of them were in the 2000 Throne Speech. He had talked about them often. Some of them were things he had been planning to do for more than a decade. Most of them were already on the drawing board and ready to go.'[131] As a result of this ongoing work, it was possible for Chrétien to implement what appeared to be a large number of policy initiatives in the last year of his mandate, several of which had simply been delayed by the national security crisis.

What was different about the final year in policy terms, as both Percy Downe and Marjorie Loveys noted, was the extent to which the policy agenda was driven by the prime minister rather than individual ministers. In addition, there was a heightened sense of urgency about completing the agenda given the shortened time period available to Chrétien. Put another way, many of his closest advisers agreed that, had he not been obliged to announce his departure date so soon, he would likely have proceeded at a slower pace with his policy priorities and might not have completed some of them. However, they also noted that a number of external events, including key court decisions concerning same-sex marriage and marijuana, drove other aspects of the agenda and would have done so regardless of when Chrétien stepped down.

As both supporters and critics of the prime minister have commented, there was considerably less discussion of issues in caucus. As one of Chrétien's closest confidants later explained, 'What was the point? He knew who was opposed to certain bills, and he knew they couldn't muster enough votes to defeat him. Since they had already "won" the battle about his leaving, what levers did they have left to use against him? He could basically ignore them, and he did.'[132]

The Throne Speech that would be Chrétien's last was read by the governor general on Monday, 30 September 2002. The speech committed the government to spending on health care, infrastructure renewal, and implementation of the Kyoto Protocol for five years. The following day Chrétien spoke in the House of Commons, laying out his plans for the remainder of his term and beyond. Chrétien stressed that his agenda would not put at risk the government's hard-won fiscal health, as some Martin supporters worried. Instead, he announced the era of tax cuts was over. Surpluses would be used for the next several years to invest in important social and infrastructure programs. 'Taxes are the price one pays to live in a civilized society,' he declared, and 'Canadians will be prepared to pay the cost' of the social safety net as 'they have in the past, rather than allow an American-style system in which individuals assume risk without regard to ability to pay.'[133]

Chrétien's speech was widely reported in the media, but many in his own caucus were not present in the House to hear it. Estimates placed the number of absentees at 100 of the 170 Liberal backbenchers. Reporter Chantal Hébert commented, 'For veteran parliamentary hands, the sight of so many empty Liberal seats on the occasion of a prime ministerial command performance spoke volumes as to Chrétien's slipping control over his caucus and the stormy times that spells for the government in the coming months.'[134] One of the absent MPs – almost all of whom were Martin supporters – told journalists there was no point in showing up because 'it's just posturing, empty rhetoric, continuation of the same.'[135] As he and his colleagues quickly discovered, they were wrong.

One of Chrétien's initiatives in the fall of 2002 was the creation of ten new national parks and five marine conservation areas across the country. Funding was committed for the five-year project and additional funds were allocated to maintain or expand a number of existing parks. As Paul Genest pointed out, this plan had been outlined in both the 2000 platform and the Throne Speech. Monte Hummel of the World Wildlife Fund added that negotiations to establish some of the new parks were already well advanced.[136] For Chrétien, this was the completion of the national network he had pursued for more than thirty years, having first established a string of ten national parks during his time as minister of Indian and Northern Affairs under Trudeau. Yet various Martin disciples described the initiative as a bolt from the blue and a determined attempt to spend away the surplus before they took over.

Shortly before, while attending the World Summit on Sustainable Development in Johannesburg, South Africa, Chrétien announced Canada would ratify the Kyoto Protocol by the end of the year. Although Canada had signed the original agreement, the protocol would not come into force until ratified by a sufficient number of member states. Chrétien reiterated his determination to ratify the protocol in a speech on 4 November in which he said, 'I do not pretend that achieving our objectives will be easy. It will not. [But] we have ten years to meet our obligations under the treaty. We can make progress together.' Chrétien also stressed that the final Climate Change Plan adopted by the government in late 2000 would 'spread the costs of meeting commitments evenly across the country and across sectors of the economy.'[137]

Despite the government's pledge, there were still a number of concerns expressed by the energy sector in Alberta and by the Klein government, as well as some business groups. They feared the implementation of the plan would leave the Canadian economy at a competitive disadvantage relative to the Americans and result in significant job losses. Some went so far as to argue there had not been sufficient consultation, despite two years of negotiations with provinces and the private sector, and the various sectoral agreements that had already been reached with key industries such as the automotive sector.

Among those who shared these concerns was Paul Martin. According to several of his former colleagues, in cabinet Martin had always expressed serious reservations about the Kyoto Accord. Some believed it was due in part to his dependence on western support in the party, as evidenced by the Dinning/Prentice fundraising letter. The split in cabinet over Kyoto was particularly relevant given Martin's earlier position as environment critic before the party's return to power in 1993, and his frequent public statements during his time in cabinet about the importance of sustainable development. Former Trudeau environment minister Charles Caccia was particularly sceptical: 'He talked about it all the time but he did very little. I wrote him many letters explaining how he needed to do something about the perverse tax subsidies to the oil and gas industries that are so counterproductive if we are to have any hope of putting the economy on a sustainable footing, and year after year he would seem to agree but nothing would happen.'[138]

Martin's supporters claimed the Climate Change Plan adopted by the government was too restrictive and ambitious. Immediately after Chrétien's South African announcement, Martin said: 'I don't think we should kid ourselves. There are costs to dealing with climate change and Canadians are entitled to know what those costs are. What they're going to be asked to bear and that it is going to be done in a way that is equitable and fair right across the country, region by region.' He also stressed, 'we have to work with the provinces on this, it's their jurisdiction to a large extent,' and then, in what would become a standard line for the next year, he seemed to agree with other critics that there was no plan at all. 'In order to have a national debate as to whether or not we're going to be able to achieve Kyoto, how and within what period, you have to lay out the plan.'[139] Despite these reservations, Martin voted with the government and the Kyoto Protocol was officially ratified by Canada. A few months later, John Manley's first budget as finance minister committed $1.7 billion to the Climate Change Plan for Canada, increasing Martin's concern that the surpluses he had worked so hard to achieve might be committed for years to come.

Martin's Policy Dilemma

The policy differences between Martin and Chrétien became more apparent as time went on. This was not because Martin, now unconstrained by the principle of cabinet solidarity, felt free to criticize his own government. Instead, with a Liberal leadership race underway it was obvious early on that Martin would actually say less than before so as to avoid antagonizing anyone. It was Martin's reluctance to comment on many of the key issues of the day, despite the media's efforts to draw him out, that led many observers to conclude he did not share Chrétien's views.

Canada's participation in the Iraq war was a case in point. Chrétien pursued the Liberals' traditional multilateral approach, including supporting the United Nations. On 13 February 2003 in a major speech to the Council on Foreign Relations in Chicago, Chrétien stated, 'Today's United Nations needs a committed United States and I would argue the world needs an effective United Nations.' He also acknowledged the increasing likelihood that the Bush administration was preparing to act unilaterally, and to refuse UN inspector Hans Blix more time to locate alleged weapons of mass destruction. Urging the United States to give the UN team more time, he said: 'It is imperative to avoid the perception of a clash of civilizations. Maximum use of the United Nations will minimize that risk.'[140]

Martin said very little publicly about his views on a possible U.S.-led invasion of Iraq. On several occasions he ignored reporters' direct questions on the subject. But there were at least two instances in which he let his discomfort with Chrétien's position be known. Before a final decision was taken by the government, he said 'I think that we really are dealing with, you know, someone [Saddam Hussein] who ... personifies, you know, evil in every way, and that ... he has ... he does have biological weapons. He does have chemical weapons. And he has demonstrated in the past his preparedness to use them. And so while I believe that he's contained, you know, for how long? And is it going to take 200,000 troops on his borders forever in order to do this? So I ... I mean I think that this issue has got, you know, there's much more that has to be played out before this issue is ... will come to an end ... It ... has to be resolved and it has not been won.'[141]

A week later, Chrétien categorically rejected Canadian participation in the American expedition. He told the House of Commons: 'The diplomatic process was bringing positive results. That was the view of the Canadian government. It was not, obviously, the view of the American government.' He also suggested that forcing a regime change would not be a good idea. 'If we change every government we don't like in the world, where do we stop? Who is next?'[142] With this formal decision, Martin fell in line and indicated his support for the government.

Similar disagreements emerged over the legislation introduced on the decriminalization of marijuana in May 2003 and on the same-sex marriage issue in August of that year. Both of these, it should be noted, resulted from court decisions that compromised existing legislation. In the first instance, however, Chrétien pointed out that he had already contemplated such a measure when he was justice minister twenty years earlier. Moreover, both a Senate and a House of Commons committee had studied the issue of illicit drug use in the past year and recommended similar changes.

The same-sex marriage bill was an entirely different matter. Describing it as a 'very difficult issue for someone of my generation, born and brought up in Catholic, rural Quebec,' Chrétien went on to say, 'but I have learned over forty years in public life that society evolves and that the concept of human rights evolves often more quickly than some of us might have predicted ... But at the end of the day [the government has] to live up to our responsibilities. And none of these are more essential than protecting the Constitution and the fundamental rights it guarantees to all Canadians.' Noting that the Alliance had attacked the Supreme Court and 'judicial activism' for years, he warned Liberal MPs and senators not to forget this term was a 'code' for the new party's underlying antipathy towards the Charter of Rights and Freedoms. 'Let us not fall into their trap on this issue,' he urged. 'This is not about weakening Parliament. It is not about weakening traditional religion ... It is about giving force and effect to Canadian values. We need to be guided by how court after court has been interpreting the Charter of Rights. And the courts have been telling us that separate but equal has no place in Canada.'[143]

At the same time, Chrétien was aware of the problems the marriage bill posed for Liberal MPs from rural ridings. For this reason he asked Justice Minister Martin Cauchon to refer the matter to the Supreme Court, to provide those MPs with a legal basis to defend the bill.[144] There was nevertheless considerable resistance to both bills by a vocal minority in caucus. The dissenters came primarily from Martin's supporters in the 'family values' group, who had been arguing unsuccessfully for the government to submit an expanded reference to the Supreme Court to see if alternatives to the term 'marriage' such as a 'registered domestic partnership' or 'civil union' would be deemed constitutional.

Caught between his desire to support government policy and his reluctance to disagree with caucus backers, Martin initially refused to discuss the issue or give his personal opinion, despite firm declarations of support for the legislation offered by Allan Rock and Sheila Copps, two of his probable leadership opponents. At an editorial board interview the following week, Martin said, 'How do we deal with the evolution of society's attitudes? How do we deal with the very legitimate views that are held on both sides of the issue? If you're going to build consensus, if you're going to find answers to these things, you don't do it by imposition.'[145]

Martin's comments led one of Pierre Trudeau's former press secretaries to remark, 'It's one thing to be imprecise. It's another to be confusing, frankly, when you have a lot of MPs looking to you for direction.'[146] Chrétien also responded to Martin's comments, declaring, 'Even if the bill is defeated, the law stands. That's the reality ... We don't act with elections in mind. We react to the problems we have.'[147] When Martin's advisers began suggesting that a referendum might be another possibility, Chrétien did not hesitate to reject that view publicly. 'To have a referendum to decide the fate of a minority, it's a problem. It's why we have constitutions to protect the minority, that's why we have charters of rights. If it is always the majority vote, who will defend the minorities?'[148]

A similar situation developed with the bill to decriminalize small amounts of marijuana. At a weekly meeting of national caucus in early June 2003, the unhappiness of many rural and socially conservative Liberal MPs was once again front and centre. Policy differences had been playing out for months in the caucus, but disagreement was now becoming increasingly public. One article published after the 1 June 2003 weekly caucus meeting referred to a 'riot-type atmosphere,' a term which seemed to be confirmed by statements offered to the media by known Martin supporters. In an article in the *Hill Times* in which several of them were interviewed, Pickering MP Dan McTeague, for example, declared that 'Chrétien knows it's a political minefield ... It's another burden we have to bear in the next election.' Mr McTeague suggested the prime minister would not have introduced the legislation had he been planning to run in the next election, a point picked up by fellow MP Jim Karygiannis, who told the *Times* reporter 'a lot of my colleagues share the frustration ... that we're facing an administration that is sunsetting and saying "Damm the torpedoes."' Meanwhile, Toronto MP Joe Volpe, ignoring the recent court decisions and the two parliamentary committee reports, maintained the bill 'came right out of the blue.' Fellow Martin supporter Roger Galloway agreed. 'A clear majority of legislation is emanating from who knows where,' Mr Galloway said. 'There is no caucus request for this legislation. Yet this stuff is flowing into the Chamber. In my view it's governance by bureaucracy.'[149]

Chrétien supporters argued this was simply another example of the Martin forces causing difficulties where none needed to exist. 'This bill is a non-event for most Canadians,' one backbencher said. Former defence minister Art Eggleton agreed: 'I haven't heard anybody say that their riding is close in terms of vote counts and so they have to be careful about this [marijuana] bill ... There are a lot of other issues out there that people care far more about.'[150]

Still, a growing number of Martin MPs began calling for Chrétien's departure ahead of his pre-determined schedule. Jim Karygiannis's remark that 'the sooner he leaves, the better' was echoed by a number of his colleagues. The almost complete abandonment of the Liberal tradition of party discipline and solidarity was heightened by growing controversy over the centrepiece of Chrétien's policy agenda, legislation to reform the financing of political parties.

Election Reform: The Final Legacy

In January 2003 Jean Chrétien tabled legislation on party financing that he had first promised in the spring of 2002 as part of his eight-point ethics package. The bill represented the first major reform to national electoral and campaign finance laws since those of Pierre Trudeau nearly twenty years earlier. That legislation focused primarily on spending limits for parties in its attempts to ensure a level playing field for all political parties. Chrétien's legislation took the concept to the next stage, namely, introducing limits on contributions by individuals and corporations. And while the 1974 legislation introduced a measure of public financing through the rebate system, Chrétien's legislation enhanced the public funding component to make up for the revenues that parties would lose through the limitations on contributions. In addition, Bill C-24 expanded the coverage of government regulations to the activities of constituency associations, leadership contests, and nominations.

All of these measures had been discussed for some time in Canada. A decade earlier the Royal Commission on Electoral Reform and Party Financing tabled a report which raised several issues regarding electoral financing. At the provincial level, Quebec introduced legislation in 1977 to limit political contributions, and Manitoba followed suit in 2000. Nearly every member state of the European Union already had similar legislation and some type of provision for public funding as an alternative.

More recently, the controversy over the financing of the Liberal leadership candidates, and indeed of the Alliance campaign which preceded it, renewed public interest in the issues of transparency and accountability in the political process. The public's concern that big business or even big unions were unduly influencing the political process through their support for certain parties or candidates was growing. It was this concern that led Chrétien, in his speech in Chicoutimi, to argue that campaign financing was 'the real democratic deficit' that the government needed to address.

Among the measures proposed in the bill were a virtual ban on political donations by corporations and unions, limitations on contributions by individuals, enhanced public financing of political parties based on a formula related to popular support, and the extension of electoral regulations to constituency associations, nomination, and leadership campaigns, including contribution limits. At the same time, the bill stopped short of telling political parties how to run such campaigns, requiring instead registration and reporting mechanisms.

The bill ran into difficulties almost immediately. Perhaps not surprisingly, opposition parties worried that the larger the party, the more public funding it would receive, even though this was a well-established principle. After considerable debate and study by a House of Commons committee, the amount provided was raised at their suggestion from $1.50 to $1.75 per vote, a solution which placated all of the opposition parties and, incidentally, resulted in a substantial windfall to the Bloc Québécois.

The concerns of Liberal MPs were more specific. Many feared that they would have little financial support to run a campaign if the ban on corporate contributions was allowed to apply at the constituency level as originally proposed in the draft. Others felt the public would not accept more funding for political parties from general tax revenue. Martin and his supporters were concerned about the significant corporate contributions they had already accumulated and those they expected to receive in the future. Delaying the bill's implementation, they believed, would at least alleviate some of that difficulty.

In an extraordinary move, party president Stephen LeDrew waded into the controversy by criticizing his own party's plans. Denouncing the legislation as 'dumb as a bag of hammers,' LeDrew insisted on appearing as a witness before the parliamentary committee to demand a series of amendments. In addition to his concern that the party still had not mastered the concept of individual donations and remained dependent on corporate contributions, he argued the draft provisions for public funding would have produced a significant shortfall in revenue for the Liberals. Le Drew went so far as to lobby both the NDP and Conservatives to join with him in making proposals for amendments to the bill at the committee stage, a move that was widely viewed as inappropriate by Liberals in the Chrétien camp who accused him of being 'Martin's mouthpiece.' Ironically, it was the opposition parties' demands for an increase in the contribution level per vote that convinced LeDrew the legislation would be revenue neutral for Liberals. In the end, national director Terry Mercer, and not LeDrew, was invited to testify before the committee and defend the bill at the express request of the PMO. As one journalist reported, 'In an unusual move that highlights the battle over the bill between the outgoing prime minister and others in his party, [PMO] told Liberal Party president Stephen LeDrew that it did not want him to testify.'[151]

Yet several prominent Liberals did support the bill, including former chief financial officers Mike Robinson and Lloyd Posno. Posno, despite being a longtime Martin supporter, later described it as 'one of the most far-sighted and important pieces of legislation' that Chrétien put forward.[152] Another Martin supporter, Winnipeg MP John Harvard, said 'I think it's good legislation. It's time has come.'[153] A number of other groups were enthusiastic about the legislation, including Liberal women. With money viewed as the principal stumbling block for greater participation, and the major source of money being the corporate donations that women were often unable to obtain, the legislation was considered a significant step towards levelling the playing field between the genders in nomination battles.

Nevertheless, as the bill approached its third reading in June 2003, the intensity of opposition to Chrétien's legislation on the part of certain Liberal caucus members grew and became more leadership centred. The fact that the leader insisted on the bill becoming law by January 2004 was seen by many of Martin's supporters as a deliberate strategy to once again cause them difficulty after Martin succeeded Chrétien as leader. Chrétien, however, refused to yield to opposition from within his own caucus, even as the day of the vote approached. 'This bill has to be in effect for the next election,' he told reporters. 'What's the use of having a bill that will not be in effect then?'[154]

To get the bill to pass, Chrétien agreed to a number of proposals for amendments from within the caucus, and from Stephen LeDrew. The bill was finally passed in late June. As one journalist noted, the vote 'capped several months of heated infighting within the Liberal caucus … Last night the bill received final approval … despite the absence of Paul Martin and several other Liberal MPs.'[155]

And so, one year after the fateful Chicoutimi summer caucus, Chrétien addressed the national caucus one more time. With the leadership race to succeed him about to kick into high gear, he acknowledged the deep divisions within his caucus and his party. His concluding remarks were seen by some Martin supporters as a defiant admonition to his successor to leave the 'legacy agenda' in place, and by others as the mark of a true Liberal, putting party considerations ahead of his own. Regardless, it contained a clear warning that preserving the party's majority would require considerable skill and political acumen:

> Let me finish this evening by telling you something that is very important for me. Only two prime ministers in Canadian history – Mackenzie King and Lester Pearson – have turned the party over to a new leader who has won the next election. I want to be the third. And I will do everything to make sure that the new leader will have the best conditions possible to

win a fourth consecutive Liberal majority government. We have a great record for my successor to build on. A record which the candidates for the leadership and each and everyone of you is part of and can be proud of. A record of liberalism and of building a new Canada for the 21st century. A record we will complete in the fall session of parliament.[156]

11 The Long Leadership Race, 2002–2003

I want to lead a new government with a renewed sense of purpose, with a sharper focus and a clearer plan – a government unafraid to change and eager to turn the page and look to the future.

– Paul Martin[1]

The leadership race to succeed Jean Chrétien was the seventh in the party's history, yet it proved historic in many ways. To begin with, hardly any Liberals were interested in the job. After the hotly contested campaigns to succeed Pearson, Trudeau, and Turner, the lack of Liberal leadership hopefuls in 2003 was stunning. This was even more astonishing considering the party was in power and the opposition was still hopelessly divided. Then there were the new constitutional rules, in force for the first time, which produced a number of unexpected consequences. Lastly, Chrétien's August 2002 announcement that he would not be leaving until February 2004 made this the longest Liberal leadership race ever.

Unfortunately for the party, the conflict between Martin and Chrétien supporters did not diminish during the race. For another eighteen months Canadians saw the typical jockeying between leadership contenders, but also the ongoing spectacle of a Liberal leader openly challenged by caucus and party members with his supporters retaliating in kind. This remarkable scenario did not have an immediately negative impact on the Liberals' standings in the polls. Still, many veteran observers predicted that, unless action were taken to restore the party's famed internal cohesion, the long-term consequences would be severe.

In hindsight, the campaign failed to achieve the two key objectives of leadership succession. First, there was hardly any public interest in the race since Paul Martin was the obvious and indeed the only possible winner. This deprived the party of its traditional boost in popular support in preparation for the next election. Second, and equally significant, the 2003 leadership race once again failed to generate the fundamental renewal and reform that had always been the hallmark of the Liberal Party.

Overture to the Race

Paul Martin was initially content with the time frame laid down by Chrétien in Chicoutimi, but many of his caucus supporters were not. Several of them wanted to put an end to Chrétien's agenda, believing it would hurt their chances of re-election. For others, the long wait to finally make it to the cabinet table had already been frustrating. Another eighteen months seemed an eternity. Yet neither group of MPs was in a position to make a difference despite their public discontent. It was the party's national executive that would make the decision on the timing of the next leadership convention.

As it turned out, the executive also was not prepared to accept an eighteen-month delay simply because the leader had asked for it. Indeed, there were some who believed the leader had reneged on an implicit agreement to leave before the February 2003 date negotiated for the leadership review. As Stephen LeDrew later recalled, 'Many of us assumed in January 2001 that he would leave before February 2003, and we would simply cancel that convention and reschedule a leadership for June.'[2] Instead, with Chrétien announcing a departure date of February 2004, the party executive would have to both cancel the February 2003 meeting and hold off on the leadership convention until early 2004.

A majority of the executive were Martin supporters, although most insisted loyalty was not their primary consideration. Certainly there was a convergence of views since the Martin supporters were also those most concerned with party reform. In fact, 'even some Chrétien supporters believed it was asking too much,' one of them later declared. 'They could see how it would look if he stayed that long, and they knew it would cause trouble politically.' Stephen LeDrew later recalled several members of the executive arguing that 'the situation was simply unacceptable. On top of everything else, it meant we would not have held a national convention for four years!' It also meant that LeDrew himself would stay on as party president for five years.[3]

Much debate took place behind the scenes among various members of the executive, who were concerned that their refusal to accept Chrétien's proposed timetable looked like yet more evidence of internal strife. Searching for legal or historic precedents to justify their decision, LeDrew actually contacted former party president Michel Robert. Robert had in his possession the original letter written by John Turner in 1989 announcing his intention to step down as leader. As Robert later confided, it was clear those who wanted to push for an earlier date had hoped the letter would provide a useful precedent.[4] But Turner, like Chrétien, had merely announced his *intention* to resign. He had also suggested the party hold a convention the following year, which they did.

Since the party's constitution required a leadership convention within twelve months of a leader's resignation or death, this distinction was crucial. By signalling their *intent* to step down without actually resigning, both Chrétien and Turner believed they had provided the party with sufficient time to organize a campaign and plan a smooth transition. Among the Martin supporters, however, Chrétien's move to delay the convention as long as possible had sinister overtones. Given the level of mistrust, his decision was viewed as one more way to thwart Martin and assist other potential candidates.

In the end, Stephen LeDrew emerged from a fractious two-day meeting of the executive in October 2002 to announce the leadership race would officially begin in February 2003. The convention would be held between 10 and 16 November 2003, and the actual leadership vote would take place on 15 November, meaning that Chrétien would still be prime minister for three months after his successor was chosen. Several members believed it might still be possible to put pressure on Chrétien to move up his timetable, a notion that the prime minister was quick to quash in his comments to the public.[5]

With the date of the convention determined, Chrétien announced that he would lift the ban on ministerial campaigning and fundraising, a move considered essential by potential candidates. They would have less than eight months under the party's new rules to put together a winning campaign, while Paul Martin had effectively been organizing for a decade.[6] As one supporter of Industry Minister Allan Rock's candidacy said at the time, 'It's a heck of a challenge, but it's still possible.' However, Rock's adviser also noted that it was not simply the huge lead held by Martin that would prove a daunting challenge. More important still was 'the stranglehold on party memberships held by Martin through his control of provincial and local executives.'[7]

The Membership Forms Crisis

The loosening of constraints for ministers was not sufficient to encourage others to join the race. As predicted by Rock's organizers, the key challenge was the restrictions placed on access to membership forms and the overall control of the party by Martin loyalists. Brian Tobin evaluated his prospects and abandoned the field in January 2002 because of this very problem. Nevertheless, three of Tobin's former cabinet colleagues – Allan Rock, John Manley, and Sheila Copps – still planned to enter the race. All three immediately began to recruit organizers and raise funds to flesh out their existing operations, which had been on hold since May. Right off the bat, however, it was clear Martin's lead was insurmountable.

Allan Rock, widely seen as Martin's chief opponent, was considered the only viable choice of social Liberals. Despite some difficulties in both the Health and Justice portfolios, his public image remained fairly positive. On several occasions he had demonstrated his commitment to the Trudeau vision of federalism, most notably during the 1995 referendum campaign. Of the three likely candidates Martin would face, Rock consistently polled the strongest and, as David Herle later confirmed, was the only candidate the Martin team considered a serious opponent.[8]

Almost immediately after Chrétien's August announcement, Rock made a series of policy statements designed to position himself as the alternative to Martin. It was no accident that he began with federal-provincial relations, an area in which the differences between himself and the frontrunner were most noteworthy. In November 2002, for example, Rock gave a widely reported speech to university students in Ottawa that indirectly criticized Martin by declaring that the CHST (which Martin had introduced in 1995) was a 'black hole' into which federal funds were poured without credit or accountability. 'No one knows exactly what's being transferred for what purpose or what's being spent for what purpose,' Rock declared. 'In my view the CHST is a device which has served its purpose.' He warned that post-secondary education and welfare were being 'crowded out' by some provinces because they were spending most of the money on health care and then criticizing the federal government for cutting back on education spending. Rock recommended a return to the pre-1995 system of three specific transfer payments for the three programs. He also concluded funds 'should be targeted' so 'taxpayers know where the money is going ... Everybody is better off. That's better public policy.'[9]

Despite his aggressive campaign, Rock was the first to recognize the futility of his efforts. His advisers assumed that, with Chrétien gone and the leadership review cancelled, they could expect the rules to be relaxed. When this did not happen Rock threw in the towel in January 2003, before the race had officially begun. Rock informed Chrétien of his decision to withdraw from the contest on 13 January, almost one year to the day after Brian Tobin had done the same. Unlike Tobin, though, Rock did not plan to leave public life. On the contrary, he announced that for the remainder of the race he would be neutral and continue to serve as industry minister.

Despite the outcome of his leadership bid, Rock's support was stronger than many had expected. Money was not an issue either when it came to his candidacy. Rock's campaign had begun in earnest in 1999, when he and others assumed Chrétien would not wage another election campaign. Complying with disclosure requirements, Rock revealed that he had received $1.2 million by July 2002, far surpassing the $171,900 raised by Manley or the $54,500 received by Copps. The issue was really the limited access to membership forms, which Rock felt was 'turning the Liberal Party into a country club for elites.'[10] He concluded that it was not possible to win under the rules for membership forms established in key provinces controlled by Martin executives (notably British Columbia, Alberta, and Ontario). Interestingly, Rock also voiced his belief that the grassroots genuinely wanted to see Martin become the next leader. 'Paul Martin is the most popular politician in the country. He's a tough candidate to beat. That's the reality.'[11]

The reality for the Liberal Party was that the leadership race was quickly becoming a non-event. As one journalist put it, 'The Liberal Party has the Air Canada Centre booked ... They have the forms printed and the rules laid out for the leadership race to begin in February. All they lack is a plausible candidate to run against former finance minister Paul Martin to make a race of it.'[12] Unlike the pattern of many previous leadership races, there were no likely candidates outside the caucus, either from the party's elites or from the public service, business or academe, to step forward and present a challenge. The only two remaining hopefuls set to face Martin both had significant image problems to overcome.

Two Challengers Emerge

Sheila Copps entered the race in March 2003 with her usual upbeat manner and single-minded determination to win. 'I'm in it for the long haul,' she declared when announcing her candidacy. She also stressed that she saw herself as a standard-bearer for the Left. She would attempt to hold Martin accountable for a number of social policy decisions taken during his time in Finance.

Although she was certainly viewed as a social Liberal, Copps's principal challenge would be to shake off her reputation as a fiery orator who lacked substance. Another problem to overcome was her earlier ardent support of Meech Lake, which had alienated some of her natural grassroots constituency. With scant funds, her organization depended primarily on volunteers as opposed to the many paid operatives in the Martin camp. Her small team proved highly professional, though, and ultimately delivered a strong performance far exceeding what their numbers or resources would have suggested. Much of this was due to her key organizers like Joe Thornley, Isabelle Metcalfe, Beatrice Raffoul, and Scott Sheppard. Several other veteran Liberals worked for her in spite of her problematic reputation and slim chance of winning, precisely because she was the only social Liberal candidate in the race and they wanted to make a statement. With a populist appeal designed to recruit new members to the party from ethnic groups as well as the gay and cultural communities, Copps's organizers believed she could attract a large number of new members to the party and make a good showing.

For John Manley the question was not whether he could win but whether he could make a creditable showing. Immediately after Rock's departure, Manley's chief organizers publicly criticized rule changes that had just been adopted in BC at the urging of the national executive. The new regulations allocated one hundred membership forms per riding to a candidate rather than the previous limit of only five forms, even though the maximum number of forms available was one thousand for the entire province, enough for only ten ridings. Both Manley and Copps argued that the changes were still woefully inadequate given that there were thirty-four ridings in the province. Joe Thornley, Copps's campaign manager and a member of the national executive, pointed out that the agreement had been that two hundred forms would be made available for each of the 301 ridings across the country. That this decision was never implemented led many Liberals to criticize the party's president for his failure to take a firm stand. Unhappiness with LeDrew's laissez-faire attitude grew when Alberta and Ontario soon followed suit, adopting the BC model rather than the executive's recommendation.

Within days, Manley was publicly decrying the 'unfair' nature of the new rules. In an interview on CTV's *Question Period*, Manley said he was convinced Martin's own candidacy would be damaged if the rules were not relaxed. 'He's not a stupid politician,' Manley stated. 'I think it would be pretty stupid of his team to shut down democracy in the Liberal Party on the eve of a leadership convention. And I think they're not stupid.' Linking the issue to Martin's policy announcements concerning a parliamentary 'democratic deficit,' Manley continued, 'I believe it's in Paul's interest to see that we have an open process, that it's run properly, in a disinterested fashion. Otherwise, how can he talk about democracy in the course of this campaign?'[13]

Manley's criticism drew an immediate response from Stephen LeDrew. 'I think it's a bit of posturing, quite frankly, and let people posture. But I'm satisfied that candidates can sell memberships.' Although he admitted that the changes introduced after the executive meeting did not go as far as he would have liked, he 'was not prepared to go to war over the issue' at the next meeting.[14] In this, at least, LeDrew was supported by his national policy chair. In an interview with the *Hill Times*, Akaash Maharaj said 'it is my sense that all provinces have adopted eminently reasonable guidelines for the distribution of forms … It simply is that in some cases, they must return some forms before obtaining others. I cannot see how that constitutes a restriction on access to forms. What it does constitute is a restriction on the ability of any one candidate to surreptitiously sign up large numbers of members.'[15]

Manley remained unconvinced. He commented on the one-sided approach to membership sales even after Martin's official campaign launch in early March. As a result of this concern, Manley delayed his official entry into the race until 10 April, when he was assured of sufficient funds and organizational support to mount a national campaign.

Unlike Copps and Martin, Manley had to organize a leadership campaign from scratch. His support came from business Liberals, some of whom viewed him as a highly credible candidate while others admitted they were determined to support a candidate other than Martin. Many of his supporters found it refreshing that Manley had not been involved in the internal warfare of the past few years. Although most of John Turner's former supporters were now working for Paul Martin, some found themselves in Manley's camp. Among his key advisers were former Turner aide Doug Kirkpatrick and former Turner fundraiser Herb Metcalfe, Leo Kolber's one-time assistant. Also on Manley's team were Ian Davey, the son of Senator Keith Davey, and Toronto lawyer Alf Apps, the original young Liberal rebel.

Manley's image problem was the complete opposite of Copps's. Although widely considered a solid candidate, he was viewed by many as simply another business Liberal. He shared the same centre-right space as Paul Martin but was decidedly less attractive to the average voter. Thus Manley's most important challenge was to differentiate himself from the frontrunner, a challenge he tackled with uncharacteristic assertiveness, using media interviews and policy debates as his primary platforms. His target was not Martin's policies, many of which he agreed with. Rather, Manley seized on the fact that Martin continued to withhold the sources and magnitude of his campaign funding.

As he later stressed, Manley viewed this issue as a crucial one for the party. In the first of the party's debates, held in Edmonton, Manley took on Martin directly. 'There are three of us on this stage who have raised money while in a ministry. Two of us have declared these sources,' he said. In an interview following the debate he called for full and open disclosure of all candidates' accounts. Martin retorted that he had complied with the party's guidelines (in revealing the $2.6 million raised since July 2002) and was not obliged to follow those of Chrétien. At issue, once again, were the funds accumulated in the blind trust created in 1998 as 'Project 2000.' By the party's rules, the total amount and contributors would not be revealed until thirty days before the leadership convention. Manley did not accept Martin's explanation, however, stressing that the origin of the funds, suspected to be largely from corporate Canada and the oil patch in Calgary, could have a significant impact on the thinking of the former Liberal finance minister and might well influence convention delegates.

Manley's strategy was not successful with many senior Liberals or even within his own camp. By late May 2003 both Alf Apps and Ian Davey had resigned from Manley's campaign, soon to be followed by Alex Sheppard, one of his few caucus supporters, in early June (Sheppard would go on to support Martin). Countering rumours that Manley would withdraw from the race itself, key organizer Doug Kirkpatrick paid the final instalment of the $75,000 registration fee to the party.

A day later, Allan Rock unexpectedly abandoned his position as a neutral observer and declared his support for Paul Martin. Initially unfazed, by the end of June Manley was heard to comment that he would be pleased to serve as foreign affairs minister in a Martin-led government. Informed by reporters that some Martin advisers were saying there was no place for him in a Martin cabinet after his personal attacks, Manley replied that conciliation was the traditional Liberal approach and he believed it would continue. If the situation were reversed, he assured reporters, he would naturally include Martin in his cabinet. 'It's important to heal the party after a spirited race,' he declared.[16] (At the same time, as several Martin advisers later stressed, Copps's focus on policy rather than personal attacks during the race had pleasantly surprised them, and most observers believed she had secured a place for herself in a future Martin cabinet by virtue of her restraint.)

Not long after, John Manley admitted defeat. Many of his remaining supporters were stunned when he withdrew from the race on 22 July 2003 stating that he believed he could not win. The recently concluded leadership debates had not provided the surge in interest for his campaign, or for the party, that he had hoped. Although this was undoubtedly true for Sheila Copps as well, she answered reporters' questions about her own plans defiantly. 'I'm in this race to the end,' she declared. 'You can take that to the bank.'[17]

Once Manley pulled out of the race the Martin camp saw many of their worst fears materialize. As one senior adviser later confided, they believed the media would not treat the event seriously with only Sheila Copps in the race. This was especially true since Copps's position on many issues was the same as Jean Chrétien's. As a result, Martin would actually be forced to run against Chrétien until November, effectively becoming an unofficial opposition to the government. They feared the increasingly obvious differences of opinion between Martin and Chrétien would wound him further for the election which they hoped to fight shortly afterwards. 'Our honeymoon was the leadership race,' Tim Murphy said, and 'we didn't even have all of that.'[18]

The Formidable Martin Organization

Paul Martin once remarked that he had not really understood the nature of a leadership campaign in 1990. 'In 1990 we were clearly the underdog,' he said. 'I had no idea just how important Jean Chrétien's organization was. It was overwhelming. I may have had far better people than he did, but he had a much better organization.'[19] That statement explains much of what happened during the 2003 leadership race, a race Martin and his advisers were determined to win at all costs. At age 64, Martin had no time left to lose.

What Allan Rock referred to as 'the Martin steamroller' was unprecedented in the history of the party and, without doubt, in the history of any Canadian political party. The sheer size of Martin's organization and the massive amounts of money raised to maintain it began to resemble an American leadership campaign rather than a Canadian one. His support within the party was also unprecedented. When he filed his nomination papers on 6 March 2003, Martin had the backing of more than 100 MPs as well as 259 of the 301 riding presidents, all provincial presidents, the presidents of the Young Liberals, and all members of the national women's commission.[20]

Martin's key personnel, both paid and voluntary, were largely holdovers from the 1990 campaign, forming a close-knit network of friends and advisers that had never really been dismantled. Many were former Turner supporters. Almost as many came originally from western Canada or rural Ontario, a reality which would take on increasing importance. Members of his inner circle – known as 'the Board' – included John Webster and David Herle, Terrie O'Leary, Mike Robinson, Michelle Cadario, Tim Murphy, Ruth Thorkelson, and Richard Mahoney, all of whom handled various aspects of the national campaign, while Karl Littler intensified efforts in Ontario. Newer arrivals included Mark Marissen, who was responsible for BC, John Bethel as the Alberta chair, and former Turner chief of staff Doug Richardson, who organized Saskatchewan. Pietro Perrino again assumed a lead role in Quebec, assisted by former MP Denis Dawson. Scott Reid, Brian Guest, Mike Robinson, and his Earnscliffe partner, former CBC reporter Elly Alboim, handled various aspects of communications. Another former westerner, Kevin Bosch, was in charge of policy at the national headquarters. Some estimates placed the total number of paid staff at more than twenty-five as early as December 2002. By the end of the campaign, most observers placed the number at more than two hundred.

There were so many dedicated volunteer workers at the grassroots level that keeping them occupied became a major task. As national campaign director Michelle Cadario later said, 'Part of the challenge was that we had so much support. We felt we had to utilize it all and make everybody feel involved.' Cadario herself had been national director of the leadership campaign since March 1999. 'After Paul was fired,' she said, 'the organization changed a lot. We ramped up the activities for him. There was even more work done with Liberals now that the Finance responsibility was gone.' In short order a national office was opened in Ottawa and regional offices were set up across the country. Cadario organized the membership sales activities and a training exercise for the workers handling these sales. 'This was key. Under the new rules, with proportional representation, we had to win big, and in all the right places.' In response to these new rules, Cadario established a riding captain model for each of the ridings as well as the roughly seventy student clubs, eighty-five women's clubs, and the various Aboriginal meetings.[21]

Another important task was encouraging Liberals who were Martin supporters to run as candidates in the next election. Ruth Thorkelson pointed out that the party held virtually every seat in Ontario. 'It was a real dilemma. When you hold all the seats you can't bring in any new blood without allowing people to challenge sitting members. And some of them had been there for a very long time.'[22] Martin's opponents, however, saw this as a form of bribery. Support for the frontrunner in the leadership race would be exchanged for support for a candidate in a future nomination battle, usually against a sitting MP who was pro-Chrétien. One MP scornfully remarked that 'there are two or three future Martin MPs in every Toronto riding and more prospective Senators than Ontario has seats.'[23]

All of this activity required a coordinated approach and numerous volunteers. Susan Delacourt highlighted this aspect of Martin's leadership drive, noting that 'the sheer size of Martin's organization was most evident when he travelled. He had an official "Tour Operation" headed up by another staffer at Earnscliffe, Charles Bird ... whose job was to manage all the logistics.'[24] Bird was assisted by Jim Pimblett, who travelled everywhere with Martin as his personal assistant, and by a vast network of local organizers. Over the course of the campaign this abundance of resources became a problem. As one Manley adviser said, 'you'd think this was a leader's tour. We fought elections with less support than this.' At the various policy debates organized by the party, Martin's huge entourage was a source of discussion and no small amount of aggravation for the other candidates and their workers. 'In Edmonton, they had a fleet of SUVs ready to take him from the hotel to the conference centre just across the street. In Charlottetown, they had an "advance man" check out the restaurants and book all the best ones a week before the debate,' a disgruntled Copps adviser complained. 'It seemed like "in your face" arrogance to most of us. They all stuck together, never socialized. Some of his people wouldn't even ride in the elevators with us. It was like no other leadership race I'd ever seen.'

Not surprisingly, this massive organization required significant amounts of capital. This was particularly the case since Martin employed a large number of his workers. As Michelle Cadario recounted, the decision to retain the dozen political staff from his ministerial office was based partly on loyalty, but also on the practical need for Martin to continue to appear as prepared as he had been in office. Cadario also noted that, while the party's official spending limit was $4 million, this restriction did not kick in until the official launch of the race in February 2003. Much of the $10 million they eventually raised was spent between May 2002 and the official start of campaigning. Several Martin organizers took pains to dispel the widely held view that Martin's fundraising activities crowded out potential revenue for the party. Stressing Martin's major contribution to the party's finances through his many fundraising efforts while a minister, Cadario pointed out that 'the remaining balance of $3.8 million from our leadership fund was donated to the party to pay down the more than $4 million in debt. We donated our computers and other hardware, and worked hard with the executive to minimize convention costs.'[25]

Another unusual feature of this race was the exclusion of travel and polling expenses from the $4 million spending cap established by the party. Party officials later explained they felt the travel exemption was necessary to level the playing field in the event that any non-cabinet ministers entered the race. Since Martin was the only non-cabinet contender, he clearly benefited most from this situation. No explanation was given for the polling exemption, which created another unfortunate impression of bias and again prompted the other camps to speculate that it was introduced for Martin's benefit.

The final disclosure of donations was made on 15 October as required by the party. Canadians learned that Paul Martin's fundraising campaign raised an astonishing $10.2 million compared with $891,000 for Sheila Copps. The contributors to Martin's blind trust were also finally revealed. They included $100,000 contributions from major accounting firms KPMG and PricewaterhouseCoopers, as well as $100,000 from Newfoundland Capital Corp. owner Harry Steele and $250,000 from Gerry Schwartz of Onex Corp. While questions were raised about potential conflicts of interest in light of such large donations, federal Ethics Commissioner Howard Wilson declared that once donations were made public it was no longer a problem.

To the dismay of many grassroots Liberals, the most important re-sult of this relentless focus on the sources of candidate funding and membership forms was an almost complete lack of attention paid to the policy process. Although a series of candidates' debates were held in advance of the November convention, the way in which these debates were organized and conducted left little doubt that money and organi-zation, not policies, were the driving force behind the Liberal Party's leadership race.

Policy Renewal Denied?

After ten years in power, many Liberals felt that whoever succeeded Jean Chrétien would have to present a coherent new vision for the fu-ture. A change in leadership was a golden opportunity for candidates to outline their visions for moving the party forward. A leadership tran-sition was also a time for grassroots Liberals to make their voices heard, and for the party to consider much-needed reforms. Despite all of this potential, however, little time and effort was spent on policy debate in 2003.

Looking to fill the void created by the cancelled review convention or at least to establish some of the parameters of the future debate, former Trudeau adviser Tom Axworthy began organizing an intimate gather-ing of senior Liberal thinkers. The by-invitation-only event, held in To-ronto, became the hottest ticket in the Liberal universe. Some eighteen formal papers were presented by well-known Liberal policy experts and commentary was provided by twelve 'independent' experts from business and academe. A small number of former and current members of the party elite were invited to attend as participants. In an effort to appear neutral, leadership candidates were not invited. Axworthy had hoped the event – to be held only days before the final Chrétien Throne Speech – would be seen as an impartial 'thinkers conference.' Perhaps it might even provide new insights and policy directions in time for Chrétien to adopt some as part of his 'legacy agenda.'

The 'Searching for the New Liberalism' conference took place at the University of Toronto on 27–9 September 2002. Media coverage was extensive. Advance reports described it as a 'high-powered intellectual summit' and a 'meeting of political heavyweights,' a 'response to critics who accuse the Liberals of lacking direction.'[26] Combining an eclectic mix of the old guard and the new, the event was widely discussed in Liberal circles. An edited collection of the papers was eventually published and soon sold out.[27] Not everyone was supportive of the event, however, and some critics accused Axworthy of elitism. 'Just before the PM unleashes a repackaging of old ideas ... Tom Axworthy and Co. will be launching the quest for meaningful new policy visions that will have greater relevance in the new century,' one senior Martin strategist snorted.[28]

Potential leadership contenders more or less ignored Axworthy's attempt to exclude them. Allan Rock and John Manley sent senior staff as observers. Sheila Copps attended one of the evening receptions. Paul Martin arrived Sunday morning and attended much of the discussion during the day. The surprise media star of the event was former Pearson adviser Tom Kent. Asked to address the topic 'Can the System Be Moved?' Kent argued that it could, but only if certain measures were taken, foremost among them being the introduction of legislation on the financing of political parties. Kent reminded attendees that Pearson's leadership campaign in 1958 had cost $3,000 while the Ontario Liberal leadership race earlier in 2002 had cost $3 million and the upcoming federal race could easily top $10 million. 'The Liberal Party is now a dependency of corporate finance,' Kent declared. He reminded the audience that Lloyd Axworthy could not run in the 1990 leadership race 'as I know many would have liked – because he could not raise the seven-figure amount needed to be even in the running. He was not popular with big business.' Arguing that reform of political financing was now crucial for party and government credibility, he concluded with a strong declaration of support for Jean Chrétien's proposed new legislation, expected to be announced in the Throne Speech the following week. No doubt the keynote left a sour taste in the mouths of many Martin supporters.

While Kent's support may have strengthened Jean Chrétien's resolve to persevere with his election financing legislation, the Axworthy conference had little or no impact on the party. When the announcement of the November 2003 convention date was made, many expected that the party would also schedule a series of candidates' debates similar to those held in 1990. This possibility, however, was not mentioned. With no declared candidates by the end of 2002, and even less willingness on the part of Paul Martin to challenge the government or launch new policy ideas in advance of the next election, the leadership race seemed to be drifting aimlessly.

There were a number of calls for more policy debate within the party, but outside of the leadership race. In theory, this would allow the grassroots membership to give direction to the new leader, whoever that might be. National columnist Jim Travers predicted that, as the leadership frontrunner, 'Paul Martin will only offer as many reforms and make as many promises as are necessary to distance himself from Jean Chrétien.' Travers made a persuasive case in favour of a second Aylmer conference, modelled on the one that allowed Jean Chrétien to establish a policy base. Referring to the party's ability to re-invent itself in opposition, Travers argued that the need was even more pressing after a decade in power. 'With an elusive fourth straight majority at stake,' he observed, 'it is incumbent on Liberals and on Martin to demonstrate that … they will know what to do if they again catch the bus. It is time to go back to Aylmer to find new ideas.'[29] His support for policy debate within the party, if not always his preference for the Aylmer model, was shared by others. Party president Stephen LeDrew, for one, put forward the idea of a second Kingston conference based on the Pearson-Kent model.

One prominent Liberal calling for policy discussion *within* the leadership race was heritage minister and potential candidate Sheila Copps. Copps had participated in the 1990 leadership race and knew that the series of six policy debates organized during that contest had been thought of as a template for future contests. She was 'amazed' that they had not been automatically factored into the leadership race this time around. On at least two occasions before officially launching her campaign, Copps publicly urged the party to organize such events, stressing that 'open debate is necessary for a party that aspires to continue to form the government.' For his part, Stephen LeDrew later stated that 'there was never any doubt there would be candidates' debates. But, after the huge fight within the executive over the convention date, I saw no need to rush into this.'[30] With the race officially underway in February 2003, LeDrew noted, there was plenty of time for the executive to meet again and finalize a series of times and venues for the debates.

Martin's Policy Dilemma

Long before the official leadership race began, Paul Martin had identified two specific policy areas in which he was prepared to outline proposals, or at least concerns: his 'cities agenda' and the so-called 'democratic deficit.' He had addressed the first issue in some detail in the Toronto speech which had led to his departure from cabinet. By contrast, his views on the democratic deficit were a mystery. Caucus supporters such as Tony Ianno had been speaking for some time about the issue, but Martin had done little more than express his concern and agree that parliamentary reform of some type was needed. Again he was torn between the frontrunner's natural tendency to say as little as possible, and the growing need to reassure his own supporters – especially in the caucus – that he had not forgotten their concerns. For them, the 'democratic deficit' was more than a theory. Its appeal was personal. For Martin and his advisers, it also was considered as safe a topic as possible for someone who did not want to be seen criticizing the government.

In this respect, Martin faced two problems not encountered by his opponents. First, he was no longer in the cabinet and was technically free to speak out on issues where he disagreed with the Chrétien administration. Reporters, therefore, could pursue him much more aggressively than they could Manley or Copps. Yet Martin strongly believed he should not engage in criticism. As a lifelong Liberal, he knew only too well how such behaviour would be seen by other members of the party and possibly by Canadians. 'I take a position and immediately it becomes a wedge issue,' he complained. 'I don't want to hurt the government, so why would I create a wedge issue?' When Martin supporter Joe Volpe speculated the governor general might ask Martin to form a government rather than allowing Jean Chrétien to call a snap election, Martin felt he had no choice but to discipline Volpe. Responding to reporters' questions, Martin categorically rejected the idea. 'That's just not going to happen,' he stated.[31]

The second difficulty facing Paul Martin was more fundamental. His genuine policy differences with Chrétien were far greater than almost anyone except those who spent time with him in cabinet apparently realized. This ignorance was particularly surprising in the case of the national media. Certainly there was ample evidence of these conflicting views ever since the Liberals returned to power in 1993. The reality was that on both the left-right axis *and* the federalism axis, Chrétien and Martin had important areas of disagreement. At one point early in the campaign Martin acknowledged this situation himself. 'I obviously have a wide range of areas in which I don't agree with the government,' he stated with uncharacteristic bluntness. He quickly returned to the theme of party loyalty, concluding, 'I don't think it's in the country's interest that I be out there for a year and a half as an alternative government.'[32] Still, the media continued to paint Martin as simply an ambitious man, a victim of hubris driven to seek the leadership his father never achieved.

Martin laid out his thoughts on the subject of the democratic deficit in a speech at Osgoode Hall on 21 October. He began by stating that 'this is no time for decision-makers or for decision-making to be isolated from the reach of the public ... what we must do is to strengthen the engagement of Canadians as we focus on the choices going forward.' He suggested that the growing apathy of citizens towards politics was caused in large measure by a dysfunctional, adversarial parliamentary system in which 'the authority of the individual Member of Parliament has been eroded while the power of the executive has grown.'[33] He offered six specific remedies for this perceived problem: decreased party discipline; greater use of legislative referral after first reading; enhanced priority for private members' bills; the selection of committee members by caucus executives rather than party leaders, and the election of chairs by committee members, rather than appointment by the leader; review of major governor-in-council appointments by a parliamentary committee; and, finally, the appointment of an independent ethics commissioner reporting to Parliament rather than to the prime minister.

Martin anticipated problems if his ideas were implemented, but surely did not anticipate how quickly they would surface. In a masterful display of House procedural tactics, the Alliance Party forced a vote on the issue of the election of committee chairs, knowing this would cause dissension in the Liberal ranks. Martin supporters in caucus were in favour of the motion, as was Martin himself. Yet Chrétien was still in charge, and publicly opposed to the idea. In caucus the PM predicted that such elections would cause endless problems for his successor. 'We don't want to be like the United States,' Chrétien warned. 'There the members have to defend themselves against every interest group. They can't say they have no choice because it's their party's position. They're on their own.'

When caucus chair Stan Keyes called an emergency meeting of the caucus to debate the issue, the problem escalated into a major public relations disaster. In the end, Chrétien allowed a free vote on the motion for his backbenchers, but not the cabinet. The result was almost inevitable. The Alliance motion passed by a margin of 174 to 87, with 57 Liberal MPs, including Paul Martin, voting with the opposition in favour of the motion. The former finance minister's discomfiture was plain for all to see, as was the fury of some of his colleagues who supported Chrétien. 'He played right into the Alliance's hand,' fumed Charles Caccia.

'We needed that kind of negative publicity like a hole in the head. Even if I had agreed with the motion, which I didn't, I would not have given the Alliance the satisfaction.'[34]

The remainder of 2002 saw more such incidents, and it was clear that the media's appetite for controversy within the Liberal Party had not declined. Commenting on the issue of party dissension directly, Martin insisted that 'candidates for the leadership have got to be free to express their views on where they would take the country … In the coming months, all of us as Liberals are going to be confronted with this challenge: how do you champion new ideas without damaging the integrity of the government?'[35]

Behind the scenes a huge team of volunteers, led by Ottawa lobbyist Mark Resnick, laboured to produce proposals for Martin's consideration. According to Resnick, there were twenty-two separate policy roundtables, at one time involving more than 300 individual experts. In addition, John Duffy was asked by David Herle to work on policy speeches in four broad target areas: health care, lifelong learning, the democratic deficit, and cities.[36] Duffy, who had written Martin's convention speech in 1990 and assisted him with the editing of the Red Book in 1993, had since worked as a consultant in Toronto and was instrumental in helping the Mike Harris government roll out their Common Sense Revolution.

Herle's four focus areas kept expanding as the policy groups reported their conclusions on internal campaign websites. Resnick recounted how Martin often went online and engaged in vigorous debate with group members. As Tim Murphy later stressed, 'one of Paul Martin's massive strengths is his ability to accommodate new views. In a veteran politician, this ability is unheard of … Paul is simply phenomenal.'[37] But not everyone was as enthusiastic about Martin's interest in all aspects of policy. Asked later about the 2003 policy assignment, Duffy diplomatically described it as 'not for the faint of heart.'[38] A former cabinet colleague of Martin's went further: 'Paul loves talking about policy. He never met an idea he didn't like. But he hates to choose among them. Instead he wants to have endless committee discussions. Try to pin him down and he'll say "Some people say this, some people say that, let's strike a working group to look into it in more detail."'

Despite all of these efforts, Martin did not outline any new policy ideas when he officially entered the leadership race on 6 March 2003. His supporters said he was sticking to the game plan outlined by the Board, keeping his powder dry for the election. Tim Murphy confirmed this: 'Throughout the leadership campaign we had our eye on the long haul. We wanted the flexibility to think about the electorate, not just the Liberal Party. Of course, knowing we would win helped.'[39]

The formal campaign launch on 27 April produced more of the same. In a ninety-minute town hall meeting organized by his staff, Martin read a prepared text in which he pledged to correct a 'drift' in government. 'In recent times a kind of complacency – a certain amount of drift has set in,' he told the assembled group. 'We've lost some of the energy and enthusiasm that Canadians are looking for.' This implicit criticism of the Chrétien regime was not followed by any specific new proposals. Instead Martin made what was rapidly becoming a standard statement of intent. 'I want to lead a new government with a renewed sense of purpose,' he declared, 'with a sharper focus and a clearer plan – a government unafraid to change and eager to turn the page and look to the future.'[40]

The day after Martin entered the race, an editorial appeared which was highly critical of this strategy. Pointing out that 'his opponents have complained for months that Martin has been trying to avoid the media spotlight and the possibility that he might trip on some political landmine,' the editorial warned that 'in the weeks to come, Martin will be asked to spell out in much more detail his vision of Canada in a dramatically changed world.' The article went on to describe Sheila Copps as 'a tough opponent for Martin. She's a no-holds-barred street-fighter.'[41] Indeed, the debates were on.

Leadership Debate Tactics

On 16 April 2003, Stephen LeDrew confirmed that six candidates' debates would be held across the country in May and early June. Superficially, at least, the party embraced the concept wholeheartedly. 'These policy sessions and the ensuing debates between the Leadership Candidates are absolutely crucial to the renewal now underway within the Liberal Party,' LeDrew said, 'and will bring clarity to the issues that are being discussed among Canadians today.'[42]

But in a precursor of things to come, the timing of the debates immediately became an issue. While the Martin team wanted them as early as possible, his rivals preferred dates closer to the convention in the fall. Ruth Thorkelson, Martin's negotiator for the debates, later stated she was 'never enthusiastic' about the debates, seeing them as 'one more complication' on the road to the ultimate goal of winning a federal election.[43] Party officials stressed that the most logical option was to hold all of the debates before the cut-off date for memberships in late June since under the new rules the delegates selected by the membership in September would have to commit to a candidate at that time.

At first glance the structure of the debates appeared to be closely patterned on the 1990 format. However, as representatives from the Copps and Manley camps soon discovered, there were several ways in which these events would differ significantly from the earlier ones. To begin with, major centres such as Toronto, Calgary, Winnipeg, and Montreal were conspicuously absent from the line-up. Instead, the debates were slated to take place in Edmonton, Whitehorse, Charlottetown, Vancouver, Ottawa, and Laval. Martin's opponents felt this was not just politically unwise but a deliberate attempt to limit the impact of the events. They argued that many more Liberals would attend in person in larger urban centres. There would also be much better media coverage and access. Moreover, the party's decision to schedule them for early Saturday afternoon meant attendance and live media coverage would be even lower. As Copps's campaign chair Joe Thornley later commented, 'It was hard to see how they could have made them any less attractive as events. When I saw the list of venues I knew right away it was going to be an uphill battle to get the media and the public to pay attention.'[44] Party officials were, of course, quick to defend their choice of venues, citing regional representation and other factors.

The national executive selected Bobbi Ethier, the Manitoba party president, and Marcel Proulx, a Quebec MP, as co-chairs for the convention along with president Stephen LeDrew. When it came to selecting an appropriately neutral moderator, all of the leadership camps were involved, finally deciding on Senator Serge Joyal, whose handling of the debates was widely praised afterwards. Other aspects of the events were negotiated by the candidates' representatives in meetings with Gordon Ashworth, who had been hired by the national executive to run the entire leadership process. Ashworth, the former national party director and Chrétien campaign director, consulted with policy chair Akaash Maharaj and, on occasion, with Stephen LeDrew. While negotiations on logistics had taken place in 1990 as well, the extent to which Martin's representatives concerned themselves with the technical details was something none of the other participants had seen before. Nevertheless, they went along in a spirit of cooperation, and agreement was reached among the principals – Martin's chief representative Ruth Thorkelson, Joe Thornley for the Copps campaign, and Doug Kirkpatrick representing the Manley camp – on all the issues raised.

Unfortunately much of the civility disappeared the day before the first debate when organizers from the Copps and Manley camps arrived in Edmonton to find that the actual arrangements bore little resemblance to what they had agreed upon. Party officials did not deny this was the case but insisted it was out of their hands given that implementation of the arrangements was the responsibility of the local and provincial party executives at each venue. One of the most controversial changes came to symbolize what Martin's opponents viewed as a bad faith scenario. 'Having spent hours on the placement and height of the podiums in our discussions in Ottawa,' one adviser fumed, 'we arrived in Edmonton only to find there were three TABLES, not podiums, on the stage, and the candidates were expected to sit behind them like schoolchildren. It was just crazy,' Doug Kirkpatrick recalled.[45] Local party organizers claimed the reason for the last-minute change was a practical one – they simply could not find three identical podiums in the city that weekend – an explanation scoffed at by the two candidates who threatened to withdraw their participation.

In the end they decided to proceed, but saw such changes as proof that provincial executives were supporting Martin for the leadership. 'It was just the Martin people doing what they had wanted to do all along,' one adviser declared. 'They didn't want their man standing for so long, they didn't want him too close to the other two candidates in case he might appear threatened, and they wanted him to have plenty of room for his piles of papers without them being seen or getting mixed up.' Copps's advisers saw another particular disadvantage for their candidate in the arrangement. 'Isn't it just typical that no one thought about the fact Sheila would be wearing a skirt,' Isabelle Metcalfe noted at the Vancouver event.

As the number of changes from the original agreement mounted, the feelings of hostility among the participants grew as well. One individual caught in the crossfire was the party's national policy chair. Akaash Maharaj had publicly supported the debates and taken some of the credit for their organization. As Sheila Copps later recounted in her autobiography, her perception of bias on Maharaj's part appeared to be confirmed when he spoke with her late in the race, after the last-minute announcement by London lawyer Mike Eizenga that he would be running for party president. Eizenga had the support of many of Paul Martin's workers, although senior advisers such as David Herle insisted that Martin himself was taking no position on the race. 'Akaash was crushed,' Copps wrote. 'He told me that he even considered quitting the party, so discouraged was he by his own shortsightedness and by the fact that he had been duped.'[46]

The debates also differed significantly in policy terms from the 1990 series. Instead of segments devoted to economic, social, and foreign policy at each venue, the 2003 debates focused on only one policy topic per venue – economic policy in Edmonton, social policy in Charlottetown, and foreign policy in Vancouver. Here, again, lack of confidence in party organizers led both the Manley and Copps camps to question the format. They noted that Edmonton, as the first and most accessible venue, would likely receive the most media coverage. Coincidentally, it was the venue chosen for the issue most closely identified with Martin's policy strength, while the environment, a specialty of Sheila Copps who had served as minister of the environment, was scheduled for Whitehorse.

In addition, there would be a series of locally derived questions coming out of workshops held the morning of the debates. There had been a small regional component to the 1990 format, but nothing this extensive. Sheila Copps complained, 'We actually spent more time ... debating Placer mining than we did missile defence. Health care was accorded a total of three minutes per candidate.'[47]

Conversely, the level of policy direction and information provided to the grassroots was much less in 2003. In 1990, the Liberal Research Bureau director had served as secretary general, reporting to the co-chairs. Documents prepared by Bureau researchers were compiled and published as a policy primer for delegates to review in advance, providing background information and FAQs on current issues to guide the discussion. In the absence of any LCRB participation in 2003, delegates received no such policy assistance.

The regional questions were supposedly provided only an hour in advance to the three camps. Concerns came to a head in Charlottetown when a question on an obscure local matter flummoxed the policy advisers for both Copps and Manley. Yet Paul Martin easily responded to the question during the debate, appearing to read from a lengthy prepared text. Perhaps not surprisingly, given the pre-existing level of mistrust, this led many in the opposing camps to question yet again the impartiality of the party organization.

The Uneventful Leadership Debates

Despite the range of topics covered, nothing particularly new came out of the debates. As several journalists reported, the three candidates agreed with each other much of the time. Martin agreed with Copps on a number of occasions. In fact, as the debates progressed it appeared that Martin became more comfortable with Copps than Manley. Assuming that the heritage minister would live up to her reputation for aggressive behaviour, Martin strategist Tim Murphy told Joe Thornley they were all 'shocked' that 'Sheila is taking the high road' and 'actually wants to discuss policy.'[48]

Apart from John Manley's focus on the fundraising issue, little controversy emerged either. When it did, it was often not reported. In both Vancouver and Charlottetown, for example, Copps raised the issue of Martin's conversion of the three social program transfers into the CHST. Echoing Allan Rock, she described what she and many others viewed as the negative consequences. Citing several studies by voluntary groups such as the National Council on Welfare and the government's own Human Resources Department website, she criticized Martin's prized Child Tax Benefit as an overrated program that had failed to provide expected benefits to the poorest of the poor. 'We can't simply write cheques to the provinces and assume the job is done,' she argued.[49] Martin, clearly taken aback, seemed genuinely shocked by the accusations and unfamiliar with the studies cited. Yet no media reports of the exchanges focused on this substantive issue.

Similarly, little media coverage was devoted to formal policy statements released by Copps and Manley. The Copps campaign issued lengthy press releases, some quite innovative, before each event but received almost no attention from the media. 'It's frustrating,' she told reporters, arguing that her views were being discounted because 'senior Liberals have written off my chances ... We need to have this friendly debate within the party,' she warned presciently, 'because it will take on a whole other tone when we start debating other parties in an election campaign.'[50]

Instead, Martin's opening remarks at each debate reflected the caution of the frontrunner. He referred to the need for change in vague terms and expressed optimism about the future of the country. An indication of the seriousness with which the Martin team approached the debates was the effort devoted to such innocuous statements. Asked on the flight to Edmonton what he was working on, a senior Martin scribe replied, 'the twenty-first draft of the opening remarks.'

There were, of course, unscripted events, but nothing like the Meech Lake protests that had marred the Montreal debate in 1990. The only criticism Paul Martin received came from interest groups rather than party members. Some demonstrators were unhappy with his defence of free trade and his cutbacks to social programs. The most controversial issues for Martin were the same-sex marriage legislation and the proposed American missile defence initiative (MDI). Both Copps and Manley were on record as supporting the former, which placed Martin in a difficult situation since he had tried hard to avoid making a definitive statement on the issue. Copps, meanwhile, attempted with some success to place the MDI on the agenda at every debate. As a strong opponent of the plan, she wanted to force Martin to commit himself one way or the other, an effort that proved impossible.

One of the few occasions in which Martin deviated from his text was in an exchange in Charlottetown. Both Martin and Manley tried to curry favour with east coast fishermen during that debate. Manley suggested giving provincial governments a role in fisheries management, an idea that was promptly dismissed by federal fisheries minister Robert Thibault because it would 'lead to chaos and paralysis on Canada's coasts.' Not to be outdone, Paul Martin vowed to extend the 200-mile limit to protect east coast fish stocks from overfishing by foreign trawlers. 'For too long we've asked our fishermen to bear the burden while allowing foreigners to get away with sheer irresponsibility and murder,' he said. 'I will not stand by ... while a weak-kneed multilateral organization fails to live up to its obligations.' Although he supported Martin, Thibault insisted that the candidate's idea would 'breach international law and cause a confrontation on the high seas.' Urging continued diplomatic action, he pointed out that Martin's approach would anger Canada's European Union trading partners and was legally impossible.[51] There were no further unscripted statements from Martin, and little interest in the remaining debates. One journalist concluded: 'Copps and Manley tried to probe, to challenge the king ... but they were frustrated at every turn, utterly sidelined, if not silenced, by the courtly party protocols surrounding this alleged leadership race.'[52]

Sheila Copps's Red Book

Undoubtedly the most significant policy initiative to come out of the 2003 Liberal leadership race was Sheila Copps's Red Book. Entitled 'Foundations: An Action Plan for Canadians,' the twenty-page document was released at a press conference in Ottawa on 28 July, four weeks after the last debate. In the introduction, Copps wrote: 'My campaign for the leadership of the Liberal Party is about ideas and idealism.' In a veiled reference to Paul Martin's business Liberal philosophy, she declared: 'I believe Canadians want a leader who will build on the legacies of Laurier, Pearson, Trudeau, and Chrétien.'[53] The text outlined more than seventy proposals in the areas of economic, social, and foreign policy, sustainable development, human rights, and cultural identity. One national columnist, clearly impressed by the document, wrote: 'Copps has done her homework ... Regardless of whether one agrees with her critique of Mr. Martin or with her proposed policies, she has cogent arguments behind them and the numbers to back them up.'[54]

Several newspaper articles acknowledged the lack of real policy debate in the party, and one well-known columnist suggested, 'Maybe, just maybe, there will now be a debate on policy directions before Paul Martin becomes prime minister.' Describing Copps's launch of the document as 'throwing down a progressive centre-left gauntlet in what is now a much clearer duel for the soul of the Liberal party with the centre-right,' veteran journalist Graham Fraser concluded: 'While no one should expect the document will put Copps any closer to 24 Sussex, it should at least provoke some discussion about what it means to be a Liberal in 2003.'[55]

Fraser's views were echoed by Susan Delacourt, who noted that Martin had been instrumental in the highly successful Red Book of 1993. But now, ten years later, 'it was left to Sheila Copps, his last remaining rival in the race, to issue the only platform in this long, somewhat strange leadership race.' Delacourt highlighted the party's apparent lack of interest in policy debate: 'If Copps hadn't released her own platform, would anyone have noticed that Martin was marching to almost-certain victory with no Red Book in hand?'[56]

Strategists in the Martin camp were quick to respond to Copps's initiative by criticizing the cost of her proposals. Ignoring the substance of the various policy initiatives, they argued instead that her 'tax and spend' approach would put the federal government back in a deficit position. Copps replied that she had used figures from the Finance Department itself, as well as predictions by Don Drummond, Martin's former deputy minister at Finance who was now chief economist of the Toronto-Dominion Bank. With the media watching, the two sides continued to trade parries and thrusts on this issue.

Martin's Western Strategy

After the debates Martin was preoccupied with a different matter. According to aides, rather than discussing policy, Martin was focused entirely on improving the party's standing in western Canada. Like John

Turner, Martin was convinced the Liberals should and could attract votes and win seats in the west by simply paying greater attention to the region. Jean Chrétien's 2000 election pledge to spend more time in the west, although a step in the right direction, had not – at least in Martin's view – been backed by any real commitment to act. After all, even as he set up a special caucus committee on western issues, Chrétien also warned that 'the federal government would create a self-fulfilling prophecy' if it acknowledged that western 'alienation' existed, or that westerners 'had a unique sense of grievance.'[57]

Martin's conviction was shared by the many key advisers on his leadership team who hailed from western Canada, including David Herle, Mike Robinson, Ruth Thorkelson, and Kevin Bosch. It was also shared by Ralph Goodale, the former Saskatchewan Liberal leader who had served for years in Jean Chrétien's cabinet and was a staunch Martin supporter. 'Paul believes western alienation is real and needs to be taken seriously,' Goodale said during the leadership race.[58]

There was evidence that much of the 'alienation' of western Canadians was based on the perception that their concerns were passed over in favour of the more delicate situation in Quebec.[59] The question for Martin and his team was how best to address the problem. One obvious way was for Martin himself to be more visible in the west. As Goodale stressed, 'The point is there has to be a presence, a personal presence, by the prime minister in a very regular way in Western Canada.'[60] As a result, much of Martin's time between June and the November convention was spent speaking to Liberals in western Canada, and media coverage became increasingly positive, leading Martin and his supporters to believe a real breakthrough was possible in the next election.

Much of the Martin team's enthusiasm for their electoral chances in the region stemmed from their success in selling memberships there. The party's BC wing alone increased its membership from 4,000 in 2002 to 37,500 by the June cutoff in 2003, as Mark Marissen was quick to note in an interview with the author. As Martin spokesperson Scott Reid put it, 'We like to believe the prospect of a Paul-Martin-led Liberal Party is attractive and has intrigued westerners.' But Reid also correctly noted that 'the challenge ... is to translate the increased interest they are showing for the first time in a long time into a deeper participation and ultimately success in the polls.'[61] Despite the membership gains, the total western membership – at roughly 76,000 – remained less than 15 per cent of the more than 500,000 nationwide Liberal members. And, as more than one expert observer pointed out, party memberships did not necessarily translate into increased popular support during elections.

Martin's efforts to translate renewed interest in the party into electoral support were hampered by his reluctance to provide concrete remedies. Although he declared himself favourable to Senate reform in theory, he would not endorse the proposal of a recent Canada West Foundation report, arguing it would lead to 'piecemeal' and 'token' reform. This position sounded much like the one taken by Jean Chrétien. Martin did, however, commit himself to delaying a federal election call until after the implementation of electoral boundary redistribution in 2004. That pledge, which would result in an increase in the number of Alberta and BC seats, was prompted by a challenge from Alliance leader Stephen Harper, who expected *his* party would benefit.

Most of Martin's commitments were more vague and fell victim to differing interpretations by supporters. More 'clout' for backbench MPs and greater federal-provincial cooperation were publicly touted by some of his caucus supporters to mean agreement with whatever their views were. The promise of an increased presence of the prime minister in western Canada, meanwhile, led to a number of bizarre suggestions, not the least of which was the idea that there would be a permanent 'western satellite PMO' probably located in Calgary. Some reports even suggested the entire PMO would be a mobile one, travelling by bus from one major western centre to another on a rotational basis. Alarmed by the number of inquiries received by the party's Calgary office about possible job openings at the phantom PMO, Ralph Goodale was eventually obliged to 'correct the record' and state that such an office was 'not part of any official plan.' Instead, drawing on a measure introduced by Pierre Trudeau more than thirty years earlier, Goodale announced that the top priority for a Martin government would be 'for Ottawa to recruit westerners for senior jobs in the public service.'[62] In the end, Martin's defining statement about the west was a symbolic one. Staking his political career on the theme of eradicating western alienation, he declared, 'No matter what else I do as prime minister, if western alienation is the same as it is at the end of my term as it is now, I will not believe I have succeeded.'[63]

One subject on which Paul Martin commented over the summer was the proposed National Health Council. Here again, his statements revealed the very different approaches of Martin and Jean Chrétien to federal-provincial relations. Chrétien's February deal with the premiers – to provide them with more funding for health care – had been conditional on their agreement to participate in this council, which had been recommended by the Romanow Commission to enhance accountability. The premiers had agreed that they would share data and results to establish benchmarks for wait times and best practices. As Finance Minister John Manley made clear in his budget, additional federal funding would not flow until the premiers followed through on these accountability measures. But in early July, as they approached the annual premiers' meeting, there were suggestions that some of them would renege. Chrétien was prepared to take a hard line on the issue. Martin was conciliatory. He issued a press release in which he stated, 'Let me be clear. I am not hung up on whether this is seen more as a federal or a provincial initiative ... If there are concerns about ... jurisdictional realities, I believe solutions can be found with a spirit of flexibility and collaboration.'[64]

Like John Turner's statements about bilingualism and the Charter during his own leadership coronation, Martin's comments sent a clear signal that the expected winner of the 2003 Liberal leadership race held very different views from his predecessor and would take the party in a new direction on the federalism axis. However, the party grassroots paid little attention to this. Much as their counterparts in 1984 had viewed Turner as a winner, so they saw Martin as a breath of fresh air who was certain to prevail in any federal election match against the Alliance.

Nor were party elites interested in such concerns. Their attention was focused on what to do about the increasingly likely scenario that the convention would be attended by barely half of the eligible delegates and that the party would run a massive deficit. They were also worried about the increasingly divisive interactions between Copps and Martin supporters, the source of a lot of negative publicity in the run-up to November. Last but hardly least, there was considerable concern that Jean Chrétien was losing control of his cabinet and caucus and was coming to be seen as arrogant in the face of challenges to his authority. Many feared Chrétien would follow through on his threat to call another snap election if he could not be persuaded to leave sooner rather than later.

The Long Goodbye

By late November, when the auditor general released her annual report indicating a huge cost-overrun on the gun registry, Justice Minister Allan Rock was not the only target of friendly fire.[65] Known Martin supporters within the Liberal camp seized the opportunity to call for Chrétien's immediate departure. 'This country cannot afford another fourteen months of legacy building,' Albina Guarnieri declared, ignoring the fact that the gun registry had not been part of the legacy. 'Not only my constituents but good friends and long-time Liberals are saying that our credibility is now starting to erode as sound fiscal managers, especially with the gun registry,' Nick Discepola, a Quebec MP and Martin supporter, maintained. Only their colleague Dan McTeague took a different approach, arguing that Chrétien should leave as soon as possible to stop the 'aimless drift' of the government.[66]

Chrétien, to no one's surprise, responded in kind. At a press conference in early December 2002 marking the ratification of the Kyoto Protocol, he answered reporters' questions on the timing of his departure in no uncertain terms. 'I am leaving in February 2004,' he stated flatly. 'I said that very clearly. I have been elected by the people of Canada to run a government.'[67] More to the point, he said, the backbenchers complaining were only doing so because they were not in his cabinet, and they would do so again under Martin because they would not all be successful. Several of them would be 'former future ministers,' he scoffed. Again, Paul Martin was obliged to demonstrate solidarity with the party leader at the expense of his caucus supporters. 'The schedule is set out by the prime minister,' he repeated, 'and the party is very clear. I'm happy with that.'[68]

In spite of this statement, rumours were rampant that the prime minister would step down in June, or September at the latest. Another rumour had Chrétien stepping down on 15 November, the day of the leadership vote. Quoting a variety of anonymous sources among MPs and ministerial aides, one *Hill Times* journalist reported growing speculation that an interim leader would be appointed to carry the government through until the November convention. 'The feeling in the Martin camp is they should wait until the budget and then after the budget, if they get a signal that he might want to leave sooner, then they will leave him alone,' a senior EA told the reporter. If not, the unnamed source continued, 'they will certainly try to push him out ... They would rather have someone else in the meantime rather than having him there.' A number of Chrétien sources were quick to deny rumours of an early departure. Quebec Liberal senator Raymond Setlakwe, a staunch Chrétien supporter, warned that if Martin MPs caused too much trouble – or voted against a money bill or confidence motion – 'I don't know what alternative the prime minister would have to calling an election,' which they surely would not want.[69]

Nothing came of the rumours, and Chrétien continued with his eighteen-month plan. On the eve of the summer recess in late June, he stood in the House of Commons to report on the status of his Throne Speech commitments from the previous October. He enumerated thirty-six separate measures that had already been taken to meet those commitments, in what he described as 'one of the most productive sessions of Parliament.' Deliberately adding fuel to the fire, he served notice that he intended to continue with his activist program in the fall.[70] For those who doubted his desire to complete his agenda the message was clear.

Chrétien did not stop there. In an obvious effort to define his record himself before his departure, he began giving major speeches across the country. The most significant was an address in Quebec City in early September 2003, at the Annual Meeting of the Canadian Chamber of Commerce and the Third World Meeting of Chambers of Commerce. There he drew attention to the very different economic and political situation the delegates were seeing in Canada from what they had encountered nine years earlier. He reminded his audience that when he last addressed the Chamber in Quebec City in 1994, the Parti Québécois was in office, a referendum was looming, the federal government was running massive deficits, and unemployment was rampant.

By contrast, he pointed first and foremost to the fact that 'there is now a federalist government in Quebec. Federalists have the majority of seats from Quebec in the House of Commons ... My party is looking forward to the next federal election much, much more than the Bloc Québécois.' On the economic front, 'in the space of four years we eliminated the total federal deficit. We have now had six balanced budgets in a row. We have cut our debt to GDP ratio from 71 per cent to just over 40 per cent and we have paid down 55 billion dollars of debt.' For average Canadians, the results of these measures were concrete. 'The economy has generated nearly three million new jobs since we have been in office ... our standard of living has increased by 20 per cent since 1997 ... our public pension system is on a sustainable footing for the first time in fifty years and ... we have made the structural reforms that Europe wishes it could make.' He went on to praise the various programs established by his government to support post-secondary education, research, innovation, and infrastructure renewal, as well as the many new social initiatives the government had launched, such as parental leave, childcare, disability, and family benefits. As a result of all these measures, he said, 'I believe my successor will inherit a country in a very, very strong position.'[71]

In his conclusion, Chrétien sent a thinly veiled message to his likely successor. Convinced Paul Martin would be inclined to take a different policy direction, Chrétien underlined his conviction that the time had come for more massive federal investment in social programs and physical infrastructure, in part because 'if these investments are not made, Canada will not be competitive in the long run.' He referred to a letter he had recently received from some two hundred business leaders, local government, and social action groups from Toronto, calling on the federal government to adopt just such an activist agenda. It was an agenda he had been following since the deficit was eliminated in 1997, he argued. 'It is an agenda I agree with. An agenda that will require government to continue to be focused. Not to be all things to all people. It is an agenda of large public investment. None of which will be cheap.' As a result, he warned, his successor 'must also recognize the implications of this agenda ... these new public investments inevitably mean that there cannot be any new large tax cuts in the near future ... Our budget deficits have been eliminated. Now the challenge for the future is to eliminate social, environmental, and infrastructure deficits.'[72]

Addressing the Montreal Board of Trade a few days later, Paul Martin outlined his economic vision for the country in the twenty-first century. His speech covered many of the same issues mentioned by Jean Chrétien, providing an unprecedented opportunity for comparison. Although Martin stated that he too believed Canada was in excellent economic shape compared to most of its competitors, he argued three things were needed urgently to ensure the country retained its competitive edge. Instead of investments in social programs or infrastructure, Martin believed that 'first and foremost, it is absolutely essential that we lower our national debt load.' Chrétien had indicated he was proud of the existing reduction from 70 per cent to 40 per cent of GDP, but Martin insisted more payments were needed to lower the rate 'back towards the 25 per cent level that Canada had in the 1960's.' While he agreed with Chrétien that 'when we strengthen our social fabric, we also strengthen our economy,' he placed more emphasis on health care and immigration policy than on welfare, childcare, or disabilities. His emphasis on research and development focused less on promoting post-secondary education and funding university research, and more on private-sector capital markets, technology transfer, business investment in research and technology, and government partnerships with small and medium-sized businesses.

Even more revealing were the two men's differing perceptions of the role of the federal government. Where Chrétien stressed that government should be a 'force for good,' Martin instead argued that 'government is about change – good governments don't react to change, they anticipate it.' In practical terms, Chrétien clearly assumed direct government intervention in the economy would be required, while Martin concluded that 'if government has a role to play, it must only be as a catalyst.' Finally, Martin countered the view that social and environmental deficits were the next fiscal priority by insisting that 'our objective is clear: to be a true land of innovation. A market teeming with new products and services, where the quality of life never ceases to grow.'[73]

Although it was delivered in Montreal, Martin's speech did not mention the political situation in Quebec. Yet, as Chrétien had noted in Quebec City only two days earlier, the political picture had changed as dramatically as the economic one during the Liberals' time in office. From the near-death experience of the 1995 referendum, the federalist cause had rebounded to heights of popularity not seen since the 1970s. With support for separatism plummeting, Lucien Bouchard had resigned as premier, and his successor, Bernard Landry, had declared there would not be another referendum in the foreseeable future. As for the Bloc Québécois, columnist Chantal Hébert had recently declared they were 'facing electoral disaster.' With polls putting the Bloc in last place in the run-up to the next federal election expected in early 2004, she noted that the party had already seen several of its MPs resign in despair, either to run in the provincial election or return to the private sector. Many in the province questioned whether the Bloc had any future in federal politics. Hébert concluded that 'the recent Chrétien agenda is even more popular in Quebec than elsewhere in the country' and in the next election 'the Bloc will be fighting for its life.'[74]

For Jean Chrétien, these were sweet words indeed. In his view, his success on the national unity front was due to his classic mix of Trudeauvian firmness in federal dealings with the provinces coupled with his delivery of good government. In stressing both the economic and political well-being of the country, Chrétien was reminding not just fellow Liberals but, most importantly, the man he knew would succeed him that this was achieved through toughness and political will, two qualities he feared Martin lacked. For their part, Martin and his advisers were forced to watch as the man they saw as an albatross around the party's neck continued to pursue a direction they considered outmoded and counterproductive.

Despite the public's unrest and apparent eagerness for Chrétien to depart, the Liberal Party remained in first place in the polls by a wide margin. For ten years the party had been at 43 per cent or better for most of every year, dipping only briefly to a low of 37 per cent and reaching 50 per cent on more than one occasion, while its nearest opponent barely managed half that level of support. Pollster Michael Marzolini put this into stark perspective in one memo: 'To hold the electoral support of between 37 per cent and 50 per cent of the Canadian public for an entire decade is unprecedented,' he wrote. 'No democratically-elected nation's leader, president or prime minister, past or present, can make a similar claim. Only the current Canadian government would have been re-elected on every single day of its ten-year mandate.'[75] Chrétien's critics argued it was Canadians' rejection of the new right-wing conservatism that had made this possible. Marzolini concurred that Chrétien had benefited from the divided right-wing vote during most of his tenure, but he also concluded that Chrétien's adept handling of the Reform/Alliance party had been instrumental in maintaining that division.

A week before the leadership convention began, one of the final chapters in the Chrétien era unfolded in the House of Commons as members on all sides of the House paid tribute to the departing prime minister. Television images revealed a painfully smiling Paul Martin listening while his seat mate, Charles Caccia, delivered the address for the Liberal side, an address apparently designed to criticize Martin while praising the departing Chrétien. Referring repeatedly to Chrétien as a 'man of infallible political instincts,' Caccia highlighted many of the Liberal leader's personal policy initiatives which had originally been opposed by Martin, including the Clarity Act, the ratification of the Kyoto Accord and the Law of the Sea, the G8 NEPAD agreement, legislation on same-sex marriage and the decriminalization of marijuana, and the decision not to send Canadian troops to Iraq. He also referred to Chrétien's unprecedented record of appointments of women, visible minorities, and aboriginal Canadians. In what appeared to be a direct rebuke to Martin, Chrétien's former cabinet colleague and ally concluded, 'If the Liberal government shows up so well in public opinion polls, it is in large part due not to deficit elimination or debt reduction, but to the courageous and timely leadership by the Prime Minister on so many issues over the past ten years.' The icing on the cake was the declaration that '[Chrétien] is a man of infallible political instincts who could have led the Liberal Party to a fourth consecutive majority victory.'[76]

The Super Weekend and the Foregone Conclusion

It was the desire for a fourth consecutive majority that drove many grassroots Liberals and elites to turn to Paul Martin. The heir apparent to the Liberal throne was hugely popular with the general public, as Michael Marzolini noted in his analysis. And, under the new rules, Martin's leadership victory seemed all but assured. At the so-called 'Super Weekend' in late September, when delegate selection took place in ridings across the country, Martin won the support of some 90 per cent of the delegates to the convention.

Martin's overwhelming victory posed a number of problems for the party. It was the first time the rules had been used for a leadership race since they were put in place in 1992. No one had anticipated such a scenario, primarily because no one had foreseen either a two-person race or one in which the frontrunner amassed such an overwhelming lead. Simply put, by the end of the Super Weekend, Paul Martin had already won the leadership and everyone knew it. With three candidates there would still have been a mathematical possibility of a second ballot, but with John Manley's departure from the race the die was cast. The winner needed 61 per cent of delegates' votes to win, or 2,902 votes. Martin had obtained 3,664, while Sheila Copps finished a distant second with 415 delegates. No second ballot would be necessary.

The Super Weekend results almost immediately led Stan Keyes, still the national caucus chair, to question whether Sheila Copps should remain in the race. As one parliamentary reporter noted, Keyes was also 'a long-time rival [of Copps] who also represents a riding in Hamilton,' and suggested personal motivation may have played a part in Keyes's proposal. Keyes denied this but informed reporters that he would raise the issue with the national executive at their scheduled meeting the following weekend. Suggesting Copps could 'concede now, rather than having to go through a vote at the convention,' Keyes added, 'If the national executive decides that this is an option, then I think the bearer of the message would probably be the president of the party, Stephen LeDrew, who would make the call to Sheila and suggest it to her.' Although he acknowledged Copps was 'entitled' to stay in the race to the end, Keyes concluded she would have to decide 'what's in the best interests of the delegates, the party and the convention.'[77] Stephen LeDrew picked up the argument, informing the media that Copps and her advisers were 'assessing the situation and looking at whether they want to go through a vote or not. I mean, the fact of the matter is it's not even close.' LeDrew stressed that if Copps were to withdraw from the race, he would 'strongly and positively recommend to the organizing committee that she still be allowed to make a speech.'[78] Copps's campaign manager, Joe Thornley, reacted swiftly to LeDrew's comments, referring to them as 'silly,' 'absurd,' and 'distressing.' Thornley also pointed out that a leadership vote would still have to be held at the convention for constitutional purposes even if there was only one candidate (the Michael Ignatieff situation would demonstrate this a few years later). Copps herself reacted angrily to the suggestion that she quit. 'I've run a vigorous campaign,' she said, 'with a whole lot of people who support my vision for the Liberal Party, and I owe it to them to put forward that vision at the convention.'[79]

LeDrew had already been chastised by the national executive in late June for suggesting that the race was already over. Both the Manley and Copps camps had filed complaints over his public statements then, and the national executive had met to discuss his comments and determine whether he should be removed as a co-chair of the convention. In the end, party vice-president Jack Graham informed reporters that 'Stephen's comments were regrettable and inappropriate.' At the same time, he said, the executive concluded that 'Mr. LeDrew has been fair in his handling of the convention organization' and would not be asked to step aside. In letters sent to both the Copps and Manley camps, LeDrew wrote: 'I regret that my comments stirred consternation, but you can rest assured that the leadership race and the convention will continue to be conducted in an impartial, fair, and responsible manner.' The apology did not assuage the concerns of Manley spokesperson Susan Smith, who told reporters 'the president of the party is trying to circumvent the democratic process.'[80] Joe Thornley agreed. 'Mr. LeDrew has lost the confidence of party members who believe he has become partisan in favour of Paul Martin.'[81]

In addition to respecting the constitution, the executive grappled with the fact that the new rules for delegate selection were likely to have perverse consequences. In many ridings, the requirement for delegates to be selected in each category – general membership, women, and youth – could mean a candidate would win the majority of votes but still not have the total number of delegates allowed for the riding. If Sheila Copps won the vast majority of votes in a riding but there was no Copps delegate slated in the youth category, for example, there would simply be no youth delegate from that riding. The votes would be wasted and there would be far fewer delegates than expected.

There were also a number of high-profile controversies over the legitimacy of many youth clubs and the memberships of new Liberals, a scenario that unfolded across the country in advance of the Super Weekend. In BC, Copps supporters were accused of having forged membership forms. Her organizers responded that the members were legitimate even if the forms were not. They argued that they had been forced to photocopy forms because they could not obtain real ones from the Martin-dominated riding associations. Meanwhile, Copps organizers reported that many of her 'new Canadian' recruits to the party were being routinely challenged at delegate selection meetings across the country. Copps recounted how members of her own family were challenged when they attempted to vote in their respective ridings.[82] As well-known left-wing author and Martin critic Murray Dobbin put it, 'the whole campaign looked more like a hostile corporate takeover than a genuine party contest.'[83]

Another perspective was provided by Scott Reid, the communications adviser who had been recruited by the Martin organization because of his reputation as a first-rate organizer who could deliver delegates. Reid later insisted, 'All I can say is, if we were overzealous, it was because it looked a lot closer to us at the time than it turned out. When you're in the middle of something it's hard to see things objectively.'[84]

In a tacit recognition of these problems, president Stephen LeDrew's report on the Super Weekend results concluded: 'The enfranchisement of all members of the Party is more democratic ... However, the process can always be improved and I am certain that the new National Executive will appoint a committee to review the leadership process under this new system so that further constitutional changes can be considered.'[85] Such changes would have to take place further down the road. Meanwhile, fewer than 25 per cent of the party membership cast their ballots at the delegate selection meetings, and the obvious lack of interest in the race among Liberals was one of the most important issues facing LeDrew and the national executive.

With some 531,000 eligible party members (the largest number of any party in Canadian history), the convention organizers expected a better turnout on the Super Weekend. They also assumed that more of the delegates elected on the weekend would actually attend the convention. But with convention fees and expenses easily topping $1,500, organizers worried that many of those who had been elected would not bother to attend, especially since the outcome was a certainty. Media interest was also declining rapidly.

To address this issue, Stephen LeDrew suggested the convention could be 'spiced up' by the invitation of internationally prominent figures such as Nelson Mandela or Tony Blair, another controversial idea which led many disgruntled executive members to question their earlier decision to support him. 'Why would we invite people who aren't Canadians?' one frustrated senior party official exclaimed. 'These people aren't even Liberals!' said another. As of 4 November only 1,800 of an eligible 5,569 delegates had pre-registered for the convention. For the first time in the party's history, the leadership convention risked posting a loss. As a result of these developments, the party executive decided to change the rules concerning leadership review. Like the leadership race, the review process was divided into two parts: the vote of rank-and-file members across the country, and the vote of delegates at a convention. It was the threat that he would lose the rank-and-file vote in September 2002, not the convention vote in February 2003, that convinced Jean Chrétien to step down in August of that year. Now, with Paul Martin's leadership victory a certainty, the executive moved to institute changes to the review system, expecting him to call an election shortly after the convention, which in turn would trigger another two-part review vote.

Referring to the system as 'a strange two-headed beast,' Akaash Maharaj was among those members of the executive who enthusiastically adopted a recommendation to eliminate one of the 'heads.' However, despite the decade of efforts by many in the party to introduce direct democracy and work towards the elimination of the delegated convention, it was not that 'head' that the executive chose to remove, but rather the universal suffrage aspect. As one member of the executive explained it, the problem was the lack of standardized national rules for party membership. As a result, 'the existing system could create, under certain circumstances, a race to the bottom, where different jurisdictions who felt differently about a sitting leader would progressively lower the threshold for membership until they could effectively take over the vote.'[86] Put another way, if Martin's opponents could capture one province or region they might be able to dethrone him.

The Anticlimactic Convention

The Liberal Party's national biennial convention of November 2003 was actually three separate events: a tribute to the departing leader, the culmination of a fifteen-month leadership race with the crowning of the heir apparent, and a meeting of the party's grassroots delegates to elect a new national executive. In some respects, the third function was the most significant since the outcomes had not all been determined and actual contests between contenders occupied many of the participants. From the perspective of most Canadians and the national media, however, it was clearly the first two events that held their attention.

Even at the convention, the chasm between the two camps in the Liberal Party was clear. For the first time ever, the president and the national executive engaged someone other than the national director to organize the convention, arguing that it was an obvious conflict of interest for longtime Chrétien supporter Terry Mercer to be involved. As a result, Gordon Ashworth served as general secretary and organized the convention events involving the leadership race and Paul Martin's victory evening. Mercer was put in charge of the Chrétien tribute, which took place the previous evening, aided by John Rae and Senator Ross Fitzpatrick, who also served as fundraisers for the event. (Fitzpatrick later stressed the tribute was paid for entirely by private donations and no funds were requested or received from the party.)[87]

The prime minister's tribute took place on 13 November at the Air Canada Centre in Toronto, televised nationally and attended by all of the party's current and past elites as well as the delegates. Here, as well, the audience was divided into sections supporting Chrétien and Martin, with a small buffer zone for the uncommitted. As David Collenette commented, 'Compared to the Trudeau farewell, which I think brought us all together for the evening in spite of our differences, this was more like a ceasefire.'[88] The symbolism of the seating arrangements did not escape the media either. One CBC reporter commented, 'Jean Chrétien had kind words for Paul Martin, calling him a "great Liberal" ... but the two men sat on opposite sides of the stadium, like leaders of two opposition parties.'[89]

When Chrétien took the stage to deliver his final address to the Liberal Party, he reiterated many of the points made in his earlier speech to the Chamber of Commerce in Quebec City. While he received polite applause throughout, there were three occasions when he received enthusiastic standing ovations. The first – and arguably most sustained – came when he referred to his introduction of the Clarity Bill after the 1995 referendum. The audience erupted a second time when he stated that 'it was because of our deep belief in the values of multilateralism and the United Nations that we did not go to war in Iraq.' A poll released a week earlier revealed that more than 70 per cent of Canadians identified that decision as one of Chrétien's greatest legacies.

The third ovation came near the end of his speech. Chrétien first warned Liberals and Canadians to 'beware of those on the right who would weaken our national government because they do not believe in the role of government,' those who 'put profit ahead of community and ... do not care about reducing the social or environmental deficit.' Building to his conclusion, he told party members, 'If you remember one thing that I say tonight, remember this ... we must never ever lose our social conscience.'[90]

The response to Chrétien's speech was particularly striking in light of the very different positions taken by the man chosen to succeed him. As national columnist Hugh Winsor asked in his column the following day, how could the same delegates who had just demonstrated their support for those three policy decisions have chosen as their next leader a man who initially opposed the first two and whose commitment to the third was problematic?[91]

Events the following day reinforced the image of a party still divided. It began with the speech Sheila Copps was finally allowed to deliver, after considerable behind-the-scenes negotiations between her campaign manager and various party officials. An angry Joe Thornley remembered that this was actually presented as a major concession, and one which was only approved after several personal interventions. It appeared her earlier refusal to concede defeat before the convention had led to a lack of interest in 'allowing' her to speak at all. The party's official reason was different. 'I was told no one would come,' he said. 'Finally I met with one of the senior Martin team members,' he said, 'someone I had known for years. I had already told them Sheila would be using the speech to call for party unity and to throw her support behind the new leader publicly. Even so, I was originally told "we see no need for that," as if they were in charge and not the party.'[92] Copps did use the speech to offer her support to Martin, but also to reiterate her left-of-centre agenda. In a dramatic flourish she noted that his father had been the author of many of the social programs with which the Liberals had become so identified. She also noted that, contrary to expectations, the room was packed.[93]

Later that afternoon the results of the formal leadership vote were announced. In the end, some 3,455 delegates attended the convention, or roughly 65 per cent of those eligible. With 3,242 votes, Paul Martin officially defeated Sheila Copps, who received only 213 votes. Regardless of any irregularities that may have occurred along the way, his victory was a resounding one.

Despite this overwhelming success, some members of the Martin organization continued to impose a rigid discipline on the remaining convention events and especially on the evening's scheduled speech by Martin. While national television cameras rolled, an unseemly public battle over reserved seating in the Copps section was narrowly averted by the intervention of several of Copps's unaligned cabinet colleagues. The symbolism of the event was, however, plainly visible, with Copps's delegates occupying a small outlying area while rank-and-file Martin supporters appeared to be in every corner of the room. Sitting immediately beside Martin and his wife, Sheila, was former prime minister John Turner.

In his acceptance speech, Martin began by saying he believed Canada was now in a position to take advantage of the political and economic successes of the past decade. He described the current situation as similar to the one Canada experienced in the aftermath of the Second World War. 'There can be little doubt that we have again arrived at a moment of great opportunity,' he declared, which must be seized by Canadians and their leaders to achieve 'transformative change.'[94] This opportunity had come about for at least four reasons. First, there was the reversal of economic decline (for which he thanked Jean Chrétien, insisting that without the prime minister's unequivocal support he could not have accomplished any of his objectives as finance minister). Second was 'the presence of a federalist government in Quebec for the first time since 1994,' a development on which he did not elaborate. Third, there was a decrease in western alienation as demonstrated by the huge increase in party memberships in that region and by 'the fact that Albertans are clearly rejecting the notion of building firewalls around their province.' The fourth factor, Martin said, was the presence of 'a new guard taking the centre of the political stage – one that has politically come of age since the constitutional and jurisdictional wars of the 70s and 80s.' Taken together, he concluded, 'Canada is positioned to make history.'[95]

The new Liberal leader identified three broadly based goals for his administration. The first two were to 'secure the social foundations' and to 'build a twenty-first century economy.' The third (foreign policy) goal was to 'ensure Canada's place in the world,' which Martin argued 'means coming to grips with a world where our closest friend and nearest neighbour – the United States – has emerged as the lone superpower.' He argued that the relationship between the two countries had been needlessly strained in recent times, and 'for the benefit of both countries we must work to confirm and strengthen it.' In conclusion, Martin returned to the theme of the democratic deficit, promising specifically to relax party discipline, enhance the role of committees, and create an independent ethics commissioner who would report directly to the House of Commons rather than to the prime minister. True to his decentralist convictions, he stressed the need for a more collaborative and less formal approach to relations between the federal government and the provinces as well as municipalities. 'New times require new approaches,' he stated.

At the end of his speech Martin broke with tradition by failing to recognize either of his two leadership rivals or to invite them onstage. He specifically invited John Turner to join him, after which everyone watched anxiously to see whether Jean Chrétien would join the two men on stage. The suspense continued as Chrétien first stood and applauded with everyone else, but eventually he made his way to the stage and the three men stood together, arm in arm, in an obviously forced effort to convince their followers and the Canadian people that the Liberal Party was still the party of internal unity.

The effect was somewhat diminished the following day when latecomer Mike Eizenga – backed by Martin organizers and endorsed by key Martin supporters such as Bill Cunningham, Helene Scherrer, Anne McLellan, and Jack Graham – eventually prevailed in the race for party president after a lengthy delay in the counting of the ballots. Unlike the leadership vote, the final numbers for the presidential ballot were never officially disclosed. Spokespersons for both camps, however, agreed that the margin of victory for Eizenga over his popular challenger, Akaash Maharaj, was fewer than fifty votes.

One insider speculated that the decision by most of Martin's team to support Eizenga was spurred by the fact that '[Martin's people] were afraid Akaash would speak out as if there were two prime ministers.' Some support for that thesis – for the view that the parliamentary and extra-parliamentary wings of the party are more often in conflict when the party is in power – came from Maharaj himself, who had delivered a strong convention speech. After stressing that his campaign 'looks towards a vision of a more inclusive party that is able to act as the conscience of the government, rather than as an apologist for the government,' the presidential hopeful also warned Paul Martin not to become 'imprisoned in a bubble of backroom cigar smoke.'[96]

Departing president Stephen LeDrew's performance over the course of the leadership race, combined with his outspoken opposition to the election expenses legislation, earned him few supporters in any camp. Despite the apprehension of bias on the part of the Copps and Manley advisers, even Paul Martin's organizers did not feel they had benefited from any of LeDrew's actions. As Tim Murphy commented, 'We didn't see him as supporting either side. He just wasn't a player. He had no troops.'[97] And so, in yet another of the many unprecedented developments related to the leadership transition, LeDrew became the first 'outsider' party president not to be rewarded with a Senate seat or other appointment for his services. LeDrew himself saw this as proof of his impartiality and effectiveness. 'I was doing my job as I saw it. I'm a party person. My responsibility was to the party membership, not any one leader.'[98]

One who did not agree with LeDrew's self-assessment was former Trudeau aide Jim Coutts. In a lengthy opinion piece outlining the various ways in which he believed the party was losing its way, Coutts called LeDrew 'the weakest party president in memory,' lambasting his efforts to block the party finance legislation, his failure to rein in provincial organizations and implement the executive's agreement on membership forms, and his handling of the 'lighter than air' convention which sacrificed policy debate for 'a US-style show-biz spectacle on prime time TV.'[99]

For most of those who attended the convention, however, it had been a distinct success. As in 1984, the vast majority of the delegates who attended the November 2003 convention were convinced the party was well on its way to another electoral victory under a new and promising leader, one who would demonstrate both change and continuity in the natural governing party. As Michael Marzolini reported, the public expectations surrounding Paul Martin were even higher than they had been for Turner. In fact, they were the highest he had ever seen.

12 From Glory to Grief: The First Martin Mandate

By the time this book is published, the tension between Martin and Chrétien will have waned, if not disappeared. Grudges are a big part of politics, but they usually evaporate upon victory. There will be a huge temptation on the part of Liberals – and especially Martin and his supporters – to simply forget a struggle that was a fascinating and important all-but-inevitable ingredient of his success.

– Susan Delacourt, *Juggernaut*

Paul Martin may have become the new Liberal leader in November 2003, but he was still a prime minister in waiting. Chrétien was determined to stay long enough to represent Canada at two international events in early December. In a pre-convention interview, the prime minister reiterated his intention to leave later rather than sooner. 'You know this is the only suspense you guys have,' he told one reporter, referring to the date of his departure.

To keep him in the public eye, Martin and his advisers continued staging high-profile events while he waited to take over. They seized the opportunity provided by the Grey Cup celebrations in Regina to arrange an informal meeting between the leader-elect and the provincial premiers. Martin was criticized by opposition leader Stephen Harper for jumping the gun, but Chrétien himself dismissed the event as 'just a football game.' Nevertheless, the significance of the venue (western Canada) and the subject matter (federal-provincial relations) could hardly have demonstrated more clearly the priorities Martin intended to pursue as prime minister.

Initially the strategy was a success. Coverage of the mini first ministers' meeting was almost uniformly positive. 'Martin, premiers begin new era with pledge,' one report declared.[1] For some, though, the image of Martin and the premiers happily declaring an end to their conflicts was unsettling. It was eerily reminiscent of the Valentine's Day meeting Brian Mulroney had organized with provincial premiers in Saskatchewan shortly after his election in 1985. For Mulroney, the goodwill lasted barely two months. Some seasoned observers feared Martin was repeating this mistake. For his part, Martin was convinced his flexible, collaborative approach would be more likely to succeed than Jean Chrétien's Trudeauvian one. 'I have always been in favour of regular meetings with provinces,' he said, indirectly criticizing Chrétien for his decision to avoid such meetings for most of his tenure. 'If you're going to establish national objectives and national priorities, you've got to establish it jointly with the provinces. And that is what I'm looking forward to.'[2]

Shortly after, Chrétien made the surprise announcement that he would leave office in December after all.

Even Chrétien's decision to leave early became a source of controversy, albeit an internal one. Much like the very public dispute between John Turner and the departing Pierre Trudeau over patronage appointments, so Chrétien's departure proved a source of contention with Martin and his advisers over the auditor general's report. One side maintains an offer was made to stay on until February in order to handle the government's response to the report, but it was not taken up. The other side insists they had no reason to suppose a delay in the turnover was necessary because they were unaware of the damaging contents of that report.

Negotiations on the exact timing of Chrétien's departure were handled by intermediaries. A meeting was arranged between Chrétien and Martin on 6 December to discuss the transition, and they agreed on 12 December as an appropriate date. Like much else about the leadership race, the transition was unprecedented in many ways. Certainly the least expected development was the apparent vendetta that Martin and his supporters conducted against Liberals who had supported Chrétien, and even those who had remained neutral. Contrary to Susan Delacourt's prediction, the rift in the party did not heal quickly, or at all. In fact, few attempts were made to paper over it. The two sides would later blame each other for their failure to come together in the name of party unity, but the entire party would pay dearly for this failure.

The Uneasy Transition

Paul Martin's transition process actually began long before 6 December. Despite some of his advisers' claims that they were not sure they would win, in March 2003 Martin asked Michael Robinson to head his transition team. Robinson in turn invited Senator Jack Austin, a former adviser to Pierre Trudeau, and Arthur Kroeger, a former senior bureaucrat, to assist him. Their meetings with Martin over the summer set the stage for the more intense round of discussions that began shortly after the party's Super Weekend in September, when convention delegates had been selected and Martin was assured of victory. This was also the point when Jean Chrétien authorized the Clerk of the Privy Council, Alex Himmelfarb, to begin speaking with Robinson about the machinery of government.

The early discussions of the transition trio focused on the structures of government, such as cabinet and its committees. After the convention, the transition team was expanded to include David Herle, Tim Murphy, Terrie O'Leary, Francis Fox, and Dennis Dawson, the latter two men providing much-needed experience as former parliamentarians. The full transition team met daily from the convention until Martin's swearing in as prime minister. In this second stage, the transition took on a far more political tone as the actual appointments to cabinet and other posts were discussed in detail.

A driving force behind the transition team's efforts was the perceived need to demonstrate change. Martin's pollster and election co-chair David Herle recounted, 'We felt there was a tremendous desire for change in the country.' But he also admitted polls showed Canadians 'were not fundamentally dissatisfied with our policies.' Herle therefore concluded that electoral success would depend on the Martin administration 'being more ambitious' in their policy objectives and in 'stylistic change. We were trying to look different.'[3] His views were shared by all of Martin's key advisers. John Duffy told journalist Paul Wells that 'change was everything. It was always at the heart of what I saw as our challenge ... to be the agent of positive, manageable, safe change. That was Paul's cachet.'[4] Unfortunately, the definition of this safe and manageable change proved elusive. Like John Turner's advisers in 1984, Martin's team believed a change of leadership also required the appearance of a significant change in policy direction for the party, rather than a minor course correction.

Their assumption that substantial change was necessary to achieve a fourth Liberal majority was accompanied by the paradoxical assumption that Paul Martin was on the verge of obtaining a massive majority of 200 seats. As Dennis Dawson emphasized, 'after the Convention, we were basically hitting the roof as far as polling was concerned.'[5] Indeed, at the time most political pundits agreed with the Board's assumption that there would be yet another Liberal majority. With the Right still in disarray and the Bloc's support essentially collapsed, it was difficult for anyone to imagine how Martin's government could *not* maintain or even improve the Liberal standing in the next election. But the Martin team's continued expectation of 200 seats long after they took office, and, more importantly, the crafting of a one-dimensional strategy to achieve that end, proved to be grievous strategic errors.

The focus of Martin's advisers was definitely on expanding the Liberal Party's representation. David Herle explained that Martin, like John Turner, wanted a 'widening of the tent' for two reasons: first, to bring the west back to the Liberal fold, and, second, to increase the party's support among so-called soft nationalists in Quebec. Many of the structural and political decisions taken by Martin and his team over the next six months were intended to further his two-pronged expansion strategy, often at the expense of other considerations. Similarly, Martin's high standing in the polls led Dawson and others to conclude, incorrectly, that the Liberals' support 'was based on Paul being anybody but Chrétien.' As subsequent events demonstrated, their attempts to ignore or disown much of the legacy of the Chrétien era would have serious consequences.

None of this thinking was evident at the time of Martin's meeting with Chrétien on 6 December. Since there had been no public meeting between Turner and Trudeau, this was the first opportunity for Canadians to observe the transfer of power within the Liberal Party in more than thirty-five years. As such it was widely covered by the media. Predictably, many reporters were specifically looking for signs of a rapprochement between the two men. In one sense they were not disappointed. When a smiling Martin arrived for the meeting in the Centre Block, he was greeted at the door of the prime minister's office by Chrétien himself, also smiling. When the two emerged from the office an hour later they were still smiling. But the brief press scrum afterwards suggested Chrétien had more to smile about than Martin. Taking the lead in the media encounter, a jovial Chrétien outlined how the two of them had agreed (evidently in exchange for Chrétien's early departure) that Martin would follow through on the initiatives Chrétien had yet to complete, notably same-sex marriage and marijuana legislation.

The day of the transition, Chrétien visited the governor general to submit his resignation several hours before Martin and his new cabinet arrived to be sworn in. The ceremony itself was another bone of contention, but this time the disagreement was between Martin's team and Governor General Adrienne Clarkson. Martin's senior advisers requested a change of venue from the traditional setting at Rideau Hall – the residence of the governor general – to the main hall in the Centre Block of the Parliament Buildings, known as the Hall of Honour. 'We wanted to modernize it, make it more relevant ... and show Paul was serious about making changes,' one adviser recalled. But Clarkson refused, arguing the symbolism of the prime minister coming to see the head of state, rather than the reverse, was an important tradition in a parliamentary democracy and one that had never before been breached. Moreover, she noted, the governor general is only allowed in Parliament for the reading of the Throne Speech in the Senate, not in the House of Commons where the Hall is located. As she later wrote, 'the idea of having a big ceremony at the Hall of Honour seemed to me to be imposing a presidential-type installation on our unpresidential system. I refused three entreaties from the Prime Minister's Office, including one from Mr. Martin himself ... I believe in modernization, I believe in Canadianization, but I do not believe in Americanization.'[6]

The ceremony took place at Rideau Hall but with a number of innovations, including an aboriginal cleansing ceremony. Undoubtedly the most poignant image was that of Martin being sworn in as Canada's twenty-first prime minister while holding the flag that had been lowered to half mast on the day his father died.

The prime minister's oath of office was followed by the swearing in of his ministers. The cabinet was huge by recent standards, equalling the largest of Brian Mulroney's cabinets. This was primarily because Martin, unlike Chrétien, decided to include ministers of state in his cabinet.[7] Apart from the need to reward loyalists, his advisers argued the large number was necessary to include posts for all the new priorities Martin outlined in his leadership acceptance speech. Certainly the optics of the large crowd of thirty-nine ministers assembled for the obligatory photograph represented another symbolic change from the more spartan approach of Chrétien.

Normally this would have marked the end of the installation ceremony, but on this occasion a new event was added, the swearing in of parliamentary secretaries as privy councillors. This too represented a departure from the past. Some critics suggested it was simply a means of rewarding more supporters who did not find a place at the cabinet table. However, transition team members insisted that Martin believed parliamentary secretaries could and should play a more important role in the policy process and that this was the reason for their inclusion. Jack Austin explained: 'The starting point for any transition is the personality of the prime minister and his management style. This prime minister believed in consultation and in broadening the base of policy-making, particularly after the more imperial style of Chrétien.'[8] Proof of this conviction was Martin's decision that secretaries should have access to cabinet committee meetings when necessary, a move the bureaucracy opposed, citing cabinet confidentiality. Austin's solution was to make the parliamentary secretaries privy councillors.

The two dozen parliamentary secretaries received a specific written mandate. Three were particularly noteworthy. This prime minister would have not one but three parliamentary secretaries supporting him, in the areas of cities, science, and Canada-U.S. relations. All of the secretaries attended at least some cabinet committee meetings and some, such as Sue Barnes (who served as parliamentary secretary to Andy Mitchell on the challenging Indian Affairs portfolio) attended almost all of them.

The swearing-in ceremony was also noteworthy for policy announcements. Mike Robinson pointed out that the many press releases and background documents made available to reporters constituted 'the most detailed set of papers that have ever been released at the swearing in of a prime minister.'[9] Some twenty pages of announcements covered the key priorities of ethics and democratic reform, Canada-U.S. relations, and federal-provincial relations, and outlined significant structural changes to the machinery of government designed to facilitate those priorities. Under democratic reform, for example, specific promises were made to provide for more free votes in Parliament, to provide greater research support for parliamentary committees, and to allow a House of Commons committee to vet governor-in-council appointments. In retrospect, the most significant commitment was that which required 'Ministers to actively engage with Private Members and to meet regularly with House committees in their portfolio area to discuss priorities and receive input on legislative initiatives.'[10]

The ceremony was designed to demonstrate that leadership change had produced real change in the government. In this context, Paul Martin's remarks to the media after he emerged from Rideau Hall take on particular significance. 'As Prime Minister,' he declared, 'I look forward to the opportunity to rally Canadians towards a new sense of purpose and around a new agenda of change and achievement.' Then he concluded, 'We are going to change the way things work in Ottawa in order to re-engage Canadians in the political process and achieve demonstrable progress on our priorities.'[11]

The Martin Cabinet: New Faces, New Issues

Apart from the prime minister, the most visible image of a government is its ministers. Paul Martin wasted little time demonstrating that – unlike John Turner in 1984 – he was able to make dramatic changes in cabinet to put a new face on his government. Twenty-two of Chrétien's ministers were dropped from the Martin cabinet, a move which came as quite a surprise to rank-and-file Liberals, not to mention those who found themselves once again on the backbenches. It was widely understood that Martin needed to reward his large coterie of faithful caucus supporters, but most Liberals assumed the new leader would balance his desire to reward loyalty with the need to ensure party solidarity. Instead, the few survivors from the Chrétien cabinet were actually Martin supporters like Anne McClellan and Ralph Goodale.

More surprising still was the fact that *none* of Martin's leadership rivals – John Manley, Allan Rock, or Sheila Copps – was included in his cabinet. This move was in striking contrast to the efforts of Pearson and Trudeau, to say nothing of Chrétien, to keep their former rivals involved in the government. One national reporter had already expressed the opinion that Sheila Copps's record and recent efforts meant 'Paul Martin will have to reward her with a cabinet gig and buy into elements of her left-wing agenda.'[12]

Events would soon prove how wrong they were.

Even among Martin supporters the omission of John Manley and Allan Rock from cabinet was viewed askance, particularly when both men had stated categorically that they would serve if asked. Instead, Rock was offered a diplomatic posting at the United Nations and Manley was offered (but refused) the position of ambassador to the United States, leading some critics to conclude that Martin was intent on ensuring his rivals' departure from Canadian politics entirely. One senior Martin aide later admitted that the decision to exclude leadership rivals 'went against the Liberal idea of bringing people back into the fold' which he had always supported, 'but there were scores to settle and the prime minister had amassed a lot of IOU's over the years.'[13]

The composition of Martin's cabinet reflected his desire to shore up Liberal support in western Canada. Longtime Martin supporters Ralph Goodale of Saskatchewan and Anne McLellan of Alberta were promoted to two of the most important cabinet posts – finance minister and deputy prime minister, respectively. Veteran Manitoba MPs Reg Alcock (Treasury Board) and Rey Pagtakhan (Western Economic Diversification) were promoted to cabinet, BC MPs Stephen Owen (Public Works) and David Anderson (Environment) retained their positions, while Senator Jack Austin of BC was named the Leader of the Government in the Senate. Although he was demoted, even Chrétien supporter Herb Dhaliwal, the former minister of natural resources from BC, made favourable comments to the media about the fact that so many key posts went to western Canadians.

A consequence of Martin's heavy reliance on his caucus supporters was a lack of experience in cabinet. As Jack Austin pointed out, however, many of those appointed by Martin had been in the Liberal caucus for more than a decade. 'They knew how government worked. They had all been parliamentary secretaries, or committee chairs, or had some other roles in the policy process.'[14] Martin felt it was important to bring along a new generation of Liberals, and Mike Robinson concurred: 'He wanted to make sure there were more people gaining the kind of experience that would be necessary to take on leadership roles in the future.'[15]

Somewhat surprisingly, there was a decrease in the representational nature of the cabinet. Although Martin appointed almost as many women as Chrétien (ten versus Chrétien's twelve), they were all, with the exception of McClellan, assigned very junior posts. Half of his female cabinet ministers were, in fact, ministers of state.[16] There were also fewer visible minorities. As one caucus critic commented, 'The people around Martin are almost all white males. That's reflected in this cabinet, and in his close advisers.' The imbalance was eased, however, with a large increase in the number of ministers representing ethnic communities, primarily from Ontario. Several staunch Martin supporters fell into this category, including Judy Sgro, Tony Valeri, Albina Guarnieri, Stan Keyes, Tony Ianno, and Joe Volpe. While some Liberals saw the presence of such a large contingent of ministers from ethnic groups as merely another result of Martin's leadership campaign obligations, CBC commentator Larry Zolf concluded that 'Martin's large ethnic cabinet component is a long overdue recognition of how much the Liberals owe immigrants and ethnic groups in Canada.'[17]

A second, even more surprising change in Martin's cabinet was the overall lack of fluency in French among anglophone ministers. Despite their prominent positions and years in Ottawa, neither Anne McLellan nor Ralph Goodale could communicate effectively in French. This problem was compounded by the many non-French-speaking southern Ontario MPs Martin promoted to cabinet. Various members of the transition team were quick to note that the lack of French competence at the cabinet level was to be compensated by the appointment of bilingual parliamentary secretaries, but this refinement was not well understood. Instead, the predominantly unilingual anglophone image of Martin's cabinet was underscored in Quebec by both Parti Québécois leader Bernard Landry and the Liberal intergovernmental affairs minister, Benoît Pelletier, who remarked about Goodale and McClellan that 'these two people will have to have a better knowledge of French if they want their careers to evolve.'[18] For a government intent on expanding its core support in Quebec, this image was cause for concern.

The only senior francophones in cabinet were Lucienne Robillard (promoted to Industry) and Pierre Pettigrew (who received both the Health and Intergovernmental Affairs portfolios). Cabinet newcomer Helen Scherrer – the first MP to call publicly for Chrétien's resignation – received the Heritage portfolio. High-profile Chrétien ministers from Quebec such as Martin Cauchon and Stéphane Dion returned to the backbenches. One former Chrétien adviser warned, 'Martin may think he's from Quebec but he needs to have more credible francophones on his team if the Liberal brand is going to make strides in the province. This is crucial now that we have the Bloc on the run. It's our big chance to wipe them out.' These comments were echoed by other Chrétien supporters and demonstrated once again the significant difference of opinion between the two camps concerning the best approach to Quebec.

But 'credible' was clearly in the eye of the beholder. The complexion of Martin's cabinet had shifted from one of strong federalists to one dominated by soft nationalists. Dennis Dawson was blunt: with too few Quebec MPs, Dawson complained they had been obliged to keep Chrétien people they would have preferred to demote. 'You build your cabinet with the wood that is given you,' he said later. 'We had to have ministers who would second-guess everything Paul (or Paul's people) were saying, or would in some cases just object to it completely. So you can imagine this was not the ideal scenario.'[19]

Another consequence of Martin's determination to reward his supporters was that the cabinet shifted from left-leaning to decidedly right of centre. Virtually none of the social Liberals from the Chrétien era were still in the cabinet. Apart from Copps and Rock, notable departures included David Collenette, Martin Cauchon, Don Boudria, Jane Stewart, Bob Nault, and Elinor Caplan. Many of the new ministers who replaced them were well-known business Liberals. Several of Martin's new cabinet ministers were also from the social conservative group that opposed Chrétien's recent bills. Since Martin had agreed to follow through on those measures, the opposition of several of his cabinet ministers would prove an unusual challenge.

The cabinet's shift to the right did not go unnoticed by other Liberals, the opposition parties, or the media. The Martin cabinet was described by one senior Liberal as 'a plane with only one wing.'[20] The shift ultimately encouraged former NDP leader Ed Broadbent to return to public life. 'It isn't just the issues,' Broadbent said, 'it's all that room on the centre left that's been vacated, indeed abandoned, by the Liberals.'[21] Arguing that the NDP had originally been worried Martin would move to the left on taking power (so as to run on his father's record in the next election), one media commentator concluded it was Martin who should be worried. 'No Liberal prime minister from King to Pearson to Trudeau to Chrétien has ever decided he could govern without a left wing to keep him on his toes. Martin is evidently planning to do so. So far, at least, he's prepared to pay the price for amputating his own left wing.'[22]

Changing the Way Government Works

In addition to the dramatic change in players, Martin made some significant modifications to the structure of government. First, in an effort to close the file on perceived scandal from the Chrétien era, he reorganized Human Resources Development Canada (HRDC), a sprawling, unmanageable Tory legacy. It was split into two separate departments: Human Resources and Skills Development, and Social Development, a move most Liberals felt was long overdue.

More controversial was the decision to split the Department of Foreign Affairs and International Trade (DFAIT). Critics saw the plan as an attempt to accommodate Martin's former college roommate and longtime supporter, Jim Peterson, who was assigned the international trade portfolio and would otherwise have been a junior minister with no department to administer. Martin's people, and Peterson himself, were quick to counter the accusation, claiming that the decision had the support of the public service. It was only later that they learned a key player, DFAIT deputy minister Peter Harder, opposed the idea, as did several other senior mandarins.[23]

Like Chrétien, Martin made considerable use of ministers of state. In his case, though, the positions were used less for regional representation and more often to address a number of specific agenda issues that came under the umbrella of large departments. For example, increased concerns about public health and safety spawned by the SARS and BSE crises led to the appointment of a minister of state for public health. Other new positions included a minister of state for infrastructure and a minister of state for new and emerging markets.

Those who disliked the business Liberal tilt of the new administration were quick to note the abolition of the position of minister of state for housing and the creation of another new minister of state position for privatization, given to Martin supporter John McKay. As one national columnist concluded, 'In a cabinet shake-up as bold and extensive as the one Prime Minister Martin conducted, something was bound to fall between the cracks.'[24] For those most affected, the signal sent by the assignment of the Housing portfolio to Environment Minister David Anderson was certainly not positive. 'Housing has been downgraded,' the chair of the National Housing and Homeless Network, Michael Shapcott, concluded, 'at a time when Canada urgently needs leadership from the federal government.'[25]

More favourably viewed measures included changes to accountability procedures and the cancellation of problematic programs such as the sponsorship program in the Public Works Department. According to several members of the transition team, Ralph Goodale seized on the transition process, arguing that it was an ideal opportunity to close a file that had already caused considerable damage to the Liberals' image as competent managers. Similarly, the creation of an independent ethics commissioner reporting to Parliament rather than the prime minister and a new series of conflict-of-interest guidelines for ministers, their staff, and parliamentary secretaries were also part of Martin's effort to heighten the Liberals' reputation for honesty and integrity in government. All of these measures were generally well received. Perhaps inevitably, though, the press releases announcing these new measures went to great lengths to emphasize areas where the government of Jean Chrétien had been considered remiss.

Last but not least, Martin added several new cabinet committees to the decision-making mix, a move that Michael Robinson confirmed had its roots in Martin's experiences in the Chrétien cabinet.[26] Like his predecessor, Paul Martin had definite ideas about how cabinet should work. He was determined to have more consultation among ministers before decisions were made, and more consultation between ministers and backbench Liberals as a means of correcting the democratic deficit. First and foremost, he wanted to establish an Operations Committee to oversee the day-to-day operations of government. It would be an entirely separate exercise from the traditional Priorities and Planning Committee, now relegated to medium- and long-range planning on policy matters. The sixteen-member Operations Committee would be chaired by the deputy PM, Anne McClellan, while the prime minister would continue to chair P&P.

These were all matters Martin was passionate about, and he maintained an active interest in ensuring they were implemented fully and completely.

As a result of commitments made during the leadership race, Martin created and chaired three new cabinet committees, one on cities, one on aboriginal affairs, and a third on Canada-U.S. relations. According to Mike Robinson, the move was largely symbolic, an attempt by the prime minister to demonstrate the importance he placed on these issues.[27] In the face of criticism that the new system was too complex, Jack Austin insisted that the prime minister would not chair the cabinet committees on a regular basis. Deputy chairs were to act as de facto managers, although Austin noted that he himself would act as chair of the Indian Affairs committee.[28] Some academics and opposition politicians did not see these moves as symbolic of Martin's priorities or his ambition to decentralize power away from the PMO. Rather, they viewed the changes as a blatant attempt to centralize power. Critics argued that ministers were essentially being disenfranchised. 'The Prime Minister, his unelected aides and advisers in the PMO and his friends in Ottawa lobbying firm Earnscliffe are the true holders of power,' Alliance leader Stephen Harper argued, 'not the former backbenchers who are now members of the Paul Martin cabinet.'[29] Given the often strained relations between Martin's advisers and his caucus, many Liberal MPs were inclined to agree.

Another factor that heightened suspicions of the intention to centralize power was the major role Martin and his advisers played in the organization of ministers' offices. Straightaway they upgraded the position of the most important political adviser in each office. Under Pearson and Trudeau that position had been designated executive assistant. Under Mulroney (who argued that ministers needed more experienced and better qualified advisers) the title was changed to chief of staff. Also during Mulroney's time, the size and total budget of ministers' offices increased exponentially. When the Liberals returned to power a decade later under Jean Chrétien, ministers' offices were dramatically downsized and their senior political adviser was again referred to as an executive assistant.

Several of the incumbents during the Chrétien era resented the reversal, but it was two women in Martin's inner circle – former executive assistants Terrie O'Leary and Ruth Thorkelson – who objected the most vehemently. Once Martin was in charge, these same women pushed hard to have the position reclassified as chief of staff. 'No one outside government understood what we did,' Thorkelson complained. 'They heard EA and they thought "glorified secretary" because they were looking at a woman.'[30]

Another more invasive change – also drawn from Mulroney's practice – was the creation of an 'acceptable' list of candidates for the chief of staff positions. Chrétien's PMO had reserved the right to veto a minister's choice for this top position, but only one example of this occurred during the first two Chrétien mandates.[31] However, in the early Chrétien years, several Martin supporters believed they had been passed over because of their allegiance. Scott Reid, for example, specifically noted that he had been led to believe 'something would materialize' for him in a minister's office following the 1993 election. It never did.[32] Under Martin the PMO went much further, providing ministers with approved lists of individuals from which to choose. Now it was Chrétien's supporters who felt they were being frozen out.

Ruth Thorkelson maintained that it had been difficult to recruit good people for many of the ministers' offices. She gave several reasons why many Chrétien-era aides were not retained. Among them, a lack of partisanship figured prominently. 'I was shocked at the lack of commitment to the Liberal Party demonstrated by some executive assistants during the Chrétien years,' she recalled. 'These were political positions – exempt staff, not public servants – but many of them did not want to get their hands dirty with political activities.' Thorkelson argued that their refusal to work on an election campaign or to contribute to the Laurier Club proved that they were not prepared to put the party's interests above their own. 'Some of them were not even card-carrying party members,' she exclaimed, and 'we needed skilled political tacticians,' especially because 'some of the tools provided to the opposition and our own backbench by the democratic deficit plank proved a serious problem for us in government.'[33]

As part of the plan to address the democratic deficit, each ministerial office was instructed to establish a new position of director of parliamentary affairs. Regular consultations with the Liberal caucus and parliamentary committees became obligatory for ministerial initiatives. Greater emphasis was placed on regional ministers and on regional offices to assist them, particularly in western Canada. In BC, for example, Jack Austin co-shared regional ministerial responsibilities with David Emerson over and above their cabinet roles as government leader in the Senate and industry minister respectively.

Revitalizing a concept that had been dormant under Chrétien, Martin re-introduced a Political Committee of cabinet comprised of regional political ministers as well as Tim Murphy and Francis Fox. The PMO's Michelle Cadario served as the secretary with Martin himself chairing. David Herle was frequently invited to attend these monthly meetings to report on polling data and other research intelligence. Defending the committee, Scott Reid argued that 'Jean Chrétien was his own political adviser' and had, in effect, functioned in isolation on many important political decisions.[34] By contrast, Martin's reliance on close advisers and pollsters raised the ire of some of the ministers in attendance. 'At least Chrétien had good political instincts,' one of them remarked afterwards, 'whereas Paul just relied on Herle and those polls of his, no matter what we said.'

In order to follow through on his ambitious agenda, Martin needed a tightly organized, professional, and efficiently run office with experienced aides. With a federal election pending, it was a need that became more obvious every day. Unfortunately, this aspect of the transition team's planning was hampered by a number of factors, first and foremost being Martin's emphasis on personal loyalty. Like Brian Mulroney, Martin was determined to reward or retain those responsible for his election, people who were not only aides and advisers but also personal friends.

The Martin PMO: Change at the Centre

The organization and staffing of the Martin PMO were quite different from those of his predecessors. One of the most remarkable aspects of

Martin's office was the fact that the entire team of senior staffers consisted of former leadership campaign workers who knew each other well. Most had worked together for more than a decade and were charter members of the Board. The same was also true of senior appointments at the Caucus Research Bureau and the party's National Office.

Another unusual feature of this PMO was the number of individuals who had previously worked as government lobbyists, particularly for Earnscliffe or for Martin's own firm, Canada Steamship Lines. Several had also worked in Martin's ministerial office. In contrast to Turner's and Chrétien's offices, where only one individual had worked so closely with the PM, Martin's PMO included seven former ministerial aides.

On paper, the key player in the new PMO was Tim Murphy, the Toronto lawyer who had served as Martin's last executive assistant before leaving cabinet. Murphy was asked to fill the crucial role of chief of staff, a position he was widely seen as ideal for, given his talent for coordination and efficiency. He faced two challenges: changing the structure of the PMO to reflect the management style of the new prime minister and finding appropriate roles and titles for the Martin loyalists who would be part of that structure. The latter task in particular represented a nearly impossible challenge of coordination and control.

In a striking departure from the standard hierarchical structure of his predecessors, Martin's PMO was a loose horizontal organization. It contained no fewer than four deputy chiefs of staff. One was Karl Littler (Martin's former legislative assistant and Ontario campaign organizer), who was given responsibility for the new concept of cabinet affairs. Ruth Thorkelson (Murphy's predecessor as executive assistant) assumed the second deputy role with responsibility for parliamentary affairs, another new function. Interestingly, the position of director of appointments (filled by Martin supporter Karen Martin) was downgraded, becoming part of the line responsibilities handled by Thorkelson. A third deputy chief of staff position (operations) was filled briefly by Mario Cucanato and then, following the June 2004 election, by Michelle Cadario, who would serve as national director at the party headquarters until then.

Another unusual feature of Martin's PMO was its heavy concentration of unilingual anglophones. To rectify the imbalance and make room for francophones, the post of deputy chief of staff (policy) was created, and Paul Corriveau, a Quebec lawyer who had also worked in the Chrétien PMO, was appointed to the post. Another former Martin finance aide, Peter Nicholson, was appointed senior policy adviser under Corriveau. Immediately after the 2004 election Corriveau left to return to the private sector, and Nicholson took over as the fourth deputy chief of staff.

Mario Lague, a career public servant, was another temporary appointment as director of communications. Martin's key strategist and former communications director at Finance, Scott Reid, was named senior adviser under Lague. With the election over, Lague returned to the public service and Reid became director of communications. He also remained in charge of issues management. As Reid himself noted later, the title did not reflect the real nature of his duties or degree of access to the prime minister. In addition to attending the senior staff meetings, Reid attended the meetings of the PCO clerk and PMO chief of staff with the prime minister. (Asked by President George Bush what he did, Reid famously replied 'I can't really say sir. It's not that I don't want to tell you, it's just that I don't really know from day to day.')[35] Another former Martin staffer at Finance, Melanie Gruer, was named assistant director of communications and press secretary. Brian Guest, who replaced Reid at Finance as Martin's communications director, became deputy principal secretary under Francis Fox.

One of the few senior positions filled by an outsider was that of principal secretary. Although Fox had supported Martin's leadership bid and served on the transition team, the former Trudeau-era minister had not expected to be part of the Martin PMO and originally declined the position when it was offered to him by Mike Robinson. Fox later explained it was only Martin's personal appeal that caused him to change his mind. 'Paul was very persuasive, and in the end I agreed. But it was always understood I would only stay until the election, which we thought was imminent. My role was primarily to deal with Quebec.'

Despite his age and experience, Fox never came to exercise the influence in PMO that Jean Pelletier had done under Chrétien. It was Tim Murphy who chaired senior staff meetings and met with the clerk and prime minister. Fox explained that there was 'an inner circle in PMO which operated informally much of the time. I came late to the organization and I wasn't part of that inner circle that had been with him from the beginning.'[36]

Like Jean Chrétien's appointment of career diplomat James Bartleman as foreign policy adviser, the new prime minister appointed two bureaucrats to serve as special advisers to his PMO. A national security adviser and a national science adviser were defended as 'long overdue' specialized support for the prime minister in key emerging issues. Just as Chrétien's aides had explained the addition of a foreign policy adviser by pointing to the common practice of European heads of state, one Martin adviser said, 'American presidents have had these for years.'[37]

The careful planning of PMO positions was soon undone, however, by a seemingly endless string of resignations. As he explained several years later, Tim Murphy knew about the planned departures of some senior PMO staffers after the 2004 election but this was not widely known at the time. Moreover, several other individuals left following the June election because, as Murphy admitted, they were 'not a good fit with the requirements of the office.' Not surprisingly, the departures were seen as proof of unrest in the Martin government's command centre, a stark contrast to the stability of the Chrétien PMO.[38]

Martin's Horizontal Management Style

The close relationships of most of the senior staff in PMO could conceivably have led to a situation in which the new 'centre' was operational and effective almost immediately, but this did not happen. Instead it led to serious problems of communication and oversight. The Martin PMO never actually formed a coherent operational unit in the months leading up to the federal election of June 2004. Even some of those who lived through the period agreed that it did not gel. As Scott Reid later concluded, 'For sure, at a minimum we never got the policy function right.'[39]

Tim Murphy and Mike Robinson both agreed in retrospect that the familiarity of the inner circle in PMO was actually a problem. Their years of interaction in the Martin campaign led many of the PMO staff to take for granted that they would consult with each other and the prime minister regularly, regardless of official titles.[40] One of their number, Dennis Dawson, later referred to their near constant interactions as 'groupthink.'[41]

The more egalitarian attitudes of western and rural Canada, the culture of the business sector from which many of them came, and of a younger generation to which most of them belonged, contributed to an informal managerial style that seemed, to many parliamentary veterans, simply unprofessional. 'They called him "Paul" even in public!' one shocked senior bureaucrat exclaimed. 'How can anyone think of him as the prime minister when he lets them do that?' This laid-back approach was reinforced by Paul Martin's own dislike of hierarchical organizations and his highly consultative management style. Virtually everyone involved with Martin referred to his preference for a 'flat' organizational structure. David Herle once commented that Martin was 'an entrepreneur, not really a manager at all.' As Robinson put it, 'Paul Martin is not a big fan of hierarchical structures. He wanted to interface directly with many people in the PMO.'[42]

Terrie O'Leary pointed out that a more consultative approach was how Martin operated in Finance, a portfolio in which he had achieved considerable success.[43] At the same time, the much broader scope of responsibilities of a prime minister, coupled with the lack of experience of Martin and his senior staff in other government departments, meant this horizontal managerial style was unlikely to succeed in PMO. Combined with the problems caused by unclear reporting relationships, Martin's PMO was virtually certain to be dysfunctional.

The consequences of Martin's managerial style were significant. Tim Murphy revealed that it was not unusual for Martin to pick up the phone and call 'any one of fifteen to twenty close advisers,' including senior public servants, to ask for advice or information. 'It made it very difficult to know where we stood on an issue, both for us and for the bureaucrats. In PMO there were at least eight people who could legitimately claim they were speaking for the prime minister.'[44] Initially the senior bureaucrats in PCO were sceptical of this consultative approach and of the inner circle in general. Although relations between Murphy, Fox, and Himmelfarb were, by all accounts, quite positive once the new managerial style was accepted, an important consequence of this approach was that ministerial staff and senior bureaucrats in other departments were frequently unsure what the position of the 'centre' was on a given issue. 'You knew who to talk to in Chrétien's PMO,' one former EA said. 'And if Eddie told you something was a done deal, you knew it was. With these guys, you never even knew who it was you should call. There didn't seem to be any logic to it at all, and they kept changing their minds every ten minutes.'

Lastly, the close-knit group around Martin was seen to have huge influence with the prime minister. In fact, despite his consultative style and the many procedural changes made to enhance the role of MPs, many backbenchers now felt they had less input than ever, victims of 'the Board's' closed shop. The irony of this new, more centralized role for the PMO was not lost on many of Jean Chrétien's former supporters. Widely criticized for centralizing power in the PMO himself, Chrétien's ministers and advisers marvelled at the degree to which ministerial decision-making power seemed to be usurped by the centre, although the lack of efficiency in PMO decision making tended to obscure what they viewed as the huge power shift taking place.[45]

This perception was reinforced by the treatment accorded to both MPs and senior public servants by some of Martin's advisers. One former bureaucrat recalled: 'These people thought they could call up deputies and demand things for the same day. Then they'd call back a few hours later and announce it was all off. No apologies. No recognition that they were only staff, and the politicians and bureaucrats had real authority. It was amazing. We started losing key people to resignations within months.' Even Terrie O'Leary, the Martin adviser best known for her professional approach and ability to maintain good relations with members of the opposing camp, readily conceded that some of her colleagues 'could have been more careful of people's feelings.'[46] Jack Austin reinforced and expanded on this view, noting that 'the fierce protectiveness that surrounded the staffs of Martin and Chrétien' had existed since 1993.[47] Dennis Dawson went further. Blaming the 'arrogance' of their 'tight knit group' on the fact that they had been together for so long, Dawson observed their often cavalier treatment of caucus members. 'There were advantages to being a small group. But one of the disadvantages was that we did become arrogant. And that made us not nice to caucus members, not nice to a bunch of people. And we paid for it in 2004, we paid for it in 2006, and God knows we're still paying for it today,' Dawson concluded.[48]

The Caucus Research Bureau and the National Party Office: More Centralization

The personnel in the PMO were also in very close contact with the key players in the Caucus Research Bureau and the party's National Office, most of whom were former Martin campaign workers and charter members of the Board as well. Long before Paul Martin took over the leadership it was known that Kevin Bosch was to become the new director of the Liberal Caucus Research Bureau. As a westerner and a supporter of John Webster's 'take no prisoners' attitude, Bosch was considered ideal for the post. An Albertan who had worked for the provincial Liberals, he had been instrumental in prompting two separate ethics investigations of premier Ralph Klein before leaving for the national scene. He had made his reputation in Ottawa during the 2000 election campaign, working in the war room, where his detailed knowledge of the Alliance Party and its leaders proved invaluable.

Then in 2002 Bosch became policy director for the Martin leadership campaign. It was Bosch who promoted the democratic deficit theme during the leadership race. He believed 'there are planks of Klein's strategy you can steal. The standing policy committees he set up in Alberta had real power ... it was strategically intelligent to create a system where backbenchers had some influence.'[49] Bosch also reinforced David Herle's argument that Martin's government needed to demonstrate change. 'It's crucial he differentiate himself from Chrétien,' Bosch argued, 'otherwise people will wonder why we've gone through this whole exercise.'[50]

When he assumed the role of LCRB director in December 2003, Bosch felt the Bureau needed to change its emphasis. Revisiting the long-standing debate over the relative importance of the research and communications functions – one that had been largely dormant under Chrétien – Bosch came down squarely on the side of communications. 'It was almost like a think tank,' he said later about the LCRB. 'Very academic and insular. We moved quickly to develop and emphasize practical communications strategies, and of course I attended the daily communications meetings in PMO with Scott Reid.'[51]

This was something no previous director had done, and clearly spoke to the increased emphasis on communications. Bosch continued to report to the national caucus chair, but it was clear that the relationship between the Bureau and the PMO became even more tightly controlled than it had been under Chrétien. Bosch's close relationship with so many of the key staff in the PMO allowed the Bureau to play a more prominent role. On the other hand, the Bureau's capacity to provide policy advice declined as more emphasis was placed on communications and the 'opposition watch' function. In addition, Bosch was hampered by the flat organizational style of the PMO. 'The prime minister's management style didn't translate well to PMO,' Bosch confided. 'He would call me directly, even on weekends,' but at the same time 'almost anyone could go to him ... there was a lack of a single funnel' to channel all of the information, he concluded.[52]

Although the budget of the Bureau had grown steadily during the years the party was in power (rising from $1.05 million in 1993–4 to $1.77 million in 2003 when Martin took over, and $2.3 million after the 2004 election), the number of researchers employed under Martin actually fell. As in 1984, a major turnover of personnel occurred with the change in leadership, causing the predictable problems of continuity and lack of institutional memory. Of the remaining policy researchers, two were assigned expressly to western issues. Bosch argued that there was far more sensitivity to western issues in the Martin PMO. As an example he indicated that Martin's hesitation over Chrétien's Kyoto plan was a direct result of that sensitivity, and of David Herle's concerns about increasing the party's electoral support in Alberta.[53]

Over the next year a number of new communications positions were created at the Bureau, as well as the position of official demographer. This latter position was enthusiastically promoted by Bosch, who noted that it was now technically possible for Bureau documents to be targeted to ridings, ethnic communities, and regions where a particular issue had the most resonance. After the 2004 election, a new position of director general was created to handle the overall administration of the Bureau. This post was filled by Toronto reporter Derek Ferguson, once again emphasizing the much greater importance of communications over research. Two new positions, chief (communications services) and chief (policy and research) were also added to the organizational structure. In many ways, the Research Bureau became a more hierarchical organization at the same time that the PMO was becoming more horizontal.

Election readiness was the Bureau's primary concern throughout the eighteen months of the Martin government. 'We were in a constant state of code red,' Bosch recalled.[54] Between November 2003 and May 2004 the Bureau filled a pre-writ function that would transfer smoothly into the war room of the election itself. Given their minority status after the 2004 election, this situation essentially continued until the second election in January 2006. What the LCRB did not do, to any significant degree, was participate in the platform exercise, a marked departure from past practice but one easily explained by the shift in emphasis to communications.

After the 2006 election, when the party found itself in opposition for the first time in nearly fifteen years, the Bureau was confronted with the consequences of its altered emphasis. Its research capacity was severely constrained as it had been in 1984. However, one huge advantage was that funding actually increased despite the minority status of the government. The merger of the Conservatives and the Alliance created a unique situation which unbalanced the funding formula used for both parties. Rather than reduce funding for themselves, the new Conservative government increased the total amount available for research, which resulted in an increase from $1.8 million to $2.37 million in the LCRB budget. Such largesse allowed the Bureau to begin rebuilding its research capacity, although there was still a conviction that communications products were more important. Ironically, given its original mandate, Bosch noted that the Bureau did less work for caucus than ever before.

At the party's national headquarters, election readiness was virtually the only preoccupation after December 2003. Michelle Cadario, appointed national director, was expected to build on Martin's leadership campaign machinery and put in place the necessary support structure for an imminent federal election. Cadario brought Martin's New Brunswick leadership campaign coordinator, Steve MacKinnon, to Ottawa to be her second in command and, after the election, to take over as national director. A former director of the New Brunswick Liberals' provincial wing and adviser to Premier Frank McKenna, MacKinnon was credited with having the type of in-depth knowledge of the party and its operations that would be necessary for the long haul.

Several senior staff members at the headquarters were also replaced following the arrival of Martin's team. In addition to Martin's choice of president, Mike Eizenga, several other key supporters such as Richard Mahoney (national revenue chair) and Lloyd Posno (chief financial officer) returned to elected and/or volunteer positions with the party almost immediately. Also among them were former Turner fundraiser Gerry Schwartz and his wife, Heather Reisman, who had served on Turner's platform committee.

Relations between the National Office and the PMO were extremely close. First Cadario and then MacKinnon participated in senior staff meetings on a regular basis, but they were also consulted by phone and email several times a day. The party headquarters counted on a favourable response from PMO about their pre-election needs. And, like the Research Bureau, the influence of the National Office could be said to have increased due to the close personal relationships among those in charge. But, also like the Bureau, the impact of party advice was diluted by the large number of players with access to the prime minister. This lack of policy filter was a primary reason why the new government had such difficulty launching its agenda.

Early Missteps and the Democratic Deficit Agenda

Just days after he was sworn in, a flurry of negative news stories began taking the shine off Paul Martin's new government and his attempts to demonstrate change. Most were relatively minor issues, but, taken together, the succession of unflattering revelations began to affect Martin's image. This was more than a little ironic. It was John Turner's rush to call an election shortly after he took over from Pierre Trudeau that led to the disastrous 1984 election campaign. Drawing from that experience, the Martin team assumed it was important to take enough time to convince Canadians that the new Liberal government was not the Chrétien government. As a result, they delayed calling the election several times. Instead of the competent, self-assured former finance minister, Canadians increasingly saw a prime minister who appeared uncertain, ill at ease, and overwhelmed by the task of governing.

Unreasonably high expectations undoubtedly played a role in public perception of the new PM, but there were self-inflicted wounds as well. These included an ineffective communications strategy, Martin's highly consultative management style, and excessive delays in providing concrete details of the new government's agenda. In the absence of that agenda, the policy vacuum was filled by a series of negative stories that the Liberals seemed powerless to counter.

Martin's attempts to provide backbench MPs with 'real' powers and influence, for example, ran into practical difficulties. No sooner had he announced that a parliamentary committee would review all senior order-in-council appointments (including those of Supreme Court judges) than an avalanche of criticism erupted from provincial bar associations and legal scholars, forcing Martin to clarify that the committee's role would be advisory and that he himself would have the final say.

Another issue hampering Martin's democratic deficit agenda was controversy over his $12 million leadership campaign war chest. On 10 December 2003, Martin attended a major party fundraiser in Toronto that attracted much of the Canadian business elite and raised over $2 million. With Jean Chrétien's political financing bill about to come into force on 1 January 2004, Martin argued that the corporate fundraiser was essential. 'The fact is that the Liberal Party is deeply in debt and this is going to really help a great, great deal,' he told reporters. Organized by his own supporters rather than the party, the event and Martin's comments were widely seen as further criticism of Chrétien's legislation.[55] They were also seen as proof that the leadership race had been more costly than the party expected and that Martin's fundraising efforts had drained off many of the party's traditional sources of funding. In early January, Martin's campaign organizers confirmed that they would be contributing a surplus of $3.8 million to the party, an announcement met with enthusiasm by new party president Mike Eizenga.[56]

A different controversy had arisen in the meantime over Martin's decision to increase the salaries of senior political staff in ministers' offices. The optics of the decision once again cast doubt on his concern for accountability and fiscal prudence, particularly as it was taken at the same time that pay increases for the public service were frozen. The underlying rationale for the decision was the reclassification of ministerial positions from executive assistant to chief of staff, an argument that failed to impress critics. PMO communications director Mario Lague maintained that the new positions were more demanding, but former ministerial assistants under Chrétien disagreed. 'There's no new tasks,' one of them told reporters. 'And who did they think *used* to meet with parliamentary secretaries and committees?' Opposition politicians seized on the issue as well. Alliance MP John Williams concluded that 'the optics for the prime minister are not good ... especially when 175,000 public servants got their own classifications frozen.'[57]

Without a doubt, Martin was in trouble with public servants, the very people responsible for implementing his agenda. The freeze on salaries and capital expenditures was announced without consultation with senior bureaucrats or union representatives, and conflicted with the Public Service Modernization Act adopted in November 2003. Moreover, Martin's newly appointed president of the Treasury Board, Reg Alcock – the minister responsible for the public service – angered many of his employees with comments that appeared to question their competence and integrity.[58] 'He is the chief mechanic and he keeps throwing monkey wrenches into the government machinery,' one expert said. Another described Alcock's 'bull-in-a-china-shop style' as a dramatic change from the approach of his predecessor, Lucienne Robillard, who 'impressed the officials she worked with through her innovation, ability to listen, skill in managing a department, and competence.'[59]

The salary freeze also led the head of the bureaucrats' prestigious professional employees' union, Steve Hindle, to announce that he would no longer be a candidate for the Liberals in the next federal election. 'I wasn't concerned about not winning,' Hindle said. 'I was more concerned I *would* win and have to be part of a government that wasn't interested in the public service.'[60] In the end, the pay freeze for public servants was lifted, but the general public had lingering doubts.

Duelling Agendas

In addition to problems launching his own agenda, Martin's handling of several bills associated with the Chrétien legacy created more image problems. Although he had agreed to follow through on the legislation, Martin came up against ongoing opposition from some of his most loyal caucus supporters, several of whom were in his cabinet. His response to such opposition was to stall, thus increasing his reputation as someone who tried to please everyone rather than make difficult decisions.[61] On the same-sex marriage bill, for example, he delayed implementation and attempted to allay his supporters' fears by extending the judicial review process.

The timing of the election call weighed heavily on the minds of Martin's strategists. According to David Herle, the reason for not calling an election immediately was Martin's leadership commitment to allow the implementation of the new riding boundaries. With both Alberta and British Columbia set to receive more seats, Martin and his advisers felt they could not justify calling an election before those boundaries took effect. Otherwise their claims to give greater weight to western Canadian concerns would be dismissed. As a result, the earliest they could hope for was a spring election.

Still, the boundaries problem was rectified once Parliament resumed. Legislation had been introduced in the fall of 2003 after consultation with the chief electoral officer, Jean Pierre Kingsley, who confirmed that it was technically possible for Elections Canada to be ready for a spring vote on the new boundaries. As a result, among the first orders of business on the return of the House of Commons in February 2004 was the reintroduction of that legislation. A vote was held on 14 February which set the stage for Martin to call an election any time after 1 April.[62]

By then it was apparent to Martin's advisers that the new Liberal government would have to develop a more comprehensive policy package if it were to demonstrate the degree of change they felt was essential for electoral success. Not only had their decision to delay put a damper on Martin's image, the former Alliance and Progressive Conservative parties had taken advantage of the delay to stage a leadership race for the newly merged Conservative Party. Stephen Harper became leader of the new party in early March, creating more concern in the Liberal ranks – cerebral and disciplined, Harper was a much less attractive adversary than Stockwell Day. Nevertheless, as Brian Tobin later emphasized, Liberals on both sides of the Martin-Chrétien divide were still prepared to put the past behind them in the name of party unity.[63] Many eagerly anticipated the Throne Speech, which they expected would rally the troops around a positive and well-defined agenda.

The 2004 Throne Speech and the Agenda of Change

Those expecting a silver bullet that would guarantee a fourth majority were disappointed by Paul Martin's first Throne Speech. It began on a high note, emphasizing the theme of change. 'This Speech marks the start of a new government; a new agenda; a new way of working.'[64] But much of what followed was familiar and predictable. No dramatic or bold new programs were outlined, certainly not what critics and Martin supporters expected from an 'agenda of transformative change.' One senator summed up the feelings of many in the caucus when he said, 'We still don't know why he couldn't wait to be prime minister, do we?'

Many observers agreed. Columnist Jeffrey Simpson wrote, 'Although it offends the Paul Martinites who now rule, their agenda has more in common with Jean Chrétien's than they would care, or dare, to admit.'[65] Political scientist Bruce Doern's assessment was similar. Doern concluded that the wording of the speech, although devoid of many specifics, had a left-leaning tendency and in many respects 'was a continuation of the last Chrétien STF.'[66]

The speech was written by PMO policy adviser Peter Nicholson, a fact which originally caused consternation in PCO. Nicholson recalled that Clerk Alex Himmelfarb informed him that the speech was always written in PCO. According to Nicholson, this very concrete example of the Martin government's new centralization was easily accommodated, however, 'because we got along well, and the new role for the PMO proved not to be a problem in the end.' Both Himmelfarb and Tim Murphy were consulted on various drafts. 'Many people in PMO and from the various policy roundtables had some input,' Nicholson noted, 'but it was ultimately an internal exercise in which I held the pen and Tim was the only other major player, apart, of course, from the prime minister.'[67]

In the crucial area of the democratic deficit, the speech focused on parliamentary reform rather than Senate or electoral reform, a point made by the opposition parties when criticizing the proposals. Unhappily for Martin, such criticisms were echoed by Liberal party icon Tom Kent. Agreeing that Senate and electoral reform were more important, Kent warned that 'Martin's words have roused considerable expectations. To fulfill them, he must let go some of the patronage and commanding control now centered in the prime minister's office.'[68] This was clearly something Martin was not prepared to do. His definition of the democratic deficit was focused on the role and powers of MPs. The promise of more free votes, an enhanced role for parliamentary committees, and more consultation with individual MPs on the shape of legislation were intended, according to the speech, to 'return Parliament to the centre of national debate and decision-making.' These changes were also expected to 're-engage citizens in Canada's political life ... by making Parliament work better,' and to 'restore the public's faith and trust in the integrity and good management of government.'

The surprises in the speech were few, but they were significant. Critics pointed to a lack of promises of further tax breaks or increased support for the military. Others noted that there was little or no discussion of agricultural or transportation policy, despite major crises in the former and proposed initiatives of the previous government on the latter. Perhaps the most significant surprise of the Throne Speech, though, was the degree to which it failed to go beyond Martin's earlier statements. The comments of the opposition parties reflected a broader public frustration with the lack of specifics. 'Where is the plan?' Jack Layton asked, while the new Conservative Party's interim leader, Grant Hill, suggested that 'Canadians will be cynical about promises that don't have any specifics tied to them at all.'[69]

Despite the sketchy outline, several policy areas covered in the Throne Speech were significant as indicators of Martin's new approach to federal-provincial relations. The section on 'Changing the Way Things Work in Ottawa' included a commitment to 'a new partnership with provinces and territories, focused on the interests of Canadians, that means greater transparency ... and financial accountability in how we govern.' The section on health care reiterated the need to reduce wait times and spoke of 'fundamental reforms' required to achieve this objective. 'The government will work with its provincial and territorial partners on the necessary reforms and long-term sustainability of the health system,' it concluded.

Similarly, on sustainable development the speech stressed that the federal government would only move on Kyoto implementation 'in partnership with provincial and territorial governments and other stakeholders.' The government promised to 'respect its commitments to the Kyoto Accord ... in a way that produces long-term and enduring results while maintaining a strong and growing economy,' a position many environmentalists considered unfeasible. Virtually everyone agreed it would allow the government considerable 'wiggle room.'[70] Still, the emphasis on provincial consultation hardly seemed revolutionary and raised few eyebrows among the traditional federalists in the caucus.

One area that did reflect substantive change from earlier policy statements was the cities agenda. Following vigorous internal lobbying by rural and western Liberal MPs and senators in his caucus, this was suddenly converted to 'a new deal for *communities*' (emphasis added) in the speech. With no mention of the gas tax that had been part of his proposal from the beginning, the speech instead offered a 'down payment' in the form of a rebate on the federal portion of the GST. Some of those most affected, such as Toronto's new mayor, David Miller, pronounced himself 'delighted' with the announcement of some $7 billion in additional revenues over a ten-year period. More importantly, in terms of the federal-provincial relations issue, Miller stressed that he saw Martin's approach as a 'huge advance' from the position of previous federal governments. 'He has moved beyond the traditional sort of grant program and is treating us seriously as another order of government,' Miller declared.[71]

In Quebec, however, where Martin seemed peculiarly insensitive to provincial concerns over the cities agenda, the reaction was quite different. Quebec Finance Minister Yves Séguin immediately asked where the federal government would find the money to pay for the GST exemptions, pointing out that the tax breaks would coincide with planned reductions in equalization payments to the province. Séguin told reporters he 'wanted to know why Ottawa can find more financial aid for cities, towns and villages but not for the provinces,' predicting that 'the tax break will generate "lively" debate on revenue sharing at the next first ministers meeting.'[72]

The 2004 Throne Speech was forgotten sooner than most. A week after it was delivered, the auditor general's second report on the sponsorship program was tabled in the House of Commons. The ensuing political crisis can be seen as the defining event of the Martin mandate for several reasons. First, with the report's release, all of Paul Martin's previous attempts to make progress on his democratic deficit agenda were effectively neutralized. Second, the crisis irrevocably tied Martin to the Chrétien era at the precise moment when he and his advisers were attempting to demonstrate major change. Martin's highly controversial response to this perceived crisis must therefore be viewed through the prism of a leader and his advisers desperate to reassert control over their agenda. Finally, the fact that the crisis arose out of measures taken by Jean Chrétien to deal with the fallout from the 1995

Quebec referendum – and to promote the role of the federal government – inevitably meant that the two central cleavages plaguing the party for nearly twenty years came together in one place. Rightly or wrongly, by criticizing the sponsorship program and disowning the resulting problems, Martin and his advisers would be seen to be criticizing Jean Chrétien and his supporters on a personal level, and also for their Trudeauvian view of federalism. The combination of the two was devastating, raising the level of distrust between the two wings of the party to new heights and guaranteeing the next election would be fought without the help of many longtime Liberals.

The Sponsorship Crisis

According to David Herle, one of the most frustrating aspects of the December 2003 transition was the total absence of any reference to the impending crisis of the auditor general's report. 'Almost no one mentioned it,' he said. 'The briefing we had from the public service said there was no problem. You can imagine what a shock it was to actually read the thing. It was explosive.' Herle added that the report, completed in November 2003, was not seen by Paul Martin's team until after he became prime minister. 'We were blindsided.'[73]

Some Liberals and bureaucrats have disputed this version of the story. As one senior public servant later exclaimed, 'I know of no one who did not think the response to the AG's report would be intense and serious!' A former MP was more direct. 'How could they be "blindsided"? Didn't they watch Question Period all fall? The opposition were hounding us for weeks in advance of the tabling, because they sensed it would spell trouble.'[74] His point was well taken. Opposition leader Stephen Harper even alluded to the fact that Jean Chrétien was refusing to hold a public inquiry despite the impending report. In one exchange, Harper specifically stated: 'Mr. Speaker, I gather from that answer the Prime Minister still refuses to hold an independent judicial inquiry into this ongoing Liberal scandal. Since the Prime Minister will not be staying around to be accountable for this, has he had the opportunity to discuss this with his successor? Does he know whether a full public airing of this matter would be supported by the member for LaSalle-Émard?'[75]

The auditor general's report was tabled in the House of Commons on 10 February 2004, immediately following the Throne Speech. This meant that, in addition to fighting the various fires outlined above and preparing the Throne Speech, members of Martin's inner circle were forced to develop a response to the report from the time they learned of its contents until the day it was made public.

Sheila Fraser had actually undertaken her first study at the request of then minister of public works Don Boudria. At the time, Boudria made clear to Fraser that the prime minister himself was requesting 'should her audit bring to light information suggesting criminal activity, the matter was to be referred to the Department of Justice for recovery of funds and to the police for investigation.'[76] Her subsequent findings of serious irregularities did lead to an RCMP investigation and to many structural and procedural changes in the program and the department. These changes were implemented by Boudria and his successor, Ralph Goodale, in consultation with their cabinet colleague, Lucienne Robillard, then president of the Treasury Board.

Despite this, the auditor general decided to launch a second, more comprehensive audit on her own, and it was this second report that she provided to the government in November 2003. The report found 'up to $100 million' of the $250 million sponsorship program funding had been awarded to advertising firms with Liberal connections in Quebec and to crown corporations with little evidence of work performed. A visibly angry Sheila Fraser expressed 'shock' and 'outrage' at the findings, declaring among other things that 'virtually every rule' in the government's procedural handbook had been broken. 'I am actually appalled by what we found,' she told reporters.[77]

Fraser's unexpectedly emotional language caused some concern among bureaucrats and academics.[78] The negative impact of her comments on the public's image of government was profound. Asked later whether she felt her initial criticism had been too harsh and had damaged the image of the public service, she replied, 'Yes, very much so,' but went on to place the blame squarely on the media for failing to provide context for the findings.[79] In her annual report of 2005, Fraser, taking a different tack, advised the government 'not to react to her damming reports by automatically adding more controls' because 'public servants need space to do their jobs.' Her words, however, would not be heeded.[80]

Martin's Response

Anticipating controversy, Paul Martin's advisers crafted a multi-pronged strategy that went into action immediately after the report was tabled. According to David Herle, he and other PMO advisers agreed

with Martin that 'this was a genuine scandal. We had a moral obligation to follow through on this.'[81] Giving it to the RCMP would not do,
Scott Reid added, partly because they themselves were being investi-
gated as participants. 'We all felt it was explosive. And everyone could
predict the response of Jean Chrétien if he had still been in power. He
would have been dismissive and authoritarian. Paul Martin, on the
other hand, would be open and transparent.'[82] In short, those close to
Martin saw the calamity of the auditor general's report as both a serious problem and a potential opportunity.

Because Martin acted out of personal conviction, he was determined
to confront the issue head on as opposed to trying to downplay the seriousness of it. Scott Reid emphasized that the government's response
was decided upon more than a month in advance. Their course of action had been debated within the Board and approved by the cabinet's
Operations Committee. 'We had thought this through and everyone
was on side. We didn't just dream this up overnight on our own,' Reid
said pointedly. Not surprisingly, perhaps, the issue remained Reid's
'dominant preoccupation' up to the election.[83]

The day after the report became public, Martin ordered a public commission of inquiry to be headed by Justice John Gomery. The commission was one of the last elements of his response plan to be finalized.
Intense debate swirled within the kitchen cabinet as to the appropriate
forum, with some supporting the idea of a blue ribbon panel of experts
and others insisting on a public inquiry. Interestingly, no one proposed
to defend the extensive changes to contract procedures already made
under Boudria and Goodale, the RCMP criminal investigation, and
Martin's own cancellation of the sponsorship program as one of his
first acts of government.

Among those who argued against a public inquiry was Francis Fox,
the conspicuously isolated Quebec voice within the inner group of advisers. Fox worried that governments had lost control of inquiries in the
past and that such a thing could happen again with disastrous consequences. According to Steve MacKinnon, however, such concerns were
not widely shared. 'I can't remember a parliamentarian from Quebec
who wanted a public inquiry,' he joked.[84] It was the prime minister
himself who chose the inquiry option.

Justice Gomery appointed Bernard Roy, a respected Montreal lawyer but also a former principal secretary to Brian Mulroney, to be his
chief counsel. Roy's past Conservative affiliations raised eyebrows
among Liberals and proved to be the source of considerable difficul-

ty throughout the process. Even more problematic was the inquiry's mandate. As Francis Fox had anticipated, Gomery ended up expanding his hearings to cover matters such as the involvement of the Quebec wing of the Liberal Party, a move that the rest of Martin's advisers did not expect. 'You have to remember, we still thought it was a scam between bureaucrats and businessmen when we set it up,' one of them said later. 'Who could possibly have known it would go as deep into the party as it did? And, of course, we didn't expect him to subpoena the prime minister!'

Another problem with the public inquiry was that it would take several months to set up and more than a year to report. Meanwhile the public was clamouring for information. If Martin hoped to call an election in the near future there had to be a temporary resolution. As a result, he invited the Public Accounts Committee of the House of Commons to hold hearings on the issue as well, an idea quickly taken up by the committee's chair, Alliance/Conservative MP John Williams.[85]

In addition, Martin announced that former public works minister Alfonso Gagliano was being recalled from Denmark and dismissed. Over the next few weeks, Martin either suspended or fired the heads of three crown corporations mentioned in the report – Business Development Bank president Michel Vennat, Via Rail president Marc Lefrancois and chairman Jean Pelletier, and Canada Post president André Ouellet – all of them appointments made by Jean Chrétien.

For his own part, Martin stressed that he had had no prior knowledge of the scandal before reading the auditor general's report. Public and media response to the first two measures – the public inquiry and the firings – was generally positive, but the reaction to Martin's claim of total ignorance ranged from incredulity to sarcasm. Few believed that someone who had not only been the minister of finance but one of the most powerful ministers in the cabinet, and the most senior minister from Quebec, would not have been aware of the program or its problems. Since the entire thrust of the communications strategy was to distance Martin from the issue, such public scepticism was rightly seen as a serious and potentially fatal setback. As Mike Robinson later admitted, 'it was counterintuitive for the public to think a finance minister – especially a hands-on guy like Mr. Martin – wouldn't know where all the money went.'[86]

Exacerbating public opinion was the fact that explanations of Martin's ignorance seemed to change hourly. In the Wednesday caucus meeting, Martin described the culprits as 'a small group of fourteen rogue public servants,' a charge he repeated the next day. When this accusation was widely ridiculed, he conceded that there must have been 'political direction' to create such a broad network of bureaucrats, crown corporations, and private sector ad companies. PMO aides backed up the prime minister, publicly criticizing the Chrétien Liberals for practising 'porkbarrel politics' and describing Chrétien himself as the 'poster boy' for such practices. The belief that Canadians would share their view of two separate, clearly distinguishable groups within the party was fatally flawed, and public critiques of certain members only worsened the situation for the Liberals as a whole.

Not surprisingly, this new line of attack drew irate responses from Jean Chrétien's supporters and former advisers as well as several backbenchers, one of whom warned it would start a 'civil war' in the party if it continued. Another, Senator Sharon Carstairs, warned that 'before people start libelling people, and that's what they're doing, they had better be very, very careful.'[87] The potential for a lawsuit against one or more Martin aides was raised by a senior Chrétien loyalist who said his former boss would 'use every conceivable measure – legal and political' to defend himself. 'You know him. He'll defend his reputation because he has a good reputation to defend. And all of us will defend his reputation because he – the man who called in the auditor general, the man who called in the RCMP – does not deserve to now be handed the blame,' the loyalist argued.[88]

Such inter-party criticism of the new Liberal prime minister was deeply troubling, especially as he had just taken over. To many it seemed reminiscent of difficulties encountered by John Turner, even before Meech Lake emerged as the key issue of his leadership. Scott Reid later insisted that the criticism was misplaced. 'There was no jihad to "get" them; we were on a mission to survive. You have to consider the context. We expected fierce criticism but not an 18.2 per cent drop in the polls. That was unprecedented!'[89]

For his part, Martin insisted that 'the leadership race is over' and that he would 'root out everyone involved in the sponsorship affair' regardless of who would be implicated.[90] He used hostilities between himself and Chrétien to explain his ignorance of the sponsorship program, stating that he had not been consulted on any Quebec matters while he was in cabinet. As Winnipeg journalist Frances Russell argued, this line of reasoning was not helpful, since it 'confirmed voters' suspicions that Mr. Martin's perennial leadership quest really *had* gotten in the way of good governance.'[91] At the same time, Martin's argument provided support for the view that Quebec was indeed a *terra incognita* for Martin and most of his advisers.

Martin faced another internal party problem when the *National Post* reported that he had received a letter from the then party policy chair, Akaash Maharaj, while he was still finance minister. The February 2002 letter had urged Martin to investigate 'rumours that funds are being diverted for partisan purposes' from the sponsorship program in Quebec. The letter's contents attracted considerable media attention, forcing Martin to stress that his correspondence unit had issued a standard reply to the letter and that he had not seen it. Further, he underlined that, although he knew vaguely about the program, it was only with the publication of the auditor's first report and cabinet's authorization of an RCMP investigation that he became aware of specific problems. 'This is when I began to understand that what had occurred went far beyond administrative failures and involved possible criminal conduct,' Martin said. 'But even then, no one understood the full scope of what was involved until the Auditor General's second report came out recently.'[92]

The 'Mad as Hell' Tour

The second phase of Martin's response to the Adscam scandal was launched soon after. It was an intensive public relations exercise in which the prime minister crossed the country at a frenetic pace, giving interviews and taking questions on open-line shows. Determined to demonstrate his hands-on approach to issues management, Martin repeatedly declared that he too was personally outraged by the findings of the auditor general's report. As public criticism mounted, his assertions became more emphatic. On the CBC's *Cross Country Checkup* program of 15 February he declared that anybody who knew anything about the affair 'should resign immediately. I've made that very, very clear.' He then pledged to resign himself if he were found to have had prior knowledge.[93] Two days later, he told another interviewer 'Let me tell you, we're going to get that money and we're going to get the facts out. There should be no doubt just how strongly I feel about this.' And finally, in a bizarre and not altogether careful choice of words, Martin bluntly stated that 'the Liberal Party is not corrupt.'[94]

This public relations offensive was soon dubbed the 'Mad as Hell' tour by Martin's critics. Before long, there were even some supporters who were increasingly unhappy with the strategy, urging him to return to the Liberals' priorities. 'I think the idea was that it was good for Paul to be out there this past week but it's time for him to stop now and get on the government's priorities,' one longtime Martin MP told reporters after the divisive national caucus meeting of 18 February. Another agreed: 'He felt quite strongly that he'd do it because he's committed to open, transparent government ... but now other ministers [should] start to take the heat.'

Another Martin loyalist described the adverse effect of raising the 'Chrétien factor.' Even MPs who had long opposed the former leader admitted that 'Chrétien has pretty much stayed out of the fray ... It came up a few times that we've got to stop pointing fingers and just try to work together ... [Martin's] spin doctors have got to tone down their messages.'[95] In his concluding remarks at the caucus meeting, Martin was quoted by several backbenchers as saying 'It was a good thing, but too much of a good thing is not necessarily a good thing,' leaving many in the room shaking their heads. 'The thing is,' one former supporter joked, 'he will always agree with everybody.'

Interestingly, many caucus members were prepared to take the fall-out from the auditor general's report much more calmly than Martin and his advisers. Although the party's support had fallen from 48 to 35 per cent in the previous week, several MPs told reporters they believed the impact could be contained. 'We have to be positive and start getting our own message out,' one commented. Another said, 'Sure, we've lost a lot of points but it's not the end of the world. We should be out there talking up the government's agenda.'[96] The message seemed abundantly clear: it was time to step back from the issue and consider other things.

Yet Martin, who had promised his caucus he would heed their advice, continued to take questions on the matter in the House of Commons and spoke at length about the issue in response to reporters' questions for several more weeks. When Martin fired Jean Pelletier in early March, the deposed chair of Via Rail raised the stakes again by publicly charging that he was the victim of 'a summary execution by a Paul Martin government bent on waging civil war in the Liberal Party and inflaming the current "climate of hysteria" over the sponsorship scandal.'[97] Both Pelletier and Alfonso Gagliano subsequently testified before the Public Accounts Committee in late March, and both described the problem as an administrative one compounded by the illicit activities of one key public servant, Chuck Guité, who was subsequently arrested and charged by the RCMP. Pelletier insisted there was no 'political direction' as Martin claimed.

When asked about Pelletier's testimony, Martin simply replied. 'Well, he would know.' This surprising about-face led several reporters to conclude that 'when challenged, Martin has a tendency to fold.' Others speculated that Martin and his advisers knew the party was being decimated by internal warfare.[98] This theory gained credence when Martin attempted to clarify his change of heart, saying that he had been speaking about crown corporations rather than the PMO in his highly critical remarks about political direction. 'I don't have all the facts,' he concluded, 'that's why we've asked for an inquiry.'[99] He was careful to say that 'the former Prime Minister, Mr. Chrétien, is a man of unquestioned integrity and I am sure he had nothing to do with this.'[100] But many Chrétien supporters felt this was too little, too late.

Years later, virtually everyone involved in shaping Martin's response to the sponsorship crisis argued in favour of the measures, describing them as necessary and effective. Some, like policy adviser Mark Resnick, pointed out that Martin firmly believed it was 'the right thing to do. He couldn't possibly just sweep it under the rug.'[101] Martin's election campaign co-chair, David Herle, maintained that the various measures provided a 'shield' for the prime minister in the 2004 election. 'Whether it was the right or wrong thing to do remains a vigorous debate in the Liberal Party,' he admitted. 'But we would have lost the 2004 election if we had taken that approach of sweeping things under the carpet.'[102]

For Herle, the Martin government's response epitomized the new approach of doing politics differently. As for the growing backlash within the party, Scott Reid responded emphatically that 'it isn't about [the Chrétien camp] any more – that's over. It's arrogant and egotistical of them to think they're the centre of the universe and our thinking.'[103] Reid conceded that Martin's response plan 'was less successful than it could have been' due to 'self-imposed restrictions' based on their respect for the party and for Martin's predecessor. Nevertheless, thoughts of vendetta continued to plague the inquiry and affect the public's image of the Liberal Party.

Just days before a federal budget was to be brought down, Martin spoke to the Chamber of Commerce in Quebec City, as Jean Chrétien had done the previous year. Instead of highlighting the government's remarkable fiscal record and the healthy state of the economy, as many anticipated, the prime minister spent most of the speech outlining further commitments to deal with the sponsorship crisis. Vowing to 'convince the skeptics, through our actions and our behaviour,' Martin declared that 'politics as usual and outmoded ways of thinking are no longer acceptable.' One commentator argued that Martin's promise to 'handle taxpayers' money with care and respect' and 'curb waste and mismanagement' actually suggested that Martin was 'agreeing that waste and mismanagement had been rife during his years as Finance Minister.'[104] More to the point, the speech served notice that Martin's strategy for the next election had shifted. Instead of demonstrating progress and change within the party, he would run *against* the record of his own party. National columnist Jeffrey Simpson referred to Martin facetiously as the leader of the opposition, describing him as the head of a 'breakaway group, the Martin party.' Since the speech was delivered in Quebec where the scandal had hurt the Liberals the most, Simpson pointed out that the speech was only 'the latest in a string of attacks [Martin] has delivered lately against the government in which he served for nine years as Minister of Finance.'[105]

The Adscam Budget

In the midst of the many claims and counterclaims levelled against the government by parliamentary reporters, the PMO attempted to divert attention to the upcoming federal budget of 23 March. With the Throne Speech having failed to deliver the silver bullet needed in advance of the spring election, the budget was now seen as the potential saviour of the agenda of change.

For only the second time in ten years, Paul Martin did not draft the budget of the Liberal government. Instead, he took a back seat to his newly appointed successor, Ralph Goodale. Goodale, the Saskatchewan lawyer better known for his skill at obfuscation in Question Period, was seen by many as a Martin clone who would carry on the tradition of fiscal prudence just as John Manley had done before him. It was an assumption that proved correct.

Several factors assured a cautious approach to the federal budget. First, the Finance Department projected that the surplus for the year, although significant, would be smaller than in the past. Second, there were a number of commitments made by the previous government which Martin was obliged to honour. Last, but arguably the most important, there was a strong sentiment among Martin's cabinet and political advisers that this budget should emphasize fiscal rectitude in light of the Adscam debacle. As a result, the first budget under Paul Martin's leadership contained almost no new initiatives or pre-election promises.

In his 23 March budget speech, Goodale outlined two objectives: one, 'to demonstrate unequivocally the principles of financial responsibility and integrity,' and, two, 'to begin to give tangible shape to the goals presented in the Speech from the Throne.' The first objective was clearly paramount. The initial paragraphs of the budget speech actually addressed the sponsorship crisis directly. Referring to 'the kinds of financial abuses that have so understandably angered Canadians,' Goodale went on to say that 'as a government, we not only accept our responsibility for what went wrong, we also accept our responsibility to get it right.' He introduced a number of administrative measures to 'strengthen financial management and operational integrity.' These included the development of a new expenditure management and spending oversight program to be supervised by the Treasury Board, the re-creation of the Office of the Comptroller General of Canada, the appointment of comptrollers in each line department, the purchase of real-time information systems to track spending across the board, and the introduction of new corporate governance rules for crown corporations. 'Taken together,' the finance minister concluded, 'these measures will enhance transparency, improve administration and help ensure taxpayers' dollars are wisely spent.'

The problem was that it was all highly technical. Many experts agreed with the measures but few ordinary Canadians understood or cared for them. An even more important political problem was that, where the speech should have been an opportunity for the Liberals to distance themselves from the sponsorship scandal, it instead drew attention to the scandal yet again.

The lack of positive benefits for individuals was equally problematic. The next section of the budget speech focused on 'fiscal prudence' despite the fact that the government enjoyed a $4 billion surplus. Goodale promised to maintain the $3 billion contingency fund and committed the government to cut $3 billion from program spending through another expenditure review process like the one initiated during the deficit. Even more surprising, the finance minister pledged to reduce the debt-to-GDP ratio to 25 per cent within a decade. Goodale announced that he would axe a variety of 'legacy' measures promised by the Chrétien government, including the improvement and capital expansion of Via Rail, the creation of a Political History Museum, and the funding of a National Unity Reserve. By the time the speech finally arrived at spending announcements, its negative tone and tenor were firmly established. Apart from the pre-existing commitments to the cities agenda and the clean-up of toxic waste sites as outlined in the Throne

Speech, the budget offered only very modest 'down payments' on a small number of outstanding issues.

The response was almost universal indifference. Patricia Lovett-Reid, a vice-president at TD Waterhouse, summed up the feelings of many when she declared: 'For the most part, it's probably a yawn for the average Canadian.'[106] Former leadership rival John Manley, recently returned to the private sector, commented, 'there are a lot of things in the government's agenda that aren't there. I think in the election campaign it'll be very important for the Liberal Party to remind people of the Speech from the Throne, to remind people of the intention they have to deliver on those commitments … not simply to run on the budget.'[107]

Perhaps most telling was the criticism summed up by Montreal columnist Lysiane Gagnon in an article titled, 'Where Was the Emergency?' Arguing that the Throne Speech and the budget failed to answer why Martin felt obliged to replace Chrétien prematurely, she continued: 'We're left with piecemeal measures that are not substantially different from what would have been announced under a Jean Chrétien government.'[108]

The budget was a disappointment to Liberals as well. Some of Martin's key supporters immediately began to downplay it, trumpeting the impending election platform as the real payoff. Meanwhile, the lack of concrete policy alternatives to the daily menu of scandal and opposition attacks was becoming critical. The sponsorship scandal was preoccupying everyone's attention precisely because there was an ongoing policy vacuum. The PMO's apparent inability to separate the Adscam crisis from other policy matters – as Jean Chrétien had done so successfully with the 9/11 crisis – proved crucial to this dilemma. One national columnist stated the problem succinctly: 'Martin's lack of focus is eroding his credibility,' Jeffrey Simpson warned. He also pointed out what insiders in Ottawa already knew: that 'many senior public servants remain mystified by the lack of policy focus in a government that had so long to think about governing before taking office.' Equally revealing was the consensus inside the beltway that the centre was paying 'excessive attention to spin, communications, and political manoeuvring.'[109] More than one observer noted the similarities with the early days of the Mulroney government.

Election Readiness: Change and 'the Martin Party'

While the party's parliamentary wing was fully absorbed in the Adscam crisis and the day-to-day activities of running the country, the party headquarters and volunteer wing were gearing up for an election from the day Paul Martin was sworn in as prime minister. 'We were in a constant state of election readiness,' Michelle Cadario said, a point reinforced by LCRB Director Kevin Bosch. 'My title actually became Director, Pre-Writ Services,' he noted.[110]

As the national campaign committee consisted of the same players who had orchestrated Martin's leadership victory, they were ready to go. Unfortunately, this meant that many of the Liberals' most experienced campaign veterans were sidelined. Indeed, almost no one in the Martin leadership team had significant federal election experience, a problem that presented itself once the campaign was launched. Apart from John Webster, who had served as John Turner's national campaign director in 1988, the key Liberal players in the 2004 election were more expert at organizing membership drives and nomination battles than in working with other Liberals to defeat their political opponents.

David Herle and John Webster were named campaign co-chairs almost immediately after Martin took office. John Webster's experience with the 1988 Turner campaign proved to be a key factor since it led him to conclude that co-chairs should not be the traditional figurehead positions filled by members of the parliamentary wing. Instead, as David Herle later recounted, Martin's top advisers were determined to ensure they had the authority to make decisions rather than having to rely on others.[111] (The subsequent addition of MP Hélène Scherrer as a third co-chair, although a deviation from this plan, was primarily symbolic and intended to address the lack of a Quebec presence and to achieve gender balance.) While this new approach may have improved efficiency, it also led to further criticism from the parliamentary wing, which, again, felt Martin's advisers were taking over roles inappropriate for non-elected officials.

There were also significant changes at party headquarters. Instead of bringing in outsiders to run the campaign (as had been done during the Chrétien era with John Rae and Gordon Ashworth), it was decided that Michelle Cadario would act as the national campaign director in addition to her role as national director of the party. Similarly, her new deputy director at the party HQ, Steve MacKinnon, was given the role of deputy campaign director. MacKinnon would run the war room and be involved in other aspects of the campaign, including the party's television commercials. Several former Martin leadership organizers in the PMO such as Scott Reid and Brian Guest assumed prominent roles as spokespersons during the campaign.

Efforts to ensure that the parliamentary wing was on side with election planning began with a pre-election briefing of the caucus executive on 24 February. The briefing involved David Herle, Kevin Bosch, and senior parliamentary officials such as the house leader and government whip. This was followed by a memorable briefing of the national caucus on issues and party standings presented by David Herle. According to several of those present, Herle told Liberal MPs and senators that the priority issues for Canadians included debt repayment and increased defence spending, conclusions which many in the audience found unconvincing. Demonstrating once again the friction between Martin's advisers and his caucus, several of those present raised pointed questions and criticized the methodology, which was based on focus group findings rather than national polls. 'You seem to want us to take this on faith,' one Martin MP said. 'Marzolini would never have made such an unprofessional presentation,' another commented *sotto voce*.

But it was Herle's projection of Liberal prospects in the upcoming election that caused the most consternation. Sounding confident and authoritative, Herle announced that the Liberals stood an excellent chance of making major gains in British Columbia and would more than make up for possible losses in Ontario through successes in Quebec. 'We tore him to pieces over that presentation,' one veteran Ontario MP, Charles Caccia, said. 'Many of us had concerns about his findings on some of the policy issues, but the BC and Quebec people could hardly believe their ears when he predicted those huge gains.'[112] Caccia's views were echoed by a sceptical western senator who pointed out, 'We're always ahead in the polls in BC before the election, and then that support just disappears once the writ is dropped. What makes you think this time will be different?'

For his part, Herle defended the decision not to provide polling data. This was partly due to an ongoing concern about caucus leaks, he said later. But it was also a pragmatic decision. 'Do you suppose Marzolini presented numbers that Eddie Goldenberg and Chrétien had not already seen and approved?' he asked. Herle also maintained that he had always cautioned not only the caucus but also Martin and his inner circle that 'we *could* lose. I said that before the leadership race was over and many times afterwards ... Running against one's own party is almost never successful, especially after more than ten years in power. That's why we had to emphasize positive change.' Before the sponsorship scandal, this approach, Herle argued, was proving quite successful. 'Certainly on the democratic deficit we were making a real impact with the public.'[113]

Martin also pursued his democratic deficit agenda within the party. Faithful to his pledge to open up the party to grassroots decision making, he set in motion the process for platform development immediately after taking over as leader. Marva Wisdom, the newly elected chair of the party's national policy committee, was approached by David Herle at the first meeting of the national executive after the convention. In his new role as campaign co-chair, Herle asked her to be a co-chair of the platform committee. 'I knew that was unusual in terms of the recent past,' Wisdom said. 'Being on the platform committee was one thing, but chairing it was quite another. I thought that sent a really positive "walk the talk" signal to the party that they were taking the volunteer wing seriously.'[114]

According to Wisdom, their deliberations were based on party priority resolutions, the various documents produced by the policy roundtables organized by Mark Resnick, and even the previous Red Book. 'It was a really consultative process,' Wisdom said. 'Extremely collaborative, and it re-engaged the party after more than a decade of isolation.' Although Peter Nicholson held the pen for the exercise, Wisdom stressed that he consulted regularly with her and other members of the committee, and the end product was something they were all happy to support. 'Of course it had to take into account Mr Martin's campaign promises, and his priorities,' she noted, 'but there were several planks that we specifically developed on our own that were very significant in the document.' Wisdom cited the child development package as a prime example of the committee's input.

The content of the final document closely followed Martin's convention acceptance speech and the Throne Speech. In most respects, it lacked the detail and precision that had come to be expected from earlier Liberal platforms. In format, however, it did resemble previous Red Books, with sections on various policy areas and a costing section at the end. There was one exception. The Liberals' vaunted Red Book for the 2004 election would not actually be red. In another symbolic demonstration of the theme of change, the Red Book was white. The title was also significant. Rather than referring to the Liberal Party, it focused on the leader. With the choice of 'Moving Canada Forward: The Paul Martin Plan for Getting Things Done,' his team could hardly have found a more direct method of demonstrating the break between the old and the new.

An article in Montreal's *La Presse* summed up the situation succinctly: 'Exit the Liberal Party's Red Book,' it proclaimed, 'Martin gets rid of the last vestige of the Chrétien heritage.'[115] Martin's brief introduction to the White Book reinforced this theme. 'I think the time is right for meaningful changes and important fixes,' he wrote. Implying yet again that the past ten years were unproductive, he continued, 'Canadians have been telling their governments to get serious about dealing with issues like health care, learning and the quality of life in communities. This document lays out how a Liberal government will respond.'[116]

There were other ways in which change was emphasized, the party's campaign materials being an obvious example. In effect, the Liberal Party did become the Martin Party. Repeating the same strategy used (unsuccessfully) by John Turner in 1984, the election readiness team authorized lawn signs, posters, and advertising campaigns that featured Team Martin rather than the party. Every document had a large photo of Martin. Liberal party logos were conspicuous by their absence, or relegated to a small corner of the documents. Given the connections of Martin's many advisers to the Turner era, the decision to adopt this approach is difficult to explain. The strategy had not worked for Turner in 1984 and it would not work for Martin in 2004. Political scientist Nelson Wiseman anticipated the failure, arguing that the emphasis on Martin actually exceeded what the party did in 1968 'at the height of Trudeaumania.' He predicted that 'with all the eggs riding in one basket, the campaign will be left in tatters if Martin falters or fails to meet expectations.'[117]

At the riding level, the use of Team Martin material proved fatal for several of Martin's preferred candidates. In the safe seat of Ottawa-Orléans, for example, Eugène Bellemare – an undistinguished backbencher who had served for a decade and remained a virtual unknown – was being challenged for the nomination by Martin supporter and backroom organizer Bruce Murdoch. But as Martin's popularity waned, Murdoch's candidacy faltered as well, since he was irrevocably tied to Martin by his campaign material. He eventually lost the nomination to a third candidate, Marcel Godbout, a newcomer to the party who campaigned on his lack of attachment to either Martin or Chrétien.

The most revealing and controversial campaign material was to be found in the party's Candidates' Handbook. The two-hundred-page document emphasized that candidates should refer to the leader rather than the party, essentially abandoning the Liberal brand that had been so successful for so long. It even provided a model speech in which candidates were urged to use phrases such as 'this party and this country are fortunate to have at their helm a political leader with such deep convictions, who is so extremely dedicated, and who possesses the ability to seize the moment.'[118] As Wiseman concluded, 'it reinforces that the Liberal team is not the Liberal candidates, it's Martin's coterie of unelected officials.'[119]

Nomination Battles: Progress or Regression?

Candidate selection was another area in which the Martin Liberals' election preparations resembled the Turner era. Before Turner and then under Chrétien, it was understood that Liberals did not challenge sitting MPs. 'Within the party, we had a culture that you didn't challenge MPs unless you absolutely had to,' Senator David Smith recalled. 'By and large, it was "If they're doing a good job, you leave them alone."'[120] As an earlier chapter detailed, John Turner's decision to allow sitting members to be challenged, coupled with the advent of special interest groups targeting riding associations and nominations, led to a chaotic period in which the Liberal Party seemed unable to control its own fate.

But after more than a decade of Jean Chrétien's more traditional, hands-on, indeed autocratic approach to the issue – appointing candidates to avoid messy nomination battles or to increase the representation of women and visible minorities – the problem appeared to have been eliminated. Throughout three elections, there were few instances of public embarrassment concerning nomination battles.

Despite this, Paul Martin reopened the debate on the 'democratization' of the party immediately after he became leader by allowing MPs to be challenged. Asked about his decision to move in the opposite direction from Chrétien, Martin argued: 'Essentially we are a democratic party and a democratic party says you win a nomination. There's no doubt in my mind the vast majority of members of Parliament who have worked very hard are going to be able to hold on to their seat if some of them are contested.'[121]

On one level, this was a straightforward debate between two sincere but competing visions of the role of the extra-parliamentary wing and its rank-and-file party members. Martin steadfastly defended his decision not to interfere even when it involved conflicts between two of his own MPs, a situation faced by many Liberal MPs in the upcoming election (Sheila Copps was one) given the redistribution of riding boundaries after the last decennial census. Martin insisted it was a matter for local riding associations to resolve and that he would not intervene. 'This is a battle that is taking place locally,' he declared. 'I wish it wasn't

happening, but I'm not interfering in any of these battles between incumbents.'[122]

On another level, the situation under Martin was more complicated
than it had been under Turner, mainly because of the intervening decade of internal strife. Given the many allegiances and conflicts evident
among candidates at the riding level, some Liberals and Canadians
viewed the 'local autonomy' argument with scepticism. Such doubts
were reinforced by news stories claiming that Martin supporters (BC
MP Hedy Fry, for example) were offered party support to fight off their
challengers while those who did not support Martin (such as Ontario
MP John Bryden) were left to fend for themselves.

There were also practical differences between Turner and Martin.
Where Turner's bottom-up candidate selection process was undertaken
at a time when the party was in opposition and had only forty sitting
MPs, Martin had just taken control of a majority government. Moreover, Turner, whose leadership was constantly under attack, had little
chance of imposing his will on individual riding associations, even if
he had wanted to. Instead, he allowed sitting MPs to be challenged
rather than risk further confrontations that, in all likelihood, he could
not win. Martin, on the other hand, was in near complete control of
the two wings of the party. His decision to allow MPs to be challenged
prompted many to question his motives.

A predictable consequence of his decision was that attendance in the
House of Commons and in committees declined as MPs felt compelled
to spend more time in their ridings. Liberal MP and Martin backer Paul
Szabo summed up the problem after a national caucus meeting on 18
March. Asked about his colleague John Bryden's recent nomination difficulties and defection, Szabo replied, 'I can't say I'm thinking clearly
on the whole thing. For myself, you know, I can't say because I'm in a
seriously contested nomination right now.'[123]

Another practical consequence of Martin's policy of open nominations was a decrease in the number of women candidates. Roughly half
of the Liberal MPs who did not run again were women, and many were
replaced by men. Coupled with Martin's appointments, the result was
still a political slate with only seventy-six women candidates, or eight
fewer than had run in 1997.

It was with Martin's decision to appoint star candidates as a means
of reinforcing the party's new image that his insistence on non-inter-
ference in local matters came back to haunt him. In BC, for example,
his successes in recruiting high-profile candidates like former NDP pre-

mier Ujjal Dosanjh, businessman David Emerson, senior public servant Shirley Chan, and union leader Dave Haggard were overshadowed
by negative coverage of the appointments. First, there was the forced
exit of Herb Dhaliwal to make way for Dosanjh. Even more damaging was the coronation of Bill Cunningham, a Martin supporter, in the
Burnaby-Douglas riding. With two Chinese-Canadian hopefuls having
campaigned in Burnaby-Douglas for some time (a riding comprised of
nearly 50 per cent Chinese Canadians), the idea of the former BC provincial president parachuting in as the party's official candidate raised
the ire of many longtime Liberals in the area. David Herle later admitted that the Cunningham episode 'undoubtedly hurt us in BC,' and
several members of the Board agreed.[124]

Martin's appointments provided fodder for his political opponents.
Former BC NDP provincial minister Ian Waddell, David Emerson's opponent, called the moves 'profoundly anti-democratic,' while leader
Jack Layton ridiculed Martin's earlier defence of local autonomy. 'It's
very odd to see Mr. Champion of the Democratic Deficit appointing
candidates rather than having them go through grassroots local processes,'[125] Layton opined as reporters noted that two of Martin's star
candidates had been earlier associated with the NDP. Only two of Martin's BC 'stars' – David Emerson and Ujjal Dosanjh – won seats in the
2004 election, a dismal showing which many analysts attributed to the
Cunningham factor.

In addition to BC's star candidates, Martin had members of his so-
called dream team elsewhere in the west, including former provincial
NDP minister Chris Axworthy in Saskatchewan; the president of the
Canadian Federation of Agriculture, Bob Friesen, and former Winnipeg
mayor Glen Murray in Manitoba; and the head of the Canadian Cattle-
man's Association in Calgary. Once again, many of these appointments
came at a cost. As University of British Columbia political scientist Norman Ruff concluded, 'the dream team has turned into a nightmare ... I
think the only ones still dreaming here are the strategists. It has backfired very badly.'[126] In the end, none of the candidates outside BC was
able to win a seat.

A slightly more positive situation developed in Atlantic Canada. In
Nova Scotia, former Tory leadership candidate Scott Brison came over
to the Liberals and was able to hold his riding of Kings-Hants for his
new party. Martin was also able to convince former New Brunswick
premier Frank McKenna to run for the Liberals, something Jean Chrétien had tried but failed to do. Martin's success was fleeting, however.

News of McKenna's intentions spread quickly and organizers were unable to find a riding to put him in. They originally expected former Chrétien minister Claudette Bradshaw to step aside but, when she refused, decided not to challenge her directly given her strong local organization and huge popularity in the riding. When no other MP came forward to offer a seat, McKenna decided to withdraw rather than tarnish his reputation with a bitter nomination battle. The resulting fiasco caused many other potential candidates to rethink their interest.

Apart from hockey legend Ken Dryden, who captured a seat in Toronto, the situation in Ontario was particularly bleak, with well-known former MPs replaced by low-profile newcomers who had been Martin supporters and Martin MPs defeating their non-Martin colleagues in merged ridings. Battles involving MPs Ivan Grosse, Steve Mahoney, and Ruby Dhalla gained widespread notoriety. In Dhalla's case, the entire riding executive not only resigned but announced they would support the NDP candidate.

In several cases, nomination battles were later seen as key reasons why the Liberals lost seats in the province. In a potentially high-profile clash between former Chrétien staffer Penny Collenette and Martin loyalist Richard Mahoney in Ottawa-Centre, for example, Collenette decided not to run rather than provoke another lengthy and messy internal battle. But it was too late. The situation had already attracted significant publicity. Mahoney went on to lose the riding to Ed Broadbent.

Martin's New Quebec Strategy

In Quebec, Martin's interference in local riding associations caused consternation not only in light of his earlier position of non-intervention, but also because, in several cases, it conflicted with his stated support for women candidates. A case in point was the decision to provide a 'safe' riding for longtime supporter and former MP Dennis Dawson. Despite a year-long campaign by three women in the riding, they were suddenly informed that it was 'reserved' for Dawson and unceremoniously told to step down. One of the candidates, Lisette Lepage, told reporters she was urged to run in another riding, a Bloc Québécois stronghold where she had no chance of winning. Dawson went on to lose the 'safe' seat by a margin of two to one.

Martin's efforts in Quebec were already undermined by his decision to welcome former Liberal MP Jean Lapierre back into the fold. Lapierre was the Martin supporter who tore up his Liberal Party card at the

1990 convention after Jean Chrétien won and Meech Lake died. Lapierre went on to co-found the Bloc Québécois with Lucien Bouchard and sat as a Bloc MP until 1993. To the amazement of many Liberals, Martin not only encouraged Lapierre to run but provided him with a safe seat. To compound the situation, Martin announced that Lapierre would be his Quebec lieutenant. The choice was encouraged by advisers who believed Martin could build on the existing Chrétien majority by taking more seats in the west and in Quebec. In Quebec, this meant taking seats from the Bloc, winning over soft nationalists to the Liberal cause. They viewed Lapierre as a role model for those voters and therefore a logical choice for Quebec lieutenant. 'Jean's role was to turn forty seats into sixty,' David Herle confirmed.[127]

The announcement was greeted with varying degrees of shock and disbelief by Trudeau Liberals across the country. For some, Martin's announcement was seen as a deliberate provocation. 'It's like waving a red flag in front of a bull,' one Liberal senator shouted in the next caucus meeting. 'Even in BC people know who Lapierre is,' another senator declared, 'and they don't have any time for him.' For some it was the final straw. 'It's official. I will not be voting Liberal in the next election,' declared Chrétien diehard Warren Kinsella on his website.[128] Some of Martin's own backbench supporters expressed concern at the decision. Martin's BC campaign chair, Mark Marissen, later revealed that he had sent an email to David Herle immediately after hearing of the appointment, arguing it would be 'a serious mistake.'[129]

Lapierre himself only added to the controversy. When asked about separatism at the press conference announcing his appointment as Quebec lieutenant, Lapierre astonished reporters by asserting, 'I never saw myself as a separatist ... I saw myself as somebody who wanted to bring about a level playing field for Quebec.' To a question about the Clarity Act, he declared, 'It's useless,' and, when asked to elaborate, he added, 'It's useless because it wouldn't change anything. If there was a will in Quebec to separate, they would not be able to stop a will like that by having tricks.'[130] His future colleague Stéphane Dion responded incredulously when asked about Lapierre's comments. 'That's completely wrong. That's not the view of the federal government. It's the most important thing we have done for the unity of the country.'[131]

The Lapierre situation demonstrated once again the fundamental difference of opinion between the two camps and the extent of their division along the federalism axis. Martin's willingness to appeal to 'soft' nationalists and his consistent belief that the party could expand its support in Quebec by doing so was eerily close to John Turner's doomed appointment of Raymond Garneau. Chrétien loyalists spoke out almost immediately. 'This is a huge and terrible mistake for the party of Pearson and Trudeau and Chrétien to make,' Warren Kinsella wrote. 'It didn't work for Brian Mulroney when he brought former separatists into a federalist party … and it's not going to work for the Liberal Party.' Senator Jim Munson, Chrétien's former communications director, concurred: 'It raises the question with the new government, is this what their claims of renewal really mean?'[132]

Martin's strategy of accommodation continued with Lapierre's recruitment of six more former Bloc and PQ members as Liberal candidates, a move which Martin defended in the face of criticism from within the party. 'The fact is that none of those people are separatists,' he insisted. 'They're nationalists but they're not separatists and they have committed themselves very, very strongly to the unity of our country … Some of them had a brief flirtation [with separatism]. Others had a slightly longer flirtation,' he told reporters. 'But I can tell you that every single one of those people is a strong Canadian.'[133] This argument was substantially weakened by the comments of one of the six recruits, former PQ MNA Lévis Brien. Asked why he had decided to defect to the Liberals, Brien described Martin as 'un winner.' He added, 'I believe in the long term. Quebec loses by being in the opposition. Let's be part of a team of winners and go and get the maximum for Quebec … my political experience has taught me that being in the Opposition means watching cheques passing by to go elsewhere.'[134]

A Cut-Throat Purge?

Nomination conflicts were widely reported, creating bad publicity in the run-up to the federal election. But such publicity was nothing compared with the growing public perception that more than just arbitrary appointments or opportunistic challenges of MPs were taking place. Most ominous for the party's electoral fortunes was the belief that a cut-throat purge was taking place in the bosom of the Liberal Party. Critics such as Ontario MP John Bryden, a former Manley supporter, insisted there was a 'coordinated and determined effort' by Martin's organizers to rid the caucus of 'dissenters.' Bryden told reporters he had been warned that party officials were actively searching for candidates to run against him for the nomination. 'This is the Liberal establishment trying to make sure that absolute Martin supporters are in place … I haven't sufficiently passed the Martin loyalty test.'[135] A senior Quebec party organizer agreed, describing the open nominations as 'political vengeance cloaked as democratic reform.'

There was considerable evidence to support the claim. In Ontario, at least fifteen MPs were challenged, all but one of whom had not supported Martin. The 'victims' included former cabinet ministers and many long-serving backbenchers. Eleven of the fifteen were women. In Ontario, it was common knowledge that two of the party's most popular MPs and best-known environmentalists, Charles Caccia and Karen Kraft Sloan, were being deposed.[136] In Quebec, the MPs being challenged included Raymonde Falco and Clifford Lincoln, another well-regarded environmentalist and former provincial cabinet minister, as well as strong federalist cabinet ministers like Stéphane Dion and Martin Cauchon. An astonishing thirty-six sitting Liberal MPs did not run again in 2004.

Prominent Saskatchewan Liberal Tony Merchant (who had lost a close nomination battle to Ralph Goodale several years earlier, in large part due to the hardball tactics of David Herle, Goodale's campaign manager at the time) had already expressed concerns about the potential for political fallout. For Merchant, the aggressive stance of many of Martin's key advisers towards other Liberals, not just opposition MPs, suggested that they would have trouble moving from a leadership race mindset to one more suited to governing. 'If they don't run the government like the hugely important, to some extent apolitical operation that it is, they won't be there for very long,' he warned several months before Martin became leader.[137]

His concerns were apparently justified. As the Sheila Copps/Tony Valeri battle unfolded, more and more Liberals and ordinary Canadians began to see it as a personal vendetta by Martin against Copps, despite his many efforts to distance himself from the contest.[138] As the situation deteriorated, belated efforts were made to salvage the Liberals' image. Copps was offered a UN posting (extended by none other than John Turner) as well as a seat in the neighbouring riding of MP Beth Phinney, both of which she refused. After losing the nomination to Valeri, Copps immediately filed a party appeal, citing voting irregularities and describing the result as 'massively orchestrated fraud.'[139] She also began to speak publicly about the number of female MPs and candidates being 'pushed aside ... There are women across the country whose ridings are at risk. And Mr. Martin – who claims to care about the under representation of women in the party – continues to say it's a local matter.'[140] The fallout from the Copps affair, both inside and outside of the party, was widespread and persisted throughout Martin's tenure as leader.

Delaying the Election Call

Rampant controversy and infighting between the new and the old guard complicated the timing of the election call. David Herle later confided that the large number of nomination battles as well as the unhappiness of many former cabinet ministers now relegated to the backbenches made Martin and his advisers feel that they were operating as a minority government. 'Could we count on Sheila Copps or Herb Dhaliwal to vote with us all the time?' he asked. 'We thought not.'[141] Virtually all of Martin's close advisers mentioned the fact that Stephen Harper was making remarkable progress unifying the two wings of the Conservative party. 'He was obviously a more serious opponent than Stockwell Day or Preston Manning,' Scott Reid noted, 'and we knew we would not be able to take advantage of the same off-the-wall Reform/Alliance antics Chrétien had benefited from in the last two elections.'[142]

Having delayed the election from January until April to allow the riding redistribution to take effect, Martin's team unexpectedly found themselves submerged in the Adscam scandal. Their original hopes for a 4 April election were dashed after the party's precipitous and unprecedented thirteen-point drop in national polls. They had gone from a strong majority to minority status in a month. Worse still, the national polls' findings were duplicated by a CROP poll in Quebec that predicted a return for the Bloc Québécois, largely a result of Adscam and Martin's handling of it. Jean Lapierre attempted to downplay the poll but with little success. 'The CROP poll which places us in second place in Quebec has no scientific basis,' Lapierre declared. Since their original strategy was based on the assumption of more seats in Quebec, Martin's advisers were flummoxed.

At the Liberals' combative 18 February national caucus meeting, MP after MP called on Martin to delay the election until May. Describing the discussions as 'polite and constructive,' some Martin MPs nevertheless told reporters that the mood was extremely anxious. Their anxiety was heightened by Martin's closing remarks, which seemed to suggest an 18 April election call (for a 25 May election).[143] Despite their concerns, most MPs insisted publicly that they were ready to go to the polls whenever the prime minister decided to call the election, demonstrating that some vestiges of party unity remained, even after the serious internal divisions.

A lot changed in the following weeks. Chrétien supporters in caucus and in the extra-parliamentary wing became increasingly incensed by Martin's response to Adscam. *Globe and Mail* columnist Jeffrey Simpson stated that the Liberals' hopes for a majority government had effectively disappeared in the interim. 'That was yesterday, before the sponsorship scandal, and before the Martinites bombed the bridges to their party's past ... They gambled that by making a bad situation worse, by inflating the whole affair into the biggest scandal ever to hit Canadian politics, they would ultimately be redeemed by a grateful public.' Instead, Simpson concluded, they had discredited the Liberal brand and the result was that 'almost half the country tells Ipsos Reid they now won't vote Liberal under any circumstances.'[144]

As columnist Lysiane Gagnon pointed out, this exacerbated Martin's problems in Quebec. 'The chickens are coming home to roost,' she wrote. 'Paul Martin is paying a high price for his putsch against Mr. Chrétien ... The crude way the Martinites then tried to get rid of all the Chrétien loyalists has ripped the party apart.' Many of those Chrétien supporters, she concluded, 'blame Martin for having overreacted to the sponsorship scandal – a real scandal to be sure, but one that Mr. Martin's horrified reaction overdramatized.'[145] Her views were shared by none other than the Conservatives' former pollster Allan Gregg. In an op-ed published in the *Globe and Mail*, Gregg likened the Adscam scandal to a tempest in a teapot, particularly in light of so many more serious policy issues that had yet to be resolved, involving much larger sums of money. To great effect he calculated that the amount of money involved in Adscam would be equivalent to a $15 shortfall in a $100,000 stock account or .015 per cent of the federal budget from 1995 to 2000.[146]

Neither the budget nor Martin's increasingly frenetic efforts to focus on health care made a difference. From the high of 49 per cent nationally just days before the auditor's report was tabled, the Liberals had settled at roughly 38 per cent. An Ipsos-Reid poll had killed any real prospect of going to the polls, demonstrating as it did that the Grits were not simply in minority territory but could lose massively in Quebec. While most MPs were still talking about waiting until May for an election call, others suggested that Martin delay the vote until at least the fall. Noting that the Liberals were only in the third year of their mandate, former Chrétien minister Herb Dhaliwal told reporters, 'The conventional thinking is it was going to be this spring but there's no reason why it can't happen in the fall or next spring.' He then added to Martin's image problems by commenting, 'We don't hold a lot of seats in British Columbia as it is and I think there was some hope that we could add more. Now, if we hold what we have, we'll be doing well.'[147]

Compounding the Liberals' problems was the fact that Chuck Guité, the key witness in the scandal, was due to testify before the Public Accounts Committee on 22 April. Since many of Martin's advisers believed he would be helpful to their cause, they felt they must once again put off a call. This led to a rather embarrassing scenario in which some $750,000 was spent by the party on an ad campaign featuring Martin, launched on 18 April despite the lack of an election announcement.

Martin continued his cross-country tour, announcing major government expenditures and anticipating that he would drop the writ any day. In seven weeks more than $8 billion in program spending was announced by either Martin or his regional ministers, although, as critics were quick to point out, not all of the announcements involved 'new' money but simply 'recycled' previously committed funds. University of Calgary political scientist David Taras delivered a particularly telling critique of these activities when he told reporters: 'All this flies in the face of the claim that this government is going to be different, that it has a different style, but most importantly that ... particularly after the sponsorship scandal, Paul Martin is going to be careful with public money.' Asked to compare Martin's spending with Jean Chrétien's decision to offer tax reductions before the 2000 election, Taras made matters worse for Martin by insisting, 'That was a different story because that was taking the Canadian Alliance policies away from them. This is not taking policies away [from the opposition], this is just the kind of spending that makes voters cynical.'[148]

By now the media were focusing on the prospects of an election to the exclusion of almost all other issues. On 21 April, a scathing editorial in the *Globe and Mail* accused a 'dithering' Martin of campaigning when he should have been running the country, spending taxpayers' money in an effort to improve the party's fortunes before dropping the writ. 'Pick a date, any date,' it urged, all the while stressing that it need not be soon, and either the fall or spring would be acceptable, 'so that the Liberals can now get on with governing.'[149]

At this point the idea of a lengthy delay would seem to have been attractive. With eighteen months left in his mandate – and a comfortable majority in spite of some caucus dissidents – Martin might easily have decided to wait out the impending storm of Gomery by implementing his own agenda before going to the electorate for a verdict. After all, the window of opportunity for an immediate election had passed. Instead, much like John Turner before him, Martin and his advisers were determined to proceed with an election as soon as possible, regardless of the dangers that move now implied. Once fixed on that objective, they seemed incapable of altering their plan in any major way. Afterwards, several of them admitted to the mistake: 'I don't think we ever got out of that mindset,' Steve MacKinnon later admitted. 'We were still built to win 220 seats, as opposed to built to win 135, which is what we won.'[150]

Certainly they were concerned about 'getting their numbers up,' and they knew they would not enjoy the near 50 per cent range support in the polls again anytime soon. Nevertheless, the only considerations outlined involved minimal delays due to logistical and political concerns. These, too, are instructive. With Martin scheduled to visit President Bush in Washington on 29 April, it was decided that it would be better to avoid a 25 April election call. Martin explained the delay publicly by declaring, 'Some time ago, I decided what's important is for us to govern.' As a result, 'the meeting with President Bush is going ahead with that in mind. The election will be held when it will be held.'[151]

The next potential date of 2 May for the election call (with the election on 7 June) was publicly ruled out from the start because the prime minister would be away from the country the day of the election. The sixth of June marked the sixtieth anniversary of the D-Day invasion, and Martin would be expected to attend ceremonies commemorating the event in Europe. Privately, however, another reason was also uppermost in the minds of several Martin organizers. The seventh of June would also mark the seventy-fifth birthday of former prime minister John Turner. For many key members of Martin's team, this event had particular significance since they had also been strong Turner supporters in the past, and many expected to attend a special dinner in his honour. Despite their best efforts, it became clear over the next several weeks that the Adscam scandal had badly affected the Martin Liberals' standing in Quebec. But the worst appeared to be over in the rest of the country. Their own internal polling showed them at 41 per cent nationally, and most observers believed the Adscam issue had already been factored into those numbers. As a result, Martin's advisers felt they should not wait for even the Public Accounts Committee to release a report. The Gomery Inquiry's hearings would begin in the fall, and they believed they must have the election out of the way before then as their situation might deteriorate again. As a result, in early May the

Public Accounts Committee's Liberal majority voted to end its hearings and begin work on an interim report. The Liberals emerged relatively unscathed from those hearings, in large measure due to the lacklustre performance of opposition committee members and the bizarre testimony of some witnesses such as Miriam Bédard.[152] With the credibility of the parliamentary committee in tatters, the Martin advisers were convinced the situation was as favourable as possible and it was finally time to pull the plug. On 26 May, Paul Martin called an election for 28 June.

13 Fall from Grace: From Majority to Minority

Given what we were up against, it's unlikely anyone could have achieved a majority.

— Martin strategist David Herle[1]

When Paul Martin delivered a minority government on 28 June, it marked the beginning of the end of his brief career as Liberal leader. It was a remarkable turnaround in Martin's personal fortunes, which had seemed almost limitless only six months earlier. But it was also a most unusual fall from grace for any Liberal leader. This was especially true since the party had not suffered anything like the humiliating defeat of 1984. In fact, it had not been defeated at all. Despite a campaign that sometimes verged on incompetence, Martin and his team actually salvaged a victory for the party. Their minority was substantial, and many pundits felt the Liberals would be able to govern for some time.

However, in other ways, the election was a classic example of history repeating itself. Like John Turner in 1984, Martin had shown a surprising lack of ease on the campaign trail, and he did not have Turner's excuse of a ten-year absence from politics. Perhaps equally surprising, Martin suffered by comparison with his immediate predecessor almost as much as Turner. Then too, Martin's campaign highlighted policy differences with Jean Chrétien in the same way the 1984 campaign had exposed Turner's differences with Pierre Trudeau. As well, both Turner and Martin were determined to ignore the record of the previous Liberal government. And, as in 1984 when Bourassa's provincial Liberals spurned Turner despite his support for Meech Lake, so the Quebec Liberals in 2004 rewarded Martin's efforts to woo soft nationalists by working for the Conservative Party. Finally, like Turner's campaign team in 1984, Martin's senior advisers were humiliated by having to request last-minute assistance from the very predecessors they disdained.

The 2004 election also revealed the deep divide within the party that the recent leadership race had exacerbated. The Martin Liberals' near brush with defeat was the subject of considerable criticism within the party even before the election was over. In their defence, Martin supporters immediately claimed the minority was actually a victory in the circumstances. 'Given what we were up against, it's unlikely anyone could have achieved a majority,' David Herle maintained afterwards.[2] He and other senior strategists quickly identified several key problems that they believed were beyond their control, some of which they felt bordered on betrayal.

First and foremost, several of them spoke of the media's seeming determination to compensate for their earlier uncritical acceptance of Martin as the heir apparent. Tim Murphy concluded 'the media needed a new story line, and "giant falls from grace" was the one they chose.'[3] Scott Reid pointed to various incidents during the campaign which, in his view, demonstrated media bias, including one on the leader's campaign plane when a well-known national reporter was overheard telling colleagues he planned to 'bring down' Martin just as he had John Turner two decades earlier.[4] Subsequent analysis of the media's election coverage suggested the Liberals' concerns were not without substance. One prominent academic study concluded that fully 22 per cent of Liberal coverage had a negative rather than neutral slant in the first half of the campaign, compared with 12 per cent for the Conservatives.[5]

While the impact of media coverage on voter intentions is debatable, Martin's supporters certainly could (and did) point to the challenging new *political* reality that confronted the Liberal Party in the 2004 election. Jean Chrétien had fought three elections against a fragmented opposition comprising four political parties. Chrétien himself was the first to admit he had benefited enormously from the division on the right between the Progressive Conservatives and the Reform/Alliance parties, and from the inept leadership of Preston Manning and Stockwell Day. Paul Martin, by contrast, was faced with a united Right, under the leadership of the more skilled, knowledgeable, and determined Stephen Harper. As well, Martin was confronted with the long-standing tradition of voters growing tired of *any* governing party after a decade or more in power. Only two incoming Liberal leaders had managed to overcome this tendency when they succeeded long-serving leaders.[6]

In these circumstances, the timing of the election call was a key factor. Critics argued the call should have been delayed for months and probably until the following spring. Several academics noted that Martin's pre-writ support of 38 per cent was very unlikely to go up. Past experience strongly suggested whatever support the Liberals entered the campaign with would most likely decline over the course of the campaign. 'In over 40 years, no party going into the election with the lead has managed to finish ahead of their immediate pre-writ standing,' political scientist Barry Kay of Wilfrid Laurier University pointed out, 'with the single exception of Pierre Trudeau in 1974.'[7] Kay's colleague Steven Brown concurred, adding 'I can't recall a situation analogous to this one, where the governing party has decided to go ahead with the election despite the fact they are still reeling from a major hit.'[8]

Nevertheless Martin's key advisers were determined to proceed with an election as soon as possible. Afterwards their concerns about the timing of the election call centred on the question of whether they waited *too long*. None indicated they might have chosen to wait longer. Virtually all of them also argued their decision to delay the call until June only posed a problem because of the sponsorship scandal. 'Here we were keeping our promises, like our commitment to the west to wait until the new boundaries came into effect, and look what happened,' one of them complained. Although his views were not shared by many Liberals, they were strongly supported by a senior Conservative organizer, who later said the Liberals had been 'too nice' and 'too intent on playing fair.' In his view, 'the time to call the election was early February,' when the Conservatives had no leader and the scandal had not taken flight. 'He lacks the killer instinct,' the Tory adviser concluded about Martin, and many Liberals secretly feared he was correct.[9]

Friendly Fire Strafes the Campaign

Like John Turner, Martin also suffered from friendly fire, some of which revealed the depth of the ongoing divisions in the party that had been reinforced by the leadership race and the internecine warfare of the previous two years. Days before the Liberals dropped the writ, Martin's former cabinet colleague Lloyd Axworthy (who was about to be installed as the president of the University of Winnipeg) delivered a scathing criticism of Martin's handling of the post-secondary education file as finance minister. Stressing that he had fought unsuccessfully at the cabinet table against Martin's plans, Axworthy denounced the 'two-tier, American-style university system' that resulted from Martin's 1997 decision to create a private body, the Canada Foundation for Innovation, to fund university research. Fairness and regional balance, Axworthy claimed, were being pushed aside in favour of public–private sector research partnerships with a few elite universities. He noted that his own university had received only 6 Canada Research Chairs, while the University of Toronto had been given 267. 'One of the great strengths of this country was that you had a variety of universities in every region, each of whom had strong faculties and research bases,' Axworthy stated, 'but now the system has been geared to five or six universities ... you don't have the capacity for balanced development.'[10]

Axworthy's comments echoed those of Sheila Copps during the 2003 leadership debates, but his timing was far more damaging. Indirectly, Axworthy had also once again questioned Martin's commitment to the Trudeauvian vision of federalism, including the role of a strong central government in nation-building. This concern was taken up by journalist Adam Radwanski (a well-known supporter of the Trudeau/Chrétien approach to federalism). Radwanski actually urged opposition parties and the media to 'target Martin's soft federalism' during the election campaign. He denounced Martin's decision to follow the tactics of Brian Mulroney and court the Quebec nationalist vote 'to save his political skin,' citing among other moves the new prime minister's promotion of Jean Lapierre, 'who has stated that his commitment to the Liberal Party this time will last only as long as Mr. Martin is leader.' Radwanski even went so far as to argue opposition leaders 'should be reminding Canadians, on a daily basis, of Martin's "soft federalism"' and 'run on a message of "one Canada," pitting their patriotism against Mr. Martin's willingness to jeopardize national unity in order to win a few extra seats in Quebec.'[11]

Then, on the eve of the election call, Ontario Liberal premier Dalton McGuinty's budget created a furore when he reneged on a key election promise not to raise taxes. Blaming his actions on the deficit left by the Harris Tories, McGuinty introduced a special health care levy and cut health services in order to deal with the revenue shortfall. Public reaction was swift and overwhelmingly negative. But Martin's campaign team disagreed as to how much impact, if any, this highly unpopular move might have on federal Liberal fortunes. There was even heated debate about whether to postpone the election call yet again. One senior adviser insisted 'it's premature to come to any conclusions on whether the impact would warrant a delay.' David Herle confirmed that Earnscliffe was in the field polling after a CanWest poll showed the Conservatives only three points behind the Liberals in vote-rich Ontario, where Martin's strategists had been planning to win their majority after the sponsorship scandal dashed their hopes in Quebec. Nevertheless deputy campaign director Steve MacKinnon declared the CanWest poll invalid, and Herle insisted: 'There's no consideration of a change of plan. We remain as utterly confident today as we were a week ago.'[12]

Martin's caucus was less sanguine. One veteran MP complained, 'How could they think it *wouldn't* affect us?' a view shared by many Ontario MPs who were Martin supporters.[13] Their frustration was heightened when they learned David Herle had advised the McGuinty government on their budget strategy at the same time he was serving as the party's national campaign chair. The party's former national director, Senator Terry Mercer, was quick to criticize Herle's involvement in the provincial sphere so close to an election call. 'You can only have one master in this business. The Liberal Party of Canada is a big enough job in itself ... It's a serious game we are playing here.'[14] Even Martin was apparently taken aback by the revelation. 'I'm not sure that's where he was involved,' the prime minister told reporters, suggesting Herle might have worked on issues other than the budget.[15] According to a McGuinty aide, the plan had been to coordinate their efforts so that criticism would be avoided. 'We wanted to make sure we were in lock-step with them as they went into their campaign,' he said. The aide also noted that McGuinty had personally informed Martin of the planned increases. Martin in turn had used the occasion of his campaign launch to reinforce McGuinty's position by stating that Stephen Harper 'wants to do to Canada what Mike Harris did to Ontario.'[16]

Many Liberals were sceptical that this strategy would work. 'You can't keep blaming the previous government for everything,' Maurizio Bevilacqua said. 'Voters get tired of hearing this.' His view received early confirmation when a poll the day of the campaign launch showed the party's support had fallen to 36 per cent – largely due to a decline in support in Ontario – a result which would mean a minority government. Only three days after the election call, another poll showed the Liberals had fallen to 33 per cent in Ontario, their core base of support.[17] Senator David Smith suggested the polls underestimated the party's support. Smith argued that Martin's personal popularity would allow them to achieve a fourth, albeit reduced, Liberal majority if they stayed the course and stayed out of trouble. 'That would mean to ensure a majority we'd have to go up a bit during the campaign,' he told reporters, 'but I think the chances are quite good for that.'[18]

Last but hardly least, there was the continuing fallout from the sponsorship scandal. Certainly the huge lead they inherited in the polls nationally and in Quebec was gone by the time Martin dropped the writ. Whether this was the fault of Chrétien and the sponsorship scandal – or of the Martinites' overwrought response to it – remains a major source of contention within the party. Carleton University journalism professor Paul Attallah, for one, argued Martin's publicly expressed outrage and 'identification with the most aggrieved members of the general public' meant that 'rather than project prime ministerial authority, he projected disorientation and supplication.'[19] But according to Steve MacKinnon the polls were no longer relevant. 'Everything had been ready to go for weeks. The buses were ready. The ads were already done. The spending announcements had been made. It was almost impossible to put the brakes on at that point. And Mr. Martin was, as I recall, determined to get this thing out of the way.'[20]

Despite their problems, the Martin Liberals arguably entered the campaign with at least three advantages over their opponents. First, they had a ten-year record of accomplishments. From the Clarity Act and the decision to stay out of Iraq, to the ratification of the Kyoto Accord and Martin's own role in the elimination of the deficit, Canadians continued to view the overall record of the Chrétien era in a very positive light.[21] Perhaps even more significant, considering Martin's strategy of trying to increase the party's support in the west and Quebec, polls showed Chrétien was not a handicap, but was actually *more* popular in the west and Ontario than Martin, and almost as popular in Quebec.[22] In addition the economy – always a key factor in elections – was the strongest of the G8 countries, with low unemployment and interest rates and a string of seven balanced budgets.

A second, related advantage for Martin should have been the fact the Liberal Party had long been seen as the party most competent to govern. As well, the party had traditionally been perceived as the one whose positions were 'closest to those of Canadians' on the national unity and social policy files. With Martin entering the election as the champion of medicare, it seemed assured that the party would maintain its priority status as guardian of those Canadian values. Indeed, a poll only a week before the election had confirmed that 44 per cent of Canadians still believed Martin and the Liberals 'would provide the best overall government for Canada' compared with only 28 per cent who chose the Harper Conservatives.[23]

A third and final advantage for the Martin Liberals was the ongoing challenge faced by Stephen Harper to curtail extremist eruptions among his candidates and advisers, and to convince Canadians he was sufficiently moderate to serve as prime minister. Simply put, Stephen Harper might be more of a threat than Stockwell Day or Preston Manning, but he was not the serious opponent that Brian Mulroney had been for John Turner. Nor was Harper able to rid himself of a number of troublesome backbenchers from the early Reform era in time for the election. Many observers believed this meant that during the campaign Harper's Conservatives were likely to live up to their image as being too extreme to govern.

Nevertheless, when Paul Martin called the election on 23 May the party was hovering near minority territory and it was clear the race would be much closer than anyone had expected only a few months earlier. Still, there was a certain early confidence among Liberals that came from having won the last two elections handily, despite initial misgivings about Jean Chrétien's timing of the call. But when Martin and his organization came close to losing the election, the near disaster suggested to many Liberals that Martin lacked the political instincts of his predecessor, a fatal flaw in any leader but especially a Liberal one.

The Campaign Launch and Early Problems

The similarities between the Liberals' 2004 election and John Turner's catastrophic 1984 campaign are striking. The first half of the 2004 election saw the newly crowned leader stumble badly, the Liberals' early lead dissipate, and panic set in among the untested advisers who had only recently taken the heir apparent to the prime minister's office.

Although several of Martin's advisers had been involved in previous campaigns, none had been in charge, and the responsibility proved a heavy burden. Their lack of experience was compounded by the fact they were accustomed to commenting on any and all Liberal developments in the media. This was a practice Chrétien's election strategists had religiously avoided, leaving public comments during an election campaign to the party's assigned – and almost always elected – spokespersons.

Another problem for Martin was the willingness of the parliamentary wing to publicly criticize the non-elected campaign team, a development clearly stemming from the long-standing tension between Martin's supporters in caucus and the PMO. Similarly, the vendetta against Chrétien supporters that continued during the first six months in office soon spilled over into the campaign. Spurned former Chrétien MPs and advisers wasted little time criticizing the Martin team's handling of the campaign once it appeared to be in difficulty.

David Herle apparently recognized the potential for some of these problems before the campaign began. In an interview several days before the writ was dropped, Herle took the blame for 'failing to reach out to those Liberals who remained faithful to former prime minister Jean Chrétien,' and acknowledged that other 'rookie mistakes' had cost the Martin team as well.[24] Yet, despite their awareness of a simmering problem, surprisingly little was done to remedy the situation until the campaign was well underway.

Equally problematic was the fact Martin ended up with an election strategy almost identical to Chrétien's, given the concerted efforts to demonstrate major differences between the two men. Martin's game plan in a nutshell was to stress Liberal values and attack Stephen Harper as an extremist. In this he was evidently hoping to replicate Chrétien's successful attack on Stockwell Day in 2000. From the beginning, though, this plan was fraught with difficulties. First, Paul Martin was an unconvincing spokesman for many of the Liberal values they were promoting. Second, Stephen Harper was not Stockwell Day. For at least the first half of the campaign the new Conservative leader succeeded in keeping his own and his candidates' statements firmly on track in the mainstream.

Nevertheless, Martin looked confident when he left Rideau Hall on 23 May after requesting the governor general dissolve Parliament. He wasted no time in outlining what issue the Liberals planned to fight the election on. 'I believe the question is this. Do you want a Canada that builds on its historic strengths and values, such as medicare, generosity and an unflinching commitment to equality of opportunity,' he asked, 'or, do you want a Canada that departs from much of its history, a Canada that rejects its valued tradition of collective responsibility?'[25]

A pamphlet for candidates to distribute door to door was designed to reinforce those questions. Like the new-look Martin Red Book, its front cover was white and featured a large photo of Paul Martin and a very small Liberal logo. Inside it stressed the five key platform themes: 'fixing health care for a generation, giving cities a new deal, supporting our families, caring for our children, developing Canada's role on the world stage.' The pamphlet had two advantages over the full platform. First, it highlighted issues with which Martin was very comfortable, and, second, it was used to wrap the themes in a blanket of Liberal/Canadian values. Entitled 'Choose Your Canada,' it showcased Martin's quote from the campaign launch: 'As Liberals, we believe in a Canada that is generous and just, prosperous and proud.' The back cover contained another Martin quote: 'To those who share our values as Canadians, to those who see Canada as we do, we ask for your support.'

Unfortunately for Martin, Stephen Harper immediately delivered a stinging rebuke to the Liberals' approach which many Canadians found all too convincing. 'My Canada will be as Canadian as any other candidate's,' he declared. 'You know, in this country you can be a Canadian without being a Liberal. This government seems to forget that.'[26] Several pundits observed that one reason Harper was able to make this criticism stick was the progress he had made in appearing prime ministerial. Another was the difficulty Martin faced in selling some of the arguments related to the Liberals' values strategy. On foreign affairs, for example, the PM used the campaign launch to tell reporters 'I love the United States, but I love far greater that we are Canada, and we're going to stay that way.' Not content with this, he argued the Conservatives were launching 'American-style attack ads' against him and had an 'American-style' plan to slash taxes that would 'turn Canada into the 51st state … You can have a country like Canada. You can have a country like the United States. That's a choice you can make.'[27] But the memory of Martin's recent visit to Washington, where he stood beside George W. Bush and promised a 'revitalized' relationship 'with our good friends and neighbours' was fresh in Canadians' minds, and Martin's sudden electoral conversion to a more nationalistic perspective seemed too great a stretch. Moreover, historian Michael Bliss warned the 'divisive' strategy of 'America-bashing' was not only a 'tired replay' of the free trade debate, which was unlikely to impress voters, but could have negative repercussions after the election.[28]

Soon after the campaign launch the Liberals rolled out their entire platform. Unlike previous Red Books, this one received scant attention from the media. A frustrated David Herle recalled: 'They said we had already released many of the platform planks in the Throne Speech and the Budget, so it wasn't news. We didn't expect that, frankly.'[29] When the media *did* pay attention to the platform, it was to highlight the Liberals' problems with their health care plank. According to Herle, health care had been deliberately left out of the budget because Martin had decided he could not negotiate a deal with the premiers until he had a mandate. At the same time, Martin and his advisers were concerned that some voters might downplay the importance of the Liberal health

care plank because of similar promises made in previous Liberal platforms. Since health care was now the top election issue, they were determined to highlight it, but they needed a new approach. This time,
the pledge was to 'fix health care for a generation.' Martin's team were
convinced their unique emphasis on a long-term solution would serve
to distinguish them from the Conservatives, and they expected it to be
their most successful wedge issue on the values front. The platform
committed an immediate $3 billion in additional funds and a five-year,
$9 billion plan to reduce wait times, as well as promising – once again –
to establish national home care and pharmacare programs.

Herle admitted Liberal strategists did not expect the Conservatives
to address the health care issue seriously. Nor did they anticipate the
rash of criticism of their own position by provincial premiers and health
care experts immediately following their announcement. This included
a CBC TV 'Reality Check' segment that described Martin as the 'architect' of the funding shortfall his pledge was now trying to remedy.[30]
Worse still was Dalton McGuinty's casual dismissal of the plan as 'a
promise made in the thick of a campaign.'[31] Pressed the following day
by reporters, the Ontario premier compounded the problem: 'I don't
think we should rush into a health care deal for the purposes of short-
term political imperatives,' he snapped when asked if he trusted Martin's promise.[32]

The situation deteriorated rapidly. Stunned by McGuinty's comments, Martin responded by attacking the premier personally. First
he stated pointedly that he would never have reneged on a promise
not to raise taxes if he had been in the premier's shoes. Then, on 31
May in Sault Ste Marie, Martin made a dramatic pledge to resign as
prime minister in two years if he were to break any of his three major
campaign promises (on health care, cities, and social programs). His
aides also suggested to reporters that Martin would not want to be seen
campaigning with McGuinty. 'Well look, I fully expect the premier will
want to help out his brother (a first-time Liberal candidate in the Ottawa area) ... but there are no immediate plans to have Mr. McGuinty
and Mr. Martin campaign together,' a frustrated Steven MacKinnon
told reporters.[33]

The damaging image of the two Liberals sniping at each other in
the early days of the campaign was only partly papered over when
McGuinty told reporters the next day: 'I have every confidence the
prime minister is making the right decision with respect to the financing
of his health care plan.'[34] But longtime Martin supporter Anne McLel-

lan, now deputy prime minister, reopened the feud when she told reporters in her Edmonton riding later the same day, 'there's no question the Dalton McGuinty budget in Ontario has hurt us. I mean, I'm not going to pretend that was a neutral event.' McLellan even confided that she viewed McGuinty as a worse threat than Stephen Harper.[35]

Meanwhile the Conservatives under Harper had been moving swiftly towards the centre of the left-right spectrum, abandoning their ambivalence to the welfare state in the face of overwhelming public support. Their platform actually offered $2 billion more than the Liberals over five years. With his platform centrepiece neutralized, and no record of his own to trumpet because of his determination to rush into an election, Martin now had only the values strategy left to fall back on.

The depth of the Liberals' difficulties became clear when an Ipsos-Reid poll revealed only 34 per cent of Canadians felt they were the best party to deal with health care problems. This in turn reflected the party's loss of credibility in the broader category of 'party whose values are closest to mine' on social policy, where they were reduced to a mere six-point advantage over the Conservatives. Similarly the Liberals' other traditional advantage – as the party best able to manage the federation – had declined dramatically because of their problems in Quebec over the sponsorship scandal. The Conservatives had actually achieved a five-point *advantage* as the party 'best able to run an ethical and scandal-free government.'

The one area in which the Liberal Party scored better than usual was 'best steward of the economy,' a clear recognition of the role Paul Martin had played as finance minister in balancing Canada's books.[36] Yet Martin and his advisers remained fixated on the health care plank in the early part of the campaign to the exclusion of almost all other issues. Their refusal to change course was accompanied by a fierce determination to avoid discussing the decade-long Liberal record, including Paul Martin's successful deficit-reduction battle. According to several of the key players, this decision was based on the belief that raising their record would open the door to more criticism of Martin and his perceived role in the sponsorship scandal.

Many *individual* Liberals were also being ignored by the Martin organization. By the end of May virtually no one from the Chrétien camp had been asked to participate in the election campaign. Some of the spurned veterans, such as Terry Mercer, Peter Donolo, and John Rae, responded to media queries with the neutral comment that they had done everything they had been asked to do. Others avoided public comments, while a few said openly that they planned to 'sit on their hands' during the campaign.[37]

Campaign Problems and Infighting

By the end of the first week of the campaign the Liberals were in serious difficulty. Their ten-point lead had fallen to a mere four points. Statistically they were in a dead heat in Ontario, where the McGuinty budget – not the sponsorship scandal – was indeed taking its toll. Equally troubling, Paul Martin's image as a leader (both nationally *and* in Ontario) had 'somewhat worsened or strongly worsened' among 47 per cent of respondents, compared with only 15 per cent for Stephen Harper and Jack Layton.[38] Worst of all, political scientist Barry Kay of Wilfrid Laurier University had projected a Liberal minority, using a model that successfully predicted the outcome in the six previous national election campaigns.[39]

Within hours of its release, disgruntled Liberals publicly called for Martin to replace David Herle as a national campaign chair, or, at a minimum, to bring in additional expertise. (Interestingly, no one referred to Herle's co-chairs – John Webster and Hélène Scherrer – demonstrating that it was widely recognized within the party that neither had the influence Herle did.) Some Liberals called for Martin to replace Herle with Senator David Smith, while others argued that Gordon Ashworth should be brought back to run the day-to-day operations as campaign director. The following day, Martin categorically ruled out any such personnel changes. 'We are not making any changes in our campaign team,' he declared. 'I knew it was going to be a tough fight,' he told reporters, 'but I'm very, very confident that we are going to come back with a majority government. And as far as I'm concerned, David Herle is going to be the one most responsible.'[40]

Herle had declared he was 'pleased' with the way the first week had unfolded, but he also indicated a number of new initiatives would be unveiled to 'step the campaign up a notch.'[41] Almost immediately the Martin team launched a three-pronged, and somewhat contradictory, strategy. First, Martin personally adopted an apologetic tone and accepted responsibility, if not blame, for the sponsorship scandal on behalf of the previous Liberal government. Speaking in Vancouver on 2 June, the Liberal leader acknowledged 'the degree of unease and concern that exists' among voters and described it as 'perfectly legitimate.' He then promised to do better, and unexpectedly admitted the Liberals might actually lose the election. 'Let me tell you,' he concluded, 'I understand clearly that Canadians don't just give you their vote. You must earn their vote.'[42]

Second, Martin's Ontario chair, Karl Littler, went on the offensive against the Conservatives. In a bizarre and highly controversial move, Littler sent two of Martin's cabinet ministers into the fray to challenge Stephen Harper directly. First Immigration Minister Judy Sgro accosted Harper at a Conservative rally in Scarborough. Referring to a Tory MP's recent comments advocating limits to abortion access, she shouted, 'Whose rights are you going to take away next?' as he passed her in the crowd. Then, at an event in Markham, Defence Minister John McCallum challenged Harper to debate the costing of his platform. The hapless Liberal minister was forced to yell repeatedly to get the attention of Harper and reporters before declaring the Tory numbers did not add up and their proposed spending cuts would 'gut' social programs.

Neither incident had the desired effect. Far from casting a negative light on the Tories' alleged hidden agenda, polls showed Harper's description of the Liberal 'ambushes' as 'desperation measures' was one shared by most voters. 'It's not only desperate but it's a bit strange,' he said. 'When you send senior cabinet ministers to street protests, I think they're pretty worried ... Usually what you normally do is you get ordinary people to go out and protest and make it look like it's not your party ... you don't send out your own front bench.'[43]

The third prong of the Martin team's strategy was to demonstrate reconciliation within the party. This was becoming increasingly urgent, as the impact of their earlier harsh treatment of Liberal opponents began to be felt almost daily. The lawsuits launched by Jean Pelletier in March and Michel Vennat in April were soon followed, just days after the campaign began, by the announcement that Alfonso Gagliano – the former Chrétien minister whom Martin had recalled from his ambassadorial post in Denmark – was now suing the federal government for $4.5 million for wrongful dismissal. Gagliano's lawsuit specifically accused Martin of 'deliberate acts motivated by political aims' and indecent haste in 'describing events as a scandal without waiting for any light to be shed on the whole affair.'[44]

In the same vein, former industry minister Brian Tobin came back to haunt the Martin team shortly after the writ was dropped. Now a regular media commentator, Tobin (whom Martin essentially had driven from the cabinet and the Liberal leadership race by refusing to fund Tobin's broadband initiative) began predicting a Liberal minority barely a

week after the campaign began.[45] His views were being privately reinforced in Quebec by several former Liberal MPs who had been shunted
aside, further damaging the party's image there as well as in Ontario.

Meanwhile public works minister Stan Keyes was forced to admit
that he had effectively buried an audit ordered by Martin on the expenditures of Canada Post president André Ouellet (another former
Chrétien minister) as part of his response to the sponsorship scandal.[46]

In Quebec, lieutenant Jean Lapierre apparently was marching to a
different drummer. Instead of reconciliation, he deliberately accelerated the conflict. Lapierre's description of the Adscam scandal as a
'rotten fish' that Paul Martin's team would 'wipe clean with Spic and
Span'[47] left Chrétienites speechless. Not only did these developments
once again draw attention to the internal feud, but it focused public
attention on the very sponsorship scandal that Martin and his advisers
were desperately trying to make them forget.

Then the 3 June announcement by Toronto Liberal MP Charles Caccia that he would not be running as an Independent in his longtime
riding of Davenport reminded all Canadians of the many vicious nomination battles that had plagued the party throughout the previous
year. Caccia, the well-regarded former Trudeau-era minister, was the
longest-serving MP at the time the writ was dropped and his margins
of victory in ten straight elections had been among the highest in the
country. His press release pointedly reminded everyone that his departure from politics, like that of Sheila Copps, was not voluntary. 'After
the nomination of someone who supported Mr. Martin in the recent
leadership race as the official Liberal candidate,' he wrote, 'the only
option open to me was to present myself as an Independent candidate.'
Moreover, Caccia made it clear he believed he could have won the seat
as an Independent: 'Support in the riding for my candidacy as an Independent appears very strong, and I am naturally appreciative of the
large number of my constituents who urged me to consider doing so.'
But, ever the loyal Liberal, he had decided against the move in the best
interests of the party.[48]

The potential damage to the party's image in Ontario was of particular concern to Martin's advisers, who now needed to retain every seat
in that province to hold on to their majority. Consequently, several initiatives were launched by Martin's team to bring disgruntled Liberals
onside and prevent further damage. In Quebec, Jean Lapierre was instructed to try harder to build bridges to former Chrétien minister Martin Cauchon and Stephen Hogue, the former Chrétien adviser who had

been denied the nomination in Chrétien's former riding by Lapierre. John Manley was approached to campaign in western Canada. Advisers said Chrétien himself was 'expected' to campaign in his old riding on behalf of the Martin candidate, Marie-Eve Bilodeau. The Martin team also made it known that various Chrétien supporters, including Peter Donolo and Senator Jim Munson, as well as Allan Rock's former adviser Cyrus Reporter, were being asked to participate in the twice-weekly campaign conference calls. Munson stressed that Liberals were putting their rivalry aside for the good of the party. 'I think the polls have been a wake-up call to all Liberals that we should work together to try and build a Liberal majority,' Munson said.[49]

Following Munson's lead, veterans David Smith, Tom Axworthy, and several other senior Liberals outside the Martin camp reacted to the troubling polls by preparing a lengthy memo on campaign strategy. They suggested Martin's speeches begin emphasizing the Chrétien record and Martin's own record on deficit reduction, a plan they felt was not only politically astute but likely to be favourably received by Martin's advisers. However, like most of those approached by the inner circle, they soon became convinced their input was not being taken seriously. Donolo later described the whole exercise as a 'smokescreen' so that Martin's advisers 'could claim they had consulted.'[50] Axworthy later recalled their memo 'went nowhere.'[51]

Martin's campaign also suffered a number of 'own goal' gaffes caused by the lack of experience in the senior ranks. In Quebec, for example, Martin minister Liza Frulla responded to Barry Kay's projection of a Liberal minority by warning that the Liberals needed a majority in order to maintain national security, a threat that backfired almost immediately when Gilles Duceppe as well as Stephen Harper ridiculed her comments.[52] A few days later, national co-chair Hélène Scherrer mused publicly, 'I don't think Paul Martin is a good politician.' Stunned reporters listened in amazement as she continued: 'It's hard for him in an election that's being fought below the belt. He is not good when it comes to playing that game ... He wants everybody to love him.'[53] Yet another Liberal MP, Carolyn Parrish of Mississauga, referred to the entire campaign as a 'comedy of errors' in a widely quoted CBC Radio interview on 9 June. 'It was like the Keystone Cops running around,' Parrish declared. This in turn led Montreal-area MP Raymonde Folco, who had successfully fended off a Martin challenger, to comment that she was quizzed on only two issues when going door to door: the sponsorship scandal and Liberal infighting.

This image of incompetence and internal dissent intensified the next day when David Herle held a conference call with Liberal MPs and candidates. Responding to new polls showing the Liberals only one point ahead of the Conservatives nationally, and running neck and neck with them in much of Ontario outside Toronto, Herle declared the Liberals were 'in a (downward) spiral that we have to arrest.' Unfortunately for Herle, the call was monitored by a journalist, who promptly reported the details of Herle's briefing and various 'desperate' MPs' criticism of his handling of the national campaign. The fact someone on the call had provided the journalist with access was another blow to party unity, but the incident also reinforced the notion among veteran Liberal strategists that Herle was out of his depth. They argued he should never have made such a comment regardless, since his role as national campaign chair was to inspire confidence, not send candidates off in a panic. Herle angrily responded that it was important for candidates to know the real state of play and understand the rationale for the next stage of Liberal tactics, which would include attack ads.[54]

The most problematic of Martin's team was unquestionably Jean Lapierre. Widely disliked in Liberal circles outside Quebec, he quickly became equally controversial within the province. From his early comments about the 'useless' Clarity Act to his insistence that the sponsorship scandal would not affect Liberal fortunes in the province, Lapierre was rapidly becoming a major impediment to the party's prospects there. Even in his own safe riding of Outremont, lifelong Liberals were talking of voting for the Conservatives or the Bloc to send a message. 'He'd better start looking for another job,' one prominent Liberal told reporters who were following Lapierre as he canvassed door-to-door.[55] However, as Michael Robinson pointed out, the former Bloc MP had been recruited at a time when the Martin team still believed they could increase their hold on the province from forty to sixty seats by capturing the soft nationalist vote. 'We expected him to deliver another twenty seats for us,' Robinson stressed, 'and then we found ourselves trying to hold on to the forty. That wasn't his job.' As a result, Herle and fellow chair John Webster decided to ask Lapierre to 'step aside' from active campaigning and allow others 'to carry the ball, and he did so with real class. Keep in mind he could have pulled out before the writ was dropped and he did not.'[56]

Lapierre's replacement was Stéphane Dion. The significance of this move could hardly be missed. Dion – whom Martin had relegated to the backbenches – had launched a letter-writing campaign during the election on his own initiative. Already he had skewered Jack Layton and the NDP regarding their ambivalent position on the Clarity Act and taken Gilles Duceppe to task on the fiscal imbalance.[57] He was, in short, one of the few success stories for the Liberals in Quebec. By relegating Lapierre to the wings and showcasing Dion, Martin had apparently turned – at least for public consumption – to the promotion of the Trudeau vision of federalism. Martin's defence of the Clarity Act, once Layton and the NDP had attacked it, reinforced this perception. In a well-received op-ed published in the *National Post*, Martin also declared 'I know that, if we are dragged into another unity fight by the opposition parties, the Liberal vision of this country will prevail once again.'[58]

The Lost Opportunity of the Leaders' Debates

Given the Liberals' steep drop in the polls and his recent spirited defence of the Clarity Act, Paul Martin might have been expected to use the occasion of the nationally televised leaders' debates to defend both the Liberals' economic record of the past decade *and* the traditional Liberal approach to federalism. Certainly this was the advice now being given to him privately by many of his own supporters as well as the Chrétienites. Still, he hesitated. 'It's Herle and Webster,' one longtime Martin MP complained. 'They are so determined to see Martin presented as … a leader of a brand new government as opposed to year 11 of the original Liberal government. [But] it just doesn't relate to reality.'[59] Montreal MP Nick Discepola, a strident Martin supporter in the past, argued that Martin needed to regain public confidence by reminding voters of his own record as finance minister. 'He exuded confidence because everybody knew that when he said something, it was going to come to fruition,' Discepola declared. 'The challenge now is to regain that trust.' Michael Robinson agreed, adding that Martin needed to look 'prime ministerial' and adopt the role of nation-builder.[60]

Martin took neither of these approaches. Instead, in the French-language debate Martin attempted to play the values card by arguing Quebeckers should vote for the Liberals in order to prevent the election of the far-right Reform/Alliance/Conservative party under Stephen Harper. In English the following night, he aggressively pursued Harper on the issue of minority rights and the Charter, an issue that Jack Layton promptly reminded viewers had hardly been Martin's strength in the recent past. Nevertheless Martin declared, 'I would never use the notwithstanding clause to take away the rights that are enshrined in the Charter,' and challenged Harper to say whether he would use the clause to ban abortions or gay marriage. Harper replied that he would have free votes in the House of Commons on several of these contentious issues but would not invoke the notwithstanding clause, with the possible exception of child pornography legislation. Although this response appeared to deflect some of Martin's arguments about the Conservatives' extreme values, most observers nevertheless agreed that Martin had made an impact on this issue. But it was not enough to counter his increasingly negative image as a desperate politician rather than a prime minister.

While Martin was focusing on values, virtually all of his opponents were raising issues related to federal-provincial relations and the sponsorship scandal. In the first night's debate in French, an ill-at-ease Martin allowed Gilles Duceppe to repeatedly raise the sponsorship scandal, denigrate the Clarity Act, and criticize the Chrétien government's reduction in funding of social programs, all without serious rebuttal. Martin also allowed Duceppe's opening declaration that sovereignty was not an issue in the campaign to go unchallenged. Since many of the former Trudeau and Chrétien advisers who had volunteered their advice on debate strategy had specifically suggested that Martin needed to play the national unity card to warn of a possible Conservative minority that would be propped up by the Bloc, his failure to respond was all the more puzzling.

The following night in English saw a repeat of Martin's passive performance regarding federalism, but this time with the Conservative leader as his main opponent. When Stephen Harper promoted a decentralized approach to health care in which each province would be allowed to implement health services differently if it chose ('What's wrong with letting them decide how they want to go about this? Why do we care how they are managed?' Harper asked rhetorically),[61] Martin stood mute and did not deliver the obvious Liberal rebuttal – that medicare was a national program based on minimum national standards to ensure all Canadians received the same level of care across the country. As historian Michael Behiels commented, Canadians were left to conclude that little now separated the Liberals from other parties along the federalist axis.[62]

In the end, no clear winner emerged from either debate, although Duceppe was considered to have done the best in French and Stephen Harper in English. Several commentators concluded this was likely due to Harper's success in appearing ordinary rather than frightening. In addition, the public's low expectations about Harper had allowed him to 'win' the debate by avoiding errors, while the unfairly high expectations placed on Martin once again caused him to fall short. The polls confirmed this analysis. Immediately after the debates, an Ipsos-Reid poll showed that 42 per cent of viewers now had a worse opinion of Martin, while only 20 per cent said their opinion had improved, producing a negative rating of 22 points. By contrast, Stephen Harper received a 25-point positive rating.

Political scientist Nelson Wiseman told reporters, 'It means the election is decided. It's over. The only question left is how far down will they [the Liberals] go and how big will the Conservative minority be.'[63] UBC political scientist Philip Resnick concurred, stating that Martin had needed a clear win and did not get one. 'This is not 1984,' Resnick said, 'This still could result in a Liberal minority ... But my own instinct tells me it's going to be a minority Conservative government.'[64] Across the country in Quebec, political science professor Robert Bernier of UQAM declared a minority inevitable and warned 'we're heading for an Italian-style parliament.'[65] These academic views were reinforced by news that the federal public service was now preparing in earnest for a Tory victory. At a party in Ottawa a few days later, celebrating John Turner's seventy-fifth birthday (an event attended by both Herle and Webster), the most popular line of the evening was suitably pessimistic: 'Who knew the Titanic was a CSL ship?' made the rounds of prominent Liberals gathered at the Chateau Laurier to fete Turner in the same venue where many had watched the depressing election night results in 1984.

The Liberals' Election Crisis

Martin's uneven performance, and especially his continued refusal to defend either his own or the extended Liberal record, left many senior Liberals stunned. Most confined their criticism to internal channels, but not all. Several well-known Chrétien Liberals voiced their concerns publicly, reminding many of the tumultuous Turner era. Former Chrétien adviser Peter Donolo's column the following day specifically highlighted Martin's failures, as did Warren Kinsella's blog.[66] Kinsella argued it was the fault of Martin's advisers in overselling his leadership that had caused such a steep decline in voter support. 'One thing I learned at Jean Chrétien's knee,' Kinsella declared, 'is that it's always better to undersell and over-perform. These guys have not done that and that is one of the biggest problems they will have [with Liberals] if they are in a minority situation. People will say you promised us 220 seats and where are those seats?'[67]

Perhaps the unkindest cut of all came unintentionally from none other than John Turner, Martin's erstwhile mentor and role model. In an interview on CTV's *Question Period*, Turner first praised Martin as 'easily the best candidate' and declared the electorate was 'extremely volatile,' arguing Martin could still win a majority. He too argued that Martin needed to defend his record as finance minister and 'hone his message to three or four priorities,' rather than the all-encompassing scattergun approach for which Martin was well known. Then Turner unexpectedly warned that Martin would likely risk internal revolt if he attempted to stay on as leader if he failed to obtain a majority. 'It's unpredictable, of course, but there's no doubt about it that the pressure's on him and a minority situation would be difficult,' Turner said. After referring to his own problems with the patronage appointments made by his predecessor, Turner once again raised the spectre of the sponsorship scandal. Trying to demonstrate sympathy for Martin's position, Turner instead launched a new wave of speculation when he said, 'Grievances build up, and he inherited some bad baggage too … It's hard to shake off, especially when people are legitimately thinking to themselves "Is it time for a change?"'[68]

Along with the devastating polls, Turner's comments prompted several of Martin's potential successors to begin discussing the fate of the party *when, not if*, it either lost to the Conservatives or was reduced to a minority. Amazingly, Martin was now seen as a liability for the party, less than a year after taking over as leader. The headline of one major newspaper actually trumpeted 'Liberals Make Pact Not to Oust Martin.' A senior Liberal confided 'there's a lot of interest in the post-Martin era … Potential candidates have already decided amongst themselves – it's a pact – that they won't use the same tactics that Martin used on Chrétien because that has the potential of destroying the Liberal Party.' Another insider stressed, 'Nobody wants to be seen dancing on the grave of Paul Martin,' and added that the party was 'too fragile' to go through another leadership race so soon, nor could it afford one. 'It is having difficulty raising money for this election,' the insider pointed out, 'let alone another leadership convention.'[69]

The situation deteriorated to near-chaos when a poll two days later showed the Conservatives with 36 per cent of decided voter support (as compared with only 31 per cent for the Liberals) and heading for a strong minority. The poll had been conducted by Michael Marzolini and Pollara, the Liberals' pollster for a decade before being dropped by Martin in favour of David Herle and Earnscliffe. A furious Herle immediately released results of the Liberals' internal polling showing the party still two points ahead of the Conservatives and poised to return with a strong minority. But Herle did not stop with this understandable attempt at damage control. In what one journalist described as a 'stunning accusation,' Herle told reporters: 'There appears to be a completely fallacious and mischievous poll in the public domain today.' He went on to question whether the reporter had seen the Pollara poll, which he noted Marzolini had refused to discuss. Pointing out that it was apparently 'leaked by senior Liberal party insiders,' Herle concluded it 'makes me think like it's a bit of internal sabotage rather than a legitimate poll.'[70]

When he learned of Herle's accusations Marzolini privately sent a copy of the poll to Herle and John Webster. His immediate public reaction was to say he found Herle's comments 'surprising and shocking.' Although he said he understood the pressures of a difficult campaign, where 'you might tend to overreact,' Marzolini added, 'I'm sure that when the dust settles ... he'll review those thoughts and find them wanting.'[71] Sources close to both men later confirmed the possibility of a lawsuit had been raised. Herle quickly responded with a letter of apology for comments he claimed had been taken out of context. His letter appeared on the Pollara website for nearly a week and stated in part: 'Media reports today inaccurately portrayed my sentiments ... At no time did I intend to imply you were engaged in undermining the campaign. Nor did I intend for people to believe that your work was anything other than high quality.'[72]

The two-day debacle sidelined any positive news of Liberal events and led former Chrétien minister Herb Dhaliwal to claim, 'What we're seeing here is really a meltdown in the Liberal Party.' Although Dhaliwal also said 'there's still time to turn it around,' the Liberals had to react quickly if they were to have any hope of stemming the bleeding.[73]

Salvaging the Campaign

Their first response was to make major changes to the itinerary of the leader's tour. Instead of focusing on western Canada, Martin's schedule now included many more trips to Quebec (unthinkable only a few months earlier in the province considered a Liberal bastion) and to parts of Ontario outside Toronto that had been Liberal strongholds for years. This included Hamilton, where the negative coverage from the Copps affair was putting the future of several Liberal candidates, such as prominent Martin supporters Tony Valeri and Stan Keyes, in jeopardy. With all of their handpicked 'dream team' candidates in serious trouble, it seemed highly unlikely the party would make any type of western breakthrough. And, with many of their star candidates in Quebec – including Dennis Dawson, Lucienne Robillard, Pierre Pettigrew, and Liza Frulla – in danger of losing formerly safe seats, it was clear to Martin's team that 'we needed to be there.' As another senior Liberal put it, 'we were in a dogfight on our own territory.' The luxury of additional trips to the west, or to the Atlantic where their support was still relatively strong, was something they simply could not afford.

The Martin team's new strategy also involved a direct appeal to NDP supporters to vote Liberal in order to stop the Harper Conservatives. This unusual plea for strategic voting, which even involved phone calls to known NDP supporters in some ridings, was repeated by Martin on several occasions. The Liberals also brought together three former New Democrats, who were now running as Liberal candidates, to press the case for strategic voting. Ujjal Dosanjh and Dave Haggard of BC and Chris Axworthy from Saskatchewan all made impassioned pleas for traditional NDP voters to 'stop shouting from the sidelines' and 'get into the real act to make sure there is a difference in the kind of government we have. I want voters all over the country to consider that.'[74]

The tactic clearly worried Jack Layton and his advisers. The NDP spent considerable time and effort in the last third of the campaign countering the Liberal argument. Yet media coverage tended to portray this new tactic solely as a desperation measure, emphasizing the dire straits the Liberals were in by noting there were many ridings in Ontario where the race was too close to call because of the presence of the NDP. The Liberals' effort to target NDP voters in the Ottawa-Centre riding (where Martin's close friend, Richard Mahoney, was running a distant second), lent credence to this view since Mahoney's opponent was NDP candidate Ed Broadbent.

Another new tactic which was not well known at the time, but would have serious long-term consequences, was Martin's attempt to bring Newfoundland premier Danny Williams on side by making a commitment to change the equalization formula. Although Liberal support in the Maritimes was still reasonably strong, there was concern that seats could be lost in Newfoundland, where traditional Progressive Conservatives had been convinced to run again under the new Conservative banner. And Atlantic Canada, like Ontario, was an area where the Liberals were reduced to core support they could hardly afford to lose. Admittedly Martin's offer, conveyed in a phone call to the premier, was hastily conceived, but once again it was at odds with the traditional Liberal approach to Canadian federalism. As columnist Jeffrey Simpson foresaw, by 'agreeing to all the premier's demands,' Martin 'essentially destroyed the underpinnings of equalization policy.'[75]

Although their financial resources were running out, another concrete decision taken by Martin's team in the second half of the campaign was to change their advertising approach, which until the debates had featured a 'high road,' policy-oriented, but ineffectual series of television ads. Desperate to halt and hopefully reverse the party's ever-deepening slide in the polls, they turned to the type of attack ads they had already criticized the NDP and the Conservatives for using. The NDP had begun the trend by appealing to anti-American sentiment and indirectly attacking U.S. president George W. Bush as a way of demonstrating that both the Liberals and the Conservatives could not be trusted to defend Canadian interests. The Conservatives, meanwhile, had launched a series of ads at the beginning of the campaign which either referred specifically to the sponsorship scandal or accused the Liberals of generally wasting taxpayers' money. When polling data suggested the Tories' ads were having an effect, and that the Liberals' 'values' message was not making an impact, Martin's inner circle decided a more direct and aggressive attack on Conservative values was necessary.

Like much else about the Martin campaign, this decision was controversial in Liberal circles. David Herle and Scott Reid took pains to point out the Liberals' new ads were not attacks on Harper personally. Although they were forceful, Martin's advisers argued the ads referred to actual policies and statements of the Conservatives or their leader. Certainly the Liberal ads invoked the 'values' threat by demonstrating through his own words that Harper, unlike the Liberals, was prepared to send troops to Iraq, abrogate Canada's agreement to the Kyoto Accord, limit a woman's right to access abortion, oppose the gun registry, and curtail federal spending on health care. However, the ads also made use of more general threats. One argued vaguely that Canada would be a dramatically different place if Harper were elected, and another warned that Harper's 'hidden agenda' was both real and dangerous. One media report described the Liberal ads as 'the most negative ever,' although others were quick to note the Conservative ads in 1993

– and especially the infamous ad depicting Jean Chrétien's face – actually could be seen as far more negative and personal.

According to Tim Murphy, the plan was to keep Martin above the fray and 'have the ads speak for themselves. Let the ads do their work, let him do his.'[76] This approach was directly related to another decision the Martin team had finally taken, namely to allow Martin to highlight his successes as finance minister over the previous decade. After an emergency meeting of senior advisers with several veteran Chrétien strategists, the widespread consensus of party activists outside Martin's inner circle was finally acknowledged. Martin's record, they now believed, could be used to defend the promises in their election platform from Conservative attacks, warning voters that they could not count on those promises being implemented. For example, Martin's success in eliminating the deficit, as he had promised, could be used to counter claims that his new health care commitment was merely an election ploy that would disappear once the Liberals returned to power.

Martin also began to speak about the broader record of the Liberal government over the past ten years. In one interview he even indicated that 'if Mr. Chrétien wanted to come and campaign with us, he'd be welcome.'[77] In addition, as several former Chrétien advisers including Peter Donolo had urged for some time,[78] Martin began to discuss the perils of a Liberal minority government for national unity, and for his health care agenda. He argued the Liberals would need a majority to implement many of their health care and social program proposals, comments denounced as a 'scare tactic' by the Tories but which polls nevertheless showed were striking a chord with Ontario voters.

The ads, meanwhile, appeared to be quite effective. David Herle later claimed the Liberals' internal polling showed they had an immediate and significant impact on Harper's numbers, especially in Ontario. While some analysts have argued Herle may have overstated the case somewhat,[79] his argument was supported by the findings of academics such as Paul Attallah and Jonathan Rose in post-election analyses.[80] At the same time, many experts also stressed that the efficacy of the Liberal ads, like any negative ads, was due in large measure to the context in which they were placed. As Jonathan Rose put it, 'Good negative ads do not persuade as much as they are able to reinforce existing opinion and translate that into sowing seeds of doubt about one's opponent. The Liberal ads did just that. They raised sufficient questions about Stephen Harper and the Conservatives … in voters who already had concerns.'[81]

Certainly the ads would not have been nearly as effective if Harper, and many of his candidates, had not spent the second half of the campaign reinforcing the Liberal claims by their own actions. Harper may have been an improvement over Preston Manning and Stockwell Day but, in the final analysis, he did not prove to be the consummate politician that Brian Mulroney had been in 1984. This was perhaps the single most important difference between the situations faced by John Turner and Paul Martin, who was able to salvage a narrow victory as a result of the startling number of gaffes made by Harper in the latter part of the 2004 campaign. As a result, the Liberals were able to argue that Harper and his party were simply too extreme for Canadians.

Conservative Blunders

Jack Layton may have done some damage to his party early in the campaign, with his accusation that Paul Martin was responsible for homeless people in Toronto, but at least Layton's concern for the social welfare of Canadians fell within mainstream Canadian values. As a result, this incident paled in comparison with the string of bizarre accusations and extreme opinions offered by many Conservative candidates, all of whom played into the Liberals' hands.

Stephen Harper's problems with his backbench and other candidates actually began almost immediately after the writ was dropped, but the number and severity of the extremist eruptions increased significantly in the latter part of the campaign. The first of these came from an unexpected quarter. One of Harper's closest and most senior confidants, MP Scott Reid, suggested in an interview in Moncton on 26 May that administrative changes to the Official Languages Act, including the withdrawal of federal bilingual services in some areas, might be considered by a Harper Conservative government. The Martin Liberals immediately seized on the comments as evidence of the 'values' differences they were targeting. As a result, although Harper himself had made similar comments in the past (notably as a signatory to the infamous Alberta 'firewall' letter), he immediately responded by stating that Reid was expressing personal opinions, not those of the party. With Reid's prompt resignation as the party's official languages critic, the matter appeared to be closed.

But the furore over those comments had not yet died down when Harper was confronted with a second and more serious problem. Again it was an experienced MP, party health critic Rob Merrifield, who landed his party in hot water. Merrifield's comments about abortion included the view that it might be desirable for the state to introduce a type of mandatory counselling for any woman considering an abortion. This time, Harper argued Merrifield had also expressed a personal view, but one that did not conflict with the party's official position that it would not table legislation on abortion. Nevertheless the Liberals' Anne McLellan drew widespread coverage to the issue, demanding Harper fire his critic. He refused. 'The notion of state-imposed, third-party counselling as if we are children, as if we are not able to make our own decisions about our health and our bodies is, to me, at the beginning of the 21st century, profoundly disturbing and dare I say it is very frightening,' McLellan charged.[82]

Harper was unable to brush off the abortion debate as easily as the one on bilingualism, particularly after another Conservative MP, Cheryl Gallant, compared abortion to the beheading of an American journalist in Iraq by a terrorist cell group. Harper was obliged to repeat his position on several occasions, including during the leaders' debates. Exasperated, he finally told reporters, 'I have no intention of supporting abortion legislation, so there's no way that abortion rights are going to be overridden by my government.' In response to questions about the possibility of private members' bills, he added 'The chances of any legislation being passed in this Parliament are virtually non-existent.'[83]

By now the idea of the Conservatives' 'hidden agenda' was nevertheless gaining momentum. Several Conservative candidates were reported making anti-gay and anti-same-sex marriage arguments in their local campaigns. Then Tory MP Randy White, the party's justice critic, said 'to heck with the judges,' when asked how his party would deal with a future court striking down some proposed family values legislation. In an interview that was part of a documentary on the subject of same-sex marriage, White declared that Charter rights could (and should) be overridden by the notwithstanding clause. 'It's the politicians that should make the laws, not the courts, not the judges,' White said. 'If the Charter of Rights and Freedoms is going to be used as a crutch to carry forward all the issues that social libertarians want, then there's got to be for us conservatives a way to put checks and balances in there.'[84] Alarmed by his comments, several traditional Conservative candidates, including former Progressive Conservative leader Peter MacKay, immediately disowned White's remarks. Harper, however, once again stressed that White's views were his own and went no further, despite growing public concern and repeated calls from Paul Martin to fire White as a critic.

No sooner had Harper dismissed White's comments than Conservative MP Vic Toews, another outspoken critic of the Supreme Court and many of its decisions regarding Charter rights, enthusiastically told reporters he would like to see two court vacancies filled within two months of a Conservative government taking power. He also proposed that an all-party committee 'ratify' the nominations of the prime minister. With a third judge scheduled to retire within less than a year of the election, many legal experts began to worry the Conservatives, if elected, would be able to 'pack' the court with Charter sceptics. Several began to speak out publicly. Constitutional lawyer David Stratas, for example, told reporters: 'If Harper is too overt about this, there will be a whole host of people concerned about court-packing. Until now, Supreme Court appointments are seen to have been made entirely on merit. Court-packing is alien to our culture.'[85] Coming as it did on the heels of Harper's release of his law-and-order planks – which included ending the gun registry, hiring more Mounties, introducing a national sex-offender registry, watering down hate crimes legislation, and eliminating the Court Challenges Program – the impression created by Toews's comments was once again extremely helpful to the Liberals.

Then Harper was sideswiped by a provincial premier, as Paul Martin had been by Dalton McGuinty. Alberta's Ralph Klein said that he planned to table a health care reform package two days after the federal election, and some of his proposals – such as charging user fees and allowing more private facilities – might violate the Canada Health Act. Since Stephen Harper had just said in the debates that he would adopt a 'hands off' approach to provincial administration of health care, he was reduced to arguing that Martin's attack on Klein's proposals constituted an anti-western bias.

By contrast Paul Martin, in one of his strongest performances of the campaign, defended medicare with passion as well as rational arguments and scored many political points. 'This might well be why Premier Klein wants to wait until after the election to reveal his plans to change health-care,' Martin warned Canadians. 'He's hoping he'll have a silent partner in Ottawa by the name of Stephen Harper – someone who will not speak up for the Canada Health Act, someone who will be propped up by the separatist Bloc Québécois, and someone who doesn't care [about national standards].'[86]

A similar fate befell Gilles Duceppe, whose Bloc Québécois was poised to sweep Quebec on the coat-tails of the sponsorship scandal. That sweep was halted dramatically by Bernard Landry, the separatist premier of Quebec. Since Duceppe had just argued in the leaders' debates that this federal election was not about separation, he too was unable to respond effectively to the premier's argument that 'with about 60 Bloc MPs in Ottawa … sovereignists will be stronger than ever and there will be a referendum in five years.'[87]

The Liberals' freefall was halted but apparently not reversed. Indeed, by early June a confident Stephen Harper told reporters he had already consulted former prime minister Brian Mulroney and hired Hugh Segal, a prominent Conservative from the past, to head up a transition team. By 11 June, Harper was beginning to speak not simply of forming a government but of winning a majority. 'There are no safe seats for the Liberals anymore, anywhere,' he crowed.[88] Veteran Conservative strategists were becoming increasingly uneasy about these bravura comments. 'Canadians don't like this kind of stuff, it makes us seem arrogant, and it's not helpful,' one said. Another noted presciently, 'The big problem is that (Harper's) strategists are mistaking Liberal disaffection with affection for us.'[89]

More bad news followed. The Harper strategists were concerned that their own numbers suddenly seemed to have stalled short of victory, and the Liberals were gaining ground. Building on comments made by Harper in the leaders' debates about the notwithstanding clause, the Conservatives' election headquarters issued a press release on 19 June titled 'Paul Martin supports child pornography.' The press release was immediately condemned by the Liberals and within hours a revised version with a different headline was sent out on the instructions of Harper himself. 'I thought the headline was a bit strong, so I asked them to change it,' he told reporters. However, Harper did not disown the contents or pull the ad. Nor did he offer an apology to Paul Martin, who had demanded one shortly after learning of the Tories' press release. 'Look, this is personal,' Martin said. 'I'm a father and I'm a husband. And he has crossed the line. He should apologize.'[90] Despite growing evidence that public opinion was on Martin's side, Harper went on the offensive. 'Paul Martin and the Liberal Party have, in fact, been soft on porn and they haven't taken the time to clamp down on child pornography,' he asserted.[91]

Being handed this huge electoral gaffe by the Conservatives so late in the campaign appeared to rejuvenate Martin. In the final days, he made herculean efforts to tour all parts of the country yet again. As Mark Marissen was quick to note, Martin ended his public appearances in Vancouver, where he had started his campaign five weeks earlier, 'to demonstrate just how seriously he took the issue of western alienation and the need for the Liberal Party to rebuild its support there.[92]

Martin also delivered some of his strongest performances of the campaign. Defending the role of a strong central government (an argument that polls showed resonated strongly with voters), he told one interviewer: 'On every single issue, Stephen Harper has a view of the role of the national government which essentially erases it. And I believe overwhelmingly in the role of the national government.'[93] After telling a Liberal audience in St Catharines that 'the wind is with us,' he reiterated his theme that a Harper government would 'erase' the role of the federal government. Then he urged potential NDP voters to switch to the Liberals 'for the good of the country.' At the same time, he continued to speak of the importance of national unity and 'constructive' intergovernmental relations.

The Results: Liberal Minority Government

In the end, the dream of a massive 220-seat majority proved ephemeral. Not only had their huge majority faded away, but the Liberals had lost all hope of a majority of any kind and come dangerously close to losing power. When the ballots were counted on 28 June, the Liberals had been returned with a strong minority, but a minority nevertheless. Canadians would have a minority government for the first time in twenty-five years, and the Liberal Party would find itself in a minority position for the first time since 1972. Paul Martin would soon pay the price for this stunnning setback, lasting barely two years as Liberal leader, compared with John Turner's six years at the helm.

The extent of the Liberals' decline was plain to see. Their share of the popular vote fell from 41 per cent in 2000 to 36.7 per cent. Political scientist André Belelieu noted this represented the fourth-smallest share of the popular vote for the Liberal Party since Confederation.[94] Similarly, their total seats in the House of Commons fell from 172 to 135. In the west they took no more seats than in 2000. In BC Mark Marissen's hopes of increasing the province's clout had been dashed. The popular vote actually fell from 32 per cent to 28 per cent. And, although the party had elected two more MPs, to bring the total to 8, one of these two new seats was the result of the defection of Keith Martin, already a longtime sitting MP, from the Conservatives. (The other was prominent business-man David Emerson, who would soon defect to the Conservatives.)

In Ontario, they fell to only 75 seats. Indeed, Liberal support fell in all parts of the country, but nowhere more so than in Quebec. There, after three successive elections in which their support had increased, the Liberals were reduced to only 21 of 75 seats, their second-worst showing. Not surprisingly, only John Turner in 1984 had fared worse in the province, taking a mere 17 seats. As the Canada Election Study concluded, 'the sponsorship scandal hurt the Liberals in Quebec, but no more than elsewhere ... the Liberals lost significantly more support in Quebec largely because of Mr. Martin's failure to match Gilles Duceppe in the debates.'[95]

More than ever, the Liberals were dependent on Ontario for their government, salvaging enough seats there to make up for their huge losses in Quebec. And since they simply retained their already strong representation in the Atlantic, Belelieu pointed out the painful reality that 'their inability to make inroads in western Canada had cost them a majority.'[96] This failure was one that Mark Marissen, David Herle, Tim Murphy, and Kevin Bosch all specifically noted in post-election interviews.

Most of the Liberals' handpicked dream team failed to win their seats. Only David Emerson and Ujjal Dosanjh overcame the stigma of internal feuding in BC, while all of the prairie stars, including former NDP minister Chris Axworthy in Saskatchewan and former Winnipeg mayor Glen Murray, fell to earth. Sheila Copps's opponent Tony Valeri managed to hang on to her seat in Hamilton, but his neighbour and staunch Martin booster Stan Keyes went down to defeat, as did star candidate Richard Mahoney in Ottawa and several of Martin's other Ontario recruits. In Quebec, Jean Chrétien's riding was taken by the Bloc, leaving Martin's former organizer Marie Eve Bilodeau in the dust. Other Martin supporters who had been handed choice ridings, such as Dennis Dawson, also fell to the Bloc, as did the ridings of several incumbent Martin supporters such as Hélène Scherrer and Nick Discepola. Even Jean Lapierre won by a severely diminished margin in the supposed Liberal fortress of Outremont.

Yet some comfort could be taken from the fact the Liberal Party had indeed received a strong minority. Luckily for Martin and his team, there was no immediate threat to their hold on power since the Conservatives took only 99 seats, while the Bloc held 54 and the NDP retained 19. With little likelihood that these philosophical polar opposites could form any stable or sufficiently large alliance to bring down the government, Martin and his caucus could expect to govern for at least a year or more, based on previous minority experience.

Martin indicated almost immediately that he would not consider forming any kind of coalition, but would govern by depending on different groupings of opposition support on an issue-by-issue basis, a strategy most Liberals and academic observers agreed was the safest course. As University of Toronto political economist Stephen Clarkson put it, the challenge for Martin now was to decide on his overall approach to governing: 'Would he take the lead from Lester Pearson and, negotiating support for every issue with the opposition, produce a creative, highly productive government?' Or, Clarkson wondered, 'would he follow Pierre Trudeau's model and govern just long enough to regain his political footing, then provoke another election on his own terms?'[97] In the end Martin followed neither course, embarking on his minority mandate with no apparent long-term plan in mind, a scenario which became all too apparent shortly after the 38th Parliament began.

14 Freefall: The Martin Minority

It's time to cast off the dead hand of history.
                                        – Martin adviser Tim Murphy[1]

Like John Turner, Paul Martin was given a second chance. When the dust settled on 29 June 2004, no Liberals openly called for his resignation, but the writing was on the wall. The discrepancy between what happened, and what had been expected of him when he took over from Jean Chrétien, was too great. Liberals were prepared to wait and see if Martin could turn things around, but they were not hopeful. And nothing short of a majority in the next election would save his precarious hold on power.

Events soon proved this was highly unlikely. Despite having obtained a strong minority, the Martin government lurched from one crisis to another, its key actors looking like deer in the headlights from the beginning. The Martin team's obsession with their minority status was surprising and likely unnecessary. Governing in a minority situation is always a challenge, but the circumstances in which Martin found himself were better than many Liberals had feared during the course of the campaign. Party veterans felt his government could be as successful as Lester Pearson's, and the comparison with Pearson's situation was made frequently in the early days. Many Liberals assumed Paul Martin, who was so keen on policy and had promised 'transformative change,' would attempt to emulate this earlier role model. Pearson's minority governments, after all, had been highly productive. As Liberal senator and former party president Dan Hays was quick to note, 'Pearson's two minority governments (1963–8) passed a total of 265 government bills, including the Canada Pension Plan, Medicare, the Canada Assistance Plan, Student Loans and the Canada Labour Code.'[2] Others pointed to the Canadian flag, the Canada-U.S. Autopact, and the Royal Commission on Bilingualism and Biculturalism.

The similarities between Martin's situation and Pearson's were certainly striking. Both men faced a badly divided opposition unlikely to make common cause against them. Martin's House leader, Tony Valeri, recognized this. 'There's a lot of talk by the opposition leaders that they have the majority in the House,' Valeri said. 'Well, if that's the case, then they should come forward with the coalition that they've struck.'[3] As well, both Liberal leaders had a sufficiently large minority that the aid of only one of their three opponents was necessary.[4] It could also be argued that both were virtually guaranteed a minimum of a year in power. Their opponents were not prepared to face the electorate before then, and voters were likely to punish any party that failed to cooperate in making the minority Parliament work. By October 2004 an EKOS poll found 60 per cent of Canadians 'want the parties to cooperate' and 'would most likely blame the Conservatives if the minority government collapses.'[5] Former NDP leader Ed Broadbent went so far as to tell journalists: 'I think the prospects are there for a very constructive two-year period.'[6]

The senior Martin staff did not see things that way. In fact, they rejected any suggestion that their situation was comparable to Pearson's. According to Tim Murphy, 'We had to calculate *every day*, how can we wend our way through these shoals?' This attitude was based on the belief that the opposition parties were 'vitriolic' in their opposition to Martin's government and 'none of them was afraid of an election.'[7]

Whether this perspective was accurate is debatable. NDP leader Jack Layton, having lost seats and popular vote share, seemed an unlikely candidate to bring down the government quickly. Stephen Harper was hardly in a position to do so either. He had arguably cost his party the election and had spent the summer considering his options. Although he decided to stay on as Conservative leader, he needed time to rethink his strategy and to eliminate loose cannons from his caucus before engaging the Liberals in battle again. Nor could he form a coalition with the Bloc Québécois to bring down the government, since this would be anathema to his western base. Moreover, by October the Liberals had already regained their pre-election support level (at 38 per cent) and Conservative fortunes were on a downward trend.

Accurate or not, however, this 'circle the wagons' mentality led to a parliamentary session in which almost no consultation took place with the opposition. This was in stark contrast to the consultative style of the Pearson government. According to his senior policy adviser, Tom Kent, Pearson's success was based on 'a great deal of discussion, negotiation and consensus-building with the opposition parties,' beginning long before a bill was unveiled in the House of Commons.[8]

The lack of consultation in the Martin era was obviously influenced by the poisoned atmosphere in the Chamber. But another, largely unrecognized difficulty facing Martin's team was their philosophical bent. Pearson and a majority of his cabinet and caucus were social Liberals. Business Liberals had been marginalized, largely because they had abandoned the party during its period in opposition. Not surprisingly, the Pearson Liberals' negotiations with NDP leader Tommy Douglas were relatively smooth, since Pearson was proposing to build much of the social policy infrastructure Douglas supported.

The same could hardly be said of Paul Martin's government. Martin, like Turner, was a business Liberal. So were many of his closest supporters in PMO, cabinet, and caucus. Negotiations with Jack Layton and the NDP would not be a natural fit. At the same time, the presence of the Bloc as the party holding the balance of power was a dilemma Pearson did not face. Not only did every policy initiative need to be considered from the perspective of Quebec nationalism, but Gilles Duceppe and most Bloc MPs were philosophically left of centre, making them far closer to the NDP than the Conservatives.

Nevertheless Tom Kent pointed out that Pearson's legislative record had not been achieved without difficulty. Both Diefenbaker and Créditiste leader Réal Caouette were prickly and often confrontational adversaries. Few provincial governments were on Pearson's side. Perhaps most important, 'Quebec, the only substantial ally, was an awkward friend.' According to Kent, Pearson disliked the constraints imposed by his minority situation and found the never-ending negotiations stressful. But Kent also noted that despite Pearson's travails, 'it is widely agreed the 1963–68 government was one of the best Canada has ever had.'[9]

Pearson's record was also accomplished despite a series of scandals and other political storms that plagued his two minorities. This point was made more than once by Liberal veterans in light of the Martin team's oft-repeated assertion that they were sideswiped by a scandal from the previous Chrétien administration. In addition to the sponsorship crisis, however, several Martin advisers would later fix much of the blame for their demise on the media's lack of interest in the Liberals' positive agenda and 'perverse' determination to paint Martin as a ditherer. Equally problematic was the public perception that the government was drifting aimlessly during its second mandate, even though it launched several major policy initiatives. As Tim Murphy declared, 'Despite sponsorship and a minority situation, we had an activist agenda that accomplished as much or more than any government, and in only eighteen months.'[10] But, Murphy noted, 'against the backdrop of the scandal, even the Health Care Accord, a singular achievement, provided no respite from media criticism.'[11] Indeed, the failure of Martin's government to receive credit for its initiatives remains an open wound for his senior advisers, who believe they were the victims of a perfect storm.

Regrouping: The 'New' Martin Cabinet

Paul Martin's first priority after the 28 June election was to form a cabinet, and the composition revealed much about the likely direction of his second mandate. Filling ministerial portfolios was a demanding exercise. He had lost six ministers in the election. Most of his handpicked candidates had been defeated. He had failed to make inroads in the west and lost most of Quebec outside Montreal. Across the country the Liberals were strong in large urban centres, but weak in rural areas. Ensuring equitable regional representation would be a significant challenge. Combined with the need to balance gender, ethnicity, and language concerns, his cabinet calculations became far more complicated.

Then there was the problem of those star candidates who *had* been elected. To find places for them meant demoting some existing ministers, particularly if Martin wanted to refrain from expanding his already large cabinet. There were also several long-standing supporters in caucus who had not been promoted to the front benches in the first mandate. They would likely become difficult to control if they were passed over again. Last but hardly least, there was the problem of the deeply divisive split in the party with the Chrétienites. Having removed twenty-two of his predecessor's supporters from cabinet when he took office, Martin now had an opportunity to make a conciliatory gesture if he chose. Underpinning all of these issues was the question of whether he should stand pat with as many experienced ministers as possible, or shake up his cabinet dramatically.

When Paul Martin announced his new cabinet on 20 July, it was immediately evident what his priorities were. First and foremost, he chose to stick with the status quo. In fact, very little was 'new' about Martin's second cabinet. In a thirty-nine-member ministry (one more than his first cabinet), only eight new faces emerged. In addition to experience, Martin was obviously relying on those individuals he knew would support him personally. There was not even much movement among the returning ministers. Many stayed where they were. Others, such as Tony Valeri, Bill Graham, and Pierre Pettigrew, simply changed places. Most of the 'new' faces at the table were veteran MPs and Martin supporters such as Joe Fontana and Tony Ianno, who had failed to make the cut earlier and were now being elevated to the front benches. The remainder were Martin's successful star candidates, who clearly owed their allegiance to him.

Martin's second priority was western Canada. The portfolios assigned to BC alone increased to five, partly as a result of the electoral success of David Emerson and Ujjal Dosanjh. With Senator Jack Austin and Stephen Owen retaining their cabinet seats, the influence of BC on policy development was expected to be significant. Similarly, with the deputy prime minister and ministers of finance, health, industry, and the Treasury Board all coming from west of Ontario, the importance of western Canada was clearly top of mind.

The BC appointments also confirmed Martin's lack of concern about rapprochement with Chrétien loyalists. Environment minister David Anderson, one of the few surviving ministers from the Chrétien era, was dropped from cabinet to make room for the BC newcomers. Anderson's replacement at Environment was Stéphane Dion, the only Chrétien supporter to make it into Martin's second cabinet. The other remaining Chrétien veterans were also dropped. In Quebec, Denis Coderre and Denis Paradis were dropped to make room for new Martin supporters such as Jean Lapierre and Liza Frulla.

Politically, Dion could not be ignored. Everyone acknowledged his successful efforts to salvage Liberal support in Quebec in the wake of Jean Lapierre's wave of destruction. At the same time, the Environment portfolio was an unlikely post, far removed from his previous responsibilities for Quebec and intergovernmental affairs under Chrétien. Meanwhile, caucus resentment of Lapierre's handling of the Quebec campaign was running high. Not only could Martin not hand Lapierre the Intergovernmental Affairs portfolio, he was hard pressed to justify *any* place for Lapierre at the cabinet table. In the end, after much internal debate in the PMO, Lapierre was given the Transport portfolio vacated by Tony Valeri, who was moved to the post of House leader. The low-profile but generally gaffe-free Lucienne Robillard was moved to the Intergovernmental Affairs post, which would prove largely symbolic since Martin planned to handle his federal-provincial policy agenda himself.

The trouble with Lapierre did not end there. The media soon realized the former Bloc MP was now third in line to replace Martin as prime minister in an emergency. Apart from Anne McLellan (who was automatically the first to replace the prime minister by virtue of her role as deputy prime minister), parliamentary protocol dictated the succession be determined by length of service as a privy councillor, a term awarded on becoming a minister. Thus Jack Austin, who had first served as a minister under Pierre Trudeau, was second in line, and Lapierre, who was very briefly a minister under John Turner, was next. The opposition parties made much of the fact a former separatist was now so close to the reins of power. In caucus, furious backbenchers and senators decried the appointment as yet another example of the Liberal Party losing its way on the federalist axis.

By contrast, almost no one seemed concerned about Martin's willingness to accept defectors from other political parties. Only some Trudeau-era senators and a few veteran backbenchers were heard to mutter unhappily about the new approach. Martin enthusiastically promoted his cross-party recruits and referred frequently in national caucus to 'the need to spread our tent as wide as possible.' Already in his first mandate he had welcomed Scott Brison (the former Conservative MP and leadership candidate) and made him a parliamentary secretary. Martin appointed him to cabinet as minister of public works immediately after the 28 June election. Similarly, Martin eagerly brought former NDP premier Ujjal Dosanjh into his cabinet as minister of health. (A few months later he would also recruit an NDP MP from Saskatchewan and another former Conservative leadership candidate, MP Belinda Stronach, whom he rewarded with a cabinet post as soon as she crossed the floor to the Liberals.)

As Carleton University political scientist J.P. Lewis pointed out, 'With the appointment of a former New Democratic premier, a former PC leadership candidate and a former Bloc Québécois member to the cabinet, Martin may have created a new representational factor – the non-partisan factor.' In addition, in doing so 'Martin not only broke with tradition ... by handing cabinet posts to individuals who only recently had been members of other parties, but he appointed them to historically attractive and influential posts.'[12] Although the long-term consequences of floor-crossing for voter identification with political parties has not been examined in much detail in Canada, some preliminary analysis suggests such activities may well have had a negative impact. At a minimum, Martin's attempt to distance his government from his predecessor, coupled with his defensive minority mindset, may actually have led to an increase in floor-crossing because ambitious opposition MPs realized there was a real possibility of becoming a Liberal minister. Some observers have also suggested the wide-open tent approach may also have blurred rather than reinforced the distinction between Liberals and Conservatives in the post-Chrétien era.[13]

There were a number of other anomalies in Martin's second cabinet, which his advisers blamed on a lack of good cabinet material. 'There were unintended consequences, if you will,' one said, 'but they were unavoidable. The caucus had been reduced to only 135 people, don't forget.'[14] Not everyone agreed. Many Liberals found the lack of women in Martin's cabinet particularly troubling. Despite his rhetoric about the need to increase representation, and the significant number of experienced women MPs in his caucus, Martin's new ministry contained fewer women than before. All of the newcomers were men. One national columnist pointed out that when Carolyn Bennett was a backbench MP under Jean Chrétien she had complained that 'only' ten of thirty-eight ministers were women. 'Now there are nine in a cabinet of 39. What does Ms. Bennett say now?'[15]

Another concern was the lack of representation from the Ottawa area. Martin's former defence minister, David Pratt, had lost a west Ottawa riding. Martin's close friend Rick Mahoney, who would certainly have received a speedy promotion to cabinet, was defeated in Ottawa Centre by the NDP's Ed Broadbent. Only Ottawa-Vanier MP Mauril Bélanger, who had been deputy House leader in the first cabinet, remained at the table at all and he was far below the salt, still only a junior minister. Instead of promoting the bilingual Bélanger, Martin turned to Sheila Copps's nemesis, the unilingual Tony Valeri, to fill the top spot as House leader. This was especially noteworthy since House leaders must negotiate with their counterparts from all parties, and, in a minority situation, the importance of establishing a good working relationship with the Bloc Québécois House leader was crucial. (In response to Quebec media criticism, Scott Reid explained that Bélanger would 'assist' Valeri in his work, and handle liaison with the Bloc. Asked directly about his role, Bélanger curtly told reporters to speak to the prime minister.)

The remainder of the Liberals' Ottawa seats were held by Chrétien loy-alists (or in one case the brother of Ontario Premier Dalton McGuinty), so there was little likelihood the capital would receive its fair share of senior ministers. Even Chrétien's whip, Marlene Catterall of Ottawa West, was demoted in favour of Martin supporter Karen Redman from southern Ontario. Under Pearson, Trudeau, and Chrétien, Ottawa had been represented by senior ministers such as Jean-Luc Pépin, George McIlraith, John Turner, and John Manley. 'It's quite a comedown,' said Alex Cullen, an Ottawa councillor. 'It's hard to believe that the fifth-largest city in Canada only gets such a junior position at the cabinet table.'[16] As one of Martin's advisers later admitted, 'it was simply a matter of spite. His candidates in the Ottawa area were defeated and he had no intentions of putting Chrétien people in the cabinet. Period. So Ottawa paid the price.'

Unfortunately, it was the Liberal Party that would pay the price in the next election. Several traditionally safe Liberal seats across the re-gion, including Catterall's, Boudria's, and Bellemare's, unexpectedly fell to the Conservatives. Perhaps equally telling, the Martin cabinet's relationship with the public service deteriorated dramatically during its second mandate.

Retrenching: The 'Stand Pat' Martin PMO

If Paul Martin's cabinet choices demonstrated a preference for conti-nuity over change, his commitment to his long-standing advisers re-inforced that tendency in spades. The day after the election, the prime minister confronted those caucus members who had called for a major overhaul of his office. He made it clear he 'intended to stick with the team that had helped him win (the leadership).' Barely three months later, at a special meeting of national caucus in October, he confirmed David Herle and John Webster would be national campaign co-chairs for the next election. Herle, who attended the caucus, was roundly criti-cized by many of those present. One MP confided 'Herle was taken to task for everything from campaign lawn signs to the strategy of dis-tancing themselves from the Chrétien record.' However, the same MP admitted that Herle was 'quite contrite.' At one point Herle told caucus members, 'We all learned a lot in the last election. And I have to say I'm going to try and do a better job next time.'[17]

As for Martin's PMO, although it had been widely criticized by cau-cus during the first mandate almost all the personnel changes that occurred were the result of planned departures. Principal secretary Francis Fox, tour director Mario Cucanato, and communications director Mario Lague had all indicated their intention of returning to government or the private sector after the election. But senior members of Martin's leadership team such as Scott Reid (now promoted to communications director), Tim Murphy (chief of staff), Peter Nicholson (policy), Ruth Thorkelson (parliamentary affairs), and Karen Martin (appointments) all remained in place. In addition, Michelle Cadario left her position as national director at party headquarters as planned to become deputy chief of staff (operations). As well, Martin's Ontario organizer and former aide at Finance, Karl Littler, moved into PMO as deputy chief of staff (cabinet affairs).

One of the few outside additions to PMO was defeated Quebec MP Hélène Scherrer, who took over the position of principal secretary from Francis Fox. On a positive note, her appointment served to maintain the presence of at least one francophone in the heavily anglophone Martin PMO, while also adding to the number of women in the overwhelmingly male office. But Scherrer, although an outsider to the Board, was hardly seen as a neutral appointment within the party. She had been the first MP to call publicly for Jean Chrétien's resignation. She had also served as co-chair of the 2004 campaign alongside David Herle and John Webster. Her appointment was a surprise for many Liberal insiders for other reasons as well. Traditionally the post would go to someone who not only had close personal ties to the prime minister but possessed excellent political and policy credentials. Scherrer, they noted, did not have anywhere near the depth of political experience or knowledge of government as Jack Pickersgill (King), Marc Lalonde (Trudeau), or Jean Pelletier (Chrétien), to say nothing of Fox himself. As one Ottawa journalist put it, 'This job, described by history professor Michael Behiels as being one "at the centre of power,'" that can "make or break a prime minister," has gone to a Quebec City social worker, sports enthusiast and public relations officer who was defeated in two of the three federal elections she contested ... She was co-chair of the election campaign, but lost her own seat.'[18]

Certainly the minor personnel changes in the PMO served to heighten the perception that Martin either lacked options (because no one would come to work for him in a minority situation) or was sufficiently unnerved by the election results that he, too, felt the need to circle the wagons. Journalist Adam Radwanski described Martin's failure to act as 'puzzling,' although he admitted: 'A case can be made that cleaning house in the middle of the campaign would have looked panicky. Now Martin has the chance to do a quick post-mortem and make the necessary changes, and instead he's merely shuffling the deck chairs.' Like many other critics, Radwanski identified two key problems with the existing set of advisers: 'What Mr. Martin needs are some veteran operatives with more experience in government,' he argued, 'and he needs a few diplomatic types willing to build bridges rather than burn them.'[19]

Nor did the changes in Martin's office address the need for more policy input. Although widely respected as an economist, Peter Nicholson was viewed by many Liberal insiders as someone who lacked the breadth of policy experience necessary for the PMO rather than Finance. As one ministerial adviser said, 'His intellectual ability was unquestioned ... No one doubted he understood the issues, but he didn't "feel" them in a way that previous occupants of PMO would have. And, as a business Liberal his orientation was productivity and prosperity, not poverty.' Nevertheless, his background was in policy, unlike most of his colleagues. Former policy adviser Tom Kent, always a thorn in Martin's side, soon pointed this out. 'I don't get the impression, frankly, that these people are policy people at all,' Kent told one reporter. 'Unkind critics call them assassins. That's certainly an exaggeration, I'm sure. But they are essentially organizers, promoters, spin doctors – not policymakers.'[20]

Kent's views were later echoed by none other than Nicholson himself. Another self-described 'outsider' within the PMO, Nicholson was becoming increasingly frustrated by his lack of influence with the prime minister. 'I would meet with him and we'd agree on several things and then, the next thing I knew, this was all up in the air again because one of the Board had spoken with him afterwards and expressed doubts, or talked about poll results. They were heavily conditioned by polling, and very parochial.'[21] Martin spokesperson John Duffy actually told reporters they intended to 'govern on the numbers.'[22]

Nicholson also recounted a conversation with Tim Murphy before he joined the PMO but after Martin had told him he would like him to come to Ottawa and work closely with him. Murphy warned Nicholson that 'Paul is always saying he wants to work directly with someone ... my job is to prevent that and make sure we all sing from the same hymn book.'[23] Yet Murphy's task became even more daunting in the minority situation. On paper no fewer than five senior staffers – Scherrer, Littler, Cadario, Reid, and Nicholson – reported directly to Martin rather than to Murphy as chief of staff. In reality the number who had direct access to the PM, as Murphy himself later admitted, was more likely twice that. Rumours abounded that internal strife in the PMO was rampant. Senior staff vied for control of the agenda and junior staff found themselves caught in the crossfire. At the lower levels, the high turnover in the second Martin PMO was a source of constant concern.[24]

Then there was the problem of the Board's high profile. As one backbench MP who had long been a Martin supporter remarked disparagingly, 'These guys are household names! I mean, Trudeau and Chrétien had that part right. Staff should be seen and not heard. Who knew most of the senior people in Chrétien's office? And when did they ever speak publicly?' Inevitably there were comparisons with Chrétien's personnel, and especially with his communications team. Where Peter Donolo had been seen as helpful but unobtrusive, Martin's new communications director, Scott Reid, was rapidly becoming a news story of his own. Bright, hard-working, and highly knowledgeable about the party, Reid had actually worked with Donolo on earlier election campaigns. But like many of the Board, his overweening personal confidence and direct access to the prime minister proved a devastating combination.

Reid's failure to recognize the limitations of his role as an unelected staffer was evident in a series of exchanges with Newfoundland Premier Danny Williams. With much of Paul Martin's agenda dependent on the cooperation of provincial premiers, Reid's antagonistic approach to Williams was even more surprising. In advance of a first ministers' meeting in Ottawa on equalization, Williams had attempted to arrange a meeting with Martin to finalize a deal on offshore resources. When that meeting did not materialize through a series of missed communications, Williams stormed out of Ottawa without attending the equalization sessions, and Reid publicly declared the premier 'had made a mistake of historic proportions' in not accepting the federal offshore offer. Reid was soon obliged to apologize for those remarks, and many caucus members called for his dismissal, but Martin took no action. The situation was particularly sensitive since many in caucus noted that Françoise Ducros, Chrétien's press secretary, had been obliged to resign for comments she had made about president George Bush, even though those comments were intended to be private and confidential. Barely two weeks later, *in advance* of another first ministers' meeting, Reid told reporters there was 'absolutely no possibility of a deal' coming out of the meeting because of Newfoundland's position. An incensed Williams referred to 'another Scott Reid fiasco' and told reporters his government would insist on dealing with someone else from PMO in future.[25]

Meanwhile at the Liberal Caucus Research Bureau, many changes were taking place. A new position of director general was created after the 2004 election. To the surprise of many Liberals and other Ottawa insiders, this post was filled by former *Toronto Star* reporter Derek Ferguson. Like Kevin Bosch, Ferguson had worked on the Rapid Response Team in the Liberals' war room during the election, and this, rather than formal research credentials or policy experience, was his entrée to the Bureau. (According to several insiders, Ferguson was also considered to be a competent administrator with good people skills, something which Bosch was felt to lack.)

Asked about the role Ferguson would play in research, Bosch stressed communications. 'We're trying to provide more and different types of communications and research products ... Derek is a former journalist and comes with all sorts of experience on the communications side. So he's coordinating the effort,' Bosch told bemused reporters.[26] In the minority situation, Bosch confirmed, the concept of research was directed almost entirely to Opposition Watch material and election readiness, a situation epitomized by the decision to have a former crime reporter handle the Justice portfolio rather than a lawyer.

Given the limited policy capacity of the Martin PMO, the Bureau was expected to provide research support for the PMO as well. A common complaint of staff in ministers' offices was that PMO officials would tell them to have the Bureau look into something, or refer questions there directly. 'It was bizarre,' one senior departmental policy adviser confirmed. 'They had no clue about policy and even less interest. If it wasn't important in the polls, they didn't care and didn't think they needed to have a position. They had no one in house to do briefings or anything like that.' The irony of this was that the Bureau had almost no one left capable of providing policy advice either. As another frustrated ministerial aide commented, it sometimes seemed as if decisions in PMO were taken 'based on who could produce the fastest or most amusing comment' in the rapid-fire Blackberry exchanges that were the stock in trade of the Board.

Concrete support for this claim surfaced in a mistakenly leaked string of Blackberry correspondence which circulated widely among Liberals on the Hill. Prompted by a news story that Immigration Minister Joe Volpe was proposing to dramatically increase Canada's intake of immigrants, this exchange between senior Martin advisers focused entirely on polling results. When they learned the polls showed the proposal would not help Liberal election fortunes (14 per cent somewhat less likely to vote Liberal, 30 per cent much less likely), their response was swift and negative. Scott Reid's input – 'Well, that's the f—g end of that, let's get out of this now!' – was representative, if somewhat more graphic than most.[27]

The correspondence was also instructive about the key players being consulted in the decision-making process. It clearly demonstrated that several members of the Board outside the government were being routinely consulted on matters of government policy. While some held formal positions within the larger Liberal organization, others did not. As a result, Martin's criticism of the Chrétien government – 'It's who you know in PMO that counts' – rang increasingly hollow. Not surprisingly, Martin's office was being viewed at one and the same time as a closed shop and as dangerously aggressive. Yet Martin himself remained determinedly consultative, calling ministers, caucus members, and even junior bureaucrats at home at night and second-guessing almost all of their policy proposals. As one Ottawa veteran joked, 'No one can get anything done. They're swamped by calls from the PM.'[28]

The Centre Tightens Its Grip: PMO versus Caucus and the Bureaucracy

Whether it was primarily the siege mentality of his advisers, or Martin's tendency to micromanage issues, the end result was that Martin's PMO soon alienated most of its natural allies. This was a dangerous development at the best of times, but especially serious in light of their minority situation. To begin with, the long-standing tension between Martin MPs and PMO advisers was intensified. What was more, the famed Liberal virtue of a unified public front appeared to have disappeared entirely. Even Martin supporters in caucus felt free to discuss the feud in public. They asked why Karl Littler had been 'promoted' to PMO. They wondered why Earnscliffe consultants still seemed to be in the picture. And they complained that Scott Reid was still in PMO at all. Perhaps most important, they made clear to reporters that they believed the unelected officials in PMO were running the government while they – loyal Martin MPs – were increasingly being treated as props for government announcements.

As one Martin MP complained to journalists at the caucus retreat in August 2004, 'Who are these guys to tell us what to do?' Another declared, 'The war is on ... some people are really stinging over the election results, and they feel it is this crew that created the mess.' Others were even more direct. 'The centre is in total control,' one frustrated

MP lamented, adding that 'they are even meddling in senior appointments in ministers' offices again.' Still another pointed out that Martin had failed to call his new and returning MPs personally to congratulate them after the election, leaving it to his aides. 'He might hate your guts, but Mr. Chrétien would place the calls nevertheless,' the MP reluctantly conceded. More damaging still, one of Martin's most senior caucus members publicly reinforced the view that the prime minister was a ditherer, trying hard to avoid coming down on one side or the other of an issue. 'Love him or hate him, you knew where Jean Chrétien stood,' the MP recalled. 'And with Paul, well, he wants to please everybody.'[29]

Perhaps Martin's team believed the support of Liberal MPs could be taken for granted since they, like Martin, did not want to risk another election any time soon. But the cooperation of the bureaucracy, which had been so important during the Chrétien era, could not. This was especially significant because the largest public service union, the Public Service Alliance of Canada (PSAC), which represented some 125,000 employees, would soon be in a legal strike position. Yet the government was refusing to negotiate. (In fact, Treasury Board president Reg Alcock had already been the subject of a labour grievance for 'bad faith bargaining' after threatening to bring in back-to-work legislation to avoid just such a strike.)

Despite the looming labour conflict, the Martin government proceeded with a planned spending review it had first announced in December 2003. Then, Reg Alcock was in charge of the exercise to recover some $12 billion out of current expenditures over a five-year period. Little progress was made before the election, primarily because the government was increasingly distracted by the Adscam scandal. But in August 2004 Martin returned to the charge. He announced Revenue Minister John McCallum would now direct the cost-cutting exercise, which would have its own Spending Review Secretariat in PCO, not Treasury Board. Both McCallum and Martin insisted there was no similarity between this effort and the massive 1995–7 deficit reduction exercise, which had led to the biggest downsizing of the federal bureaucracy in Canadian history, eliminating some 50,000 positions. Nevertheless they insisted that despite a projected $43 billion surplus over the coming five years, they still needed another $12 billion in savings – to come from the elimination of outdated or low-priority programs in all departments – to pay for their new health care and municipalities initiatives. Although they acknowledged some jobs would be lost, they also maintained the rationalization of programs would result in minimal cuts.

Their arguments were immediately rejected by Steve Hindle, the disgruntled president of the Professional Institute of the Public Service (PIPS), who had decided not to run for the Liberals in the recent election. 'It's deja vu all over again,' Hindle declared. 'There's lots of expectations out there that the government is going to cut the size of the public service again. Even though we have a surplus now.'[30] Like other union leaders, Hindle suggested that politics played a role in the government's intransigence. Faced with the fallout from the Adscam debacle, Martin's advisers appeared to feel a firm stand against the unions would lend the appearance of renewed fiscal probity to the governing Liberals. Certainly the combination of a projected $9 billion surplus (more than three times the original estimate) for the 2004–5 fiscal year, coupled with a healthy $1.6 billion contingency fund already set aside for wage settlements, led many observers to wonder why the federal government allowed the public service labour dispute to escalate, when it could easily afford to settle. Yet in the face of three separate conciliators' reports favouring the union's position, and repeated attempts by PSAC president Nycole Turmel to return to the bargaining table, the federal government refused to budge.

As a result the fall of 2004 was punctuated with work stoppages and walkouts by various bargaining units, including the highly visible Parks Canada and Border Services officers. Other public service unions, such as PIPS and the Foreign Service Officers, watched with growing apprehension as the tone and tenor of the conflict grew increasingly hostile. On 11 October, PSAC's entire 125,000 employees went on strike. Eventually union and public pressure forced the government's hand and separate deals were finally struck with each of the units. However, the employees' hostility towards the government did not dissipate quickly, if at all.

Meanwhile the senior public servants who were dealing directly with the Martin PMO on a regular basis were increasingly unhappy with the conflicting directions and aggressive tone of requests coming from the centre. 'This was nothing like Chrétien's operation,' one very senior bureaucrat confided. 'We never knew what these people would ask for, or how long it would be before they changed their minds again. And when they did, they expected everyone to jump to it.' Another recently retired deputy with forty years in the service privately described the Martin minority as 'the worst government I had to deal with in my entire career.'

Not everyone went quietly. In a widely circulated keynote address to assistant deputy ministers in Ottawa in the fall of 2005, former DM Harry Swain declared, 'all my friends tell me that this town has never been so miserable. Ridiculous and surreal impositions are raining on the public service from ... politicians seeking to bury Gomery.' Warning the hapless ADMs in the audience that the worst was not yet over, Swain continued by demonstrating his disdain for several of the deals the Martin government considered its most substantial policy accomplishments, the details of which were negotiated over the objections of their senior public servants. 'The last two years,' Swain said, 'have been a quite amusing combination of dumb things done just to make the Martin government look different from Mr. Chrétien's – splitting DFAIT for one – and huge lurches to deal with minor problems.' Among those 'lurches,' Swain saved his most cutting comments for the health care and equalization deals. 'Taking an axe to equalization for the chance of a few Atlantic seats, or committing $41 billion – $41 billion dollars – to solve ... the wholly provincial problem of wait times are good examples.'[31] (Not surprisingly, after Stephen Harper's Conservatives replaced Martin's government in early 2006, one senior parliamentary journalist confirmed 'there is in fact a large reservoir of goodwill within the senior ranks of the mandarinate towards this incoming government. Relations between the Martin administration and the upper levels of the bureaucracy had become toxic, marred by indecisiveness on the one hand and political interference from PMO on the other.')[32]

The extent of the PMO's interventions on issues large and small was exemplified by a tempestuous caucus meeting in early December 2004, when MPs launched a 'holy war' over the role of PMO advisers in the distribution of tickets for a dinner with visiting U.S. President George Bush. Not only had some MPs received tickets while others had not, but lobbyists, party officials, fundraisers, and even some staff in ministers' offices had been in attendance. When veteran Toronto MP Derek Lee asked who had been in charge of the invitation list, Foreign Affairs or PMO, 'everyone in the room knew the answer,' one MP said. Frustrated Foreign Affairs officials later confirmed they had nothing to do with the list, which traditionally would have been drawn up by them using a well-established set of criteria for determining priorities.[33]

The larger problem was the constant meddling in budgetary planning and policy matters by communications and other non-policy advisers in the PMO, something which Peter Nicholson admitted 'drove him to distraction.'[34] Then, of course, there was Martin's own penchant to act decisively on certain occasions when least expected. In the end the deal struck by Martin with the premiers to 'fix health care for a generation' would demonstrate conclusively that federal bureaucrats had little influence with the Martin PMO.

The Health Care Accord: Martin's Controversial 'New Federalism'

Throughout the summer of 2004, federal bureaucrats were working on proposals and costing for the new health care deal promised by the prime minister during the election campaign. Meanwhile the premiers were making it clear they expected Paul Martin to deliver on his election promise to 'fix health care for a generation' when they met with him at the first ministers' conference (FMC) on 13 September.

In July, Ontario Premier Dalton McGuinty launched a major offensive to obtain more federal funding. As chair of the annual premiers' conference, McGuinty announced he had toured the country to present a concrete proposal to his counterparts in advance of the premiers' meeting in Niagara-on-the-Lake. In addition to more federal dollars, McGuinty's proposal recommended provinces be held accountable to their own voters, not to Ottawa or to 'rigid' federal standards. This position ran directly counter to the views expressed by Martin's health minister, Ujjal Dosanjh, who declared Ottawa was not prepared to 'throw more money' at the problem without receiving provincial guarantees. Dosanjh argued there was a pressing need to establish a clear set of national guidelines, a schedule for reducing wait times, and a dispute-resolution panel. The war of words escalated when McGuinty responded the federal government 'has a junior role' in health care and was in no position, given its decreased funding, to demand that provinces report their progress to Ottawa. McGuinty's views were reinforced by Manitoba Premier Gary Doer, who unashamedly told reporters after the premiers' meeting: 'I sense the consensus around the table was that the funding should be unconditional.'[35]

The stage was set for tough bargaining when the two sides met in Ottawa in September, but the federal government possessed a number of strong bargaining chips. As Dosanjh argued, Ottawa had the moral support of Canadians after winning an election on the issue of 'fixing' health care. It also had a surplus which the premiers coveted. (Premier Gordon Campbell of BC was remarkably straightforward about this. 'I think we have a real window of opportunity here [to extract] more money from Ottawa,' he declared. In his view, the minority would not last longer than eighteen months, so there was no time to waste.)[36] Former

Saskatchewan premier Roy Romanow's report was also helpful to the federal side, since it had called for most of the measures Dosanjh was proposing, and several more. Romanow spoke out publicly in advance of the FMC, urging the prime minister not to 'cave in' to provincial demands, and to ensure that any deal required provinces to make key changes in the delivery of health care, establishing common guidelines in exchange for additional funding.

The FMC was to be a symbol of Martin's positive new relationship with the premiers. The meeting was televised to demonstrate the openness and accountability he had promised. There would be no more closed-door sessions and no more behind-the-scenes deals. Unfortunately for Martin, things did not go according to plan. Instead, after the two scheduled days of meetings, and despite the federal offer of increased long-term and stable funding (ultimately $41 billion over a ten-year period, or substantially more than federal bureaucrats and the finance minister had originally told Martin he could safely offer without endangering federal finances), no agreement was reached. Quebec Premier Jean Charest's insistence that no federal conditions would be acceptable was a key sticking point. At this point the cameras were turned off and the meeting moved behind closed doors. Federal and provincial negotiators from Quebec spent another twenty-four hours attempting to hammer out a deal. When that approach also failed, Martin intervened personally and simply agreed to Charest's original request. For Quebec, there would be no conditions at all except the ones it decided upon itself. And then, following Brian Mulroney's lead in the Meech Lake Accord, Martin appeased Alberta and other provinces by declaring that any one of them could have the same side-deal as Quebec if they wanted. Even for the other provinces, the agreement was merely to develop 'comparable' indicators (not 'common' ones) and to agree on priority 'benchmarks' within three years, leaving many observers, bureaucrats, and anxious Liberals wondering if Martin had given away the store. Several of his own supporters also wondered what had happened to the new, transparent, and amicable federal-provincial process that Martin had promised.

Martin, however, was exuberant. Speaking with reporters after the accord was clinched, he described it as 'a deal that really embraces the reality of Canada and I am very, very proud of it.' He further described it as 'a deal for a decade,' and declared 'asymmetrical federalism would henceforth be the order of the day.'[37] Martin stressed 'there is no devolution of power. Quebec is acting within its own jurisdiction.' He also argued such side-deals were 'nothing new.' At the same time, he insisted: 'This is a different way of operating. We have got great challenges and great opportunities in front of us, and our role as a federal government is to set out those challenges and bring the country together.' In addition, following once more in Brian Mulroney's footsteps, he suggested 'what happened with the accord is an important building block ... in getting Quebec to sign on to the 1982 constitutional amendment.'[38]

The agreement was certainly consistent with Martin's long-standing preference for a more decentralized, less structured federation, evidenced by his own ardent support so many years earlier for the Meech Lake Accord. As Tim Murphy explained, 'Martin's support for asymmetric federalism (was based on) the sensible view that in a country 5,500 kilometers across, it is simply more efficient to define national goals at the federal level but leave it to the provinces to determine how best to achieve them.' It was a view Murphy described as 'post-modern' and 'incredibly innovative.' In practice, this meant 'dealing with one issue at a time and avoiding sweeping gestures.'[39] Indeed, Martin quickly indicated he would use a similar approach to fund childcare and cities.

There was considerable relief in caucus that a deal had been reached. The opposition parties suggested Martin had been desperate to sign a deal at any cost, but the most vocal critics were often Liberals. In what by now had become a common occurrence, they did not hesitate to express their views publicly. Some, such as former finance minister John Manley, were primarily concerned that the federal finances might have been badly overcommitted. Although Martin's advisers attempted to dismiss this criticism as 'sour grapes' from a defeated leadership candidate, Manley was hardly alone. Among those who agreed with him was the editor of the *Globe and Mail*, who wrote: 'The prime minister promised to fix health care for a generation, but he has dug so deeply into the federal pocketbook that Ottawa may indeed find itself in a fix for a generation.'[40] Then former minister David Anderson complained the deal had not received any firm guarantees that the provinces would keep their part of the bargain. This too was rejected as the biased assessment of a deposed cabinet minister.

Sheila Copps, meanwhile, worried that one of the five principles of the Canada Health Act – portability – would be seriously jeopardized, if not eliminated, by the patchwork arrangement that was sure to follow if other provinces took up the Quebec option as well. She too was dismissed by Martin and his advisers as simply another thwarted leadership contender, despite the fact most social policy experts agreed with her.

These concerns about policy paled in comparison with the criticism levelled at Martin's plan along the federalist axis. Given his spirited defence of asymmetrical federalism, Martin should hardly have been surprised that some of the harshest criticism came from Trudeau federalists within the Liberal Party. For them, asymmetry was philosophically incompatible with a healthy federal system and something to be avoided whenever possible. While virtually everyone acknowledged that there were already some asymmetrical aspects to some federal-provincial arrangements, these were few in number and did not affect key principles.[41] The health care accord, in their view, was quite different and could have far-reaching consequences. They saw Martin's trumpeting of asymmetrical federalism as a direct challenge to the orthodox Liberal vision, and they said so loudly and publicly. In effect, they accused him of implementing administratively what Meech Lake had failed to do constitutionally. Some argued it provided special status for Quebec, others that it made a mockery of the concept of minimum national standards, still others that it abandoned the role of a strong central government. All of them were convinced it would lead to a patchwork quilt of different services and degrees of access that would destroy the welfare state and undermine the federal government's nation-building efforts.

Liberal Senator Serge Joyal did not mince words: 'A pandora's box has been opened. Asymmetry means the federal government doesn't have an important role to work for the good of every Canadian. That is, in fact, left to the provinces. That is not the kind of country we want to build.'[42] Another Liberal senator, Jerry Grafstein, warned presciently that 'Federal Liberals could suffer the same fate as the Ontario Liberals under David Peterson when he abandoned Mr. Trudeau's One Canada policy. He [Peterson] was against the Trudeau vision of the country and he lost.'[43] Once again former Pearson adviser Tom Kent waded into the debate, accusing Martin of 'Sugar-daddy federalism' that was neither innovative nor post-modern, but old-fashioned and out-of-touch with the times. 'The popular will for a Canada-wide social union is now stronger, not weaker, than before,' he argued. 'The federal government has the ability to give effective leadership. It needs the ability to fit its policies to the times.'[44]

Not all of these Liberals were former Chrétien supporters, although Martin's advisers were continuing to dismiss internal party criticism as the result of the ongoing feud. Their argument lost ground, however, when several national columnists including James Travers of the *Toronto Star* argued Martin was 'changing Canada by stealth ... sliding significant change past the public in the dead of night ... piecemeal, incremental administrative change' rather than constitutional change, and leaving in his wake 'a confused bureaucracy, caucus and country.'[45]

Quebec journalist Chantal Hébert concurred, and also underlined the seriousness of the rift in the party. 'It is no coincidence that the first public rumblings of yet another federal Liberal leadership battle in the making are surfacing in the immediate wake of last week's federal-provincial health accord,' Hébert wrote. She noted that no other issue, and not even the delivery of a minority government when a majority was expected, had prompted disaffected Chrétienites or would-be leadership candidates to speak out publicly in this manner. But 'Paul Martin's decision to embrace asymmetrical federalism has predictably flushed into the open' those who oppose his position on that issue. 'Martin's approach to the health accord was always bound to divide his own Liberal house more deeply than the House of Commons,' she concluded, correctly pointing out that 'all three opposition parties partly or wholly support asymmetrical arrangements and a decentralized federation,' and only the Liberals (historically) do not.[46] To this Martin's point man on the intergovernmental file, Tim Murphy, replied aggressively that it was time to forget Trudeau. 'It's time to cast off the dead hand of history,' Murphy declared, creating even more furore in Liberal ranks.[47]

Another blow to the credibility of Martin's deal came from colleagues and supporters. No sooner had the agreement been signed than Quebec Premier Jean Charest (in a move strikingly reminiscent of Robert Bourassa's damaging decision to invoke the notwithstanding clause at the height of the Meech Lake debate) announced he would be joining French Prime Minister Jean-Pierre Raffarin's trade mission to Mexico and meeting formally with Mexican President Vincente Fox, an unprecedented move. As Jeffrey Simpson noted, this was completely unlike earlier trade missions organized by Quebec and other provinces to another country. 'For Quebec, or any other province, to participate in a trade mission organized by another country (and a trade competitor) ought to be completely unacceptable from every point of view to a Canadian government.' Simpson concluded the problem was a weak government that would not defend the national interest. 'Here we have a federal government that is intruding everywhere in areas of provincial jurisdiction – cities, child care, health – throwing around tens of billions of dollars that will cripple the federal government for years to come,' Simpson wrote. 'But one that lacks the backbone to defend an area (trade and foreign affairs) that is clearly within federal jurisdiction.'[48]

Martin's intergovernmental affairs minister, Lucienne Robillard, and his foreign affairs minister, Pierre Pettigrew, were at a loss for words when asked to comment. Other Liberals were not. Liberal Senator Terry Mercer immediately jumped into the fray: 'We were the party of national unity and, while I'm a huge fan of Jean Charest and his Liberals in Quebec, I'm just very concerned about the message we are sending,' he told reporters at a press conference. 'You can't give this authority away.' Mercer asked the obvious question. Would Martin and his ministers allow a separatist Quebec premier to travel abroad independently and meet with heads of state? Then he linked this directly to Martin's championing of asymmetrical federalism. 'Asymmetrical federalism is far more worrisome than Conservative leader Stephen Harper's flirtation with Belgian federalism,' Mercer declared. 'I am concerned that the Harper thing is going to distract us because it's funny and he's an easy target.' But, he argued, 'the Trudeau-Chrétien vision of One Canada is being jeopardized by Mr Martin's embrace of so-called asymmetrical federalism espoused by Quebec nationalists led by [transport minister] Jean Lapierre.'[49]

Lapierre himself was adamant in his defence of the health accord and asymmetrical federalism. But for once he was not the principal source of the Martin government's self-inflicted wounds. Instead, it was Heritage Minister Liza Frulla who blindsided Martin with her off-the-cuff remark that her good friend Line Beauchamp, Quebec's minister of culture, could speak for Canada at UNESCO meetings in Paris if she were unable to attend. Former Martin supporter Maurizio Bevilacqua wasted little time in denouncing Frulla's comments. 'We as Canadians need to recognize who speaks for Canada,' the Toronto MP said. 'In my world it's the federal government … That is our domain and it should stay our domain and there really can be no opening in that area.'[50]

Journalists were quick to make fun of Frulla's comments. One scathing article by columnist Paul Wells offered a number of hypothetical scenarios for her consideration. 'If Line is tied up at the National Assembly or maybe stuck late at the orthodontist's,' he wrote, 'will you be filling in for her at meetings of provincial ministers?' Or, equally devastating, 'If Liza and Line are stuck some weekend at a hunting lodge and there's a big meeting on cultural matters in Geneva, is it fine with both of them if Newfoundland's culture minister (Al) or Alberta's culture minister (Stu) goes off to defend Quebec and Canadian culture in their place?'[51]

The *Toronto Star*'s James Travers concluded: 'Instead of quietly demonstrating the wisdom of this new form of federalism ... the Martin administration has needlessly stirred up the animosity of an overwhelming majority of Canadians outside Quebec.' Travers added: 'If Martin is to put this genie back in the bottle, as Liberals desperately hope, he must take the time and make the effort to fully explain his vision for a federalism that he claims is both strong and flexible.'[52]

Martin did not follow that advice. Although there were references to the Health Accord in the Throne Speech a few weeks later, the opportunity to engage his own caucus, and Canadians, in a meaningful debate about the nature of Canadian federalism was lost. Critics within the party argued that Martin had blinked again. Others suggested it was a fight he could not win, since Canadians were overwhelmingly opposed to anything that appeared to grant special status to Quebec. His senior policy advisers, however, said later that there was simply no time to undertake something which could not produce concrete results in the near future. The accord, they argued, was an accomplishment in its own right and demonstrated the new approach to federalism more clearly than lengthy debates and rhetoric about where Martin wanted to take the country. Indeed, Tim Murphy went so far as to stress that Martin's major concern was actually the national economy in an era of globalization. 'He wanted to put the constitutional issue to rest so that he could look outward, not inward,' Murphy said.[53]

Buying Time: The 2004 Throne Speech

Given their anxiety about their minority status, the extent of the 'centre's' unilateral approach to governing was surprising. It was demonstrated almost immediately after the return of Parliament in October 2004, when the Speech from the Throne simply repeated the Liberals' campaign promises. The narrow cast of the speech was deliberate. Martin's team was intent on buying time. 'Originally we thought we would be lucky to have six months,' Tim Murphy confided. As Scott Reid recalled, their approach was based on the belief the opposition 'could hardly criticize the government for sticking to its election promises. We didn't want to add any surprises.'[54]

Nevertheless the government's failure to consult was raised immediately by all parties. On the eve of the Throne Speech, opposition leader

Stephen Harper told the media he would oppose it, leaving the other opposition parties to prop up the government. Harper made specific reference to the government's failure to consult. 'If the Liberals think they can walk in and make parliament not work because they refuse to cooperate or consult, they're in for a rude awakening.' Even more instructive were the comments of NDP leader Jack Layton, who announced that 'NDP MPs have been trying to speak with Liberal cabinet ministers for weeks' about the NDP's wish list, but 'we've had virtually no response back.'[55] (This was surprising since many issues the NDP wanted to see in the speech were already part of the Liberals' campaign platform. As such, reassuring their most likely ally would surely have been a simple matter for Martin's team. In the end, however, the NDP and the other parties were only shown a draft of the speech a few hours before its delivery.)

Martin was unapologetic. 'We ran on a very specific program in terms of what we believe the priorities of Canadians are. The Speech from the Throne will reflect those priorities.' His view was reinforced by House leader Tony Valeri, who warned 'the government can only water down its major campaign promises so much to meet opposition demands,' despite the fact no opposition parties had been able to make demands.[56] The immediate consequence of the government's failure to consult was a highly charged beginning to the 38th Parliament, which from the outset was marked by unusually deep partisan hostility. In addition, the Liberals' 'inexplicable failure to seek more support for their agenda strengthens the opposition case that Governor General Adrienne Clarkson should give them a chance before plunging the country into an early, unwanted election.'[57]

Convinced that their safest course was to proceed with their platform, they made sure the text of the Throne Speech echoed the Red Book almost word for word in many places. The health care commitment, already taken care of by Martin's federal-provincial deal in September, was also spelled out in detail in the speech. Other campaign promises concerning children, seniors, aboriginals, and cities were equally prominent. Interestingly, each of these areas required the cooperation of other levels of government if they were to be implemented.[58] Indeed, the prominence of the terms 'federal-provincial negotiation,' and 'intergovernmental cooperation' in the speech was striking. On their proposed national childcare system, 'the Government will put the foundations in place with its provincial and territorial partners.' Foreshadowing Martin's decentralist approach to the federation, it then hurried to stress 'within this national framework, the provinces and territories will have the flexibility to address their own particular needs and circumstances.' The 'New Deal for Cities and Communities' section was also careful to note the federal government would be 'working with the provinces and territories ... to make available, for the benefit of municipalities,' a portion of the federal gas tax (rather than the GST as earlier promised).[59]

Even more significant was a passage that was *not* included in the final text of the speech. In an earlier draft, several paragraphs specifically sang the praises of asymmetrical federalism. As journalist Richard Gwyn reported, one cabinet minister had even called him 'to explain how creative the new approach would be,' shortly before the offending segment was abruptly removed from the text at the insistence of several Ontario Liberal MPs. The MPs, many of whom were newcomers, were all Trudeauvian federalists. In caucus they had expressed serious concerns that 'asymmetric federalism would lead either to special status for Quebec, or to everyone being special so that no one was left to speak for Canada.'[60] Martin backed down, fearing another highly public internal party feud would break out over his views.

By contrast Martin's ambivalence about the Kyoto Accord was plainly visible. While the speech declared the government 'reiterates its commitment to the Kyoto Accord on climate change,' this was conditional on several points. Martin's scepticism about climate change measures producing economic benefits meant his government's approach to Kyoto would only proceed 'in a way that produces long-term results while maintaining a strong and growing economy.' His desire to secure federal-provincial harmony at all costs meant federal action would only be taken 'by refining and implementing an equitable national plan in partnership with provincial and territorial governments and other stakeholders.' The message was clear. For Martin and his advisers, the potentially negative impacts of any emission reduction plan on western Canada, and particularly on Alberta and the energy sector, were ongoing and high-priority concerns.

The predictability of the contents did not prevent the speech from being controversial. In fact, the vote on the Throne Speech marked the first challenge to the government's continued existence. With opposition leader Stephen Harper determined to vote against it, and Bloc leader Gilles Duceppe demanding major changes before he would support it, there was furious speculation that the government might fall immediately. Votes against a government's Throne Speech, or in favour of amendments to a Throne Speech, would traditionally be considered non-confidence votes. To avoid this, the wording of both the Bloc and Conservative amendments was modified through negotiations between the government and opposition House leaders. Among other items, the Bloc's assertion of a fiscal imbalance between Ottawa and the provinces was watered down. But wording that required Ottawa to 'fully respect' provincial jurisdiction – an area that would include health care – surprisingly was left in place.

Then the Martin government stunned observers by announcing it would support the amendments. Although there was nothing in parliamentary procedure to prevent the government from taking this approach, it was unprecedented, as many critics within and outside the party noted. Considerable concern was expressed that this course of action would set a dangerous precedent for future minority governments. At a minimum, it suggested the Martin Liberals were more concerned about losing power than in pursuing their own agenda. Martin's growing reputation as a weak leader was also heightened by the move. Even journalists often viewed as favourable to Liberal policies roundly criticized the decision not to stand and fight on the Throne Speech. Richard Gwynn warned 'the real point of concern is more immediate. We seem to have as Prime Minister a leader who, oddly for a businessman, has no bottom line.' Gwynn's conclusion was equally damaging: 'Each time Martin commits himself to some bottom line,' he wrote, 'he blinks as soon as he comes under pressure.'[61]

Democractic Deficit Woes

If the government had been ready to proceed with a number of important pieces of legislation shortly after the Throne Speech, the opposition parties (and the media) might have been distracted from their criticism of Martin's controversial new approach to federalism, to say nothing of Liberal infighting and the ongoing saga of the Gomery Inquiry. But that did not happen. Instead, House leader Tony Valeri announced the first order of business for the 38th Parliament would be to 'start from scratch' on several bills which died on the order paper when the election was called. Rather than reintroducing them at whatever stage they had reached before the writ was dropped, bills left over from the Chrétien era – such as decriminalization of marijuana, same-sex marriage, and the prevention of animal cruelty – as well as bills introduced in Martin's first mandate, such as child pornography and whistleblower legislation, would have to begin the parliamentary process all over again. Valeri argued that nearly one-third of MPs were new to Parliament and had not had a chance to express their views on the issues. This position was not without merit. However, critics noted that several of the bills had been controversial within the Liberal caucus and now were likely to be conveniently stalled indefinitely in a minority situation.

Aware of the growing criticism that the Martin Liberals lacked a concrete agenda of their own, Valeri promised some forty new bills would be introduced before the Christmas recess. But when the first group of eleven bills was announced, the opposition parties were quick to declare them mere housekeeping measures. For the most part they were. 'There's nothing really exciting or new here,' said Conservative House leader John Reynolds. 'I'm anxious to see the other 29 bills.'[62]

Most of the remaining bills were equally innocuous. Seven of them dealt exclusively with the implementation of organizational changes Martin had begun as soon as he took over as prime minister. Liberal Senator Terry Mercer told reporters he 'saw little evidence of the major change Mr. Martin and his supporters had promised' as the reason for their takeover of the Liberal leadership. Although his motives were suspect, Mercer insisted, 'I'm not the only one' in the Liberal caucus who was concerned. 'I think that the minority government has set in place a little paralysis in the system and, quite frankly, I think we should do just the opposite.'[63] Valeri responded that his first priority had been to ensure the smooth operation of the minority government in the House, and he planned to use the lengthy Christmas recess to 'work on a more ambitious agenda.'[64] This comment was greeted with scepticism by opposition parties as well as some Liberals. One former Chrétien minister was overheard at the caucus Christmas party saying, 'What were they doing for the past ten years? Don't they have any game plan at all?'

Among the non-legislative priorities of the Martin government were the firing of several more Chrétien-era appointees to crown corporations and the nomination of several Martin supporters to key positions. It appeared as if their minority status had galvanized Martin and his advisers into acting quickly on these matters, rather than on a legislative agenda, in case they should be defeated sooner rather than later.

The first to depart was Canada Post chair André Ouellet, a former Chrétien minister, whose expenditures had been criticized by the auditor general and whose corporation had been linked indirectly to the Adscam scandal along with the RCMP. Ouellet first had been suspended from his duties with full pay. Then, days before Revenue Minister

John McCallum was scheduled to announce his decision on Ouellet's fate in August 2004, the famously wily Ouellet made public a letter to McCallum in which he announced his 'retirement' from the position 'in the best interest of Canada Post.' Nevertheless, Ouellet also submitted a seventeen-page letter to McCallum in which he defended his expenses as legitimate. His message was clear. He believed his firing was imminent, prompted by political rather than administrative concerns. 'I am conscious you have a minority government,' he wrote. '*Even if you would like* to make a business decision in my case, it is very clear to me that at the end you will have to make a political decision.'[65]

McCallum attracted more negative publicity when the media learned of his decision to personally appoint a replacement for Ouellet, bypassing the new appointment procedures that had only recently been announced by Treasury Board President Reg Alcock. The new rules, Alcock had trumpeted, were part of Martin's democratic deficit plan to 'clean up government.' Despite this, McCallum initially defended his decision to fast track the appointment of bank executive Gordon Feeney as the new president of Canada Post. He cited the superior credentials of his appointee (a former colleague at the bank) and his willingness to serve. 'He's perfect for the job,' McCallum said. But critics argued this was beside the point. Soon the PMO's Scott Reid took over the file, and he too defended McCallum's move by pointing out (correctly) that no one disputed Feeney's excellent qualifications for the post. He also said 'the rules were bent in this instance because a new chair was urgently needed.' But Reid's explanations could not overcome the expectation created by Martin that his government would handle patronage appointments differently. 'So much for the dawn of a new era,' NDP MP Judy Wasylycia-Leis commented. According to public opinion polls shortly afterwards, many Canadians agreed with her.[66]

This incident might have been seen as a minor misstep had it not been for the appointments Martin had already made before and during the election campaign to secure the candidacies of his supporters, and the series of new patronage-related controversies that followed the election. For example, Martin appointed former Winnipeg MP John Harvard as Manitoba's lieutenant governor immediately after the election, apparently in exchange for Harvard having stepped aside for Martin's star candidate in that province, Glen Murray, who ran in a losing cause. Similarly, Quebec MP Yvan Charbonneau, who had not sought another term so that Martin supporter Pablo Rodriguez could run in Charbonneau's riding, was appointed Canada's representative to UNESCO in

Paris. And former Chrétien minister Art Eggleton, who had agreed not to run again in York Centre in favour of Martin recruit Ken Dryden, was soon appointed to the Senate.

In all, Martin made some seventeen Senate appointments during his short term of office. Some were non-partisan choices such as high-profile Conservatives Hugh Segal and André Champagne, and former general Roméo Dallaire. The majority were not only Liberals but Liberals who had worked on Martin's leadership campaign. Most noteworthy were two of Martin's long-standing supporters, defeated Liberal candidate Dennis Dawson and former principal secretary Francis Fox. The moves were widely criticized, not least because Martin was simultaneously professing his support for Senate reform. Here too, the issue of raising too many expectations appeared to have caught up with the Liberal leader. 'I have long been an advocate of Senate reform,' he told the House of Commons, 'but I do not believe that doing (it) piecemeal would really bring us the desired result,' he explained.[67] This was a long-standing Liberal position, but difficult for Martin to maintain in the face of comments by Alberta Premier Ralph Klein, who told reporters Martin had promised him earlier that he would look favourably on the idea of appointing Alberta's so-called 'senators-in-waiting' to fill the Alberta vacancies in the Red Chamber. As a result, Martin received little or no credit for his principled stand against Klein's plan, despite the fact he took the position in full realization that it would not help his efforts to improve the party's standings in the west.

Then there was the fateful decision to ignore a vote in the House of Commons in which the government's legislation to formally separate the departments of Foreign Affairs and International Trade was actually defeated. Although not a confidence vote, the government's cavalier announcement that it would proceed with the reorganization regardless was almost universally viewed as shocking and something that would reflect badly on Martin's future efforts to stress parliamentary reform or the increased importance of backbenchers.

More unfortunate still for Martin's democratic deficit agenda was the appearance of a continuing vendetta against Jean Chrétien and his supporters. This image persisted even after Martin found himself in a minority government situation, where the importance of Liberal Party unity would logically have been a major concern. In fact, the infighting between the two camps, now heightened by the recent asymmetrical federalism debate, appeared to be no closer to resolution. But it was the government's handling of various order-in-council appointments that cast a further pall on its attempts to demonstrate a new openness and transparency in decision making, even calling into question its capacity to serve as a role model for employers in the private sector.

Liberal Infighting Continues

The image of an ongoing Liberal vendetta was reinforced when André Ouellet's departure was followed by that of David Dingwall, another former Chrétien minister, who had been serving as head of the Royal Canadian Mint. Dingwall's case was quite different from Ouellet's. Despite the support of his board of directors as well as the employees' union, both of whom described his efforts in glowing terms, Dingwall also 'resigned' over alleged spending irregularities. In his case, though, he had negotiated a severance package with the government that soon proved as controversial as his expenditures. Indeed, the government subsequently reneged on its commitment to honour the severance package. This in turn resulted in a lengthy legal battle which only heightened the public's awareness of the conflict. In the end, the federal arbitrator who found in Dingwall's favour – awarding him substantial back pay and damages – delivered a stinging rebuke of the Martin government's handling of the affair:

> There was no basis to the criticisms leveled against him (about spending irregularities) but no one in the government was prepared to listen to him or inquire fairly. Several former Chrétien ministers had already lost their jobs and were involved in very public and expensive litigation. No one disagreed with his assessment that he was next. No one suggested that he would be defended, or that the allegations would be the subject matter of a rational resolution process.[68]

The Martin government's subsequent decision to appeal a court ruling reinstating Jean Pelletier as the chair of Via Rail seemed to take this vendetta to a new level. Rejecting the Federal Court's ruling that Pelletier's firing was 'hasty and done in an opaque manner' which denied Chrétien's former principal secretary due process, Transport Minister Jean Lapierre promptly told reporters that he had started a process 'to fire him all over again.'[69] Not content with this, Lapierre also fired a broadside at the entire Chrétien wing of the party, who reportedly had been asking for an apology for the derogatory comments Lapierre had made about their alleged involvement in the Adscam scandal before the election. Instead, Lapierre poured oil on the flames by declaring he had no intention of apologizing for remarks he had made in the past. 'That's ancient history,' he said. 'I think people who are concerned about the future will take all that with a grain of salt ... people who want the best for the Liberal Party and the country will work for us, regardless of what camp they were part of in the past.'[70]

In this poisonous atmosphere, even Martin's attempts to respond to legitimate concerns about the implications of some of the measures in the party financing legislation were seen primarily as an attack on Chrétien's legacy. Ironically, this perception was especially true in Quebec.[71] A similar round of negative publicity followed Martin's expulsion of MP Carolyn Parrish from caucus, despite the fact her departure was approved by the majority of her fellow caucus members. As an outspoken critic of the Martin camp's attempts to remove Chrétien as leader, her departure inevitably was seen as a settling of accounts. In addition, Martin chronicler Susan Delacourt concluded, 'the focus ... quickly shifted to what the whole controversy revealed about Martin's leadership skills – or lack of them.' As Delacourt noted, none of the Martin supporters who had called publicly for Chrétien's resignation was ever disciplined, let alone removed from caucus. 'The most provocative question is whether Martin has turned out to be less tolerant of dissent than Chrétien was.'[72]

The cumulative effect of all of these incidents was important. Just as Brian Mulroney's attack on patronage during the 1984 leaders' debates ultimately came back to haunt him in light of his own record number of patronage appointments, so Paul Martin's efforts to portray his new Liberal government as more open, accessible, and accountable created an environment in which no appearance of 'old style' politics would be acceptable, even if justified by circumstances. In the 2006 election these various controversies, taken together, arguably created an image of the party which lent credence to the claims of insider trading regarding Finance Minister Ralph Goodale's announcement on income trusts in November 2005, claims which polling data suggested were a key factor in the Liberal government's demise.[73]

The Party in Disarray

The 2004 election had not simply reduced the Martin Liberals to a minority government. As party president Mike Eizenga later noted, it highlighted many of the financial and organizational problems continuing to plague the Liberal Party. On the financial side, for example, the party was still operating with a divided fundraising structure and no comprehensive central membership list. The first election fought under Jean Chrétien's new party financing legislation had resulted in a serious funding shortfall. 'It was an expensive election,' Eizenga told reporters at the time. 'We ... have spent very close to the limit. That's what we planned to do and that's what we did. [Our debt] will certainly be in excess of $4 million and I would be surprised if it is less than $5 million.'[74] And the party's financial situation was likely to worsen. In addition to repaying the debt and covering the ongoing costs of the national party office, the Liberal government's minority status meant the party would need additional funds to finance the cost of yet another election campaign, one that likely would be held in less than two years. Worse still, because the Liberals had received fewer votes in the June 2004 election than in the previous 2000 election, the new legislation also required the party to repay some $250,000 to Elections Canada. Moreover, the reduced support in the June election meant the party would receive no new public funding until April 2005. Even then, the payment would only be a drop in the bucket at $2.2 million.

Referring to the party's dire straits, the director of the Federal Liberal Agency, Ben Hutzel, predicted 'the party's debt could rise as high as $9 to $10 million,' although he cautioned that this was a ballpark figure.[75] Hutzel's comments were almost immediately contradicted by Eizenga. Insisting that 'I've never heard that number,' he denied the party's debt could possibly reach $10 million because of a second election. The party president also now argued that '$4 to $5 million is kind of a wild estimate, given we don't have invoices in yet.' In addition Eizenga pointedly mentioned that 'Ben stopped being the chief financial officer in November,' and his own conversations with the new CFO, Lloyd Posno, had convinced him the concerns about the debt were overstated. Eizenga also touted the $8 million in election expense rebates the party could expect to receive from individual candidates.[76] Reporters, however, noted that almost all of that money would be required to pay off the last election campaign's debt and ongoing office expenses. There would be nothing left to pay for another election, which could cost up to $16 million, without additional fundraising. Adding to the Liberals' concerns, the Conservatives announced they were in the black after the 2004 election and possessed ample funds to fight another election at any time.

Not surprisingly, a number of articles concerning the Liberals' financial woes and fundraising efforts appeared in the fall of 2004. Paul Martin's decision to continue to host cocktail parties at 24 Sussex Drive for members of the Laurier Club was highly controversial, because once again it appeared to contradict his commitment to more open and accountable decision making. Opposition parties had always criticized this practice, which both Brian Mulroney and Jean Chrétien had carried on, but the Conservatives were able to target Paul Martin much more effectively. Referring to Martin's 'alleged' commitment to eliminating the democratic deficit, Conservative MP Monte Solberg declared, 'There's absolutely no difference between Chrétien and Martin on this front – it's the old perception that access to the prime minister is closed unless you've got deep pockets.'[77]

Then in November the Conservatives lobbed another grenade at the Liberals, telling reporters that Liberal Party officials had approached them about the possibility of amending Chrétien's financing legislation to ease the limits on individual donations. 'We are very very pleased with the new system and we know the Liberals are hurting because they have already approached us about raising the personal donation limits. But we're not interested,' said Geoff Norquay, the communications director for Stephen Harper in the opposition leader's office. His claim was promptly dismissed by Scott Reid in PMO, who told reporters the government had 'no plans' to change the legislation and Norquay's allegation was 'utterly groundless.'[78] However, Reid's denial was tempered by the fact that Liberal House leader Tony Valeri had already mused publicly about changing the limits. A number of Liberal MPs had also been complaining publicly about their difficulties raising money in their ridings.

Clearly the nature of the Liberals' financial problems had changed little since John Turner's time. Despite two decades of reform efforts, the Liberals were still unable to canvass individual members effectively. Nor had they made any significant progress on direct mail campaigns. Instead, as virtually everyone on the national executive acknowledged, the party remained dependent on corporate contributions – which were now banned – and on a relatively small number of very large donations – which were now limited – from wealthy individuals.

The party's response to this dilemma was slow in coming, but the minority government situation prompted a rethinking of several traditional approaches. First, rather than raise the amount of a membership in the Laurier Club from $1,000 to $2,000 or $5,000 as some had suggested, it was eventually decided to leave the rate where it was and attempt to broaden the base of membership. Laurier Club president Daryl Friedlander told reporters the plan was to increase membership in the club from 2,000 to 5,000. 'The whole new finance regime is something that is going to drive things more towards the grassroots,' he said. His views were echoed by Toronto Laurier Club chair Gregory King, who said, 'We're better off as a Liberal party, the party of the people so to speak, to keep the fees modest and work at involving more people.'[79] A second effort, the 'Liberal-Leaders campaign,' was an email canvass sent under the signature of president Mike Eizenga. Here the request was for 'as little as $15 a month (that's 50 cents a day) … will provide us with a steady source of funds throughout the year to mount winning campaigns.'

Yet the party's move towards broadening the base was not universally adopted. This became clear in November when Martin's former leadership fundraisers, Diane Mitchell and Gerry Schwartz, unveiled the party's alternative to replace the large corporate fundraisers known as leader's dinners, which were now illegal. The new 'Prime Minister's Receptions,' to be staged across the country in late November and December 2004, were the vehicle at least part of the party elite was pinning its hopes on to attract 'individuals' who would contribute the maximum $5,000 allowed under the new rules. Few doubted that most of the tickets would be sold to the same individuals who had attended the corporate fundraisers in the past.

Meanwhile Martin and his advisers were leaving nothing to chance with respect to the leadership review vote that would take place at the first party convention after the election. With former Chrétien ministers John Manley, Martin Cauchon, and Maurizio Bevilacqua reportedly laying the groundwork for future leadership bids, should Martin fail to deliver a majority government in the next election, he adopted Jean Chrétien's strategy. Martin pushed the National Executive to schedule a convention as soon as possible, preferably in early 2005. Remarkably, members of the executive – almost all of whom had been Martin supporters – talked openly of the prime minister's need to 'fend off leadership challengers and prepare for the next election.' Demonstrating conclusively how much the traditional Liberal culture of solidarity and support for 'the leader, right or wrong' had eroded, one senior official told journalists, 'they're going sooner rather than later because there is a risk of things turning sour by waiting.' According to another member of the executive, the same man who had been selected leader of the party in a landslide in November 2003 was, by November 2004, in need of every procedural advantage he could get. 'It makes sense to hold this convention as soon as possible,' the official bluntly told reporters.

'The earlier time frame gives Paul the advantage. Just coming out of an election, people don't have time to organize (against him in a leadership review), so the quicker you can get through the review question, the better.'[80] Still another stressed that the decision on the convention timing needed to be made before Martin's control of the executive was lost once their terms of office expired, because they could not count on their re-election.

Confirmation of the executive's view of Martin's precarious hold on power came from former Chrétien minister David Anderson, who declared publicly: 'What's sauce for the goose is sauce for the gander.' Arguing that Martin had no right to complain if people were organizing to succeed him as leader, Anderson concluded, 'After all, what did he do from 1990 on? Thirteen years of the Martin organization doing exactly the same.'[81] Ultimately Martin was successful in having the convention scheduled for 6 March 2005 and, with some effort from his team, he received the support of some 88 per cent of delegates.

This open criticism of the leader may have also been the impetus for Martin to take action on another front. In late October he suddenly announced he would reverse his position from the 2004 election and protect his sitting MPs from nomination challenges next time. Martin and his supporters described this as the 'politically responsible' thing to do. 'This announcement allows MPs to focus on their parliamentary duties,' Tony Valeri said. But Valeri's opponent for the nomination in Hamilton-East in 2004, Sheila Copps, suggested there were other motives. 'I'm sure he (Martin) was under enormous pressure,' she said, noting that this time it would also be much easier for Martin to take this move since the incumbents would largely be Martin supporters. One national columnist recalled that Martin's 'nomination experiment led to divisive feuds marked by threats of libel lawsuits, accusations of ballot-stuffing and many party stalwarts either quitting or being turfed out,' something to avoid at all costs in the next election. Other journalists were quick to remind voters that Martin's earlier decision to allow MPs to be challenged 'soon began smelling like a purge of those who didn't support his leadership.' One noted 'Caccia was one of the few Liberal MPs who supported Copps' leadership bid, and both were gone within months of Martin's coronation.'[82]

In what increasingly appeared to be evidence of an opposition party mindset (as if the Liberals had *lost* the last election rather than been reduced to minority status), one prominent party spokesman after another felt free to join the debate and analyse the party's difficulties in public. First to do so was former Trudeau adviser Jim Coutts, who delivered a scathing critique of the entire Martin era in an article published in *Policy Options*. Coutts's complaints began with the leadership convention where, he underlined, no policy debate had taken place and a leader who had campaigned for the job for ten years had been crowned through a 'hostile takeover' of the party apparatus. He also lamented the fact that Martin's leadership opponents had been untypically 'shown the door.' In Coutts's view, this had led inevitably to the 'disastrous June election campaign,' in which the traditional Liberal brand was replaced with the Team Martin approach, 'abandoning a trademark that has governed Canada for most of the last century' and ignoring the party's major policy tenets for a 'dangerously blurred' set of policy options. 'The question now,' Coutts wrote, 'is whether Martin has the talent, the team and the desire to get the Red Machine back on the road.' Summing up, Coutts warned: 'If he fails, the Liberals could lose their cohesion as a broad centrist party.'[83]

This devastating critique was followed by the negative and highly public assessment of Martin by his perpetual nemesis, former Pearson adviser Tom Kent. On the first anniversary of Martin becoming leader, Kent described Martin as a 'huge disappointment' who lacked focus and had difficulty defining his policy objectives. Agreeing with Jim Coutts, Kent concluded: 'Unless there is some big change,' then 'disillusionment will come. Unquestionably,' and the party 'will be in serious trouble.'[84]

Not long after, former Turner party pollster Martin Goldfarb added to the dismal assessment of Liberal prospects. Like Coutts, Goldfarb stressed the need for the parliamentary wing to be receptive to the views of the broader party membership. In his article, Goldfarb pulled few punches: 'After one year Paul Martin's government seems to be floundering,' he wrote. 'It lacks clear direction. It has moved on health care with an approach akin to asymmetrical federalism – the same approach Canadians turned down in Meech Lake and the Charlottetown Accord.' Moreover, the pollster claimed, 'the Liberal Party has not endorsed such an approach. The government's strategy on health care is just one example of how it has moved forward without the consent of its own grassroots.'[85] Goldfarb also argued that the Martin Liberals had strayed from the fundamental values and tenets of Liberalism. While a change in party policy was always possible, he argued, any such change would need public debate, and consultation with Liberal grassroots members, if it were to be legitimate and/or successful.

In short, barely one year after Paul Martin had taken power, three veteran policy advisers from previous eras of Liberal government had all spoken publicly of their concern that the Martin Liberals were taking the party in a new direction, without the consent of the membership or the support of Canadians. At the same time, they had urged the minority government to take decisive action on areas of traditional Liberal policy strength, rather than appearing to be rudderless. Their concerns seemed to have found some resonance with Martin and his advisers, although perhaps not in the manner they anticipated. By the time Ralph Goodale prepared to table the government's first minority budget in February 2005, the PMO had decided to ignore the opposition and proceed as if they had a majority.

The 2005 Budget Crisis

If the Martin government's weak-kneed reaction to the 2004 Throne Speech did anything, it emboldened the opposition parties to raise the threat of an election to obtain concessions in the first minority budget. Both the Conservatives and the Bloc indicated in advance that they would likely table amendments. By then the Liberals had decided they would take a different tack this time and stand firm. House leader Tony Valeri gave an interview the day before Finance Minister Ralph Goodale brought down the budget, confirming the new tough approach and stating there had been no discussions with opposition parties. 'No one has said to me how they will vote,' he confided. 'It's not a coalition budget, it's not a coalition government … The opposition will have a choice. They can work and see Canadians achieve things … or they can drag Canadians to the polls out of their own political ambition.'[86] Valeri also indicated no amendments to the budget would be accepted. They would be considered non-confidence motions this time, he stated categorically.

As Tim Murphy later explained, Martin's strategists expected the opposition parties to wait and see what the budget contained. 'We knew Canadians wanted our programs to be carried out, and they didn't want an election.' And, despite his earlier belief that the opposition would bring down the government without hesitation if they could, Murphy believed the risk was now much less. 'We thought we could count on the NDP,' Murphy recalled, and he also believed the Conservatives would make sure enough of their MPs would be absent for the vote that they could safely oppose it without bringing down the government. If not, then the Martin team felt the Liberals could run on the budget and probably win a majority.[87]

The approach initially seemed to work. Conservative House leader Jay Hill expressed predictable outrage that he had not been consulted in advance, but told reporters: 'We're trying to do the responsible thing. We're waiting for some overtures from the Liberal government to suggest what it is going to take to ... work together, the four parties, to try and get this budget passed.'[88] His counterpart, Michel Gauthier of the Bloc, concurred: 'If we find a certain number of the things that we have asked for, we could vote for it ... if the budget is a good budget, we will vote for it.'[89]

Certainly the budget tabled on 23 February 2005 appeared to have something for everyone. In addition to details of the health care deal, it offered $5 billion over five years for childcare, $5 billion over five years for the cities agenda, some $4 billion for initiatives to meet the Kyoto Protocol commitments, and a $12.8 billion increase in defence expenditures over the same five-year period. A personal income tax cut was introduced, and a 2 per cent corporate tax cut was planned by 2010. In total, the budget represented over $42 billion in new expenditures over five years. While this would be partially funded from the $11 billion in savings achieved by the Expenditure Review exercise chaired by John McCallum, political scientist Bruce Doern noted the budget still 'contained the largest spending increases seen in decades.'[90]

Several commentators described it as a pre-election budget filled with goodies, and more than one questioned whether Martin and the Liberals had abandoned their once-cherished mantra of fiscal prudence. However, one of the reasons for the huge numbers, as Doern pointed out, was Goodale's decision to use five-year projections rather than the traditional two-year term. Goodale stressed this shift in his budget speech, insisting it was a sensible decision 'given that many of the government's newest and largest program obligations represent commitments of five years or longer.'[91] These commitments, of course, were federal-provincial agreements. In the end some experts expressed concern that 'the huge medium-term expenditure increases ... undoubtedly pose new risks if the economy falters or if other large unforeseen needs arise in these longer timeframes,' but the fiscal probity and prudence of the budget were not challenged.[92]

Indeed, the budget initially appeared to be a non-event. This was largely due to the speedy decision by the Harper Conservatives to support it. The Conservatives' declining support in the polls was undoubtedly a factor in their decision, as Harper's comment on budget day made clear. 'There's nothing in this budget that would justify an election at this time,' he said.[93] Meanwhile, NDP leader Jack Layton called it a Conservative budget and said his nineteen MPs would oppose it.

Long before the budget was passed the initial support of the Conservatives and the Bloc had turned to determined opposition. This change of heart was, not surprisingly, directly linked to the dramatic reversal of fortune of the Liberals and Conservatives over that period. The Liberals' decline was tied to the constant barrage of negative news stories coming from the Gomery Inquiry throughout March and April. Polls showed the chances of a Conservative victory were increasingly likely, and this prompted Harper to reconsider his options. On 25 March the opposition leader – evidently looking for ways to retract his hasty support for the budget – caused consternation in Liberal ranks when he told reporters he would not vote for the Liberal budget if the government included an amendment to the Canadian Environmental Protection Act.

Over the next several weeks Liberal numbers declined precipitously, the Gomery revelations continued, and the mood of all the opposition parties in the House shifted towards the attack. As a result, when the NDP approached Martin's advisers about possible budget amendments that would guarantee their support, their proposal received serious consideration rather than the curt dismissal they would have received in early March. In the end, the NDP was able to negotiate the elimination of the proposed corporate tax cut and a $4.6 billion package of additional measures on housing, public transit, post-secondary education, and foreign aid, all of which was announced by NDP leader Jack Layton, not the prime minister, on 26 April.

Media coverage of this side agreement was almost universally positive. But there was little good news in this for Martin, since Layton received the credit. Reporters began referring to 'the NDP budget.' A *Globe and Mail* editorial on 27 April underlined this, saying 'NDP Leader Jack Layton was looking positively prime ministerial when he announced yesterday's agreement with the Liberals.' Martin's willingness to cut a deal to remain in power, meanwhile, was criticized by everyone from Richard Gwyn ('Only Jack Layton and the New Democrats have gained in stature, politically and morally, from all the cynicism and opportunism')[94] to Don Martin ('Why would Canadians vote for a tired, stale-dated, corrupted, unprincipled Liberal party when the New Democrats have an untainted guy calling the shots in an acting prime ministerial capacity?').[95] Perhaps the unkindest cut of all came from Jane Taber, who pointed out, yet again, how the centre was making decisions without consulting its bureaucrats or its own supporters: '[Jack Layton] has had so much influence now on a budget, more influence than members of the Liberal caucus, for instance. He has totally changed Martin's agenda. He's had more influence than [Liberal finance minister] Ralph Goodale.'[96]

Despite their deal with the NDP the Liberals were increasingly unsure they would win the second-reading vote on the budget. The Conservatives and the Bloc were likely to vote against it en masse, and so every vote counted. The sudden defection of Liberal MP David Kilgour to sit as an Independent meant they now were several votes short of a majority even with the nineteen NDP votes. The earlier expulsion of Carolyn Parrish from the Liberal caucus was beginning to look like a serious mistake. Her vote as an Independent could not be guaranteed either. A third Independent MP, Chuck Cadman, was an unknown quantity. The former Reform/Alliance MP had won his seat in the 2004 election as an Independent, running against the Conservative candidate who had defeated him for the new party's nomination when Harper refused to intervene to protect Cadman. Now that Cadman was seriously ill, his attendance in the House for votes was in doubt.

By mid-April a number of national polls showed the Liberals were imploding. Then on 21 April, Prime Minister Paul Martin delivered an extraordinary nationally televised address, pleading with Canadians to wait for the Gomery Inquiry to complete its report before an election. Noting that 'the Parliament you sent to Ottawa less than a year ago is preoccupied with election talk and political strategy, not with the job you sent us here to do,' Martin declared he would take full responsibility for Gomery's findings but 'I believe before there is an election … Canadians deserve a full and frank accounting of all the facts. Fairness and due process require nothing less.' Then he committed to calling an election 'within thirty days of the publication of the commission's final report and recommendations. Let Judge Gomery do his work. Let the facts come out. Then let the people have their say.'[97] Martin's plan would have resulted in an election in early spring of 2006. A first report assigning blame was due in late November, and the final report, with recommendations to prevent future incidents, was scheduled for release at the end of January 2006.

Response to the speech was mixed. Some observers felt the gambit had allowed the Liberals to buy time to implement their agenda. Others felt it had only made the Martin Liberals appear more desperate. A CRIC poll revealed most Canadians agreed with Martin that there should be no election until Gomery had released his report, but an Ipsos-Reid poll done for Canwest showed a spike in support for the Conservatives. It was in this context of rising expectations that Stephen Harper moved a motion on 11 May urging the Finance Committee to reject measures in the budget and call for the government's resignation. That unexpected motion passed in the House by a margin of 153 to 150, but the Liberals – supported by several expert opinions – dismissed it as an unimportant procedural matter and certainly not a non-confidence vote.

This rejection led the Conservatives, with the help of the Bloc, to organize a three-day filibuster, forcing the House to adjourn. Finally a deal was struck. The Martin government agreed to bring forward the budget and the NDP budget amendment package for a second-reading vote on Thursday, 19 May. Although Harper had promised the Conservatives would support the Liberal budget, he made it clear his party would oppose the NDP amendment package. Defeat on that second budget vote would also be fatal for the Martin minority.

The week that followed was nothing short of chaotic. In addition to wild media speculation about an imminent election if the government fell on the budget vote, there were new revelations about the involvement of the Quebec wing of the Liberal Party in the Adscam debacle. On 17 May Conservative MP and former leadership contender Belinda Stronach shocked everyone by crossing the floor to sit as a Liberal. It soon became known that her defection had only come about after lengthy conversations with a number of senior Liberals, and she was immediately appointed to the cabinet as minister for human resource development. The drama turned to comedy the following day when another Conservative MP, Germant Grewal, held a press conference in which he produced tape recordings of conversations between himself and Martin's chief of staff, Tim Murphy, discussing his possible defection as well. However, Grewal did not defect, and a number of bizarre claims and counterclaims by the BC MP, his leader Stephen Harper, and others involved in the affair soon led many Canadians to conclude their parliamentarians had become totally preoccupied with political gamesmanship. Several of Grewal's claims soon proved groundless and the disgraced MP eventually left Ottawa for his riding on indefinite 'stress leave.' Nevertheless the incident reflected the Martin government's obvious determination to remain in power at all costs and did little to bolster their image.

The day of the actual votes was equally dramatic. The NDP and Conservatives supported the first budget vote as they had promised, and it passed without difficulty. However, the second vote on the NDP amendment package was incredibly close. Both Carolyn Parrish and Chuck Cadman voted with the government, but David Kilgour voted with the opposition. The result was a rare tie, broken by the Speaker in favour of the government. The budget was brought forward for third reading on 15 June, after the Liberals had added another seat by winning a by-election in Newfoundland. Although there were no fewer than sixteen separate votes on opposition amendments to the legislation, none were close, and the budget, at last, was adopted. This meant the Liberals were safely out of danger until the fall session, allowing them to plan a new strategy over the summer. For the most part, this strategy involved negotiating more federal-provincial agreements.

Martin's Asymmeterical Federalism in Action

One reason Paul Martin's government did not receive credit for their major policy initiatives was because they took place outside of Parliament. Michael Robinson later acknowledged: 'For reasons that are unclear to me, negotiations with the provinces are evidently not something people see as the federal government taking action.'[98] Another part of the explanation may lie in the fact that the policy areas being addressed were ones Martin had identified many times before as top priorities. As a result, when the actual deals were announced they appeared anticlimactic. Yet another reason may be the lack of concrete, nationwide deals. Instead they were often only agreements in principle, followed by a series of bilateral deals spread over a much longer period of time, defusing their impact.

At the time, though, Martin's advisers certainly expected much more credit would be earned for their efforts. Martin had wasted little time in the fall of 2004, negotiating a series of federal-provincial deals beginning with the dramatic and controversial health care accord in September. By 1 November, less than two months later, a national agreement in principle was struck on childcare. But the actual deals with individual provinces did not materialize until the following spring, and then only with certain ones. In late April 2005 Manitoba and Saskatchewan signed on, followed by Ontario on 5 May, Newfoundland on 12 May, and Nova Scotia on 16 May. But major players such as Quebec, Alberta, and British Columbia were still not part of the plan. Nor was New

Brunswick, where Martin and HRDC Minister Ken Dryden had been scheduled to make an announcement similar to that of Newfoundland. Martin's team was humiliated by Conservative Premier Bernard Lord's last-minute statement that there was in fact no deal, and had to cancel the scheduled press conference in Fredericton at the eleventh hour.

As a result, one of the lasting images of the childcare arrangements was confusion. According to political scientist Don Desserud of the University of New Brunswick, the Liberals appeared to be in disarray and 'crisis management' mode. 'They recognize that the end is nigh and they have to do things as quickly as possible,' Desserud said. 'They can't wait. So even if they smell a deal, they're willing to jump into action and formally announce that it's at least imminent. It speaks to the fact that the government is looking at a very short calender.'[99] Similarly, as both Jean Chrétien and Sheila Copps had warned, Martin's approach to his 'cities agenda' was a singularly unrewarding one for the federal government. Instead of funding specific programs, the budget's allocation of gas tax revenue meant the public was unaware of the initiative. This was particularly true since the money would be given to provinces, and only after another series of bilateral negotiations. Moreover, the amount committed in the 2005 budget was actually less than the cost of the Chrétien government's highly successful trilateral infrastructure program, which had been introduced in 1994 and extended twice at the urging of the Federation of Canadian Municipalities (FCM). This time, rather than a $9 billion federal contribution over three years as provided in that earlier plan, the same amount of $9 billion was allocated over a five-year period. Nor was there a requirement for matching funding from the other two levels of government, so that there was no certainty a total of $27 billion would be spent. While both the FCM and several urban mayors expressed their guarded approval of the federal measure, it was far from enthusiastic. Perhaps most striking was the fact that if fell to Jack Layton, in his side amendment to the 2005 budget, to insist that some federal funding be targeted specifically to urban public transit, a move which received far more positive and widespread coverage.

Undoubtedly the most successful of Martin's major federal-provincial policy initiatives – at least from the standpoint of public awareness and support – was the Kelowna Accord. Martin's dramatic meeting with provincial and aboriginal leadership in late November 2005, and the positive message communicated at the conclusion of the negotiations by all of the actors, provided a significant boost to the Liberal leader's image just days before his government fell. The accord was referred to by Assembly of First Nations Grand Chief Phil Fontaine as a 'historic' agreement, while BC Premier Gordon Campbell compared the presence of aboriginal leadership at the meeting to 'a seat at the confederation table,' and PEI Premier Pat Binns declared the implementation of the accord 'will be the modern test of our nationhood.'[100]

Perhaps one reason for the public's heightened awareness of the Kelowna deal was that Martin was not normally identified with aboriginal issues. Yet his sincerity and commitment to the process had been obvious during the televised sessions. In addition his government negotiated directly with national aboriginal leaders along with premiers and territorial leaders, making it a more credible and noteworthy event. Paradoxically, in other respects the Kelowna process marked a return to the more traditional Liberal approach to federal-provincial negotiations. The deal reached in Kelowna on 25 November 2005 was national and comprehensive. It resulted from detailed negotiations at the bureaucratic level over the previous eighteen months, and of two previous federal-provincial meetings held in September 2004 and May 2005. In short, it was the opposite of the ad hoc deals recently concluded by Martin in some other policy areas, in the pressure-cooker environment of a one-time federal-provincial meeting of politicians. Moreover, the objective of the negotiations – to 'close the gap' in living standards between aboriginal peoples and other Canadians – had been clearly spelled out in advance. Less ambitious than 'fixing health care for a generation,' it was also more likely to be achieved. Avoiding any discussion of constitutional issues or land claims, the accord focused on four key areas: education, housing, health, and 'a new relationship,' and committed the federal government to provide some $5 billion over ten years.

The Kelowna Accord succeeded in uniting Liberals, something which none of Martin's other federal initiatives had done. In fact, most had reinforced the internal schism along the federalist axis. By far the most controversial was his handling of equalization, where widespread expert criticism was accompanied by intense and highly public disagreement among Liberals.

The importance of the equalization program – the second-largest intergovernmental transfer program in Canada – can hardly be overestimated. Indeed, it was considered so important that it was entrenched in the constitution in 1982 as a fundamental principle of Canadian federalism. By then, the program had long been accepted as the most appropriate way to deal with the horizontal imbalance – the difference in wealth and revenue-raising capacity among provinces – in order to ensure all Canadians had access to a minimum level of public services. Moreover, as the report of the expert panel commissioned by Martin later concluded, the program worked and there was widespread support for it. 'Without equalization payments the fiscal capacity of the least well-off province was between 58 and 68 per cent of the national average,' the report noted, whereas 'with equalization the fiscal capacity of that province was raised to between 91 and almost 100 per cent of the national average.'[101]

True, there had been growing provincial concern that the formula for determining the amount of federal payments had become overly complex and, at the same time, increasingly unfair due to changing economic realities in some of the have-not provinces. But no one was questioning the concept of equalization per se. The primary concern was that the transfers, which had been growing steadily throughout the 1990s, had begun to decrease in the new millennium. This was due to the impact of a declining Ontario economy and a surge in other provincial economies, producing a significant (and some argued perverse) result based on the existing formula. Among 'have-not' provinces with natural resource revenues, a second concern was the way the existing formula treated those revenues when calculating payments, since they were reduced by a comparable amount and prevented them from 'getting ahead.'

As with other transfer programs, the equalization formula was scheduled to be reviewed and revamped every five years to allow for changing demographics and other factors. This renewal had taken place in April 2004. Yet only six months later, at a first ministers' conference in October 2004, Paul Martin surprised almost everyone by announcing that he was essentially abandoning the concept of a formula based on provincial revenue. Instead, he was committing the federal government to absolute amounts of funding, with a guaranteed floor of $10 billion in total, and minimum amounts per province. And, after the initial year, increases were to be determined on a per capita basis, which again was a new development.

Simply put, the program suddenly moved from one in which funding depended on a needs-based, standardized formula, to one where the federal government would simply provide fixed amounts of funding. Although this may have resulted in greater certainty, it was, as several experts on fiscal federalism concluded, apparently ad hoc and not based on any formula at all. This made it vulnerable to claims of even greater potential imbalance and unfairness. A study by the Library of Parliament noted that 'the new framework guarantees that every qualifying province will receive more equalization money under the new framework than it would have under the old system.' However, the same study went on to highlight the fact that 'some provinces benefit more than others from the new arrangement ... Saskatchewan, Manitoba and Prince Edward Island will receive less equalization in 2005–6 than in 2004–5, while payments will rise in Quebec and the three Atlantic provinces.'[102]

In the end, the bizarre result of these cumulative changes was that there would be almost no correlation between the calculation of federal payments and the objective of equalizing the horizontal imbalance. One expert analysis concluded bluntly: 'The new framework fundamentally changes the nature of the equalization program ... Equalization is no longer "equalizing" what it once did.' In addition, it argued national standards would be lost. 'Another significant change is that, at least until 2007–2008, the new framework no longer attempts to align all have-not provinces to one standard.'[103]

Then there was the issue of natural resource revenue. Without waiting for the expert panel report which he himself had commissioned, Martin was driven by his rash 2004 election promise and the intimidating tactics of Newfoundland Premier Danny Williams[104] to cut a bilateral deal with that province in February 2005. When PMO advisers realized a similar deal would have to be struck with Nova Scotia for political reasons, this task was given to the regional minister, Geoff Regan, who eventually settled an $800 million lump-sum deal with the province. In their defence, Martin's advisers noted that the deals officially were to compensate the two Atlantic provinces for their concerns about off-shore oil revenues and correspondingly reduced equalization payments. As such, the eight-year agreements were not technically part of the equalization program, but instead provided offsetting federal payments to compensate for the lost equalization revenues.

Nevertheless the side deals almost immediately provoked widespread criticism. On the one hand, other 'have-not' provinces with resource-based revenue, such as Saskatchewan, immediately demanded the same type of bilateral deal. On the other hand, the 'have' province of Ontario, along with Quebec, immediately decried the side deals as subverting the entire purpose of the equalization program. Ontario Premier Dalton McGuinty demanded further federal funding for his province – the only one to have always been classified as a 'have' province – insisting there was a $23 billion 'gap' between what Ontario sent to Ottawa and what it received in federal payments. Martin initially dismissed McGuinty's claims as specious and based on erroneous calculations, a position supported by the vast majority of economists.[105] But he eventually gave in to the political pressure yet again, fearing an imminent federal election in which the Ontario Liberal machine would not be onside. By May 2005 Martin had reached an agreement to transfer an additional $5.75 billion to Ontario, ostensibly for a variety of specific programs, including immigration and labour market development. Although the prime minister described his settlement as fair and reasonable, McGuinty served notice that he viewed it as only a downpayment, with more provincial demands likely to surface after the next federal election.

Gomery Redux

While the various federal-provincial negotiations were taking place in the fall of 2004, Ottawa was continuing to be rocked by the sponsorship scandal. It soon became apparent that Paul Martin's plan to refer the Adscam scandal to a public inquiry, rather than waiting for the RCMP to conclude their criminal investigation, was indeed opening a Pandora's box as Francis Fox had feared. The Gomery hearings took on a life of their own and plagued the Martin government, which was unable to control the direction of the inquiry or limit its interpretation of its mandate, throughout the fall session. One unanticipated consequence was the public airing of vignettes from the internal party feuding between Martin and Chrétien supporters. These included the disputes over contracting guidelines between Public Works Minister David Dingwall and Finance Minister Paul Martin, and the accusations and counter-accusations by Chuck Guité, Warren Kinsella, and Terrie O'Leary concerning the role played by the finance minister's office in the awarding of contracts to the Earnscliffe Strategy Group. As both Tim Murphy and David Herle lamented on several occasions, every time the Martin government made a major policy announcement, it would be sideswiped by another Gomery revelation. Another unexpected shock came in early October with Justice Gomery's demand that the prime minister testify, likely in early February. This represented another precedent, but Martin immediately indicated that he would comply. 'I've always said it will be a pleasure ... I *want* to testify before the Gomery inquiry.'[106]

Before Martin could testify, however, former prime minister Jean Chrétien was scheduled to appear before the commission. Already known to be unhappy about Gomery's selection of former Mulroney adviser Bernard Roy as his chief counsel, Chrétien and several other witnesses became even more concerned by comments Justice Gomery made in an interview with the *National Post* in December, while the inquiry was in recess. For the judge to comment publicly in the middle of the proceedings was unusual, but the real problem stemmed from the nature of Gomery's remarks. Specifically, his comments appeared to suggest he had formed conclusions about the case long before the hearings were completed. Among other things, the judge referred to a key player who was under criminal investigation, former bureaucrat Chuck Guité, as a 'charming scamp,' and described the government's administration of the sponsorship program as 'catastrophically bad.' Lawyers representing Guité, Jean Pelletier, and Alfonso Gagliano all questioned the judge's objectivity in light of the comments, which Gomery defended, declaring 'my objectivity is the same as it always has been.'[107]

Jean Chrétien's lawyer, David Scott, finally tabled a twenty-five-page brief on 25 January demanding that Gomery step down. Scott argued Gomery's comments clearly suggested he had 'lost his objectivity.' Moreover, Scott protested that the judge had taken an 'adversarial' tone in talking about Chrétien, whose practice of presenting golf balls to visiting dignitaries was described by Gomery as 'small town cheap.' Gomery eventually admitted it had been a mistake to speak with the media, but he refused to step down. In the end the hearings continued even while Scott indicated he would consider taking the matter to the Federal Court.[108]

Jean Chrétien testified before the inquiry on 8 February 2005. There he aggressively defended the sponsorship program as 'necessary and right' in the fight against Quebec separatism and made it clear he believed the inquiry was a mistake. In stark contrast to the repeated apologies offered by his successor, the former prime minister made no concessions. Instead, he reiterated his earlier position that he knew nothing about the details of the program, and that those who had committed crimes would be punished, which was why he had called in the RCMP as soon as he learned of possible wrongdoing. Rejecting any notion that Martin had been in the dark about the sponsorship program, he asserted 'the Minister of Finance and I always agreed to set aside $50 million a year for expenditures related to national unity.' Near the end of his testimony Chrétien also took direct aim at Gomery, opening a briefcase and pulling out golf balls given to him by other heads of state and VIPs, including one from U.S. President Bill Clinton, whom he pointedly described as 'another small town boy.'

Chrétien's performance was viewed by his supporters and many in the media as a tour de force. Several MPs told the *Toronto Star* they felt he had 'saved the Liberal brand.' In national caucus the following day Martin said he 'loved Chrétien's performance.' Veteran journalist Larry Zolf summed up the irony of the situation well: 'It was a great day for Chrétien and for the Liberal Party,' he said. 'No better defence for the sponsorship fiasco will come from anyone else. Chrétien has revived the Liberal brand so effectively that it is possible for even Paul Martin to run under its banner.'[109]

Only two days later Paul Martin appeared before the inquiry, the first time a sitting prime minister had testified before any public inquiry since John A. Macdonald more than 130 years before. Although different in tone and content from Chrétien's testimony, Martin's performance was also viewed by most observers as highly successful. He delivered a wide-ranging and convincing explanation of the role he had played as finance minister, insisting he had no involvement in the sponsorship program. He also maintained he did not know that the program's budget came from the special unity fund Chrétien had mentioned. Yet Martin's success in distancing himself from the program came at a price. On numerous occasions, in direct reply to questions posed by Gomery, Martin declared that he had always been 'out of the loop' on anything to do with Quebec, thereby confirming the impression that Jean Chrétien had not trusted his finance minister's judgment on issues relating to national unity. Equally important were Martin's clearly implied views that the program – not the inquiry – had been a mistake, and that he blamed Chrétien for the entire scandal and saw himself as an innocent bystander.

Certainly Martin and his advisers had consistently attempted to convince Canadians that there were two different groups, the new Liberal team and the old. As one insider blatantly put it, 'the storyline was we versus them.' However, with the testimony throughout March and April by various ad agency executives (two of whom were facing criminal charges along with Chuck Guité), the Martin team's narrative collapsed. Or, as David Herle admitted, 'it blew up in our faces.'[110] First, it became increasingly clear that the scandal was not limited to one rogue public servant and a few private sector executives who personally benefited. There was growing evidence that the Quebec wing of the federal Liberal Party also had been involved in the scandal through a complicated kickback scheme, apparently organized by at least one former Chrétien organizer and prominent Quebec Liberal, Jacques Corriveau. As a result, the ongoing spectre of various Quebec party officials heatedly contradicting each other, based largely on whether they had been Chrétien or Martin supporters, meant the public was even less inclined to view the problem as Martin's advisers had hoped. Instead, more than ever the scandal was seen to be a Liberal issue and all Liberals were tarred with the same brush.

Martin subsequently redoubled efforts to establish himself as the man who cleaned up the mess. A lawsuit was launched by the government to recoup some $40 million in excess payments from private sector contractors, and a $750,000 trust fund was established by the Liberal Party of Canada to be used to repay the government if the Gomery Inquiry found the party had indeed received funds destined for the sponsorship program. Martin's televised address to the nation in late April, pleading for the inquiry to be allowed to complete its work and report, was yet another effort to reassert his image as someone who planned to 'get to the bottom of this.'

Yet as the hearings drew to a close in early June 2005, a major nationwide poll conducted for the Institute for Research on Public Policy (IRPP) showed that his efforts had been in vain. It concluded 'by a margin of two to one, Canadians are more likely to blame Mr. Martin – not Mr. Chrétien – as being solely responsible for the mess,' despite the fact the events took place while Chrétien was prime minister. Adding insult to injury, the poll's findings demonstrated two major reasons for the unexpected result. First, nearly 70 per cent of Canadians believed that Martin, as finance minister during that period, *should* have known about the funds channelled to Liberal-friendly ad firms, despite his comprehensive explanations as to why this was not so. Secondly, as SES-Research president Nik Nanos explained, 'by being proactive, Martin has taken ownership of the issue ... The impact of the Gomery inquiry on the public perception of Prime Minister Martin should give political leaders pause. It appears that the best of motives and a proactive open approach are no guarantee of gaining public confidence.'[111] Martin and his supporters argued this was a lose-lose situation which Martin had been handed. Other analysts and Liberal insiders suggested that, had there not been such serious and public infighting throughout the entire period, the results might have been different. As Peter

Donolo later commented, 'They never seemed to realize that other Liberals weren't the enemy.'[112]

Martin's Last Chance

Over the summer, with Justice Gomery retiring from public view to write his first report, the Martin Liberals had another opportunity to define their agenda and shift public opinion from scandal to policy matters. Why they were unable to do so is something which none of his senior advisers was able to explain, particularly given their exhaustive preparations before taking power. Even the selection of a new governor general proved to be a public relations problem for Martin, something which should have automatically been a good-news story. Instead, the August announcement that Michaëlle Jean would be the new governor general managed to become highly controversial and created another tempest in a teapot for the Martin government. Jean's loyalty to Canada came into question not only because of the dual citizenship acquired by virtue of her French husband, but also because of persistent rumours that she and her husband had supported the separatist cause in the last referendum. Martin and Jean herself took action to defuse the situation, but Martin's image was not helped by the explanation of his principal secretary, Hélène Scherrer, of the haphazard way in which Ms Jean was selected. 'Once [Mr Martin] was in love with the name and in love with the woman, he wanted her appointed as soon as possible,' she blithely told journalists. 'I remember one Friday morning while we were just informally discussing it with the senior staff. I think he watches Radio-Canada and had seen her on TV. It did not take long. I did not have to convince him. He said yes right away.' Then, on the following Monday, she said Martin asked her if Ms Jean had been approached about the job. 'I said, "No, I didn't think you were that serious on Friday," or that it was a rush. And he said, "Yes, I want you to see her." I said, "This is it?" And he said, "Yes it is. That's the one."'[113]

As one editorial concluded, luckily for Martin the general public was very supportive of Ms Jean's appointment. However, once again he received almost no credit for his inspired choice. Instead, 'the entire situation, to any political veteran, is taking on the appearance of a rushed decision, now being massaged in a massive damage control project to lesson any political fallout for the prime minister.'[114]

A few days later the entire Liberal caucus met in a special three-day retreat in Regina, ostensibly to prepare for the upcoming fall session of

Parliament. But there was no mention of any policy agenda. Instead, senior ministers and backbenchers were quoted extensively discussing only two topics: their reaction to the Gomery Inquiry and their need for a majority government to deliver on their commitments. Jean Lapierre, still designated as Martin's Quebec lieutenant, insisted that the worst was over in terms of Gomery revelations, and 'I'm not afraid' of the final report. 'It's not daily conversation any more,' he declared, 'and in Quebec it's like the end of a TV season ... we're just waiting for the new fall season now.'[115] His colleagues Reg Alcock of the Treasury Board and Belinda Stronach of HRDC were scheduled to make one of the few 'policy' presentations, outlining the changes introduced by the Liberal government to eliminate the bureaucratic problems that had led to the scandal.

Meanwhile Foreign Affairs Minister Pierre Pettigrew and Finance Minister Ralph Goodale told reporters that they were being hampered by the way the minority government was unfolding. Goodale argued 'it's not that minorities can't work, but this particular parliament has been especially "rancorous,"' while Pettigrew maintained that instead of being more responsive, the minority situation had made government less so. 'What Canadians have lived through under the leadership of Harper and Duceppe is politics, politics, politics,' he said. Both men argued voters should give the Liberals a majority to correct the situation, now that the backlash from Gomery had subsided.[116]

The following month the prime minister did attempt to lay the groundwork for some proactive Liberal policies in a much-heralded speech to senior public servants. On 20 September, Paul Martin delivered the 'vision' speech for which his supporters – and many Canadians – had been waiting. Written by Peter Nicholson and endlessly revised by the prime minister, in many respects it was a classic Martin speech. It surveyed the waterfront in terms of new and emerging policy ideas. It highlighted a number of key issues that would need to be addressed by Canadian policymakers, including the aging population, the emerging economic ascendancy of India and China, the new era of global terrorism, and the growing threat of climate change. It also targeted specific demographic (aboriginals and immigrants) and regional (the west and the north) concerns as important elements of the solution. Last but hardly least, it referred again to health care, childcare, and the cities agenda, and 'the need to give Canadians the tools they need to compete.' Then the prime minister concluded enthusiastically: 'That's the plan, both the long term goals and the priorities we'll be primarily focusing on this fall. That's what we're doing to address where we're going.' As for the public servants, 'Our job together is to get there,' he declared, citing 'the need to respond broadly, across government departments, to succeed.'[117]

For many the speech was a disappointment. There was no discernible 'plan' and no real indication of how the government intended to proceed. Many senior mandarins left the meeting mystified as to what this would mean for them and their specific responsibilities. 'I'm no further ahead than I was before,' one deputy was heard muttering as they left the room. Neither were the media. Columnist Jeffrey Simpson described Martin's speech as an attempt to 'filter his many priorities through a prism' and pull them all together. Instead, the prism 'came toward the end of a very, very long list of apparently equally urgent priorities. Depending on how you count such things, 20 to 25 previous policies were mentioned before Mr. Martin got around to the prism.'[118] Not surprisingly, the speech sank without a trace in official Ottawa.

The backlash re-emerged soon after when Gomery submitted his first report on 1 November 2005. Although he absolved both Martin and Chrétien of any personal responsibility for the scandal, making it clear that he did not believe either man knew anything about it, Gomery did attach indirect blame to Chrétien's office. He particularly faulted Chrétien's chief of staff, Jean Pelletier, for what he saw as the failure to insist the program be subject to the same accountability rules as other funding programs in government, and for their 'political interference' in awarding contracts.

The prime minister held a press conference the same day, appearing at the event flanked by his Quebec lieutenant, Jean Lapierre, and Public Works Minister Scott Brison. Martin's message was blunt. The report was 'troubling,' he said, but 'it needed to be written' so that Canadians would have faith in the system and in politicians. He admitted, 'when I first established this inquiry, I didn't know what the investigation would uncover.' Nevertheless, Martin said he accepted the findings of the report without question. Asked repeatedly whether that included the indirect blame attached to Chrétien and his advisers, the prime minister replied the report 'speaks for itself' and did not defend his predecessor. He pointed out that even before Gomery's findings he had taken decisive actions to correct the problem, including cancelling the program the day he took office.

Martin announced four new measures, namely: turning the matter over to the RCMP as Jean Chrétien had done, adding a dozen names to the list of individuals and companies the government was suing for recovery of funds, instructing affected crown corporations to take disciplinary action against any employees who participated in the scheme to transfer sponsorship money to other purposes, and, finally, requesting the Liberal Party of Canada to repay the government some $1.14 million (or nearly twice the $750,000 the party had already put aside in a trust fund for such an eventuality). In addition, he informed reporters that he had 'instructed' the party president to revoke the party membership of ten individuals named in the report, including Alfonso Gagliano and Jacques Corriveau. Finally, Martin reiterated that he would call an election thirty days after Gomery tabled his second report in late February. 'I will call a general election,' he promised, 'and Canadians will have an opportunity to pass judgement on my response to the facts about the sponsorship, on the reforms I've taken, and on the overall performance of the government I lead.'[119]

The fallout from the report was significant. It provided more ammunition to opposition parties and also rekindled the smouldering ashes of the Martin/Chrétien conflict. At Chrétien's press conference the same day, he flatly rejected Gomery's findings of blame, arguing the judge had either misunderstood or distorted the facts. He specifically questioned why the judge would accept the word of Chuck Guité, a man facing criminal charges, over that of Jean Pelletier, whom he described as a man of impeccable character. Chrétien also admitted he felt 'betrayed' by former supporters such as Jacques Corriveau, who had apparently taken advantage of their role in the party for personal gain. Chrétien's lawyer announced that he would challenge the report in Federal Court, arguing among other things that the judge was clearly biased, as evidenced by his hiring of Mulroney adviser Bernard Roy.[120]

A few days later Chrétien's former principal secretary, Eddie Goldenberg, publicly called on the Martin forces to call a halt, a plea which was rejected with disdain by PMO adviser Scott Reid. Martin's former leadership opponent, Sheila Copps, also came to Chrétien's defence. 'Why rush to exonerate Martin and blame Chrétien?' she wrote in an initial column about the report. 'Could it be the allegations leveled by the former prime minister against Gomery are true? Why *did* he hire Bernard Roy as his chief legal counsel?'[121] Copps also pointed out the obvious when she noted that Martin had been flanked by a former separatist and a former Conservative at his press conference, sending an even more confusing message to Liberal grassroots members about party loyalty. In another column, she made a crucial point about the state of the party: 'As the current prime minister hangs the former prime minister out to dry, Liberals find themselves caught in the middle. Their loyalties are torn.' Noting that Martin's move to expel party members ignored the same due process he was asking Canadians to respect by waiting for Gomery's final report, Copps argued Martin was adding insult to injury. And, having claimed in the past that he had no authority over party membership, she asked: 'How, then, does he suddenly have the authority to expel ten members in good standing?'[122] This second point was underlined by none other than Jean Chrétien, who responded to reporters' questions on Martin's move by commenting that he never thought he had the power as leader, or he might have used it to remove other members he felt were troublesome, such as Jean Lapierre.

Former Conservative pollster Allan Gregg put the entire exercise into context. In an opinion piece the following day he wrote: 'After 14 months of hearings, and a budget of $32 million ... it is now clear that the full sum of public funds that could possibly have been put to illegitimate or illegal ends adds up to an average of $6.3 million per year for the nine years in question.' As Gregg pointed out, 'in the end – considering the federal government manages $200 billion of taxpayers' money every year – this scandal accounts for .0003 per cent of the total ... The fact is that our governments manage our tax dollars with the utmost of professionalism and that systems of compliance, control and audit are more stringent than any private-sector enterprise.'[123] Gregg also reiterated the argument made by many of Chrétien's supporters that the exercise had produced a perverse and unintended consequence, namely the vilification of all party officials, politicians, and public servants as incompetent or corrupt.

Certainly the opposition parties were quick to continue their attack on Liberal politicians. Jack Layton initially indicated he would not force an election, hoping instead to win more concessions from the government on issues such as health care. Both the other opposition leaders made it clear they felt the days of the minority Parliament were numbered. Bloc leader Gilles Duceppe was forthright about his intentions: 'They no longer have the moral authority to govern,' he told reporters. Stephen Harper stopped short of calling immediately for an election, but came close: 'I can't think of any other parliamentary democracy where a scandal of this magnitude and of this nature ... could pass without the fall of the government,' he said. In little more than three weeks, this would translate into a non-confidence motion that called for the government to resign.[124]

The Fall

An SES Research poll published on 31 October, the day before Gomery's report was released, had provided both good and bad news for the Liberals. On a positive note, the party was in majority territory with the backing of 40 per cent of decided voters, as opposed to only 28 per cent for the Conservatives and 15 per cent for the New Democrats. On the negative side, nearly 20 per cent of voters indicated they would remain undecided until the final Gomery report was released. Evidently the Conservatives felt this was encouraging news for them. 'There's room for us [to grow],' Tory MP John Williams told reporters. 'This demonstrates the government is still vulnerable, and rightly so, on what happened in the sponsorship scandal.'[125]

Gomery's hard-hitting criticism of various Liberals was made public on 1 November, and it soon became apparent the Conservatives saw this as their best chance to bring down the Martin government. The Bloc, meanwhile, saw this as an opportunity to come back from the brink of oblivion. Support for sovereignty had fallen to its lowest level in thirty years by the time Jean Chrétien left office, but thanks to the Gomery debacle the Bloc now enjoyed the support of some 60 per cent of Quebeckers, compared with only 29 per cent for the Liberals. Both Harper and Duceppe now indicated they wanted to pull the plug on the minority Parliament right away. Harper went so far as to put the onus on Jack Layton to agree with them immediately in order to have the election before Christmas.

The NDP, on the other hand – without whom the other two opposition parties could not bring down the government – saw this as an ideal chance to extract more concessions from the Martin Liberals. Jack Layton had already met privately with Martin on 25 October to discuss health care. Layton had left the meeting describing Martin as 'in denial' about the extent to which private health care alternatives were being created across the country, despite the prime minister's $41 billion solution. On 2 November, Layton called on the prime minister to adopt several measures proposed by the NDP in exchange for his party's ongoing support. Among these measures was a declaration that the federal government would not allow health care to be 'privatized.' Although Martin's team prepared a package of options for Layton to consider, he rejected them a few days later, saying they fell far short of his demands. Layton also warned the government he would not support them on any non-confidence motions in future. By then, however, it was too late to call an election which would be concluded before Christmas, and all three opposition leaders were leery of being held responsible for a campaign that would take place over the holidays.

As an alternative, on 12 November the three leaders demanded that Martin agree to call an election in January, even though the final Gomery report was not due to be released until early February. Martin categorically refused, saying he had already promised Canadians he would call an election in February. Behind the scenes, his advisers were optimistic. They had the polling numbers. They had public opinion on their side about waiting for the report. And they would not be the ones to force a Christmas election. Apart from their problems in Quebec, which they realized were serious, they believed the prospects of a Liberal majority were quite good. And, as Tim Murphy later noted, 'we had already lasted longer than most minority governments. We couldn't expect to hold on much longer, and having the election *before* the second Gomery report came out was looking more and more like a good idea.'[126]

As a result, the Martin team began to plan for what they now saw as an inevitable holiday election. On 14 November, when Finance Minister Ralph Goodale released the traditional fall economic update, the document included new initiatives such as an increase in spending on post-secondary education and a massive $30 billion tax cut. These measures would not normally have been found in an update, but Goodale argued they were the result of the 'unexpected' massive surplus. The opposition, meanwhile, accused him of underestimating the surplus deliberately and of offering pre-election bribes to electors.

Two days later, Stephen Harper announced that all three opposition parties had agreed to introduce a non-confidence motion in the House on 24 November, forcing an election campaign over the holidays. 'The agreement is that if the prime minister has not clearly agreed … to call the election in January, then a non-confidence motion will go ahead on Thursday November 24.' But on 21 November, the NDP introduced a different motion, calling on the government to dissolve Parliament in January for a 13 February vote, which would be after the release of the second Gomery report. This motion, supported by the other two opposition parties, passed by a vote of 167–129. At the time, Layton said he felt this 'compromise' was a good idea, since it would not only allow the second report to be released in advance, but prevent the campaign from taking place over the holidays.

The Martin government immediately said it would ignore the non-binding motion. 'It's not really a compromise,' House leader Tony

Valeri told reporters, because Martin would still have to call the election in January and the vote would come only a week or so after the release of the second Gomery report, rather than in late February or early March as he had planned. Valeri, who appeared confident and feisty, suggested 'the leader of the NDP is so fearful of the fact that so many people have come out and said there is absolutely nothing wrong' with the prime minister's timetable, 'he's attempting to backtrack because he's afraid.'[127]

In the meantime the Liberals began to make major spending announcements in a campaign-style swing by ministers across the country. They included $46 million in aid to the auto industry, $920 million for immigrant reception programs in Ontario, and nearly $15 million for redress measures for Chinese head tax victims and Italian Canadians interned during the Second World War. Other seemingly random funding announcements included money for farmers, the softwood lumber industry, victims of residential schools, and the military. One estimate put the total at nearly one-seventh of the government's total budget, and a Liberal cabinet minister was heard joking in the Government Lobby, 'I hope they defeat us soon. The country can't afford us.'[128]

Then on 23 November Ralph Goodale made a surprise announcement about the tax implications of income trusts, a long-standing concern of the pension industry. After months of intense speculation as to the government's likely approach, Goodale stated that 'given the uncertainty surrounding how long this session of Parliament will last, as well as the need for greater certainty and stability in the income trust market, there is a clear case for immediate action.'[129]

The election mania gripping Ottawa in light of these announcements soon spread to the rest of the country. In an unexpected twist, Alberta Premier Ralph Klein boosted Liberal morale when he told journalists in Halifax, where he was on a speaking tour of eastern Canada, that he thought the likely outcome of a federal election would be another Liberal minority. 'It's a damn shame,' Klein said. 'Maybe the Conservatives might make some gains, but unfortunately I don't think they're going to do well in Ontario.' Making matters worse, he concluded that Stephen Harper was 'a bright, articulate individual but he's perhaps seen as too much on the right.'[130]

Undeterred by this friendly fire, the Conservatives tabled a non-confidence motion the next day condemning the government for its 'culture of entitlement,' its 'arrogance' and 'corruption.' Harper tabled his motion saying: 'This is not just the end of a tired, directionless scandal-plagued government, it's the start of a new future for this great country.' Jack Layton, by contrast, sought to place the blame for the election on the Liberals, not the NDP, knowing his party could have propped the government up if he had wanted to. 'As a result of the stubbornness of the Liberals and the inflexibility we've seen,' he declared, 'we will be starting an election campaign tomorrow.' Paul Martin, in an upbeat mood given polls which now showed his party at 35 per cent compared with 30 per cent for the Conservatives, told his caucus: 'Stephen Harper sees no positive role for government, not in improving the lives of Canadians, not even in standing up for Canada.'[131]

In the end the vote on the non-confidence motion passed easily on Monday, 28 November, marking the first time ever that a minority government had fallen on a straight non-confidence motion unconnected to a money bill, Throne Speech, or major piece of legislation. The following day Martin visited the governor general and emerged to announce the election would take place some fifty-six days later, on 23 January. Canadians were faced with the prospect of an election campaign that would span the holidays, and a rare vote in the dead of winter. The parties were faced with the prospect of another minority government, with some 70 per cent of Canadians telling pollsters they believed the result of the election would be a House of Commons that looked almost identical to the one that had just been dissolved.

15   Back to the Wilderness

It's too bad, but the Liberals simply need to go stand in the corner for a while.

> – a former Liberal voter[1]

During the caucus retreat in Regina in August 2005, David Herle declared, 'Either we win a majority or we could lose entirely.'[2] At the time, he made it clear he thought the odds were good the Liberals would win. Certainly nothing in their preparations for the next election suggested the Martin team felt they needed to change course dramatically. In fact, their plans for the next election closely resembled those in 2004.

In fairness to Herle and his team, the polls leading up to the 2006 election consistently suggested he was right. Virtually none of them foresaw a significant change in the parties' standings. Instead, the polling data predicted the real question was whether Martin would be able to move from a minority to a majority. On that, opinion was divided.[3]

Unfortunately for the Liberals, the ground beneath their feet was shifting rapidly. Many of the advantages they would normally have been able to rely on going into an election were no longer there. To begin with, it was embarrassingly obvious the party's reputation for competence and trustworthiness had been compromised by the Gomery affair. The Liberals' leader, once seen as untouchable, now clearly had feet of clay. And although Stephen Harper seemed to be an even greater handicap to his party, Martin's approval ratings were falling fast.

Then, too, the Martin Liberals were not expected to play the national unity card. It was an issue that badly divided the party, and it was thought they would avoid it entirely if they could. With their difficulties

in Quebec over Gomery, a decision to downplay what had traditionally been their party's greatest strength was seen by many as merely
prudent. As one insider later noted, 'we had enough trouble recruiting
workers in Quebec. The last thing we needed was more trouble over
Martin's views on federalism.' Indeed, it was widely rumoured in Liberal circles that Marc Lalonde had agreed to serve as an election adviser
only if Martin avoided the term 'asymmetrical federalism.'

Not surprisingly, then, the Liberals' primary strategy for the election
was to highlight the one remaining traditional Liberal strength, namely
their perceived status as the party most in tune with Canadian values.
On the one hand, they would focus on what they saw as Paul Martin's
successes in health care, childcare, and aboriginal peoples. On the other
hand, they would focus on Steven Harper's perceived distance from
mainstream values and his lack of commitment to the social programs
Canadians cherished. Once again, the plan was to demonstrate that
Harper and the Conservatives were simply too extreme to be trusted
with the reins of power.

Taking to heart the criticism of their 2004 campaign, the Martin team
also planned to highlight their economic record. Their good-news story
would be the prolonged economic prosperity Paul Martin had engineered for Canadians as finance minister, while their warning to voters
would be that Martin's recent progress on his social policy initiatives
would be endangered if people chose Stephen Harper's neoconserva-
tive agenda. This message was particularly important in Quebec, where
the values card was to be played to counter Stephen Harper's plan to
discredit the Liberals through accusations of corruption and arrogance
in the Gomery affair.

In this context, it might have been expected the Liberal platform
would play a crucial role. Yet the drafting of the 2006 platform was a
disjointed and ultimately chaotic process that did nothing to help the
Liberals' image in the election. In fact, although it was originally ready
shortly after the writ was dropped, the party's centrepiece only appeared late in the campaign and many Canadians never knew it existed.

The Top-Down Platform

If more evidence were needed to demonstrate the growing concentration of power at the centre under Paul Martin, the evolution of the 2006
platform was surely a case in point.[4] In the PMO, Peter Nicholson was
beavering away at a draft document almost from the moment the previ-

ous election came to an end. His work on the 2004 Throne Speech and the prime minister's February 2005 budget speech, followed by the 'vision' speech to senior public servants in September 2005, was all directed towards that end. Yet those very efforts prevented him from turning his attention to the actual platform document until late October. 'At the point, there was really no time to consult anyone,' Nicholson said later.[5]

And almost no one *was* consulted. Certainly not the extra-parliamentary wing. As for the caucus, or even cabinet ministers, the PMO's request for their input was purely pro forma. The much-hyped plans to eliminate the so-called democratic deficit did not extend, it seemed, to the party's platform. Graphic evidence of the lack of consultation emerged on 19 October when one minister told his staff he had just learned in regional caucus that the deadline for submission of platform recommendations was the same day. 'I'm not sure what the process is for this, or whether the regional chair is supposed to assemble them or what,' he told his floored policy adviser.

Nevertheless Nicholson produced what many Liberal insiders considered to be his best effort. 'Securing Canada's Success' contained the same type of carefully planned and clearly laid out policy options for which the Liberals had become known since 1993. Like its predecessors, it was also fully costed. Silently jettisoning the white cover of 2004, and with the Liberal logo far more prominently displayed this time, the 2006 platform document returned to the familiar Red Book format.

The document was divided into five parts and covered much of the material raised by Martin in his September speech to public servants, which in retrospect appeared to have been a dress rehearsal for the election.

A first section, 'Meeting Canada's Demographic Challenge,' addressed policies related to seniors, health care, aboriginals, and immigrants. 'Succeeding in a New World of Giants' covered the education, research, trade, and cities issues flowing from the emergence of new international economic powers like China and India. Then the section on economic growth and prosperity reiterated the personal income tax cuts promised in Ralph Goodale's economic update, and a fourth section on 'Accountable and Efficient Government' underlined the number of concrete measures taken by Martin in response to the Gomery Report. Finally, a section on 'The Canada We Want' spoke to the values issue while addressing crime-prevention, environmental, and cultural policies.

As political scientist Stephen Clarkson commented, technically it was one of the very few strengths of an otherwise disastrous Liberal campaign. 'Securing Canada's Success' was, in Clarkson's view, a 'comprehensive document that highlighted the Liberals' record of achievement and presented a strong vision for the future.'[6] Nevertheless the bulk of the national media would go on to criticize the document for being a rehash of many already announced government policies.

However, the main problem with the Liberals' platform was that it was invisible. Peter Nicholson hastened to point out that 'it was ready and could have been released in mid-December.' According to Nicholson, there was a clash between those like himself who considered a platform to be essential to the campaign, and those who argued it might be unnecessary. 'The "brain trust" didn't believe a policy platform was important,' Nicholson recalled. 'They felt we needed something more mainstreet, what they called "retail" policies. So no one in the campaign paid any attention to it.'[7]

While the platform waited to be released it was vulnerable to endless tinkering. As the pre-Christmas segment of the campaign unfolded, it became increasingly clear that Stephen Harper's Conservatives were making inroads with Canadians by announcing a large number of their own 'retail' policy initiatives. Consequently the platform fell victim to 'emergency' planks, most of which were added in direct response to Conservative announcements. Devised on the fly, sometimes overnight, they ranged from eliminating the immigrant landing fee, allocating infrastructure funds for sports facilities and the purchase of icebreakers, to additional measures for seniors and housing. As one disenchanted insider observed, 'they [the Board] really didn't understand the discipline of policy-making, and they were often ready to make changes based solely on focus groups.' Another lamented 'the platform grew from a manageable size to some 85 pages; a manageable number of priorities soon became unmanageable and the platform became a phonebook.'[8]

Déjà Vu: The Martin Campaign Team and Election Strategy

While the platform expanded, the team in charge of the campaign grew smaller. Paul Martin stuck to his guns and insisted David Herle and John Webster would again be his campaign co-chairs. In addition, Herle would once again double as the campaign pollster. The small group around Herle and Webster was even more closely knit than before. Terrie O'Leary and Tim Murphy once again were key players on the leader's tour, along with Senator Francis Fox and party president

Mike Eizenga. Scott Reid as communications director was also part of the tour team, and, as in 2004, he was the chief spokesperson for the campaign on the ground, aided on occasion by John Duffy. This doubling up on communications functions, like the polling situation, was repeated from 2004 even though that, too, had been problematic. The Red Leaf advertising team under Jack Fleischman of ROB TV in Toronto was also the same. Even the campaign slogan, 'Choose Your Canada,' was resurrected from 2004.

One significant change occurred on the ground, where Karl Littler took on the role of national campaign director, replacing Michelle Cadario. This represented a somewhat surprising promotion for Littler, whose strategy of having Liberal cabinet ministers accost Stephen Harper during the 2004 election was widely seen to have backfired. On a more positive note it did mark a return to the traditional approach of separating the positions of campaign director and national director of the party. In 2004, Michelle Cadario had served in both capacities. This time her successor as the party's national director, Steven MacKinnon, was on the plane with the leader while Littler chaired the daily campaign meetings on the ground.

Otherwise little had changed. Cyrus Reporter again ran the war room, Kevin Bosch coordinated the Bureau's efforts, and Scott Feschuk wrote the leader's speeches. Regionally, Mark Marissen was again in charge of BC, Jean Lapierre incredibly was still in command in Quebec, and in Ontario – due to Littler's promotion – former Turner staffer and Earnscliffe lobbyist Charles Bird was now the provincial chair.

In short, no Chrétien veterans were involved in the day-to-day operations of the campaign, and virtually no one outside the tightly scripted group of longtime Martin supporters was being asked for advice. To prevent the damaging leaks that occurred during the 2004 campaign, even national conference calls were eliminated. Many of Martin's grassroots supporters were disenchanted with his handling of the reins of power and were planning to sit out the campaign entirely, and even the Young Liberals, a traditional source of support for Martin, had been marginalized from the campaign organization. Worse still, a significant group of the party's elites were hoping to lose the election in order to change leaders. As one observer put it, 'Many actually wanted what they called the Martin Party to lose because it had gone astray and needed to be put out of its misery so that the real Liberal Party could rebuild itself.'[9]

Although Martin's advisers insisted they had wanted to stay in power and 'in no way engineered our own defeat in Parliament,' the team's strategy for the campaign was set well in advance. They called an unusually long eight-week election, assuming most of the action would take place after the holidays. According to David Herle, they also assumed the longer the campaign lasted the more likely it would be that Stephen Harper, whom they viewed as one of their best assets, would self-destruct. 'We were ahead by roughly eight points at the start of the campaign and we saw no cause to change tactics, especially with Harper.'[10]

The Liberal campaign was to be divided into three separate segments: the four-week period before Christmas, when only an advertising campaign or 'air war' was contemplated; the week of the holiday break, when nothing was scheduled by mutual consent with the other parties; and the three-week post-Christmas period, in which most of the heavy lifting would be done. Not until after Christmas would the Liberals release their platform or schedule the major leader's tour events, since they were convinced few Canadians would be paying attention to the campaign until then. For the same reason, a second set of leaders' debates was scheduled in January.

The Liberal platform may not have been considered important, but both Herle and Webster were counting on their 'retail' items to highlight Harper's extremism. This would prove to be a significant challenge for the Liberals once they began what they saw as 'the real election' after the holidays, since the Conservatives had taken a completely different tack and decided to release substantive policy announcements from the very beginning. Hardly 'liberal' in tone or tenor, their planks nevertheless looked far more reasonable than the Liberal strategists had ever imagined. Moreover, Harper was not the man he had been in 2004. He was increasingly successful in presenting himself as calm and rational, rather than a dangerous, wild-eyed radical. The Liberal campaign team was ill-prepared to make significant changes to their strategy to accommodate these surprising developments, some of which David Herle insisted did not register in their polling until well after the Christmas break.[11]

Early Setbacks

Only two days after his government fell and the winter election began, Paul Martin was campaigning in Quebec, the one place the Liberals were prepared to spend time before Christmas, since they still believed they could make gains at the expense of the Bloc. But whatever the Liberal leader had been planning to say was quickly lost in the media feeding frenzy over reports his predecessor, Jean Chrétien, had just launched a challenge to the Gomery Report in Federal Court. Chrétien's lawyers said the timing was a coincidence, but journalists covering Martin's campaign bombarded him with questions about the challenge. The thirty-page document pulled few punches, claiming Gomery's findings were 'erroneous, perverse, capricious and ... completely contrary to the uncontested evidence.'[12] Martin had little choice but to defend the report he had commissioned, and whose recommendations he had only recently accepted in full. 'It is clear enough that we are backing Justice Gomery's report and his conclusions,' Martin stated repeatedly. 'Mr. Gomery spent a lot of time working on this inquiry. He read all the documents, he was there six days a week ... We back what he found.'[13] The upshot was that Martin found himself discussing the one topic he had hoped to avoid at his campaign launch, and in the province where he least wanted it to be raised.

In this first segment of the campaign, the Liberals' strategy had been to highlight their economic good-news story. Martin expected to deliver a strong defence of his fiscal record that reminded Canadians 'you never had it so good.'[14] Unfortunately, the time for this strategy had passed. Economic issues, no doubt because of the Liberals' very success in managing them, now ranked low on the list of voters' concerns.

The Liberals' inability to define the key issues of the election – and their lack of overarching 'vision' or election theme – could also be seen in their ad campaign. In the first four weeks of the campaign, they aired only five ads compared with the Conservatives' fourteen. Three of them focused on the economic good-news story that fewer than 10 per cent of Canadians were now interested in. Then Stephen Harper raised the bar by promising to cut the hugely unpopular GST by 2 per cent, a move which *did* catch the attention of the ordinary voter. In response, Paul Martin and Ralph Goodale could only repeat their pre-election commitment to lower personal income tax. While this was sound economics, it was a much more difficult sell than Harper's simplistic offer.

In short order, Stephen Harper seized control of the campaign agenda and kept it for the first four weeks, making an announcement almost every day while the Liberals simply waited for the Christmas break. As columnist Jeffrey Simpson pointed out, the Conservatives' 'Gainesburger' approach to policy announcements was in sharp contrast to the Liberals' comprehensive Red Book approach, which had become the gold standard. But the Red Book was nowhere in sight. Few journalists questioned the costs or details of each new Conservative announcement, and Harper was never forced to answer difficult questions about the promises.[15]

Harper also tackled the Liberals' strategy to demonize his values on the first day of the campaign when he announced he would hold a free vote on the same-sex marriage issue. This was largely because his party's opposition to the legislation had been used by the Liberals in the last campaign to make their case about the 'dangerous' new Conservatives. Although some believed Harper had made a tactical error by referring to the issue at all, it soon became clear that he had actually scored a direct hit on the Liberals. Not only had he put the issue to rest at the start of the campaign, but his promise merely to hold a free vote (as virtually all observers were quick to point out) meant that the plans of the social conservatives in his caucus to undo the legislation had virtually no chance of success.

Harper's next step was to demonstrate that Conservatives could have social policies too. Although his initiatives were grounded in different values, in many cases his more modest and often simplistic proposals were also more easily understood by ordinary Canadians. Instead of Paul Martin's huge transfer payments to the provinces to 'fix health care for a generation,' Harper promised a 'patient wait time guarantee.' Instead of an $11 billion national childcare program, he offered $1 billion in childcare tax credits directly to families. His success was reinforced by Martin adviser Scott Reid's comment on national television that Harper's 'paltry' childcare proposal – which was estimated to provide families with less than $25 per week – would likely be spent by parents 'on beer and popcorn.' This time it was the Conservatives who were quick to seize on a Liberal mistake. Reid promptly apologized, but Canadians remembered Tory MP Rona Ambrose's outraged response that Reid's remarks were 'offensive' and demonstrated the Liberals 'don't trust people with their own money. They don't trust Canadians to do what is best for their children.'[16]

Playing the National Unity Card, Part 1

Evidently rattled by Harper's progress in defusing the Liberals' values issue, Paul Martin suddenly abandoned that strategy during his Quebec tour. On 2 December he made a remarkable statement on the national unity front, the very area he had been expected to avoid. Noting that Bloc leader Gilles Duceppe and the new provincial PQ leader, André Boisclair, had agreed to pursue the sovereignty option as quickly as possible, Martin declared: 'This is really a referendum election, certainly according to the duo of Duceppe and Boisclair ... We will fight to defend Canada. The battle begins now.'[17]

Veteran Liberals questioned the sudden shift in strategy. For one thing, only 3 per cent of Quebeckers and 2 per cent of Canadians had identified the national unity issue as an important issue in the election. For another, a recent Léger poll had indicated some two-thirds of Quebeckers 'had put the Gomery report behind them and might be open to what the Liberals had to say,'[18] suggesting the values card might have been effective. Some reporters dubbed Martin 'Captain Canada' after the remarks, but not everyone was impressed. The *Toronto Star* actually published a highly critical editorial on 3 December, accusing Martin of playing with fire for political ends and concluding, 'Let's not drown out Santa's sleigh bells with apocalyptic talk of national ruin if the Liberals lose big. Politicians' futures may be riding on this election, Canada's is not.'

Then Gilles Duceppe put the cat among the pigeons by releasing an old tape of Martin's Quebec lieutenant, Jean Lapierre, speaking at a large separatist rally enthusiastically telling militants how to defeat the federalists. Duceppe's ploy appeared to energize Martin. In the first English-language debate, held in Vancouver on 15 December, Martin gave a passionate defence of Canada that was well received by viewers. Then he added, 'I'm ready to meet him (Duceppe) on every street corner, in every city and every town and village in Quebec' to debate the merits of Canadian federalism. But when Duceppe rapidly accepted Martin's offer, the prime minister demurred. His handlers later described the challenge as a figure of speech, and insisted that there would be plenty of opportunity for a rematch between the two men in January. Paul Wells of *Maclean's* described the move as an ignominious retreat. 'That vanishing dot in the distance? That would be the PM's butt.'[19]

On 19 December, Stephen Harper stepped into the breach and offered to debate Duceppe himself when he released his party's platform for Quebec. Its purpose was patently obvious: to replace the Liberals as *the* federalist alternative in Quebec. The Liberals had admittedly lost some of their cachet as the party of national unity. But, as the Léger poll had demonstrated, this was a temporary setback courtesy of the Gomery affair. Until then they remained the only credible federalist option in Quebec, even if their halo had been tarnished. Certainly there was no evidence the Tories had made inroads in the same province that had been barren ground for them since 1993.

Harper's plan changed all that. His bold announcement that he supported a new decentralist version of federalism, which he called 'open federalism,' was accompanied by cleverly targeted criticism of the Liberal Party as 'paternalistic and arrogant' while the Bloc was described as 'blindly obstructionist and sterile.'[20] His offer to allow the government of Quebec to attend international fora such as UNESCO, and his declaration that there was indeed a fiscal imbalance between Ottawa and the provinces which he would remedy, turned the tables on the Martin Liberals overnight. In one fell swoop he had beaten them at their own game of appealing to soft nationalists, just as Brian Mulroney had done in 1984 when he assumed the federalist mantle after John Turner stumbled.

In Quebec, the implications of Harper's move were seen immediately. Veteran *La Presse* journalist Alain Dubuc concluded, 'Harper's articulation of his vision of Canada has ended the Liberals' monopoly on national unity by proposing a credible alternative.'[21] Both Liberal Premier Jean Charest and Action Démocratique leader Mario Dumont were quick to welcome Harper's moves. Dumont actively threw his support to Harper and Charest played a coy game of indirect support, reminiscent of Robert Bourassa's treatment of John Turner. Harper finished by suggesting the Liberals were actually hoping for a separatist win in the next Quebec election, an accusation which left a furious Martin demanding an apology and many Canadians wondering.

The Catastrophic Christmas Break

For the Martin camp the holidays could not come soon enough. Tim Murphy recalled there was already 'a nagging feeling we were losing ground,'[22] although their polling repeatedly suggested there had been very little movement in voter intentions over the first four weeks of the campaign. No one was prepared for the events that took place during the one-week break and arguably changed the course of the campaign. As Pammett and Dornan note, in that one week 'the Liberals and Conservatives more or less reversed places in party standings and they maintained those positions, with minor ebbs and flows, up to the final result.'[23]

On Boxing Day a teenaged girl was accidentally killed in the crossfire during a gang-related shooting in downtown Toronto. Coincidentally, the Martin Liberals had already unveiled a crime prevention plan in one of their few concrete initiatives during the early part of the campaign. The package had received good coverage and enthusiastic support from both the premier of Ontario and the mayor of Toronto. As a result, the Liberals felt they were well positioned in the aftermath of the nationally reported tragedy and at first did nothing more. But the Harper Conservatives seized the opportunity to emphasize their extensive law and order platform, and in particular their plan to crack down on violent crime. More importantly, they accused the Liberals of being 'soft on crime.' In the days immediately following the tragedy, when public attention and sentiment were running high, this approach garnered considerable support for the Conservatives in Ontario and across the country.

Among the many punitive measures proposed by Harper was an expanded minimum mandatory sentence for crimes in which a gun was involved. Rather than pointing out that Canada already had such a minimum sentence, Martin and his team appeared to give in to this public pressure. They eventually introduced their own new proposal to *increase* the minimum mandatory sentence. This seeming capitulation only served to weaken the prime ministerial image of the leader and erode the party's reputation for moderation.

Three days later, in a highly controversial move, the RCMP announced it had launched a criminal investigation into leaked information and insider trading connected with the finance minister's November announcement on income trusts. Responding to a complaint from NDP MP Judy Wasylycia-Leis, the Mounties actually issued a press release saying they had decided to undertake an immediate criminal investigation 'into a possible breach of security or illegal transfer of information … due to the seriousness of the situation.' In a bizarre twist, they also took the unusual step of emphasizing 'at this time there is no evidence of wrongdoing or illegal activity on the part of anyone associated to this investigation, including the Minister of Finance, Ralph Goodale.'[24] (It later transpired the decision to include Mr Goodale's name in the press release had been the personal decision of Commissioner Giuliano Zaccardelli and was 'not in keeping with past practice' according to the report on the RCMP's actions released by the chair of public complaints, Paul Kennedy, nearly a year after the election. The report also noted Zaccardelli had refused to provide any statement of explanation to the committee. Moreover, Kennedy concluded the RCMP moves had a 'direct impact' on the election results.) The motives behind the RCMP's extraordinary behaviour continued to be debated long after the election was over, with many observers suggesting political considerations could have played a part, although Kennedy found no evidence to either support or reject that thesis.[25]

This explosive development caused consternation in Liberal ranks. David Herle pointed out the RCMP had not merely sent a letter to Wasylycia-Leis announcing the investigation, they also had faxed a copy to her campaign office when they realized the original letter had been sent to her parliamentary office, where she would be unlikely to see it in the middle of an election campaign. The stated reason for their actions was to alert her to the fact that the 'review' they had promised had now been upgraded to a criminal investigation. As a former solicitor general, Francis Fox believed the entire procedure followed by the RCMP in this instance was unprecedented. 'Normally, even if they were asked, they would simply respond that they could neither confirm nor deny that an investigation was taking place,' Fox commented.[26]

Both Goodale and Martin immediately responded to the implied accusations by indicating they themselves were blameless and were convinced nothing untoward had taken place. Goodale referred to his lengthy unimpeached record of public service, and Martin defended his finance minister as a man of 'impeccable character and integrity.' All to no avail. The NDP and the Conservatives called for Goodale's resignation, and the media went into overdrive. By 5 January the Liberals took the extraordinary step of announcing that Paul Martin would take no more questions on the income trust matter. 'I am not going to be responding to questions on a daily basis to an investigation ... that's being handled by the RCMP,' he declared in Vancouver.[27]

The intensity of public reaction to the accusations was undoubtedly heightened by the fact that the sponsorship scandal was still fresh in everyone's minds. Then there were Paul Martin's many promises to ensure open, transparent, and accountable government. As journalist John Ibbitson concluded, the new accusations were being seen as only the latest in a lengthy list of apparent Liberal transgressions. 'How many times can the Liberal Party ask us to suspend judgment on its moral worth?' Ibbitson asked. 'The most the Liberals can hope for now is that this is as bad as it gets.'[28] This was wishful thinking. Two separate polls by SES and the Strategic Counsel between 22 December and 5 January found support for the Liberals had fallen at least 7 percentage points, to 29 per cent, while the Conservatives had risen from 30 to 38 per cent. Another poll found Paul Martin's leadership rating had fallen an incredible 20 points, from 88 per cent to 68 per cent.[29] Most ominous was a Strategic Counsel poll of 3 January which revealed fully 34 per cent of Canadians believed the Conservatives now had the momentum, compared with only 23 per cent who picked the Liberals. These numbers represented an exact reversal from five days earlier and spelled the beginning of the end for the Martin Liberals.

A Perfect Storm

The first week back in action after the Christmas break was intended to be a showcase for Liberal policies. But the fate of Paul Martin's first platform announcement demonstrated only too clearly how far the mighty Liberals had fallen. On 5 January, Martin's announcement of a key social policy plank – a multi-billion-dollar post-secondary education package – was plagued with organizational problems, including a lengthy delay. In addition, Martin had offered an apology for the Chinese head tax the previous day in Vancouver, something both he and his minister, Raymond Chan, had steadfastly refused to do for months. Journalists accompanying the leader's tour had not been apprised, and they were livid. Taken together, the predictable result of these gaffes was that Martin's plank was lost in the wash. Hardly any mention was made of the Liberals' education policy the next day, while the Tories garnered front-page headlines for their 'tough on crime' package.

Nevertheless Martin made a valiant attempt to appear upbeat. He declared he was happy with the direction the campaign was taking to date and remained confident.[30] And in fact his next two announcements – on caregiver benefits for the disabled (7 January) and a massive $1 billion water clean-up package for the Great Lakes and St Lawrence River (8 January) were generally well received by experts. So was his robust criticism of Conservative spending promises to date (9 January), which he argued would throw the federal government back into a deficit situation. Martin was backed up by his beleaguered finance minister, who argued the cost of the promises to that point would mean a huge deficit unless 'something else gives. It's either tax increases on one side or program cuts on the other ... So I think it's important, before people buy a pig in a poke, to ask the specific question "Which is it? And how much?"'[31]

But the Liberals' rollout of policy announcements was soon interrupted by another crisis. A new book levelled more accusations of Liberal corruption and incompetence. It claimed the federal government had been involved in financing the activities of a group called Option Canada, which had championed the NO side during the referendum campaign. According to allegations contained in the book, Option Canada had secretly received several million dollars from the federal Heritage Department, none of which had been included in the final tally of NO side expenditures. The authors claimed a close aide to Paul Martin, Claude Dauphin, had been in charge of Option Canada. Not surprisingly, *The Secrets of Option Quebec* became an overnight cause célèbre in Quebec.

As Paul Martin's Quebec lieutenant, Jean Lapierre quickly responded to media questions about the book by noting 'the timing is very suspicious,' given its release the same day as the leaders' debates. He also said 'the book is so partisan the cost of publishing it could be included in the Bloc's election expenses.'[32] Former Ottawa-area Liberal MP Marlene Catterall added the authors 'are avowed separatists, who admitted they conceived of the book only a few days ago.'[33] Others pointed to a 1997 Supreme Court ruling that had already determined the provincial referendum legislation limiting expenditures did not apply to the federal government.

Yet the damage had been done. As former NDP MP Dick Proctor commented, 'the timing could hardly be worse for the Liberal Party. Whether there is any substance to the allegations is almost beside the point.' Like other analysts, Proctor also noted that both the Option Canada furore and the RCMP investigation would not have been as serious a blow to the Liberals if their reputation had not already been in tatters thanks to the Gomery Inquiry. 'It's just another reason not to reward Liberals with a vote on January 23. As one longtime Liberal supporter told me this weekend, "It's too bad, but the Liberals simply need to go stand in the corner for a while."'[34]

Behind the scenes the Martin team were working frantically to add items to their platform to counter some of the Tory initiatives. This led them to delay the release of the Red Book until 11 January – the day after the leaders' debates – at which point the Liberals' apparent lack of policies had been emphasized by the media so often that the platform 'launch' passed with little or no public comment. As one analyst noted, even the Liberal-leaning *Toronto Star*'s editorial the following day endorsed Martin without even mentioning the release of the Red Book.[35] Columnist James Travers went further and argued the same day that Martin was simply the lesser of two evils. 'This election isn't about Stephen Harper,' he declared. 'It's about expectations Martin couldn't meet.'[36]

The lack of attention paid to the Liberal platform was striking. Paul

Martin rarely referred to it, nor did most of his candidates. This stunned the document's author and other Liberal insiders, who felt it contained invaluable information that could have proven useful in the campaign. Several of them singled out a table entitled 'By the Numbers: That was Then ... and This Is Now.' Originally prepared for the 2004 election and rejected by the campaign team (who did not want to refer to the Liberal record), the material was updated for 2006 and included in the platform introduction. 'It's a graphic good news story of Canada's progress,' one veteran campaigner sighed. Peter Nicholson concurred: '"By the Numbers" should have been a major source of pride and it should have been a big part of our ad campaign as well,' he said later.[37]

As the Conservatives' numbers continued to rise, the Liberals turned to two options they had so far deliberately avoided. The first was a series of negative advertisements. All of them featured an image of Stephen Harper, with a voice-over quoting some of his earlier, more extreme statements before concluding with the phrase 'We're not making this up.' Political scientist Fred Fletcher of York University stressed the ads technically were not 'attack ads.' They were not personal and they were factual, based on actual statements made by Harper, although they did interpret those statements very broadly. However, Fletcher also described the ads as 'risky' because Canadians were likely to dislike their tone.[38]

In fact many voters did not like the tone, but many more found the ads ludicrous and they soon became an object of ridicule. The entire 'We're not making this up' series became a campaign issue in itself. Ordinary Canadians and frustrated Liberals from coast to coast called the national party office to express their distaste for one segment in particular, which suggested the Conservatives were planning to deploy the army in urban areas for unstated nefarious ends. Making matters worse, Martin's team originally said he had not approved the ad. Then they insisted that he had approved it but it had been released in error, even as they reserved the right to release it again at a later date.

Nevertheless the ads were described by prominent advertising executive Don Masters as 'the most effective of the campaign from any party ... They are very well done, simple, and will make people stop, think and reconsider.'[39] Other analysts agreed the ads could be effective, even if they were unpopular. Both David Herle and Allan Gregg had noted earlier that negative advertising was effective in the United States. 'It works,' Herle said, 'whether you like it or not.'[40] Still, most analyses of the 2006 election concluded the ads were unsuccessful, partly because the rest of the Liberal campaign was failing badly, and partly because they came too late in the campaign to make a difference. Queen's University political scientist Jonathan Rose explained the failure of the Liberals' 2006 negative ads by pointing out that they pictured the same 'scary' Stephen Harper as 2004. Yet Harper had changed his image dramatically in the interim, and the Liberals had allowed him to do so for weeks with impunity. 'The scary Stephen Harper in the ads was nowhere to be seen,' Rose said. 'Instead, Harper was inoculated against the demonizing effects by his calm, measured demeanour during the Conservative policy rollouts in the first half of the campaign. By the time the Liberals delivered their ads to market ... it was too late.'[41]

One forum where Harper had demonstrated this calm and almost prime ministerial bearing was the second set of leader's debates. Here the full extent of the Liberals' panic became evident. With polls showing the Conservatives had a ten-point lead nationally and were likely to win a minority, the Liberals, as David Herle later confided, were 'patently desperate.'[42] Not only did they suddenly decide to play the national unity card once more, but they did so by making one of the most unlikely announcements of the campaign.

The National Unity Card, Part 2: Martin's Hail Mary Play

For several days before the leaders' debates, Martin insiders were trying to reassure nervous Liberals. They insisted the leader would fire a silver bullet into the Conservatives' campaign, one which would stop them in their tracks and ensure a Liberal turnaround. Speculation was intense, but few imagined this coup de grâce would be a promise to unleash another round of constitutional reform.

The debates began with Martin attacking the Conservatives on the values issue. He argued this 'value gap' was demonstrated by Stephen Harper's ten-year-old speech criticizing the welfare state, a gambit that failed to make an impact, as did his warning that a vote for the Bloc would allow Harper to implement those right-wing plans. Then he attempted to discredit the Conservatives' abilities as fiscal managers, referring to Harper's recent statement that he would repeal the Liberals' proposed income tax cuts for low-income Canadians if elected. Martin asked pointedly what other services or programs might be sacrificed. However this, too, failed to find its target as Harper simply dismissed the claim and then scored a palpable hit when he retorted that 'the Conservative party does not start from the premise that it has a "divine right" to rule.'[43]

Then Martin moved on to the national unity file. Evidently recognizing that Harper now posed the greater threat, the Liberal leader ignored Gilles Duceppe entirely, focusing on Harper and reminding Quebeckers, 'I supported the Meech Accord and the distinct society, Mr. Harper was against both.' This was an unusual lead-in to his much-heralded statement, namely that 'the first act of a new Liberal government will be to strengthen the Charter' by removing the option for the federal government to use the notwithstanding clause. This, he said, would be done through a unilateral federal constitutional amendment. Interestingly, the 'first act' of the new Liberal government was nowhere to be found in the platform released the following day, as several commentators promptly noted. Nor did Liberal candidates – ranging from a nonplussed Justice Minister Anne McLellan to Toronto area MP and lawyer Derek Lee – hesitate to inform anyone who cared to listen that they had not heard of the plan until Martin made the announcement during the debates. Lee also made it clear what he thought of the idea: 'If it ain't broke, don't' fix it,' he told reporters before leaving for an event in his riding.[44]

As David Herle explained, the logic of the announcement had been to emphasize the values gap. 'We wanted to demonstrate that Stephen Harper *would* use the clause to eliminate the same-sex marriage legislation, introduce abortion legislation, or overturn court decisions on other minority rights issues.'[45] The actual effect of the statement was quite different. For many Canadians, it was a meaningless promise. For others was it was seen as a mere technicality. In short, politically Martin had fired a blank.

For constitutional experts, however, Martin's pledge was a serious concern, and one they believed would once again be leading Canada into a potential quagmire. Most did not agree with the Liberals' apparent assumption that only the federal government needed to be involved in such an amendment. Noted constitutional scholar Peter Hogg summed up those views when he declared the Liberals could not simply pass a law through Parliament. 'It would have to have the support of 7 provinces representing half the population,' Hogg said. 'The change would have to be done through section 38. There isn't any escape from that.'[46] One of the few scholars who supported the Liberal interpretation was Patrick Monaghan, dean of Osgoode Hall Law School, who argued the change could be made unilaterally under section 44. Unfortunately Monaghan's blessing was a mixed one, since he also pointed out that by the same token any future federal government could just as easily reinstate the clause through the same means.

The failure of the Liberals' desperate tactic to resurrect their fortunes served to increase their leader's image problems. Within days Paul Martin's approval ratings had fallen another six percentage points and he now found himself trailing both Harper and Jack Layton. Martin's poor performance on the hustings, described by the media in terms of flailing arms, odd syntax, and wild-eyed intensity, had already been factored into his ratings. The principal explanation for this most recent plunge in popularity was Martin's apparent lack of political sense, and his equally apparent willingness to change his position to garner votes.

As Martin himself had reminded voters, he had supported Meech Lake, the initiative Pierre Trudeau had rejected out of hand because it would override the Charter. In addition, the opposition leaders were quick to remind voters that Martin himself had mused earlier about the possibility of using the notwithstanding clause to protect churches if the courts found that they would be obliged to perform same-sex marriages against their will.

In a similar vein, voters were constantly reminded by the Conservatives and the media that Paul Martin's defence of a strong federal government – and his attacks on Harper's vision of open federalism – flew in the face of his own earlier hesitation over the Clarity Act, his acceptance of Jean Lapierre and eight former Bloc candidates in Liberal ranks, and his embrace of asymmetrical federalism, to say nothing of his willingness to allow Quebec to participate in international events. As journalist Graham Fraser concluded, 'The angry exchanges of insults this week between Martin and Harper … was a reminder that the fundamental fault line of Canadian unity that has run through domestic politics (for several decades) … is still a significant factor in this election.'[47] This time, though, it was not the Liberals who were profiting from it.

The Opposition Saves the Day

The debates took place on 9 and 10 January, barely two weeks before election day. On 14 January an Ipsos-Reid poll predicted the Tories – with a ten-point lead – were 'unstoppable' and would win a minority. By 17 January, a Strategic Counsel poll suggested the Tories might be on the brink of achieving a majority. Despite this, on 20 January Martin repeatedly told reporters he believed his party was about to make a 'remarkable comeback' because voters were beginning to see the 'real' Stephen Harper and his 'extreme' right-wing agenda.[48]

To some extent the beleaguered Liberal leader was right. But it was not so much a Liberal resurgence that saved the party from a much more serious electoral disaster. Rather it was the help they received from both opposition parties in the dying days of the campaign. In particular, Martin benefited from the same over-confident behaviour on the part of Stephen Harper that many believed had cost the Conservatives a minority in 2004.

In the 2006 election, Harper kept that bravado closely in check for much longer. As his party took the lead after Christmas and their numbers continued to rise, Tory spokespersons were careful to tell reporters they would never underestimate their Liberal opponents. Harper himself had stuck to a tightly scripted message. His remaining 'loose cannon' candidates had been kept under even tighter wraps.

Then, in the final days, Harper began to make critical errors. In order to downplay the 'scary' label Martin was still pushing, Harper actually tried to reassure voters by saying he would never have 'absolute power' since there would never be a Conservative majority in the same way as a Liberal one. Apparently hoping to secure a majority with this argument, Harper declared: 'We will have checks on us, and limits on our ability to operate that a Liberal government would not face.' When he tried to clarify his meaning for reporters, he made matters worse. 'The reality is that we will have, for some time to come, a Liberal Senate, a Liberal civil service ... and courts that have been appointed by the Liberals,' Harper said.[49] In short order he had confirmed for many Canadians the truth of Martin's accusations. It appeared that the Conservatives really *did* have a hidden agenda, which only the institutions of government prevented them from implementing. This suspicion was reinforced the next day when Harper declared it would be 'an abuse of power' for a Liberal-dominated Senate to block Conservative legislation 'that would scrap same-sex marriage rights or deal with other controversial issues that have been raised in the course of the campaign.'[50]

With one stroke Harper had managed to question the impartiality of judges and public servants. His comments produced a flood of negative coverage. As former senior public servant Arthur Kroeger commented, Harper's 'extraordinary' remarks were especially ill-timed since relations between bureaucrats and politicians under the Martin government 'have never been worse.' Referring to Martin's 'heavy-handed and even abusive PMO,' as well as the highly unpopular raft of

200-plus new rules and reforms introduced by Martin's Treasury Board president Reg Alcock, in light of the Gomery affair, Kroeger concluded: 'In view of what the public service has been through at the hands of the present government, if those were friends, I'd hate to see enemies.'[51] Harper attempted to repair the damage by issuing a statement offering 'an open hand' to the public service, but the suspicions remained.

Meanwhile Paul Marin had been attacking the NDP to considerable effect. He accused the party and its leader of giving the Conservatives a 'free pass' and 'abandoning their principles' in order to ensure the Liberals did not benefit from strategic voting. Jack Layton's angry response – 'Join with the NDP, because the Liberals haven't earned your vote and they are not going to be successful in stopping the Conservatives'[52] – perversely served to remind voters about the impending Conservative victory, and arguably convinced some of his usual supporters to switch their votes in an attempt to hold the Conservatives to a minority.

The split between Layton and the charismatic but independent-minded head of the Canadian Auto Workers, Buzz Hargrove, had further complicated the NDP's fortunes. On the fourth day of the campaign Hargrove had appeared with Martin at a rally in southern Ontario, giving the Liberal leader a CAW leather jacket and a hug, and urging NDP voters to carefully consider their choice. A memo from Hargrove to his members urged them to support NDP candidates where they had a good chance of winning, but to vote strategically for Liberals in other ridings in order to stop the Conservatives. Hargrove's 'defection' was viewed by many in Layton's camp as an angry response to the NDP leader's role in bringing down the government, something that gained credibility when other prominent NDP supporters such as Jim Laxer and Maude Barlow publicly sided with Hargrove.

The accusations and counter-accusations continued for several days. Bloc leader Gilles Duceppe, concerned about his party's fading fortunes and the unexpected rise in Conservative support in Quebec, called a vote for Harper a 'big risk.' He suggested the Tories were a threat to the province's language law, Bill 101, a transparent move designed to shore up francophone support. Citing Harper's comment several years earlier that 'the affirmation that special status is necessary to protect the French language in Quebec is simply false,' Duceppe added: 'Mr. Harper has never revisited or withdrawn those remarks.'[53] Duceppe's attack may have served to save some Bloc seats, but a number of analysts argued it could also have stemmed the flow of federalist votes from the Liberals.

In yet another twist in the unexpected 'national unity campaign,' Buzz Hargrove had told Quebeckers to vote for the Bloc to stop the Conservatives, a position Paul Martin was forced to disavow in the dying days of the campaign. Worse, the Liberal leader found himself obliged to defend Stephen Harper's patriotism as a result of Hargrove's comments.[54] And so, as the election wound down, it was obvious that Martin's efforts to expand the Liberals' appeal in Quebec had failed. Merely holding on to existing seats was now a challenge. His last-minute embrace of Trudeauvian federalism had come too late and been unconvincing, and the Conservatives appeared poised to seize the mantle of the Liberals as the real federalist option in the province.

End of the Line

By the time election day finally arrived on 23 January, it was clear Stephen Harper would be the next prime minister. The only remaining question was whether he would be in charge of a minority or a majority government.

In the end it was a Conservative minority, and a slim one at that. Where the 2004 Martin minority had obtained 135 seats and received 37 per cent of the popular vote, the Harper Conservatives were limited to only 124 seats with 36 per cent of the vote. The Tories had made a stunning breakthrough in Quebec by electing 10 MPs, but they had not made the strides they had hoped for in Ontario. They had actually lost seats to the NDP in the west. Most important, they had formed a government with no support from the country's three largest cities. The rural-urban divide was starkly evident in the split between the Liberals and the Conservatives, and cause for considerable concern.

The NDP, meanwhile, fared the best of the opposition parties, increasing both its seat count (from 10 to 29) and its popular vote. The Bloc, which had entered the race fearing it would lose many seats to the Liberals, had managed to retain all but three.

Instead, it was the Liberals who were the big losers in Quebec, reduced from 21 to 13 seats and, far more importantly, from 34 per cent to 20 per cent of the popular vote. Still, they retained much of their support in Atlantic Canada and kept their small base in the west, despite being widely portrayed as a party whose support was now based almost entirely in Ontario. In fact, Ontario was the scene of the Liberals' greatest losses in terms of seats, falling from 75 to 54.

And so, two decades after John Turner led the party to its worst electoral defeat just months after taking over the helm from Pierre Trudeau, history had repeated itself. The Liberals were back in the opposition wilderness.

Several reasons for the Liberals' loss have been identified by election studies.[55] Volatile voters, prepared to switch their allegiance to demonstrate their unhappiness with the Liberals despite their ongoing concerns about the Harper Conservatives, were clearly a major factor. At the same time, as Stephen Clarkson has underlined, the Liberals were the authors of much of their own misfortune. The party's defeat, he declared, 'spoke to the unerring propensity of its leader and his clique for strategic miscalculation and tactical ineptitude.'[56]

One measure of the importance of the Liberals' self-inflicted wounds was the sharp decline in Paul Martin's approval ratings. The former 'saviour' of the party had seen his popularity decline in every region of the country. The drop was dramatic in Atlantic Canada, the Prairies, and, of course, Quebec. As political scientist André Turcotte concluded, in those regions 'the Liberal candidates and incumbents who once looked to Martin as their main electoral asset managed to win their seats in 2006 despite him.'[57]

Yet the party had not been humiliated. There was no 1984-style rout. One interpretation of the results – which like 2004 were much better than insiders had feared – was that Harper was on borrowed time. 'Even at rock bottom, when practically everyone wanted a change, they couldn't bring themselves to vote for him,' one veteran organizer commented at an election night party. But among Liberals the animosity towards Martin and his inner circle was visceral. Unlike John Turner in 1984, many party insiders had made it clear weeks before election day that they were expecting a resignation and a leadership race within the year. Hopefuls such as John Manley, Martin Cauchon, and Maurizio Bevilacqua had already begun contacting members and testing the waters. Frank McKenna was reported to be waiting in the wings.

They were not disappointed. Only a few hours after the results were in, Paul Martin not only conceded defeat but announced his intention to resign as leader of the party before the next election. One insider's comments summed up the feeling of many Liberals. 'It was a classy thing to do,' he told reporters. 'Tonight's results show that Martin and not the Liberal Party was defeated.'[58]

Although Martin planned to stay on as an MP, he asked to be replaced immediately in the House of Commons by an interim parliamentary leader. The choice was Toronto MP Bill Graham, who, like

Herb Gray in 1989, had made it clear he had no interest in seeking the party leadership. However, such was the degree of mistrust in Liberal circles that Martin's stated *intention* to resign as party leader at a later date, rather than his actual resignation, soon became a bone of contention even though this procedure had been followed by Turner and Chrétien. His detractors worried that, if an election were called suddenly, Martin would still be the leader and there might be no time to select a successor to lead the party in the next campaign. Some saw this as a deliberate ploy by the Board to retain power at all costs. Tensions mounted and public comments became increasingly pointed. The matter was only resolved when Martin submitted his formal resignation as leader, paving the way for a convention within a year as spelled out in the party's constitution. The party executive met to determine the timing of yet another leadership race within the space of less than three years, an extraordinary development for the natural governing party.

The 2006 Leadership Race: The Divisions Continue

If ever the Liberal Party should have taken the opportunity to renew itself in its traditional fashion – debating and developing new policies, revamping and modernizing its organization, and selecting a leader who represented mainstream Liberal values – the 2006 leadership race was surely the time. In fact, as many veterans repeatedly stressed, party renewal was long overdue. Having set themselves an entire year for the race, there was both time and opportunity. But little party renewal occurred. Only in the area of organization and structural reform did the Liberals manage to make significant progress, and even there they were playing a game of catch-up with the other federal parties.

There are many reasons for this failure, including a lack of resources and a very crowded field of candidates. But the ongoing federal cleavage, personified by the Martin/Chrétien vendetta, was also an important factor. And problems erupted almost immediately. On the one hand, the party apparatus continued to be controlled by Martin supporters. On the other hand, virtually everyone involved in the party was intent on demonstrating publicly that the divisive internecine warfare was a thing of the past. As a result, many of the leadership camps were loath to take on supporters from either side. Others went out of their way to ensure they had a 'rainbow coalition' of supporters. Senior Martin adviser Mike Robinson stressed, 'There is no likelihood whatsoever that Board members will come together to support a particular candidate in the next leadership race.'[59] Instead, they had come to a tacit agreement that some of them would remain outside the event entirely, while others would fan out and support the wide range of candidates who were coming forward. In theory this seemed to be a satisfactory solution, but in reality the distribution of former 'Martin' and 'Chrétien' supporters among the various leadership camps continued to be a source of discussion and contention throughout the entire race.

The timing of the convention was easily determined, since the party had already scheduled a biennial policy convention in early December. After a meeting of the national executive, party president Mike Eizenga announced they had decided to convert the event into a full-fledged leadership convention, with the actual vote taking place on 2 December. The convention would take place in Montreal, a fact that now seemed more significant in light of the election results.

By 20 March the executive had decided on the rules for the race, such as a $50,000 entry fee and a $3.4 million cap on spending by candidates. Although the cap was higher than the $1 million suggested by some potential candidates such as Carolyn Bennett, it was much lower than the total spent by Paul Martin in 2003. In addition, there was a new option to sign up members online in order to avoid the problem created by the Martin camp's almost total control of membership control of forms in 2003.

Eizenga told reporters New Brunswick MP Dominic LeBlanc and party executive member Tanya Kappo would co-chair the convention and Steven MacKinnon, the national party director, would serve as secretary of the convention. The race was officially set to begin on 7 April 2006. Until 1 July, candidates would be expected to devote their time and energy to signing up new members. From July until the Super Weekend in late September, when delegate-selection meetings would be held, candidates would focus on winning the support of riding members and hence delegates. Then, after the Super Weekend, there would still be an eight-week period until the 1 December convention in which candidates could attempt to convince delegates who were committed to someone else on the first ballot to switch to them on the second ballot.

Unlike 2003, this race attracted a large number of potential candidates. Then the unexpected happened. One by one the high-profile Liberals who had been considered leading contenders declined to enter the race. Allan Rock, Brian Tobin, John Manley, Martin Cauchon, and Frank McKenna – all of whom were not active in politics at the time –

demurred. Most cited personal reasons, but it was widely understood in Liberal circles that the prospect of taking on a disorganized and divided party, and sitting on the opposition benches for an indeterminate period of time, had proven too discouraging.

This surprising development inevitably led to a period of reflection. Then a number of leadership hopefuls emerged from the backbenches of caucus, including veteran but relatively unknown MPs Joe Volpe, Hedy Fry, Carolyn Bennett, and John Godfrey. A surprising entry was Ken Dryden, whose name recognition as a former hockey great was high, but not as a Liberal MP. More surprising still was the decision of newly minted Liberal Scott Brison (the former Conservative MP) to throw his hat in the ring. Less surprising was the candidacy of newly elected MP Michael Ignatieff, even though he had only joined the party a few days before contesting the 2006 election. Ignatieff's return to Canada after a lengthy absence had been promoted by a group of senior Liberals, including Alf Apps and Ian Davey, for this eventual purpose.

However, none of these entries could compare with the unexpected decision of Bob Rae, the former NDP premier of Ontario, to enter the race. Rae's move was generally attributed to the urging of his brother, John Rae, the longtime adviser to Jean Chrétien. As such, Rae soon came to be seen by many Liberal insiders as the preferred candidate of the Chrétien camp, just as Michael Ignatieff eventually emerged as the perceived stalking horse for the Martin Liberals. That this occurred despite the pains the two men took to ensure a broad representation from both camps in their campaign organizations spoke volumes about the depth of the ongoing conflict which had simply gone underground once more.

Along with these two obvious frontrunners, two more candidates entered the race who would eventually emerge in the top tier. The first, former Chrétien minister Stéphane Dion, was originally viewed as a very dark horse, lacking the requisite political skills or roots in the party. Nor did people know where he stood on issues other than the environment. The second was a provincial education minister in the McGuinty government, Gerard Kennedy. Apart from Bob Rae, Kennedy – a well-known former Toronto food bank director – was easily the most left-leaning or 'social' Liberal in the group. For Kennedy, though, this too was an uphill battle, albeit for different reasons. His ties to the federal party were few and far between, despite his deep Liberal roots in his native Manitoba. Even more problematic was his limited ability to communicate in French.

Given the large number of lesser-known candidates in the race this time, it was evident they would need a forum to raise their profile, and most assumed the series of leadership debates would be the logical venue. However, the combination of a difficult format due to the large number of candidates, the party's lack of resources following so closely on a national election campaign, and the apparent lack of interest on the part of the media all combined to produce a lacklustre set of meetings in which very little was learned about the candidates or a new vision of the Liberal Party. As one report on the first such debate concluded, 'Liberal leadership debate fails to ignite.' Journalist Linda Diebel went on to note that 'the 11 leadership candidates bored their audience with consensus and politeness,' and the format virtually ensured no actual debate would take place.[60] Moreover, very few Canadians saw the debates or were even aware they were taking place, since the major networks had declined to carry them. It became apparent that any efforts to highlight the party's interest in policy reform would have to focus on other venues.

Policy Interrupted: The LPC Policy Renewal Commission

The December convention was originally intended to be a biennial national policy convention where policy resolutions from the provincial wings would be prioritized and debated. As usual, there would be meetings of each of the provincial wings in advance, to finalize their resolutions. Despite this, the national executive decided the party needed to attract greater attention to its policy deliberations. As a result, Mike Eizenga announced the creation of a unique consultative body, the Liberal Party of Canada Policy Renewal Commission.

Former Trudeau adviser and policy guru Tom Axworthy was asked to serve as overall chair, and some thirty-two separate policy groups were identified, each with their own appointed chair. In almost every case the chairs were prominent Liberals, some retired from active politics, some still engaged. Well-known veterans such as David Collenette, Anne McClellan, and Frank McKenna were joined by newcomers such as Justin Trudeau. The chairs were instructed to choose a small number of knowledgeable Liberals and outside experts to work with them and produce a report. Although it was not obvious at the time, the most important would prove to be 'The Federation: Shaping Canada,' a group chaired by former justice minister Martin Cauchon.

The stated purpose of the commission and its task forces was 'to assist the party in policy development.' Evidently aware that the novelty of the process could be a cause for concern, the press release announcing the Renewal Commission expressly noted: 'The reports [will] not represent party policy; that is a matter for rank and file activists to establish through our policy development process.' Nevertheless, the release declared: 'Liberals have always been prepared to discuss, debate and consider ideas from a breadth of perspectives.'[61]

One problem with this entire structure, as many grassroots Liberals and party officials commented sotto voce, was that it lacked a source of authority grounded in the party. Why, they asked, were members of the national policy committee not conducting this exercise? Apart from the initial response that many of those members had been included in various groups, the public answer appeared to be that it was an attempt to expand the party's base. Privately, many Liberals believed the continued domination of the party machinery, including the policy committee, by the Martin camp was a factor as well. Another problem was what to do with the reports when they were completed. The executive announced they would be placed on the party website. In December, they would be given to the new leader for consideration. Party officials stressed the reports would have no formal role, only an advisory one like the party's resolutions, since the new leader could not be seen to be tied down by decisions taken before his or her selection.

The relative merits of this approach were debated for some time behind the scenes. Some longtime party members refused to serve on a committee in protest. Still, Chair Tom Axworthy was originally enthusiastic about the entire procedure, which he saw as a grassroots exercise. However, as summer came and went, and many committees had not submitted a report, it became apparent that internal conflicts raged even within these small groups. Nevertheless by late autumn several reports had been made public on the LPC website, and one – the Cauchon report on Canadian federalism – had received widespread media coverage.

Axworthy himself had prepared a comprehensive report summarizing the group's activities, along with proposals for further study and research. Originally he was expecting to present this report as the centrepiece of the party's policy process at the convention. However, when he arrived in Montreal and was given a copy of the program, it was obvious that other political considerations had intervened. Although he said nothing publicly, Axworthy was known to be fuming about the decision to downplay his efforts and those of the countless commission members. His own presentation had been unceremoniously moved to a site far removed from the convention centre where the main activities were taking place, virtually ensuring a sparse turnout. (One volunteer recalled arriving at his assigned room to serve as a rapporteur and found no one there at all. 'I had my coffee and read the paper, and eventually went back to the convention hall,' he said in resignation.)[62] Meanwhile at the convention site, during the time originally allotted to Axworthy, former Martin adviser and consultant John Duffy was given considerable time to make a presentation on environmental issues.

The reports, and in fact the entire Reform Commission file on the party website, disappeared soon after the convention. Axworthy subsequently submitted his report and the reports of the various task forces to the new Liberal leader, Stéphane Dion, and the newly elected party president, Senator Marie Poulin, on his own initiative. In his accompanying letter, Axworthy reiterated his commitment to the process: 'I both insist that the Party should follow through on its commitment to use this product of the volunteer wing of the Liberal party to assist ridings and activists in their policy work,' he wrote, 'and I suggest a plan for the months ahead that would see the Party commit to a thinker's conference, extended policy discussion in the ridings, an e-mail vote by the whole party membership on platform priorities, and the use of the new mechanism of the Council of Presidents to give legitimacy to the platform effort.' Axworthy concluded his comments by noting, 'My argument is that Party renewal and success in the next election go hand-in-hand.'[63] He later confided that nothing came of these suggestions, or of the work done by the various commission groups.

Although Dion had undoubtedly been bombarded with suggestions in the early weeks of his leadership, another reason for his seeming reluctance to consult widely on policy might well have been the problems caused by the national unity debate which had plagued the leadership race almost from the beginning, and which Stephen Harper was continuing to use to frustrate Dion's attempts to enforce caucus solidarity in Parliament.

The Ongoing Federalist Cleavage: Same Issues, Different Players

As one member of the Cauchon Task Force on the Canadian Federation learned first-hand, the national unity debate within the Liberal Party was alive and well during the 2006 leadership race. Out of the country for two weeks in late April 2006, the committee member returned to find the committee's draft report (which all members had essentially approved a month earlier) was now in revision and contained a major new section discussing 'Is Quebec a Nation?' This transformation had come about as a result of Prime Minister Stephen Harper's recent comments in Quebec, and leadership candidate Michael Ignatieff's subsequent enthusiastic embrace of the concept of Quebec as a nation. By June, Ignatieff was repeating this theme regularly and adding that he was 'open to new discussions to bring Quebec fully into the Canadian constitution, something Quebec refused to accept at the time of the last constitutional revision in 1982.'[64] Deliberations within the Cauchon task force took on more confrontational tones as efforts were made to resolve the dilemma this bombshell posed for a group that until then had been concerned with revisions to the equalization formula and transfer payments.

This latest public manifestation of the party's federalist cleavage led to months of serious infighting within the party, among not only candidates but also the party executive. Ignatieff's proposal was described by one national columnist as 'a lose-lose proposition that is derailing the Liberals' leadership race.'[65] The debate also brought about comments from several Liberals who had remained on the sidelines until then, including former prime minister Trudeau's son Justin. Arguing strenuously against Ignatieff's proposal and the Quebec resolution, Trudeau's comment that 'nationalism builds up barriers ... and has nothing to do with the Canada we should be building' received national coverage.[66]

Among the candidates, much evasion and soul-searching took place, but few openly expressed their views. Most hoped the issue would go away. In the end Stéphane Dion felt obliged to make a statement. The apparent heir to the mantle of Trudeau and Chrétien by virtue of his work in the trenches against the separatists and in drafting the Clarity Bill, Dion in his ambivalence surprised many. He laboured long and hard to produce the complicated statement that yes, he felt Quebec was a nation 'sociologically,' but not politically or legally.[67]

The Cauchon committee laboured long and hard to resolve the dispute. As a result, despite the report's useful material on other issues, media coverage focused almost exclusively on the section on Quebec's status. After discussing the 'sociological' definition of a nation, the report pointed out that there were many other nations within Canada by that same definition. Then it stressed that Quebec's identity, however defined, had flourished because it had been protected within the Canadian federation. The report concluded: 'The Liberal Party must find the right balance, respecting provincial wishes but continuing to build a Canada that is greater than the sum of its parts.' Media response to the report was overwhelmingly favourable. Alain Dubuc of *La Presse* concluded that the report 'provides a thoughtful but practical assessment of the situation' which any new Liberal leader would be wise to adopt.[68]

Meanwhile in Ottawa, interim leader Bill Graham was working hard to 'avoid a train wreck' in caucus and at the upcoming convention of the Liberal Party's Quebec wing, where a controversial resolution on the same issue was planned. Indeed, journalist Don Macpherson of the *Montreal Gazette* declared 'the Liberal Party is preparing to rip itself apart over Quebec nationhood.'[69] The resolution, widely believed to have been promoted by Ignatieff supporters, not only called for the recognition of Quebec as a nation but recommended reopening the constitution to entrench the concept. 'Virtually everybody wants to keep this thing (the resolution) in a workshop,' one senior Liberal admitted, explaining that if it remained in a workshop it would not become a priority to be debated on the floor of the national convention. Since all of the frontrunning leadership candidates but Ignatieff opposed the resolution, this was becoming a crucial issue.[70]

Sensing that the Liberals might be able to prevent a public relations disaster, Prime Minister Stephen Harper took matters into his own hands. On 27 November parliamentarians were forced to vote for or against a surprise motion put forward by Harper declaring that Quebeckers did in fact form a nation. Like Brian Mulroney before him, Harper was about to throw a spanner into the Liberal works. And like Mulroney, his weapon was a flawed document. The resolution, as Harper's own intergovernmental affairs minister, Michael Chong, pointed out before resigning, did not even say the same thing in English and French. Several Conservative cabinet ministers admitted they had no idea what it meant. Nevertheless the optics were clear. Conservatives voted in favour en masse. Liberals, although Bill Graham had tried hard to exert control, did not. Shortly after a heated debate in caucus about the need for the appearance of party unity, veteran MP Diane Marleau publicly lashed out at Michael Ignatieff for 'causing the stupidity we've gotten into.' Later in the House, some fifteen Liberal MPs voted against the motion. They included leadership candidates Ken Dryden, Hedy Fry, and Joe Volpe, all avowed Trudeau federalists. Meanwhile Ignatieff and Bob Rae (still a staunch supporter of the Meech Lake and Charlottetown deals according to his candidate website) supported the motion, as did an uncomfortable-looking Stéphane Dion.

The most dramatic move came from someone who was not there. Leadership candidate Gerard Kennedy, who was not yet an MP, held a press conference at his Toronto campaign headquarters the day of the vote to state expressly that he did not support the motion. 'I'm here today to say I can't support the Harper-Duceppe motion,' Kennedy declared. 'I don't think it's good for Canada.' What's more, Kennedy argued, 'it's politically motivated and we need and should expect better'[71] from the federal government. Shortly thereafter Justin Trudeau publicly announced that he would be supporting Kennedy for the leadership.

Of course the 'Quebec nation' issue was only part of the larger problem. As Paul Martin's flirtation with decentralization and asymmetrical federalism had demonstrated, the distance between the Liberals and their opposition was seriously narrowed if the federalist axis was removed. With all of the other parties already favouring decentralist versions of federalism, the Liberals' ace in the hole was their pan-Canadianism. This dilemma was clearly perceived by at least one journalist outside Quebec. *Globe and Mail* columnist John Ibbitson raised the issue at the start of the leadership race. 'Here is the first question a card-carrying Liberal should ask each candidate who comes to the door: Do you agree with Stephen Harper and Jean Charest that Ottawa should retreat from all areas of provincial jurisdiction and transfer sufficient funds to allow the Quebec government to manage its own affairs?' As Ibbitson pointed out, if the candidate answered 'Yes,' then the next question should be 'What makes you any different from the Conservatives?'[72]

Despite this, no serious discussion of the issue ever took place among the frontrunners at the leadership debates. And, with the rules placing so much emphasis on the recruitment of new members before the fall cutoff date and Super Weekend, no candidate was willing to devote much time and effort to a lengthy policy debate with his opponents elsewhere. After the weekend results were known, a renewed competition for delegates continued to preclude serious policy debate. In fact, as the repercussions of the vote and the subsequent eight-week hiatus before the convention became evident, more and more grassroots Liberals were becoming convinced that the type of structural reform Mike Eizenga was promoting had become essential.

Party Renewal: The LPC Red Ribbon Task Force

More than twenty years after John Turner and Iona Campagnolo had attempted serious structural and constitutional party reform, very little had changed. Repeated efforts to streamline the composition of the national executive, standardize the candidate selection and leadership processes, and modernize membership and fundraising had resulted in what Steven MacKinnon described as 'baby steps,' each change having been debated and fought at every stage along the way. By the spring of 2006 MacKinnon – still the party's national director – announced that he and party president Mike Eizenga intended to push through a major series of reforms at the national convention in December. MacKinnon lamented the party's 'patrician attitude, the arrogance of power, and wanton blindness to changes in the world' that had prevented these changes from taking place earlier. 'Now is the time,' he declared. 'The party is not just in opposition. The Liberal Party is broken beyond repair. It needs to be completely restructured to survive.'[73]

Certainly the Liberals had taken a beating in the past two years. The transition to a new leader had been difficult. The staging of a full-blown national convention in March 2005 along with two sets of nomination meetings and two federal elections had left both paid party workers and volunteers exhausted. The cost of two election campaigns, the party's repayment of $1.1 million to the federal government as promised by Paul Martin, and the implementation of Jean Chrétien's election finance bill and its subsequent modification by the Harper government had left the party nearly $2 million in debt.[74] Then the Gomery Commission had left the party humiliated. Steven MacKinnon stated flatly that Gomery had 'shaken the party to its very foundations.'[75] Moreover both he and Mike Eizenga had spent nearly half of their time on Gomery-related issues for months, since the party had official standing at the commission hearings.

Now he and the president were organizing a leadership convention, and they intended to take advantage of the situation to drag the party into the twenty-first century. Their efforts began in earnest in May, when Eizenga delivered an address to the Ontario wing's annual meeting. In a hard-hitting presentation, Eizenga declared the party 'is institutionally unable to provide us with an electoral advantage.' He stressed that the 'competitive environment' had changed totally over the past two decades and failure to act would leave the party at a significant disadvantage. Most important, he identified the disconnect between party priorities – policy development, revenue generation, and election readiness – and the structures of the party.

He produced charts comparing the state of the Liberal Party with the Conservatives, including the 'top-heavy' but underfunded national executive and the failure of provincial and territorial wings to accomplish the goals originally intended for them. Finally, after noting that the party's federal structure made reform more difficult, Eizenga argued earlier reform attempts had failed in part because of the desire to accommodate as many elements of the federal structure as possible. 'Our first approach was to pull more chairs up to the table,' he said. 'But this did not enable better decisions, even though participation increased.'[76]

Eizenga reminded delegates that the executive had already appointed a Red Ribbon Task Force comprising Liberals from both the parliamentary and extra-parliamentary wings. The group, chaired by Annie Claude de Paoli and Michael Hilman, was also advised by veteran Liberals Jack Graham and Andy Scott.

The issues of fairness, equity, and representation which had preoccupied reform efforts for decades were tangential. The mandate of their task force was expressly practical, namely to 'evaluate how the current operational and decision-making structure of the Party can be streamlined and made more efficient.'[77] Recommendations in the form of a consensus report were to be submitted in advance of the national convention.

The final report of the task force was released in August. 'A Party Built for Everyone, A Party Built to Win' offered twenty-four recommendations including proposals to adopt a truly national membership, with a national fee and standardized rules; a major redistribution of responsibilities between PTAs and the national office; the abolition of existing standing committees and the creation of a revamped national policy committee, a permanent election readiness committee, a national revenue committee, and a management committee of the national executive. In addition, the national executive would be reduced from more than sixty members to roughly twenty. The controversial Commission clubs for youth and seniors were to be limited to those with more than fifty members. A Council of Presidents composed of all riding presidents was proposed, which would meet once per year.

Several significant changes were proposed with respect to conventions and leadership, all of which clearly stemmed from problems the party had encountered in the recent past. To begin with, the task force recommended a leadership review take place only after an election in which the party did not form the government. Second, the call for a leadership convention would take place when a leader announced his or her intention to resign, rather than waiting for a formal resignation letter. The task force also recommended the writ period be reduced from one year to six months. The fate of leadership conventions themselves was a matter of debate. The report recommended that delegates to the Montreal convention be asked whether the structure of those conventions should be significantly modified, to deal with the problems created by the dual system of riding votes and national convention, or if conventions should be replaced entirely by a direct one-member, one-vote system.

The task force concluded with a call to arms to hand the party back to the members. 'We strongly urge the National Executive … to oversee forthwith the drafting of constitutional amendments to be put before delegates at the upcoming [Montreal] convention,' they wrote. Acknowledging that each amendment would require the support of two-thirds of delegates to pass, a threshold which had proven insurmountable in the past, they nevertheless argued it was time to solicit the views of members. 'The Liberal Party belongs to all of us, and we must collectively agree to change it.'[78]

To that end Eizenga and MacKinnon spent the fall crossing the country and urging Liberals to support the recommendations. Interim leader Bill Graham also became deeply engaged in the exercise, urging both caucus and leadership candidates to support the proposals. At the convention, Graham spoke before the voting began, telling Liberals, 'I want to be the last party leader who cannot say "I am a member of the Liberal Party of Canada."' In the end he and the party task force were well rewarded for their efforts. Delegates adopted almost all of the proposed amendments, rejecting only one major proposal by deciding not to eliminate leadership conventions. A new era in party structure and organization was about to begin. At the same time the election of the new party president (Senator Marie Poulin), from within the parliamentary wing, suggested that delegates were prepared to retain some aspects of the traditional system as well. And of course the 2006 leadership race itself operated under the old rules, proving by example the merit of the party's proposed reforms.

The Race and the 'Upset' Result

After the Super Weekend in late September, the party experienced the first real fallout from its existing leadership rules. It was readily apparent that four candidates – first-place finisher Michael Ignatieff, second-place candidate Bob Rae, and the two candidates essentially tied for third place – Gerard Kennedy and Stéphane Dion – were the only ones who could win the contest. Moreover, Ignatieff, who his own advisers had said would need at least 35 per cent of delegates in this vote in order to win on the first ballot, did not reach that goal. With only 30 per cent of committed delegates, he was far short of the mark. Given his low rating as the second choice of delegates, he was evidently in some difficulty. Meanwhile Rae (20 per cent), Kennedy (17 per cent), and Dion (16 per cent) were so closely grouped that the results said very little about their chances. Rae, too, was seen by many delegates as a controversial figure who did not rate highly as a second choice, as opposed to the two 'new school' candidates Kennedy and Dion. In fact, informed discussion among insiders put Kennedy in the role of kingmaker almost immediately, given his strong second-place finish in Canada outside of Quebec (ahead of Bob Rae in Ontario, and in first place in BC and Manitoba).

As a result, a number of developments took place that altered the course of the race, developments that would not have been possible without this two-part process and the lengthy period in between. First and foremost, several of the second-string candidates withdrew from the race. Second, and far more important, supporters of Dion and Kennedy began to work behind the scenes to form a strategic alliance, determined to ensure that neither Rae nor Ignatieff could win. In the end, an agreement was reached that whichever of the two finished in fourth position would move to the other on the next ballot.

Yet despite the weekend results, many in the media – either genuinely ignorant of the situation or determined to promote the idea of a horse race with their preferred candidates as frontrunners – consistently reported that it was still a race between Rae and Ignatieff. Ignatieff's advisers knew his momentum had stalled. Like Rae, his candidacy had been viewed from the start as representing one of the two old-school camps from the years of internecine warfare. In addition, both men were carrying baggage that made them unacceptable to a significant number of longtime Liberals. As one senior Liberal put it, 'These are outsiders. Who are they to tell us how to run the party?' Kennedy, by contrast, although a provincial Liberal, was accepted as a legitimate candidate from the beginning because of his deep roots in the party.

Of far more importance than was generally recognized, both Ignatieff and Rae were also supporters of the decentralist Turner/Martin vision of federalism which was opposed by the vast majority of grassroots Liberals. Indeed, many left-wing Liberals and former Chrétien supporters who would otherwise have been logical Rae supporters – such as Sheila Copps, Charles Caccia, and Terry Mercer – formed the core of Kennedy's elite support. Among his staunch caucus supporters were newer MPs who also supported the Trudeau vision of federalism and had played a key role in opposing Martin's asymmetrical vision, such as Mark Holland, Nahdeep Bains, and Scott Simms. Like the support of Justin Trudeau, their presence in the Kennedy camp, as everyone but the media appeared to recognize, was not an accident.

In a similar vein, Stéphane Dion's eventual victory at the convention, while surprising to some of the media, was not unexpected for many grassroots Liberals. The defeat of Bob Rae and Michael Ignatieff was no surprise at all. Nor was the fact that Kennedy did play the role of kingmaker. He had acquired a large number of committed Liberal youth, new members from Ontario, and strong western support. In an extraordinary display of candidate loyalty, Kennedy was able to deliver more than 95 per cent of his committed delegates to Dion on the second ballot, when he finished fourth behind Dion by a handful of votes. The move, surprising given Kennedy's third-place finish on the first ballot and the desire of many of his supporters that he stay on the ballot for the third vote, was a determining factor in Dion's eventual victory over Ignatieff on the fourth ballot.

Nevertheless delegates had chosen a largely unknown quantity. Dion's speech at the convention had been lengthy, uninspired, and theoretical, as opposed to the polished, partisan speeches delivered by Rae and Kennedy. His three-pronged policy agenda, while encouraging to many who felt the party had been without a vision for too long, was not easily communicated. As the green scarves worn by his supporters during victory celebrations demonstrated, the primary focus was on the environment, and this theme was widely picked up by the media in the days and weeks after the convention. They began to extol Dion's virtues as an anti-leader whose lack of charisma and political skills was actually an advantage and represented a 'new beginning' for the Liberal Party.

Whither the Party?

Nearly two years later, the new beginning had not materialized. This was nowhere more true than in the area of party finances. Clearly the party's ongoing difficulties with fundraising were made worse not only by Stephen Harper's changes to Jean Chrétien's election finance legislation, but also by the costs of debt repayment for the many leadership candidates. Dion himself had not repaid his leadership debt by the summer of 2008, nor had eight of his former opponents. Money raised to pay off these debts, in turn, was money not available to the party.

More than four years after the introduction of the new financing legislation, the Liberal Party had made only modest progress in increasing its contributions from individuals. Its total revenue in the first quarter of 2008 was a mere $846,129 from 10,169 contributors. This was barely one-fifth of the total raised by the Conservatives (at $4.95 million from 44,345 donors), and, for the first time, it was also less than the amount raised by the NDP ($1.1 million from 13,329 contributors). As one report concluded, 'Once Canada's most efficient political money-raising machine, the dismal results suggest the Liberals, traditionally the party most reliant on corporate largesse, have still not adapted to the prohibition on corporate donations imposed in 2004.'[79]

The party's ongoing financial troubles significantly affected the party's state of election readiness. Another factor in the Liberals' apparent organizational problems was the lack of machinery Dion could deliver in the aftermath of the convention. His shallow roots in the party meant that he had depended on others. Many insiders believed his victory had been secured partly by the recruitment of environmentalists as new Liberal members, and with his success most of those activists had left, unprepared and unequipped to work within a party organization.

Throughout 2007 and early 2008 the Harper Conservatives had introduced a number of measures that would typically have caused the Liberals to consider bringing down the government. Instead, debate raged within the caucus and the party over their perceived inability to fight an election. Prime Minister Harper's frequently observed skill in causing further dissension in Liberal ranks resulted in a series of retreats on the part of Dion and his caucus. On several occasions they were obliged to abstain in order to avoid defeating the government. Not surprisingly, the result of this behaviour was the public image of an emasculated Liberal Party, fearful of its own shadow and unwilling to take firm positions on any issue. This produced an unprecedented situation in which a precarious minority government was able to function as a majority, while opposition parties – normally keen to bring down the minority and wage another election – were instrumental in keeping it in power.

There could be little doubt that, after nearly two years, Stéphane Dion had not shown the type of growth in political or communications skills and personal leadership style that his supporters had originally hoped. In addition, having served almost all of his time in the Chrétien cabinet as the minister of intergovernmental affairs, Dion, like Paul Martin, had almost no experience in managing a line department. Last but hardly least, Dion's apparent determination to rely on only a handful of close advisers, most of whom had been with him in his ministerial office or even at university, continued to cause consternation among the larger party hierarchy, both parliamentary and extra-parliamentary, who felt more rather than less isolated from the centre of power. The conflict between the two wings exploded with Dion's appointment of a former adviser as the party's youngest national director ever, an appointment that soon proved problematic and was rescinded. But within PMO the fortress mentality continued unabated throughout 2008.

At the same time, supporters of both Michael Ignatieff and Bob Rae continued to cause problems for Dion, despite his efforts to engage caucus members from all camps in the parliamentary process. Ignatieff was immediately made deputy leader in the House of Commons, where he proceeded to outshine the leader in Question Period on a regular basis. Outsiders Bob Rae and Martha Hall Findley, before their subsequent election as MPs in 2008 by-elections, were assigned platform development duties, and virtually all of the other MPs who had been leadership opponents were assigned specific responsibilities as well. These moves did not compensate, however, for Dion's tendency to make decisions on his own, with little or no consultation.

Public manifestations of discontent with Dion's leadership erupted in Quebec in the spring of 2008. Clearly the divisions within the party along leadership lines had not healed and were reinforced by the federalist cleavage. After the unexpected loss of two Liberal seats in March 2008 by-elections – one of which was the former Liberal fortress of Outremont in Montreal, where Jean Lapierre had resigned along with Paul Martin and Dion had appointed his own choice as a candidate – a substantial number of party organizers and MPs in Quebec began a concerted campaign of dissent. Their theme was simple. Dion's leadership was impossible to sell in Quebec because of his support for the Clarity Bill and his Trudeauvian vision of federalism. Among the discontented, almost all of whom were known Ignatieff supporters, were former Turner and Martin supporters such as Jean Lapierre and Raymond Garneau. Shortly after, Dion announced that Gerard Kennedy (the nominated candidate in a Toronto riding held by the NDP, but not yet an MP) would assume the role of critic for intergovernmental relations.

The subsequent events surrounding Dion's disastrous 2008 election campaign and the party's humiliating defeat, followed by Dion's prompt resignation as leader – and replacement by Michael Ignatieff through problematic means in terms of the party's constitution – have been described in detail elsewhere.[80] And so, some fifteen years after the party's return to power in 1993, the Liberals find themselves once again in the wilderness, in circumstances strikingly similar to those of John Turner's small band in 1984. As this study comes to an end, the Liberal Party is much further from resembling the natural governing party than ever, despite the unpopular Harper minority. In fact, continued Liberal infighting has led more than one analyst to conclude that the Liberals are exhibiting the symptoms of a party destined to remain in opposition for some time.[81] What seems certain is that the party will not be able to regain its vaunted internal cohesion until it resolves the philosophical federalist cleavage in its midst. Divisions on the left-right axis between social and business Liberals have always existed and have been accommodated successfully for generations, although, as Jean Chrétien was fond of noting, one group has been conspicuously more successful at winning elections than the other. Those left-right divisions also played out primarily within caucus, as internal dissent was kept under wraps for the good of the party. The newer federalist cleavage, on the other hand, appears to be of a different order. As a result, it has frequently emerged in full public view throughout the past two decades. Internally, the federalist conflict causes more angst for the Liberals precisely because it has been such a fundamental element of the party's identity. Publicly, the issue causes serious political problems for the Liberals because, once again, the party has historically positioned itself at one end of the federalist axis while all of its opponents were at the other. In an era of a united right and a crowded left wing on the other axis, this distinction is even more critical.

Only time will tell if the Liberals can overcome their significant operational and philosophical challenges and return to power in the near future. Nevertheless, this analysis of the rise and fall of the Liberal Party over the past twenty-five years suggests a return to some semblance of the pan-Canadian Trudeauvian vision would be a major step forward. There can be little doubt the party will continue to have difficulty differentiating itself from its opponents if it strays too far from its traditional place on the federalist axis. Conversely, a return to that approach would likely ensure its status as the party most able to handle the national unity issue and best represent the values of Canadians, a significant move towards regaining its place as the natural governing party.

List of Interviews

(Date format: Year-Month-Day)

Apps, Alf	2004-10-26
Ashworth, Gordon	2006-05-09
Austin, Hon. Jack	2006-10-19
Axworthy, Hon. Lloyd	2004-09-30
Axworthy, Tom	2006-04-18
Bosch, Kevin	2006-09-13
Boudria, Hon. Don	2005-10-28
Caccia, Hon. Charles	2004-10-26; 2006-04-03
Cadario, Michelle	2006-07-26
Cauchon, Hon. Martin	2007-03-13
Collenette, Hon. David	2004-10-04; 2006-02-06
Collenette, Penny	2005-08-09
Coutts, Jim	2006-03-08
DeVillers, Hon. Paul	2005-11-23
Donolo, Peter	2004-12-03
Downe, Hon. Percy	2006-04-03
Eizenga, Mike	2007-04-24
Fitzpatrick, Hon. Ross	2007-03-21; 2007-04-19
Fox, Hon. Francis	2006-09-27
Francolini, Geno	2006-04-03
Frith, Hon. Doug	2004-10-25
Frith, Hon. Royce	2005-03-01
Genest, Paul	2006-04-18
Hays, Hon. Dan	2005-12-19
Herle, David	2006-07-13; 2006-10-19

Johnson, Patrick	2005-03-01
Johnston, Hon. Don	2005-09-26
Kaplan, Hon. Bob	2005-01-21
Kirkpatrick, Doug	2005-07-25
Lalonde, Hon. Marc	2006-03-07
LeDrew, Stephen	2005-10-19
Loveys, Marjorie	2006-05-06
Macdonald, Nicky	2006-04-03
MacKinnon, Steve	2006-06-23
Manley, Hon. John	2005-02-03
Marchi, Hon. Sergio	2005-10-19
Marissen, Mark	2007-03-07
McCarthy, Dan	2005-06-08
McCauley, Gary	2005-07-12
McCauley, Randy	2006-11-17
Mercer, Hon. Terry	2005-12-14
Metcalfe, Isabelle	2006-06-09
Moore, Sean	2004-11-18
Murphy, Tim	2006-03-22; 2006-09-15
Nicholson, Peter	2006-03-28; 2006-11-08
O'Leary, Terrie	2006-08-15
Paul, Jeff	2005-01-17
Peterson, Hon. Jim	2007-03-21
Posno, Lloyd	2004-12-02; 2006-02-19
Reid, Scott	2006-07-12
Resnick, Mark	2005-02-02; 2005-06-28
Richardson, Doug	2005-01-10
Robert, Hon. Michel	2004-09-30
Roberts, Hon. John	2004-10-26
Robinson, Mike	2006-03-10; 2006-09-13
Ryan, Craig	2006-01-19
Schwass, Rodger	2005-05-24
Shaw, Andy	2005- 06-09
Siegel, Jack	2004-12-03; 2007-05-03; 2008-05-25
Stanbury, Hon. Richard	2006-02-01; 2006-02-06; 2006-03-03
Stollery, Hon. Peter	2005-03-30
Swift, John	2005-01-15
Thorkelson, Ruth	2006-07-13
Thornley, Joe	2004-10-08; 2005-07-06; 2006-04-27
Tobin, Hon. Brian	2005-11-16

Wisdom, Marva	2006-11-10
Young, George	2005-07-27
Zalusky, Taras	2008-05-13
Zussman, David	2005-08-15

Declined to Be Interviewed:

Fairbairn, Hon. Joyce
Maharaj, Akaash
Metcalfe, Herb

Notes

Introduction

1 John Meisel, *Working Papers on Canadian Politics* (Montreal: McGill-Queen's University Press, 1972).
2 Christina McCall Newman, *Grits: An Intimate Portrait of the Liberal Party* (Toronto: Macmillan, 1982), 356.
3 Stephen Harper, comments at press conference, Ottawa, 23 May 2004.
4 G. Bruce Doern, 'The Chrétien Liberals' Third Mandate,' in *How Ottawa Spends: 2002–2003*, ed. G. Bruce Doern (Don Mills: Oxford University Press, 2003), 3.
5 Susan Delacourt, *Juggernaut* (Toronto: McClelland and Stewart, 2003), xi.

1: Into the Wilderness

1 Hon. Brian Tobin, interview with author.
2 Ibid.
3 Hon. Doug Frith, interview with author.
4 See, for example, Christina McCall-Newman, *Grits: An Intimate Portrait of the Liberal Party* (Toronto: Macmillan, 1982), 97–119.
5 Ibid.
6 Hon. Marc Lalonde, interview with author.
7 Several earlier accounts incorrectly state that LeBlanc was the only cabinet minister to support Chrétien, a point underlined by both Caccia and Collenette in interviews.
8 Rt Hon. Jean Chrétien, *Straight from the Heart* (Toronto: Key Porter Books, 1985), 202.
9 Ibid.

10 Greg Weston, *Reign of Error* (Toronto: McGraw-Hill Ryerson, 1988), 58.
11 Ibid.
12 Ron Graham, *One-Eyed Kings* (Toronto: Collins, 1986), 236.
13 Lalonde, interview with author.
14 Jeffrey Simpson, 'The Vincible Liberals,' in *The Canadian General Election of 1984*, ed. Alan Frizzell and Anthony Westell (Ottawa: Carleton University Press, 1985), 20.
15 Lalonde, interview with author.
16 As quoted in Weston, *Reign of Error*, 68.
17 Ibid., 69.
18 John Swift, interview with author.
19 Some parliamentary systems now have fixed election dates. This is a practice that is now spreading to Canadian jurisdictions, and was introduced at the federal level by the Harper government.
20 Weston, *Reign of Error*, 73.
21 Simpson, 'The Vincible Liberals,' 16.
22 Frith, a Sudbury-area MP first elected in 1980, may have been secretly relieved to be replaced by Erola as one of the campaign co-chairs. Ms Erola, a prominent Turner supporter and also from the Sudbury region, went down to defeat in the election.
23 Lalonde, interview with author.
24 Simpson, 'The Vincible Liberals,' 17.
25 Rt Hon. Pierre Elliott Trudeau, *Memoirs* (Toronto: McClelland and Stewart, 1995), 188.
26 Graham, *One-Eyed Kings*, 282.
27 In 2003 the Liberal Party still had no such list, for reasons outlined in a later chapter.
28 Graham, *One-Eyed Kings*, 284.
29 Ibid., 291.
30 Ibid., 292.
31 Hon. Gerry Grafstein, confidential memo to Rt Hon. John Turner; emphasis added.
32 Hon. Doug Frith, interview with author.
33 Hon. Charles Caccia and Hon. Don Boudria, interviews with author.

2: Life in the Opposition, 1984–1987

1 Hon. Doug Frith, interview with author.
2 See, for example, Greg Weston, *Reign of Error* (Toronto: McGraw-Hill Ryerson, 1988), and Ron Graham, *Promise and Illusion in Canadian Politics* (Toronto: Collins, 1986).

3 Hon. Doug Frith, interview with author.
4 Ibid.
5 Hon. Royce Frith, interview with author.
6 Douglas Richardson, interview with author.
7 Hon. Doug Frith, interview with author.
8 Hon. Jean-Luc Pépin, conversations with author, 1985.
9 LCRB director, memorandum to Caucus Executive on possible expansion of LCRB activities, 23 June 1987.
10 In the end the OLO chief of staff was also allowed to attend as a compromise.
11 Doug Richardson, interview with author.
12 Ibid.
13 See, for example, Greg Weston, *Reign of Error*, ch. 10.
14 Ibid., 159.
15 Ian Mulgrew, 'Turner on Road to Recovery from Stumbles in Campaign,' *Globe and Mail*, 16 February 1985, A1.
16 'Turner Magic Restored?' *Victoria Times Colonist*, 6 April 1985.
17 Letter from Rt Hon. John Turner to all caucus members, 21 January 1985.
18 'Message from the Leader of the Opposition,' Office of the Leader of the Opposition, Ottawa, 4 December 1987.
19 Paul Martin, 'Closing Statement,' Canada Conference Series I, 25 October 1987, 10.
20 Canada, House of Commons, *Debates*, 27 February 1986, 1110.
21 Transcript of press conference by the Rt Hon. John Turner, Ottawa, 27 February 1986.
22 Brooke Jeffrey, *Breaking Faith* (Toronto: Key Porter, 1992), 102–11.
23 Weston, *Reign of Error*, 237.
24 Ibid., 238.
25 Liberal Party of Canada, *Policy Resolutions Passed by the Plenary Session of the National Policy Convention*, 30 November 1986, Resolution #8(a) (ii).
26 Weston, *Reign of Error*, 232.

3: Reconstructing the Party

1 Iona Campagnolo, Address to the President's Reform Committee of the Liberal Party, 1983.
2 Iona Campagnolo, President's Address to the Reform Committee, *Towards a Better Liberal Party*, Discussion Paper (Ottawa, January 1984), 4.
3 Doug Richardson, interview with author.
4 For a detailed discussion of this issue, see Greg Weston, *Reign of Error* (Toronto: McGraw-Hill Ryerson, 1988), 173–4.

5 Hon. David Collenette, interview with author.

6 Ibid.

7 Lloyd Posno, interview with author.

8 Collenette, interview with author.

9 *Towards a Better Liberal Party*, 16–17.

10 President's Committee on Reform of the Liberal Party, *Final Report*, Ottawa, August 1985, 32.

11 Hon. Doug Frith, interview with author.

12 Rt Hon. John Turner, 'Remarks on the Occasion of the Opening of the New National Headquarters,' Ottawa, 26 November 1986, 2.

13 John Swift, interview with author.

14 J.L. Granatstein, *The Ottawa Men: The Civil Service Mandarins, 1935–57* (Toronto: Oxford University Press, 1982).

15 See, for example, Colin Campbell and George Szablowski, *The Superbureaucrats* (Toronto: Macmillan, 1979).

16 The selection of Pierre Trudeau as leader in 1968 – although it involved nine candidates and required four ballots – has been described not so much as a demonstration of the elite's lack of control but rather as an indication that the elites were divided. For a detailed description of the deal making that evolved during that leadership race, see Christina McCall-Newman, *Grits: An Intimate Portrait of the Liberal Party* (Toronto: Macmillan, 1982), 103–16.

17 Joseph Wearing, *The L-Shaped Party: The Liberal Party of Canada, 1958–1980* (Toronto: McGraw-Hill Ryerson, 1981), 235.

18 The self-imposed names for the wings are revealing in themselves. The volunteer side sees itself as the core of the party and refers to the 'parliamentary wing,' while parliamentarians see themselves as the central element of the party and refer to the 'volunteer wing.' Tom Axworthy's celebrated term was the 'lay' wing of the party.

19 Liberal Party of Canada, *Transcript of Plenary Session* (Ottawa: 1966 National Convention).

20 Richard Stanbury, interview with author.

21 Wearing, *The L-Shaped Party*, 79.

22 Jim Coutts, interview with author.

23 Rt Hon. Pierre Elliott Trudeau, 'Notes for Remarks by the Prime Minister,' 10 November 1968, 3–5. See also Richard Stanbury, *The Liberal Party of Canada: An Interpretation* (Ottawa: The Liberal Federation of Canada, June 1969), 40–2.

24 Richard Stanbury, interview with author. See also Wearing, *The L-Shaped Party*, 141.

25 For more detail, see Trudeau's own account of his motives in his *Memoirs* (Toronto: McClelland and Stewart, 1993), 117–18.

26 Ron Graham, *One-Eyed Kings* (Toronto: Collins, 1986), 241.

27 Hon. Peter Stollery, interview with author.

28 Alf Apps, interview with author.

29 Hon. Charles Caccia, interview with author.

30 Christina McCall-Newman, *Trudeau and Our Times* (Toronto: McClelland and Stewart, 1991), 317.

31 Ibid., 149.

32 Hon. Marc Lalonde, interview with author.

33 David Berger, conversation with author.

34 A 19 June 1982 Gallup poll (reproduced in *La Presse*) showed Quebeckers supported the constitutional package as a 'good thing' by a margin of more than 3 to 1.

35 Alf Apps, interview with author.

36 Ben Tierney, 'Capital Accounts,' *Ottawa Citizen*, 16 January 1982, A4.

37 Liberal Party of Canada, 'Resolution 40,' *Priority Resolutions*, National Biennial Convention (Ottawa, 1982).

38 Alf Apps, interview with author.

39 McCall-Newman, *Trudeau and Our Times*, 317.

40 Hon. Iona Campagnolo, PC, 'Remarks to the First Meeting of the President's Committee for Reform,' Ottawa, 17 June 1983.

41 *Towards a Better Liberal Party*, 9.

42 Ibid., 66.

43 One Angus Reid poll in June 1985, widely cited by Turner supporters, gave the Liberals 38 per cent of decided voter support compared with 30 per cent for the Conservatives and 27 per cent for the NDP.

44 Hon. Sergio Marchi, interview with author.

45 Weston, *Reign of Error*, 199.

46 Gary McCauley, interview with author.

47 Jacques Corriveau, 'The Case for a Liberal Leadership Review,' note distributed to Liberal caucus members, Montreal, 19 September 1986, 3–4.

48 George Young, interview with author.

49 Weston, *Reign of Error*, 199.

50 Ibid., 197.

51 Doug Richardson, interview with author.

52 Weston, *Reign of Error*, 195–6.

53 Ibid., 201.

54 Hon. Keith Davey, *The Rainmaker: A Passion for Politics* (Toronto: Stoddart, 1986).

55 Hon. Marc Lalonde, interview with author.
56 Hon. David Collenette, interview with author.
57 Weston, *Reign of Error*, 209.
58 Hon. David Collenette, interview with author.
59 Hon. Doug Frith, interview with author.
60 Weston, *Reign of Error*, 214.
61 Ibid., 222.
62 Ibid., 222–3.
63 Hon. Jack Austin, interview with author.

4: The Meech Morass, 1987–1988

1 'Liberals Stumble over Meech Lake,' *Toronto Star*, 6 March 1988, B3.
2 See, for example, Alan Frizzell, Jon H. Pammett, and Anthony Westell, *The Canadian General Election of 1993* (Ottawa: Carleton University Press, 1994); R. Johnston, with N. Nevitte, A. Blais, H. Brady, and E. Gidengil, 'Electoral Discontinuity: The 1993 Canadian Federal Election,' *International Social Science Journal* 146 (1995): 583–99; B. Jeffrey, *Hard Right Turn* (Toronto: Harper Collins, 1999), 332–4.
3 'Breakthrough: Behind the Constitutional Accord,' *Maclean's*, 11 May 1987.
4 Doug Richardson, interview with author.
5 Ibid.
6 Hon. Robert Kaplan, interview with author.
7 Canada, House of Commons, *Debates*, 1 May 1987, 5629.
8 Brian Tobin, interview with author.
9 Transcript of interview with Rt Hon. John Turner, *Canada AM*, CTV, 4 May 1987, 1.
10 B. Jeffrey, 'Briefing Note on the April 30, 1987 Meeting of First Ministers re: Quebec's Adherence to the Constitution Act, 1982,' 11. Internal document prepared for distribution to national caucus.
11 Hon. Don Johnston, letter to the Rt Hon. John Turner, 7 May 1987.
12 CTV transcript of Turner interview, 4 May 1987, 5.
13 Canada, House of Commons, *Debates*, 11 May 1987, 5934.
14 Doug Richardson, interview with author.
15 Sergio Marchi, interview with author.
16 Andrew Cohen, *A Deal Undone: The Making and Breaking of the Meech Lake Accord* (Toronto: Douglas and McIntyre, 1990), 148.
17 Stephen Scott, 'Canada's Retreat into the Parish: Rubicon at Meech Lake,' memo from Scott to Hon. Don Johnston, as distributed to national caucus, 16 May 1987, 7–9.

18 Letter dated 4 June 1987 from Ron Steele, president, Prince George Liberal Riding Association to Hon. Charles Caccia.

19 Iain Hunter, 'Opposition Greets Accord Cautiously,' *Ottawa Citizen*, 2 May 1987, A1.

20 Rt Hon. P.E. Trudeau, conversations with author.

21 P.E. Trudeau, 'Such Sleight of Hand,' letter to the editor, *Toronto Star*, 27 May 1987, reproduced in D. Johnston, ed., *With a Bang Not a Whimper: Pierre Trudeau Speaks Out* (Toronto: Stoddart, 1988), 13.

22 Jeff Sallot, 'Liberals Try to Avoid Split over Accord,' *Globe and Mail*, 29 May 1987, A1–2.

23 For more detail, see the address of Mr Rémillard, Quebec National Assembly, *Debates*, 33rd Parliament, 1st session, 19 June 1987.

24 As quoted in Liberal Caucus Research Bureau, 'Briefing Note,' 30 April 1987, 12.

25 B. Jeffrey, *Breaking Faith: The Mulroney Legacy* (Toronto: Key Porter, 1992), 104–5.

26 Management Committee of the Liberal Party of Canada, 'Confidential Memorandum to Members of the National Liberal Caucus,' 8 June 1987. Signed by President Michel Robert, party officials Rosemary McCarney, Red Williams, Lloyd Posno, Lynda Sorenson, Sean Moore, Andre Lizotte, Lise Saint-Martin Tremblay, Jonathan Schneiderman, Rodger Schwass, Ross Milne, and Bill McEwen.

27 Greg Weston, 'Grits Warned of New Dip in Polls,' *Ottawa Citizen*, 10 June 1987, A1; and Joe O'Donnell, 'Turner Admits 10 MPs Oppose Pact,' *Toronto Star*, 11 June 1987, A1.

28 Cohen, *A Deal Undone*, 148.

29 Sergio Marchi, MP (York West), 'Memorandum to Liberal Caucus,' 25 June 1987, and draft copy of article 'In Respect of the Multicultural Canada Defined by the Ottawa Constitutional Accord the Dream Still Eludes Us,' *Corriere Canadese*, 26 June 1987.

30 John Nunziata, MP (York South-Weston), confidential letter to Rt Hon. John Turner, 10 June 1987.

31 As quoted in Greg Weston, *Reign of Error* (Toronto: McGraw-Hill Ryerson, 1988), 258.

32 Ross Howard, 'Liberals Well Poised Despite Dissent,' *Globe and Mail*, 26 September 1987, A7.

33 Val Sears, 'Liberals Said Ready to Demand Major Change in Meech Accord,' *Toronto Star*, 3 September 1987, A1.

34 Special Joint Committee on the 1987 Constitutional Accord (SJCCA), *Report*, issue no. 17 (Ottawa, 9 September 1987), 76.

35 Ibid., 86
36 Ibid., 95 and 121.
37 *Toronto Star*, editorial, 4 September 1987, A20.
38 Marjorie Nichols, 'Grits Playing Cynical Game with Meech Lake Strategy,' *Ottawa Citizen*, 5 September 1987.
39 *Question Period*, CTV News, 11 September 1987.
40 Stephen Bindman, 'PM Challenges Liberals to Put Up or Shut Up on Meech Lake Accord,' *Ottawa Citizen*, 22 September 1987, A1.
41 They were Berger, Caccia, Dingwall, Finestone, Henderson, Johnston, MacLellan, Marchi, Nunziata, Penner, and Robichaud.
42 Hon. Charles Caccia, interview with author.
43 Canadian Press release, 2 October 1987.
44 Hon. Peter Stollery, interview with author.
45 Rt Hon. Pierre Elliott Trudeau, presentation to the Senate Committee of the Whole, 30 March 1988, as reproduced in D. Johnston, ed., *With a Bang Not a Whimper*, 36–105.
46 Ibid., 105.
47 Hon. Donald Johnston, interview with author.
48 Johnston, ed., *With a Bang Not a Whimper*, Introduction.
49 Sharon Carstairs, 'Meech Lake Would Balkanize Canada,' *Financial Post*, 28 August 1988, 18.
50 Memo from Hon. Don Johnston to David Berger, Charles Caccia, David Dingwall, Sheila Finestone, Russell MacLellan, Keith Penner, and George Henderson, 28 April 1988.
51 Hon. Michael Kirby, 'Meech Lake Pact Reflects Traditional Tory Views,' *Toronto Star*, 4 June 1988.
52 Michael Kirby, Hugh Segal, and Gerald Caplan, *Election: The Issues, the Strategy, the Aftermath* (Toronto: Prentice-Hall, 1989), 57.
53 Daniel Drolet, 'Leaders Line Up on Meech Lake Accord,' *Ottawa Citizen*, 15 June 1988, A4.
54 Joel Ruimy, 'Liberal Opposed to Meech Pact Indicates He'll Abstain on New Vote,' *Toronto Star*, 17 June 1988, A10.
55 Tim Naumetz, 'Grits Rebel on Meech,' *Toronto Sun*, 23 June 1988, 4.
56 'Liberals Stumble over Meech Lake,' *Toronto Star*, 6 March 1988, B3.

5: The Fight of His Life: The 1988 Election

1 Graham Fraser, *Playing for Keeps: The Making of the Prime Minister, 1988* (Toronto: McClelland and Stewart, 1989), 199.
2 Ibid., 143–5.
3 Memo from Senator Michael Kirby to Rt Hon. John Turner, 9 June 1988.

4 Hon. Brian Tobin, interview with author.

5 Fraser, *Playing for Keeps*, 101.

6 *La Presse*, 15 August 1988.

7 David Vienneau, 'Bourassa Says Turner Was Wrong on Trade,' *Toronto Star*, 14 August 1988, A1.

8 Interestingly the strategy failed. Although right-to-life groups did capture several ridings, they had no impact on the outcome of the debate as sitting MPs. The bill subsequently introduced by the Mulroney government was far more moderate than they had hoped and was, in any event, defeated by Conservative senators before the next election. The Chrétien government never introduced legislation during its ten-year mandate.

9 Hon. Doug Frith, interview with author.

10 Fraser, *Playing for Keeps*, 163.

11 Gerald Caplan, Michael Kirby, and Hugh Segal, *Election: The Issues, the Strategy, the Aftermath* (Toronto: Prentice-Hall, 1989), 63.

12 Patrick Johnson, interview with author.

13 Redistribution occurs after a decennial census. However, the 1981 census, which resulted in revised legislation in 1985, was not implemented until the 1988 election. For more detail, see James Robertson, *The Canadian Electoral System*, Library of Parliament, BP147E, revised May 2004.

14 Hon. Michel Robert, interview with author.

15 Hon. Marc Lalonde, interview with author.

16 Michael Robinson, interview with author.

17 Lloyd Posno, interview with author.

18 Hon. Michel Robert, interview with author.

19 Ibid.

20 See, for example, the successive analyses of Andre Siegfried, *The Race Question in Canada* (Ottawa: Carleton University Press, 1978), 130–42; M. Kirby and I. McKinnon, 'Political Knowledge in Canada,' in Jon H. Pammett and J-L Pépin, *Political Education in Canada* (Ottawa: IRPP, 1988), 21–4; and Harold D. Clarke et al., *Absent Mandate: Canadian Electoral Politics in an Era of Restructuring* (Toronto: Gage, 1996).

21 See, for example, Clarke et al., *Absent Mandate*. Ironically, by the 1988 election the leadership factor was actually on the decline, as Pammett later demonstrated in his work on the 1993 election, but at the time it was still believed to be a crucial factor. 'Tracking the Votes' in A. Frizzell, J. Pammett, and A. Westell, *The Canadian General Election of 1993* (Ottawa: Carleton University Press, 1994).

22 Memo from Dr Rodger Schwass, chair, National Policy Committee to the LPC executive, June 1990.

23 Mark Resnick, interview with author.

24 Patrick Johnson, interview with author.
25 R. Schwass, interview with author.
26 Memo from the director of the Liberal Research Bureau to all nominated candidates, 27 June 1988.
27 Notes for a Speech by Rt Hon. John Turner, 15 July 1988.
28 Fraser, *Playing for Keeps*, 199.
29 Author interview with senior Tory election organizer.
30 Fraser, *Playing for Keeps*, 175.
31 Press release. Notes for a speech by the Leader of the Liberal Party, Ottawa, 1 October 1988.
32 Ibid.
33 Caplan, Kirby, and Segal, *Election*.
34 See, for example, A. Frizzell and A. Westell, 'The Media and the Campaign,' in A. Frizzell, J. Pammett, and A. Westell, *The Canadian General Election of 1988* (Ottawa: Carleton University Press, 1989), 75–91, esp. 76.
35 Peter Maser, 'On the Hustings,' in ibid., 57.
36 David Vienneau, 'Confusion Reigns as Turner Unveils Child Care Plan,' *Toronto Star*, 5 October 1988.
37 Andy Shaw, interview with author.
38 Caplan, Kirby, and Segal, *Election*, 126.
39 Tom Axworthy and Martin Goldfarb, *Marching to a Different Drummer: An Essay on Liberals and Conservatives in Convention* (Toronto: Stoddart, 1988), 127.
40 Caplan, Kirby, and Segal, *Election*, 217–18.
41 An excellent summary can be found in A. Westell and A. Frizzell, 'The Media and the Campaign,' in Frizzell, Pammett, and Westell, *The Canadian General Election of 1988*.
42 Hon. Bob Kaplan, interview with author.
43 Senator Michael Kirby, chair of Strategy Committee, memo to Rt Hon. John Turner, 14 October 1988. See also Kirby's detailed explanation of his role in Caplan, Kirby, and Segal, *Election*, 131–3.
44 Doug Kirkpatrick, interview with author.
45 Michael Robinson, interview with author.
46 Kirkpatrick, interview with author.
47 See Peter Connolly's lengthy comments as quoted in Fraser, *Playing for Keeps*, 238–41.
48 Author interviews. See also Fraser, *Playing for Keeps*, 238–40.
49 For a detailed description of Chrétien's role and that of other Quebec Liberals, see Fraser, *Playing for Keeps*, 260–3.
50 Mark Resnick, interview with author.

51 Hon. Charles Caccia, interview with author.
52 Caplan, Kirby, and Segal, *Election*. 148.
53 *Montreal Gazette*, 22 October 1988, and repeated in his address at a confer-
    ence at Queen's University in February 1989 that was organized by the
    School of Policy Studies and the CBC to review the campaign.
54 As cited in Frizzell and Westell, 'The Media and the Campaign,' in Frizzell,
    Pammett, and Westell, *The Canadian General Election of 1988*, 83.
55 Caplan, Kirby, and Segal, *Election*, 149.
56 Maser, 'On the Hustings,' 61.
57 A complete video of the 25 October 1988 leaders' debate can be found on
    the CBC website (www.cbc.ca) under Digital Archives/Politics/Federal
    Elections.
58 Caplan, Kirby, and Segal, *Election*, 220.
59 Maser, 'On the Hustings,' 67.
60 A detailed description of Wilson's speech to the press corps in Ottawa on
    31 October 1988 can be found in Fraser, *Playing for Keeps*, 323–4. It was this
    speech that paved the way for the Tories' Ten Big Lies ad campaign.
61 Robert Krause, 'The Progressive Conservative Campaign: Mission Accom-
    plished,' in Frizzell, Pammett, and Westell, *The Canadian General Election of
    1988*, 24.
62 A study by political scientist Janet Hiebert for the Lortie Commission,
    set up to look at this issue, eventually led to several attempts by the gov-
    ernment to ban third-party advertising, which were opposed by single-
    issue groups like the Taxpayers Federation and the National Citizens'
    Coalition.
63 Jeffrey Simpson, 'Overnight Redemption,' *Globe and Mail*, 12 November
    1988, D6.
64 Allan Gregg, Riding Report Memorandum, Progressive Conservative
    Party of Canada, Decima Research, 13 November 1988, as cited in Krause,
    'The Progressive Conservative Campaign,' 25.
65 Ibid., 23.
66 Jon Pammett, 'The 1988 Vote,' in Frizzell, Pammett, and Westell, *The Cana-
    dian General Election of 1988*, 131.

6: Transition: Chrétien Takes the Helm, 1989–1992

 1 Interview with author.
 2 Hon. Sergio Marchi, interview with author.
 3 Brooke Jeffrey, memo to National Caucus chair (Brian Tobin), 1 December
    1988, 2.

4 David Unruh, *Manitoba Chair's Report*, 6; Gord McKenzie and Barb Mac-Nevin, *Saskatchewan Federal Campaign Report*, 2.
5 Carol Young, *Nova Scotia Election Report*, 4.
6 Rémi Bujold, *Report of the Chair of the Quebec Electoral Campaign*, 3.
7 Derek Lewis and Norman Whalen, *Report of the Newfoundland Co-Chairs*, 3.
8 Norman McLeod, *Report of the Federal Campaign Committee for Ontario*, 2.
9 Russell Brink, *Report on the British Columbia Federal Election 1988*, 4.
10 David Morton, *Red Leaf Communications Election 88 Report*, 4.
11 Ibid.
12 Brooke Jeffrey, *Report on the Platform and the Role of the Research Bureau in the '88 Campaign*, 2.
13 Douglas Kirkpatrick, *Summary Report, Leader's Tour*, 4.
14 Hon. Sergio Marchi, interview with author.
15 Susan Delacourt, *Juggernaut: Paul Martin's Campaign for Chrétien's Crown* (Toronto: McClelland and Stewart, 2003), 51.
16 Ibid.
17 Brian Tobin, interview with author.
18 John Gray, *Paul Martin: In the Balance* (Toronto: Key Porter, 2003), 93–7.
19 Delacourt, *Juggernaut*, 42–3.
20 Tim Murphy, interview with author.
21 Hon. Terry Mercer, interview with author.
22 Joe Thornley, interview with author.
23 Hon. Michel Robert, interview with author.
24 Brian Tobin (Chair of Liberal Caucus), memo to Hon. Herb Gray, Opposition House leader, and Peter Connolly, principal secretary to Rt Hon. John Turner, 26 July 1989.
25 Brooke Jeffrey, 'Introduction to the Policy Primer: Purpose and Organization' (Ottawa: Liberal Party of Canada, 3 January 1990).
26 Mark Resnick, interview with author.
27 Bruce Wallace, 'Waiting for a Leader,' *Maclean's*, 6 November 1989, 21.
28 As quoted in Bruce Wallace, 'Waiting for a Leader,' 24.
29 Michael Robinson, interview with author, March 2006.
30 Wallace, 'Waiting for a Leader.'
31 Jean Chrétien, 'A Challenge of Leadership,' speech delivered to the Faculty of Law, University of Ottawa, 16 January 1990, 7.
32 Ibid., 12.
33 Ibid., 16–18.
34 Rosemary Speirs, 'Chrétien, A Man Back from Exile,' *Toronto Star*, 19 June 1990, A12.
35 Sheila Copps, 'On the Importance of Liberalism,' *De Novo*, January 1990, 20.

36 Paul Martin, 'Nationalism without Walls,' *De Novo*, January 1990, 23.
37 Terrie O'Leary, interview with author.
38 Lawrence Martin, *Iron Man: The Defiant Reign of Jean Chrétien* (Toronto: Penguin, 2003), 25.
39 Mark Resnick, interview with author.
40 Speirs, 'Chrétien, A Man Back from Exile,' A9.
41 Sean Durkin, 'Chrétien's under Fire,' *Calgary Sun*, 20 June 1990, 5.
42 Michel Robert, *President's Report: A Renewed Commitment*, 22 June 1990.
43 Sean Moore, memo to members of the National Executive, 28 November 1989, 3.
44 Liberal Party of Canada, *Forum Primer I: Party Issues*, 12.
45 Moore, memo to members of the National Executive.
46 Sean Moore, interview with author.
47 Sheila Gervais, 'The Democratic Deficit in the Liberal Party of Canada: A Prescription for Reform,' Ottawa, February 2005, 10.
48 Originally Roberts's only opponent was a professional fundraiser, D'Arcy Barrett, who had few ties within the party. Cathy Richardson, a former party vice-president, and Don Johnston, the former MP and Meech Lake opponent who had left the Liberal caucus over the issue, were late entrants.
49 John Gray, *Paul Martin: The Politics of Ambition* (Toronto: Key Porter, 2003).
50 John Gray, *Paul Martin: In the Balance*, 189.
51 Marg Leguilloux, 'No Holds Barred in Grits' Debate,' *Calgary Sun*, 21 June 1990, 4.
52 Bill Kaufman, 'Trudeau Trashes Meech,' *Calgary Sun*, 22 June 1990, 4.
53 Sean Durkin, 'Turner Takes Parting Shot,' *Calgary Sun*, 22 June 1990, 4.
54 Hon. Don Johnston, interview with author.
55 Martin, *Iron Man*, 26.
56 Geoff White, 'We Have Work to Do,' *Calgary Sun*, 24 June 1990, A2.
57 Martin, *Iron Man*, 26.
58 Mark Resnick, interview with author.
59 The author attended this event.
60 David Vienneau. 'Chrétien Meets Ex-Rivals to Mend Leadership Rifts,' *Toronto Star*, 5 July 1990.
61 Ibid.
62 Speirs, 'Chrétien, A Man Back from Exile.'
63 Rodger Schwass, interview with author.
64 Joe Thornely, interview with author.
65 Joan Bryden, 'Chrétien Rejects Lure of Early House Seat,' *Ottawa Citizen*, 27 July 1990.

66 Geoffrey Stevens, 'Jean Chrétien: PM's Only Asset,' *Toronto Star*, 12 August 1990, B3.

67 Hon. Sergio Marchi, interview with author.

68 Shortly after Chrétien became prime minister, Robichaud was appointed to the Senate.

69 Ibid., 29.

70 George Young, interview with author.

71 William Walker, 'Liberal MPs Fuming over Martin's Unity Pitch,' *Toronto Star*, 16 February 1991, A8.

72 Hon. Jean Chrétien, 'Submission to the Commission on the Political and Constitutional Future of Quebec,' 17 December 1990, 42–3.

73 Lise Bissonnette and Alain Dubuc, as cited in Martin, *Iron Man*, 50–2.

74 Stephen Clarkson, 'Yesterday's Man and His Blue Grits,' in Frizzell, Pammett, and Westell, *The Canadian General Election of 1993* (Ottawa: Carleton University Press, 1994), 27–8.

75 Carol Goar, 'Liberal Strategists Hope Chrétien Will Quit,' *Toronto Star*, 9 May 1991, A27.

76 Peter Donolo, interview with author.

77 As David Collenette later noted, Penny Collenette's appointment resulted in the first husband and wife team ever to hold the same position within the Liberal Party.

78 Jon Pammett, 'Tracking the Votes,' in Frizzell, Pammett, and Westell, *The Canadian General Election of 1993*, 149.

79 David Berger, 'Let's Remember Our Roots,' speech to the General Assembly of the Montebello Conference, 14 April 1989, 5.

80 Martin, *Iron Man*, 17.

81 Ibid., 46.

82 Kenneth Courtis, 'Globalization: The Economic Impact,' in *Finding Common Ground*, ed. Jean Chrétien (Hull: Voyageur Press, 1992), 22.

83 Peter J. Nicholson, 'Nowhere to Hide: The Economic Implications of Globalization for Canada,' in ibid., 34.

84 Chrétien, *Finding Common Ground*, 10.

85 Ibid., 7.

86 E. Greenspon and A. Wilson-Smith, *Double Vision* (Toronto: Penguin, 1997), 22.

87 Based on interviews with several research officers involved in the exercise.

88 In 1988 there were separate background documents for each plank, in addition to the widely distributed summary pamphlet. Although the possibility of one large background book was briefly discussed, factors of cost and concerns about possible errors being difficult to correct

precluded any serious discussion of this option. In 1993, a single, more comprehensive background book was prepared and distributed to all candidates as well as the media. This 112-page background document is the one often referred to by the media as the Red Book, although the one widely available to the public was in fact the ten-page pamphlet similar to that of 1988.

89 Clarkson, 'Yesterday's Man and His Blue Grits,' 35.
90 Canada, House of Commons, *Debates*, 25 May 1992.
91 For a detailed outline of these various developments, see B. Jeffrey, *Strange Bedfellows, Trying Times: October 1992 and the Defeat of the Powerbrokers* (Toronto: Key Porter, 1992), 48–54.
92 Susan Delacourt and Graham Fraser, 'Pro Canada Crusade Begins,' *Globe and Mail*, 29 August 1992, A1.
93 It is unclear where Rizzuto might have obtained the information on Liberal voting intentions. However, several public opinion polls had indicated roughly 70 per cent of Canadians were inclined to support the deal.
94 Delacourt and Fraser, 'Pro-Canada Crusade Begins.'
95 *Ottawa Citizen*, 19 October 1992.
96 Jeffrey Simpson, 'The Trudeau Vision Triumphed,' *Globe and Mail*, 29 October 1992, A26.

7: Return to Power: The 1993 Election

1 Jon Pammett, 'Tracking the Vote,' in Alan Frizzell, Jon Pammett, and Anthony Westell, *The Canadian General Election of 1993* (Ottawa: Carleton University Press, 1994), 1.
2 Peter Donolo, interview with author.
3 Gordon Ashworth, interview with author.
4 Joe Thornley, interview with author.
5 Sheila Gervais, 'The Democratic Deficit in the Liberal Party of Canada: A Prescription for Reform' (Ottawa: February 2005), 11.
6 Jack Siegel, interview with author.
7 Gordon Ashworth, interview with author.
8 Isabelle Metcalfe, interview with author.
9 The nine included three who became MPs, namely Jean Augustine, Elinor Caplan, Anne McLellan, and Georgette Sheridan. In 1997 he appointed six candidates, of whom four were women. In the three elections during which he was leader, Chrétien appointed a total of twenty-one candidates, fourteen of whom were women.
10 B. Kent, Letter from the Office of the Prime Minister, 27 February 2002.

11 Hon. Don Boudria, interview with author.

12 L. Martin, *Iron Man* (Toronto: Penguin, 2003) 57. (In the end, Cloutier replaced Hopkins on his retirement in 1997 and served as the Liberal MP for two terms.)

13 Carol Goar, 'Liberal Candidates Give Substance to Leader's Bravado,' *Toronto Star*, 13 May 1993, A23.

14 Hon. David Collenette, interview with author.

15 Hon. Charles Caccia, interview with author.

16 Kim Campbell, *Time and Chance* (Toronto: Doubleday, 1996).

17 Peter Woolstencroft, 'Doing Politics Differently: The Conservative Party and the Campaign of 1993,' in Frizzell, Pammett, and Westell, *The Canadian General Election of 1993*, 19.

18 Ibid., 18.

19 Hon. Bob Kaplan, interview with author.

20 Gordon Ashworth, interview with author.

21 Woolstencroft, 'Doing Politics Differently.'

22 For a detailed account of these debates, see Lawrence LeDuc, 'The Leaders' Debates: Critical Event or Non-Event?' in Frizzell, Pammett, and Westell, *The Canadian General Election of 1993*, 127–41.

23 Ross Fitzpatrick, BC campaign chair, memo to National Campaign Committee, 7 October 1988.

24 Gordon Ashworth, interview with author.

25 Editorial, *Globe and Mail*, 12 October 1993.

26 Frizzell, Pammett, and Westell, *The Canadian General Election of 1993*, 2–4.

27 Jon Pammett, 'Tracking the Vote,' 153.

28 Ibid., 1.

29 Rodger Schwass and Hon. Bob Kaplan, interviews with author.

30 Pierre Drouilly, *L'année politique au Québec: 1993* (Montreal: UQAM, 1995).

31 Frizzell, Pammett, and Westell, *The Canadian General Election of 1993*, 6.

32 Ken Carty, William Cross, and Lisa Young, *Rebuilding Canadian Party Politics* (Vancouver: UBC Press, 2000).

8: Return to Governing: A Tale of Two Crises

1 Rt Hon. Jean Chrétien, Speech to Confederation Dinner, Toronto, 31 October 1995, as cited in Eddie Goldenberg, *The Way It Works* (Toronto: McClelland and Stewart, 2006), 222–3.

2 See, for example, Chrétien's recollections of his time as secretary of the Treasury Board in his autobiography, *Straight from the Heart* (Toronto: Key Porter, 1985), 82–90.

3 John Gray, *Paul Martin: In the Balance* (Toronto: Key Porter, 2004), 110.

4 David Zussman, interview with author.

5 Hon. John Manley, interview with author.

6 Hon. Brian Tobin, interview with author.

7 Lawrence Martin, *Iron Man: The Defiant Reign of Jean Chrétien* (Toronto: Penguin, 2003), 58–9.

8 For a detailed discussion of the operation of the Mulroney PMO and PCO, see P. Aucoin, 'The Machinery of Government: From Trudeau's Rational Management to Mulroney's Brokerage Politics,' in *Prime Ministers and Premiers*, ed. L. Pal and D. Taras (Scarborough: Prentice-Hall, 1998), 50–68; and Colin Campbell, SJ, 'Mulroney's Broker Politics: The Ultimate in Politicized Incompetence?' in *Canada under Mulroney: An End of Term Report*, ed. A. Gollner and D. Salée (Montreal: Vehicule Press, 1988), 309–34.

9 A detailed discussion of this approach is found in B. Jeffrey, *Breaking Faith* (Toronto: Key Porter, 1990), 50–3.

10 Zussman, interview with author.

11 James Bartleman, *Rollercoaster* (Toronto: McClelland and Stewart, 2005), 32.

12 E. Greenspon and A. Wilson-Smith, *Double Vision* (Toronto: Doubleday, 1996), 6.

13 Hon. John Manley, interview with author.

14 Hon. Lloyd Axworthy, interview with author.

15 Marjorie Loveys, interview with author.

16 Penny Collenette, interview with author.

17 Bartleman, *Rollercoaster*, 16.

18 See, for example, Bartleman's account in *Rollercoaster*, 39–42.

19 Dan McCarthy, interview with author.

20 Dan McCarthy, note to author, 25 May 2008.

21 Brooke Jeffrey, memo from the Coordinator of the Western Communications Project to the Director of the Liberal Caucus Research Bureau, 15 September 1996, 3.

22 George Young, interview with author.

23 Peter Donolo, interview with author.

24 George Young, interview with author.

25 Hon. Terry Mercer, interview with author.

26 George Young, interview with author.

27 Hon. Don Johnston, interview with author.

28 Hon. Dan Hays, interview with author.

29 Hon. Terry Mercer, interview with author.

30 Hon. Dan Hays, interview with author.

31 Ibid.

32 Ibid.

33 Ibid.

34 As quoted in Martin, *Iron Man*, 95.

35 Peter Donolo, interview with author.

36 See, for example, John W. Kingdon, *Agendas, Alternatives, and Public Policies*, 2nd ed. (New York: Longman, 2003).

37 Hon. Paul Martin, 'The Canadian Experience in Reducing Budget Deficits and Debt,' *Notes for an Address by The Honourable Paul Martin, Minister of Finance,* presented to the Federal Reserve Bank of Kansas City Symposium on 'Budget Deficits and Debt: Issues and Options,' Jackson Hole, Wyoming, 1 September 1995.

38 Peter Nicholson, interview with author.

39 As cited in Greenspon and Wilson-Smith, *Double Vision*, 157.

40 Ibid., 133.

41 Peter Nicholson, interview with author.

42 During this period Martin's speeches were written by Larry Hagen, a freelance speech writer whose untimely demise a few years later seriously curtailed Martin's ability to communicate effectively for some time.

43 For a detailed description of the incident, see Greenspon and Wilson-Smith, *Double Vision*, 162–6.

44 Hon. John Manley, interview with author.

45 Goldenberg, *The Way It Works*, 145.

46 Hon. Sheila Copps, *Worth Fighting For* (Toronto: McClelland and Stewart, 2004).

47 Hon. Sergio Marchi, interview with author.

48 Hon. Don Boudria, interview with author.

49 Greenspon and Wilson-Smith, *Double Vision*, 211.

50 Copps, *Worth Fighting For*, 73–4.

51 Hon. John Manley, interview with author.

52 Manley also pointed out that, for the first time under a Liberal administration, the 1995 budget as printed did not correspond perfectly with the budget as read. This was due to a last-minute decision to remove a measure that would have severely reduced funding for the Space Agency, prompted by a personal call from U.S. President Clinton to the prime minister.

53 Copps, *Worth Fighting For*, 74–5.

54 Martin, *Iron Man*, 101–2.

55 See, for example, Greenspon and Wilson-Smith, *Double Vision*, 260–7.

56 Goldenberg, *The Way It Is*, 198–9.

57 See, for example, Martin, *Iron Man*, 119.

58 Ibid., 124.

59 For a detailed description of Copps's experience during the campaign, see *Worth Fighting For*, 139–46.

60 Ibid., 143.

61 Hon. Don Johnston, interview with author.

62 As cited in Martin, *Iron Man*, 118.

63 Canada, House of Commons, *Debates*, 19 September 1995, 14610.

64 Hon. John Manley, interview with author.

65 Ibid.

66 Copps, *Worth Fighting For*, 139–46; Hon. David Collenette, interview with author.

67 Yves Boisvert, 'Denatalité: Le Québec loin du record,' *La Presse*, 17 October 1995, B1.

68 As quoted in Greenspon and Wilson-Smith, *Double Vision*, 311.

69 Hon. Don Boudria, interview with author.

70 Ibid.

71 Susan Delacourt, *Juggernaut: Paul Martin's Campaign for Chrétien's Crown* (Toronto: McClelland and Stewart, 2003), 98.

72 Hon. David Collenette, interview with author.

73 Mario Fontaine, 'Chrétien dit non a Johnson,' *La Presse*, 22 October 1995.

74 Copps, *Worth Fighting For*, 142.

75 Hon. John Manley, interview with author.

76 Mario Cardinal, *Breaking Point: The 1995 Referendum* (Montreal: CBC / Boyard Press, 2005), 363.

77 Ibid., 365.

78 Eddie Goldenberg, 'The Day of the Vote,' *Globe and Mail*, 24 October 2005, A6.

79 Rt Hon. Jean Chrétien, Speech to Confederation Dinner, Toronto, 31 October 1995, as cited in Goldenberg, *The Way It Works*, 222–3.

80 As cited in Martin, *Iron Man*, 127.

81 David Zussman, interview with author.

82 Jean Chrétien, opening statement to the Gomery Inquiry, 8 February 2005.

83 Rt Hon. Jean Chrétien, comments at press conference in Vancouver during special National Caucus Meeting, 12 February 1996.

84 Peter Donolo, interview with author.

85 Hon. Don Boudria, interview with author.

86 Goldenberg, *The Way It Works*, 78.

87 Hon. Sheila Copps, conversation with author.

88 Copps, *Worth Fighting For*, 138.

89 Martin, *Iron Man*, 165.

90 Rt Hon. J. Chrétien, opening statement to the Gomery Inquiry.

9: Return to Liberalism: The Clarity Act and the Deficit Dividend

1 Interview with author.
2 Pollara, *Perspectives Canada Survey*, June 1997.
3 Christopher Dornan, 'The Television Coverage: A History of the Election in 65 Seconds,' in *The Canadian General Election of 1997*, ed. Alan Frizzell and Jon H. Pammett (Toronto: Dundurn Press, 1997), 151.
4 See, for example, Neil Nevitte et al., *Unsteady State: The 1997 Canadian Federal Election* (Oxford: Oxford University Press, 1999).
5 Hon. Don Boudria, interview with author.
6 Liberal Party of Canada, *A Record of Achievement: A Report on the Liberal Government's 36 Months in Office* (Ottawa, 1996), 10.
7 Dan McCarthy, interview with author.
8 Carol Goar, 'Chrétien's Touch,' *Toronto Star*, 23 April 1994, B1.
9 Editorial, 'A Clever Budget Unless You're Poor,' *Edmonton Journal*, 7 March 1996, A10.
10 Alain Dubuc, *La Presse*, December 1996; my translation.
11 Liberal Party of Canada, *A Record of Achievement*, 12.
12 Gene Swimmer, *How Ottawa Spends: 1997–98* (Ottawa: Carleton University Press, 1998).
13 George Young, interview with author.
14 Susan Delacourt, *Juggernaut: Paul Martin's Campaign for Chrétien's Crown* (Toronto: McClelland and Stewart, 2003), 107.
15 Edward Greenspon, 'Covering Campaign 2000,' in *The Canadian General Election of 2000*, ed. Jon H. Pammett and Christopher Dornan (Toronto: Dundurn Press, 2001), 168.
16 Hon. Don Boudria, interview with author.
17 Peter Donolo, interview with author.
18 Liberal Party of Canada, *Securing Our Future Together: The Liberal Plan 1997* (Ottawa, 1997), 87–9.
19 Ibid., 23.
20 Ed Greenspon, 'Following the Campaign Trail of 97,' in *The Canadian General Election of 1997*, ed. Frizzell and Pammett, 24.
21 Jon Pammett, 'The Voters Decide,' in ibid., 235.
22 Ibid., 239–42.
23 Dornan, 'The Television Coverage,' 150.
24 Pammett, 'The Voters Decide,' 243.
25 See, for example, Michael Marzolini, 'The Regionalization of Canadian Politics,' in *The Canadian General Election of 1997*, ed. Frizzell and Pammett, 193–207.

26 Pammett, 'The Voters Decide,' 225.

27 Lawrence Martin, *Iron Man: The Defiant Reign of Jean Chrétien* (Toronto: Penguin, 2003), 178.

28 PCO, Speech from the Throne, First Session, Thirty-Sixth Parliament of Canada, 23 September 1997.

29 Jacques Brossard, press release (translation) (Quebec City), 13 November 1997.

30 Hon. Sergio Marchi, interview with author.

31 Hon. David Collenette, interview with author.

32 Peter Donolo, interview with author.

33 David Herle, interview with author.

34 Hon. Stéphane Dion, 'Collaborative Federalism in an Era of Globalization,' in *Collaborative Government: Is There a Canadian Way?* ed. Susan Delacourt and Ed Lenihan, Institute of Public Administration of Canada, New Directions Series, no. 6.

35 For more detail on the theoretical underpinnings and differing expectations of the SUFA, see Thomas Courchene, 'ACCESS: A Convention on the Canadian Economic and Social Systems,' *Canadian Business Economics* 4, no. 4 (1996): 3–26; and G. Boismenu and J. Jenson, 'A Social Union or a Federal State?' in *How Ottawa Spends 1998–99: Balancing Act, the Post Deficit Mandate*, ed. L. Pal (Toronto: Oxford University Press, 1988), 57–80.

36 For an in-depth account of the evolution of the federal Liberals' thinking, see B. Jeffrey, 'From Collaborative Federalism to the New Unilateralism: Implications for the Welfare State,' in *Continuity and Change in Canadian Politics*, ed. H. Michelman and C. DeClercy (Toronto: University of Toronto Press, 2006), 117–46.

37 Boismenu and Jenson, 'A Social Union or a Federal State?' 63.

38 B. Jeffrey, 'From Collaborative Federalism to the New Unilateralism,' 135–41.

39 National Welfare Council, *Poverty Profile 2001* (Ottawa, 2001).

40 See, for example, P.E. Trudeau, *Federalism and the French Canadians* (Toronto: Macmillan, 1968), 188–204.

41 Martin, *Iron Man*, 248.

42 Eddie Goldenberg, 'The Day of the Vote in Their Own Words,' *Globe and Mail*, 24 October 2005, A6.

43 Hon. John Manley and Hon. David Collenette, interviews with author.

44 Hon. Paul DeVillers, interview with author.

45 Delacourt, *Juggernaut*, 153.

46 Paul Wells, *Right Side Up: The Fall of Paul Martin and the Rise of Stephen Harper's New Conservatism* (Toronto: McClelland and Stewart, 2006), 39.

47 Rhéal Séguin, 'Quebec Walks If Ottawa Won't Talk,' *Globe and Mail*, 24 November 1999, A4.
48 Jennifer Ditchburn and Jim Brown, 'Martin Supports Chrétien on Unity,' *Kingston Whig Standard*, 27 November 1999, 20.
49 Martin, *Iron Man*, 252.
50 A. Persichilli, 'Martin Sings Praises of Clarity Bill,' *Hill Times*, 26 June 2000, 1.
51 Delacourt, *Juggernaut*.
52 Sergio Marchi, interview with author, 19 October 2005.
53 The first caucus chair under Turner, Doug Frith, had been handpicked by the group that set about to rebuild the party, including Turner's chief of staff John Swift. Frith's successor, Marcel Prud'homme, had been a compromise choice of the Quebec caucus and the leader. Even Brian Tobin, the third caucus chair of the Turner era who had been chosen in a 'free' election with no preference expressed by the leader, had always enjoyed good relations with Turner.
54 Hon. Paul DeVillers, interview with author.
55 Hon. Dan Hays, interview with author.
56 George Young, interview with author.
57 Hon. Terry Mercer, interview with author.
58 Percy Downe, interview with author.
59 Delacourt, *Juggernaut*, 136.
60 Sergio Marchi, interview with author.
61 Hon. Terry Mercer, interview with author.
62 Tim Murphy, interview with author, 22 March 2006.
63 Delacourt, *Juggernaut*, ix.
64 Ibid., 254.
65 As cited in ibid., 175.
66 Stephen LeDrew, interview with author.
67 Ibid.
68 John Gray, *Paul Martin: In the Balance* (Toronto: Key Porter, 2003), 183–4.
69 Tim Murphy, interview with author.
70 Mark Marissen, interview with author.
71 Hon. Ross Fitzpatrick, interview with author.
72 Hon. Sergio Marchi and Hon. Brian Tobin, interviews with author.
73 Delacourt, *Juggernaut*, 127.
74 Donald Savoie, *Governing from the Centre: The Concentration of Power in Canadian Politics* (Toronto: University of Toronto Press, 2001).
75 Hon. Charles Caccia, 'Democratic Deficit? What Democratic Deficit?' *Policy*

Options (May 2004): 48–50. Caccia's committee was well known for its successes in forcing the government to accept modifications to its legislative plans, from CEPA to the Species at Risk Act, and had recently published a major report on pesticides that led to numerous municipal bylaws prohibiting their use for cosmetic purposes.

76 Tim Murphy, interview with author.
77 Mike Robinson, interview with author.
78 Hon. Percy Downe, interview with author.
79 John Gray, *Paul Martin: In the Balance* (Toronto: Key Porter, 2003), 208.
80 As quoted in Delacourt, *Juggernaut*, 175.
81 Tim Murphy, interview with author.
82 Martin, *Iron Man*, 265.
83 Michael Robinson, interview with author.
84 Delacourt, *Juggernaut*, 159–60.
85 Ibid.
86 Peter Donolo, interview with author.
87 Anne McIlroy, 'Youth Wing Cheers PM's Populist Theme,' *Globe and Mail*, 17 March 2000, A9.

10: Implosion: The Third Chrétien Mandate

1 G. Bruce Doern, 'The Chrétien Liberals' Third Mandate,' in *How Ottawa Spends: 2002–2003*, ed. G. Bruce Doern (Don Mills: Oxford University Press, 2003), 3.
2 Author interviews with Tim Murphy, Mike Robinson, and Mark Resnick.
3 Angus Reid poll, as reported in 'Alliance Surges, Tories Collapse: Day Helping Party Make Gains While Liberals Maintain Solid National Lead,' *Globe and Mail*, 29 July 2000, A1.
4 Hon. Percy Downe, interview with author.
5 B. Jeffrey, 'Should We Take Stock?' *Literary Review of Canada* (November 2000): 3.
6 Jon Pammett and Christopher Dornan, 'Introduction,' *The Canadian General Election of 2000*, ed. Jon H. Pammett and Christopher Dornan (Toronto: Dundurn Press, 2001), 8.
7 Gordon Ashworth, interview with author.
8 Michelle Cadario, interview with author.
9 A detailed description is provided by Brian Tobin in his autobiography, *All in Good Time* (Toronto: Penguin, 2002), 219–23.
10 George Young, interview with author.
11 Isabelle Metcalfe, interview with author.

12 For an analysis of the Reform/Alliance approach, see Lisa Young, 'Representation of Women in the New Canadian Party System,' in *Political Parties, Representation, and Electoral Democracy in Canada*, ed. William Cross (Don Mills, ON: Oxford University Press, 2002), 191–6.

13 See, for example, B. Jeffrey, *Hard Right Turn: The New Face of Neo-Conservatism in Canada* (Toronto: Harper Collins, 1995), 188–95; and K. Carty, W. Cross, and L. Young, *Rebuilding Canadian Politics* (Vancouver: UBC Press, 2000).

14 Marjorie Loveys, interview with author.

15 A point made in his statistical analysis of the campaign by political scientist Jon Pammett, 'The People's Verdict,' in *The Canadian General Election of 2000*, 302–4.

16 Marjorie Loveys, interview with author.

17 Ibid.

18 Author interviews with David Herle and Terrie O'Leary.

19 As quoted in Susan Delacourt, *Juggernaut: Paul Martin's Campaign for Chrétien's Crown* (Toronto: McClelland and Stewart, 2003), 182.

20 Brian Tobin, notes for a speech on the occasion of his resignation as premier of Newfoundland, 16 October 2000.

21 Liberal Party of Canada, *Opportunity for All: The Liberal Plan for Canada* (Ottawa: October 2000), 2–3.

22 Stephen Clarkson, 'The Liberal Threepeat,' in *The Canadian General Election of 2000*, 41.

23 CBC Newsworld, *Counter Spin*, 28 October 2000.

24 Hon. David Collenette, interview with author, 4 October 2004.

25 Pammett, 'The People's Verdict,' 307.

26 Edward Greenspon, 'Covering Campaign 2000,' in *The Canadian General Election of 2000*, 183.

27 See, for example, Christopher Dornan and Heather Pyman, 'Facts and Arguments: Newspaper Coverage of the Campaign,' in *The Canadian General Election of 2000*, 191–213.

28 Brian Laghi, 'Chrétien Says He'll Consider Quitting,' *Globe and Mail*, 17 November 2000, A1.

29 Paul Wells, 'After All That, Nothing Settled, Nothing Learned: Serious Debate Was the Biggest Loser in This Campaign,' *National Post*, 28 November 2000.

30 Doern, 'The Chrétien Liberals' Third Mandate,' 3.

31 CBC, *The National*, 29 October 2000, as cited in Clarkson, 'The Liberal Threepeat,' 50.

32 CBC, *The National*, 29 November 2000.

33 Clarkson, 'The Liberal Threepeat,' 50.

34 Craig Ryan, interview with author.

35 Hon. Stéphane Dion, 'The West and the Liberal Government at the Beginning of the New Mandate: The Need to Work Better Together,' University of Saskatchewan, 6 March 2001.

36 Allan Tuer, 'Towards a New Beginning? The Chrétien Liberals and Western Canada,' in *How Ottawa Spends,* 88–102.

37 Brian Tobin, interview with author.

38 Hon. Paul Martin, presentation to the House of Commons Committee on Finance, 17 May 2001.

39 Delacourt, *Juggernaut,* 205.

40 Hon. David Collenette, interview with author.

41 Percy Downe, interview with author.

42 Tim Murphy, inteview with author.

43 Delacourt, *Juggernaut,* 217.

44 Ibid., 209.

45 Hon. John Manley, interview with author.

46 Referred to in several author interviews. Dawson later insisted publicly the views were his own.

47 Tobin, *All in Good Time,* 252.

48 Government of Canada, *Budget Documents,* 'Strategic Investments: Bridging to the Future' (Ottawa, 10 December 2001).

49 Hon. Brian Tobin, interview with author.

50 Eddie Goldenberg, *The Way It Works* (Toronto: McClelland and Stewart, 2006), 153.

51 Richard Schultz, 'Dancing around the Digital Divide: The Fight for a Federal Broadband Access Policy,' in *How Ottawa Spends,* 198.

52 Marjorie Loveys, interview with author.

53 Paul Genest, interview with author.

54 Goldenberg, *The Way It Works,* 147–8.

55 The NEPAD was designed to increase foreign aid and investment to those African countries which improved their records on human rights abuses and corruption in government, two main sources of concern among donor countries.

56 As described in Delacourt, *Juggernaut,* 188–90.

57 Stephen LeDrew, interview with author.

58 Delacourt, *Juggernaut,* 191.

59 Hon. Charles Caccia, interview with author.

60 Hon. Paul DeVillers, interview with author.

61 Hon. Percy Downe, interview with author.

62 Canada, House of Commons, *Debates,* 28 February 2002.

63 Lysiane Gagnon, 'Quebec Is Why Jean Won't Let Go,' *Globe and Mail*, 10 June 2002.

64 CBC News, *The National*, 5 September 2002; see also Delacourt, *Juggernaut*, 233.

65 Hon. Brian Tobin, interview with author.

66 Stephen LeDrew, interview with author.

67 As quoted in Delacourt, *Juggernaut*, 227–8.

68 Hon. Jim Dinning (Executive Vice-President, TransAlta), letter to Mr Jim Palmer, 7 February 2002.

69 As cited in a Leger and Leger poll in 'Position Challenges Chrétien to Restore Canadians' Confidence in Government,' *Globe and Mail*, 22 April 2002.

70 Jonathan Murphy, 'Your Candle's Flickering, Jean,' *Globe and Mail*, 17 May 2002, A2.

71 Hon. Paul DeVillers, interview with author.

72 As quoted in Delacourt, *Juggernaut*, 239.

73 Tim Murphy, interview with author.

74 Hon. Percy Downe, interview with author.

75 'Time for Rough Justice: Series of Scandals Removes Moral Authority to Govern,' editorial, *Calgary Herald*, 10 May 2002, A20.

76 Institute for Global Ethics, *Ethics Newsline*, 27 May 2002.

77 As recounted in Delacourt, *Juggernaut*, 3.

78 Percy Downe, interview with author.

79 Hon. Sergio Marchi, interview with author.

80 Mike Robinson, interview with author.

81 Tim Murphy, interview with author.

82 As quoted in John Gray, *Paul Martin: In the Balance* (Toronto: Key Porter, 2003), 218.

83 Hon. David Collenette, interview with author.

84 Amy Carmichael, 'Chrétien Defiant,' *Kingston Whig Standard*, 1 June 2002, 13.

85 Tim Murphy, interview with author.

86 Hon. Paul Martin, 'Statement on Future Plans,' press release, Ottawa, 1 June 2002.

87 Delacourt, *Juggernaut*, 12–24.

88 Hon. John Manley, interview with author.

89 Tim Murphy, interview with author.

90 Rt Hon. Jean Chrétien, 'Statement on the Resignation of the Finance Minister,' 3 June 2002.

91 Hon. Paul Martin, 'Statement on Leaving Cabinet,' 3 June 2002.

92 Delacourt, *Juggernaut,* 246.
93 Peter O'Neil, 'Stay Loyal or Quit, MP Warns President of BC Wing,' *Vancouver Sun,* 2 August 2002.
94 Ibid.
95 *RDI News,* 5 August 2002.
96 Anne Dawson, 'More MPs Call for Chrétien to Retire,' *National Post,* 3 August 2002.
97 Hon. Charles Caccia, interview with author.
98 Peter O'Neill, 'Stay Loyal or Quit.'
99 Ibid.
100 Tim Murphy, interview with author.
101 'Business Leaders, MPs Meet Martin on Ontario Links,' *Globe and Mail,* 8 August 2002.
102 Hon. Sergio Marchi, interview with author.
103 'Liberal Recruiting Rules Must Be Evenly Applied: Martin Should Make His Troops Give Chrétien's People a Fair Shot,' editorial, *Vancouver Sun,* 15 August 2002, A12.
104 Mark Marissen, interview with author.
105 'Liberal Recruiting Rules Must Be Evenly Applied.'
106 Interview with Don Martin, *Calgary Herald,* 24 June 2002.
107 For more detail, see Delacourt, *Juggernaut,* 266–9.
108 Andrew Telegdi, 'I Like PM Jean Chrétien, But It's Time for a Change,' *Hill Times,* 22 July 2002.
109 Ibid.
110 Ibid.
111 Jack Aubry, 'Martin Sets Up War Room to Battle PM,' *Ottawa Citizen,* 7 August 2002.
112 Hon. Sergio Marchi, interview with author.
113 Hon. Doug Frith, interview with author.
114 George Young, interview with author.
115 Hon. Percy Downe, interview with author.
116 Ipsos-Reid poll for Globe and Mail/CTV, reported 16 August 2002.
117 Michael Marzolini, 'Viewpoint,' *Liberal Times* (Fall 2002).
118 Delacourt, *Juggernaut,* 255.
119 Ibid., 256.
120 Tim Harper, 'PM's Letter Seeking Input Dismissed by Some MPs,' *Toronto Star,* 6 August 2002.
121 Tim Naumetz, 'Senate Liberals Split over Petition for PM,' *National Post,* 14 August 2002, A6.
122 Hon. Percy Downe, interview with author.

123 Delacourt, *Juggernaut*, 269.
124 Stephen LeDrew, interview with author.
125 Tim Murphy, interview with author.
126 Joan Bryden, 'I Will Not Run Again,' *Vancouver Sun*, 22 August 2002, A1.
127 Paul DeVillers, interview with author.
128 Bryden, 'I Will Not Run Again.'
129 Delacourt, *Juggernaut*, 277.
130 Ibid., 276.
131 Paul Genest, interview with author.
132 George Young, interview with author.
133 'Chrétien's Agenda in Sharper Focus,' editorial, *Toronto Star*, 2 October 2002, A22.
134 Chantal Hébert, 'Liberals Conspicuous by Their Absence,' *Toronto Star*, 2 October 2002, A21.
135 Jane Taber, 'One Hundred Liberals Skip PM's Speech,' *Globe and Mail*, 2 October 2002.
136 CBC, *The National*, 3 September 2002.
137 Government of Canada, Department of Foreign Affairs, press release, 17 December 2002.
138 Hon. Charles Caccia, interview with author.
139 CBC, *National News*, interview, 4 September 2002, and Canadian Press, interview, 4 September 2002.
140 Rt Hon. Jean Chrétien, 'Notes for a Speech to the Chicago Council on Foreign Affairs,' 13 February 2006.
141 Hon. Paul Martin, interview on CBC Radio's *As It Happens*, 11 March 2003.
142 Canada, House of Commons, *Debates*, 8 March 2003.
143 Rt Hon. Jean Chrétien, transcript of speech to the National Liberal Caucus, North Bay, 19 August 2003, 3.
144 Hon. Martin Cauchon and Paul Genest, interviews with author.
145 *Montreal Gazette*, 20 August 2003.
146 'Martin's Ambiguous Statements Leave People Scratching Heads,' *The Guardian*, 22 August 2003, A8.
147 Canadian Press, 'Chrétien Stands Firm on Same-Sex Union,' 21 August 2003.
148 Canadian Press, 9 December 2003.
149 Paco Francoli and Angelo Perischilli, 'Riot-Type Atmosphere in Grit Caucus,' *Hill Times*, 2 June 2003.
150 Ibid.

151 Campbell Clark, 'LeDrew Prevented from Testifying on Election Bill by PMO,' *Globe and Mail*, 30 April 2003.
152 Lloyd Posno, interview with author.
153 'Finance Bill Receives Final Approval as Martin Absent from Vote,' *National Post*, 12 June 2003.
154 Joan Bryden, 'Liberals More Divided Than Ever over Election Financing Bill,' *Ottawa Citizen*, 30 May 2003.
155 Bill Curry, 'Finance Bill Receives Final Commons Approval: Paul Martin Absent for Vote,' *National Post*, 12 June 2003, A4.
156 Rt Hon. Jean Chrétien, transcript of speech to special national caucus in North Bay, 19 August 2003.

11: The Long Leadership Race, 2002–2003

1 Speech at the November 2003 leadership convention.
2 Stephen LeDrew, interview with author.
3 Ibid.
4 Hon. Michel Robert, interview with author.
5 Susan Delacourt, 'New PM Will Be Chosen November 15, 2003,' *National Post*, 21 October 2002, A11.
6 Since all delegates to the convention would be chosen on the same 'super weekend' in October, some thirty-five days before the convention itself, the cut-off date for party members eligible to vote on that weekend would consequently become late June 2003, or ninety days earlier.
7 Delacourt, 'New PM Will Be Chosen November 15.'
8 David Herle, interview with author.
9 Mark Kennedy, 'End Lump Sum Provincial Funding: Rock,' *Ottawa Citizen*, 2 November 2002.
10 Mark Kennedy and Anne Dawson, 'Rock Backs Former Rival Paul Martin,' *National Post*, 7 June 2003, A6.
11 Hon. Allan Rock, comments at National Press Club press conference, 14 January 2003.
12 'Rock Bows Out,' editorial, *Winnipeg Free Press*, 15 January 2003, A10.
13 Campbell Clark, 'Keep Race Fair, Manley Warns Martin,' *Globe and Mail*, 20 January 2003.
14 Shawn McCarthy, 'Complaints about Memberships Just Posturing, LeDrew says,' *Globe and Mail*, 21 January 2003, A5.
15 'Q&A with Akaash Maharaj,' *Hill Times*, 30 June 2003.
16 Sandra Gordon, 'Manley Would Serve in Cabinet Led by Martin,' *National Post*, 30 June 2003.

17 Daniel Leblanc, 'Copps Staying to Last Round in Liberal Leadership Contest,' *Globe and Mail*, 23 July 2003, A9.
18 Tim Murphy, interview with author.
19 Susan Delacourt, *Juggernaut: Paul Martin's Campaign for Chrétien's Crown* (Toronto: McClelland and Stewart, 2003), 263.
20 Tim Harper, 'Martin Leadership Run Official,' *Toronto Star*, 7 March 2003.
21 Michelle Cadario, interview with author.
22 Ruth Thorkelson, interview with author.
23 Hon. Charles Caccia, interview with author.
24 Delacourt, *Juggernaut*, 280.
25 Michelle Cadario, interview with author.
26 Gillian Cosgrove, 'Key Liberals to Thrash Out New Vision for Party,' *National Post*, 16 September 2002, A2.
27 H. Aster and T. Axworthy, eds., *Searching for the New Liberalism* (Toronto: Mosaic Press, 2002).
28 Cosgrove, 'Key Liberals to Thrash Out New Vision for Party.'
29 James Travers, 'Time for Liberals to Revisit Aylmer,' *Toronto Star*, 17 December 2002.
30 Stephen LeDrew, interview with author.
31 Delacourt, *Juggernaut*, 293
32 Ibid., 291.
33 It should be noted that a number of academic studies, in Canada and elsewhere, do not support this thesis. Instead, the decline of the traditional media and the growth of 'infotainment,' as well as the increasing use of alternative media including the internet as sources of information, the decrease in political literacy, the explosive growth of single-issue interest groups, and, most importantly, a demographic imbalance in which those under thirty participate less than all other age groups (skewing results), are some of the alternative explanations offered. See, for example, A. Blais, E. Gidengil, and N. Nevitte, eds., *Citizens* (Vancouver: UBC Press, 2004); J. Pammett and L. LeDuc, 'Confronting the Problem of Declining Voter Turnout among Youth,' *Electoral Insight* (July 2003); Henry Milner, 'Civic Literacy in Comparative Context: Why Canadians Should Worry,' *Policy Matters* (IRPP) 2, no. 2 (July 2001); and Paul Howe, 'Electoral Participation and the Knowledge Deficit,' *Electoral Insight* (July 2003).
34 Hon. Charles Caccia, interview with author.
35 Presumably he was referring to his specific situation as a recent former

minister, since Turner in 1984 had also been running from outside of cabinet at a time when the party was in power.

36 Mark Resnick, interview with author.

37 Tim Murphy, interview with author.

38 Delacourt, *Juggernaut*, 259.

39 Tim Murphy, interview with author.

40 'Martin Vows to Correct Government "Drift,"' CBC TV News, 28 April 2003.

41 'Martin Finally Steps into the Spotlight,' editorial, *Toronto Star*, 7 March 2003, A24.

42 Liberal Party of Canada, 'Liberals Announce Details of Leadership Forum Series,' press release, Ottawa, 16 April 2003.

43 Ruth Thorkelson, interview with author.

44 Joe Thornley, interview with author.

45 Doug Kirkpatrick, interview with author.

46 Sheila Copps, *Worth Fighting For* (Toronto: McClelland and Stewart, 2004), 179.

47 Ibid.

48 Joe Thornley, interview with author.

49 'Copps Fires at Martin for Social Spending Cuts,' CTV.ca, 25 May 2003.

50 'Liberal Leadership Contender Says It's Been Frustrating to Have Been Written Off by Senior Party Members,' *London Free Press*, 17 August 2003.

51 Richard Foot, 'Martin Vow to Extend 200-Mile Limit "Legally Can't Be Done," Minister Says,' *Ottawa Citizen*, 28 May 2003.

52 Susan Riley, 'Vote for Me, Details to Come,' *Ottawa Citizen*, 30 June 2003.

53 Sheila Copps, 'Foundations: An Action Plan for Canadians,' 1.

54 Hugh Winsor, 'Copps' Platform Shows She's Done Her Homework,' *Globe and Mail*, 5 August 2003.

55 Graham Fraser, 'Copps Red Book May Prompt Policy Talk,' *Toronto Star*, 27 July 2003, A11.

56 Susan Delacourt, 'Copps Says There's More than One Way to Run the Country,' *Toronto Star*, 2 August 2003.

57 Peter O'Neill, 'How Martin Plans to Win the West,' *Ottawa Citizen*, 10 November 2003.

58 James Baxter, 'Goodale Plays Down Western PMO,' *Saskatoon Star Phoenix*, 14 October 2003.

59 Roger Gibbins, 'The West in Canada: An Action Plan to Address Western Discontent,' Canada West Foundation, 3 September 2003, http://www.cwf.ca/V2/cnt/a04502dd17bea81a87256d960054ca13.php.

60 Baxter, 'Goodale Plays Down Western PMO.'

61 Jane Taber, 'Martin Backers Hope for Gains in House Seats from West,' *Globe and Mail*, 9 July 2003.

62 Baxter, 'Goodale Plays Down Western PMO.'

63 Peter O'Neill, 'How Martin Plans to Win the West,' *Ottawa Citizen*, 10 November 2003.

64 Martin campaign, 'Martin Issues Statement on Health Council,' press release, 10 July 2003.

65 Martin supporters such as MPs Joe Comuzzi, Judy Sgro, and Benoît Serre all called publicly for the resignation of Rock and also of his predecessor at Justice, Anne McClellan.

66 Delacourt, *Juggernaut*, 305.

67 Ibid.

68 Ibid.

69 'Grit EA Predicts Chrétien Will Step Down before September,' *Hill Times*, 6 January 2003, 14.

70 PMO, 'Prime Minister Reports on Throne Speech Commitments,' press release, Ottawa, 17 June 2003, 2.

71 PMO, 'Notes for an Address by Prime Minister Jean Chrétien on the Occasion of the 3rd World Chambers Congress,' Quebec City, 16 September 2003.

72 Ibid.

73 Hon. Paul Martin, 'Building the 21st Century Economy,' speech delivered to the Board of Trade of Metropolitan Montreal, 18 September 2003.

74 Chantal Hébert, 'Bloc Facing Election Disaster,' *Toronto Star*, 4 August 2003.

75 Michael Marzolini, chairman of Pollara, as reprinted in 'In My Opinion,' *The Liberal Times* (Fall 2003): 3.

76 Canada, House of Commons, *Debates*, 6 November 2003.

77 Jane Taber, 'Caucus Chair Wants Copps to Quit, Concede Defeat,' *Globe and Mail*, 25 September 2003.

78 Ibid.

79 CBC Online News (cbc.ca), 'Liberals Urge Copps to Step Aside,' 25 September 2003.

80 Brian Laghi, 'LeDrew Takes Rap for Remarks, Keeps Job,' *Globe and Mail*, 17 June 2003.

81 Ibid.

82 Copps, *Worth Fighting For*, 191–3.

83 Murray Dobbin, *Paul Martin: CEO for Canada?* (Toronto: Lorimer, 2003), 149.

84 Scott Reid, interview with author.

85 Stephen LeDrew, 'President's Message,' *Liberal Times* (Fall 2003): 2.

86 Bill Curry, 'Liberals to Make Review of Leader More Difficult,' *National Post*, 29 September 2003.

87 Hon. Ross Fitzpatrick, interview with author.

88 Hon. David Collenette, interview with author.

89 CBC News, *The National*, 13 November 2003.

90 PMO, 'Notes for an Address by Prime Minister Jean Chrétien on the Occasion of a Tribute to the Prime Minister,' 13 November 2003.

91 Hugh Winsor, 'New PM Should Heed Warnings,' *Globe and Mail*, 17 November 2003.

92 Joe Thornley, interview with author.

93 Copps, *Worth Fighting For*, 188–94.

94 Martin first used this term in his address to the 1990 leadership convention. The speech was written by John Duffy, who was also involved in the work on the 2003 speech.

95 Hon. Paul Martin, 'Making History: The Politics of Achievement,' speech delivered to the Liberal leadership convention, 15 November 2003, 3–4.

96 Campbell Clark, 'Martin's Organizers Spark Bitter Suggestions of Heavy-Handedness,' *Globe and Mail*, 13 November 2003.

97 Tim Murphy, interview with author.

98 Stephen LeDrew, interview with author.

99 James Coutts, 'The Tenets and Constituency Roots of Liberalism,' *Policy Options* (November 2004): 9–17.

12: From Glory to Grief: The First Martin Mandate

1 'Martin, Premiers Begin New Era,' CBC News Online, 17 November 2003.

2 Ibid.

3 David Herle, interview with author.

4 Paul Wells, *Right Side Up: The Fall of Paul Martin and the Rise of Stephen Harper's New Conservatism* (Toronto: McClelland and Stewart, 2006), 80.

5 Ibid., 78.

6 Adrienne Clarkson, *Heart Matters* (Toronto: Viking, 2006), 195.

7 Chrétien's last cabinet had consisted of twenty-eight ministers, with an additional ten ministers of state who were not part of the cabinet. Martin's cabinet consisted of an equal number of ministers but also eleven ministers of state.

8 Hon. Jack Austin, interview with author.

9 Michael Robinson, interview with author.

10 PMO, 'Prime Minister Announces Appointment of Cabinet,' press release, Ottawa, 12 December 2003, 1.

11   CBC News, 12 December 2003.
12   Don Martin, 'The Candidate Likely to Finish Second,' *National Post*, 6 June 2003, A15.
13   Hon. Francis Fox, interview with author.
14   Hon. Jack Austin, interview with author.
15   Mike Robinson, interviews with author.
16   Jeffrey Simpson, 'Where Are All the Women?' *Globe and Mail*, 14 January 2004.
17   Larry Zolf, 'Cabinet Making,' *Viewpoint*, CBC News, 16 December 2003.
18   'Martin Cabinet Too Unilingual: Quebec,' CBC.ca News, 12 December 2003.
19   Wells, *Right Side Up*, 90.
20   Hon. Charles Caccia, interview with author.
21   L. Ian MacDonald, 'Opening on the Left,' *The Gazette*, 25 January 2006.
22   Larry Zolf, 'What's Happened to Left-Wing Liberalism?' *Viewpoint*, CBC News, 26 January 2004.
23   David Herle, Michael Robinson, Hon. Jack Austin, and Hon. Jim Peterson, author interviews.
24   Carol Goar, 'Martin Continues Liberal Assault on Affordable Housing,' *Toronto Star*, 19 December 2003.
25   Ibid.
26   Michael Robinson, interview with author.
27   Ibid.
28   Hon. Jack Austin, interview with author.
29   Anne Dawson and Bob Fife, 'Day One: Martin Concentrates Power,' *National Post*, 13 December 2006.
30   Ruth Thorkelson, interview with author.
31   A considerable number of PMO staffing interventions were cited by observers in the last mandate, as internecine conflict accelerated.
32   Scott Reid, interview with author.
33   Ruth Thorkelson, interview with author.
34   Scott Reid, interview with author.
35   Jane Taber, 'Bush Prefers Our Pretty Boy to His Pretty Boy,' *Globe and Mail*, 16 January 2004.
36   Hon. Francis Fox, interview with author.
37   Michael Robinson, interview with author.
38   Larry Zolf, 'Copps and Robbers,' *Viewpoint*, CBC News, 2 October 2003.
39   Scott Reid, interview with author.
40   Tim Murphy and Michael Robinson, interviews with author.
41   Wells, *Right Side Up*, 105.

42 David Herle and Michael Robinson, interviews with author.

43 Terrie O'Leary, interview with author.

44 Tim Murphy, interview with author.

45 Strikingly, almost every Liberal insider interviewed for this book expressed amazement at the description of the Chrétien administration as highly centralized. They flatly rejected the image presented by academics such as Donald Savoie (*Governing from the Centre*) and media commentators such as Jeffrey Simpson (*The Imperial Prime Minister*), dismissing them as misguided and ill-informed. Several suggested that critics were confusing coordination and efficiency with decision-making power. Instead, they argued individual ministers were given even more autonomy than under Pierre Trudeau, while the public service and PCO were more significant than the PMO among advisers. Their views were later echoed by senior PMO adviser Eddie Goldenberg, who referred to 'the mythology about excessive centralization or inordinate concentration of power in the way in which a modern PMO exercises its coordination function across government.' *The Way It Is* (Toronto: McClelland and Stewart, 2006), 75.

46 Terrie O'Leary, interview with author.

47 Hon. Jack Austin, interview with author.

48 Wells, *Right Side Up*, 105.

49 Don Martin, 'The Shadow behind Paul Martin,' *National Post*, 17 September 2002, A19.

50 Ibid.

51 Kevin Bosch, interview with author.

52 Ibid.

53 Ibid.

54 Kevin Bosch, interview with author.

55 Louise Elliot, 'Paul Martin Says Grits in Debt,' Canadian Press, 10 December 2003.

56 James Brown, 'Martin Pumps up Liberal Coffers,' *Winnipeg Sun*, 19 January 2004.

57 Jane Taber, 'Raise Could Boost Top Aides' Pay above MPs,' *Globe and Mail*, 2 January 2004.

58 Kathryn May, 'Our System Is Broken: Alcock,' *Ottawa Citizen*, 21 February 2004.

59 'Tough Times in the Public Service,' *Globe and Mail*, 12 July 2004.

60 'Civil Servants' Union Vows to Fight Martin Cuts,' *Globe and Mail*, 29 January 2004.

61 See, for example, William Watson, 'PM's Attempt to Please All Should

Please Opposition,' *Montreal Gazette*, 30 December 2003; and 'Paul Martin's Democratic Deficit,' *National Post*, 3 April 2004.

62 As outlined on the Elections Canada website, Parliament had the authority to change the deadline in the same way it could alter any piece of legislation. This proposed change had already gone through all the normal stages and committee reviews in the House the previous year, passing third reading on 23 October 2003.

63 Hon. Brian Tobin, interview with author.

64 Speech from the Throne to Open the Third Session of the 37th Parliament of Canada, 2 February 2004, http://epe.lac-bac.gc.ca/100/205/301/pco-bcp/website/06-07-27/www.pco-bcp.gc.ca/default.asp@language=e&page=sftddt&doc=sftddt2004_1_e.htm.

65 Jeffrey Simpson, 'Punt the Problems, Score with Clichés,' *Globe and Mail*, 3 February 2004.

66 G. Bruce Doern, 'Martin in Power: From Coronation to Contest,' in *How Ottawa Spends: 2004–2005*, ed. B. Doern (Montreal: McGill-Queen's University Press, 2004), 12–13.

67 Peter Nicholson, interview with author.

68 Tom Kent, 'He Must Pluck His Power,' *Globe and Mail*, 29 January 2004, A15.

69 'Opposition Says Throne Speech Short on Details,' CTV.ca News, 6 February 2004.

70 See, for example, Murray Dobbin, 'Paul Martin from the Throne: Still Crying Poor,' Rabble.ca, 3 February 2004, http://www.rabble.ca/news/paul-martin-throne-still-crying-poor.

71 CTV.ca, News Online, 6 February 2004.

72 CBC TV News, Quebec City, 8 February 2004.

73 David Herle, interview with author, 13 July 2006.

74 Hon. Charles Caccia, interview with author.

75 Canada, House of Commons, *Debates*, 15 September 2003.

76 Treasury Board of Canada, *Final Submission of the Attorney General of Canada to the Commission of Inquiry into the Sponsorship Program and Advertising Actvities*, part III, section D, article 167, 8 August 2005.

77 'Indepth: Auditor General's Report 2004,' CBC News Online, cbc.ca, 11 February 2004.

78 Denis Saint-Martin, 'Managerialist Advocate or "Control Freak"? The Janus-Faced Office of the Auditor General,' *Canadian Public Administration*, 22 June 2004, http://www.encyclopedia.com/doc/1G1-121873238.html; Peter Hadekel, 'Fraser's Critics Off-Base,' *Montreal Gazette*, 6 May 2004.

79 Sean Gordon, Bill Curry, and Mark Kennedy, 'Spending Watchdog Tones Down Rhetoric,' *National Post*, 24 November 2004.

80 Susan Riley, 'A Kinder, Gentler Fraser,' *Ottawa Citizen*, 26 November 2004.

81 David Herle, interview with author.

82 Scott Reid, interview with author.

83 Ibid.

84 Wells, *Right Side Up*, 95.

85 Exceptionally, the chair of the Public Accounts Committee is traditionally a member of the Official Opposition, a fact Martin would certainly have known.

86 Drew Fagan, 'Martin Team Was Surprised by Depth of Public Backlash,' *Globe and Mail*, 21 February 2004.

87 Alexander Panetta, 'Back Off, Chrétien Pals Warn Martin,' Canadian Press, 14 March 2004.

88 Ibid.

89 Scott Reid, interview with author.

90 Panetta, 'Back Off, Chrétien Pals Warn Martin.'

91 Frances Russell, 'This Is Too Much of Whatever,' *Winnipeg Free Press*, 20 February 2004.

92 Michael Friscolanti, 'Martin Was Urged in 2002 to Look into Sponsorships,' *National Post*, 13 February 2004, A1.

93 *Cross-Country Checkup*, CBC, 15 February 2004. See also summary of Anne Dawson in 'Martin Vows to Resign If Implicated in Scandal,' *National Post*, 16 February 2004.

94 Interview with Kevin Newman, Global TV, 17 February 2004.

95 Jane Taber, 'Liberal MPs Tell Martin to Ease Up,' *Globe and Mail*, 19 February 2004.

96 Ibid.

97 Daniel Leblanc, 'Pelletier: Martin Waging Civil War on Grits,' *Globe and Mail*, 6 March 2004.

98 L. Ian Macdonald, 'Martin Would Be Smart to Cool It,' *The Gazette*, 10 April 2004.

99 'Martin Backtracks on "Political Direction" in Scandal,' CBC TV, 6 April 2004.

100 Dawson, 'Martin Vows.'

101 Mark Resnick, interview with author.

102 David Herle, interview with author. It should be noted that public opinion polls do not necessarily bear out this contention, with many commentators arguing the Adscam crisis had been factored into the party's standing (which had rebounded to 42 per cent) long before the writ was dropped.

103 Scott Reid, interview with author.
104 Jeffrey Simpson, 'Paul Martin Takes to Life as Opposition Leader,' *Globe and Mail*, 20 March 2004.
105 Ibid.
106 'Mixed Reaction to Goodale's Budget,' CTV.ca, 23 March 2004, http://toronto.ctv.ca/servlet/an/local/CTVNews/20040323/budget2004_commentary_20040323?hub=THO.
107 Ibid.
108 Lysiane Gagnon, 'Where Was the Emergency?' *Globe and Mail*, 29 March 2004, A13.
109 Jeffrey Simpson, 'Martin's Lack of Focus Is Eroding His Credibility,' *Globe and Mail*, 18 February 2004.
110 Kevin Bosch, interview with author.
111 David Herle, interview with author.
112 Hon. Charles Caccia, interview with author.
113 David Herle, interview with author.
114 Marva Wisdom, interview with author.
115 Joël-Denis Bellavance, 'Exit le livre rouge du PLC,' *La Presse*, 29 March 2004.
116 Liberal Party of Canada, *Moving Canada Forward* (Ottawa: May 2004), 5.
117 Canadian Press, 'Liberal Candidates to Stress Martin,' 10 May 2004.
118 Ibid.
119 Ibid.
120 'Paul Martin Machine Moving to Purge Party of Some MPs, Say Insiders,' Canadian Press, 8 December 2004.
121 Ibid.
122 Campbell Clark and Brian Laghi, 'Copps Battle Symptom of Liberal Infighting,' *Globe and Mail*, 17 January 2004, A11.
123 Paco Francolini, 'Governing Grits Feeling Uncomfortable,' *Hill Times*, 23 February–31 March 2004.
124 David Herle, interview with author.
125 Bruce Campion-Smith, 'Martin's Naming of Candidates Criticized,' *Toronto Star*, 2 April 2004.
126 Mark Hume, 'Liberal Breakout in BC Unlikely, Poll Shows,' *Globe and Mail*, 24 May 2004.
127 David Herle, interview with author.
128 Warren Kinsella, 'It's Official,' www.warrenkinsella.com.
129 Mark Marissen, interview with author.
130 CBC.ca News, 5 February 2004.
131 Ibid.

132 Bill Curry and Anne Dawson, 'Chrétien Loyalists Leery of Alliance with Former Separatists,' *National Post*, 6 April 2004.

133 As quoted by Andrew Coyne, 'Whereas This Is a Deep, Meaningful Relationship,' *Globe and Mail*, 6 April 2004.

134 Ibid.

135 Canadian Press, 'Paul Martin Machine.'

136 Kate Jaimet, 'Liberal Party to Lose Its Three Eco-Heroes,' *Ottawa Citizen*, 7 March 2004.

137 John Ibbitson and Jane Taber, 'True Grit,' *Globe and Mail*, 10 May 2003, F7.

138 In one *Globe and Mail* poll (19 January 2004), 54 per cent of respondents agreed that the prime minister 'had not treated Sheila Copps fairly.' See www.politicswatch.com/election-april12-2004.htm. In a Compass poll, 59 per cent of decided voters said they would prefer Copps to Valeri as the Liberal candidate and would vote for her. *National Post*, 21 January 2004.

139 CBC TV, *The National*, 10 March 2004.

140 Canadian Press, 'Martin Team Pushing Catterall Aside: Copps,' 24 December 2003.

141 David Herle, interview with author.

142 Scott Reid, interview with author.

143 Angelo Persichilli, 'Rattled Grits Want PM to Hold Off on Election Call,' *Hill Times*, 23 February–1 March 2004.

144 Jeffrey Simpson, 'PM Has Bombed the Bridges,' *Globe and Mail*, 27 March 2004.

145 Gagnon, 'Where Was the Emergency?'

146 Allan Gregg, 'Get a Grip Canada,' *Globe and Mail*, 2 November 2005.

147 Ian Bailey, 'Dhaliwal to PM: Postpone Election,' *Ottawa Citizen*, 15 February 2004.

148 Janice Tibbetts, 'Liberals' Pre-election Spending Spree Hits $8 billion,' *Ottawa Citizen*, 23 May 2004.

149 'Pick an Election Date, Mr. Martin,' editorial, *Globe and Mail*, 21 April 2004, A22.

150 Wells, *Right Side Up*, 122–3.

151 Rt Hon. Paul Martin, press conference, Rimouski, Quebec, 26 April 2004.

152 Chantal Hébert, 'Bédard Cameo Casts Shadow on Probe,' *Toronto Star*, 26 March 2004.

13: Fall from Grace: From Majority to Minority

1 Interview with author.

2 David Herle, interview with author.

3 Tim Murphy, interview with author.
4 Scott Reid, interview with author. While some other reporters on the Liberal campaign plane later acknowledged such an incident informally, none was willing to confirm it for the record.
5 McGill University, Observatory for Media and Public Policy, '2004 Newspaper Coverage Content Analysis: Cumulative Results May 17–June 25, 2004,' 25 June 2004.
6 Louis St Laurent succeeded Mackenzie King and remained PM from November 1948 to June 1957; Pierre Trudeau succeeded Lester Pearson and remained PM from April 1968 to June 1979.
7 Paco Francolini, 'Is Paul Martin Poised to Defy History?' *Hill Times*, 3 May 2004, 1.
8 Ibid.
9 Drew Fagan, 'Martin Chasing Trudeau's Ghost,' *Ottawa Citizen*, 24 May 2004.
10 Sarah Schmidt, 'Liberals Pushing Two-Tier Universities: Axworthy,' *Ottawa Citizen*, 25 May 2004.
11 Adam Radwanski, 'Opposition Should Target Martin's Soft Federalism,' *Ottawa Citizen*, 8 April 2004.
12 Anne Dawson, 'Liberals Weigh Delaying Election,' *Ottawa Citizen*, 22 May 2007.
13 Gloria Galloway, 'Ontario Liberal MPs on the Defensive,' *Globe and Mail*, 24 May 2004.
14 Robert Fife, 'Liberals Hold Herle Responsible,' *Ottawa Citizen*, 1 June 2004.
15 Lee Greenberg, 'Martin Aide Advised Ontario on Budget,' *Ottawa Citizen*, 26 May 2004.
16 Robert Benzie, 'Ontario Liberals Hired Martin Adviser,' *Toronto Star*, 25 May 2004.
17 COMPAS poll, 21 May 2004, reported in Robert Fife, 'Poll Points to Liberal Minority,' *Ottawa Citizen*, 21 May 2004, A1; and Decima/Navigator poll, 27 May 2004, reported in Glen McGregor, Shawn Gordon, and Bill Curry, 'Liberals Could Feel the Big Squeeze after Redrawing the Electoral Map,' *Ottawa Citizen*, 28 May 2004, B1.
18 Anne Dawson, 'It's Official: PM to Drop Writ Today,' *Ottawa Citizen*, 23 May 2004, A1.
19 Paul Attallah, 'Television and the Canadian Federal Election of 2004,' in *The Canadian General Election of 2004*, ed. Jon H. Pammett and Christopher Dornan (Toronto: Dundurn Group, 2004), 281.
20 Steve MacKinnon, interview with author.

21 See, for example, Pammett and Dornan, 'Election Night in Canada,' in *The Canadian General Election of 2004*, 12–14.
22 Ibid., 20.
23 'Canadians Find Grits Most Capable to Govern,' *Report of Strategic Counsel/ CTV/Globe and Mail Poll*, 17 May 2004.
24 Anne Dawson, 'PM's Adviser Admits to Making "Rookie" Mistakes,' *Ottawa Citizen*, 21 May 2004.
25 Rt Hon. Paul Martin, 'Statement on the Calling of the Election,' Ottawa, 23 May 2004.
26 Stephen Harper, comments at news conference, 23 May 2004.
27 Janice Tibbets, 'When You're in Doubt, Bash the Americans,' *Ottawa Citizen*, 26 May 2004.
28 Michael Bliss, 'Taking the Low Road Already,' *National Post*, 25 May 2004, A1.
29 David Herle, interview with author.
30 'Reality Check,' CBC, *The National*, 25 May 2004.
31 Lee Greenberg, 'Fallout from Ontario Budget Still Hurting Martin,' *Ottawa Citizen*, 27 May 2004.
32 Robert Fife, 'McGuinty Puts PM on the Spot,' *Ottawa Citizen*, 26 May 2004, A1.
33 Ibid.
34 Greenberg, 'Fallout from Ontario Budget.'
35 Drew Fagan, 'Ontario Budget Bigger Concern than Harper, McClellan Says,' *Globe and Mail*, 2 June 2004, A7.
36 Drew Fagan, 'Liberals Losing Initiative on Health Care,' *Globe and Mail*, 22 May 2004.
37 Dawson, 'Liberals Weigh Delaying Election.'
38 Ipsos-Reid poll, reported in Drew Fagan, 'Poll Puts Martin's Stumbling Liberals Ahead by Four Points,' *Globe and Mail*, 1 June 2004, A1.
39 Details of the Kay methodology and projections were reported nationally in an article by Robert Fife, 'Liberal Knives Out for Martin Adviser,' *Ottawa Citizen*, 1 June 2004, A1.
40 Robert Fife, 'My Team Is Just Fine: Martin,' *Ottawa Citizen*, 1 June 2004.
41 Campbell Clark, 'Poll Prompts Liberal Shift,' *Globe and Mail*, 2 June 2004, A1.
42 Ibid.
43 Anne Dawson, 'Liberal Ambushes Show Liberal Desperation,' *Ottawa Citizen*, 2 June 2004, A6.
44 Tu Thanh Ha, 'Gagliano Sues for $4.5 Million,' *Globe and Mail*, 28 May 2004.
45 CTV, *Question Period*, 30 May 2004.

46 Andrew McIntosh, 'Ouellet Audit Quietly Moved to PM's Office,' *Ottawa Citizen*, 26 May 2004, A6.
47 Joël-Denis Bellavance, 'Jean Lapierre ne s'excusera pas auprès du clan Chrétien,' *La Presse*, 27 September 2005, A8.
48 Hon. Charles Caccia, press release, Toronto, 3 June 2004.
49 Kate Jaimet, 'Chrétien Backers Put Rivalry Aside, Pitch in to Help,' *Ottawa Citizen*, 2 June 2004, A6.
50 Peter Donolo, interview with author. Donolo also made the point that, having been 'used' for spin, it would be even more difficult in future for Martin's advisers to establish any positive rapport with a significant segment of the party.
51 Tom Axworthy, conversation with author.
52 Anne-Louise Champagne, 'Les libéraux ont besion d'une majorité, croit Liza Frulla: La securité nationale en dépend, dit-elle,' *Le Soleil*, 27 May 2007, A9.
53 Daniel Leblanc and Rhéal Séguin, 'Attacks Haven't Allowed Martin to Be Himself, Liberals Feel,' *Globe and Mail*, 3 June 2004, A4.
54 Jane Taber, 'Liberals "Are in a Spiral," Top Martin Adviser Says,' *Globe and Mail*, 10 June 2004, A1.
55 Ingrid Peretz, 'Big Trouble for Martin's Quebec Star,' *Globe and Mail*, 17 June 2004, A1.
56 David Herle and Michael Robinson, interviews with author.
57 Hon. Stéphane Dion, 'An Open Letter to NDP Leader Jack Layton,' Ottawa, 28 May 2004, as published on Info@liberal.ca.
58 Rt Hon. Paul Martin, 'Steer Away from the Politics of Division,' *National Post*, 1 June 2004, A20.
59 Anne Dawson, 'Blow Your Own Horn, Martin Told,' *Ottawa Citizen*, 17 June 2004, B1.
60 Campbell Clark, 'Martin's Longest Four Hours,' *Globe and Mail*, 14 June 2004, A1.
61 Robert Fife, 'Harper Put on Defensive over Divisive Social Issues,' *Ottawa Citizen*, 16 June 2004, A1.
62 www.forums.cbc.ca/roundtable (30 January 2006).
63 Michael Valpy, 'Voters' Opinions on Martin Worsen after Debates, Polls Show,' *Globe and Mail*, 17 June 2004, A7.
64 Mark Kennedy, 'A Desperate Sandbox Fight with Martin in the Middle,' *Ottawa Citizen*, 16 June 2004, A2.
65 Brian Laghi, 'Leaders Drop Restraint and Go for Blood,' *Globe and Mail*, 15 June 2004, A4.
66 Peter Donolo, 'The Strategists,' *Globe and Mail*, 17 June 2004, A8.

67 Robert Fife, 'Liberal Knives Out,' *Ottawa Citizen*, 1 June 2004, A1.

68 Mark Kennedy, 'Win Majority or Risk Revolt, Martin Warned,' *Ottawa Citizen*, 14 June 2004, A1.

69 Anne Dawson, 'Liberals Make Pact Not to Oust Martin,' *Ottawa Citizen*, 11 June 2004, B1.

70 Anne Dawson, 'Martin's Man Cries Sabotage,' *Ottawa Citizen*, 18 June 2004, B1.

71 Ibid.

72 Anne Dawson, 'Liberal Chief Apologizes for Rant on "Sabotage,"' *Ottawa Citizen*, 19 June 2004, A1.

73 Jane Taber, 'Confident Harper Talks Majority,' *Globe and Mail*, 11 June 2004, A5.

74 Anne Dawson, 'Voting for NDP Helps Tories, Liberals Warn,' *Ottawa Citizen*, 12 June 2004, A4.

75 Jeffrey Simpson, 'Equalization Politics 101: Dumb Promises Will Bite You,' *Globe and Mail*, 13 June 2007, A7.

76 Drew Fagan, 'Martin Plans to Emphasize His Successes as Finance Minister,' *Globe and Mail*, 11 June 2004, A1.

77 Robert Fife, 'Martin Says He'd Welcome Chrétien's Help,' *Ottawa Citizen*, 4 June 2004, A1.

78 Peter Donolo, 'What Should the Liberals Do Now?' *Globe and Mail*, 1 June 2004, A6.

79 Elisabeth Gidengil et al., 'Down to the Wire,' *Canadian Election Study*, Institute for Social Research, York University, 2005. While the authors agree Harper's lead 'evaporated in four days' after the ads were launched, they also claim 'the story is not so simple.'

80 Attallah, 'Television and the Canadian Federal Election of 2004,' 268–73; Jonathan Rose, 'Television Attack Ads: Planting the Seeds of Doubt,' *Policy Options* (September 2004): 92–6.

81 Rose, 'Television Attack Ads.'

82 Jill Mahoney, 'Harper Stands by MP in Abortion Furor,' *Globe and Mail*, 2 June 2004, A1.

83 Jonathan Fowlie, 'Harper Tries to Allay Fears on Abortion,' *Globe and Mail*, 10 June 2004.

84 Comments excerpted from *Let No One Put Asunder*, video documentary by Vox Veritas Pictures (Jerome de Luca interviewer), 19 May 2004.

85 Kirk Makin, 'Tories Would Act Fast to Fill Court Vacancies, Toews Says,' *Globe and Mail*, 16 June 2004, A6.

86 Mark Kennedy, 'Harper, Klein Will Strip Medicare: PM,' *Ottawa Citizen*, 18 June 2004, A1.

87 Rhéal Séguin, 'Landry Says Bloc Sweep Will Hasten Referendum,' *Globe and Mail*, 25 June 2004, A1.

88 Kate Jaimet, 'Harper Blasts Liberal Attack Ads,' *Ottawa Citizen*, 12 June 2004, B1.

89 Sean Gordon, 'Top Tories Seek to Muffle Talk of Majority,' *Ottawa Citizen*, 18 June 2004, B3.

90 Brian Laghi, 'Tories Try to Connect Martin to Child Porn,' *Globe and Mail*, 19 June 2004, A1.

91 Ibid.

92 Mark Marissen, interview with author.

93 Mark Kennedy, 'Martin: The Wind Is with Us,' *Ottawa Citizen*, 19 June 2004, A1.

94 André Belelieu, 'The 2004 Canadian Federal Election,' *Canada Election Studies* 1, no. 4 (8 July 2004): 1–9.

95 Patrick Fournier et al., 'How the Liberals Lost Quebec,' extracted from the findings of the Canada Election Study 2004, *Globe and Mail*, 21 July 2004, A13.

96 Belelieu, 'The 2004 Canadian Federal Election.'

97 Stephen Clarkson, 'Disaster and Recovery: Paul Martin as Lazarus,' in *The Canadian General Election of 2004*, 61.

14: Freefall: The Martin Minority

1 Speech to Young Liberals, March 2005.

2 Hon. Dan Hays, interview with author.

3 Hon. Tony Valeri, interview on *Question Period*, CTV, 3 October 2004, as reported in 'Parliament on Knife Edge for Minority Session,' *National Post*, 4 October 2004, A4.

4 Pearson's two minorities were first five, and then three, seats short of a majority, so that only the support of the NDP or, in the case of the second mandate, either the Social Credit or Créditistes, was sufficient to keep him in power. While Martin's minority was twenty seats shy of a majority, either the NDP and one of several Independents, or the Bloc Québécois, could keep him in power in the face of Conservative opposition.

5 Susan Delacourt, 'Public Wants Parties to Work Together,' *Toronto Star*, 10 November 2004, A3.

6 Campbell Clark, 'Ottawa Power Struggle Erupts,' *Globe and Mail*, 5 October 2004, A6.

7 Tim Murphy, interview with author.

8 Hon. Dan Hays, *Speaker's Report* (Ottawa: Fall 2004), 3.

9 Tom Kent, 'The Pearson Decade: How Defeat Foretold Victory,' *Policy Options* (February 2006): 13.

10 Tim Murphy, interview with author.

11 Tim Murphy, 'Noble Ambition,' *The Walrus*, December–January 2007, 59.

12 J.P. Lewis, 'Another Representational Factor? An Analysis of Paul Martin's Contribution to the Evolution of Federal Cabinet Composition,' paper presented to the Annual Meeting of the Canadian Political Science Association, June 2005. (Of course floor-crossing had existed before, as in the case of Trudeau's appointment of former Alberta Conservative Jack Horner to the cabinet, but the extent of Martin's willingness to accept defectors, without the impetus of rationales such as a lack of western representation, made this qualitatively different.)

13 Jeffrey Simpson, 'Not Exactly a Brave New Cabinet,' *Globe and Mail*, 21 July 2004, A13.

14 Tim Murphy, interview with author.

15 Simpson, 'Not Exactly a Brave New Cabinet.'

16 Jack Aubry, 'A Capital without Clout,' *Ottawa Citizen*, 21 July 2004, A1.

17 Jane Taber, 'Red-Faced Liberal Campaign Strategist Apologizes to Caucus,' *Globe and Mail*, 28 October 2004, A7.

18 Joanne Laucius, 'Right at the Very Centre of Power,' *Ottawa Citizen*, 19 August 2004, A4.

19 A. Radwanski, 'Martin's Blind Loyalty May Be His Downfall,' *Ottawa Citizen*, 9 July 2004.

20 Mark Kennedy, 'Precarious Perch of Martin's Disciples,' *Ottawa Citizen*, 14 November 2004, A5.

21 Peter Nicholson, interview with author.

22 As cited in Michael Marzolini, 'Public Opinion and the 2006 Election,' in *The Canadian General Election of 2006*, ed. Jon H. Pammett and Christopher Dornan (Toronto: Dundurn, 2006), 258.

23 Peter Nicholson, interview with author.

24 F. Abbas Rana, 'A Total of 11 PMO Staffers Have Left in Less than Five Months,' *Hill Times*, 15 November 2004, 3.

25 Ibid. See also Kennedy, 'Precarious Perch.'

26 F. Abbas Rana, 'Ferguson Joins Liberal Research Bureau as Director General,' *Hill Times*, 18 October 2004, 32.

27 Email correspondence among D. Herle, T. Murphy, S. Reid, P. Nicholson, J. Webster, T. O'Leary, J. Strauss, V. De Passille, K. Littler, M. Cadario, M. Robinson, Easton, R. Mahoney, S. Feschuk, H. Chalifour Scherrer, J. Leffler, S. MacKinnon, E. Alboim, D. Ferguson (24 September 2005, 8:02 A.M.–10:41 A.M.), re: 'Ottawa Throws Doors Open: Canada to Welcome 100,000 More

Immigrants Each Year,' *Toronto Star*, 24 September 2005. The time shows how little thought (two hours) was devoted to major policy decisions.

28 Martin's penchant for telephone conversations was well known through-out official Ottawa. See, for example, James Travers, 'Hold the Phone: It's the PM Calling,' *Toronto Star*, 2 October 2004, A2.

29 Jane Taber, 'Martin Faces Backlash over PMO Powers,' *Globe and Mail*, 25 August 2004, A9.

30 Kathryn May, 'Spending Review Spurs Fears of PS Job Losses,' *Ottawa Citizen*, 23 August 2004, A1.

31 Harry Swain, 'Turning the Tide,' speech to the Annual ADM Update, Ottawa, 9 November 2005, 1–2.

32 John Ibbitson, 'Tories Must Win Bureaucrats' Trust,' *Ottawa Citizen*, 6 February 2006, A5.

33 Jane Taber, 'Holy War Sparked by Dinner Invitations,' *Globe and Mail*, 2 December 2004, A11.

34 Peter Nicholson, interview with author.

35 Jill Mahoney, 'Show Us the Money, Premiers Tell Martin,' *Globe and Mail*, 9 July 2004.

36 Ibid.

37 Allan Gregg, 'Quebec's Final Victory,' *The Walrus*, 3 February 2005, 17.

38 Rhéal Séguin, 'Health Accord's Separate Deal First Step toward Quebec Signing Constitution, Martin Says,' *Globe and Mail*, 25 September 2004, A4.

39 Tim Murphy, 'Noble Ambition,' *The Walrus*, January 2007, 54.

40 'The PM Pays Dearly for Medicare Promises,' editorial, *Globe and Mail*, 18 September 2004, A18.

41 An excellent analysis of the nature of asymmetrical arrangements in Canada can be found in Michael Behiels's 'Asymmetrical Federalism in Canada: Magic Wand or Breaking the Ties That Bind?' presentation to the Canadian Constitutional Affairs Conference, Quebec City, 18 January 2008.

42 Robert Fife, 'PMs New View of Federalism Fractures Party,' *Ottawa Citizen*, 22 October 2004, A4.

43 Ibid.

44 Tom Kent, 'Paul Martin's Sugar Daddy Federalism, Donating to a Favoured Cause – Health Care,' *Policy Options* (November 2004): 34.

45 James Travers, 'Changing Canada by Stealth,' *Toronto Star*, 21 October 2004, A2.

46 Chantal Hébert, 'Shark Fins Spotted in Liberal Waters,' *Toronto Star*, 24 September 2004.

47 Susan Riley, 'Glimmers of Harmony and Hope Fuel Liberals' Sense of Victory,' *Edmonton Journal*, 5 March 2005, A15.

48 Jeffrey Simpson, 'Ottawa, Please Stop Trying to Please,' *Globe and Mail*, 15 October 2004, A17.

49 Robert Fife, 'PM Threatens One Canada, Liberal Says,' *National Post*, 21 October 2004.

50 Ibid.

51 Paul Wells, 'Ottawa Hallucinations,' *Maclean's*, 3 February 2004.

52 Travers, 'Changing Canada by Stealth.'

53 Tim Murphy, interview with author.

54 Scott Reid, interview with author.

55 Les Whittington, 'It's Up to Martin to Keep Government from Falling,' *Toronto Star*, 4 October 2004, A6.

56 Whittington, 'It's Up to Martin.'

57 James Travers, 'Liberals in Political Hot Seat,' *Kelowna Daily Courier*, 6 October 2004.

58 John Ibbitson, 'Where's the Fall Agenda?' *Globe and Mail*, 19 August 2004, A4.

59 Speech from the Throne, 38th Parliament, First Session, Ottawa, 5 October 2004, 8.

60 Richard Gwyn, 'Martin Has Bad Habit of Blinking,' *Kelowna Daily Courier*, 13 October 2004.

61 Ibid.

62 Bill Curry, 'New Parliament to Start from Scratch: Valeri,' *Ottawa Citizen*, 9 October 2004, A6.

63 Bill Curry, 'Nothing There in Liberal Agenda,' *Ottawa Citizen*, 14 December 2004, A4.

64 Ibid.

65 Hon. André Ouellet, letter to Hon. John McCallum, Minister of National Revenue, 12 August 2004 (my emphasis).

66 Gloria Galloway, 'Liberal Bent Rules to Appoint Mail CEO,' *Globe and Mail*, 2 October 2004, A29.

67 Brian Laghi, 'PM Vetoes Alberta's Senate Proposal,' *Globe and Mail*, 18 November 2004, A4.

68 Human Resource Professional Administrators of Ontario, 'Dingwall Left Hanging in the Wind,' *Employment Law Update*, 20 October 2006, 3.

69 Campbell Clark, 'Ottawa Appeals Ruling to Reinstate Pelletier,' *Globe and Mail*, 22 December 2005, A10.

70 Joël-Denis Bellavance, 'Jean Lapierre ne s'excusera pas auprès du clan Chrétien,' *La Presse*, 27 September 2005, A8 (my translation).

71 Alec Castonguay, 'Les libéraux remettent en question l'héritage de Chrétien,' *Le Devoir*, 20 October 2004, A3.

72 Susan Delacourt, 'Parrish Saga Gives Glimpse of What Makes Martin Tick,' *Toronto Star*, 20 November 2004, A4.

73 Jack Aubry, 'Majority of Canadians against Income Trust Levy,' *Vancouver Sun*, 8 November 2006, A5.

74 Anne Dawson, 'Liberals Saddled by $5 Million Debt,' *Ottawa Citizen*, 2 September 2004, A6

75 Ibid.

76 Anne Dawson, 'Our Debt Isn't $10M, Liberal Boss Insists,' *Ottawa Citizen*, 5 September 2004.

77 Anne Dawson, 'Martin to Fete Liberal Donors at 24 Sussex,' *Ottawa Citizen*, 21 August 2004, A4.

78 Sean Gordon, 'Debt Ridden Liberals Deny They're Trying to Rewrite Rules,' *Ottawa Citizen*, 13 November 2004, A3.

79 Anne Dawson, 'Cash-Strapped Grits Eye Grassroots,' *Ottawa Citizen*, 15 November 2004, A5.

80 Anne Dawson, 'Early Review of Martin's Role a Bid to Block Rivals,' *Ottawa Citizen*, 1 October 2004, A5.

81 Ibid.

82 Nicole Macintyre, 'Martin Protects MPs from Riding Challenges,' *Hamilton Spectator*, 28 October 2004.

83 James Coutts, 'The Tenets and Constituency Roots of Liberalism: Retooling the Red Machine,' *Policy Options* (November 2004): 9–17.

84 Mark Kennedy, 'A Huge Disappointment,' *Ottawa Citizen*, 13 November 2004, A3.

85 Martin Goldfarb, 'My New Years' Wish for the Liberal Party,' *Globe and Mail*, 29 December 2004, A15.

86 Bill Curry, 'Liberals Advise Opposition to Wait and See,' *Globe and Mail*, 22 February 2005.

87 Tim Murphy, interview with author.

88 Bill Curry, 'Liberals Advise Opposition.'

89 Ibid.

90 Bruce Doern, 'The Martin Liberals and the Harper Conservatives: The Politics of Governing Precariously,' in *How Ottawa Spends: 2005–2006*, ed. B. Doern (Montreal: McGill-Queen's University Press, 2005), 9.

91 Government of Canada, Department of Finance, *The Budget Speech 2005*, 23 February 2005, 4.

92 Doern, 'The Martin Liberals,' 10.

93 http://www.cbc.ca/news/background/parliament38. See entry for 23 February 2005.

94 Richard Gwyn, 'Get Set for Long, U.S.-Style Election Campaign,' *Toronto Star*, 24 May 2005, A17.

95 Don Martin, 'Prime Minister Jack Layton,' *National Post*, 28 April 2005, A20.

96 Jane Taber, *Canada AM*, CTV, 27 April 2005.

97 Hon. Paul Martin, *Text of an Address to the Nation* (Ottawa: PCO, 21 April 2005), 3.

98 Michael Robinson, interview with author.

99 'PM Cancels Visit to N.B. for Daycare Signing after Province Says No Deal,' Canadian Press, Fredericton, 11 November 2004.

100 Canadian Intergovernmental Conference Secretariat, Ottawa.

101 *Report of the Expert Panel on Equalization (O'Brien Report)*, Ottawa, 4 June 2006, 30.

102 Michael Holden, 'Equalization: Implications of Recent Changes,' PRB 05-91E (Ottawa: Library of Parliament, January 2006), 8.

103 Ibid., 9.

104 At one point in December 2004 a furious Williams ordered all Canadian flags removed from government buildings in Newfoundland. He also took out full-page ads in national newspapers declaring the Martin government had failed to live up to their election promise.

105 See, for example, the incisive analysis produced by Hugh Mackenzie, 'Dalton McGuinty's Fiscal Problems: Made in Ontario,' *Behind the Numbers* 7, no. 2 (Ottawa: Canadian Centre for Policy Alternatives, 7 April 2005); and Michael Holden, 'A Closer Look at Ontario's $23 Billion Gap,' PRB 05-15E (Ottawa: Library of Parliament).

106 Kathryn May, 'Martin to Be Called before Inquiry,' *Ottawa Citizen*, 27 October 2004, A1.

107 Katherine May and Joe Paraskevis, 'Gomery Defends Remarks about That "Scamp" Guité,' *National Post*, 17 December 2004, A4.

108 http://www.cbc.ca/story/canada/national/2005/01/31/gomery.

109 Larry Zolf, 'Saving the Liberal Brand,' CBC News, *Viewpoint*, 15 February 2005.

110 David Herle, interview with author.

111 Mark Kennedy, 'Gomery: Poll Shows People Hold Martin Accountable,' *Ottawa Citizen*, 3 June 2005, A6.

112 Peter Donolo, interview with author.

113 Jack Aubry, 'Jean Victim of Rushed Screening by PMO,' *Ottawa Citizen*, 27 September 2005, A5.

114 James Murray, 'Decision over Governor General Looks Like Martin Jumped before Thinking,' *The Infozone*, 17 August 2005.

115 Campbell Clark and Jane Taber, 'Liberals See Past Gomery to Majority in Next Vote,' *Globe and Mail*, 26 August 2007, A4.

116 Ibid.

117 Rt Hon. Paul Martin, 'Address by Prime Minister Paul Martin,' Gatineau, Quebec, 20 September 2005, 10–11.

118 Jeffrey Simpson, 'The Future Is Scary: So Are the PM's Priorities,' *Globe and Mail*, 23 September 2005, A27.

119 Rt Hon. Paul Martin, 'Statement on the Release of the Gomery Report' (Ottawa: PCO, 1 November 2005).

120 In July 2008 the Court ruled the judge was in fact biased and that segments of his report concerning Chrétien should be quashed.

121 Hon. Sheila Copps, 'Martin Knew Nothing? C'mon!' *Ottawa Sun*, 2 November 2005.

122 Hon. Sheila Copps, 'Liberals Torn by Internal Strife,' *Ottawa Sun*, 6 November 2005.

123 Allan Gregg, 'Get a Grip, Canada,' *Ottawa Citizen*, 2 November 2005.

124 'Opposition Leaders Hand Martin an Ultimatum,' 12 November 2005, http://www.cbc.ca/news/background/parliament38.

125 'Gomery Report to Sway Voters: Poll,' Reuters, 31 October 2005.

126 Tim Murphy, interview with author.

127 'Opposition Eyeing Christmas Campaign,' 16 November 2005, http://www.cbc.ca/news/background/parliament38.

128 As cited in Marzolini, 'Public Opinion and the 2006 Election,' in Pammett and Dornan, eds., 161.

129 Department of Finance, 'Minister of Finance Acts on Income Trust Issue,' news release, Ottawa, 23 November 2005.

130 'Klein Predicts Second Liberal Minority,' 23 November 2005, http://www.cbc.ca./news/background/parliament38.

131 'Liberals Lose Confidence of the House,' 29 November 2005, http://www.cbc.ca./news/background/parliament38.

15: Back to the Wilderness

1 Interviewed during the 2006 election.

2 Jane Taber, 'Liberal Majority in Sight, Chief Strategist Tells MPs,' *Globe and Mail*, 25 August 2005, A1.

3 See, for example, Stephen Clarkson, 'How the Big Red Machine Became the Little Red Machine,' in *The Canadian General Election of 2006*, ed. Jon H. Pammett and Christopher Dornan (Toronto: Dundurn, 2006), 24–5.

4 Donald Savoie, *Governing from the Centre: The Concentration of Power in Canadian Government* (Toronto: University of Toronto Press, 2004).

5 Peter Nicholson, interview with author.

6 Clarkson, 'How the Big Red Machine,' 38.

7 Peter Nicholson, interview with author.

8 Dan McCarthy, interview with author.

9 Although no one interviewed by the author would confirm for attribution that this had been the thinking, it was a widely discussed strategy in internal party circles and one that Stephen Clarkson alluded to publicly in his assessment of the Liberal campaign. 'How the Big Red Machine,' 31.

10 David Herle, interview with author.

11 Ibid.

12 Jack Aubry, 'Chrétien's Gomery Brief Mars Grit Launch,' *Ottawa Citizen*, 1 December 2005, A14.

13 Ibid.

14 Jon Pammett and Christopher Dornan, 'From One Minority to Another,' in *The Canadian General Election of 2006*, 12.

15 Jeffrey Simpson, 'Let's Put a Price on Those Conservative Treats,' *Globe and Mail*, 7 January 2006, A17.

16 Faron Ellis and Peter Woolstencroft, 'A Change of Government, Not a Change of Country,' in *The Canadian General Election of 2006*, 79.

17 Carol Ryan, 'Playing the Quebec Game,' Canada Votes 2006, http://www. cbc.ca/canadavotes/leadersparties/quebec_game.html.

18 Ibid.

19 As cited in Paul Wells, *Right Side Up* (Toronto: McClelland and Stewart, 2006), 199–201.

20 Robert Dutrisac, 'Harper courtise le Québec,' *Le Devoir*, 20 December 2005, A1; my translation.

21 Alain Dubuc, 'Back to Quebec's Bleu Roots,' *National Post*, 20 January 2006, A15.

22 Tim Murphy, interview with author.

23 Pammett and Dornan, 'From One Minority to Another,' 13.

24 Steven Chase, 'RCMP Launch Trusts Probe,' *Globe and Mail*, 29 December 2005, A1.

25 Brodie Fenlon and Omar Akkad, 'Top Mountie Amended Media Alert to Include Goodale,' *Globe and Mail*, 31 March 2008. A year later, no one had been charged in Martin or Goodale's office, and in fact only one individual – a middle-level public servant – was ever charged. Zaccardelli's role in several other events caused him to become a target for opposition parties. Eventually the Harper government abandoned its dogged defence of the commissioner and he resigned.

26 Hon. Francis Fox, interview with author.

27 Campbell Clark, 'Martin Won't Take Questions on RCMP Income Trust Probe,' *Globe and Mail*, 5 January 2006.

28 John Ibbitson, 'For Liberals, It's a Matter of Trust,' *Globe and Mail*, 29 December 2005, A6.

29 CPAC-SES polling, http://www.sesresearch.com.

30 Campbell Clark, 'Setbacks Aside, Martin "Happy" with Campaign,' *Globe and Mail*, 6 January 2006.

31 Mark Kennedy, 'Martin Brands Tories as Fiscal Fumblers,' *Ottawa Citizen*, 6 January 2006, A3. (It is instructive to note that the Conservatives were able to delay releasing their own platform document until 15 January without paying any price in the media, apparently due to their steady string of earlier announcements. As a result, the total cost of their promises – some $75 billion, or far more than either of the other two parties – was not actually known until days before the vote, when little could be done to effectively analyse it.)

32 Kevin Dougherty, 'Quebec Considers Option Canada Probe,' *Ottawa Citizen*, 10 January 2006, A3.

33 Panel commentary, 'Option Canada: Will It Have an Impact?' *Ottawa Citizen*, 10 January 2006, A3.

34 Ibid.

35 Clarkson, 'How the Big Red Machine,' 40.

36 James Travers, 'Liberal Party's Scattered Campaign a Reflection of Martin's Leadership,' *Toronto Star*, 12 January 2006, A1.

37 Peter Nicholson, interview with author.

38 Chris Cobb, 'Grits Unleash Stinging Attacks,' *Ottawa Citizen*, 11 January 2006, A2.

39 Ibid.

40 David Herle, interview with author.

41 Jonathan Rose, 'The Liberals Reap What They Sow: Why Their Negative Ads Failed,' *Policy Options* (March 2006): 80.

42 David Herle, interview with author.

43 Norma Greenaway, 'Passions Flare over Unity Issue,' *Ottawa Citizen*, 10 January 2006, A4.

44 For more detail, see Clarkson, 'How the Big Red Machine,' 40–1.

45 David Herle, interview with author.

46 Daniel Leblanc, 'Martin's Charter Promise Easier Said Than Done,' *Globe and Mail*, 11 January 2006, A10.

47 Graham Fraser, 'About Face,' *Toronto Star*, 24 December 2005.

48 Mark Kennedy, 'Martin Predicts Remarkable Comeback,' *Ottawa Citizen*, 20 January 2006, A1.

49 Gloria Galloway, 'Harper: Don't Fear a Conservative Majority,' *Globe and Mail*, 18 January 2006, A1.

50 Mark Kennedy, 'Using Senate to Block Tories "An Abuse of Power":
Harper,' *Ottawa Citizen*, 20 January 2006, A4.

51 Kathryn May, 'Harper's Suspicions of PS Hint of Rocky Relations to
Come,' *Ottawa Citizen*, 18 January 2006, A4.

52 James Gordon, 'Layton Blasts Liberals' Fear Tactics,' *Ottawa Citizen*,
19 January 2006, A5.

53 Nicolas van Praet, 'Duceppe Calls Harper a Threat to Language Law,'
Ottawa Citizen, 20 January 2006, A4.

54 Paul Vieira, 'PM Apologizes for Buzz,' *National Post*, 19 January 2006, A1.

55 See, for example, André Turcotte, 'After Fifty-Six Days … The Verdict,' in
The Canadian General Election of 2006, 283–304.

56 Clarkson, 'How the Big Red Machine,' 51.

57 Turcotte, 'After Fifty-Six Days … The Verdict,' 299.

58 Jane Taber, 'The Knives Came out Quickly for Martin,' *Globe and Mail*,
24 January 2006.

59 Mike Robinson, interview with author.

60 Linda Diebel, 'Liberal Leadership Debate Fails to Ignite,' *Toronto Star*,
11 June 2006, A3.

61 See http://epe.lac-bac.gc.ca/100/205/300/liberal-ef/06-10-26 and
www.liberal.ca/renewal_e.aspx.

62 Ron Lemieux, conversation with author.

63 Tom Axworthy, letter to the Hon. Stéphane Dion, 18 February 2007.

64 Hubert Bauch, 'Quebec Is a Nation within Canada: Ignatieff,' *The Gazette*,
28 June 2006, A9.

65 Don Martin, 'Ignatieff Proposal Derailing Liberals' Leadership Race,' *Calgary Herald*, 27 October 2006.

66 Justin Trudeau, interview on *Canada AM*, CTV, 26 October 2006.

67 Joan Bryden, 'Le Québec est une nation … "sociologiquement," dit
Stéphane Dion,' *Le Devoir*, 27 June 2006.

68 Alain Dubuc, *La Presse*, 27 October 2006 (translation).

69 Don Macpherson, 'Liberal Party Preparing to Rip Itself Apart,' *The Gazette*,
24 October 2006.

70 Sean Gordon, 'Liberals Work to Avoid Train Wreck,' *Toronto Star*, 15 November 2006.

71 'Kennedy Takes Stand,' *The National*, CBC TV, 27 November 2006.

72 John Ibbitson, 'Choosing Montreal Is Portentous,' *Globe and Mail*, 20 March
2006, A5.

73 Steven MacKinnon, interview with author.

74 Nevertheless by 1 July 2006 party president Mike Eizenga announced the
party was officially out of debt. According to Steven MacKinnon, this was

accomplished through spending cutbacks, some $7 million in donations and fundraising, and more than $9 million in government funding resulting from the new Elections Act.

75 Steve MacKinnon, interview with author.
76 Mike Eizenga, 'Notes for a Presentation on Red Ribbon Task Force,' LPC(O) Annual Meeting, 6 May 2006, and author interview.
77 LPC Red Ribbon Task Force, *Final Report: A Party Built for Everyone, A Party Built to Win* (Ottawa: 6 August 2006), 8.
78 Ibid., 29.
79 http://www.cbc.ca/canada/story/2008/05/01/party-fundraising.html.
80 Brooke Jeffrey, 'The Invisible Liberals,' in *The Canadian General Election of 2008*, ed. J. Pammett and C. Dornan (Toronto: Dundurn Press, 2009), 63–97.
81 James Travers, 'Liberals, Conservatives Swapping Core Traits,' *Toronto Star*, 19 April 2007.

Index